Modern Wales

Modern Wales:
Politics, Places and People

KENNETH O. MORGAN

UNIVERSITY OF WALES PRESS
CARDIFF
1995

British Library Cataloguing in Publication Data

A catalogue record for this book is available from the British Library.

ISBN 0-7083-1317-5

Typeset at the University of Wales Press, Cardiff
Printed in England by Bookcraft, Midsomer Norton

For Sue and Denis Balsom
Jane's friends – and mine

Contents

Preface

In September 1995 I leave the service of the University of Wales. I first joined it in September 1958 as (temporary) Research Fellow in Welsh Social History at Swansea, at the princely stipend of £650 p.a.; I leave it as Vice-Chancellor and Principal of Aberystwyth. In the course of the intervening thirty-seven years (most of which were spent in Oxford) I wrote, among other things, a considerable number of articles, chapters and occasional papers on the modern history of Wales, in addition to various monographs. It has been suggested to me that, since many of the academic articles, at least, appeared in relatively local or perhaps obscure places, it might be useful to collect them together in a single volume. The present book is the result, and I wish warmly to thank the editors and publishers in each case for permission to reprint. The book may also be taken as a kind of token of appreciation to our national federal university, whose history is so deeply intertwined with the experience and aspirations of the people of Wales, and to which I personally owe so much. Long may it endure.

The thirty-seven years which these articles span have unquestionably seen an astonishing renaissance in the history of Wales, as the experience of the *Welsh History Review* (which I have edited with Professor Ralph Griffiths since 1965) bears testimony. In the late 1950s, Welsh history (unlike Scottish or Irish) was commonly regarded as relatively marginal, local history and little more. It made scant impact on the wider public. But since then there has been a massive upsurge in all periods and aspects of the subject, with particular emphasis on the history of the past two hundred years.

There have been flourishing journals, exciting television and radio

series, important monographs and authoritative projects like the
Oxford History of Wales. It is entrenched in the schools' core
curriculum. In many ways, Welsh history, like Irish, has been
innovative and pioneering, not least in exploring the relationship
between culture and social change, or the nuances of the Welsh
mentalité. It has helped ensure that our collective story is viewed as
truly British, multi-cultural and pluralist, the convergence of a variety
of national experiences, rather than a Whiggish commentary on the
path of ascendancy trodden by the imperial English. The devoting of a
special meeting of the Anglo-American Historical Conference in June
1994 to the varieties of British history is but one indication of the
breakthrough in understanding that we have achieved.

There is now anxiety that this remarkable intellectual momentum
should be carried forward by younger scholars. The assaults on
university funding in the eighties had a particularly serious impact on
the University Colleges of Wales, and on specific humane disciplines
like Welsh history. The diminution of graduate studentships in the
humanities in the United Kingdom at large has meant that the mass of
graduate students, the seed-corn for the academic future, has been
seriously reduced. It must be hoped that the new Humanities Research
Board, set up by the British Academy, will address this problem.
Otherwise, the great progress in Welsh history achieved in the past four
decades will peter out. There are already signs that too many of our
creative and productive Welsh historians are in their fifties, sixties or
seventies. Their successors, the basis for renewal, must emerge now.
The immediate future of Welsh history, therefore, causes me concern. I
only hope that it proves to be misplaced.

These disparate articles have common themes. They focus partly on
political issues, partly on different areas of Wales, partly on key
personalities. Underlying them all, perhaps, are two major concerns.
One is the dynamic of democratic politics, including its social,
cultural, religious and ideological contexts, from the 1860s to the
present time. The other is the idea of nationhood, still an aspiration
unfulfilled by this 'unhistoric' nation, yet surely a mainspring of Welsh
history in the industrial and post-industrial periods. Much of my work
has focused on the half-century from the 1860s down to the end of the
First World War, a unique era of national achievement and socio-
political transformation in the history of what Gwyn A. Williams has
called 'imperial' Wales. This period still seems to me to provide the key
to most of the changes that have affected, or perhaps afflicted, the
Welsh people in the past century and more. Even with the total
transformation of the Welsh economy, major changes in the fabric of
politics and the moral climate, and the relentless advance of
anglicization, we still live and work under the shadow of Henry

Richard, Tom Ellis and Lloyd George. The era of *Cymru Fydd* still provides the basic mould for shaping the Welsh identity.

However, over the years, my interests have moved on into the period beyond the First, and now well beyond the Second, World War. Indeed, one of the ways in which Welsh historians have been pioneering figures of late has been in the projection and justification of contemporary history. My writing evidently reflects this, as it undoubtedly does the fact that most of my work over the years, as teacher and author, has concerned wider areas of British, European and American history. This developing range of interests will no doubt continue. To adapt Robert Frost, I hope I have a few more miles before I sleep.

Over the years, I have surely been influenced by changes in the Welsh and British scene, including particularly the upsurge of nationalism in the sixties, the debate on devolution in the seventies, and the troubles of the British left in the eighties. I find it difficult now to recapture the Fabian confidence in British institutions and their Welsh offshoots that I held in the early sixties. But many things are better. Thus, the changes in the moral and artistic climate since the early sixties seem to me to have left Wales and Britain generally a more humane, tolerant and civilized society as a result. Some of these wider concerns impinge more obviously in other writings of mine. Thus some of my major interests as an historian, and indeed as a citizen (for instance, Britain's international role, especially its relationship with Europe) hardly appear in these essays at all. Only a part of me appears here, but maybe that is as well.

The academic and scholarly influences that have affected me as an historian are harder still to determine. I have never been particularly attracted by the more doctrinaire versions of socialism or nationalism, two visions with which I have some sympathy. On the other hand, Welsh historians, the medievalists no less than the modernists, have been pre-eminent in showing that empiricism, like patriotism, is not enough. The late Professor David Williams of Aberystwyth, my old mentor, showed in his masterpiece on the Rebecca Riots that a *pointilliste* display of rich local detail could offer a way of understanding profound movements of social and political change. As one whose socialism has never been Marxist, I do feel that the glib rejection of Marxist approaches to the humanities and social sciences in the current post-modernist (and post-cold war) atmosphere is narrowing and deadening the range of historical inquiry. I hope and believe that the Welsh historians of the future will break free from this atlanticist strait-jacket as they have done from other conventional wisdoms in the past. Let us continue to be (as Alan Taylor delighted to call himself) men and women who 'stir things up'.

One historical influence upon me is beyond question. For me and many others, the experience of being in the history department at Swansea under Glanmor Williams, the doyen of our craft, was an inspiration and an awakening. The intellectual vitality and personal comradeship that bound together Glanmor Williams, Ieuan Gwynedd Jones, Rees Davies, Ralph Griffiths, John Davies, Prys Morgan, Peter Stead, myself and others in pursuit of a common cause was unforgettable. Aberystwyth, Bangor and Cardiff all produced major scholars and important scholarly achievements in this period. But by common consent it was Swansea that became (to use Glanmor Williams's description of working-class Merthyr) 'the matrix and crucible' of Welsh historical writing in the sixties. It has been a decisive stimulant in the self-understanding and perhaps self-confidence of modern Wales.

I hope that these essays will be of interest, not only in themselves, but also as showing how one individual responded to the course of later twentieth-century Wales as it unfolded in the historical profession. They are the product of far too many friendships and partnerships, not only with historians in Wales, but in England, Ireland, the United States and elsewhere, to be listed here. The main debts are clear enough. Professionally, as I have shown, they are to the Swansea history department, staff, students and academic leader, in the years 1958–66. Personally, they are to another former Welsh historian at Aberystwyth and one-time researcher for the Board of Celtic Studies. I hope very much that my beloved Jane would have liked this book.

Plas Penglais, Aberystwyth   *KENNETH O. MORGAN*
July 1995

Acknowledgements

The papers printed here first appeared in the following works and are reprinted by kind permission of the original publishers.

1. R. R. Davies *et. al.* (eds.), *Welsh Society and Nationhood* (University of Wales Press, Cardiff, 1985), 232–50.
2. *University of Wales Review* (1964), 7–10.
3. *National Library of Wales Journal*, XVI (2) (1969), 163–71.
4. *Welsh History Review*, 4 (4) (1969), 367–80.
5. *Welsh History Review,* 6 (3) (1973), 288–312.
6. *Welsh History Review*, 10 (4) (1981), 398–430.
7. *Bulletin of the Society for the Study of Labour History*, 30 (1975), 22–37.
8. Church in Wales publications (Penarth, 1966).
9. Jay Winter (ed.), *The Working Class in Modern British History* (Cambridge University Press, 1983).
10. *Journal of Contemporary History*, 6 (1) (1971), 153–72.
11. *Ceredigion,* V (4) (1967), 311–46.
12. *Welsh History Review*, 16 (1) (1992), 93–109.
13. Glanmor Williams (ed.), *Merthyr Politics: The Making of a Working-Class Tradition* (University of Wales Press, Cardiff, 1966), 58–79.
14. David Butler and Anthony King (eds.), *The British General Election of 1966* (Macmillan, 1966), 245–9.
15. David Butler and Anthony King (eds.), *The British General Election of 1964* (Macmillan, 1965), 265–77.
16. Ralph A. Griffiths (ed.), *The City of Swansea: Challenges and Change* (Alan Sutton, Gloucester, 1990).

17. *Transactions of the Honourable Society of Cymmrodorion* (1960), 35–52.
18. *Transactions of the Honourable Society of Cymmrodorion* (1984), 149–71.
19. Geraint H. Jenkins (ed.), *Politics and Society in Wales, 1840–1922* (University of Wales Press, Cardiff, 1988).
20. *Transactions of the Honourable Society of Cymmrodorion* (1972), 65–85.
21. Judith Loades (ed.), *The Life and Times of David Lloyd George* (Headstart publications, Bangor, 1991), 1–16.
22. Stewart Williams (ed.), *Glamorgan Historian* III (1966), 35–51.
23. Kenneth O. Morgan, *Labour People: Leaders and Lieutenants, Hardie to Kinnock* (Oxford University Press, 1987), 69–77.
24. National Library of Wales, Aberystwyth, 1989.
25. Paul Barker (ed.), *Founders of the Welfare State* (Heinemann, London, 1985), 105–13.
26. *The New Welsh Review*, 3 (1988), 31–9.

I
Politics

The Welsh in English Politics, 1868–1982

The growing centrality of Wales in English and British public life has been a pronounced feature of the history of the United Kingdom from the later Victorian period onwards. During the hundred years that have passed since then, the idea and the impact of Welsh nationality have become far more precisely defined and recorded – ever since Matthew Arnold apparently buried the Welsh without trace in the swirling mists of the Celtic twilight, in his eloquent and profoundly misleading lectures given in 1866 while he held the chair of Poetry at Oxford University. From the 1870s, indeed, the Welsh, like the Scots, have surged on relentlessly to fill major voids in British social and cultural life. They have added substantially to the cosmic consciousness of the British people in the twentieth century, a process which still continues.

This growing impact of the Welsh upon English society between the 1870s and the 1980s could, indeed, be illustrated in a great variety of ways. It could be demonstrated, for example, in terms of education. As is well known, the national cultural revival within Wales, and the total restructuring of its system of elementary, intermediate and higher education between 1889 and 1902, led, well before the First World War, to an immense export to England of schoolteachers and other academics. The effect of this, both through institutions such as the National Union of Teachers and more generally, in shaping the intellectual framework within which a popular culture could evolve, was far-reaching and something in which Welsh people took legitimate pride. The impact of the Welsh was also evident in many of the professions, notably in the law courts where the forensic and dialectical skill of Welsh judges and barristers was frequently noted, quite apart from the unique talents of one 'little Welsh attorney'. In the medical profession also, stimulated by the founding of the National School of Medicine at Cardiff, the Welsh produced surgeons and specialists of great distinction, to serve the hospitals and medical schools of England. In the world of industry and commerce, of course, the advent of the Welsh was immensely influential both upon management and on the trade unions. From the troubles of the mining industry in the 1920s, when the Coalowners' Association headed by Sir Evan Williams confronted the Miners' Federation led by Arthur Cook, down to the crises at British Leyland in the early 1980s, Welshmen were frequently to the fore, both as capitalist employers and, far more characteristically, as officials of major trade unions. Again, in the field of literature and the arts, the emergence of the ill-named 'Anglo-Welsh' school of poets, novelists and short-story writers from the 1930s onwards, through such periodicals as Keidrich Rhys's *Wales* and Gwyn Jones's *Welsh Review*, had a powerful influence upon the cultural sensibilities of the English-reading world. And no account of the contact of the Welsh with their English neighbours in the present century would be complete without reference to popular sport and to rugby football in particular, whose emotional messianic appeal has been traced by David Smith and Gareth Williams in a splendidly evocative official history of the Welsh Rugby Union.[1]

In all these varied areas, the impact of the Welsh upon England, and the English-speaking world, has been consistent and penetrating. Yet there is justification for elevating politics above all other aspects in this context. For the changes that galvanized Welsh life and the relations of the principality with England from the 1870s onwards – that process of interlinked social, economic and cultural transformation that went on well beyond the end of the Second World War in 1945 – took place within a largely political framework. Many of the decisive landmarks in modern Wales were political. There were the franchise reforms of 1867, 1884, 1918 and 1928; the advent of democracy at the parliamentary and the local government level; the framing of new Welsh political aspirations and objectives; the growing recognition not simply as a region, another Yorkshire or Kent, but as a nation. The very concept of what it meant to be Welsh, from the days of Gladstone onwards, was conditioned in large measure by political change. The growing impact of the Welsh in other areas of English, British and transatlantic life – educational, professional, industrial, literary or sporting – was projected against a political background which gave new meaning to the sense of Welsh identity, from the era of Tom Ellis and David Lloyd George to that of James Griffiths and Aneurin Bevan.

[1] D. Smith and G. Williams, *Fields of Praise* (Cardiff, 1981).

It was this truth that was indeed perceived by Aneurin Bevan himself when he declared that 'the most revolutionary power in the world is political democracy', the explosive force of which doctrinaire Marxists never understood.[2] So no apology need be offered here for adopting a largely political perspective in examining the impact of the Welsh upon various strata of English life from the late-Victorian era down to the early 1980s. For through adopting such a method the very concept of Welsh nationhood can be most fully understood.

The advent of the Welsh, their invasion of English political space in the modern period, was first located in that remarkable era of Liberal party ascendancy that lasted from the 'great election' of 1868 down to the end of the First World War. Until then, the Welsh impact upon English politics had been almost non-existent since the age of the Tudors. Wales provided simply occasional 'noises off' from a forgotten hinterland or a drowned landscape, as in the mysterious eruption of the Scotch Cattle in the 1820s, the Merthyr rising of 1831, or the attacks on tollgates by the Rebecca rioters in the early 1840s. Matthew Arnold in those same lectures in Oxford maintained that the Welsh were 'ineffectual' in politics, in eternal revolt against 'the despotism of fact', including presumably political fact.[3] His views were paralleled by those of a Welsh radical contemporary in 1866, the pacifist Henry Richard of Tregaron, who wrote that Welsh electoral politics were almost 'feudal' in character, redolent of Celtic clansmen struggling for their respective chieftains.[4] The Welsh members of Parliament were largely obscure squireens. In the words of a later Welsh MP, Stuart Rendel, they were 'in an inferior category, a cheaper sort of member'.[5] There was only one well-known native politician, Henry Richard himself – and he was the exception that proved the rule. For Henry Richard was really an international celebrity, a cosmopolitan free trader, Cobden with a Cardiganshire accent, 'an inveterate peace-monger' to adopt Michael Foot's self-description. Richard had left Cardiganshire in his early twenties and viewed the politics of his native land, until the mid-1860s, very much from the outside.

Then, in the decades following the famous election of 1868, with its sweeping Liberal gains and political evictions after the poll, all this changed, very rapidly and dramatically. The whole tempo of Welsh politics from the 1870s onwards followed a unique rhythm,

[2] A. Bevan, *In Place of Fear* (London, 1952), 39; speech in the defence debate, 15 February 1951 (*Parl. Deb.*, 5th ser., Vol. 484, 734).

[3] M. Arnold, *On the Study of Celtic Literature* (London, 1867), 102, 106.

[4] H. Richard, *Letters on the Social and Political Condition of Wales* (London, 1867), 80.

[5] F. E. Hamer, *Personal Papers of Lord Rendel* (London, 1931), 313.

significantly different from that of England. Long before the outbreak of world war in 1914, Wales had been transformed into a populist democracy and into an impregnable stronghold of the British left. As a result of this process, the effects of this Welsh regeneration upon English politics were sweeping and conclusive.[6]

First, there emerged in English politics a unique Welsh presence and style. A cluster of new themes arose, largely concerned with the social and civic grievances of Welsh Nonconformists, that were forced upon the sluggish attention of hitherto indifferent English party politicians. There was reform of the system of land tenure on the model achieved in Ireland in 1881, a demand that reached its climax during the Welsh Land Commission that held its sessions between 1893 and 1896. There was temperance reform, a priority symbolized by the passage of the Welsh Sunday Closing Act in 1881, the first statute to apply a separate legislative principle to Wales as distinct from England. There was the sweeping revamping of the Welsh educational system through the Intermediate Education Act of 1889 that set up over a hundred 'county' schools, the university colleges of Bangor, Aberystwyth and Cardiff that led to the creation of the national University in 1893, the emergence of the Central Welsh Board and, finally in 1907, the launching of the Welsh Department of the Board of Education. Above all, there was the contentious and persistent issue of the disestablishment of the Church of England in Wales. To the later twentieth century, Welsh disestablishment may appear a time-worn and parochial matter, of little wider concern. But it involved major principles of religious, civic and national equality. It embodied all the aspirations of the Nonconformist majority. In 1868, disestablishment in Wales was a virtual non-issue. When it was first raised in the Commons in 1870, it gained a derisory forty-seven votes, in marked contrast to the triumphant passage of Irish disestablishment a year earlier. But twenty-one years later it had gained such momentum that it was a major item on the Liberals' Newcastle Programme of 1891. By 1914, aided by the 1911 Parliament Act which had curbed the House of Lords' veto, Welsh disestablishment was on the point of becoming the law of the land. Its fulfilment came shortly after the armistice, with the enthronement of the first archbishop of Wales in June 1920. Disestablishment was a quiet, undramatic revolution. It lacked the fire and fury of Home Rule and the other demands of the Irish Nationalists. But its successful accomplishment was part of a peaceful process of social equality and democratization that helped reconcile

[6]For fuller discussion and documentation of this theme, see my *Wales in British Politics* (Cardiff, new edn., 1980), chaps. II–VI, and also my *Rebirth of a Nation: Wales 1880–1980* (Oxford and Cardiff, 1981), ch. II.

denominations and classes within Wales, and helped consolidate the
status of the principality within the United Kingdom.

Long before 1914, in fact, through disestablishment and other
issues, there is a detectable change in the rhetoric and dialogue of
English politics. In the daily and weekly newspaper press, in the
quarterlies and the literary reviews, on platform and pulpit, Welshness
had become a distinct and respectable political theme.

This process was closely linked with an important, yet little
regarded, change in the structure of English, or more specifically
Liberal, party politics. Until the mid-1880s, there was no coherent
mechanism for Welsh political demands to be presented before the
Liberal party leadership. The historic transformation took place
between 1886 and 1892.[7] In those years of Liberal parliamentary
opposition, the strategy of Stuart Rendel, the Englishman who sat as
member for Montgomeryshire, for the Welsh members to become
more effective as a pressure-group and to achieve far greater political
effectiveness, chimed in with the desire of Francis Schnadhorst and
the machine men of the National Liberal Federation to recast British
Liberalism at its foundations after the disastrous schism over Irish
Home Rule in 1886 which had led to the secession of Joseph
Chamberlain, Hartington and other Liberal Unionists. In 1886–7, new
Liberal Federations were formed for north and for south Wales,
represented together in a Welsh National Liberal Council. Most
significant, these new bodies were affiliated directly to the National
Liberal Federation (NLF) based in party headquarters in London.
This move was ratified at the annual conference of the NLF at
Nottingham in October 1887 – when, revealingly enough, Welsh
disestablishment was first adopted as a plank on the Liberal party
programme. Conversely, the Scottish Liberal Association was not
directly affiliated to the NLF in London, and it is not fanciful to
explain the greater political success of the Welsh in influencing the
national Liberal party in 1886–1914, compared with the Scots,
through their organic relationship with the parent body. The Scots, by
contrast, suffered from their own exclusion. The legacy for Wales of
this historic development in the late-1880s is writ large upon
subsequent passages of the history of Wales, with perhaps the
University itself, which owed so much to the sympathy shown by
Gladstone and other Liberal leaders, as the main landmark. *Si
monumentum requiris . . .*

[7]See K. O. Morgan, *Wales in British Politics*, ch. III; M. Barker, *Gladstone and
Radicalism* (Hassocks, Sussex, 1975), 117–28; G. V. Nelmes, 'Stuart Rendel and
Welsh Liberal political organization in the late-nineteenth century', *Welsh History
Review*, 9 (4) (1979), 468–85.

A second feature of this period of Liberal ascendancy was that the human instruments of Welshness thrust themselves aggressively upon English political consciousness as the alien outsiders they were. Some of these Welsh Liberals operated within English constituencies in London, Birmingham and Middlesbrough. The London Welsh, with their intensely-developed chapel life, became a leading pressure-group in promoting the *Cymru Fydd* brand of nationalism in the later 1880s. They became a powerful support for the later political advance of Lloyd George.[8] Most important of all was Liverpool where, by the end of the century, there were many thousands of first- or second-generation Welshmen encamped on Merseyside.[9] By 1900, there was a score of Welsh-language chapels (at least 20,000 first- or second-generation Liverpudlians were said to be Welsh-speaking), a Welsh publishing house was soon to be formed, while a leading Welsh newspaper, *Y Cymro*, was launched in 1890 by Isaac Foulkes, a publisher and novelist from rural Denbighshire. The North and South Wales Bank, founded in Liverpool in 1836, lent financial assistance to builders and small businessmen from Anglesey and elsewhere. The Liverpool Welsh were prominent, then, in the business, commercial and religious life of that troubled city. Inevitably, too, they were active in Liverpool Liberal politics, notably in the Toxteth, Walton and West Derby divisions, where the chapel-going, temperance-minded Welsh worked most uneasily alongside their Irish papist allies. Birkenhead, across the Mersey, also boasted a large Welsh community: an important national eisteddfod was held there in 1917, celebrated for the posthumous award of the bardic chair to the Trawsfynydd shepherd, Hedd Wyn.

Apart from the role of the Welsh in English constituency politics, many Welshmen emerged as members of Parliament for English or Scottish seats. In the halcyon year of 1906, over a dozen were recorded as representing English constituencies after that Liberal electoral landslide (some highly authentic like Leif Jones in Appleby or Timothy Davies in Fulham, others distinctly anglicized like John Simon in Walthamstow or Donald Maclean in Bath).[10] One prominent Welsh-born MP in Scotland was J. Wynford Philipps, later Viscount St David's, who defeated Keir Hardie in the famous by-election at Mid-Lanark in April 1888. Oddly enough, despite his base in

[8]For example in his famous address on the war and 'the little five-foot-five nations' to a London Welsh audience at Queen's Hall, 19 September 1914.

[9]P. Waller, *Democracy and Sectarianism. A Political and Social History of Liverpool, 1868–1939* (Liverpool, 1981), 9–10, and biographical notes; J. R. Jones, *A Welsh Builder on Merseyside* (Liverpool, 1946); O. Thomas and J. M. Rees, *Cofiant y Parch. John Thomas D.D.* (London, 1898).

[10]*South Wales Daily News*, 5 February 1906.

Pembrokeshire and his close attention to the Welsh tithe riots at the time, Philipps referred to himself repeatedly before the Mid-Lanark electors as 'an Englishman who lived in Wiltshire'.[11] It is noticeable that the same amnesia afflicted Roy Jenkins of Abersychan when campaigning as Social Democratic candidate in Hillhead, Glasgow, in February 1982. Maybe the northern air produces some curious effect on the chemistry of Welsh candidates in Scottish by-elections.

But the main human agents of Liberal Welshness, of course, operated from within Wales itself. They were backed up by a powerful community presence, a thriving newspaper press in both languages, a buoyant Nonconformist pulpit, a vigorous cultural revival in music and literature, and a mass working-class involvement in politics in industrial and rural areas alike. From this stimulating background, there emerged a new generation of radical middle-class Non-conformist Liberals within the Welsh Parliamentary Party, adroitly presided over from its formation in 1888 by the Englishman, Stuart Rendel, a close personal friend of Gladstone himself. These new Welsh MPs were very different from the old style of mid-Victorian survivors like Henry Richard (died 1888) Lewis Llewelyn Dillwyn (died 1892) or Sir Henry Hussey Vivian (died 1893). They were younger, more aggressive, more politically sophisticated, more avowedly national or nationalist in their ideological approach.

This was a half-forgotten generation which deserves to be re-surrected and honoured anew. There was Ellis Griffith, an eloquent barrister who represented Anglesey from 1895 to 1918. There was Herbert Lewis, a modest, constructive Clwyd solicitor, who repres-ented the boroughs and county of Flintshire between 1892 and 1918, and who also achieved much effective work on behalf of public education in partnership with the historian, H. A. L. Fisher. There was the schoolteacher, Willliam Jones, member for Arfon between 1895 and 1915, whose 'silvery tones' captured the fancy of *Punch*. There was Llewelyn Williams, a barrister, journalist, historian, man of letters and politician of almost limitless talent, who sat for Carmarthen Boroughs from 1906 to 1918. There was Samuel Evans, another lawyer who sat for Mid-Glamorgan from 1890 to 1910 before serving with much distinction as president of the Court of Admiralty. And in the depths of the industrial coalfield, there was D. A. Thomas, Lord Rhondda, the coalowner of the Cambrian Combine, the 'Czar of Tonypandy' in 1910, but also MP for Merthyr (and briefly for Cardiff) for twenty-two years between 1888 and 1910, and a brilliantly creative figure at the

[11]K. O. Morgan, *Keir Hardie, Radical and Socialist* (London, 1975), 28; *The Scotsman*, 6 April 1888.

local Government Board during the supreme crisis of the First World War in 1917.

There were two others, more notable still. Tom Ellis, a reflective cultural nationalist of beguiling charm, member for Merioneth between 1886 and 1899, was a politician of real charisma who became Liberal chief whip at thirty-five and died of tuberculosis at the age of forty, his talents largely unfulfilled. Ellis was New College on top, Bala and Cefnddwysarn underneath. It was wholly characteristic that some of his most memorable addresses should be given before the Welsh Guild of Graduates, and that he should occupy his leisure moments by studying the works of the seventeenth-century puritan and mystic, Morgan Llwyd. For many in the Darwinian age, Tom Ellis was the very embodiment of the Celtic genius in politics.[12] And finally there was David Lloyd George, who represented Caernarfon Boroughs without a break from his famous narrow by-election victory in 1890 until just before his death in 1945. Lloyd George was a politician from his turbulent school-days and his childhood instruction at the feet of 'Uncle Lloyd' – perhaps even from the age of five when, as a junior onlooker, he attended Liberal election demonstrations during the great contests of 1868. From the time of the Boer War, if not earlier, he became the very personification of Welsh radicalism. In so many ways, Lloyd George was an untypical Welsh Liberal. As connoisseurs of the television screen will have observed, he was no puritan, whether at home or away. He was impatient with the constraints and the parochialism of the Nonconformist chapels, and with the petty snobberies of the 'beatified drapers' and 'glorified grocers' on the *sêt fawr*.[13] Contradictions abounded in him throughout his kaleidoscopic career. The 'big beast' contained multitudes. Yet, without doubt, he did more than anyone else in politics to bring Welsh affairs to the controversial forefront of British politics, in relation to disestablishment, tithe, education, devolution and much else besides. As a dominant figure in Liberal and coalition governments in 1905–16, and then for six years as a prime minister, he never lost his unique compelling identification with his own nation, his abiding point of reference throughout the storms that beset his long career.

These Welsh Liberals were different in many significant respects from their successors, or some of them. They were not socialists –

[12]J. A. Spender, *Sir Robert Hudson: A Memoir* (London, 1930), 24. There is a stimulating account of Ellis's career in N. C. Masterman, *The Forerunner* (Llandybïe, 1972).

[13]See David Lloyd George to his Wife, 10 June 1890 and 1 December 1890 (K. O. Morgan (ed.), *Lloyd George: Family Letters, 1885–1936* (Oxford and Cardiff, 1973), 28, 39–40, in which D. H. Evans and his wife are referred to; L. Masterman, *C. F. G. Masterman* (London, 1939), 200.

certainly Lloyd George could never be so styled, for all his frequent essays in collectivism, notably when in fruitful partnership with Christopher Addison at the Ministry of Munitions. A major objective for his brand of 'new Liberalism' was to ward off the extreme threat of socialism. Nor were these Liberals nationalists in the sense that Plaid Cymru later understood that term. They sought equality for Wales within the British and imperial framework, not exclusion from it. Welsh Home Rule was, broadly speaking, simply not on their agenda. The one occasion when it appeared to be, the *Cymru Fydd* movement of 1894–6, proved to be a massive and disastrous fiasco that divided Liberals in rural and industrial Wales almost fatally. Nor were these Welsh Liberals much concerned with the future of the Welsh language. In that optimistic age, Tom Ellis or Lloyd George felt that the Welsh language would last for ever, and the linguistic census figures from 1891 to 1911 appeared to confirm that confidence in the sense that the numbers of Welsh-speakers were steadily rising. Even so, these Welsh Liberals, with all their limitations or apparent limitations, made Wales a political reality. Indeed, as has been seen, they were distinctly more successful than the Scots in the 1886–1914 period. Even the Conservative party, unionist to the bone, was by 1914 converted to the idea of Welsh nationality which in the past it had dismissed or derided. No longer would Conservatives make political capital by bland pronouncements that 'there was no such place as Wales'. After all, the Welsh had steered clear of the separatism – and the incipient violence – of the Irish. *Cymru Fydd* and Sinn Fein were worlds apart. This was a creative, energetic generation of late-Victorian and Edwardian Liberals whose powerful legacy lives on in the Wales of the later twentieth century.

During this period of Liberal ascendancy, the perceptions of Welshness became far more subtle, sensitive and intelligent. As David Smith has argued,[14] this corresponded with the new images created for themselves by Welsh publicists and propagandists during the heyday of 'imperial Wales'. The Celtic mists conjured up by Matthew Arnold at Oxford were finally dispelled. Gladstone himself became an imaginative interpreter of the meaning of Welshness in politics – notably in a famous address to 60,000 people at Singleton Park in Swansea in 1887[15] – and where this titan led, lesser mortals followed. Down to the Edwardian high noon before 1914, the English politicians' view became far more positive and sympathetic, and all parties shared in this process. It is true that, during the fierce

---

[14]D. Smith, 'Wales through the looking-glass', in idem. (ed.), *A People and a Proletariat* (London, 1980), especially 220–5.

[15]*The Times*, 5 June 1887.

campaigning and controversy that surrounded the fight for Lloyd George's 'people's budget' in 1909–10, with its contentious taxes on land, some more traditional attitudes began to surface. A few Conservatives were prone to reflect upon the distinctive Celtic personality and methods of the Welsh chancellor of the Exchequer. Cosmo Lang, archbishop of York, denounced 'that mysterious possession affecting the Celtic temperament which is called the "hwyl" which makes the speaker say he knows not what and excites the audience they know not why'.[16] These Unionist suggestions that the Welsh were somehow not quite as British as the English were, and that some Britons were more unionist than others, gave Lloyd George admirable grist for his dialectical mill on the public platform. He delighted to point out the hypocrisy of Unionists, who emphasized the indivisibility of the empire from the Old Man of Hoy in the north to Van Diemen's Land in the far south, in attempting to isolate the Welsh in so blatant a fashion. 'They would have to reckon with the Welshman this time.'[17]

But, in general, these attacks were untypical of Conservative attitudes and assumptions. As has been shown above, the Conservative party had become increasingly more attuned to Welsh nationality. No longer would Tory spokesmen dare to ridicule the Welsh language and folk culture as little more than 'bardic fragments', as H. C. Raikes (Cambridge University) had once done in the 1880s.[18] Lloyd George and his apparent political extremism stirred up nothing remotely resembling the ugly anti-semitism excited by the implication of Rufus and Godfrey Isaacs and Herbert Samuel in the Marconi affair. For Conservatives now understood that the cases of Wales and of Ireland were clean different. They now asserted that the main argument for not disestablishing the Welsh Church was derived from its inherent Welshness. Historically and sentimentally, the Church was rooted in the age-long experience of the Welsh people since the early middle ages, whereas the Nonconformist denominations were *arrivistes* of the seventeenth century. Welshness, for Conservatives, was now safe and acceptable, as it was for a landowner like Sir John T. Dillwyn-Llewelyn who served as president of the Welsh Rugby Union. Wales now implied an accommodating, safe identity, another form of social control.

This kind of Welsh impact upon English politics was weakened fatally with the downfall of the Liberal party after 1918, and the

[16]Cited in J. H. Edwards, *Life of David Lloyd George*, Vol. IV (London, 1913), 126.

[17]A particularly effective exposition of this line of attack was in his speech at Queen's Hall on 'rural intimidation', 23 March 1910.

[18]*Parl. Deb.*, 3rd ser., CCCXXII, 482 (7 March 1988). Raikes was postmaster-general at the time.

decline of religious Nonconformity that was associated with it. It was perhaps cheapened by the crude jingoism of 1914–18 in which even great Liberal littérateurs like Sir John Morris-Jones and Sir Owen M. Edwards used the stereotypes of Welsh nationhood to abuse the 'Hun', and to sustain the war effort and the premiership of Lloyd George.[19] As a result, Welsh Liberalism underwent an erosion of morale from which it never recovered. Thereafter, the sagging fortunes of Lloyd George after 1918 were often associated with some kind of perception of Welshness. J. M. Keynes in his *Economic Consequences of the Peace,* written in 1919 (but in a passage not published until 1933 when the dust had partly settled), linked some of the weaknesses of the peace settlement to the feckless qualities of a Welsh prime minister allegedly 'rooted in nothing'. He bracketed an account of Lloyd George's mercurial personality with some colourful and far-fetched speculations on the 'hag-ridden magic and enchanted woods of Celtic antiquity'.[20] There were other critics to relate the unorthodox financial aspects of the 'honours scandal' and the Lloyd George Fund to the well-known kleptomania in which Taffy had traditionally indulged. Later on there appeared political novels which focused attention on some of Lloyd George's better-known public and private weaknesses, such as Arnold Bennett's *Lord Raingo* (1926) and later on Joyce Cary's political trilogy, of which the most notable was *Prisoner of Grace* (1952). But these novels made no attempt to associate Lloyd George's defects with a wider condemnation of the Welsh in politics. Indeed, Andy Clyth in *Lord Raingo* was a Scot, while Chester Nimmo, the central character in Cary's novels, is an Englishman apparently from Devon. Despite the First World War, therefore, despite the extraordinary decline of the public stature of the once all-powerful imperial figure of Lloyd George, the Liberal legacy, in relation to political perceptions of Wales, remained a distinctly positive one.

A new form of the Welsh impact on English politics arose with the rise of the Labour party from the end of the First World War down to the later 1960s. Wales had been a slow starter in Labour politics prior to the great six-months' coal lock-out of 1898. Until then, Labour had been but a section of a broad-based Liberal coalition; trade union leaders like Mabon (William Abraham) of the Cambrian Miners were inseparable in their outlook from middle-class Nonconformist

[19]For example Sir J. Morris-Jones in *Y Beirniad*, October 1914, 217–24, and October 1915, 191–205; Sir O. M. Edwards in *Cymru*, February 1915. I have discussed this point at greater length in 'Peace movements in Wales, 1899–1945', *Welsh History Review*, 10 (3) (1981), 405–8 (published in this volume, 84–116).
[20]J. M. Keynes, *Essays in Biography* (London, 1933, reprinted 1961), 35–6.

Liberals. Even Keir Hardie's first election for Merthyr Tydfil in the 'khaki election' of 1900 owed everything to Liberal votes and relatively little to the strength in the valleys of the Independent Labour Party (ILP).[21] But the years of Taff Vale and Tonypandy, together with the great Bethesda lock-out in the Penrhyn quarries in 1900–3, brought about a profound shift of industrial and political attitudes. By the 1918 'coupon election', the fifty-seven-strong parliamentary Labour party included ten Welsh MPS. From 1922 onwards, Labour dominated the parliamentary representation of Wales with its monopoly of power throughout the coalfield from Llanelli to Pontypool. Even in the débâcle of 1931, Labour largely retained its strongholds in the Welsh valleys, and Welsh influence within the Labour party in the 1930s was pervasive. It was reinforced before and after the 1945 election by other Welshmen serving as Labour members for English and Scottish constituencies, including Rhys Davies (Westhoughton), Elwyn Jones (West Ham South), Moelwyn Hughes (Islington) and Emrys Hughes (South Ayrshire). Alongside these political developments, in the trade union world several major trade unions had prominent Welsh figures at the helm. There were Jimmy Thomas in the National Union of Railwaymen, Bob Williams in the Transport Workers, and above all the Miners' Federation of Great Britain (MFGB), where one general secretary from south Wales, Frank Hodges, gave way in 1924 to another, the far more militant personality of Arthur Cook.

One consequence of this Labour ascendancy that now unfolded in the wake of the older Liberalism, was that a new type of Welsh politician loomed large for the English to try to comprehend. The older type of Labour man, like Mabon or William Brace, was hard to distinguish from the Liberals. Mabon lived on until 1920, and the ethic of 'Mabonism', expressing the imperatives of class collaboration and industrial harmony, survived with him. But immediately after the First World War, there was a massive transformation. The rise of a man like Vernon Hartshorn of Maesteg, prominent in the MFGB executive and a member of the first two Labour Cabinets, illustrated the rise of a new, authentic cadre of working-class leadership, conscious of its class base.[22] More powerful still, the products of the Central Labour College in Regents Park in London – Aneurin Bevan, Ness Edwards, James Griffiths, Morgan Phillips, Bryn Roberts and many others – formed a new élite as certainly as did the Aberystwyth-trained middle-

---

[21]Morgan, *Keir Hardie* . . ., 117–18; and K. O. Fox, 'Labour and Merthyr's khaki election of 1900', *Welsh History Review*, 2 (4) (1965), 364–5.

[22]See P. Stead, 'Vernon Hartshorn: miners' agent and Cabinet minister', *Glamorgan Historian*, VI (1969), 83–94; and idem, 'Working-class leadership in south Wales, 1900–1920', *Welsh History Review*, 6 (3) (1973), 329–53.

class Liberals of the *Cymru Fydd* vintage of the 1880s and 1890s.[23]
Here were new Welsh 'space invaders' in the *lebensraum* of the English
political culture – but speaking the language of class rather than of
community.

Unlike their Liberal predecessors, the Welsh Labour MPs were less
closely identified with specifically Welsh issues. Indeed, many of these
issues had passed away with the older secretarian politics of pre-1914.
Welsh disestablishment in 1920 had seemed a massive anti-climax
after a century of struggle. As time went on, many Welsh Labour MPs
were Welsh only in accent, and with greater social mobility and cultural
homogeneity after 1945 even this characteristic was often less in
evidence. By the 1960s, with such names as Callaghan, Donnelly,
Padley and McBride among their number, many of them were Welsh
by occasional residence and little more.

From the 1930s to the 1960s, much of the Welsh Labour politics
was embodied in the rival appeals of two major figures, James Griffiths
and Aneurin Bevan. They offered a twin challenge for the Welsh
political psyche. James Griffiths was, from the start of his career in the
ILP before the First World War, uniquely associated with specifically
Welsh themes. He came from a remarkable and vigorous cultural
heritage in the Amman valley in east Carmarthenshire which J.
Beverley Smith has admirably delineated.[24] From his entry into
Parliament in 1936, Griffiths was identified with the Welsh aspects of
the troubles of the coal-mining and tinplate industries, with tuberculosis in rural and industrial Wales, with the social services offered by
Welsh local and central government. Within the Attlee government in
1945–51, even when colonial secretary in 1950–1, he fought hard for
the recognition of Wales within the centralized structure of the gas,
electricity and transport industries after nationalization.[25] He fought
hard, too, for Welsh interests on the Cabinet Machinery of Government Committee from May 1946 onwards. He battled (in vain) for
effective executive powers to be given to the new Council for Wales
inaugurated by Herbert Morrison in 1948.[26] James Griffiths was from

[23]See W. W. Craik, *The Central Labour College* (London, 1964), notably the
biographical appendices.

[24]J. B. Smith et al., *James Griffiths and his Times* (Cardiff, 1977); and Professor
Smith's article, 'John Gwili Jenkins (1872–1936)', *Transactions of the Honourable
Society of Cymmrodorion*, (1974–5), 191–214.

[25]Cf. J. Griffiths, 'Note on the Electricity Bill, 17 December 1946', CP (46),
462 (PRO, CAB 129/15).

[26]Material in prime minister's files, including correspondence between Griffiths
and Attlee, 1946 (PRO, PREM 8/1569); memorandum on 'The Administration of
Wales and Monmouthshire', PRO, CP (48), 228 (CAB 129/30); correspondence
between Griffiths and Morrison, October 1948 (NLW, Griffiths papers, C/2/6–11).

the start deeply influenced by older Welsh Nonconformist radical values. He fought hard against the erosion of the Welsh Sunday Closing Act of 1881 by the 1960 Licensing Bill introduced by the Macmillan government. Significantly enough, his brother, Amanwy, was a noted eisteddfodic bard.

By contrast, Aneurin Bevan, the member for Ebbw Vale from 1929 to 1960, viewed socialism in class and international terms. Despite a warm commitment to Welsh communitarian values, derived in part from his Welsh-speaking Baptist father in Tredegar, he had no sympathy with Welsh or other particularist deviations from the socialist norm. In a famous intervention in the first Welsh day debate in the House of Commons in 1944, he inquired, sarcastically, how precisely Welsh sheep differed from sheep grazing in Westmorland or the Highlands.[27] After 1945 he argued vigorously – and successfully – against James Griffiths within the Attlee administration in opposing any recognition of Wales within the framework of centralized economic planning.[28] In addition to this, with his observations about 'vermin' and other oratorical excesses, Bevan became for a time, in the English press and on the radio, the popular symbol of the Welsh extremist of his day – an impression reinforced by the activities of other incorrigible rebels on the far left such as S. O. Davies and Emrys Hughes. To the 'Radio Doctor', Bevan represented a 'Tito from Tonypandy'. His very name was mispronounced, with heavy emphasis on the second syllable, allegedly to distinguish him from Ernest Bevin elsewhere in the Attlee government and the political spectrum, but probably just to be offensive. For a brief period, at the time of the 1950 and 1951 elections, Aneurin Bevan appeared to have aroused a kind of hostility towards 'the unspeakable Celt' unknown since Lloyd George and the 'people's budget'. However, it did not last very long or go very deep. By the time of his death in 1960, Bevan, deputy-leader of the Labour party, an old associate of Beaverbrook, a shadow foreign secretary who had warmly championed Britain's retention of nuclear weapons, almost a patriot at the time of Suez, could safely be embraced by the British establishment in Fleet Street and beyond. By the 1980s, it had become a journalistic cliché to contrast the 'legitimate' parliamentary socialism of the Bevanite left of the 1950s with the Marxist extremism of the Bennite battalions in the constituencies a generation later.

In the era of Labour dominance, the influence of the Welsh within the English political structure was far more widespread than during the period of Liberal ascendancy between 1868 and 1914. From the

[27]Welsh day debate, 17 October 1944 (*Parl. Deb.*, 5th ser., CCCCIII, 2311–14).
[28]J. B. Smith *et al.*, op. cit., 41–2.

1920s, the Welsh penetrated far into the utmost recesses of the party machine. The most notable of all within the Labour party bureaucracy was Morgan Phillips, a Welsh-speaking ex-miner born in Aberdare, subsequently active in Bargoed, the dominant apparatchik of British socialism, and from 1944 to 1962 the most powerful secretary of the Labour party since the days of Arthur Henderson. Attlee once observed to Crossman that Phillips's draft papers 'always had to be translated from the Welsh'.[29] Phillips was to be succeeded as general secretary in 1962 by a Welsh émigré from Birkenhead, Len Williams.

With the massive outflow of Welsh unemployed workers from the staple industries of the valleys in the later 1920s and the 1930s, the Welsh became increasingly assertive within English constituency politics. They were active in transforming and radicalizing the politics of Dagenham and Hounslow, of Cowley and Coventry, and of Slough with its important trading estate and government training centre which acted as a magnet for many Welsh emigrants. Industrially and politically, the Welsh became known as a militant, perhaps rebellious, element. De-skilled as coal-miners or steel-workers, they now became active in general unions of the unskilled such as the Transport Workers or the General and Municipal Workers. Herbert Austin, the car manufacturer, noted their 'bloodymindedness' and the role of Welsh unionists in leading the first-ever strike at his Longbridge works in 1929.[30] Welsh shop stewards were in the forefront in Oxford in the first strike at the Pressed Steel works in 1934.

Politically, the life of the tranquil conservative university city of Oxford was much transformed by the impact of many thousands of immigrants from the 'depressed areas'. This applied to the Welsh above all, since over 10 per cent of migrants into Oxford between 1926 and 1935 (especially in 1933–5) came from Wales.[31] Firebrands like Tom Harris and Dai Huish, both former activists in the South Wales Miners' Federation, were prominent as shop stewards for the Transport Workers and in the politics of the Labour party.[32] Welsh

[29]The best source for Phillips lies in the general secretary's papers in the Labour party archive, Walworth Road, London; J. Morgan (ed.), *The Backbench Diaries of Richard Crossman* (London, 1981), 234 (26 May 1953).

[30]R. Church, *Herbert Austin: The British Motor Car Industry to 1941* (London, 1979), 151.

[31]G. H. Daniel, 'Some factors affecting the movement of labour', *Oxford Economic Papers*, 3 (February 1940), 144–79; and idem, 'A Sample Analysis of Labour Migration into Oxford' (unpublished University of Oxford D.Phil. thesis, 1939), where a sample of 600 Oxford Welsh male workers in 1937 is used.

[32]R. C. Whiting, 'The Working Class in the "New Industry" Towns between the Wars: the case of Oxford' (unpublished University of Oxford D.Phil. thesis, 1978), especially 186ff, 251, 274ff, 353–4, 391. I am much indebted to Dr Whiting for some helpful advice on this important topic.

trade unionists were active in starting up the Cowley Labour party, in the neighbourhood of the Morris works, in 1934, shortly after the Pressed Steel strike. Several Welshmen fought key local elections in wards of Oxford previously uncontested by Labour. Emrys Roberts, a south Walian from the National Union of Railwaymen (NUR), won a major victory in Oxford's South Ward in 1937. The exact quality of the Welshness of these militants is open to some question. They did not generally participate in the more traditional aspects of cultural life in the city – in the Welsh chapels, in the Oxford Welsh male voice choirs, or in the Pressed Steel rugby team. Their national awareness expressed itself in radical politics and in industrial militancy which saw Tom Harris of the Transport and General Workers Union (TGWU), for instance, dismissed by Morris Motors in 1938 – and later reinstated after a one-day strike. The following year, the TGWU itself removed Harris as a branch secretary – which led to some car workers defecting to the Amalgamated Engineering Union in consequence. It is no surprise to see Harris and other Welshmen prominent in the Oxford Spanish Democratic Defence Committee at the same period. In their distinctive fashion, the Welsh helped break the mould of politics in constituencies like Oxford in the English midlands and some of the home counties. They acted as catalysts for political change as Irish immigrants had done before them in English and Scottish con- stituency politics, and in the 'new unionism' of the 1880s and the 1890s. The incursion of the Welsh in the depression years of the 1930s was on a smaller scale, but it was a part of the road that led inexorably to 1945.

More generally, the Welsh in major unions such as the TGWU and the Miners' Federation (the National Union of Mineworkers from January 1945), together with such figures as Bryn Roberts of Abertillery and the Central Labour College who served as general secretary of the National Union of Public Employees from 1934 onwards, added massively to the popular strength of the Labour party before and after the 1945 election. Sometimes, indeed, the Welsh emerged under other auspices. For example, there was Arthur Horner, general secretary of the NUM in 1946 after a long period as president of the south Wales miners. He was a noted Communist, as also were younger men like Will Whitehead, Will Paynter and Dai Francis. Yet Horner confirms the general argument. For all his communism, the tribune of Maerdy, 'little Moscow', lent his weight to the Labour triumph of 1945, to bringing about the nationalization of the mines, and drafting the 'miners' charter' with Emanuel Shinwell, and to shoring up the position of the Attlee government during the difficult years of the wage freeze and devaluation of 1948–50. There was a brief prospect of Arthur Horner even joining the National Coal Board, which would have been the poacher turning gamekeeper indeed.[33] Horner, understandably and probably rightly, declined in the end. Yet Arthur Horner, 'incorrigible rebel' as he proclaimed himself in his fascinating memoirs, was another paradigm example of the successful permeation of English public life by the radical culture of the Welsh valleys.

What these Labour men (there were few women of significance) contributed to politics that was distinctively Welsh is hard to define. Indeed, their very notion of Welshness was singularly elusive. The overall verdict must be that the specifically Welsh aspect of Labour politics was a limited one. Labour continued to place its emphasis primarily upon centralization and class solidarity which united the workers of all countries. That was certainly the view of Morgan Phillips who looked with intense suspicion upon ideas for a Welsh secretary of state, an elective council, or other symbols of particularism or quasi-nationalism.[34] The 'Parliament for Wales' campaign in the early 1950s was sternly rebuffed by the Labour leadership and the party machine. Even the creation of a Welsh Regional Council of Labour within the Labour party, uniting the efforts of all the local constituency parties under the secretaryship of Cliff Prothero, was gained only with some difficulty in 1947.[35] And yet Welshness in politics obstinately refused to disappear during the Labour ascendancy. After the fall of the Attlee government in 1951, pressure continued to mount for a secretaryship of state on the same lines as that achieved for Scotland as long ago as 1885. The record of Welsh pressure for economic regional assistance in 1945–51, while impressive and successful in many ways, emphasized the difficulty experienced by Welsh Labour MPs who had no direct voice in the Cabinet to proclaim their views. It was an attitude strongly reinforced by the powerful north Wales trade-union leader Huw T. Edwards of the TGWU, the first chairman of the Council for Wales.[36]

[33]A. Horner, *Incorrigible Rebel* (London, 1960), 182–3. There is a sympathetic and perceptive treatment of Horner in H. Francis and D. Smith, *The Fed* (London, 1979), especially 145–70. Also see the entry on Horner in J. Bellamy and J. Saville (eds.), *Dictionary of Labour Biography*, Vol. 5 (London, 1979).

[34]Goronwy Roberts to Morgan Phillips, 5 August 1950 (Labour party archives; general secretary's files).

[35]Minutes of Labour Party Organizational Sub-Committee of NEC, 15 January 1947 (Labour party archives).

[36]See the Labour parliamentary deputation on unemployment in Wales, 1946 (PRO, PREM 8/272) and the Welsh deputation to discuss unemployment, 1946 (PRO, LAB 43/1); also the correspondence between D. R. Grenfell and W. Mainwaring and Attlee, 1946, in PREM 8/1569. Grenfell and Mainwaring complained to the prime minister, 14 August 1946, that the government's attitude seemed 'to repudiate entirely the claims of Wales as a nation'; they repeated their demand for a minister for Wales, if not necessarily a secretary of state. There is

The establishment of a Ministry for Welsh Affairs by the Conservatives (admittedly under a Scotsman, Maxwell-Fyfe, in the first instance) increased the pressure for the Labour party to be more adventurous. In the end, even Aneurin Bevan, with great reluctance, accepted the pledge to create a Welsh secretaryship of state being placed on Labour's general election manifesto in 1959. Bevan's biographer and close friend, Michael Foot, was later to prove himself a warm enthusiast for devolution. The key figure was James Griffiths, eventually to be appointed the 'charter secretary' for Wales by Harold Wilson in 1964. Griffiths was the vital link, along with important north Wales Labour MPs like Cledwyn Hughes and Goronwy Roberts, connecting the class revolt of the 1930s with the very different, more diffuse political pressures that led to a Welsh Office being created in 1964, and to Welsh devolution emerging on the political agenda later in the decade.[37] By the later 1960s, the Labour party was evolving a very different outlook towards the government of Wales from that displayed during the Morrisonian centralism of the Attlee years after 1945. More indirectly, less insistently than their Liberal predecessors, the Welsh Labour MPs helped reinforce the impact of the Welsh upon the wide open spaces of English politics.

The Labour ascendancy reached a high water-mark in 1966 when Labour captured thirty-two seats out of thirty-six in Wales. More than at any other time in its history, Labour seemed the voice and conscience of Wales, as rooted in Anglesey and Conwy as in Rhondda and Ebbw Vale. Since that time, there has been a period of intense change. Indeed, the picture offered by Welsh politics in the early 1980s is scarcely recognizable compared with that of 1966. The Labour party went through great turmoil in the 1970s and, with two seats lost in the 1979 election, showed clear signs of losing its old dominance, especially in north and central Wales. Only two constituencies north of the Teifi and the Brecon Beacons returned Labour MPs in that year, East Flint and Wrexham – and the MP for the latter was later to defect to the Social Democrats. The Conservatives, who gained three seats in 1979, also showed much change, as did Plaid Cymru as the struggle for the party leadership between its two remaining MPs in 1981 suggested. The import of the Social Democratic Party (to which three Welsh Labour MPs had defected by early 1982)[38] has still to be

important material on this theme in the Huw T. Edwards papers in the National Library of Wales (general correspondence files, arranged chronologically), notably Edwards to Herbert Morrison, 27 November 1946.

[37]James Griffiths, *Pages from Memory* (London, 1969), 164–6.

[38]T. Ellis (Wrexham), E. H. Davies (Caerphilly), J. Thomas (Abertillery). No SDP candidates in Wales were elected in the June 1983 general election.

properly assessed. Its achievement in polling over a quarter of the votes in the Gower by-election in September 1982, while respectable enough, was hardly a sign that the mould of Welsh politics was being cracked asunder.

The main impact of the Welsh upon British politics in this later period, unlike the periods of Liberal and Labour ascendancy in the past, came largely from outside the mainstream of party politics. There was the resurgence of Plaid Cymru between 1966 and 1970, and the forceful (sometimes unlawful) campaigning of the Welsh Language Society. The victory of Gwynfor Evans in the Carmarthen by-election in July 1966, followed by high Plaid Cymru polls at Rhondda West and Caerphilly in 1967–8, led directly to the appointment of the Crowther-Kilbrandon Commission on the constitution. The vibrant debate on Welsh and Scottish devolution conducted throughout the 1970s was a direct consequence of this new, if temporary, stimulus from Welsh politics.

In the later 1970s, there was some evidence of Welsh infiltration at Westminster and in Whitehall on something like the old pattern. Two successive leaders of the Labour party, James Callaghan (Cardiff South East) and Michael Foot (Ebbw Vale) represented Welsh constituencies. In the years of the Callaghan government, from 1976 to 1979, the prime minister and the deputy prime minister were both Welsh parliamentary representatives. There were also a Welsh foreign secretary (David Owen), a Welsh home secretary (Merlyn Rees), a Welsh lord chancellor (Lord Elwyn-Jones), even a speaker of the House who came from Tonypandy. Within the Callaghan administration, there existed the so-called Welsh Mafia or 'Taffia', a tier of under-secretaries and other junior ministers. In addition, devolution in Wales and Scotland was a major political priority from the introduction of the two devolution bills in late 1976 until just after the fall of the Callaghan government in April–May 1979. This process of Welsh infiltration continued after the May 1979 general election, with the Conservative government of Margaret Thatcher inaugurating a Welsh Select Committee which could conduct searching inquiries into the steel industry, water, broadcasting and other important questions. The final decision to proceed with a fourth channel on television, with extended transmission in the Welsh language, also owed much to pressure in the principality from Gwynfor Evans and other leading figures.

In fact, this later prominence of Welsh affairs was wholly deceptive. The Welsh impact upon English politics was, in reality, less substantial and more episodic than in the past. This, indeed, had been the case even before Labour's electoral defeat in 1979. There were some positive gains from the new Welsh presence in national politics. There was the substantial new funding released for the Development Agency, and the creation of the Development Board for Rural Wales under Emrys Roberts in 1976. But the 'Taffia' was really a product of the labyrinthine manoeuvres within the parliamentary Labour party, and the particular position of James Callaghan. The new prominence of devolution owed everything to the existence of a minority government dependent on Liberal and Nationalist support: after all, even the Ulster Unionists enjoyed some prominence at this time, and for the same reason. Devolution also owed much to the tactical exigencies of the 'Lib-Lab' pact between James Callaghan and David Steel early in 1977, in the negotiation of which Cledwyn Hughes then the chairman of the parliamentary Labour party, was a key figure.[39] Otherwise, it can only be concluded that Wales was less central politically now than in the period of Liberal domination from 1880 to 1914, less even perhaps than in the Attlee years of Labour rule between 1945 and 1951. Wales in the early 1980s, especially under a Conservative government which looked with hostility upon manifestations of Celtic separatism, could well be returning to the periphery of English politics.

This might not necessarily be of tragic significance. By the 1980s, parliamentary pressure of the traditional type by Welsh or other pressure-groups was markedly less important, the power of members of Parliament themselves more circumscribed. The years of economic recession since the huge increase in oil prices in 1974 demonstrated the relative powerlessness of the British parliamentary system in the face of external forces, world movements of trade or of capital, the power of the multinational corporations, the crisis in energy supplies. The activities of bureaucrats in Brussels or of some remote sheikhdom in the Persian Gulf might have a greater influence upon the economic life of some Welsh constituency – and indirectly upon its long-term cultural vitality as well – than all the blandishments of parliamentary representatives at Westminster. The older forms of peaceful persuasion and of constitutional agitation through party politics might be reaching their natural close.

The ultimate significance of the Welsh impact upon English politics between 1868 and 1982 will always be a matter of some controversy. Many, indeed, may consider it a saga of failure. Some Nationalists, perhaps, may rightly point out that, despite a hundred years of parliamentary pressure and artifice, Wales has never at any stage come anywhere near to winning the prize of self-government. Welsh Nationalists or republicans had to gaze across the waters of the Irish

[39] A. Michie and S. Hoggart, *The Pact* (London, 1978), 115ff.; personal information from Lord Cledwyn.

Sea to observe the fulfilment of their ambitions. In 1982, Welsh Home Rule looked further off than ever. To this complaint, it can only be replied that the limits of the achievement accurately reflected the limits of the aspiration. There was never any decisive pressure for Welsh self-government, neither at the time of the *Cymru Fydd* movement in the 1890s, nor in the later 1970s either, as the devolution referendum in Wales on 1 March 1979 showed so cataclysmically. The entire course of Welsh politics had followed a very different pattern from the relentless thrust for national self-determination in southern Ireland. Beyond the mountain fastnesses of Welsh-speaking Gwynedd, Plaid Cymru had made no permanent inroads.

Conversely, some Unionists, across the political spectrum, may consider the entire political story to be one of deceit, a bogus concoction of an essentially fictional identity. There are those who may still see Wales as a region rather than as a nation, a mere 'geographical expression' as Bishop Basil Jones of St David's described the land in 1886.[40] This view may be endorsed by a London historian who has argued that Wales ought to be defined in terms of a multiple series of self-contained economies rather than by means of the 'metaphysical' concept of nationality.[41] Clearly, by adopting so restricted a viewpoint, the forest of nationhood would soon be obliterated by the trees of the census returns. It may well be doubted whether even the concepts of English or French nationality would survive so destructive and depressing a treatment. The clearest answer to all this is that it is simply unhistorical. Over the past 120 years, the national charac-teristics have without question manifested themselves in a growing variety of aspects of Welsh society, in education, in cultural and literary activity, in social organization (witness the Welsh TUC, founded in 1973), in religious and intellectual life, and indeed in politics, as the earlier discussion has tried to demonstrate. The process of self-discovery and of self-definition inherent in the emergence of the idea of nationhood remains, with all the failures and disappointments, and accretions of fable and myth, inseparable from the history of the Welsh as a people in the recent past.

In many ways, the Welsh invasion of English politics is highly instructive. It provides, on balance, one of the success stories of twentieth-century Britain – of which there have been precious few. Further, it may be taken to illustrate a profound, if sometimes neglected, truth – that Wales is not a revolutionary country. Its complex national evolution is not a crude product of economic determinism, and it fits most uneasily into the Marxist diagnosis, as

[40]Charge to St David's diocese, 1886.
[41]M. J. Daunton, *English Historical Review*, XCVII (1982), 161.

Aneurin Bevan amongst others pointed out. There have been, of course, important episodes of class uprising and potentially revolutionary action, which historians of great talent have rightly examined in depth and in detail, such as the Scotch Cattle, the Merthyr rising of 1831, the Chartist affray at Newport, the tithe riots of the 1880s, the Tonypandy riots of 1910, the 'stay-down' stoppages of 1935. Such episodes, fascinating in themselves, have been the exception rather than the rule. There have been occasional violent upsurges or civil disorders or ancient expressions of folk protest – usually provoked by brutal or insensitive authorities such as the Merthyr magistrates in 1831 or the Cambrian coalowners in 1910. Such episodes have been present to an equal degree in England and Scotland. Indeed, it may be suggested that Liverpool and Glasgow have shown more violence and turmoil within their societies over the past century or more than have any comparable communities in Wales. Nor did the explosive events at Bristol, Brixton or Toxteth in the recent past provoke any similar response in Wales: indeed, the last serious Welsh race riots took place in Cardiff, Barry and Newport back in 1919.[42] Apparently revolutionary documents such as the half-syndicalist *The Miners' Next Step*, published by the Unofficial Reform Committee at Tonypandy with the blessing of the Plebs League in 1912, bodies like the Workers' Freedom Groups with which Aneurin Bevan himself briefly flirted in the early 1930s, were diversions from the main theme. Their significance can be greatly exaggerated. In the two world wars, the Welsh, for all their dissenting and pacifist traditions, flocked to sustain the 'patriotic' cause as enthusiastically as their English neighbours. The dominant tendency in Welsh history is emphatically not a militant tendency.

For every act of civil disobedience or industrial direct action that several historians have so faithfully chronicled, there were countless, less spectacular, instances of legal, constitutional, peaceful protest that provided the essential stimulus for change. Even in the worst horrors of the 1930s, with its mass unemployment and near-starvation in the valleys, the main thrust of radical endeavour went towards con-structive, constitutional activity – towards building up the 'Fed' and other trade unions, working through the Workers' Educational Association and the extra-mural world revitalized by Coleg Harlech, capturing the citadels of local government, sustaining the main fabric of local social services, revitalizing the Labour party, striving to capture the commanding heights of the economy by political means. The creative genius of the Welsh has been, in reality, the total opposite

---

[42]There is an excellent account in N. Evans, 'The south Wales race riots of 1919', *Llafur*, III (1) (Spring 1980), 5–29.

of that diagnosed by Matthew Arnold. It has been businesslike and
cerebral. It has lain, not in pursuing the futile chimera of pseudo- or
quasi-revolutionary activity, but in artistry in the uses of political
power. The Welsh have seen politics as a compassionate, civilizing
force, in which, to cite Aneurin Bevan again, each freedom won was
protected only be adding another to it. They have seen, too, the limits
to political action, a point driven home by Tom Ellis in a moving
evocation of the spirit of the 'Cymric dead' in an address at Bangor in
1892.[43] They have usually viewed politics as 'power in the subjunctive
mood'.[44] They have used politics as a motor for national renewal, to
make and to change history, and thereby to change themselves.

1984

[43]T. Ellis, 'The Memory of the Kymric Dead', in *Addresses and Speeches by the
late T. E. Ellis M.P.* (Wrexham, 1912), 3–28. This fascinating volume includes other
discussions on art, a Welsh school of architecture, and the preservation of Welsh
literary and historical records.

[44]This vivid phrase appears in B. Crick, *In Defence of Politics* (paperback edn.,
1964), 146.

2

The People's University
in Retrospect

'The history of learning in Wales of which the new University is but a symbol and a manifestation, is not merely the history of a movement or of a phase of national activity. It is the history of the nation itself.'[1] The words are those of the first official history of the University of Wales, published in 1905. As a commentary on the educational movement in Wales in the later nineteenth century, it is of course romantic, even partisan. Yet it may be that it comes nearer the truth than do later, more objective studies of higher education in Wales. In 1905, the visionary idealism of *Cymru Fydd* was still a vital force, the career of Tom Ellis was still fresh in the memory, and David Lloyd George was championing Welsh radicalism with a vision that was shortly to take him into Campbell-Bannerman's Liberal government. The authors of the official history, Cadwaladr Davies and W. Lewis Jones, were themselves the products of the national movement which their book celebrated; as Liberal Nonconformists, they were acutely aware of the role of radicalism in revitalizing Welsh life in the exciting years since 1868. Their history was based on the premise that the University symbolized a native cultural tradition that dated from the Celtic saints, but which had lain dormant and unprotected until the heroic endeavours of the past forty or fifty years. Further, the attitude that Davies and Jones expressed in 1905 has since become the prevailing orthodoxy – that the ultimate validity of the University resides in the unity and the nationhood of Wales. This was stated explicitly by the

[1]W. Cadwaladr Davies and W. Lewis Jones, *The University of Wales* (London, 1905), xi.

Haldane Committee in 1918, in rejecting proposals (emanating, then as now, mainly from the Cardiff Senate) to defederalize the University. It has been accepted by Sir Alexander Carr-Saunders[2] and others that the University of Wales rests upon premises that make it different in kind from other universities, and which override administrative considerations.

It is this national awareness that has so coloured, and even embittered, current arguments for and against federalism in the University, and which makes a basic consensus so hard to achieve. On the one hand, we are given pragmatic objections, of varying substance, which allege that the University is administratively impractical. On the other hand, we hear statements to the effect that administrative convenience is not the highest criterion, and that the social and cultural values of Welsh nationality form the ultimate test. The debate seems to be conducted on different planes, and the federalists and the anti-federalists to be concerned with different scales of values. What is, however, beyond dispute is that the arguments from history, emotional and even sentimental though they may sometimes be, cannot be ignored. There is a distinctive quality to the University of Wales still, which differentiates it equally from Oxbridge and from Redbrick. In however intangible a form, it symbolizes a century of national achievement in which successive generations have taken legitimate pride. 'For', to quote Davies and Jones again, 'the University of Wales is the creation not of sovereigns and statesmen, but of the people themselves.'

Democracy

The 'People's University', *Prifysgol y werin*, is a product of nineteenth-century democracy. It forms perhaps the most glorious monument to the national revival which revitalized Wales in the later Victorian era. This period was in many ways the most exciting and compulsive in the history of modern Wales. Throughout the whole of Welsh society, there seemed to be a new dynamic mood of change. In its political life, Wales was regenerated in the years after the 1867 Reform Act. From being one of the most conservative sections of the British Isles, it had become by the 1880s a stronghold of radicalism, which it remains to the present time. The key to this process was the advance of democracy, the vast expansion of the parliamentary electorate and the growth of the new popularly-elected local authorities. Measures like the Reform Acts of 1867, 1884 and 1918, and the Local Government Acts of 1888 and 1894 formed the milestones of a profound social and

[2]Sir A. Carr-Saunders, *New Universities Overseas* (London, 1961), 111.

political revolution, with the old Anglican squirearchy displaced by a new, emergent Nonconformist middle class, the spokesmen for the excluded majority of Welsh society. At Westminster, a new Welsh Parliamentary Party became a powerful force in British politics, led by such militant young spokesmen as Tom Ellis, D. A. Thomas, Ellis Griffith and, above all, David Lloyd George. In Wales itself, new Liberal county councils overthrew the long ascendancy of the landowning justices of the peace. Until the First World War, the dominance of Liberal middle-class Nonconformity was almost unchallenged, while its very strength made it the vehicle for a growing nationalism.

These years witnessed unparalleled economic growth, with the massive expansion of heavy industry in the south Wales coalfield. By 1914 Wales had become the major coal-exporting area in the world. Immigrants poured in their thousands into the industrial south, at first from the impoverished and over-populated rural hinterland, later from outside Wales. In the decade from 1901, Wales was absorbing immigrants at a faster rate than the United States – at a time when economic activity in much of Britain generally was in decline. As the old rural Wales went into eclipse, a new, industrialized Wales was emerging, cosmopolitan yet essentially Welsh, a new 'American Wales' which was supplanting the old 'Welsh Wales' of the countryside.[3] The chambers of commerce of Cardiff, Newport and Swansea were the spokesmen of a new mercantile élite, wedded to free trade and 'finance imperialism', fiercely proud in their way of the growing power of their own regional base in south Wales as the Cardiff press bore witness. Finally, the later nineteenth century was marked by a new cultural renaissance such as Wales had seldom experienced, distinguished by the lyric poetry of W. J. Gruffydd, Silyn Roberts and T. Gwynn Jones, the literary grace of Owen M. Edwards and the academic scholarship of J. Morris-Jones and John Edward Lloyd. All were coloured by an intense patriotism, above all the patriotism of optimism and of youth. *Nid Cymru Fu ond Cymru Fydd*, wrote Morris-Jones in 1892. They communicated to a public more receptive than ever before, with the great advance of literacy and of public education. Everywhere the cultural genius of Wales seemed to be flowering anew, in the eisteddfod, in the vast expansion of newspapers and periodicals of all kinds and in the new impetus for the teaching of Welsh in schools.

In all these ways, then, Wales seemed a land in the throes of exciting and dynamic upheaval. It seemed caught up in the surge of democracy and of national self-awareness that characterized so many countries in

[3]This distinction is drawn by Sir A. Zimmern, *My Impressions of Wales* (London, 1927), 37.

Europe and the New World. It is not surprising that this phase of
Welsh history, from the 1860s to 1914, is so frequently subjected to
romanticizing and to idealization of *y werin*. In spite of all the changes
that have affected Wales since the First World War, the glow of hope
from these earlier years still lingers on.

The significance of the University

The importance of the University of Wales in the history of modern
Wales is above all that it forms a synthesis of all the different threads of
the national movement of the later nineteenth century.

It symbolizes, first, the new self-confidence of Liberal Nonconformity in its effort to create and sustain its own social institutions.
The architects of the University, it is true, included men of all parties
and of all creeds. Anglicans were active in the movement for higher
education – Lord Aberdare and Stuart Rendel being notable examples.
The Aberdare Committee in 1881 reported that Anglicans had
contributed a larger share to the college at Aberystwyth than had any
other denomination.[4] Nevertheless, the University Colleges were
peculiarly the achievement of the *pays réel* of Liberal Nonconformity,
which felt excluded by such Anglican institutions as Oxford,
Cambridge and Lampeter. Sir Hugh Owen and his colleagues, in their
campaign for Aberystwyth in the 1870s strove quite consciously to
create a new dissenting middle-class élite in Wales, to supplant the old
squirearchy and to control the rising working-class democracy.[5] It was
part of the Nonconformist entry into public life, most dramatically
shown by the career of the young Llanystumdwy solicitor, David Lloyd
George. The campaigns for public support were strongly redolent of
the voluntaryist traditions of the chapels, and *Sul y Brifysgol* became a
nation-wide institution.

The most notable products of the early days of the Welsh colleges
were such champions of the new national radicalism as Tom Ellis, S. T.
Evans and Ellis Griffith. In 1893, St David's College, Lampeter,
declined to be associated with the new University charter, rightly
regarding the University as dominated by Nonconformists, many of
whom had notoriously little love for the Church and sought its
disestablishment. It was argued that the University was creating a new
Liberal establishment of its own – a charge given some substance years

---

[4]*Report of the Committee appointed to inquire into the condition of Intermediate and
Higher Education in Wales* (C.3047, 1881), xvii.

[5]This point is stimulatingly discussed by Gwyn A. Williams, 'Sir Hugh Owen',
Pioneers of Welsh Education (Swansea, 1964), 57ff.

later when the members returned to Parliament by the University from 1918 to 1950 were almost all Nonconformist Liberals.[6] (The exception was the pacifist Maitland Lloyd Davies, and he was the grandson of John Jones of Talsarn.) The outstanding personality in the early years of the University was John Viriamu Jones, an apolitical personality himself, but the son of an eminent Congregationalist minister, and the brother of Brynmor and Leif Jones, both Liberal MPs for many years. Together with disestablishment of the Church, the new system of higher education formed the outstanding legacy of Welsh radicalism.

Similarly, the University demonstrated the economic expansion of Wales. Men like Owen and Lord Aberdare were acutely aware of the need to create a new class of technical specialists to run the new industry. Like many others of their generation, they were impressed by the technical and scientific strength of the German empire, and by the way in which its educational system served as the forcing ground for industrial expansion. To meet the growing competition from overseas rivals, Britain would have to emulate the celebrated 'Prussian schoolmaster' as well as the Prussian industrialist, and in this process Wales would have its share. In appealing for local support, the pioneers of the university colleges stressed the element of economic self-interest. This found sympathy equally from the Cardiff Chamber of Commerce and from the South Wales Miners' Federation. The University College of Swansea (1921), indeed, began life as a college of technology. In time, developments such as the departments of forestry at Bangor, of geography at Aberystwyth (with the Plant-Breeding Station founded in 1919), of engineering at Cardiff and at Swansea were to serve as testimony to the value of the colleges as a form of economic investment.

Finally, the University served as a focus and stimulus for the new cultural renaissance. Welsh studies were assiduously fostered in all three (later four) colleges, with Bangor in particular leading the way. The linguistic studies of J. Morris-Jones and the historical researches of J. E. Lloyd lent a new vigour to the growing cultural awareness of Wales – a process continued after the war with the foundation of the University Press and the Board of Celtic Studies. In the persons of W. J. Gruffydd and T. Gwynn Jones, the professor-poet joined the preacher-poet as a power in the land. Politically, economically and culturally, the University served as a symbol of national achievement. Most of its students were from Welsh homes, many of them very poor.

[6]Sir Herbert Lewis (1918–22; T. Arthur Lewis (1922–3); G. Maitland Lloyd-Davies (1923–4); Capt. Ernest Evans (1924–43); Prof. W. J. Gruffydd (1943–50). Lloyd-Davies took the Labour whip in the House.

Up to 1940, over 90 per cent of the student population was resident in
Wales. The small minority of English students tended to be
distinguished exceptions attracted to the Welsh colleges by the
academic reputation of such men as Fleure and Ethé at Aberystwyth,
Ker, Seth and Burrows at Cardiff and Sir Henry Jones at Bangor.
Further, through the pioneering of extra-mural teaching (notably at
Aberystwyth after 1920 under the direction of Herbert Morgan), the
University was able to sustain its roots in the community that fostered
it, and to offer a new self-respect to working men, victimized by the
economic system. Above all, the University was a token of national
equality. Wales had attained parity with England and Scotland, in the
provision of higher education as in other respects. The 'county' schools
of the Intermediate Education Act of 1889 ensured a steady flow of
recruits to the colleges, while as school masters and mistresses, many
of the new graduates transmitted the ethos of their University to new
generations. This, then, was the social transformation of late-Victorian
and Edwardian Wales. In 1880, a mere 189 Welshmen enjoyed higher
education of any kind.[7] By 1914, there was a federal, national
university from which thousands had already graduated. It is not
surprising that Viriamu Jones could reflect in 1896, with pardonable
exaggeration, that 'the history of Wales during the last twenty-five years
has been little else than the history of its educational progress'.[8]

The colleges

For some decades, this early fervour coloured the growth of the
university colleges. The story of their development and union has been
told often enough, and needs no repetition here[9] – the foundation of
the three colleges at Aberystwyth (1872), Cardiff (1883) and Bangor
(1884), and the final creation of a degree-awarding, teaching university
in 1893. At every stage, the colleges operated in the maximum glare of
national publicity, since their progress seemed in a special way to
demonstrate the new-found self-respect and self-confidence of
'neglected Wales'. The 'treason' of the notorious *Llyfrau Gleision* of
1847 was at last being forgotten. Much of the early aura surrounding
the University dated from the pioneering days of the college at
Aberystwyth in the 1870s. This aura may, indeed, be somewhat
deceptive. The 'college by the sea' was a struggling institution in its

[7]Speech by Sir Hussey Vivian (*Parl. Deb.*, 3rd ser., CCLXVII, 1141ff).
[8]J. Viriamu Jones, 'The University of Wales', *Wales*, January 1896, 6.
[9]The best account is D. Emrys Evans, *The University of Wales* (Cardiff, 1953).
Also helpful is T. I. Ellis, *The Development of Higher Education in Wales* (Cardiff,
1935). For the political background, see Kenneth O. Morgan, *Wales in British
Politics, 1868–1922* (Cardiff, 1963).

early days and by the 1880s of doubtful academic standing. The furore provoked by the Aberdare Committee in 1881, which threatened its extinction, gave it new life and a permanent and stable basis. It was at this time very much of a regional college, with few roots in the expanding industrial south. Nevertheless, the Aberystwyth tradition cannot be dismissed as wholly mythical: it symbolized the ethos of *Prifysgol y werin*. If the largest single contribution to its funds came from the wealth of David Davies of Llandinam, there were nevertheless the 100,000 subscriptions of under half a crown. The enthusiasm the college provoked from countless unknown farm labourers and quarrymen cannot be cynically disregarded. Further, the remarkable generation of students who congregated at the college during the days of Thomas Charles Edwards's principalship, Tom Ellis and Ellis Griffith, Owen M. Edwards and John Edward Lloyd, T. F. Roberts and Marchant Williams, illustrated the kind of hitherto untapped ability residing in the Nonconformist *pays réel* of Liberal Wales.[10] Aberystwyth was thus able to appeal to a latent national sentiment that spilled over into the later pressure for a federal university. It was a powerful force in the new Guild of Graduates, the first two wardens of which were the most eminent of Aberystwyth ex-students, Owen M. Edwards and Tom Ellis, now Liberal chief whip. Ellis's vision of the Guild as enjoying an organic relationship with the social culture of Wales as a whole was derived from those early, heady days at Aberystwyth.[11] If American universities had their 'Wisconsin Idea', Wales proclaimed the 'Aberystwyth Idea', steeped with the folk-nationalism of *Cymru Fydd*. In their different ways, the first principals of Cardiff and Bangor, Viriamu Jones and Harry Reichel (the latter at first abused as an Ulster Tory and a High Churchman), subscribed to the same vision. They gave their blessing to the movement for a national university that received its final official sanction in 1893 with the royal charter.

The twentieth century

Until 1893, therefore, the university movement seemed to show the same relentless progress as the national causes in general. But in the present century, like those causes, its character has gradually changed. As the political and religious passions that accompanied the creation of the University in the 1880s died away, so the University as an

[10]The best introduction to the history of Aberystwyth is through works dealing with its first three principals: T. I. Ellis (ed.), *Letters of Thomas Charles Edwards* (Aberystwyth, 1953); David Williams, *Thomas Francis Roberts* (Cardiff, 1960); T. I. Ellis, *John Humphreys Davies* (Liverpool, 1963).

[11]See T. E. Ellis, 'The duty of the Guild towards the literature and records of Wales', *Addresses and Speeches* (Wrexham, 1912), 143ff.

academic institution became less and less distinguishable from those other 'provincial' universities springing up throughout Britain. The kind of disillusion provoked by other achievements of the national movement came to be extended to the University also. Even in the years before 1914, complaints were heard from nationally-minded Welshmen that the University was proving a disappointment to the pioneers of *Cymru Fydd*.[12] Although created to serve the 'needs of Wales', it was apparently failing to fulfil the kind of role in Welsh society that Ellis and his colleagues had envisaged. In short, the University was becoming less and less Welsh; the pressure from some quarters for defederalization was a symptom of this process. If Wales had obtained its own Parliament in these years, perhaps the decline in the University's national characteristics might have been halted. If Wales had shown the fierce separatism of the Progressive movement in the Mid-Western states of America, then perhaps in Wales also a new kind of local university could have emerged – as the old land-grant colleges in the Mid-West could promote the 'Wisconsin Idea' and serve as laboratories of social and political experiment.[13] But the pressure for Welsh separatism was negligible then – as it is today. Why should Wales wish to return to the impotence of political isolation? Why should it wish its university to share the national insularity of the National University of Ireland?

In fact, the University of Wales had been outward-looking from the start, with many of its abler students going on to do research at Oxford and Cambridge, and even at German universities. It became clear, in fact, that the University of Wales, like the national movement that gave it birth, was a victim of its own success. It was a monument to national equality, not to national separatism. The more it was able to emulate the standards of other universities in Britain, and to create links with them, the more secure would be its status. Also, in practice, the less Welsh it would become. The very progress of the University, therefore, seemed self-defeating.

In particular, growing concern was felt at the widening gulf between the University and the secondary schools, the latter run by the Central Welsh Board, one of the bastions of middle-class Nonconformity. Partly in response to this concern, the Haldane Committee was appointed in 1916.[14] Its report two years later seemed superficially to

[12] For instance, J. Arthur Price to J. E. Lloyd, 4 December 1902 (UCNW, Bangor, Lloyd papers, MSS.314, no. 455).

[13] See Charles McCarthy, *The Wisconsin Idea* (1912); Richard T. Ely, *The Ground under our Feet* (1938); Merle Curti and Vernon Carstensen, *The University of Wisconsin* (Madison, Wisconsin, 2 vols, 1949).

[14] *Royal Commission on University Education in Wales: Final Report* (Cd. 8991, 1918).

confirm the old national image of the University. It firmly declared against defederalization. It recommended that the National School of Medicine should become a constituent college (as should the new college at Swansea). It urged that the University should be even more firmly rooted in the democratic support of the Welsh people, through their local authorities. It therefore recommended that a penny rate be levied locally, in return for which local authorities would be given a majority of one on the University Court. (The local authorities still retain their preponderance even though their contribution to the University's income had dwindled from 38 per cent in 1920 to 2 per cent in 1964.) A University Press and a Board of Celtic Studies were to be instituted to promote the national culture, as the Guild of Graduates had in the past. Yet the ultimate effect of the Haldane Committee's findings were perhaps inevitably to strengthen the pressure towards Anglicization and disunion in the University. The old academic senate, one of the very few unifying institutions in Wales, was abolished, while the reconstituted Court totally failed to act as the kind of itinerant 'educational parliament' that Haldane himself fondly anticipated.[15] From 1920, the University severed most of its direct links with the *Cymru Fydd* traditions of the past thirty years. The depression of the inter-war years, the social revolution wrought by the Second World War, and the new upheaval by expansion and the Robbins Report – these are merely commentaries on the decisive chapter written in the early 1920s.

The position in 1964

What remains of the national ideals of the University of Wales today? It is clear that the national movement of the late nineteenth century has largely lost its impetus, its work mainly accomplished. Liberal Nonconformity no longer dominates the political and civic life of Wales. Since 1918 it has represented a declining and ageing element in Welsh society, *Cymru Fu* rather than *Cymru Fydd*. With the decline of puritanism in British life, the hold of the chapels is much diminished. The decline seems irreversible, though some residual strength was shown in the campaign against Bacchus in the Sunday Closing Act agitation of 1961. Liberal Nonconformity, therefore, no longer lends its old social homogeneity to the university colleges of Wales. Still powerful in the Court (a memorial to the Haldane Committee), it seems in such issues as the opening of student bars all too often at variance with the wishes of those who work in the University.

The pattern of economic change since 1918 has also been intense

[15]Viscount Haldane, *The University and the Welsh Democracy* (Oxford, 1922).

and sweeping. The closing of railway services marks a new stage in the erosion of the populist village culture of Wales, rural and industrial, on which the University was in large measure founded. The process of rural depopulation has now been extended to the inland mining villages; while the latest phase of economic development, based on steel and oil, is confined to a narrow coastal strip in the south, linked indissolubly with the economic and social complex of England. Young Welsh men and women are drawn more and more to the 'subtopian' sprawl of south-east England, to study in English universities and to teach in English schools.

Finally, native Welsh culture is much attenuated since the 1890s. In 1964 barely 25 per cent of the Welsh people speak their own language – among the students at the Welsh university colleges the proportion is below 20 per cent.[16] The inter-collegiate eisteddfod is a shadow of what it once was. The struggle to preserve Welsh culture and the Welsh language becomes more desperately defensive every year; all the resources of BBC (Wales) cannot turn back the tide of Anglicization and Americanization. It is this sense of erosion and decline that lends desperation to the controversy about the federal structure of the University. In a rapidly changing world, the University survives as a grand monument to the past, and a surviving focus of national unity. The defence is a rearguard action – though not necessarily an unsuccessful one. The University can arouse immense sympathy from the most divergent sources – as a glance at the supporters of the 'Friends of the University of Wales' will confirm. Nevertheless, there is prevalent a feeling that the arguments of the federalists and anti-federalists alike are less academic than in a broad sense, political. Should the University be preserved as a part of a decaying national tradition, a last ceremonial *recherche du temps perdu*?

It may be, however, that the current pessimism about the University and the Welsh nation will prove as exaggerated as was the uncritical optimism of the 1890s. Just as the hopes of the radicals of the late nineteenth century were inflated by Victorian beliefs in the inevitability of progress and the certainty of moral values, so the current disillusion and defeatism may also prove a passing vogue. It ought to be possible to respect the Welsh past, without becoming its prisoner. Welsh society is indeed rapidly changing, yet many of the changes might well be welcomed since they are likely to enhance the Welsh nation rather than to erode it. The glorious achievements of the nineteenth century should not obscure the physical poverty and intellectual isolation that marked so much of Welsh life then. Some of the recent changes in

---

[16]*Council for Wales and Monmouthshire: Report on the Welsh Language Today* (Cmnd. 2198, 1963), 89ff.

Welsh culture are the product of a much increased prosperity, diffused far more equitably than ever before throughout working-class sections of society. Others are the product of a cultural enrichment that is likely to leave Welsh (particularly Anglo-Welsh) culture freer from the dangers of being inward-looking and self-contained. Above all, the new transformations in Wales are largely the product of that very national equality for which the pioneers of Welsh education laboured, in the face of such heavy odds. The same is true of the University of Wales. In a world of large international units and assimilated cultures, it occupies an honoured place in a new and expanded pattern of higher education and social opportunity. The issue of federalism or defederalism is undeniably an important one, which rightly occupies the attention of the graduates of the University.[17] They are right to emphasize the historical antecedents of the University and to attack those critics who ignore them. But what is more important is that the University should not be dominated by a past tradition, however glorious. As it was able to triumph over poverty and failure in the past, so now it should be able to come to terms with affluence and success.

1964

[17]This article was written before the publication of the findings of the Commission on the University of Wales on 24 April 1964.

3

The Liberal Unionists
in Wales

Gladstone's first Irish Home Rule Bill of 1886 produced an immense crisis of conscience for the Liberal party. Whigs like Hartington on the right of the party, and radicals like Chamberlain on the left were fundamentally alienated. Ninety-three Liberals eventually voted against their own government on the second reading of the Irish Bill on 7 June: a new dissident 'Liberal Unionist' party was born. As a result, Gladstone's third government was ejected from office and the divided Liberals were heavily defeated at the subsequent general election. Some commentators have even claimed to detect the ultimate decline of the Liberal party in these events surrounding the Home Rule schism in 1886. In Wales, the divisions within the party were as painful as they were elsewhere. Seven Welsh members were among the ninety-three Liberals who voted against the second reading of the Home Rule Bill;[1] another, Richard Davies (Anglesey), abstained. Leading Welsh Liberals like Sir Robert Cunliffe, David Davies and Sir Hussey Vivian joined the Loyal and Patriotic Union which was committed to outright opposition to Irish Home Rule.[2] Several leaders of radical Nonconformity, among them Thomas Gee, editor of the influential *Baner ac Amserau Cymru*, and the Revd J. Cynddylan Jones, the eminent Methodist theologian, joined their Whig colleagues in the

[1]They were H. G. Allen (Pembroke District); David Davies (Cardiganshire); Sir J. J. Jenkins (Carmarthen District); H. Robertson (Meirioneth); C. R. M. Talbot (Mid-Glamorgan); Sir H. H. Vivian (Swansea District); Colonel W. Cornwallis-West (West Denbighshire). The four Welsh Conservatives also voted against the bill.

[2]*Baner ac Amserau Cymru*, 5 Mai 1886.

groundswell of protest against Gladstone's measure, on political, economic and especially on religious grounds. Nowhere was it felt more keenly than amongst Welsh Liberal Unionists that 'Home Rule was Rome Rule' and that the Protestants of Ulster must be sustained by their brethren elsewhere. In Wales truly the Orange card seemed the one to play. The growth of Liberal Unionism is, then, a significant episode in the evolution of Welsh politics in the late nineteenth century. Yet it remains almost totally forgotten or else ignored. Now, however, papers deposited in the National Library of Wales, especially those of Sir Hussey Vivian, later the first Lord Swansea, and those of Henry Tobit Evans of Aberaeron, illuminate some important facets of Welsh Liberal Unionism.[3] They shed important light upon a crisis of Welsh Liberalism in its crucial Gladstonian phase.

Sir Henry Hussey Vivian, a Swansea industrialist, the Liberal member of Parliament for Swansea District since 1885 (and previously member for Truro, 1852–7 and for Glamorgan from 1857 to 1885), was amongst the seven Welsh Liberals who voted against the second reading of the Home Rule Bill on 7 June 1886. He agreed with C. R. M. Talbot, the octogenarian member for Mid-Glamorgan and another rebel, that the Welsh people were allowing their 'infatuation' with Gladstone to overrule their political judgement.[4] 'The only logical course would be to appoint the G.O.M. Dictator or Czar', Vivian sarcastically commented.[5] In the July general election, Vivian was returned unopposed as a Liberal Unionist after the Swansea Liberal Association had voted by eighty to thirty to endorse him. Even so, his radicalism was too deep-rooted for his defection from his party to be enduring. During the critical days in May, he had been much involved in attempts to try to create a compromise between the Liberal factions over the exact powers to be accorded to the new Irish legislature. Hartington was frigid towards Vivian's overtures, but he went on to try to enlist support from Joseph Chamberlain and from Gladstone as well, though without success.[6] During the general election campaign, Vivian conspicuously refrained from coming out in opposition to old

[3]Only a section of the Vivian papers is concerned with politics: the majority are concerned with Vivian's industrial interests. There are several small collections of Tobit Evans's papers in the National Library; those which contain material of relevance here are MSS. 18,438B, 18,618C and 18,882B. Much the most valuable for the study of Liberal Unionism, however, is a collection acquired in 1968 and uncatalogued at the time of writing (July, 1969). Several other collections indicate Tobit Evans's interests in genealogy and other historical and cultural matters.

[4]C. R. M. Talbot to Sir H. H. Vivian, 18 June 1886 (NLW, Vivian papers).

[5]Vivian to Talbot, 20 June 1886 (ibid.).

[6]Hartington to Vivian, 16 May 1886 (ibid.). Vivian noted on this letter, 'Take to Mr. Chamberlain'. Also Vivian to Gladstone, 6 June 1886 (ibid., copy).

allies like L. Ll. Dillwyn in Swansea Town and A. J. Williams in South Glamorgan.[7] When the Liberal Association for the Maintenance of the Legislative Union between Great Britain and Ireland called for an all-out crusade against all Gladstonian candidates, Vivian announced his withdrawal from that body on 12 June.[8] He still believed firmly in the desirability of Liberal unity. Shortly after the election, it came as no surprise when it was announced that Vivian had resumed his association with the official Liberal party.[9]

Vivian's last appearance in the role of intermediary came in January 1887, during the 'Round Table' conference on Liberal reunion. He offered Joseph Chamberlain a compromise solution of the Irish question on the basis of a federal division of powers between the Irish legislature and the imperial government, on the lines of the United States, and also a state purchase of land holdings. Chamberlain was far from hostile. He thought Gladstone was now in a conciliatory mood and 'much less "Gladstonian" than his followers'.[10] However, all hopes were shattered by the collapse of the 'Round Table' discussions at the end of February. Chamberlain's angry letter in the *Baptist* claimed that Welsh disestablishment and other radical reforms were being hopelessly frustrated by Gladstone's obsessive urge to surrender to Irish separatism. After the episode Vivian's adherence to the Liberal cause was unshakeable. As an index of this, it was at Vivian's home in Singleton Abbey, Swansea, that Gladstone was to make his famous declaration to the Welsh people on 4 June 1887.[11] The bonds between the Vivians and the old Liberal cause were finally sealed and Vivian remained a firm Gladstonian until his elevation to the Lords in 1893.

The Liberal Unionist candidates in the 1886 election had had a depressing time in Wales. They failed badly in five of their eight contests – Caernarfonshire (Eifion), South Glamorgan, North Mon-

[7]Hartington to Vivian, 17 April 1886; Vivian to Hartington, 20 April 1886 (ibid).

[8]Vivian to F. W. Maude, 12 June 1886; Vivian to Sir J. T. Dillwyn-Llewellyn, 22 June 1886 (ibid).

[9]This had already seemed probable after statements Vivian had made during the campaign; for example, 'I am quite prepared to support the establishment of a legislative body in Ireland for the purpose of giving effect to the powers which the wisdom of the Imperial Parliament may confer on them' (*The Times*, 25 June 1886).

[10]Vivian to Joseph Chamberlain, 10 January 1887; Chamberlain to Vivian, 11 January 1887 (NLW, Vivian papers). This episode may be dealt with in a forthcoming article in the *Welsh History Review* by Mr Michael Hurst whose *Joseph Chamberlain and Liberal Reunion* (London, 1967) is the definitive account of the Round Table conference.

[11]Here Gladstone made an emphatic statement on the national claims of Wales (cf. Kenneth O. Morgan, *Wales in British Politics, 1868–1922* [Cardiff, 1963], 80).

mouthshire, Flint District and Cardiff. The sitting member, Sir John Jones Jenkins, a powerful local industrialist, lost his seat at Carmarthen District to Sir A. Cowell-Stepney, who was to join the Liberal Unionists himself in 1891. The only undisputed Liberal Unionist actually elected (excluding Vivian) was Colonel Cornwallis-West, returned in West Denbighshire without opposition. Only in one seat did a Liberal Unionist come close to victory in a contested election. This was in the famous contest in Cardiganshire, described by the present writer elsewhere.[12] Here David Davies, the 'railway king' of Wales and a prominent member of the dominant Methodist denomination, was defeated by the barrister Bowen Rowlands, a little-known High Churchman from Haverfordwest. Davies's defeat, even if only by the margin of nine votes, was testimony to the fidelity of Cardiganshire Liberals to the name of Gladstone. As in neighbouring Montgomeryshire, they felt 'we must go to the country on the Gladstone ticket, say as little as we can about Ireland and as much about Church and Land'.[13] During the campaign, some of David Davies's party workers had sensed the defection of old supporters of their candidate. 'Do not trust even half of the Methodist preachers in this county', Edward Davies was warned; 'they will certainly vote for Gladstone.'[14] The assistance of county Conservatives was a two-edged weapon which alienated potential Liberal support for David Davies. He was, therefore, defeated; in disgust, he terminated his official links with the county, and retired from active politics. His son, Edward, resigned from the Montgomeryshire Liberal Association the following December,[15] and not until 1906 did the Llandinam family again emerge as political chieftains in Wales.

After the 1886 election, Liberal Unionism in Wales rapidly went into eclipse. It lost men like Vivian, Talbot and, most crucially of all, Thomas Gee to the Gladstonian camp. It faced the vigorous challenge of young radicals like Thomas Ellis who identified many of the grievances of Wales with the Irish cause. The problems now confronting those constituency Liberals who still resisted Gladstone's Irish policy are illustrated by the papers of Henry Tobit Evans of Llanarth, Aberaeron. Evans, an active journalist and a former schoolmaster in

[12]Kenneth O. Morgan, 'Cardiganshire politics: the Liberal ascendancy, 1885–1923', *Ceredigion*, V (4) (1967), 323–5 (published in this volume, 216–50).

[13]A.C. Humphreys-Owen to Stuart Rendel, 20 June 1886 (NLW, Rendel papers, XIV, 293).

[14]D. J. Jones to Edward Davies, 'Sunday Noon', 1886 (NLW, Davies of Llandinam papers, 302).

[15]Edward Davies to Montgomeryshire Liberal Association, 21 December 1886 (ibid., 303).

Llechryd, was always something of a political lone wolf. Perhaps significantly, he was a Quaker, one of the very few Friends in the county of Cardiganshire. He was also that rare phenomenon, a Nonconformist justice of the peace. He had campaigned for the Liberals in the Aberaeron region during the 1885 election,[16] but had then reacted sharply against Gladstone's Irish Home Rule Bill, like his fellow-Quaker, John Bright. Even so, Evans's allegiance to David Davies's cause had long been under suspicion. He was accused of having attacked Davies anonymously in the Liberal *South Wales Daily News* for having voted against Jesse Collings's 'three acres and a cow' amendment in February 1886. He was also suspected of being much more concerned with furthering his own private ambitions than with championing the cause of the Unionist candidate.[17] This so-called 'arch-traitor'[18] was indeed a 'friend' with many foes. Nevertheless, Tobit Evans it was who attempted to pull together the shattered forces of Liberal Unionism in Wales after the 1886 election. In January 1887, he was in touch with Joseph Chamberlain about founding an organization in Wales to link up with his national Radical Union. Tobit Evans was also approached shortly afterwards by Joseph Powell Williams, a prominent Birmingham Welshman, Chamberlain's close ally and chief of staff for the next seventeen years, who urged Evans to produce a Welsh-language pamphlet in support of Unionist principles. The Birmingham Radical Union was approached with this in view. Chamberlain also encouraged Evans to found a Welsh newspaper which might champion Liberal Unionist principles.[19] Chamberlain dryly told him: 'I have great hopes that further discussion will convince the Welsh people that their interest does not lie in establishing a separate Irish Parliament in Dublin.'[20]

For the next four years Evans kept up a steady stream of propaganda and comment on the Liberal Unionists' behalf, notably a pamphlet on the Irish question, *Y Berw Gwyddelig* (the Irish turmoil) which attracted wide attention in Wales and in Ulster. Evans also came into close contact with another prominent Welsh Liberal Unionist, Thomas

[16]H. Tobit Evans to H. C. Fryer, 18 November 1885 (NLW, 19,643B).

[17]D. J. Jones to Edward Davies, 6 March 1886 (NLW, Davies of Llandinam papers, 301).

[18]Ibid., and also D. J. Jones to Edward Davies, 22 July 1886 (ibid., 302). Jones, a resident of Lampeter, was a rural sanitary inspector in the Aberystwyth region. After the 1886 election, he seems to have sidled back to the official Liberals.

[19]Joseph Chamberlain to H. Tobit Evans, 9 April 1887 (NLW, 18,882B); J. Powell Williams to Tobit Evans, 22 March 1887 (ibid.). For Powell Williams, see Julian Amery, *Life of Joseph Chamberlain* Vol. VI (London, 1969), 554ff. His death in 1904 was a severe emotional blow to Chamberlain.

[20]Joseph Chamberlain to Tobit Evans, 4 January 1887 (ibid.), 'Private'.

Marchant Williams. Evans tried to press Williams's claims for the new post of assistant commissioner for schools under the Welsh Intermediate Education Act, passed in 1889. Williams considered his main rival for the post to be Owen M. Edwards, 'Fellow of Lincoln and Tutor of Balliol, though he is a Calvinistic Methodist preacher and is one of the editors of *Cymru Fydd*'.[21] R. A. Jones and Beriah Gwynfe Evans were other radicals also thought to be in the running. Tobit Evans sought the assistance of such Liberal Unionist potentates as Lords Hartington and Wolmer, with the aim of relieving the government of 'the reproach of having done nothing hitherto for the Welsh Unionists'.[22] Marchant Williams himself exclaimed in some desperation: 'this is the first piece of patronage fairly within the reach of a Welsh Unionist'.[23] In fact, he met with another in his series of disappointments in his native land.

Tobit Evans's main political role, however, came in October 1889, when he accepted Lord Wolmer's offer of the post of Liberal Unionist agent for the whole of Wales at a salary of £200 a year.[24] At the time, there was in effect no agent active in the country on behalf of the Liberal Unionists. Their agent for north Wales, Llewellyn Jones, had died, while Leigh MacLachlan, the agent for south Wales, was moving on to Manchester. Wolmer listed nine constituencies in north Wales and twelve in the south where Liberal Unionists ought to make a special effort.[25] The other constituencies could be written off. The best prospects were thought to be in Anglesey and in Swansea Town, if Richard Davies (the lord lieutenant of Anglesey, although a Non-conformist) and Sir John Jones Jenkins could respectively be enlisted as candidates for these two seats. At the same time as undertaking his new post, Tobit Evans founded a new Welsh-language monthly, *Yr Undebwr Cymreig*, to uphold the Liberal Unionist cause. It first appeared in January 1890 and a complete file of it exists in the National Library of Wales. Its pages included a characteristically

[21]T. Marchant Williams to Tobit Evans, 17 October 1889 (NLW, uncatalogued). *Cymru Fydd* was a Liberal monthly which Edwards edited with R. H. Morgan from June 1889.

[22]Marchant Williams to Tobit Evans, 13 October 1889 (ibid.).

[23]Marchant Williams to Tobit Evans, 21 October 1889 (ibid.). Williams was incensed by the fact that leading Churchmen like the Bishop and Dean of St Asaph and Bishop Jayne of Chester were backing Owen M. Edwards. 'Why in the name of conscience do the St. Asaph folk "run" him?', Marchant Williams asked.

[24]Lord Wolmer to Tobit Evans, 15 October 1889 (ibid.).

[25]Wolmer to Evans, 23 October 1889 (ibid.) Years later, Leigh MacLachlan was to serve as principal agent of the Conservative Party, 1926–8. J. C. C. Davidson described him as 'an old Liberal Unionist of great cunning and ability, but not with any great personality or presence': see Robert Rhodes James, *Memoirs of a Conservative* (London, 1969), 266 and fn., 274–5.

vitriolic column from the anonymous pen of Marchant Williams. Evans laboured hard and long on his uphill task as agent, especially in the Caernarfon District by-election of April 1890, in which Lloyd George scraped home for the Gladstonian Liberals by only eighteen votes.

But all Evans's efforts seemed to come to nothing. *Yr Undebwr* eventually ceased publication in December 1890, amidst gratified comment by its editor that Parnell's involvement in the O'Shea divorce scandal seemed to have destroyed the Irish Nationalist party.[26] Shortly afterwards, Evans's national agency collapsed also. By October 1891, Joseph Chamberlain was trying out the alternative (and much more modest) idea of a limited agency for three Welsh rural counties 'at £6 or £7 a month'. Unionist constituency organization remained enfeebled: only Cardiganshire and Cardiff among the south Wales constituencies were represented in the 1889 Liberal Unionist annual conference. Elsewhere Unionists had to turn their efforts to providing reluctant support for the Conservatives.[27] In the general election of July 1892, only eight Liberal Unionist candidates were put up in the thirty-four Welsh seats. They included three former Liberal members, Jenkins in Carmarthen District (where Cowell-Stepney had retired), Sir Robert Cunliffe in Flint District and Morgan Lloyd in Anglesey. None of them was successful, while Cornwallis-West was defeated by well over 2,000 votes in West Denbighshire by Herbert Roberts, a youthful timber merchant. Unionist efforts to whip up Nonconformist prejudice against the sinister menace of Irish popery, a theme heavily emphasized in election addresses and other propaganda, failed completely. Indeed, one ultimate legacy was renewed division within the Unionist ranks. Welsh Conservatives, committed to Church and Queen, deeply resented Chamberlain's sponsoring of Nonconformist Unionist candidates like William Jones, the Methodist draper from Birmingham and an open supporter of Welsh disestablishment, who ran in Cardiganshire.[28] Here and all over Wales, the Liberal Unionist flame soon flickered out.

It was not quite the end of the story. In 1895, Sir John Jones Jenkins was indeed returned for Carmarthen District as a Liberal Unionist: he was later to return to the Liberal camp in 1903 when Chamberlain raised the banner of Tariff Reform, and later still moved to the Lords as a Liberal peer, disguised as Lord Glantawe. The appearance of

[26]*Yr Undebwr* (Rhagfyr 1890), 5.

[27]Joseph Chamberlain to Evans, 24 October 1891 (NLW, 19,618C); J. Andrews to Evans, 18 February 1889 (ibid., uncatalogued); Liberal Unionist list of 'correspondents' (ibid.).

[28]Kenneth O. Morgan, 'Cardiganshire politics', 325 (published in this volume, 216–50).

David Davies, the young heir to the patrimony of Llandinam, as 'Liberal–Conservative' member for Montgomeryshire and an opponent of Irish Home Rule in the 1906 election, might also be regarded as a curious echo of the controversies in the days of his grandfather twenty years earlier. Chamberlain had high hopes of capturing David Davies as a Tariff Reform and Unionist candidate in 1905 but was undone by the perennial Church question. Chamberlain wrote to Ridley, the chairman of the Tariff Reform Committee:

> I am afraid that the Bishop of St. Asaph and the Church Party lost David Davies by pressing him too hard about the Disestablishment question. I pointed out that it was really academical [sic] at the present time, as, if the other side brought it forward they would have a sufficient majority and it would matter very little whether it was increased by Davies' vote or not. If we came in of course, we should not touch the subject. On the other hand Davies would have been all right about Fiscal Reform and Home Rule. Now I am afraid he has gone over finally to the Radicals.[29]

The attitude of David Davies, an ardent Methodist like the rest of his family, serves as a parable for the entire Liberal Unionist movement in Wales.

In general, it was always a lost cause. Tobit Evans seemed to sense this when he retired from machine politics after 1892. He diverted his energies instead to editing Unionist newspapers like the *Brython* and the *Carmarthen Journal*, to the study of Welsh genealogy, and to pre-paring a history of the Rebecca riots. He died in 1908, a disappointed man. For all his efforts, the contradictions implicit in Liberal Unionism could not be reconciled. The claim that Welsh disestablish-ment and the other radical reforms in which men like Tobit Evans believed could more plausibly be gained by alliance with the Tory enemy than with Gladstone's Liberal party was one that very few Welsh radicals felt able to accept, whatever their private reservations over Irish Home Rule. How could one be Liberal and anti-Liberal at the same time? This circle just could not be squared, even by the geometry of 'our Joseph'. The logic of Liberal Unionism seemed to be confirmed in 1895 when the party virtually united with the Conservatives and when Joseph Chamberlain entered Salisbury's government as colonial secretary.

[29]Joseph Chamberlain to Ridley, 18 December 1905, quoted in Amery, op.cit., VI, 773; *South Wales Daily News*, 16 December 1905. Davies in due course was to vote for Asquith's third Irish Home Rule Bill in 1912–13; he represented Montgomeryshire until 1929. He served briefly in Lloyd George's prime ministerial secretariat, but after 1918 quarrelled with the premier and joined the Asquithian 'Wee Frees'.

Even so, the importance of Welsh Liberal Unionism during the critical years after 1886 was far from negligible. It generated vital tensions within the Liberal ranks which it required all the mediation of men such as Stuart Rendel to overcome. More significant than the relatively modest tally of Liberal Unionist votes or supporters is the impact of the Irish question upon the conscience of individual Liberals, members of Parliament like Hussey Vivian, more obscure constituency workers like Tobit Evans. Each Welsh Liberal had to ask himself whether the claims of Wales could best be met by adherence to a national party under Gladstone's unpredictable leadership or through independent action on the Liberal Unionist model. In 1886, as in very different circumstances during the *Cymru Fydd* crisis ten years later, the party regulars won the day. Until the rise of Labour, Wales was still a two-party country: there was simply no middle ground. But the failures of Liberal Unionism should not obscure the fact that, to many contemporaries, it was a fairly close-run thing.

Welsh Liberal Unionism left one more permanent memorial. Among those young Welshmen who almost joined its ranks in the spring of 1886 was David Lloyd George, then aged only twenty-three. Only his allegedly missing a train to Birmingham kept him from attending the inaugural meeting of Chamberlain's Radical Union.[30] Throughout his subsequent career, the name and the mystique of Chamberlain continued to fascinate him.[31] Certainly, Lloyd George was eventually to claim the honourable title of the man who resolved the Irish question, where Pitt, Peel and Gladstone had failed and where Palmerston and Disraeli had not even tried. In December 1921, it was Lloyd George who was to conclude the Free State treaty with the Sinn Fein leaders. Yet throughout his career Lloyd George was never a committed crusader for Home Rule. In a discussion with Tom Ellis after Gee's funeral in October 1898, he deplored the permanent loss to Liberalism of men like Chamberlain, Bright, Dale and Spurgeon, and the harm that Gladstone's Irish policies had done to the Welsh cause.[32] This attitude was to re-emerge during Lloyd George's premiership after December 1916. In his attempt to impose conscription upon Ireland in 1918, in the martial law his government enforced which fatally alienated a moderate Nationalist like John Dillon, in the

[30]J. Hugh Edwards, *Life of David Lloyd George* (London, 1913), Vol. II, 142–4 is the one source for this story.

[31]Cf. Conversations of Lloyd George with C. P. Scott, 15 September and 23 October 1922 (BL, Add. MSS., 50,906, ff. 190 and 196). I touch on this theme in a later publication, 'Lloyd George's stage army: the coalition Liberals, 1918–22', in A. J. P. Taylor (ed.), *Lloyd George Studies* (London, 1971).

[32]J. Herbert Lewis's Diary, 3 October 1898 (NLW, Penucha papers).

ruthless policy of 'retaliation' carried out by the 'Black and Tans' and the 'Auxis' during the tragic era between 1919 and 1921, in the bitter sectarian hatreds which survived the partition and which almost fifty years later could still drive men to savage, mindless violence in the backstreets of Belfast and the slums of Bogside – in all these things, Lloyd George was to provide Welsh Liberal Unionism with its ultimate, brutal legacy.

1969

4

Wales and the
Boer War

It has usually been assumed without question that the overwhelming
majority of Welshmen were opposed to the war fought in South Africa
between October 1899 and May 1902. This has been the view of most
Welsh writers on this theme, from radical Liberals before 1914 down
to supporters of Plaid Cymru a half-century later. They have invariably
claimed that Welsh people felt an instinctive sympathy for the citizens
of the Boer republics, a small, Protestant farming community under
the heel of Anglo-Saxon rule, similar in many ways to Wales itself.
Evidence for imperialist or 'jingo' sentiment among the Welsh people
during the late 1890s tends to be dismissed as a temporary aberration.
Presumably that massive support in Wales for extreme forms of
xenophobic 'patriotism' during the 1914–18 war later on has to be
explained away in the same manner. The prevailing view appears to be
that of a Wales radical and pacifist, a nation that largely rejected the
pressures of that imperialism welling up in England and Scotland at
the same time, a nation of 'pro-Boers' which, during the crisis of the
South African War, kept its conscience clean and its principles pure.
    This has also tended to be followed by English historians. Thus Mr
A. J. P. Taylor once referred to Welsh sympathy for the Boers as a small
nation struggling for self-determination: however, he acknowledged that
the Welsh 'pro-Boer' was far more moderate than his Irish counterpart.[1]
The Irish Nationalists cheered the news of the disasters of the 'Black
Week' when they were announced in the Commons in December 1899.
Unlike the Welsh, the Irish 'pro-Boers' wanted the Boers to win. Dr

[1]A. J. P. Taylor, *The Troublemakers* (London, 1957), 42, 108–9.

Henry Pelling, however, is the only English historian who has made a real attempt to assess in any precise way Welsh attitudes towards the Boer War. Dr Pelling has long put all historians of this period deeply in his debt, not only for his earlier magisterial writings on the rise of the Labour party, but even more for his invaluable pioneer study of the social geography of electoral politics between 1885 and 1910. In a most stimulating collection of essays, he has also studied in depth popular attitudes, especially among the working class, towards British imperialism. His views on this problem, therefore, command the greatest respect. Dr Pelling has, in several publications, reiterated that pro-Boer sentiment in Wales largely explains the considerable swing back to Liberalism shown in the 1900 election returns in Wales. He has pointed out the contrast between the Welsh results and the powerful support for the Unionists shown in England and, to a lesser extent, in Scotland. As the South African War was the dominant issue of the day, it was, therefore, presumably the cause of the peculiar electoral reaction in Wales. (In passing, it may be noted that Dr Pelling has also concluded that in Britain generally popular interest in imperialism was ephemeral and limited, and that it was blurred by many other issues even in the 1900 general election.) His conclusions, therefore, appear to confirm the view of Wales as a nation of pro-Boers.[2]

The present writer, when he wrote upon this subject in 1963, was unable to accept this view. I felt that Welsh sympathy for the Boers had been greatly exaggerated and that the pro-Boers were a minority in Wales in 1900, as they were everywhere else. In the mainly English-speaking areas of industrial south and east Wales, where the vast majority of Welsh people resided, I found ample evidence for Welsh sympathy for imperialism at a variety of levels, trivial and profound, and this showed itself during the 1900 general election. On the other hand, I also found that in the Welsh-speaking areas of the rural north and west, sympathy with the Boer cause was far more pronounced. This became more and more emphatic in the later stages of the war, when the 'methods of barbarism' employed in the concentration camps of the Rand aroused considerable revulsion among Welsh Non-conformists.[3] Now, on surveying his writings of several years back, the historian is inevitably confronted with passages that he might wish to amend or to excise altogether. However, I remain firmly convinced that my main conclusions on Welsh attitudes towards the Boer War still

[2]Henry Pelling, *Social Geography of British Elections, 1885–1910* (London, 1967), 370, 417; *Popular Politics and Society in Late Victorian Britain* (London, 1968), 93 and n. See also Dr Pelling's book review, *Welsh History Review*, 2 (1) (1964), 103.

[3]Kenneth O. Morgan, *Wales in British Politics, 1868–1922* (Cardiff, 1963), 178ff. The term 'methods of barbarism' is Campbell-Bannerman's.

stand. Dr Pelling's evidence is basically statistical, derived from the median electoral 'swing' towards Liberal candidates in almost all the Welsh seats contested in 1900. He has shown that, while the Unionist vote rose substantially in England and Scotland, in Wales it fell from 43.6 per cent in 1895 to an estimated 35 per cent in 1900.[4] These electoral statistics are extremely illuminating but they do not explain. They are rather a neutral framework within which historical explanations have to be constructed and to which they have to be related. They are not a real substitute for an examination of the local source material, which is what the present writer has used. In this brief compass, I will try to explain why I still consider my original view to be the correct one, and why I remain undeterred even by Dr Pelling's psephological challenge.

Welsh attitudes towards the Boer War can be studied at three different levels: the views of Welsh members of Parliament and parliamentary candidates; the views of political activists in the constituencies; and the views of the Welsh political public in general. The last of these is especially hard to assess and impossible to quantify, but even here something can be said. Governing Welsh political opinion at all these levels was the fact that since 1868 Wales had been the most overwhelmingly Liberal section of the British Isles. Its social and cultural characteristics had made its political pattern remarkably consistent, especially since the Liberal party under Gladstone managed to turn itself into the apparent spokesman for the nationhood of Wales. Even in 1895, that year of electoral disaster for Liberalism, twenty-five of the thirty-four Welsh seats remained in Liberal hands. By-election and local government results since then suggested that much of the lost ground would be made up by the Liberal next time. It is against this unique background of political homogeneity that Welsh attitudes towards the South African War must be measured.

First, as regards the attitude of members of Parliament and candidates in Wales, there is no room for doubt that the pro-Boers, however casually defined, were in a distinct minority. Only four members from Welsh constituencies prior to the 1900 general election can be strictly classified as being in this category. All of them came from rural north Wales constituencies, remote from a sense of involvement with imperial policy: David Lloyd George (Caernarfon District), J. Herbert Lewis (Flint District), J. Bryn Roberts (Caernarfonshire, Eifion) and Arthur Humphreys-Owen (Montgomeryshire). They were a very mixed group and had little in common with one another. Lloyd George and Herbert Lewis were old allies from the days of the 'revolt'

[4]Pelling, *Popular Politics*, 93.

against the Liberal whips in 1894 and the *Cymru Fydd* movement of the following year. Bryn Roberts, a highly individual 'little Englander', had been, by contrast, a virulent opponent of *Cymru Fydd* and deeply estranged from Lloyd George. Humphreys-Owen was an English-speaking squire whose only close ally in Welsh politics was Stuart Rendel, now remote in the House of Lords.[5] These four were the only Welsh members of Parliament who consistently made anti-war speeches in the country and who attended 'peace' meetings such as that held in the Cory Hall, Cardiff, on 1 January 1901. The voting record in the main test divisions in the House of Commons is suggestive here. If one takes the four main 'pro-Boer' motions – Dillon's amendment to the address (17 October 1899), Stanhope's amendment (18 October 1899), Redmond's amendment (7 February 1900) and Sir Wilfrid Lawson's amendment (25 July 1900), the picture becomes clear.[6] Of the Welsh members, only Bryn Roberts voted for all four, while Lloyd George, Humphreys-Owen and Herbert Lewis voted for two. On the other hand, five Welsh members, D. Brynmor Jones (Swansea District), J. Wynford Philipps (Pembrokeshire), Albert Spicer (Monmouth District), Ellis Griffith (Anglesey) and J. Lloyd Morgan (West Carmarthenshire), voted with the government on one or more of these motions. The other Welsh members took an intermediate position. Two of them voted for and against the government, while five never voted at all. Even allowing for the fact that formal votes in the Commons probably underestimate the number of critics of the war among the Liberals in Parliament, it can hardly be disputed that the active 'pro-Boers' among the Welsh members were a distinct minority. Indeed, even the anti-war stand of Lloyd George himself was far from being unqualified. He was by no means an unequivocal anti-imperialist and declared on more than one occasion that the Transvaal and the Orange Free State would inevitably have to be annexed by Britain.[7] In years to come he was to work closely with imperialists like Milner and products of the 'kindergarten' like Philip Kerr. He condemned Chamberlain now for having helped to bring the war about by provocative and maladroit diplomacy and for making money out of it while it was being fought. He veered towards the J. A. Hobson thesis of viewing the war as a capitalist conspiracy, often lacing his assaults with xenophobia and antisemitism. But there were distinct limits to his enthusiasm for the Boers – as for the Irish.

[5]Humphreys-Owen had often shown a profound distaste for Lloyd George: see Morgan, op. cit., 114, 197.

[6]The votes on these motions were analysed in *The Times*, 31 July 1900. Bernard Porter, *Critics of Empire* (London, 1968), estimates the total of persistent 'pro-Boer' Liberal MPs at around thirty (76, n.6).

[7]For example, *Parl. Deb.*, 4th ser., XCIV, 891–2 (4 July 1901).

In the general election of October 1900, most Liberal candidates in Wales made it clear that they accepted the necessity for the war; some gave it their ardent blessing. Five Liberal candidates only took a consistent anti-war line in their election addresses and in their campaigns: they regarded the war as unnecessary and unjust. These were the four mentioned above, together with J. A. Bright (Montgomery District), the son of John Bright. The latter's position is explained by his parentage and has no bearing on the situation in Wales. In addition, some five other Liberals were so consistently scathing in their criticisms of the conduct of the war by the British government that they might be held to be very close to the 'pro-Boer' position: D. A. Thomas (Merthyr Tydfil), S. T. Evans (Mid-Glamorgan), William Jones (Caernarfonshire, Arfon), Frank Edwards (Radnorshire), and Clement Edwards (defeated at Denbigh District). Thomas and Evans had moved and seconded a motion on 20 February 1900 demanding a new inquiry into the Jameson Raid. However, these five were anxious to clear themselves of the imputation of being 'pro-Boers'. D. A. Thomas, for instance, a scathing critic of 'Chamberlainism', made it clear that he regarded it as his patriotic duty to support the imperial cause once war did begin.[8] When his opponents issued leaflets during the 1900 election campaign linking him with Keir Hardie as a 'pro-Boer', he was justifiably indignant. It would not be correct to say that his and Hardie's positions were identical.[9] Conversely, eleven Liberal candidates, eight of whom were to be elected, unmistakably adopted the imperialist view. They included Ellis Griffith, Brynmor Jones, Lloyd Morgan and Abel Thomas (East Carmarthenshire), all Nonconformist radicals of the most traditional stripe. Abel Thomas's vehement imperialism is especially intriguing. Labouchere had alleged that it was Thomas who was the mysterious Liberal back-bencher who had kept the Hawksley telegrams in his pocket during the famous debate on Stanhope's motion concerning the Jameson Raid inquiry on 27 July 1897.[10] The other Welsh Liberal candidates in 1900, eleven in all, adopted an intermediate position, similar to that held by Campbell-Bannerman, the Liberal leader. They almost all commented in severe terms on the government's mismanagement of the war and its lack of military preparation beforehand. On the other hand, they

[8] *Western Mail*, 10 October 1899. Also see his election address in 1900.

[9] Morgan, op.cit., 206; Pelling, *Social Geography*, 352. D. A. Thomas himself strove to disseminate this erroneous version of his earlier views in the later stages of the war: see D. A. Thomas to T. J. Rice, 11 November 1901 (Glamorgan Record Office, D/D Xes 1). It is repeated by W. Llewelyn Williams in Lady Rhondda, *D. A. Thomas, Viscount Rhondda* (London, 1921), 77.

[10] Jeffrey Butler, *The Liberal Party and the Jameson Raid* (Oxford, 1968), 199, 260.

also tended to agree with Charles Morley (Breconshire) that the war was 'unavoidable' and that it must be supported to the end.[11] One or two of these eleven avoided mention of the war entirely in their election addresses. Among these was the south Wales miners' leader, William Abraham (Mabon): he was to assert during the campaign that the war had been forced upon Britain when the Transvaal invaded her territory and had issued an ultimatum.[12] He was to continue to hedge for some months after the election until the 'Chinese slavery' issue emerged. Years later in 1916, Mabon was to support the 'social imperialist' British Workers National League. The conclusion is, therefore, that at least twenty-two and arguably twenty-seven of the thirty-two Liberal candidates in Wales in 1900 were prepared to accept the necessity for the Boer War and to support its being fought out to a victorious ending. Many things can be said about the Liberals returned by the Welsh electors in 1900 but hardly that they were predominantly pro-Boer.

Secondly, we may consider constituency activists. Among Liberal Associations there is little doubt that a majority were controlled by supporters of the war. Especially was this true in industrial south Wales, where it could be political suicide for an aspirant for a Liberal candidature to be identified with a 'pro-Boer' position in the summer of 1900. Thus, Robert Bird, a respected Wesleyan and former mayor of Cardiff, was turned down by his Liberal Association there as a 'pro-Boer'.[13] Almost every leading Cardiff Liberal was an imperialist of sorts. A rare exception was Edward Thomas (Cochfarf) who, as a Welsh-speaking Baptist and *eisteddfodwr*, was an untypical figure in the cosmopolitan milieu of Cardiff. Instead, Cardiff Liberals chose as their candidate the former member, Sir Edward Reed, who was as uninhibited an advocate of the imperial cause as was Milner himself. (It may be noted that Cardiff Unionists also turned down as candidate their sitting member, John Maclean, who had been a persistent critic of Chamberlain since the Jameson fiasco in 1896, and nominated instead an ardent imperialist, J. Lawrence.) In Swansea again the local Liberals turned down a pro-Boer candidate, R. D. Burnie, in favour of the nebulous generalities of Sir George Newnes, a man unknown in the constituency.[14] In neighbouring Gower, another 'pro-Boer', Daniel Lleufer Thomas, was humiliatingly rejected by the resurrected Liberal Association there in favour of a local employer, J. Aeron Thomas, who

[11]*South Wales Daily News*, 26 September 1900.

[12]*Cardiff Times*, 6 October 1900. 'Mabon' took a noticeably less radical stand than did the TUC itself (Pelling, *Popular Politics*, 86–7).

[13]*Western Mail*, 22 August 1900.

[14]*South Wales Daily News*, 3 July 1900.

took a more benevolent view of imperial policy.[15] Clearly in Wales, as in the rest of Britain, local politicians in urban and industrial communities tended to be in some sense imperialists.

In rural Wales the pattern was very different. Some prominent radicals there were imperialists, among them Beriah Gwynfe Evans (former secretary of the Cymru Fydd League) and the Revd Thomas Johns of Llanelli. Most Liberal party workers in rural Wales, however, seem to have been hostile to the war. Influential ministers like the Revd J. Towyn Jones or the Revd Evan Jones, Caernarfon, were militantly pacifist. Yet, even in the rural heartland, remote from the pomp and pageantry of jingoism, opposition to the war was far from being universal. There were divided counsels in the Cardiganshire, Merioneth and Anglesey Liberal Associations. Lloyd George's stand provoked violent demonstrations against him in Bangor, in his own constituency.[16] Herbert Lewis's hostility to the war aroused such criticism in the Flint District party caucus that he contemplated resigning. Lewis wrote that his constituency was 'saturated by utter jingoism'.[17] Even in rural Wales, pro-Boer candidates viewed the coming elections with trepidation.

The local press sheds more light on local opinion towards the war among Liberal activists. Without doubt, the great majority of Welsh-language journals were strongly opposed to the war from the outset. Most of them took their stand on general grounds of conscience and honour, opposing the Boer War because they opposed all war. Some also expressed repeated sympathy with the aspirations, real or presumed, of Kruger and the Boer Republics. Gee's old newspaper, *Baner ac Amserau Cymru*, took this line,[18] as did *Yr Herald Cymraeg*, the Methodist *Goleuad*, the Independent *Tyst* and the Unitarian *Ymofynydd*. The Wesleyan *Eurgrawn*, a relatively unimportant publication, was a rare exception: it followed the pro-war opinions of national Wesleyan leaders such as Hugh Price Hughes and R. W. Perks, MP.[19] Of the major Welsh-language literary reviews, *Y Geninen* printed impartially articles supporting and opposing the war, whereas *Y Traethodydd* (edited from 1900 to 1905 by the Revd Evan Jones) made itself a platform for pro-Boer views alone. However, a common theme in all these journals is a lament that so many even in Welsh-speaking

[15]*Llais Llafur*, 22 September 1900; *Cambria Daily Leader*, 28 September 1900.

[16]D. Lloyd George to J. Herbert Lewis, 13 April 1900 (NLW, Penucha MSS): 'The mob was seized with a drunken madness and the police were helpless.'

[17]J. Herbert Lewis to Owen Williams, 20 July 1900 (NLW, ibid.).

[18]*Baner ac Amserau Cymru*, 14 October 1899 and subsequent issues. See also *Y Tyst*, 20 September 1899, and *Y Goleuad*, 25 October 1899, for a full discussion of the war issue, particularly the 'Uitlander' franchise question.

[19]'Y Rhyfel', *Yr Eurgrawn Wesleyaidd*, April 1900.

areas were being infected by the imperialist passions of the time. As the elections drew near in the early autumn of 1900, they attempted to deflect public attention towards a range of other issues – disestablishment, land reform and the like – instead of concentrating solely on the war. The Caernarfon *Y Genedl Gymreig*, with which Lloyd George had been closely associated in the past, took a different stand. While critical of the conduct of the war (especially on grounds of expense), it felt that it must be seen through to the end and that the Boers must be defeated.[20] It also attempted to play down the war issue in the 'khaki election'. A very different picture emerges from the English-language press. Quite apart from the 'patriotic' hysteria emanating from the Unionist *Western Mail* (Cardiff), *Daily Post* (Swansea) and *Carmarthen Journal*, the Liberal press was markedly imperialistic. The Cardiff *South Wales Daily News* and the Swansea *Cambria Daily Leader* made little effort to subdue their belief that war was righteous and necessary.[21] Not until hostilities petered out in guerrilla operations in the last eighteen months before the peace of Vereeniging did these journals turn to favour Campbell-Bannerman's compromise position rather than the imperialism of Rosebery and the Liberal League. Here again, Liberal opinion in 1900 is hardly suggestive of overwhelming pro-Boer sentiment.

Finally, and most crucial of all, there is the attitude of the Welsh people more generally. This is not easy to assess. As Dr Pelling has rightly pointed out,[22] temporary excesses such as 'mafficking' (even though they went far beyond 'surface manifestations of jingoism here and there') need not necessarily be taken as evidence for a permanent popular mood. The most that one can say is that Welsh opinion in the twelve months prior to the October 1900 general election was deeply divided by crisis of conscience about the war, as it had not been, for instance, during the Bulgarian 'atrocitarian' agitation in the period 1876–8. Even in the heartland of rural Nonconformity there was active imperialist crusading by the 'Salem chapel jingo', while glowing popular accounts of 'what Wales has done in the war' tried to exploit the alleged Celtic origins of heroes like Lord Roberts or Baden-Powell.[23] But the only really firm evidence is found in the 1900 election returns, on which Dr Pelling has rightly concentrated. Only

[20]*Y Genedl Gymreig*, 22 May, 11 September 1900.

[21]The *South Wales Daily News* summed up its position on 16 October 1899. One English-language newspaper, however, did oppose the war strongly – *The Rhondda Leader* (cf. issue of 15 September 1900).

[22]Pelling, *Popular Politics*, 89–90. Dr Pelling shows that 'mafficking' celebrations were marked by a high degree of middle-class participation.

[23]Lord Rendel to A. C. Humphreys-Owen, 29 March 1901 (NLW, Glansevern MSS, 704); *Young Wales*, February 1900, January 1901.

four of the nineteen constituencies contested by the Unionists in Wales in 1895 and in 1900 failed to show a pro-Liberal swing in the latter year. But it is very doubtful whether Welsh sympathies with the Boers were the cause of this phenomenon.

In the contests in Wales, eleven Liberals were unopposed, including Bryn Roberts in Eifionydd and all the leading 'Lib.Imps.'. Elsewhere, the Liberals regained four seats lost in 1895 – Cardiff, Swansea Town, Carmarthen District and Radnorshire – and lost Monmouth District, losing it again in 1901 when a new election was necessary after an inquiry into corrupt practices. Can these Liberal gains be plausibly attributed to pro-Boer sentiment? The evidence points the other way almost everywhere. In Cardiff, Reed, as has been seen, was the most bloodthirsty of imperialists. After the election, he was to speculate that 'in times more practical than our own' such anti-war snipers as Lloyd George and Labouchere 'would have paid for their utterances on Tower Hill'![24] In Swansea again, the Liberal vote was not obviously one cast for anti-imperialism. Sir George Newnes was at pains in speeches and in his address to make it clear that he supported the war and that 'annexation is necessary and wise'.[25] The same is true of almost all his prominent supporters there. In both Swansea Town and Cardiff, the Liberals were victorious basically because of their ability to increase their poll, regaining the votes of traditional supporters lost in the defeats of 1895. Local government elections in Cardiff and Swansea in 1897 and 1900 had already pointed to Liberal victories in the parliamentary election. In Carmarthen District, a seat lost unexpectedly in 1895 (partly through the recession in the tinplate industry resulting from the American McKinley tariff and partly because the Unionists put up a popular Liberal Unionist employer, Sir John Jones Jenkins), the victorious Liberal in 1900, Alfred Davies, was a vehement imperialist.[26] Only Frank Edwards, who recaptured Radnorshire, was critical of the war, but it seems reasonably clear that events in South Africa played only a minor part in this remote rural (and highly marginal) constituency. The citizens of Rhayader or Llandrindod Wells were far more involved with land reform or church schools than with contemplation of the illimitable veld. Elsewhere, Liberals' share of the poll returned to near their level of 1892, though in most cases still falling some way below it. Lloyd George and Herbert Lewis increased their precarious majorities in Caernarfon and Flint – a notable achievement – but it is significant that they both tried to divert

[24]Western Mail, 19 December 1900.

[25]Cambria Daily Leader, 26 September 1900; see also Newnes's election address (formerly deposited in the National Liberal Club Library).

[26]See Alfred Davies's election address; he later joined the Liberal League.

attention to a whole range of other issues (such as the Penrhyn quarry strike) and away from the Boer War. The one Welsh seat the Liberals lost, Monmouth District, was gained by Dr Rutherford Harris, the associate of Jameson in the notorious raid of four years earlier. The defeated Liberal was Albert Spicer, an imperialist now, despite his Congregational religion and his earlier condemnation of the Jameson Raid in 1897. Spicer listed the war, the Monmouthshire Sunday Closing issue and the Catholic University in Ireland (which lost him Catholic votes in Newport) as the reasons for his defeat.[27]

This evidence does not reveal that the Welsh electors voted Liberal because of an excess of pro-Boer zeal. No doubt many pacifists would have voted even for Sir Edward Reed as a protest against the imperialist policies of the Salisbury administration. The campaign suggests, however, that most Liberal candidates, rightly or wrongly, regarded a 'little Englander' position as an electoral liability. Dr Pelling's view that pro-Boer candidates in Wales suffered no marked disadvantage at the polls may certainly be accepted for the rural areas (but for different reasons, as will be discussed below). This was hardly peculiar to Wales. Dr Pelling himself has shown that in England and Scotland also 'the evidence that opponents of the war did particularly badly at the polls is by no means convincing', and has cited the successes of pro-Boer candidates in such constituencies as Shoreditch, Battersea, Northampton and Northamptonshire East.[28] However, it could be plausibly argued that imperialism cost the Liberals two possible gains in south Wales, in Pembroke District and south Glamorgan. In the former, T. Terrell, an exceptionally strident Liberal imperialist, found himself tarred with the 'pro-Boer' brush: he had the misfortune to have an elderly general as his opponent.

One Welsh constituency has often been claimed to be an outstanding instance of the electors rejecting an imperialist and returning an anti-war candidate instead. This was the second seat in Merthyr Tydfil, where Keir Hardie defeated the imperialist Liberal member, W. Pritchard Morgan. Certainly, Hardie was a notoriously bitter critic of the government and its 'capitalists' war'. Even so, the view once stated by the present author and maintained now by Dr Pelling that anti-imperialism was the main cause of Hardie's victory appears not to be correct.[29] The conclusion of Kenneth O. Fox (cited in his own support in a footnote by Dr Pelling) is that 'Hardie won Merthyr Boroughs, not as the candidate of the ILP nor as the antagonist of the war in

[27]*South Wales Daily News*, 11 May 1901; the Unionists placarded the constituency with posters which read 'Vote for Spicer and Kruger'.
[28]Pelling, *Popular Politics*, 94.
[29]Morgan, op. cit., 180; Pelling, *Social Geography*, 370.

South Africa, but as the only alternative, for the Liberals who followed D. A. Thomas, to Pritchard Morgan'.[30] Hardie, in short, won in 1900 because of second votes cast by Thomas's supporters. In my view, Mr Fox here underestimates the positive pressure for direct labour representation that had surged to the surface in Merthyr Boroughs following the massive six-month coal stoppage in 1898, but he is correct in minimizing the comparative unimportance of the imperial issue. Hardie spent 'only eleven waking hours' in Merthyr prior to the poll:[31] his three speeches there made little reference to the war, while his supporters earlier had dwelt almost entirely on social and economic issues affecting labour. No doubt some voters may have voted for Hardie through being stirred by the pacifist traditions of Henry Richard, the former member up to 1888. On the other hand, Merthyr was no more insulated from the imperialist currents of the time than was any other industrial south Wales seat, while the boom in the coal export trade had lent the war some local popularity. In general, imperialism was perhaps too intangible an issue in Merthyr to be decisive, compared with the overwhelming evidence of industrial distress nearer home, felt with special keenness in a constituency with a unique radical tradition. Even the Merthyr election in 1900 cannot reasonably be regarded as testimony to Welsh revulsion against the South African War.

How, then, can the swing to the Liberals in the 1900 elections in Wales be explained? If one takes a wider perspective, there is little difficulty in finding the answer. The really unusual election in the fifty years between 1868 and 1918 is not that of 1900 at all, but that of 1895. Then, for a variety of reasons, the Liberal poll slumped disastrously and the Unionists mounted their only serious challenge during the entire half-century, winning as many as nine Welsh seats and gaining a swing in votes ranging from 3.5 per cent in the parliamentary boroughs to as much as 5.0 per cent in the county divisions of Glamorgan and Monmouthshire. Everything weighed against the Liberals in 1895. There was depression in the industrial south, stagnation in the countryside. Welsh Liberals were deeply divided over the rise of *Cymru Fydd*, with its call for Home Rule. Organization was run down and party workers disillusioned. There was widespread bitterness at the failure of the 1892–5 Liberal governments to push

[30]Kenneth O. Fox, 'Labour and Merthyr's khaki election of 1900', *Welsh History Review*, 2 (4) (1965), 365. See also Kenneth O. Morgan, 'The Merthyr of Keir Hardie', in Glanmor Williams (ed.), *Merthyr Politics: The Making of a Working Class Tradition* (1967), 65ff (published in this volume, 268–86).

[31]Hardie's own account, *Labour Leader*, 13 October 1900. The reason for Hardie's late arrival in Merthyr was that he had also been a candidate in Preston, which he considered a more hopeful constituency.

through disestablishment of the Church and other reforms. Tom Ellis in office had been a disappointment, while the leaders of the Liberal party, Rosebery and Harcourt, Morley and Asquith, were hopelessly at odds. Frustrated expectations led to a massive falling away of the Liberal poll in constituency after constituency, from rural Anglesey to industrial Merthyr. Given the fundamental homogeneity of Welsh politics, this trend could hardly be expected to continue, especially with the new freedom of being in opposition to unite back-bench Liberals. After January 1896, the divisions over *Cymru Fydd* died away, Welsh Liberals regrouped their forces and in 1900 Welsh politics returned to normal. As a result, as Dr Pelling shows, there was a swing to the Liberals in all save four constituencies.[32] The 'khaki election' in Wales was not monopolized by a tide of anti-war feeling at all. Generally, Liberals tried to play down the war issue, while laying stress on their own impeccable patriotism. They turned instead to the old radical causes of the past – disestablishment, education, land reform and temperance – together with a new emphasis on labour questions in south Wales. Temperance may have cost the Liberals Irish votes in Monmouth District; disestablishment was beginning to lose its earlier appeal. But generally the stress on local issues was extremely effective, far more so than it could be in Scotland, where the impact of political nationalism was not so clear-cut and where an issue like disestablishment divided rather than united Scottish Liberals. A study of the 1900 campaign in Wales, therefore, does not suggest that Welsh electors were obsessed with the war in South Africa. It does indicate, however, that where the war issue was raised by Liberals it tended to be Liberal imperialists rather than pro-Boers who did so. Critics of empire suspected that too direct a confrontation with the jingo passions of the time would court electoral disaster, and with reason. Welshmen voted Liberal in 1900 not because 'the Boers were felt to be fellow-victims of English aggrandisement',[33] but because the Liberal party was the party of Wales. 'Lib.Imps.' and

[32]There were special reasons in these four constituencies. As Dr Pelling points out, the Sunday Closing issue had some effect in Monmouth District and West Monmouthshire. In Cardiganshire the local Liberal machinery was particularly run down and the sitting member, Vaughan Davies, unattractive. The Liberals were also thought to have lost votes through seasonal migration to the south Wales coalfield (Kenneth O. Morgan, 'Cardiganshire politics: the Liberal ascendancy, 1885–1923', *Ceredigion*, V (4) (1967), 326–8, published in this volume 216–50). In Montgomery District, Pryce-Jones was a popular Unionist member and the Liberal candidate, Bright, an English outsider. In any event, the anglicized boroughs of the border county of Montgomeryshire were perilous terrain for Liberals, quite apart from any residual corruption there: the Unionists won this seat in five elections out of eight between 1885 and 1910. Welshpool, where the Powis influence was considerable, was a notable Tory stronghold.

[33]Pelling, *Popular Politics*, 93.

'pro-Boers' both reaped the dividends. Voters lost in 1895 were reclaimed, the old Liberal hegemony re-established and the pattern of Welsh politics preserved for almost a generation to come.

In the later stages of the Boer War, as has been said, there was a marked disenchantment with its course throughout Wales. The impact of imperialism there was apparently a transient phenomenon and soon subordinated to local issues. Even so, it would be an error to minimize unduly the appeal of empire, however temporary. It is not in the least surprising that so many Liberals in Wales, as elsewhere in Britain, could respond to the imperial idea in all its many facets, its squalor and its idealism, its jingoism and racism, its urge to humanitarian reform and social reconstruction. After all, most of the major prophets and practitioners of the imperial movement, from Chamberlain and Dilke to Rhodes and Cromer, had grown up within the Liberal tabernacle. Tom Ellis himself had been the ardent admirer of Rhodes and the close colleague of Rosebery; for him, as for other young Welshmen, imperialism and social regeneration were closely linked. What the influence of imperialism suggested was that Welsh politics were now merging almost imperceptibly into those of the United Kingdom as a whole. For a generation, Welsh radical leaders had been advocating national equality and national involvement for their country; the imperial idea was a part of this involvement and Welsh nationalism could be held to be compatible with it (as Irish nationalism could not). Equally, when the reaction against imperialism set in after the 1900 election, when public controversy turned anew to the fascinations of domestic themes such as free trade, church schools and licensing reform, this was reflected in public debate in Wales also. The overwhelming Liberal preponderance in Wales made this transformation more pronounced than elsewhere in Britain, particularly in the 1906 election, but this was an exceptionally violent eddy in a national tide of opinion. Welsh politics certainly had their own distinctive flavour and priorities in the later 1890s; this emerged strongly during the 1900 election campaign. However, the degree of isolation should not be over-emphasized. Wales was no long a neglected backwater: the radicals of the post-1868 period had done their work too well. By 1900 Wales was an inseparable part of the wider British context; the career of Lloyd George, in which he was able to harmonize Welsh nationalism with British 'patriotism', is an index of this change. In this wider context, the feverish passion for imperial grandeur had its place. The 'khaki' election returns in 1900 only confirm this conclusion. At the high noon of Anglo-Saxon imperialism, some Welshmen, too, sought to claim their place in the sun.

1969

5

The New Liberalism and the Challenge of Labour: The Welsh Experience, 1885–1929

The decline of the Liberal party seems to have supplanted the rise of the gentry as the major area of contention for historians of modern Britain. An abundance of new sources is available; a variety of new techniques is being applied. This theme has generated a series of controversial works ever since Dangerfield postulated the 'strange death' of Liberal England back in 1936. Since the late 1960s, the debate has gathered momentum, as attention has moved from the centre of politics to the periphery. Regional investigations have raised new questions about popular involvement in the constituencies and its social and cultural bases; in particular, major studies of politics in Lancashire, London and the east Midlands have made crucial contributions to the debate on late-Victorian and Edwardian Liberalism.[1]

The Welsh experience in the late nineteenth and early twentieth centuries sheds a particularly revealing light on the fortunes of the Liberal party in this period, for politics and social change in Wales pursued a markedly different course from that prevalent elsewhere in Britain. Recent Welsh politics have been dominated by two major characteristics – first, the completeness of the Liberal ascendancy in Wales in the years down to 1914; secondly, the unrelieved nature of the Liberal decline ever since. Unlike much of England and Scotland,

[1] P. F. Clarke, *Lancashire and the New Liberalism* (Cambridge, 1971); Paul Thompson, *Socialists, Liberals and Labour* (London, 1967); Janet Howarth, 'The Liberal revival in Northamptonshire', *Historical Journal*, XII (1) (1969). There is also much helpful material on regional politics in Henry Pelling, *The Social Geography of British Elections, 1885–1910* (London, 1968).

Wales has shown no consistent sign of a Liberal revival since 1918, in
the face of the mounting challenge from Labour. There was no Liberal
recovery in Wales in the late 1950s or the early 1960s – no Welsh
Torringtons, Orpingtons or Rochdales. After the general election of
1966, the Liberals retained only one seat in Wales, that of Montgomeryshire; the 1970 election brought no further success.[2] The
Liberal party has long since been supplanted by Labour in industrial
south Wales. In the later 1960s the resurgence of Plaid Cymru posed a
new threat to what survived of Liberalism in the rural hinterland also.

There are, therefore, two related questions which the historian of
recent Welsh politics needs to examine. First, why were the Liberals so
overwhelmingly dominant in Wales, north and south, in the era down
to 1914? And secondly, why have they been so totally ineffective in
meeting the challenge of Labour since then? The answers lie deeply
rooted in late-Victorian society. Other Welsh historians have examined
aspects of these themes from the standpoint of the Labour movement.
But perhaps a more fundamental set of explanations arises from a
consideration of the Liberals themselves, and their role in the making
of modern Wales.

From the 1860s down to the First World War, Welsh politics were
dominated by the dynamic and overwhelming growth of the Liberal
party. At the national level, the Liberal party secured a massive
dominance at every general election from 1868 down to 1918, straddling the Gladstonian heyday and the era of Lloyd George. In 1906,
every Welsh member returned at the polls took the Liberal whip,
except for Keir Hardie at Merthyr Tydfil – and even he was in large
measure a symbol of the 'Progressive Alliance'. At the local level, the
Liberals were even more in command. The Local Government Act of
1888 produced a unique social revolution in Wales, especially in the
countryside, in marked contrast to the political continuity shown by
the local government elections in England. The new Welsh county
councils in almost every instance contained a massive Liberal majority,
while the landed gentry were routed almost everywhere.[3] These years
of Liberal dominance formed a period of unique character and
distinction in the evolution of the Welsh nation. They were marked by a

[2]In the 1966 general election, the Liberals put up eleven candidates in Wales:
their total poll was only 103,747, a drop of over 2,000 in the average vote.

[3]For a discussion of the change in one county, see Kenneth O. Morgan,
'Cardiganshire politics; the Liberal ascendancy, 1885–1923', *Ceredigion*, V (4)
(1967), 330–1 (published in this book, 216–50). The Liberals gained a majority of
thirty-seven to ten in the elections for the first Cardiganshire county council in
January 1889. Their thirty-seven councillors included thirteen tenant farmers,
eleven small businessmen and four Nonconformist ministers.

growing prosperity, particularly in the mining valleys and thriving conurbations of the industrial south. They formed an era of educational advance, with the new 'county' schools of 1889 and the federal, national University providing new social opportunity and new symbols of nationhood. They were a time also of a dramatic cultural renaissance, especially in poetry and in literary criticism. The eisteddfod was never more flourishing. And with all these major transformations in Welsh society and culture between the 1860s and 1914, the Liberal party and the liberal ethic were intimately associated. The advance of democracy, the economic growth, the educational progress, the new cultural and national awareness were in large measure the creation of Liberals. They were the heirs of this new Wales which they had so largely created.

The key to this Liberal ascendancy, without doubt, is the pressure for social and civil equality from the newly-emergent Nonconformist middle class. Rising to authority in the small towns of rural and industrial Wales and on the chambers of commerce of the south Wales ports, it was they who led the pressure for religious equality, for educational opportunity, for security for tenant farmers, and for free trade. They were poised in opposition to the age-old ascendancy of the gentry and of the Anglican Church. Further, the grievances and the values of these middle-class Nonconformists and their working-class supporters were associated with the national grievances of Wales as a whole. To a marked degree, Liberalism and nationalism were fused, and in a real sense the Liberals were the party of Wales and the vehicle for its growing national consciousness. And this pattern continued, despite such political crises as the schism over *Cymru Fydd* (the Welsh Home Rule League) in the mid-1890s or the fierce conflicts over the South African War, down to the outbreak of world war in 1914.

Throughout this remarkable era, the involvement of the working class in the Liberal ascendancy was largely assumed. The orthodox view was that Welsh Liberalism was socially and culturally homogeneous. A corollary was that Welsh society was not thought to be marked by the deep chasm between capital and labour that scarred industrial relations in England. The homogeneity of Welsh society was reinforced by the migration of so many Welsh-speaking Welshmen from the rural areas into the coalfield from the 1830s onwards, bringing their values and their cultural and religious institutions with them. Not until the first decade of the twentieth century did the majority of immigrants into the Welsh coalfield come from England. Until then, phenomena like the explosive growth of Nonconformist chapels and of local eisteddfodau in rural and industrial areas alike testified to, and reinforced, this prevailing sense of national unity. Mainly for this reason, the political Labour movement was held to be sectional, and made very little headway in Wales until the six-months' coal stoppage of 1898. The Independent Labour Party and the Fabian Society, proclaiming the exotic creed of socialism, struck few roots in industrial south Wales and virtually none at all in the north.

In addition, until the turn of the century, labour played very little direct part in the activities of the Liberal party in Wales. For instance, the *Cymru Fydd* League in 1895 placed 'labour and industrial' questions seventh on its programme, far behind such 'Old Liberal' themes as Welsh Home Rule, disestablishment of the Church, temperance reform and security for the tenant farmer. Indeed, the president of the Rhondda Labour and Liberal Association, the Revd O. Haelfryn Hughes, complained on this point, but quite in vain.[4] The North and South Wales Liberal Federations virtually never pronounced on industrial issues, but were largely absorbed by assaults on the gentry and the 'alien Church'. Again, like party workers in the constituencies, Welsh Liberal leaders took little part in pressing for social and industrial reform. There were, of course, a few exceptions. Tom Ellis took a theoretical interest in social questions in his Oxford days in the early 1880s, under the stimulus of Ruskin and Toynbee and his patrician friends in the 'Co-efficients'.[5] But practical urban and labour issues occupied relatively little of his attention in his subsequent career in Parliament after 1886. The coalowner, D. A. Thomas, proprietor of the Cambrian collieries and member for Merthyr Tydfil from 1888, was also, with some justice, regarded as a champion of organized labour on paternalist grounds, despite his stubborn opposition to the miners' eight-hour day. His later involvement in the violent conflicts of Tonypandy and the Cambrian stoppage in 1910–11 should not obscure his earlier concern with working-class grievances.[6] But, in general, Welsh Liberals, in Parliament and in the constituencies, so articulate and so active in pressing for disestablishment and land reform, were conspicuously silent on industrial matters, until (and in most cases, even after) the great coal stoppage of March–September 1898. Welsh Liberals, middle- and working-class alike, maintained a general adherence to a broadly-conceived Progressivism, based on assumption of the class harmony of the productive classes against the feudal pretensions of the bishop and the squire – much like the agrarian radicalism of the Jacksonian Democrats or the Southern Populists in the nineteenth-century United States. Welshmen who

[4] *South Wales Daily News*, 20 May 1895.
[5] Neville Masterman, *The Forerunner* (Llandybïe, 1972), ch. 2, for a searching and sensitive discussion of Ellis's Oxford days.
[6] Kenneth O. Morgan, 'D. A. Thomas: the industrialist as politician', in Stewart Williams (ed.), *Glamorgan Historian*, III (1966), 46–7 (published in this volume, 419–34).

proclaimed that 'labour' had a distinctive interest of its own, and that this required political and industrial recognition, stood accused of sectionalism – and, by implication, of hostility to the advance of the Welsh nation itself in the golden years that followed the *annus mirabilis* of 1868.

In general, the Welsh working class seemed well content with this state of affairs down to the end of the century. Only occasionally was there tension over the selection of candidates, when labour organizations complained that middle-class cliques were dominating local constituency associations. This occurred twice in by-elections in 1888. In Merthyr Tydfil, the gold speculator Pritchard Morgan claimed successfully to represent the local workers against a *Cymru Fydd* carpet-bagger from London. Morgan was hailed by Keir Hardie's Scottish journal, *The Miner*, as a champion of the working man who had been elected on 'a good labour programme'.[7] In Gower, David Randell was nominated and elected as Liberal member, with strong support from local miners and tinplaters, as a 'Labour and Welsh home rule candidate'. He promptly confirmed his radical credentials by sending a message of support for Keir Hardie in the famous by-election struggle at Mid-Lanark.[8] Again, in 1892, working-class endorsement helped to secure the radical R. D. Burnie as Liberal member for Swansea Town. But these candidatures were invariably resolved without conflict. Working men in urban and industrial constituencies instinctively accepted middle-class leadership, and representation by professional and mercantile men on the pattern of Alfred Thomas, S. T. Evans, Brynmor Jones and D. A. Thomas, in election after election. On only one occasion up to the turn of the century was there a direct class conflict at the polls. This came as early as 1885 in the new Rhondda constituency, when William Abraham (Mabon), the secretary of the Cambrian Miners' Association, defeated a young coalowner, F. L. Davis, in a famous contest.[9] But this was the exception that proved the rule. For Mabon was the supreme 'Lib–Lab', even more firmly dedicated to the old Liberal premise of class collaboration on behalf of the twin causes of Nonconformist radicalism and Welsh nationalism than were the middle-class Liberals themselves. Mabon's election left no legacy of direct labour representation. The Liberal ascendancy still stood secure.

In the new century, the aims and values of Liberalism in Wales showed comparatively slight change in the period up to 1914. Wales

[7] *The Miner: An Advanced Political Journal*, November 1888, 121.
[8] Ibid., April 1888, 38.
[9] For this election, see L. J. Williams, 'The first Welsh "Labour" M.P.', *Morgannwg*, VI (1962), 78–94.

remained sunk in the politics of nostalgia and of the Gladstonian past. Despite massive industrial conflicts such as the south Wales miners' stoppage of 1898 or the savage strikes of the Penrhyn quarrymen in north Wales between 1896 and 1903, Welsh politicians were still wedded to the old themes – disestablishment, education, temperance, modified Home Rule, the eternal memories of the 'great election' of 1868 and of the evicted martyrs who suffered after the polls were declared.

All this is particularly puzzling because in England the whole content of the Liberal creed changed substantially during these very years.[10] An array of brilliant intellectuals and publicists pressed successfully for new creative roles for the central government. J. A. Hobson, the searching critic of imperial expansion, urged Liberals to turn instead to remedy the evils of underconsumption at home. Herbert Samuel advocated state action as a basic means of extending personal liberty, rather than curtailing it. The sociologist, L. T. Hobhouse, called for a union of Liberalism and socialism in the pursuit of social reform, and for constructive planning in place of the indiscriminate charity of private philanthropists. Leo Chiozza Money demanded a sweeping redistribution of income, with the public ownership of major industries as one means of effecting this. C. F. G. Masterman, deeply influenced by Christian socialism, eloquently drew the contrast between the 'conquerors' in suburban Edwardian villadom and the misery of the destitute poor in urban slums, R. J. Campbell's 'new theology' called for the Christian ethic to be given a social rather than an individualistic basis, and appealed for co-operation rather than competition in social relationships. Thus by 1914, Liberal intellectuals had largely parted company with the older simplistic individualism of the Gladstonian-Cobdenite tradition. Groups like the 'Rainbow Circle' and its organ *The Progressive Review*, journals like the *Speaker* and (after 1907) *The Nation* pioneered new concepts of social planning, with David Lloyd George and Winston Churchill eventually emerging as their popular tribunes. Admittedly, much of this 'New Liberalism' was the product of small groups of London intellectuals. How far their ideas permeated to rank-and-file Liberals in the constituencies must remain doubtful. However, Dr Peter Clarke has shown that in Lancashire at least, partly through the

[10]Among the major documents for the 'New Liberalism' are J. A. Hobson, *Imperialism: A Study* (London, 1902); idem, *The Crisis of Liberalism* (London, 1909); Herbert Samuel, *Liberalism* (London, 1902); L. T. Hobhouse, *Democracy and Reaction* (London, 1904); L. Chiozza Money, *Riches and Poverty* (London, 1905); C. F. G. Masterman, *The Condition of England* (London, 1909); R. J. Campbell, *The New Theology* (London, 1907). There is a general account in Kenneth O. Morgan, *The Age of Lloyd George* (London, 1971), 29ff.

leadership of C. P. Scott and his *Manchester Guardian*, the local Liberals were by 1914 overwhelmingly committed to the policy of social reform.[11] They had bridged the gulf between John Bright and Lloyd George. And in terms of the national appeal of Liberalism as a creed, by 1914 it was largely transformed. The New Liberalism had in large measure supplanted the Old, a factor which by itself goes far to demolish the 'Dangerfield thesis' of an inevitable Liberal decline in the face of collectivism and class conflict before 1914.

But in Wales, by contrast, the New Liberalism barely existed. It met with virtually no discussion, particularly in the Welsh-language press. In a major periodical like *Y Traethodydd*, edited for a long period (1900–5) by the Revd Evan Jones, Caernarfon, a leading Methodist patriarch, the few discussions of social or economic issues were largely uninspired repetitions of the creed of Cobden. For the rest, its columns were in large measure consumed by theology of a peculiarly unreconstructed kind.[12] The analyses in *Y Geninen*, a quarterly somewhat more contemporary in its interests, were preoccupied with the materialism thought to be embodied in the socialist creed, and the dangers that this held for the essentially spiritual character of Welsh Liberalism. A Nonconformist writer on 'signs of the times' in Wales in April 1912 rejoiced that most intellectual and religious leaders there still held firm to the faith of their fathers, despite the encroachment of English newspapers, the 'higher criticism', 'the new theology' and similar threats.[13] Welsh Nonconformist writers, the very core of radical politics, gave scant indication that Liberalism in the early twentieth century was undergoing an intellectual revolution; their views were almost totally insulated, frozen almost in the mid-Victorian world of 'S.R.' and Thomas Gee.

There were, it is true, a handful of distinguished 'new theologians' in the Nonconformist ministry in Wales, inspired by the ideas of R. J. Campbell. Many of them were younger men like the Revd Rhondda Williams, Union church, Brighton, and the Revd James Nicholas, Moriah, Tonypandy, who urged the Welsh churches to turn their attention from time-worn shibboleths like disestablishment and towards the squalor and poverty in 'darkest Cardiff' or 'darkest Merthyr'. A handful of Welsh theologians wrote on the issues raised by Campbell's 'new theology', on the distinction between *mewnfodaeth* and

[11]Clarke, op. cit., particularly ch. 7.

[12]The only article dealing with current social conditions in *Y Traethodydd* between 1906 and 1912 was one by the Revd H. Barrow Williams in the issue of July 1911. Among other things it was concerned to discuss whether trade unions existed in ancient Nicodemia in the time of Pliny.

[13]D. Tecwyn Evans, 'Arwyddion yr amserau yng Nghymru', *Y Geninen*, Ebrill 1912.

uwchfodaeth, and the need to stress the immanence of God as a positive force working within society rather than a remote transcendent power. A distinguished (though conservative) theologian like the Revd David Adams strove to reconcile the contradictions between the new theology and the old, though evidently with scant success.[14]

A few Welsh Nonconformist ministers went even further. Often inspired by the apocalyptic vision of the religious revival which raged like wildfire through Wales in 1904–5, some of them lent their oratorical and other talents to the political Labour movement. The eminent Baptist preacher, Dr 'Gomer' Lewis of Capel Gomer, Swansea, campaigned for Labour and against the Liberal candidate in the 1906 election in Gower. A triumphant service was held in Capel Gomer after the election in which the victorious Labour candidate, John Williams, miners' agent and Baptist lay preacher, addressed the congregation.[15] In Merthyr Tydfil, Keir Hardie's distinctive moral appeal attracted several young ministers to his election platforms in January and December 1910. The presence of men like the Revd James Nicholas, the Revd George Neighbour of Mountain Ash, and the Revd Herbert Morgan added force to Hardie's contention that his brand of socialism was far from incompatible with Welsh Nonconformity.[16] Significantly, these three ministers were all Baptists, that denomination being particularly stirred by the 'social Christianity' released by the 1904 revival. Particularly notable was the presence of Herbert Morgan, the minister of Lloyd George's own chapel, Castle Street, London, and an ardent worker for the ILP. (Indeed, John Hinds, MP, and the other Liberal deacons of that chapel were broad-minded enough to accept another socialist firebrand, James Nicholas, as their minister from 1916 onwards.) Perhaps the most remarkable of all these socialist evangelists among the Nonconformist ministry was the celebrated eisteddfodic bard, the Revd Thomas E. Nicholas of Seion Independent chapel, Glais (1880–1971). He produced poetry as well as propaganda to further the workers' cause; his *Cerddi Gwerin* were hymns to social justice and the living wage. He became closely associated with Keir Hardie, served as the Welsh editor of the ILP's *Merthyr Pioneer* from its first appearance in 1911, was a founder-member of the Communist Party of Great Britain in 1920 and for

[14]E. Keri Evans and W. Pari Huws, *Cofiant y Parch David Adams* (Liverpool, 1924), 143–5. Also see 'Y Beibl a'r Dduwinyddiaeth newydd', *Y Geninen*, Ionawr 1908.

[15]*Cambria Daily Leader*, 29 January 1906. Also see T. Morgan, *Darlithiwr Enwocaf Cymru: sef y Parch J. Gomer Lewis* (1914); and Kenneth O. Morgan, 'The Gower election of 1906', *Gower*, XII (1959), 15–20.

[16]For example 'Open letter to the ministers of the Gospel in the Merthyr Boroughs', *Merthyr Pioneer*, 17 June 1911.

nearly seventy years (until his death in 1971) was an uncompromising but much-loved symbol of the union between Nonconformist radicalism and the extreme political left.[17]

But men like Thomas Nicholas, Glais, were very much isolated exceptions up to 1914. In the main, the Nonconformist churches, so vocal on political themes, like disestablishment, were conspicuously silent on social questions. Denominational assemblies year after year concentrated on the old issues and the old enemies: the Revd J. Cynddylan Jones, an eminent theologian, protested in vain on this point at the Calvinistic Methodist annual assembly in 1908.[18] In the monthly *Wales*, shortly before the outbreak of war, the Revd Gwilym Davies criticized the insularity of Welsh Nonconformists. He urged them to pay heed to the urban squalor, the raging phthisis, and wretched housing described in the recent inquiries of the Welsh Land Committee.[19] But such concern as there was in social problems such as these came, not from the churches, but rather from secular, non-partisan movements, admittedly many of them led by prominent Nonconformist laymen. Instances of this kind were the national crusade against tuberculosis inaugurated by David Davies, the millionaire coalowner and railway magnate of Llandinam, in 1909, and the new Welsh School of Social Service launched at Llandrindod Wells in 1911.[20] At the founding meeting of this latter body, the president, the Revd T. Richards of Newport, issued a powerful plea for the churches to devote their energies to social problems. He explicitly noted the political imperatives that dictated this policy.

> Their churches used to be made up of people who were Liberals with just a sprinkling of Conservatives, and the result was that ministers and leaders and even the churches themselves could take their place and stand on the Liberal platform.
> . . . That day, as far as Wales was concerned, was gone, and in their churches today they still had a sprinkling of Conservatives and many Liberals, but also a large number of people who called themselves

[17]T. E. Nicholas, 'Y Ddraig Goch a'r Faner Goch: cenedlaetholdeb a sosialaeth', *Y Geninen*, Ionawr 1912. There is a portrait and obituary of Nicholas on the front page of the *Morning Star*, 21 April 1971. The present writer has greatly benefited from conversations with the late Mr Nicholas about his career.

[18]*Y Goleuad*, 2 September 1908.

[19]*Wales*, March 1913, 124ff., and May 1914, 149ff.

[20]The papers of Lord Davies of Llandinam and of Daniel Lleufer Thomas in the National Library of Wales contain material on these two movements. Lleufer Thomas was chairman of the School of Social Service, 1911–23 (see a valuable sketch of him by David Williams in the *Dictionary of Welsh Biography down to 1940*, 939–40).

members of the ILP and the Socialists . . . The time had passed when
the Free Churches of Wales could be looked upon as necessary adjuncts
to any political party.[21]

Perhaps some of his audience reflected that many of these ILP zealots,
especially among the young, were leaving the chapels altogether in
pursuit of what Mrs Snowden termed 'real religion'.[22] But, in general,
pleas like those of the Revd Richards fell upon deaf ears up to 1914,
both in relation to the Nonconformist denominations and to the
Liberalism that was largely their creation.

In fact, Welsh Nonconformist Liberals made few concessions to
working-class demands in the period up to 1914, both in terms of
programmes and of personnel. There was increasing friction over the
adoption of 'labour candidates' in traditional Liberal constituencies.
This led to an early clash between Liberals and Labour in the Gower
division in 1900. Significantly, at this early stage a prominent working-
class spokesman like John Williams, miners' agent for the western
valleys (and later to be the victorious Labour candidate himself in
1906) campaigned for the Liberal employer against John Hodge, the
LRC candidate.[23] In 1903–4 there was severe friction with local
Liberal associations over the adoption of two other prominent miners'
agents, William Brace and Tom Richards (respectively vice-president
and treasurer of the South Wales Miners' Federation) for the South
Glamorgan and West Monmouthshire constituencies. With singular
reluctance, the local Liberal associations gave way in the face of severe
pressure from the party whips in London, and Brace and Richards
duly became 'Lib–Lab' MPs.[24]

But, on many more occasions, local Liberal associations, perhaps
narrower in their social composition in the 1900s than they had been

[21] South Wales Daily News, 8 September 1911.

[22] 'Socialism in south Wales', Labour Leader, 27 October 1905.

[23] John Hodge to J. Ramsay MacDonald, 17 October 1900 (Transport House,
Labour party letter files, 1/181). Cf. Kenneth O. Morgan, 'Labour's early struggles
in Wales: some new evidence, 1900–08', National Library of Wales Journal (1972).

[24] For South Glamorgan, see South Wales Daily News, September–October 1903.
Herbert Gladstone, the Liberal chief whip, decreed that Brace should receive the
nomination provided he was in sympathy with Liberals on general questions (ibid.,
29 October 1903). For West Monmouthshire, see South Wales Daily News, May–July
1904; Llais Llafur, May–July 1904; and Glamorgan Free Press, 14 May 1904, 'Some
plain talk about the West Monmouth Campaign'. Tom Richards's nomination in
this constituency was made possible only when C. M. Warmington, the Liberal
nominee, refused to oppose a Labour candidate. The local press noted the fierce
hostility of Nonconformist ministers in the West Monmouth Liberal Association to
any Labour candidature, even though Richards was an ardent chapel-goer.

twenty years earlier as the power of organized labour built up, resented and rejected pressure from the central party organization in London to let in 'Lib–Lab' or LRC candidates. A notable instance of this came in March 1910 when the master of Elibank totally failed to persuade the Mid-Glamorgan Liberals to give a free run to Vernon Hartshorn for the Labour party. At a time when cordial relations between the Liberal and Labour parties were crucial for the carrying of the government's legislation, the Mid-Glamorgan Liberals twice ran against Hartshorn and, significantly, defeated him with some ease.[25] After his defeats, Hartshorn wrote, with much bitterness, that the Liberals had ignored free trade, the Lords' veto, even the 'people's budget' recently introduced by Lloyd George, and had concentrated solely on the theme that socialism was tantamount to atheism.[26] His defeat Hartshorn ascribed, quite simply, to 'chapel influence'. Certainly, Hartshorn himself was no great advertisement for the puritan ethic, especially when locked in conflict with J. Hugh Edwards, an Independent minister cradled in the Mecca of Welsh radical Nonconformity, the university college at Aberystwyth. To countless working-class voters down to 1914, even a respected working-class leader like Hartshorn was suspect and apparently in conflict with the national values. Conversely, middle-class business or professional 'men of light and leading', the vanguard of that political revolution which had transformed Wales since 1868, were widely felt to be more appropriate representatives for industrial or urban constituencies than were comparatively unlettered and untried working men. The point was put in its most naked form by Sir Edward Reed to the electors of Cardiff in 1903. 'He had always been a labour member. Anyhow, he'd recently secured orders for Cardiff business on which over £2 million was being spent. Could a working man have achieved that?'[27] In fact, inverted Marxism of this kind helped to dissuade the struggling labour and socialist organizations in Cardiff from putting forward any parliamentary candidate at all before 1918.

[25]Hartshorn was defeated by the Liberal Quaker industrialist, F. W. Gibbins, by a majority of 2,710 in a by-election on 31 March 1910 *South Wales Daily News*, 7 March–2 April 1910). The master of Elibank urged the Mid-Glamorgan Liberals in vain that the seat had been earmarked for the South Wales Miners' Federation when the sitting member retired. For the Mid-Glamorgan Liberals, Alderman T. J. Hughes replied that Hartshorn was in fact an LRC (and ILP) candidate. Hughes added: 'The gulf between Liberalism and rampant socialism was far wider than that between Liberalism and Conservatism' (*South Wales Daily News*, 19 March 1910). In the December 1910 general election Hartshorn was comfortably defeated by J. Hugh Edwards.

[26]Articles by Hartshorn, *Labour Leader*, 8 April and 16 December 1910.

[27]*South Wales Daily News*, 19 September 1903.

In one respect, this lack of sensitivity towards working-class aspirations among the Welsh Liberals between 1900 and 1914 may seem decidedly curious. For the dominant personality in the Welsh Liberal world throughout these years was, of course, Lloyd George, the supreme tribune of the New Liberalism during his triumphant period at the Treasury from April 1908 onwards. In fact, Lloyd George's viewpoint on social issues was extremely limited until he became chancellor of the Exchequer, as was that of the Liberal government of Campbell-Bannerman generally. Lloyd George had some knowledge of the surveys of urban poverty conducted by Charles Booth and by Seebohm Rowntree, and of the writings of the Webbs on trade unionism, but they seem to have made scant impression on him. His concern for social reform in his early period in politics from the 1880s was largely an extension of the radical democracy of the Old Liberalism, with a humanitarian gloss added, perhaps, by the imaginative writings of Hugo and Carlyle. The Caernarfon Boroughs constituency, which he represented from April 1890 onwards, contained working-class electors, but Lloyd George addressed them, in the main, in traditional terms. In 1892, for instance, he urged the working men of Bethesda, mainly quarrymen and railwaymen, that 'there was no need to form a Labour party. He considered that the land question, the temperance question and the question of disestablishment were equally matters of interest to labourers as was an Eight Hours' Bill.'[28] At Bagillt in 1895, he told a Flintshire audience: 'The fact was that government had nothing to do with trade . . . No one had ever been able to discover what trade depended on: it depended on conditions which had puzzled the ablest economists of the day.'[29] This was as far as his diagnosis of the problem of unemployment went. His major preoccupation down to the 1906 election, apart from his assault on 'Chamberlainism' during the Boer War, was with such issues as denominational schools, licensing reform and an educational council for Wales.[30] In the period of Liberal recovery between 1902 and 1905, Lloyd George paid scant heed to the columns of 'New Liberal' periodicals such as *The Speaker.* He still saw the New Liberalism rather through the perspective of the Old. Thus, he advocated old age pensions as a means of denouncing the payment of tithe to the 'alien Church'.[31] Although he served on Chaplin's Select

[28]*North Wales Observer,* 28 October 1892.

[29]Ibid., 12 July 1895.

[30]For Lloyd George's involvement in educational devolution, see Leslie Wynne Evans, 'The Welsh National Council for Education, 1903–06', *Welsh History Review,* 6 (1) (1972).

[31]*North Wales Observer,* 12 July 1895 (reporting an election speech by Lloyd George in the Caernarfon Guildhall).

Committee on pensions in 1899, he largely ignored the issue thereafter. He upheld the cause of the Bethesda quarrymen as a means of assailing the 'feudal' pretensions of Lord Penrhyn.[32] The savagery of the Penrhyn strike of 1900–3 did little to enlighten him in wider aspects of the relations between capital and labour.

Certainly, in British politics generally, Lloyd George's view of social questions was fundamentally transformed after his famous visit to Germany in the summer of 1908.[33] (So, incidentally, was his outlook on international affairs.) Henceforth, he was the outstanding national voice for social reform in the period down to 1914. He pushed through old age pensions, the 'people's budget', and the great National Insurance Bill. In 1913–14 he pressed on with land and housing reform, and with the radically redistributive budget of 1914. He made direct approaches to the Labour party to seek an overt coalition with the Liberal government.[34] In England, his political priorities were largely transformed. But in Wales it was all very different. Even after his famous speech on behalf of social reform to the Welsh National Liberal Council at Swansea in October 1908 (shortly after his return from Germany),[35] his outlook in Wales was largely parochial. He continued to hammer away at such issues as disestablishment of the Church, even though privately he no longer regarded it as being of much real significance. For Lloyd George, Welsh and English Liberalism represented different worlds – the worlds, perhaps, of Dame Margaret and of Frances Stevenson. After 1908, he was a New Liberal in England, and Old Liberal in Wales.[36] In this, perhaps, he was typical of Welsh Liberalism as a whole. In 1914 Keir Hardie's *Merthyr Pioneer* lamented, as Hartshorn had done in 1910, that the nation was still largely involved 'in the little Bethel stage of Wales for the Welsh', rather than in the international movement of working-class solidarity (which, in those pre-war days, was still believed to exist).[37] If this was still largely true of Welsh Liberalism in general, it was the case even with Lloyd George, its most dynamic and creative representative during his radical high noon.

[32]For example a speech at Rhyl, 6 January 1897, in which Lloyd George attacked Lord Penrhyn's propensity to talk of 'my quarry' and 'my men' (*Rhyl Record and Advertiser*, 9 January 1897).

[33]The only first-hand account of this visit is given in Harold Spender, *The Fire of Life* (n.d. [1926]), 161–6.

[34]Ramsay MacDonald papers (8/1): report of a meeting of Lloyd George and MacDonald, 3 March 1914 (consulted by kind permission of Mr David Marquand).

[35]*South Wales Daily News*, 2 October 1908.

[36]Cf. Kenneth O. Morgan, 'Lloyd George and the historians', *Transactions of the Honourable Society of Cymmrodorion*, 1971 (1), 73–4 (published below, 380–99).

[37]*Merthyr Pioneer*, 14 March 1914.

In fact, the Welsh Labour movement was surprisingly slow to derive much advantage from this rigidity in the outlook of Welsh Liberalism. Indeed, the undermining of the Liberal ascendancy in Wales before 1914 has often been very much exaggerated. Undoubtedly, the ILP was making headway in south Wales in the years after 1898. Beyond this, there was a rising tide of class militancy in the south Wales mining valleys after the turn of the century: Tonypandy was its folk symbol and *The Miners' Next Step* its political testament. Even in rural Caernarfonshire the north Wales quarrying community demonstrated something of the same mood in the aftermath of the Penrhyn quarry strikes.[38] Wales seemed by 1914 to have become the major battle-ground for the class war; in no other part of Britain was the confrontation between capital and labour more naked and complete.

But the coherence and strength of the labour 'unrest', especially of rank-and-file protest, can be exaggerated. Earlier writers, like G. D. H. Cole,[39] grossly overstated the prevalence of syndicalism and of other theories of 'direct action', and misinterpreted their influence upon events. The roles of the Plebs League and of the Unofficial Reform Committee, for too long grossly neglected, are now in danger of being given a prominence they scarcely deserve. The Plebs League, after all, was almost entirely confined to the Rhondda valleys; by 1914 much of its energy had been transferred to the scattered tutorial classes of the Central Labour College.[40] By the summer of 1914 the Unofficial Reform Committee had largely disbanded, while Noah Ablett, the messiah of Welsh Marxism, was under fire from 'maximalists' like C. L. Gibbons and W. F. Hay ('Syndic' of the *Rhondda Socialist*) for choosing to work within the South Wales Miners' Federation.[41] The turmoil of the years 1908–14 ended with the official union leadership firmly in control of events. Even though Mabon had been eclipsed on the SWMF executive in 1911, 'Mabonism' lived on through younger men like Brace and Tom Richards.[42] Even ILP activists like Hartshorn and James Winstone, were known to be vehement opponents of syndicalism and industrial indiscipline. Almost in spite of themselves they had become symbols of the official processes of collective bargaining,

[38]See Cyril Parry, *The Radical Tradition in Welsh Politics: a study of Gwynedd Politics, 1900–1920* (Cardiff, 1970), 8–11.

[39]For example, G. D. H. Cole, *A Short History of the British Working Class Movement*, Vol. III (1927), 70–7, 101–2.

[40]There is an excellent discussion of this point in M. G. Woodhouse, 'Rank and File Movements in South Wales, 1910–26' (unpublished University of Oxford D.Phil thesis, 1970).

[41]*South Wales Worker*, 1913–14 *passim*.

[42]Brace was re-elected to the SWMF executive (at the top of the poll) in September 1912. Richards remained its treasurer until 1931.

of constitutionalism, social cohesion and the imperatives of the 'Progressive alliance'. Despite the class conflict, despite the massive influx of new immigrants from England, despite the new generation of miners represented by younger men like Ablett, Frank Hodges and A. J. Cook, 'Lib–Labism' remained a dominant and unifying creed in industrial south Wales down to the outbreak of war in 1914.

In any event, the connection between industrial activism and political action by the ILP or the Labour party was not a direct one at all. Little benefit accrued to the ILP from the miners' vote for affiliation to the Labour party in 1908 or from the massive strikes of 1910–12. Keir Hardie and the ILP, after all, were a part of the discredited political process that the Unofficial Reform Committee and the Central Labour College ridiculed. Furthermore, the ILP in south Wales was still comparatively fragile despite all the progress made since 1898, and the Labour party suffered accordingly. Even in Merthyr Tydfil, that time-honoured radical stronghold and the seat of Keir Hardie, the secretary of the Aberdare ILP could write to Ramsay MacDonald in 1907: 'The L.R.C. is really dead here. The question of putting new life into it has caused a great deal of anxiety to our comrade Hardie.'[43] In the January and December 1910 elections, in almost every instance, Labour candidates failed miserably against Liberal opponents in cases where there was a direct clash at the polls. In east Glamorgan, C. B. Stanton, a pugnacious spokesman for 'direct action', was heavily defeated by a Liberal new to this overwhelmingly working-class mining constituency.[44] Further, the Welsh Labour members returned in 1910 were wholly of the 'Lib–Lab' persuasion, almost all of them committed to Welsh national causes and to Nonconformist radicalism. The one exception, of course, was Hardie in Merthyr. Even he never came top of the poll at Merthyr in four successive contests. He owed much of his appeal to traditional Nonconformist radical sentiment in 1910, just as earlier he had, in effect, run in double harness with the coalowner tycoon, D. A. Thomas of the Cambrian Collieries.[45]

If anything, it was the Liberals who were the aggressors in the Labour–Liberal relationship in the immediate pre-war period. Liberal

[43]W. W. Price to Ramsay MacDonald, 28 April 1907 (Labour Party General Correspondence files, LPGC 14/1).

[44]The successful Liberal was Clement Edwards, formerly member for Denbigh District, 1906–January 1910. Edwards emphasized his record of involvement in trade unionism since 1891 but urged workers to free themselves from 'the Socialist-Syndicalist chariot'. His views are recorded in *South Wales Daily News*, 18 May 1914, and *Glamorgan Free Press*, 11 December 1913.

[45]In the 1900 election, 4,437 of Hardie's 5,745 votes had been cast jointly for Thomas and himself.

MPs like Clement Edwards and J. Hugh Edwards launched an anti-socialist crusade in the mining valleys. The Revd W. F. Phillips, a Calvinistic Methodist minister who had briefly (in 1910) been a member of the Newport branch of the ILP, construed it as his mission to denounce the economic and spiritual heresies of socialism.[46] He was soon locked in legal conflict with the ILP newspaper for west Wales, *Llais Llafur* of Ystalyfera. Undeterred, he set forth his creed in an ephemeral new journal, *Y Gwerinwr: The Monthly Democrat*, which he launched in 1912. Certainly, many of these anti-socialist onslaughts proved barren. The annual conference of the ILP held at Merthyr in 1912 confirmed how durable were the roots of that party in many parts of the coalfield.[47] The falling statistics for religious observance, the declining status of the Nonconformist ministry, the waning appeal of the puritan ethic in the Welsh coalfield suggested that the high noon for Nonconformist radicalism had passed some time before. The revival of 1904–5 was a short-lived one.[48] The fact remains that, in narrowly political terms, it was Labour rather than the Liberals who felt themselves to be on the defensive in industrial south Wales in 1914. The assaults of professional anti-socialists like W. F. Phillips frequently missed their mark, but not always. In particular, the accusation that the internationalism of revolutionary socialism was at variance with the Welsh national causes won much support. However much Keir Hardie might proclaim his sympathy with Welsh Home Rule and his desire to unite 'the red dragon with the red flag',[49] the

[46]Phillips's views are given in 'Cymru a sosialaeth', and 'Y Ddraig Goch ynte'r Faner Goch?', *Y Geninen*, Ionawr, Hydref, 1911, and in articles in *Y Traethodydd*, 1912–14. Phillips, the son of a Penmaenmawr worker, was a BA and BD of Jesus College, Oxford, and a member of the South Wales League of Young Liberals. He unsuccessfully contested Gower as a Liberal candidate in December 1910 and lost by 953 votes to the sitting Labour member, John Williams: his campaign there is covered in *Mumbles Weekly Press and Gower News*, 1–22 December 1910. He fiercely attacked the Swansea Liberal journal, the *Cambria Daily Leader*, for giving the impression that his candidacy was a lost cause. During the campaign, the secretary of the Newport ILP, H. Humphreys, revealed the damaging information that Phillips had been a member of the Newport ILP from 3 February to 12 May 1910 (*Llais Llafur*, 10 December 1910). He died young in 1920.

[47]Keir Hardie, 'Socialism in south Wales', *Labour Leader*, 26 February 1912; *Twentieth Annual Conference of the Independent Labour Party, held at Merthyr Tydfil, 27–28 May 1912*.

[48]There is much valuable evidence on these matters in the *Report* and *Evidence of the Royal Commission appointed to inquire into the Church and other Religious Bodies in Wales* (PP, 1910, XIV–XVII: Cd. 5432–5). See also E. T. Davies, *Religion in the Industrial Revolution in South Wales* (Cardiff, 1965), ch. IV.

[49]Keir Hardie, *The Welsh Dragon and the Welsh Flag* (Pioneer Pamphlets, No. 1, 1911); *Merthyr Express*, 14 October 1911.

appeal of the ILP basically rejected particularism. When a conference of socialists at Carmarthen in 1911 called for the formation of a distinct Welsh Independent Labour Party, Keir Hardie himself voiced the opposition to it.[50] Hardie himself was acutely aware of the growing tension between socialism and nationalism in industrial south Wales. In his own Merthyr constituency, the local Liberals in 1913 had finally jettisoned the unofficial electoral agreement, and had nominated a second Liberal candidate for this two-member seat, a Welsh-speaking Nonconformist barrister, Thomas Artemus Jones.[51] Jones, a vehement opponent of socialism, was to fight Hardie in the next general election. It is by no means unlikely that Hardie, had he lived, might have lost his seat, even without war intervening. Here and elsewhere, the deteriorating relations between Liberals and the Labour party in the years up to 1914 did not necessarily presage the 'strange death' of Liberal Wales. In some sense, they were testimony to the strength and resilience of Welsh Liberalism and the old nineteenth-century values it represented, however barren its programme and however outdated its ideology.

The First World War introduced a totally new phase. After being riven by division in the first two years, with men like MacDonald and Hardie isolated outcasts in opposition to the war, the Labour party eventually gained immensely in strength. The key to this process was the dramatic expansion of the trade unions which more than doubled in membership between 1914 and 1920. In addition, the party constitution of 1918 gave Labour a new organizational base in the constituencies, while the ideological fervour of the Russian revolution reinforced Labour's moral appeal. Many of these factors were particularly evident in south Wales as the 1917 Committee on Industrial Unrest reported.[52] Socialist propagandists, a pessimistic Liberal later recorded, had now come to regard the Welsh coalfield as 'the Eldorado of their Utopian hopes'.[53] The Labour party, even under the quiescent leadership of men such as Henderson and Clynes, could hardly fail to be the leading beneficiary.

By contrast, the Liberals underwent massive strains in organization and in morale during the wartime years. The entry of Britain into war in August 1914 drove many Liberal idealists into political isolation or

[50]*Labour Leader*, 25 August, 8 September 1911: see particularly a letter by David Thomas in the latter issue.

[51]*Merthyr Pioneer*, 26 July 1913.

[52]*Report of the Commissioners appointed to inquire into Industrial Unrest: No 7 Division* (Cd. 8668), 15–34.

[53]Sir Alfred Mond to Lloyd George, 10 August 1922 (Beaverbrook Library, Lloyd George papers, F/37/2/17), enclosing statement by W. C. Jenkins of Swansea.

exile. While John Williams, Brynsiencyn, preached in Independent pulpits in full military uniform, radicals like the Revd Thomas Rees, the principal of Bala-Bangor theological college, and the Revd Puleston Jones, the celebrated blind preacher, suffered cruelly for their anti-war views. Quasi-pacifist periodicals like *Y Wawr* and *Y Deyrnas* were bitterly assailed.[54] Some Liberal intellectuals, like the poet T. Gwynn Jones, underwent a more private torture; others joined the Union of Democratic Control or the Labour party; still others, like D. R. Daniel (the associate of Tom Ellis and the young Lloyd George in the late 1880s) went out of public life almost entirely in response to the appalling tragedy of total war.[55] Welsh Liberalism was further demoralized by the schism between Asquith and Lloyd George after the political crisis of December 1916, although the new premier's mystique in his native land largely endured. In the 1918 'coupon election', the Liberals retained an illusory strength. They captured twenty-one out of the thirty-six Welsh seats, newly redistributed; twenty of these twenty-one members were supporters of the Lloyd George coalition. Anti-war candidates like Thomas Nicholas at Aberdare were overwhelmed.[56] But the transient nature of these Liberal successes was emphasized by a succession of crucial by-elections in 1919–22. Drawing new strength from the industrial depression and mass unemployment that afflicted south Wales from 1921 onwards, Labour made sweeping inroads into Liberal territory. In August 1921, Morgan Jones, an ILP militant who had been a conscientious objector during the war, more than doubled the Labour majority. In July 1922 Gower was safely retained by D. R. Grenfell, and Pontypridd won from the Liberals by T. I. Mardy Jones with a majority of over 4,000.[57] In the November 1922 general election, in which local Liberal organizations seemed almost paralysed after the sudden downfall of the Lloyd George coalition, Labour gained eight seats from the Liberals, including Wrexham and Caernarfonshire in north Wales. In

[54]*Y Tyst*, 30 September–25 November 1914; *Y Deyrnas*, October 1916–November 1919 *passim*; T. Eirug Rees (ed.), *Y Prifathro Thomas Rees: Ei Fywyd a'i Waith* (Llandysul, 1939), 138–48; R. W. Jones, *Y Parchedig John Puleston Jones, M.A., D.D.* (Caernarfon, 1929), 186 ff; R. R. Hughes, *Y Parchedig John Williams, D.D., Brynsiencyn* (Caernarfon, 1929), 262 ff. Thomas Rees, in one celebrated episode, was expelled from the Bangor Golf Club.

[55]K. W. Jones-Roberts, 'D. R. Daniel', *Journal of the Merioneth Hist. and Record Society*, V (1) (1965), 70–1.

[56]Nicholas met with defeat by over 16,000 votes at the hands of the bellicose National Democratic Party candidate (and former militant miners' agent), Charles Butt Stanton, an advocate of hanging the Kaiser.

[57]See Kenneth O. Morgan, 'Twilight of Welsh Liberalism: Lloyd George and the "Wee-Frees", 1918–35', *Bulletin of the Board of Celtic Studies*, XXII (1) (1968), 389–91.

south Wales, every remaining Liberal seat was now clearly at risk. Meanwhile, in local government contests the calamitous defeats of Liberal nominees, whether running openly or under the label of 'independent' or 'ratepayer', provided further testimony to the political revolution that was taking place in post-war Wales.

In these dismal circumstances, it might have been expected that Welsh Liberals would at last respond to the challenge of Labour with a new awareness of the more fundamental social issues of the day. In particular, they might acknowledge the economic transformation that had occurred since the apparently limitless prosperity when Coal was King before 1914. Yet, in fact Liberals in Wales were perhaps even more doctrinaire in their hostility towards socialism than in the years of pre-war Liberal ascendancy. A key factor here was that official Liberalism in Wales was overwhelmingly dominated by adherents of the Lloyd George coalition. The Welsh National Liberal Council, presided over by Lord St David's, was the one regional council which the Asquithians failed to capture. It could well be argued that the Coalition Liberal ministers in the government – men like Addison, Fisher, Montagu, Mond and even Churchill – were active forces in promoting constructive social reform. As a result, the Lloyd George administration passed a series of radical measures dealing with education, housing, health, unemployment insurance and pensions in the period 1918–21, until the Geddes 'axe' descended.[58] But this enlightened attitude was emphatically not shared by Coalition Liberals in the constituencies, especially in Wales. Although vestiges of the old pre-war radicalism survived in protests by Welsh Liberals against the retaliatory policies of the 'Black and Tans' in Ireland, [59] their social and economic programmes largely consisted of the severest retrenchment and a dogged anti-socialism. Coalition Liberalism in Wales became increasingly impatient towards the demands of organized labour, while grass-roots constituency parties simply withered away as younger radicals and women voters defected to Labour or the 'Wee Frees'. A characteristic sample of the social philosophy of post-war Coalition Liberalism is seen in the views of Sir George Hay Morgan, after his heavy defeat in the Abertillery by-election in December 1920:

> I hammered away at Constitutionalism and Bolshevism. The mind of the Miners was, however, impervious to any national question. The

[58]Kenneth O. Morgan, 'Lloyd George's stage army: the Coalition Liberals, 1918–22' in A. J. P. Taylor (ed.), *Lloyd George: Twelve Essays* (London, 1971), 240–2.

[59]Winifred Coombe Tennant to D. Lloyd George, 31 March 1921 (Lloyd George papers, F/96/1/15).

only subjects that interested him were More Pay, Shorter hours of work, No Income Tax for wage earners, more facilities for Drinking.[60]

The social and ideological gulf that separated a wealthy barrister like Hay Morgan from the militant working-class electors of Abertillery was vividly underlined.

The erosion of Welsh Liberalism was confirmed in the general elections that followed each other in November 1922, December 1923 and October 1924. In each of them, the main programme of the Liberals was a sterile anti-Bolshevism. Alternatively, they called for 'a sane circumspect course',[61] totally at variance with the iconoclastic radicalism of pre-war years. Occasionally, there were evocations also of the old causes of Home Rule and temperance reform, together with protests at the generous financial terms accorded the Church in the disendowment settlement in 1919.[62] In several constituencies in 1923 there was a clear anti-Labour pact with the Conservatives: a notable instance was Aberavon, where Ramsay MacDonald was now the member. A Liberal like Sir Alfred Mond, a genuine voice of radical reform in the government and in the country, even in the immediate post-war period, was now a dedicated apologist for monopoly capitalism. Much of west Wales Liberalism in the Swansea area went with him. The union of the two Liberal wings, Asquithian and Lloyd Georgian, beneath the banner of free trade just before the 1923 election, in fact made the sterility of the party even more pronounced, for Welsh Asquithians had even less to say on social questions. By 1924, the traditional creed of Welsh Liberalism indeed had become anachronistic. The old programme had largely vanished with the disestablishment of the Welsh Church in 1920. Other issues such as local Home Rule or temperance legislation evoked little enough enthusiasm in the post-war world, especially among younger ex-servicemen back from the trenches. Lloyd George himself now seemed a curiously dated figure, while his unsympathetic approach to labour militancy in the 1919–21 period had seriously impaired his radical credentials. As a result, by the 1924 election the Liberals had largely been driven out of south Wales by Labour, and the change was to prove permanent. A new generation of young miners from the Central Labour College, men like Aneurin Bevan, Morgan Phillips, Ness

[60]F. E. Guest to Lloyd George, 6 January 1921 (ibid., F/22/3/2) (enclosure).

[61]See C. P. Cook, 'Wales and the general election of 1923', *Welsh History Review*, 4 (4) (1969), 392 (citing the election address of the Liberal candidate for Neath).

[62]*South Wales News*, 10 January 1921: manifesto of the (Asquithian) Welsh Liberal Federation under the presidency of Ellis W. Davies. (Cf. *Welsh Gazette*, 20 November 1922.

Edwards and James Griffiths, provided a new élite of leadership just as surely as had the young Liberals of the *Cymru Fydd* era, a generation or more back in the early 1880s.[63] Welsh Liberalism, significantly, retained much more support in more sparsely-populated and characteristically Welsh rural constituencies. For instance, in Cardiganshire the triumph of Hopkin Morris (Independent Liberal) over Ernest Evans (Lloyd George Liberal) in the 1923 election gave local Liberalism in this old radical stronghold a new lease of life, and helped it to ward off the challenge of Labour for another forty years.[64]

Perhaps the most striking result in many ways in this period was the 1923 election in the University of Wales constituency. Here George Maitland Lloyd Davies, a Christian pacifist (and ultimately Labour) candidate, who had been imprisoned as a conscientious objector during the war, was elected. Davies owed his success largely to a split vote, his majority was only ten, and he was defeated in 1924 by Ernest Evans (Liberal). But the mere fact that Labour could capture the national University, so deeply permeated with the spirit of Tom Ellis and the great days of *Cymru Fydd*, was surely a sign of a profound shift of mood in the character of Welsh politics and society. However transient, Davies's victory suggested that the university intelligentsia and professional middle class in Wales were no longer automatically or instinctively Liberal. Significantly, Davies's candidature held especial appeal for younger voters.[65] Since 1914 a generational change had occurred. The Liberals now gave every sign of being an ageing party shackled to its past. This was felt with especial keenness by the young intellectuals who came together to found the Nationalist party, *Plaid Genedlaethol Cymru*, at Pwllheli eisteddfod in 1925. They saw the alleged betrayal of small nationalities during the First World War and the 'Black and Tans' era in Ireland during Lloyd George's administration as symbols of the crisis facing the Liberal ethic.[66] Saunders Lewis, the party's first president, the son of a Nonconformist minister in Liverpool and a distinguished littérateur, poured scorn on the old 'nationalist' Liberalism – 'the spare time hobby of corpulent and successful men', who attended denominational assemblies and the dinners of the

---

[63]W. W. Craik, *The Central Labour College* (London, 1964).

[64]Kenneth O. Morgan, 'Cardiganshire politics: the Liberal ascendancy, 1885–1923', *Ceredigion*, V (4) (1967), 333–7 (published in this volume 216–50).

[65]Principal Thomas Rees to G. M. Ll. Davies, 17 December 1923 (NLW, Davies papers, 2153); *Welsh Outlook*, January 1924.

[66]J. E. Jones, *Tros Gymru* (Cardiff, 1970), 25–36. Alan Butt-Philip, 'The Political and Sociological Significance of Welsh Nationalism since 1945' (unpublished University of Oxford D.Phil. thesis, 1971) gives an excellent account of the origins of Plaid Cymru.

Honourable Society of Cymmrodorion.[67] The post-war generation would espouse nationalism of a far more intense and aggressive nature.

The last serious attempt to adapt Welsh Liberalism to meet the challenge of Labour came with Lloyd George's dramatic programmes in the later 1920s. These policies provided a stark contrast to the cautious outlook of both Conservatives and Labour in the period 1926–9. Significantly, Lloyd George's new programmes owed virtually nothing to Welsh Liberalism. All his advisers were Englishmen like Keynes, Walter Layton, Seebohm Rowntree and Hubert Henderson. Their schemes provided a total rejection of the older Liberalism of his Welsh past. They concentrated on economic issues rather than social, on unemployment and industrial stagnation rather than on democracy and civic equality. Some of Lloyd George's new programmes were not immediately popular in the principality. The 'Green Book', *The Land and the Nation*, published in 1925, was attacked by many Welsh Liberals. Its proposals for 'cultivating tenure', a form of quasi-nationalization of cultivable land, were anathema to those many Welsh freeholders who had so recently purchased their holdings in the revolution in the land market after 1918. The scheme was sufficiently redolent of socialism to drive Sir Alfred Mond out of the party entirely after a bitter quarrel with Lloyd George.[68] It was notable that the Carmarthen Liberals in a by-election in 1928 (caused by Mond's receiving a peerage) had earlier turned down a Lloyd George nominee, Captain R. T. Evans, who warmly endorsed the 'Green Book'.[69] Instead, they put up Colonel W. N. Jones, an avowed critic of the new land proposals – and, incidentally, also an opponent of free trade. In consequence, the Liberal majority over Labour fell from more than 9,000 to forty-seven.

Even so, in the 1929 general election, Welsh Liberals wholeheartedly embraced Lloyd George's dramatic new policies. They even endorsed the schemes for public works and compensatory government spending embodied in the 'Orange Book', *We Can Conquer Unemployment*. Every Liberal candidate in Wales made this dramatic document the centre-piece of his campaign. This was true even of Colonel Jones in Carmarthen, and of Hopkin Morris in Cardiganshire (who continued to reject Lloyd George's leadership of the party). Colonel Jones added the gloss that the new public works schemes might save money on the rates. Candidates like James Jenkins in Merthyr and D. L. Powell in Ogmore

[67] *The Welsh Nationalist*, January 1932, 1.

[68] For the issues that divided them, see Sir Alfred Mond to Lloyd George, 25 September 1924; Lloyd George to Mond, 29 September 1924 (Lloyd George papers, G/14/5/8, 10).

[69] *Western Mail*, 19, 21 June 1928. Jones had been nominated on 7 March 1926.

urged that the new employment to be provided by road construction, housing and other public-supported programmes, would remedy depression in the coalfield and decay in the rural communities.[70] Several Welsh industrialists signed petitions on behalf of the proposals in *We Can Conquer Unemployment*: the interests they represented included banking, construction, chemicals, electricity, engineering, insurance, iron and steel, oil, shipping and textiles, the second industrial revolution as well as the first. They gave Lloyd George's schemes the benediction of being 'economically and financially sound'.[71] In the 1929 election, indeed, for the first time, a party in Wales had a radical, progressive economic programme, a sophisticated range of policies for remedying the structural decay of twentieth-century Wales, and a positive reply to the challenge of Labour.

But it was all in vain. The 1929 election did, it is true, see Liberal gains from the Conservatives in two constituencies (Flintshire and Pembrokeshire). But there was the further loss of Carmarthen, Swansea West and Wrexham to Labour who now claimed twenty-five seats in Wales. Lloyd George's own majority in Caernarfon Boroughs, in a three-cornered contest, fell by over 3,000 votes. He claimed, wrongly, that Liberals had been 'tripped up by the triangle', that is, that they were the victim of three-cornered contests which eroded their poll.[72] In reality, the Liberals were the victims of their – and their leader's – past. Liberalism, unlike Labour, was inextricably associated with a society that was passing away. When disestablishment of the Church was finally passed in 1919, much of the essence of Welsh Liberalism seemed to pass away with it. Liberals retained their foothold in rural Wales until 1945. Thereafter, historic Liberal constituencies like Merioneth, Anglesey and Cardiganshire (captured by Labour) and Denbigh (won by the Conservatives) slipped away also. Symbolically, perhaps, Lady Megan Lloyd George joined the Labour party in the 1950s: she captured the Carmarthen seat from the Liberals in a fiercely-fought by-election contest in 1957. Nine years later, Plaid Cymru was to win this seat from Labour, with the Liberal candidate coming in third. In the years since 1929, Liberalism in Wales has become more and more attenuated. Perhaps it was, indeed, in non-party pressure groups such as the League of Nations Union in the 1930s that the resilience and the idealism of the older Liberalism found its most effective resting-place.[73]

[70]Ibid., 17, 20, 21 May 1929; *Cambrian News*, 9, 16 May 1929.

[71]*Western Mail*, 29 May 1929; *Liverpool Daily Post*, 29 May 1929.

[72]*Liverpool Daily Post*, 1 June 1929. Lloyd George's view is not supported by a comparison of the percentages of the poll obtained, and seats fought, by Welsh Liberal candidates in 1924 and 1929.

[73]See Goronwy J. Jones, *Wales and the Quest for Peace* (Cardiff, 1970).

Liberalism in Wales was uniquely well-equipped to withstand the challenge of Labour in the years before 1914. It was a broad, democratic, populistic national movement, associated with the aspirations of Welsh society and with Welsh cultural awareness at every level. It helped to inspire the history of John Edward Lloyd, the poetry of Gwynn Jones, the imaginative prose of Owen M. Edwards, no less than the rhetoric of Lloyd George. But precisely because it was so integrated with Welsh society before 1914, and so Welsh in character, it was uniquely ill-equipped to meet the Labour challenge after the war when the old society passed away. How far a vigorous programme of social reform would have delayed the rise of Labour in Wales is debatable. The enthusiasm of working-class voters for such reforming measures as the National Insurance Bill has recently been questioned by Dr Henry Pelling.[74] What is not debatable is that Welsh Liberalism, until 1929 when it was too late, never made any effort to develop a coherent social policy. The Nonconformist churches, the backbone of constituency Liberalism, were apathetic or hostile. Movements like *Urdd y Deyrnas*, founded in 1924 to consider current social problems from a Christian standpoint, had little effect. Whether Welsh Liberalism was untypical in its reactions, compared, for instance, with the vitality of the New Liberalism in Lancashire, is also debatable. It may, indeed, have been Lancashire that was untypical, in view of the existence there of a distinctive working-class Protestant Toryism. It is notable that 'New Liberal' strength in the country was concentrated mainly in Manchester, where the influence of men like Scott and Hobhouse flourished. Tory Liverpool, by contrast, the domain of Alderman Salvidge, remained impervious to reformist Liberalism and to Labour alike until 1945.[75] The Welsh experience might have been nearer the norm for Britain as a whole.

Liberalism in Wales was the product of a remarkable phase of national emergence in the late nineteenth century. By the 1920s, by contrast, the Liberals were undeniably a nostalgic party: witness the *Cambrian News* in 1923 lauding the Cardiganshire voters for 'remaining true to the faith of their fathers, true to free trade, true to the promise of 1868'.[76] In the 1880s and 1890s, Welsh Liberals were on the left of their party on most domestic and international issues – even though the widespread initial support for the Boer War in Wales,

[74] Henry Pelling, *Popular Politics and Society in Late Victorian Britain* (London, 1968), 12 *et seq.*

[75] Clarke, op. cit., especially 45–52. On the other hand, Dr Clarke does show the close relations that obtained between Liberals and Labour in such towns as Bolton, Blackburn and Preston by 1910.

[76] *Cambrian News*, 14 December 1923 (leading article).

indicated sharp limits to that radicalism.[77] By the 1920s, however, Welsh Liberals were equally clearly on the right of their party. One suspects that they remained so in the 1930s and 1940s, despite the temporary stimulus of Lloyd George's radical programmes in 1929. After all, Clement Davies, the outstanding figure in Welsh Liberal circles after Lloyd George's death, was markedly conservative in his social and economic outlook. He had supported the National Government for most of the 1930s. By then, the Liberal party in Wales, the instrument of so much democratic and progressive reform, the creator of a disestablished church and a disestablished gentry, the standard-bearer of nationhood, had become, in Arthur Schlesinger's expressive phrase, 'a party of memory'. It can scarcely be denied that Welsh political life is the poorer for it. Whether we had reached a further point of transition in the 1970s, whether the Labour party was likely to go along the same path of ossification and decay as did the Liberals before it, might provide a fruitful theme for a later colloquium. But that is to take us from history into prophecy.

1973

[77]Kenneth O. Morgan, 'Wales and the Boer War – a reply', *Welsh History Review*, 4 (4) (1969), 367ff (published in this volume, 46–58).

6

Peace Movements in Wales,
1899–1945

Accounts of Welsh radical politics in the nineteenth and early twentieth centuries are usually essays in introspection. They have invariably focused on domestic themes – on the campaigns against political and social privilege, on the struggles for religious and civic equality, educational advance and a more emphatic national status for Wales. But publicists and propagandists for Welsh radical causes, down to the First World War and beyond, frequently chose to interpret their native political traditions in external terms as well, as a crusade against war. Peace was located alongside retrenchment and reform in the Welsh radical pantheon, from the era of Gwilym Hiraethog to that of Lloyd George.

Certainly anti-war journalists during 1914–18 were able to point to the elements of a coherent peace movement during the evolution of radicalism in Wales in the century that followed the Napoleonic Wars, and it remains surprising that later historians have not made more of this theme.[1] Welshmen such as the Neath Quaker industrialist, Joseph Tregelles Price, and his fellow Quaker, Evan Rees, were prominent in the formation of the Peace Society in London as early as 1816, and in the local Peace Society formed in the Swansea and Neath district a year later. The virtues of Christian pacifism or non-resistance, and the inhumanity and obscenity of war were topics frequently echoed in Welsh local newspapers and Nonconformist periodicals such as *Yr Amserau* and *Y Traethodydd* in the 1840s and 1850s. Two of the most

[1]For an excellent general survey, see Goronwy J. Jones, *Wales and the Quest for Peace* (Cardiff, 1969).

celebrated of radical figures in their generation, William Rees (Gwilym Hiraethog) and Samuel Roberts of Llanbrynmair ('S.R.'), editors respectively of *Yr Amserau* and *Y Cronicl*, were prominent in leading the campaign for international peace in the years that followed the revolutionary turmoil of 1848. Both fought hard against British involvement in the Crimean War despite much local unpopularity. 'S.R.' even urged a peaceful resolution of the differences between North and South in the United States in 1861, for all his opposition to slavery.

Later in the century, the popular agitation against 'Beaconsfieldism' saw large sections of Liberal and Nonconformist opinion in Wales vehement in denouncing the threat of war with Russia over the troubles in the Balkans in 1876–8. Pacifism combined with a powerful prejudice against the Mohammedan Turks who had persecuted Christian minorities in south-east Europe in the recent past. These sentiments endured. Nearly fifty years on, in the 1922 general election, Sir Alfred Mond was still able to regard anti-Turkish feeling as a potent electoral weapon in rallying Liberal opinion in Swansea.[2] Lord d'Abernon noted the 'little Bethel mentality' of the prime minister, that Welsh Baptist, in handling the Chanak crisis.[3] Perhaps one man, above all others, inextricably linked Welsh radical opinion with the quest for international peace and a system of arbitration of disputes between the nations of the world. This was Henry Richard of Tregaron, elected for Merthyr Tydfil in the celebrated election of 1868, that *annus mirabilis* as it has been termed, but also a close friend of Cobden and Bright, secretary of the Peace Society from 1848 onwards and internationally revered as 'the apostle of peace'.

On the other hand, it is clear that the anti-war tradition in nineteenth-century Wales was a limited one. For all their professed radicalism and humanitarian idealism, the Welsh were reluctant to beat all their swords into ploughshares. The Peace Society was not a powerful organization in Wales, despite enjoying a temporary boom in the later 1870s. Henry Richard himself, perhaps even during his twenty years of service as a Welsh MP until his death in 1888, was regarded more as a symbol of cosmopolitan free-trade Liberationist radicalism than an authentic spokesman for radical opinion within Wales itself. At the time of his death, he was basically a revered anachronism in his native land. Just as anti-war men like the writer, E. Tegla Davies, and the socialist bard, the Revd Thomas Nicholas,

---

[2] Sir A. Mond to David Lloyd George, 5 November 1922 (House of Lords Record Office, Lloyd George papers G/14/5/2).

[3] D'Abernon diary, 25 September 1922 (British Library, Add. MS. 48954B, f. 95).

could produce in 1914–18 a kind of pedigree of Welsh involvement in earlier peace movements,[4] so Lloyd George and others could appeal to an equally convincing tradition of military achievement and celebration.[5] The roots of Welsh national sentiment from the Edwardian conquest in the thirteenth century were, in many ways, warlike ones, as the words of the Welsh national anthem bore witness. The accomplishments of Welsh bowmen at Crécy and Agincourt, or Welsh seamen during the naval encounters of the Elizabethan or Cromwellian periods, could equally be summoned up as evidence by the advocates of war. The Welsh past, like the American, was a distinctly usable one. While Welsh Liberals in the nineteenth century, following their brethren in England and Scotland, conceived their ideology against the background of a nation at peace, the pressures of wartime could all too easily transform Welsh national sentiment into a belligerent commitment to British patriotism or imperialism.

During the Napoleonic Wars, the bulk of articulate Welsh opinion had appeared to remain faithful to church and state. Jac Glan-y-Gors, 'the Welsh Tom Paine', sang in praise of Nelson and the glory of Trafalgar, and Iolo Morganwg, former publicist of the Jacobin 'Madoc', extolled the Glamorgan Volunteers. At the time of the Crimean War, 'S.R.' and Gwilym Hiraethog appear to have been minority voices in resisting the Russophobia and jingoism of the Palmerstonian heyday. The great bulk of Welsh-language periodicals, save only for some of those published by the Independents, were strongly pro-war in 1853. As British patriotism acquired new imperial overtones with the annexation of vast new tropical territories in the later decades of the century, so Welshmen, anxious that the status of their nation should be exalted within the fabric of Union and empire, concerned for their place in the sun, drew consolation from the successes of Welshmen at arms. The protests of Henry Richard and others against the Zulu War in 1879 paled by comparison with the acclaim won by the South Wales Borderers at Rorke's Drift and Isandhlwana, engagements which brought a rash of Welsh Victoria Crosses and comparisons with the stand of the Spartans in resisting the Persians at Thermopylae.[6] Indeed, the loyalism and patriotism of the Welsh was an argument widely used by Liberals from 1880 onwards to justify political concessions to Wales, in the form of temperance and land reform, education, church disestablishment, even governmental devolution. The contrast was firmly drawn between the Welsh, basically zealous for national equality within the United

[4]For example, E. Tegla Davies in *Y Deyrnas*, Tachwedd 1916.
[5]Cf. Lloyd George's address to Bangor National Eisteddfod, 5 August 1915.
[6]Frank Emery, *The Red Soldier: Letters from the Zulu War, 1879* (London, 1977).

Kingdom, and the rebellious Irish, anxious for national separatism, hostile to imperial expansion, perhaps republican in sentiment, naturally prone to applaud British defeats in the field from Majuba Hill to Magersfontein.

These two conflicting strains of militarism and pacifism asserted themselves most dramatically in Wales during the South African War between October 1899 and May 1902. It caused intense political controversy in the principality, both because the war marked a crisis of empire of a quite new kind, and also because it followed nearly two decades of political, economic and cultural upheaval in Wales. In a sense, Welsh reactions to the Boer War were a commentary on the entire evolution of the nation since 1868 and on the very concept of *Cymru Fydd*. The traditional view of events often presented by historians is that the Welsh were strongly opposed to the war, partly on general pacifist grounds, partly because they sympathized deeply with the Boers, another small Calvinist, pastoral people, grappling with Anglo-Saxon rule.[7] This interpretation owes much to the role played by David Lloyd George who, from the start, adopted a fiercely hostile attitude to the war in South Africa, and who rose to national eminence as a violent critic of the Salisbury government and of its colonial secretary, Joseph Chamberlain, in particular. Some emphasis has been laid also on Keir Hardie's election as Labour member for Merthyr Tydfil in the 'khaki election' of October 1900. Hardie's return has sometimes been seen as a vindication of the cause of pacifism in the constituency represented for so long by Henry Richard himself. The marked swing back to the Liberals in the 1900 general election, in which the party registered a net gain of three seats and ended up with twenty-eight seats out of thirty-four in Wales, has often been interpreted as a token of the Welsh revulsion against imperialism and war. The Welsh, in short, were a nation of 'pro-Boers'.

In fact, a careful examination of the political response in Wales to the South African War leads irresistibly to the conclusion that the bulk of articulate, measurable opinion in Wales was strongly pro-war and sympathetic to imperialism, at least in the first period of the war down to the end of 1900.[8] Popular sentiment focused on local contributions to British arms, including General Hills-Johnes, Dr Mills Roberts (former goalkeeper for the Preston North End 'Invincibles') who ran the Welsh field hospital, and such alleged part-Welshmen as Lord Roberts and Baden-Powell. Of the Welsh Liberal MPs, only four were

[7]For example, Henry Pelling, *Popular Politics and Society in Late Victorian Britain* (London, 1968), 93 and n.1.

[8]For a fuller treatment of this theme, see Kenneth O. Morgan, 'Wales and the Boer War – a reply', *Welsh History Review*, 4 (4) (1969), 367–80 (published in this volume, 46–58).

unequivocally anti-war up to the time of the 'khaki election'. They
were a mixed group – Lloyd George himself and his old ally Herbert
Lewis (Flint Boroughs); Arthur Humphreys-Owen, an English-
speaking Anglican squire who represented Montgomeryshire; and
Bryn Roberts, an old-fashioned Cobdenite who sat for Eifion in
Caernarfon and had until recently been a bitter opponent of Lloyd
George because of the latter's quasi-Welsh nationalism. Most of the
rest of the Welsh Liberal MPs were, to a greater or lesser extent,
sympathetic to the war; some, such as Ellis Griffith (Anglesey), Sir
David Brynmor Jones (Swansea District) and J. Lloyd Morgan (West
Carmarthen) adopted a vehemently imperialistic position. Of the
thirty-two Liberal candidates in Wales in the 1900 'khaki election',
only five were outright opponents of the war; one of these, the son of
John Bright, was defeated at the polls. Equally, much of activist
constituency opinion seems to have been largely in sympathy with the
war, especially in industrial south Wales and the coastal ports, where it
could be political suicide to stand out against the tide of war. Robert
Bird in Cardiff was but one prospective candidate dropped by his local
Liberal Association because of his pro-Boer views.[9] Prominent south
Wales Nonconformists like the Revd Thomas Johns of Capel Als,
Llanelli (editor of the children's magazine, *Tywysydd y Plant*), spoke
out strongly on behalf of the war and in favour of the superior qualities
of civilization of the British race.[10] Even in rural Wales, predominantly
Welsh-speaking, a nationalistic journalist like Beriah Gwynfe Evans
could write strongly in support of the war while deploring the excesses
of war fever.[11] Herbert Lewis lamented the 'utter jingoism' amongst
his own Liberal supporters in Flintshire in early 1900,[12] while Lloyd
George required all his reserves of moral courage to withstand verbal,
and sometimes physical, assault from his constituents in Caernarfon
Boroughs.[13]

Nor was the opinion of the Welsh people – at least, that 55 per cent
of males who possessed the vote – clearly hostile to the war at first. The
Liberal gains in the 'khaki election' were not the product of anti-war
sentiment at all. Indeed, the Liberal candidates in two of the four seats
gained, Sir Edward Reed in Cardiff and Alfred Davies in Carmarthen
Boroughs, were imperialists of extreme fervour. In general, a strongly
pro-Boer attitude was thought by most Liberals to be an electoral
liability at this time. They preferred rather to deflect interest away from
the war, if they could, and to stress the grand old causes of church

[9] *Western Mail*, 22 August 1900.
[10] *Cardiff Times*, 7 July 1900.
[11] *Y Genedl Gymreig*, 18 Medi 1900.
[12] J. Herbert Lewis to Owen Williams, 20 July 1900 (NLW, Penucha MSS.).
[13] D. Lloyd George to J. Herbert Lewis, 13 April 1900 (ibid.).

disestablishment, elementary education and land reform. On balance, these themes figured more decisively in winning election victories for the Liberals than did the cause of specific opposition to the Boer War, let alone absolute pacifism. In any case, the seats won back were ripe for recapture after the quite unusual swing to the Unionists in the previous general election in 1895. In Merthyr, Keir Hardie did indeed defeat a fanatical supporter of the war, Pritchard Morgan, but he owed his victory largely to his general position as a representative of labour in a constituency much affected by the lengthy coal-stoppage in 1898, where the Independent Labour Party was already active.[14]

On the other hand, anti-war opinion certainly remained vigorously alive in Wales, even during the first year of the war, which brought excesses of jingoism and the spirit of Mafeking. Lloyd George alone gave the critics of imperialism considerable vitality and influence, especially when he arranged for the *Daily News* to be taken over by an anti-war syndicate, with the aid of the Cadbury family.[15] It was noticeable, too, that in the Welsh-language newspaper and periodical press, opposition to the war was far more pronounced than in the industrial coalfield and the more anglicized areas of Wales. Thomas Gee's old newspaper, *Baner ac Amserau Cymru*, now managed by his son, Howel Gee, was strongly hostile to the war from the outset, and warmly endorsed Lloyd George's outspoken attacks on Joseph Chamberlain.[16] In this, it countered the Caernarfon *Y Genedl*, published in Lloyd George's own constituency, which had taken a line generally sympathetic to the war. Similarly, such important Welsh-language newspapers as the *Herald Cymraeg* of Caernarfon, the Independent *Y Tyst* and the Methodist *Y Goleuad* were generally hostile to the war, although on grounds of public policy rather than on strictly pacifist lines.[17] As in the past, the Baptist and Independent denominations were most vocal in their criticism of war, followed by the Methodists. The Wesleyans, however, including their organ, *Yr Eurgrawn*, tended to echo the imperialism of such national Methodist leaders as the Revd Hugh Price Hughes and the MP for Louth, R. W. ('Imperial') Perks.

In the later stages of the war, from the end of 1900 until the peace

---

[14]For a fuller discussion of this election in Merthyr, see Kenneth O. Morgan, *Keir Hardie: Radical and Socialist* (London, 1975), 116–18, and Kenneth O. Fox, 'Labour and Merthyr's khaki election of 1900', *Welsh History Review*, 2 (4) (1965), 351–66.

[15]Stephen Koss, *Fleet Street Radical* (Hamden, Connecticut, 1973), 30–46.

[16]*Baner ac Amserau Cymru*, 14 Hydref 1899 *et seq*.

[17]For example *Y Tyst*, 20 Medi 1899 *et seq*.; *Y Goleuad*, 25 Hydref 1899. The Baptist *Seren Cymru* and the Unitarian journal, *Yr Ymofynydd*, were also strongly anti-war throughout.

concluded at Vereeniging in May 1902, it was noticeable that Liberal opinion in Wales became increasingly outspoken in criticism of the war. Something of a turning-point came at a large peace demonstration held in Cory Hall, Cardiff, long a citadel of jingoism, on New Year's Day, 1901.[18] Vigorous attacks were launched on the war here by Lloyd George and Bryn Roberts, among other Liberals, and they were joined on the platform by the dockers' leader, Ben Tillett. The Cardiff councillor and eisteddfodic bard, Edward Thomas (Cochfarf), denounced 'the insane ravings of Mafeking Day in Cardiff' and the pro-war stance of the local Liberal newspaper, the *South Wales Daily News*. A motion supporting an immediate end to the war through conciliation was carried with only seven dissentients. Thereafter, the tone of discussions of the conflict in southern Africa showed a significant change. What was at issue now was the methods by which the war was being fought, not the underlying disputes which had led to war between the British government and the Boer republics of the Transvaal and the Orange Free State in the first instance. The 'methods of barbarism' denounced by the Liberal leader, Campbell-Bannerman, as a result of which thousands of Boer women and children (and, less publicized, many blacks as well) died in concentration camps set up by Kitchener on the Rand, caused a fierce moral outcry. Simple war weariness, too, was taking its toll. Opinion remained divided to the end. When Lloyd George sought to hold a peace demonstration in Llanelli in October 1901, he was refused the use of two Baptist chapels, Moriah and Sion, and attacked again by the Revd Thomas Johns who identified British supremacy in South Africa with 'the path of righteousness'.[19] But the tide of opinion had clearly turned. By the spring of 1902 it was rare to discover a leading Welsh Liberal as implacable in his commitment to the imperial cause, compared with two years earlier. Sir David Brynmor Jones MP, who joined the Liberal League, the vehicle for the imperialist wing of the Liberal party, was by now a distinctly unusual figure.

Welsh opinion towards the war, therefore, proved volatile. Quick to respond to the jingo passions of the later 1890s, it could respond equally rapidly to the humanitarian and moral plea for an ending of the guerrilla warfare in the last eighteen months of the war in South Africa. It is this later period, in which the Welsh largely followed Liberal currents of sentiment in England and Scotland, which has helped foster the view of the Welsh as a nation of pro-Boers. In general, it is clear that absolute pacifism as such played little part in

[18] *South Wales Daily News*, 2 January 1901.
[19] *Llais Llafur*, 12 October 1901; also ibid., 19 October 1901 for a very weak reply by Johns.

determining anti-war sentiment amongst Liberals or Nonconformists between 1899 and 1902. Lloyd George himself, a man already committed to a strong defence of British strategic interests in eastern Africa, one who had vigorously attacked the French at the time of the 1898 Fashoda crisis, was no pacifist and no extreme anti-imperialist, then or later. He was subsequently in his career to become the exponent, along with men like Milner, of a kind of social imperialism. His Garden Suburb of advisers after 1916 included dedicated prophets of empire like Philip Kerr and Edward Grigg. Lloyd George was never one of nature's isolationists or little Englanders. He attacked this particular war on policy grounds, on the inept diplomacy that had led to its outbreak and the corrupt capitalistic interests that were making money out of it during its course.[20] Gradually, though only in the latter half of the war, the majority of his countrymen came to follow his lead. But they were always reluctant pacifists.

The outbreak of world war in August 1914 posed a far more profound challenge to the pacific inclinations of Welsh radicals. Obviously, it made a far greater impact on the national life and psychology than a remote imperial conflict like that of 1899. The advent of universal male conscription in early 1916 brought home the reality of total war directly to every citizen and every household in Wales. The years before 1914 had seen little talk of war. Wales, like Britain generally, was consumed with domestic conflicts, with national insurance and the House of Lords, with free trade and Irish Home Rule, with disestablishment and other national claims of the principality. Welsh pacifists roused themselves on occasion, such as the fifth National Peace Conference held at Cardiff in 1909 or in commemorating the centenary of the birth of Henry Richard in 1912. But the Peace Society in general attracted little attention.

When war broke out so suddenly in August 1914, the Welsh responded with profound emotional intensity. From the moment that Lloyd George delivered a flamboyant address to a London Welsh audience gathered in the Queen's Hall, London, on 19 September 1914, and proclaimed it as a war fought on behalf of Liberal values and the rights of the 'little five-foot-five nations', the national response was overwhelming. Nonconformists were stung by an early charge from the bishop of St Asaph that they were less wholehearted in their rallying to the flag than were Welsh Anglicans. On 9 October 1914, twenty leading Welsh Nonconformists from all the main

[20]See John Grigg, 'Lloyd George and the Boer War', in A.J.A. Morris (ed.), *Edwardian Radicalism, 1900–1914* (London, 1974), 13–25; Kenneth O. Morgan (ed.), *Lloyd George: Family Letters, 1885–1936* (Oxford and Cardiff, 1973), 120–34.

denominations, including such influential figures as the Methodist
ministers, the Revd John Williams, Brynsiencyn, and the Revd
Gwynoro Davies of Barmouth, the Independent journalist, Beriah
Gwynfe Evans, and the Aberystwyth law professor, Thomas Levi,
issued a manifesto in the press calling on their co-religionists to enlist
in the armed services.[21] Tens of thousands of them did so. Indeed, over
the war years as a whole the recruitment rate from Wales, in relation to
the population, was higher than that for England or Scotland.[22] This
was, indeed, claimed to be a war fought on behalf of Welsh traditional
values, Liberal as well as national. Patriotic Welsh sentiment, directed
over the past twenty years towards such domestic objectives as
disestablishment, a Welsh educational council or land reform, was now
enlisted on behalf of the war effort, and in support of other struggling
small nations like Belgium, Serbia or Montenegro. Recruiting drives
for the Welch Regiment and the Royal Welsh Fusiliers, including
efforts in the university colleges, were immensely successful. Chapels
in many parts of the land were used as recruiting offices. In the face of
Kitchener's uncomprehending hostility, Lloyd George succeeded in
creating a new Welsh Division, the 38th Welsh. It was intended,
perhaps, as the basis of an entirely distinct Welsh Army Corps, as
foreshadowed in the Queen's Hall speech.[23] The Welsh Division,
commanded by General Sir Ivor Philipps from the Pembrokeshire
family of Picton Castle, saw front-line service for the first time in the
battle of the Somme in July 1916. Its first major success came with the
clearing of Mametz Wood and later the capture of Pilckheim Ridge in
1917. Welsh societies such as the Cymmrodorion and the London
Welsh Committee, run by Sir Vincent Evans, became heavily
preoccupied with recruitment.

In Welsh-language intellectual journals such as *Y Beirniad*, the great
literary figure, Sir John Morris-Jones, the very epitome of cultural
integrity and literary sensitivity who had steered clear of political
commitment for years, now called for an all-out dedication to the war
effort.[24] He and other Welsh intellectuals, even Sir Owen M. Edwards
himself in *Cymru*,[25] devoted their ingenuity to fierce attacks on

---

[21]'A War Manifesto', *South Wales Daily News*, 9 October 1914.

[22]Ivor Nicholson and Lloyd Williams, *Wales: Its Part in the War* (London, 1919):
Scotland, 13.02 per cent; England, 13.30 per cent; Wales, 13.82 per cent. It should
be noted that Wales had, proportionately, a larger male population.

[23]*The Times*, 21 September 1914. (I am indebted to valuable information here
from Mr Colin Hughes.)

[24]Cf. Sir J. Morris-Jones in *Y Beirniad*, Hydref 1914, 217–24, reviewing two
works by Bernhardi; and ibid., Hydref 1915, 191–205, where he condemns
Germany's 'new religion' of power worship, in 'Crefydd Newydd yr Almaen'.

[25]Editorial notes by Sir O. M. Edwards in *Cymru* from November 1914

German culture and the ethic of Nietzsche, Treitschke and Bernhardi, with its implied worship of military violence. The eisteddfod itself, complete with annual Thursday address by Lloyd George, became an annual forum for jingoism. In the Bangor eisteddfod of 1915 (at which the pacifist, Thomas Parry-Williams, won both crown and chair), Lloyd George paid tribute to the Welsh military tradition from the days of King John. He cited (erroneously) Welsh signatures on Magna Carta as evidence of earlier Cymric struggles for freedom.[26] During the 1916 eisteddfod at Aberystwyth, he reached new heights of pathos with his famous plea, 'Let the people sing'. The *Cymanfa Ganu* there raised £430 for war funds. At the 1917 eisteddfod in Birkenhead, national sentiment went still further with the emotional celebration of a Welsh poet, the Trawsfynydd shepherd 'Hedd Wynn'. He won the chair for his poem 'Yr Arwr' (The Hero), two weeks after he had been killed on the western front. The chair was draped in black, a kind of national consecration of Wales and the war.

The torrent of warlike hysteria continued unabated. There were many cases of individual persecution, including the eviction of the famous linguistic scholar, Dr Hermann Ethé, from the University College of Wales, Aberystwyth, solely on the grounds of his German nationality.[27] The college council and principal failed to defend him. For Wales, it appeared to be truly a good war. It brought new prosperity, both to the mines and the docks of the industrial south, and to the rural areas as well, with the growing demand for food supplies. It created a new kind of military hero, a sort of Christian warrior, like Brigadier-General Sir Owen Thomas of Carrog, Anglesey, chief training officer for recruits in north Wales. Sir Henry Jones, the eminent university philosopher, was another actively engaged in army enlistment drives. A new species of Nonconformist patriot emerged. Most spectacular was the Methodist, the Revd John Williams of Brynsiencyn, Anglesey, 'Lloyd George's chaplain' so-called, who caused a stir by preaching in the pulpit in full military uniform.[28] The ultimate symbol was Lloyd George himself, long the radical hero of his people, who ascended from the Treasury to the Munitions Office, then to the War Office and finally, in December 1916, to the premiership. No one was more closely linked with fighting the war to the bitter end, with the 'knock out blow' and the 'unconditional surrender' of the

onwards: see particularly, 'Cwymp yr Almaen', *Cymru*, Chwefror 1915, where the degeneration of German *kultur* is briefly discussed.

[26] *South Wales Daily News*, 6 August 1915.

[27] E. L. Ellis, *The University College of Wales, Aberystwyth, 1872-1972* (Cardiff, 1972), 171-3, has an excellent account.

[28] R. R. Williams, *Y Parchedig John Williams D.D., Brynsiencyn* (Caernarfon, 1929), 226-42.

Alliance powers. Into the central administration, he brought with him a veritable Welsh Mafia of advisers – men like Thomas Jones in the Cabinet office, David Davies and Joseph Davies in the Garden Suburb, John Rowlands, Clement Jones and Sir J. T. Davies in the premier's personal entourage. In key government departments were Welshmen like Lord Rhondda who took the vital portfolio of the Local Government Board, and later organized the system of food rationing. A new generation of Welsh bureaucrats, men like Sir Thomas Hughes of the National Insurance Commission, emerged to dominate the new instruments of central, collective organization which controlled social and economic life.[29] Mainly Liberals and Nonconformists, often Welsh-speaking, they seemed to confirm a novel and unbreakable link between Welshness and the fighting of total war. Wales appeared to enjoy a centrality in British life unknown since the early Tudors.

In this atmosphere, anti-war feeling in the land, rural or industrial, appeared to be smothered. Yet, in fact, the very immensity of the pressures and propaganda on behalf of fighting the war, gave the opponents of war a new strength and an influence over the political and cultural ideas of the new generation that could not have been foreseen in the heady days of 1914. From almost the start of the war, there were notable Welsh pacifists, many of them operating as isolated protesters and critics. Welshmen were prominent in the Fellowship of Reconciliation, a Christian pacifist organization formed in December 1914. Its secretary was a Welsh-speaking Welshman, the Revd Richard Roberts, minister of a North London Presbyterian chapel who would shortly migrate to the United States.[30] Among the Fellowship's inspirational figures was George Maitland Lloyd Davies, a Liverpool Welsh banker turned Methodist minister, the spiritual leader of the Welsh pacifist movement over the next thirty years and a man of immense personal charisma and courage.[31] There was also a significant organ for anti-war sentiment being published. This was *Y Wawr*, the first specifically anti-war journal to exist in Wales, and by origin a Welsh-language cultural periodical started by students at Aberystwyth university college in the autumn of 1913.[32] *Y Wawr* is a journal of

[29]For a fuller account, see the present author's *Rebirth of a Nation: Wales, 1880–1980* (Oxford and Cardiff, 1981), 166–9.

[30]*Y Bywgraffiadur Cymreig, 1941–1950* (London, 1970), 50, *sub* 'Roberts'; for some personal recollections, see Gwynfor Evans, *Non-Violent Nationalism* (Alex Wood Memorial Lecture, London, 1973), 3.

[31]See the excellent biography, E. H. Griffiths, *Heddychwr Mawr Cymru* (Caernarfon, 2 vols., 1967–8).

[32]Thirteen issues of *Y Wawr* appeared between 1913 and 1917: there is a complete run of issues in the National Library of Wales. Also see Cassie Davies, *Hwb i'r Galon: Atgofion Cassie Davies* (Swansea, 1973).

considerable interest and distinction: it is surprising that it has been ignored in histories of the University College of Wales. The authors who appeared in its pages included many of the outstanding Welsh poets and prose writers of their day, notably the towering figure of the poet T. Gwynn Jones and younger men such as Thomas Parry-Williams and G. J. Williams. Its editor was a youthful Welsh Nationalist, W. Ambrose Bebb. The comments of *Y Wawr* on the war were often indirect and allusive: T. Gwynn Jones, however, did address himself directly to combating the virulent anti-Hun hysteria of the time by analysing in a cool-headed way German cultural traditions. He clashed openly with Liberal intellectuals such as Morris-Jones and Llewelyn Williams MP on this point.[33] *Y Wawr* was also at pains to explode some of the more lurid fables of German atrocities and wartime destruction, the mutilated children, the margarine factory sustained by prisoner's corpses and so on. The journal caused much *frisson* in Aberystwyth university circles. The Welsh department was somewhat torn since two of its members, T. Gwynn Jones and Parry-Williams, wrote for this anti-war publication, while the third, Timothy Lewis, eventually enlisted in the armed forces in protest at the views of his pacifist colleagues. The Aberystwyth authorities were much alarmed and in 1917 *Y Wawr* was eventually closed down.

The anti-war tone of *Y Wawr* was largely cultural and unpolitical. Many of its contributions were distinctly rarefied. Its writers ranged from sensitive intellectuals alienated by the cult of violence, such as Parry-Williams, to more pugnacious spirits like Gwynn Jones who described himself as a 'pacifist with the emphasis on the fist'.[34] Soon, however, radical critics of the war were to find a more powerful voice. This arose almost entirely through the crusading efforts of Thomas Rees, principal of Bala-Bangor Independent College, an ex-farm servant and collier, an eminent theologian and later editor of *Y Geiriadur Beiblaidd*.[35] With almost reckless courage, he wrote to the Independent newspaper, *Y Tyst*, a letter published on 30 September 1914 in which he attacked the war on Christian pacifist grounds and urged the need for finding a common basis of humanity between the British and German people. Some of his letter contained more directly political material such as the false accusations being published about

[33]*Y Wawr*, II (1) (Gaeaf, 1914). For an impression of the influence of Gwynn Jones's views and personality on a young student at Aberystwyth in 1918, see Iorwerth Peate's recollections in *Y Llenor*, XXVIII (1949), 108-13.

[34]See David Jenkins, *Thomas Gwynn Jones: Cofiant* (Denbigh, 1973), 238-63, and *Y Llenor*, XXVIII, a memorial issue devoted to Gwynn Jones.

[35]For Rees, see T. Eirug Davies (ed.), *Y Prifathro Thomas Rees: Ei Fywyd a'i Waith* (Llandysul, 1939).

German war crimes. But the nub of his appeal was based on the
ultimate, pacific truths of the Christian message. Rees was most
virulently attacked. Two weeks later, a string of prominent
Nonconformists from all major denominations, denounced his attitude
as irresponsible and unpatriotic. Llewelyn Williams MP, a cultured and
humane Liberal littérateur, committed himself to the view that this
was a holy war on behalf of Christian virtue.[36] The editor of *Y Tyst*, the
Revd H. M. Hughes of Ebenezer chapel, Cardiff, totally dissociated
himself from Rees's heretical utterances.[37] Thomas Rees was subjected
to much personal attack and persecution, including, in a celebrated
episode, expulsion from his beloved Bangor golf club. Even so, from
this historic letter to *Y Tyst*, and from these views which he strongly
upheld in many subsequent contributions to Welsh- and English-
language publications,[38] can be seen the crystallization of a new Welsh
commitment to resistance to war. Thomas Rees's now forgotten
gesture of protest launched a new Welsh political tradition.

Throughout 1915, Liberal critics of the war, although still evidently
a small minority, were beginning to find their voice. There were other
eminent Nonconformist ministers who were speaking out against the
mass slaughter on the western front, notably the blind preacher-poet,
the Revd J. Puleston Jones, once a founder-member of the Dafydd ap
Gwilym Society at Oxford, who now stood out against harassment
from his congregation at Pwllheli.[39] In the Methodist newspaper, *Y
Goleuad*, the editor, E. Morgan Humphreys, vigorously denounced the
war passions of the time, despite criticism from many readers. George
Maitland Lloyd Davies above all, the symbol of absolutist pacifism in
its purest form, was tireless in his campaigning. He was the main
inspiration behind a new Peace Society formed at Bangor early in
1915. A conference of leading Welsh Christian pacifists was then held
at Barmouth in March 1916,[40] and the outcome was the creation of
much the most important anti-war periodical ever published in Wales.
This was *Y Deyrnas*, a monthly which appeared from October 1916 to
November 1919 under the editorship of the indefatigable Principal
Thomas Rees. The new journal made a lasting impact. From the start,

[36]W. Llewelyn Williams, 'Y Rhyfel', Y Beirniad, Hydref 1914, 153. He cited the
destruction of the University Library at Louvain by the Germans.
[37]*Y Tyst*, 21 Hydref 1914.
[38]For example, 'Yr Eglwys a'r Wladwriaeth', *Y Dysgedydd*, Gorffennaf 1915,
299. Subsequent issues of *Y Dysgedydd*, an Independent quarterly, contained
vigorous rebuttals of Rees's views by the Revd J. Lewis Williams, Baker Street
chapel, Aberystwyth, and others.
[39]R. W. Jones, *Y Parchedig John Puleston Jones, M.A., D.D.* (Caernarfon, 1929),
186ff.
[40]E. H. Griffiths, op. cit., Vol. I, 61.

it adopted a broad-based anti-war position, rather than being purely sectarian. Its contributors included both strict Christian pacifists and more politically-minded 'pacifists' who opposed the war on strict policy grounds: they comprised politicians, poets and ministers of religion, Liberals, socialists and non-party sympathizers with the Union of Democratic Control.[41] Month after month, Rees pleaded the urgent need for an immediate end to the slaughter; he supported peace terms variously proposed by President Woodrow Wilson, Lord Lansdowne and the ILP. At the same time, in his endorsement of Wilson's 'Fourteen Points' in early 1918 and in his analysis of the basis of a post-war peace settlement, Rees at times came close to admitting that there might have been some political justification for Britain's going to war in 1914.[42] Certainly, there was some evidence of editorial inconsistency.

Perhaps the most influential theme in the columns of Y Deyrnas was its emphasis on the harmful impact of the war on Welsh life – the war profiteers, press censorship, restrictions on free speech, the erosion of civil liberties. The harsh treatment suffered by many conscientious objectors in prison or elsewhere, as a result of their refusal to accept conscription into the armed services, was the subject for a regular column by the Revd E. K. Jones, a Baptist minister in Caernarfon. By 1917, Y Deyrnas had become far more than a monthly periodical. It was the nerve-centre for the general organization of anti-war movements in Wales. Through its agency, Principal Thomas Rees and his assistant, the Revd D. Wyre Lewis, a Baptist minister from Penuel, Rhos, Wrexham, sponsored the peace convention held at Llandrindod Wells on 3–5 September 1917, the most significant pacifist demonstration of the war.[43] This meeting, in addition to passing motions for the immediate entry into peace negotiations with Germany, addressed a public letter to Lloyd George to demand an inquiry into the working of the military service acts and the maltreatment of conscientious objectors who rejected the findings of local military tribunals.

By now, Y Deyrnas and its writers were no longer Ishmaels of public life, lonely voices crying in the wilderness. In 1917, anti-war sentiment in Wales was growing in intensity. There were many indications of the new mood – the peace meetings held at Bangor and addressed by Professor E. V. Arnold; the prosecution of J. H. Jones, editor of Y Brython, for being in breach of the Defence of the Realm Acts. A decisive factor was the advent of military conscription. The two Military Service Acts of January and May 1916 deeply alienated many

[41]There is a complete run of Y Deyrnas in the National Library of Wales.
[42]Y Deyrnas, Chwefror 1918 and subsequent issues.
[43]Ibid., Medi 1917.

Liberals who had originally accepted the necessity – even the righteousness – of the war but now saw universal male conscription as deeply injurious to the rights of free citizenship. The Welsh Liberal MPs offered little opposition to conscription in the House. Only a small handful voted against the two conscription acts; among them was E. T. John, the nationalistic Liberal member for East Denbighshire who was shortly to move into the Labour party.[44] The most influential rebel of all was W. Llewelyn Williams, member for Carmarthen Boroughs who, as has been seen, was in 1914 an ardent supporter of the war effort. He revolted fundamentally against conscription and developed henceforth an overwhelmingly, almost pathological, hatred for Lloyd George, long his close ally.[45] Henceforth, Llewelyn Williams was a powerful 'pacifist' recruit to the critics of the war.

The growing publicity given to the plight of the conscientious objectors also aroused concern. A significant proportion of the 16,500 conscientious objectors in the 1916–18 period came from Wales, some objecting on Christian pacifist grounds, others on political, usually socialist ones.[46] Some of the objectors, like the distinguished poet Thomas Parry-Williams, were able to continue with their professional interests, after a fashion. But many suffered for their faith. George Maitland Lloyd Davies, a man of deep humility, became the very symbol of self-sacrifice with his periods in prison in Wormwood Scrubs and elsewhere for his anti-war activities. Indeed, he was still in Winston Green prison, Smethwick, when the war ended and was not released until July 1919.[47] Even many Liberals who did not share the absolutist pacifist philosophy that inspired George Davies felt alienated by the manner in which local tribunals conducted their operations. The surviving records of the military tribunals for Cardiganshire, for instance, reveal the narrow social composition of those serving on the borough, rural and county appeals tribunals, and the haphazard way in which exemptions from service were granted on occupational or

[44]Three Welsh Liberals (Llewelyn Williams, E. T. John and G. Caradoc Rees) voted against the first reading of the January 1916 Bill, and one (John) against the second reading. John had originally endorsed the war effort as a battle for Christian civilization; see 'Y Rhyfel – ei achos, ei amcan a'i ganlyniadau', *Y Cymro*, 30 Medi 1914.

[45]Cf. W. Llewelyn Williams to Arthur Ponsonby, 12 October 1920 (Bodleian, Ponsonby papers, MS. Eng. Hist. c. 668, f.32), in which he attacks Lloyd George as 'the Dictator'. Also Lloyd George to his wife, 12 August 1919 (*Family Letters*, 190), in which he complains of Llewelyn Williams's 'intense personal bitterness'.

[46]For wartime conscientious objectors, see John Rae, *Conscience and Politics* (Oxford, 1970); David Boulton, *Objection Overruled* (London, 1967); and R. S. W. Pollard, *Conscience and Liberty* (London, 1940).

[47]E. H. Griffiths, op. cit., 100–9.

compassionate grounds.[48] The domestic servants of a squire such as
T. J. Waddingham of Hafod were treated with an indulgence not always
encountered by self-employed artisans. The rare conscientious
objector met with a hostile reception both from the tribunal and from
the assembled public audience, though several Aberystwyth students
did receive exemption from service on religious grounds. Long before
the war came to its close, it was clear that bodies like these, and the
kind of protest symbolized by the appearance of Y Deyrnas and the
activities of men like Thomas Rees and George Davies, were having a
powerful effect on the values and morale of Welsh Liberalism. No
longer would the imperatives of Welsh radicalism be instinctively
equated with those of justice and humanity. A revolt by sections of the
Welsh intelligentsia was in the making. The crisis of Welsh Liberalism,
so obvious after the war, was already apparent.

The growing anti-war passion of Welsh Liberals existed side by side
with, and to some degree was reinforced by, a growing movement
against the war within the Welsh labour movement, especially in the
south Wales coalfield. In August 1914, industrial south Wales, for all
the class tensions of the pre-war years, seemed to respond as
vigorously as elsewhere to the war-like mood. Keir Hardie's staunch
opposition to the war led to his being rejected by his own constituents.
On a notorious occasion, Hardie's self-styled 'Gethsemane', he was
howled down at a mass meeting at Aberdare on 6 August; the meeting
was broken up by a mob led by the former miners' agent and quasi-
syndicalist, Charles Butt Stanton.[49] The old ILP newspaper, Llais
Llafur, changed its name, its language and its political stance. As
Labour Voice, it was by 1915 a right-wing, pro-war 'patriotic labour'
journal.[50] Leading miners' agents, even a left-winger like Ted Gill, took
part in recruitment campaigns. Some went further still. David Watts
Morgan organized the Welsh Labour Battalion, became a major and
won the DSO at Cambrai in 1917. Left-wing minority movements
amongst the rank and file, such as the Plebs League and Unofficial
Reform Committee, largely went into dissolution; Marxist critics like
Noah Ablett and Will Hay kept their heads down and waited hopefully

[48]Records of Cardiganshire appeal tribunal, March 1916–November 1918, in
National Library of Wales, including Minute book for 15 March 1916–20
September 1918; attendance book; Clerk's draft note books, 13 April 1916–25
October 1918); correspondence; and the recollections of H. M. Vaughan. Also see
Vaughan's reminiscences in Wales (Spring 1947), 172ff. (Here and elsewhere, I am
indebted to materials accumulated by my late father.)
[49]Merthyr Express, 8 August 1914; Western Mail, 8 August 1914.
[50]Labour Voice, January 1915 et seq.

for the jingo storm to blow over.[51] For long, however, the general pro-
war enthusiasm amongst the miners and others, for whom the war
brought higher wages, improved social conditions and new forms of
collective ownership and control, remained undimmed. After Keir
Hardie died in the autumn of 1915, in a by-election that November
the electors in the old radical bastion of Merthyr Tydfil gave a large
majority of over 4,000 to Charles Stanton as a fanatically pro-war
Labour candidate at the expense of James Winstone of the ILP,
president of the South Wales Miners' Federation.[52] Winstone was no
pacifist and had a son serving at the front. But his membership of the
anti-war ILP and his invitation to critics like Ramsay MacDonald and
Fred Jowett to speak for him tarred him with the pacifist brush. Even
in radical Merthyr, the constituency of Hardie and Henry Richard, the
cradle of working-class protest from the days of Dic Penderyn and the
Chartists, the warlike passions of the time were supreme.

But in 1916 it became clear that disaffection with the consequences
of war and with the control of labour implied in the Munitions of War
Acts and then in the Military Services Acts was growing rapidly. The
official strike by the Welsh miners in July 1915 on behalf of a new
standard wage rate had been a significant portent. There were several
notable socialist rebels who were imprisoned, or otherwise harassed,
for being conscientious objectors on political rather than on religious
grounds. The case of Morgan Jones, a Welsh schoolteacher in Reading
and a founder-member of the No-Conscription Fellowship, who was
dispatched to various prisons in Wales and England for refusal to
enlist, aroused much popular attention. So did the similar fate suffered
by R. C. Wallhead, once a close ally of Keir Hardie in Merthyr. Both of
these were to be elected Labour MPs after the war: indeed, in 1921
Morgan Jones was to become the first ex-conscientious objector
elected to Parliament. Interestingly enough, surviving correspondence
seems to suggest that his unquestioning commitment to non-
conscription was somewhat undermined as a result of his prison
experiences.[53] The cases of Jones and Wallhead were paralleled by
those of hundreds of little-known south Wales workers committed to
prison for refusal to take up arms against their comrades in Germany

[51]The best account of these developments is contained in M. G. Woodhouse,
'Rank and File Movements among the Miners of South Wales, 1910–1926'
(unpublished University of Oxford D.Phil. thesis, 1970). Also see R. Page Arnot,
The South Wales Miners, 1914–1926 (Cardiff, 1975), ch. I.

[52]For a fuller account, see Morgan, *Keir Hardie*, 273–5.

[53]See Keith Robbins, 'Morgan Jones in 1916', *Llafur*, I (4) (1975), 38–43; also
the same author's *The Abolition of War* (Cardiff, 1976), especially 80–6.

or Austria-Hungary; the local press recorded a flood of such cases each week.[54]

More generally, throughout 1916–17, industrial protest merged into political, as pressure for improved working conditions fused with resentment against the endless fighting. There were many indices of unrest amongst Welsh workers now. In the quarrying areas of Gwynedd, the journal *Y Dinesydd* was resolutely anti-war; so, increasingly, was *Labour Voice*, as it gradually returned to its original socialist commitment. In the southern coalfield, the Unofficial Reform Committee re-emerged, and so, too, did the classes of the Marxist Central Labour College, under the guidance of such tutors as W. H. Mainwaring and Will Hay. A new generation of young Marxists was emerging, men like Arthur Horner and Arthur Cook, far more rebellious in their approach to the economic and social framework than were their pre-war predecessors. Horner actually went to Ireland for a time to serve in James Connolly's Citizen Army. Bertrand Russell undertook a speaking tour on behalf of the No-Conscription Fellowship throughout south Wales in 2–16 July 1916.[55] He noted the massive audiences and the intense enthusiasm that greeted his attacks on conscription and on the war more generally, from Briton Ferry in the west to Newport in the east. In 1917 the coming of revolution in Russia added a new socialist messianism to the anti-war movement.[56] The convention of anti-war delegates of workers' and soldiers' organizations held at Swansea on 29 July 1917 was violently broken up by demonstrators from outside. Arthur Horner and others were physically injured. But it confirmed the intensity of the anti-war mood in south Wales. The National Soldiers' and Workers' Council did not long survive the Swansea convention but it did encourage speaking tours by anti-war socialists such as Tom Mann and Sylvia Pankhurst. It markedly reinforced, too, the militant grass-roots socialism amongst Welsh workers, notably in the executive and other higher echelons of the Miners' Federation. It seems to have increased also the nervousness of the authorities about the anti-war crusades conducted by a man like the Revd Thomas Nicholas, the socialist minister-bard once prominent in Hardie's *Merthyr Pioneer*, now tireless in his work for the ILP and the anti-war movement, and shortly to join the Communist

[54]See an excellent detailed account by David Egan, 'The Swansea Conference of the British Council of Soldiers' and Workers' Delegates, July 1917', *Llafur*, I (4) (1975), especially 30–1.

[55]Bertrand Russell, correspondence with Lady Ottoline Morrell, July 1916 (transcripts from Russell Archive, McMaster University, Ontario, by courtesy of Ms Jo Newberry).

[56]Egan, op. cit.

Party of Great Britain.[57] In the last year of the war, the rising tide of militant passion amongst the Welsh miners, voiced now on the executive by younger men such as Ablett and S. O. Davies, not merely by 'unofficial' fringe groups in Rhondda, confirmed the dramatic impact of the war in generating a new socio-political consciousness amongst the Welsh workers. In short, just as the war helped to undermine the older radicalism, it gave impetus and vigour to the new socialism.

The impact of the anti-war movements in Wales must not be exaggerated. The bulk of the population seems to have remained 'patriotic' throughout. Lloyd George's charisma survived to the end. In the 'coupon election' of December 1918, Lloyd George and his 'couponed' supporters were swept to triumph amidst widespread nationalistic frenzy. Only 'patriotic' members were returned for Welsh constituencies as Labour MPs, men like Watts Morgan, Brace, Richards and the aged Mabon. 'Bolshevik' or 'pacifist' representatives of the ILP and the anti-war movement like Thomas Nicholas in Aberdare[58] and E. T. John in Denbigh were swept into oblivion. But this was only a short-term post-war reaction. The impact of the anti-war movements of 1914–18 was to be an enduring one. These movements were extremely varied in form. In general, the industrial protests of the coalfield remained distinct from the more traditional moral or civic protest of men like Thomas Rees and George Davies, both reared in the old Liberal tabernacle. What the anti-war pressure-groups did, as variously as in the columns of *Y Deyrnas* and the activities of the No-Conscription Fellowship, was to erode the certainties and confidence of pre-1914 radicalism. They served to discredit its leaders, both political figures like Lloyd George and literary giants like Morris-Jones. Liberal Wales was a casualty both of total war and of the enduring commitment of the peace movements of 1914–18.

For the next twenty years, opposition to war became once more a largely theoretical issue for thinking Welsh men and women. *Y Deyrnas* wound up in November 1919 after heavy financial losses. There were brief post-war episodes which served as reminders of the old wartime jingoism. One was the controversy which surrounded the appointment of the former conscientious objector, Thomas Parry-Williams, to a

[57]Deian Hopkin, 'Patriots and pacifists in Wales, 1914–1918', *Llafur*, I (3) (1973), 27–41, citing materials in HO 45 on 'the seditious and disloyal propaganda of Thomas E. Nicholas' as viewed by the chief constable of Glamorgan, Captain Lindsay.

[58]Defeated in Aberdare by 16,595 votes by C. B. Stanton (NDP): I am indebted to interviews with the late Revd Thomas Nicholas.

chair of Welsh at Aberystwyth in 1919–20.[59] But these emotions soon disappeared. In the twenties, Wales shared in the anti-war reaction, if not the pacifism, strictly defined, of Britain generally. It has been noted by Mr Tecwyn Lloyd that, just as Wales had not produced a generation of 'war poets' of the Siegfried Sassoon/Wilfrid Owen type, so memory of the war was obliterated from its literature after 1918.[60] Cynan's poem, 'Mab y Bwthyn', a rare exception by an ex-serviceman, spoke mainly of the moral rejection of war. By 1923 Lloyd George seemed almost a figure from the past, and his wartime patriotism, anachronistic. In the general election of November that year, a remarkable episode confirmed how rapidly the wartime mood had dissolved. To the universal astonishment, George Maitland Lloyd Davies was elected as Christian Pacifist member for the University of Wales. He owed much to a split vote amongst the Liberals and his majority was only ten. Nevertheless, as the supreme symbol of Christian non-resistance in the war years, he was a deeply controversial figure. The very fact of his election in this traditional academic stronghold of Lloyd Georgian Liberalism and the mystique of *Cymru Fydd* was a remarkable commentary on the shift of mood amongst sections of the Welsh intelligentsia, notably such able young men as the economist, Hilary Marquand, and the philosopher, R. I. Aaron.[61] Davies did not remain long in Parliament. He was defeated by Ernest Evans (Liberal), Lloyd George's former private secretary, in the 1924 general election. Thomas Rees had warned Davies previously that the University Court of Governors had passed a new rule 'which will enable a number of older men to qualify as voters & this will not help'.[62] Davies's time at Westminster, including the unexpected decision to take the Labour whip, proved unacceptably taxing in its demands upon the conscience of so incorrigible an individualist.[63] Nevertheless, his brief period as MP underlined his role as a talisman of post-war pacifism for the younger generation, a role fortified by his later philanthropic work amongst the unemployed of Brynmawr.

Apart from Davies's personal impact, the Welsh-language literary world received a powerful new impetus from anti-war or pacifist writers. The young poet, D. Gwenallt Jones, gained in popular acclaim

[59]E. L. Ellis, op. cit., 202–4.

[60]D. Tecwyn Lloyd, 'Welsh public opinion and the First World War', *Planet*, 10 (February/March 1972), 25–37.

[61]R. I. Aaron to G. M. Ll. Davies, 24 November 1923 (NLW, Davies papers, 585); Hilary Marquand in *Welsh Outlook*, September 1922, 217–19.

[62]Thomas Rees to G. M. Ll. Davies, 17 December 1923 (NLW, Davies papers, 2153).

[63]Ben Spoor to Davies, 12 February 1924; 'Harold' (of University of Wales Labour Party, Cardiff) to Davies, 14 December 1923 (ibid., 150, 2156).

not only as a poet of rare distinction but also as one who had suffered
months of imprisonment in Dartmoor as a socialist conscientious
objector active in the ILP. Years later, in his autobiographical novel,
Plasau'r Brenin (1934), and the poem, 'Dartmoor' (1942), he evoked
again the powerful impact upon his spirit and sensitivity of confine-
ment in prison.[64] The distinguished new literary periodical, *Y Llenor*,
founded in 1922 under the editorship of W. J. Gruffydd, reflected some
of the political as well as literary currents of the time. Gruffydd himself
had been a highly ambivalent member of the Royal Navy in 1915 and
a strong foe of conscription. His authors, though many and varied,
included prominent anti-war figures like Ambrose Bebb, Parry-
Williams and G. J. Williams, together with a writer like Saunders Lewis
who had served in the war but had totally rebelled against the ethic
that sustained it.[65] Anti-militarism played its part in attracting young
recruits for the newly-formed Plaid Cymru in 1925: its first president,
the Baptist minister, the Revd Lewis Valentine, was a pacifist, although
the party's international policy was never strictly so committed. The
famous episode at Penyberth aerodrome in September 1936 when
Saunders Lewis, Valentine and D. J. Williams burnt down an RAF
bombing school in Llŷn and were later committed to Wormwood
Scrubs for nine months, attracted widespread support in Wales for its
anti-militarist as well as its nationalist aspects, although it was
undoubtedly the latter that had the more lasting impact upon the
sensibilities of the Welsh-speaking community.

More characteristic than any of these, perhaps, as an index of the
post-war mood in Wales was the formation of the League of Nations
Union, whose powerful Welsh Council came into being at Shrewsbury
in early 1922.[66] It was in part an offshoot from the old radical conscience associated with the Liberal party. Its main patron was David
(later Lord) Davies, at the time Liberal MP for Montgomeryshire, and
a philanthropic supporter of internationalist causes; its honorary
secretary was the Revd Gwilym Davies, a Baptist minister of powerful
social conscience. No doubt, the League of Nations Union attracted
Welsh pacifists; ritual pilgrimages were paid to the shrine of Welsh
pacifism, Henry Richard's birthplace at Tregaron. But, in fact, the
Union was the very reverse of pacifist, even if many of its supporters
remained confused on the point. Its main emphasis lay on collective
security and international collaboration to preserve peace. It was

---

[64]See Emyr Humphreys, 'Poetry, prison and propaganda', *Planet*, June 1978,
17–23; also J. E. Meredith, *Gwenallt: Bardd Crefyddol* (Llandysul, 1974).

[65]Saunders Lewis made his debut in *Y Llenor* (Winter 1922) 242ff.

[66]Goronwy J. Jones, op. cit., 97ff; the monthly *Welsh Outlook* is a useful source
for the Welsh League of Nations Union.

nationalism, rather than war as such, that was the ultimate target of the Welsh League of Nations Union and its 400 branches scattered throughout Wales. David Davies himself stressed increasingly the need for controlled international disarmament, backed up by an international police force, including considerable air power. The Welsh League of Nations Union probably reached the peak of its influence in the early 1930s. The later crises of that decade, with the manifest inadequacy of the League of Nations in resolving successive international crises from Abyssinia to Munich and beyond, let alone coping with the growing menace from Hitler, led to a decline in membership and in morale.

In addition, throughout the 1930s, the Welsh League of Nations Union became disturbed at the growing challenge from 'absolutist' pacifists, especially within the Nonconformist churches. At the end of 1933, the Revd Gwilym Davies was writing to Lord Davies to express concern at the 'decided drift towards out and out pacifism in the big religious denominations of Wales'; the Baptists had become 'by resolution 100% pacifist'.[67] There was now the Council of Christian Pacifist Groups to merge the various efforts of pacifist groups in the Methodist, Independent and Baptist churches, together with traditional small bodies such as the Quakers. In addition, there was an expansion of the Peace Pledge Union in Wales after its formation in May 1936. George M. Ll. Davies became an executive member and sponsor, and a close associate of such leading Christian pacifist figures as Dick Sheppard and Canon Raven. To bolster the efforts of the PPU amongst Welsh-speakers, in 1937 there was formed *Cymdeithas Heddychwyr Cymru*, with Davies as president and the youthful Gwynfor Evans, fresh from studies at Aberystwyth and Oxford and already the articulate exponent of 'non-violent nationalism', as its secretary.[68] Its pamphlet series circulated widely. Conversely, the opening of the Temple of Peace in Cathays Park, Cardiff, in 1938 sponsored by the tireless Lord Davies of Llandinam, served as a stimulus for the waning forces of pro-League sentiment.

But much of this activity was small-scale or purely theoretical. It tended to dissolve in the face of specific crises, especially in the aftermath of the German seizure of Czechoslovakia in March 1939 and the subsequent pledge to Poland resulting from popular condemnation of the government's policy of appeasement. Sympathy with

[67]Gwilym Davies to N. Foot, 29 December 1933, NLW, David Davies papers, cited in Martin Ceadel, *Pacifism in Britain, 1914–1945* (Oxford, 1980). Dr Ceadel's book offers an excellent analysis of this entire movement, and its ideology. Also relevant is Martin Pugh, 'Pacifism and politics in Britain, 1931–1935', *Historical Journal*, 23 (3) (1980), 641–56.

[68]E. H. Griffiths, op. cit., Vol. II, 120ff.

Republican Spain also fostered anti-fascist sentiment: over 170 Welsh workers, largely miners, served in the International Brigade.[69] Pacifist or other anti-war movements tended to dissolve in Wales as elsewhere in the face of what were perceived as threats not only to national security but to the very basis of that liberty and democratic radicalism which Welshmen of all creeds had long cherished.

The Second World War in many ways did not generate the kind of crisis of conscience for Welshmen that the war of 1914 had done. Welsh opinion seems to have been overwhelmingly in sympathy with the war effort, especially when the government was transformed into a coalition in May 1940 with Labour and Liberal members prominent in it. In addition to an overwhelming response to the call to military service, Welsh people assisted in vast numbers in civil defence, arms production, Spitfire funds, war savings campaigns and the like. Apart from the general anti-fascism which united Welsh opinion as the war of 1914–18 had never done, there was also the devastating impact of the war on the home front. The bombing blitz that damaged areas of Cardiff, Newport and, above all, Swansea brought home to Welsh opinion the reality of world conflict as never before. So, too, did evacuees from bombed cities in England. Welsh opinion, then, was largely unanimous. Even a leading Communist in Wales such as Arthur Horner rebelled against the official party line in 1939: 'I believed that the need to defeat Fascism was paramount', Horner later wrote.[70] Other Communists, however, obeyed Moscow's directives. When the Soviet Union itself entered the war against the Axis powers in June 1941, of course, all ambiguities, even amongst the Communists, were removed.

   Peace sentiment of the traditional type was a minor theme in Wales between 1939 and 1945. The Christian Pacifists of *Heddychwyr Cymru* continued their operations on behalf of an immediate armistice. Their new pamphlet series in 1941 comprised a dozen distinguished contributors, including the Labour MP, Rhys Davies; Nonconformist ministers like the Revd Herbert Morgan and Professor J. Morgan Jones; the first warden of Coleg Harlech, Ben Bowen Thomas; and academic figures such as Iorwerth Peate and Hywel D. Lewis. In 1942 the Welsh Congregational Union was actually persuaded to pass, with few dissentients, a resolution in favour of immediate peace negotiations.[71] In early 1944, a new Welsh Council of Peace was formed to co-

---

[69]See an admirable article by Hywel Francis, 'Welsh miners and the Spanish Civil War', *Journal of Contemporary History*, V (3) (1970).

[70]Arthur Horner, *Incorrigible Rebel* (London, 1960), 162.

[71]*Peace News*, 15 April 1941, 26 June 1942.

ordinate the activists of different pacifist groups.[72] George M. Ll. Davies remained an indefatigable figure, campaigning tirelessly through the Peace Pledge Union, innumerable pamphlets and articles in *Peace News* and elsewhere, and through his contacts with leading politicians. He even sought the co-operation of the aged Lloyd George but the ex-premier told him pessimistically in October 1940 that

> any active public movement at this stage is premature. The reservoir of unreasoning optimism is far from being exhausted. It is replenished by the press and by other propaganda and anyone who calls attention to the realities is regarded as defeatist.[73]

Nor could Lloyd George offer anything more positive when approached by Davies in early 1943 on negotiations with Gandhi in India.[74]

Conscientious objectors were granted more sensitive treatment than before. Perhaps for this reason, 60,000 were registered in Britain, far more than in 1916–18. Under the National Service Act of May 1939, it was laid down that they could be registered unconditionally, registered conditionally to undertake work of a civilian character, or be employed in the armed services on strictly non-combatant duties.[75] Local tribunals were somewhat more alive to the consciences of those who rebelled against war this time. Two of the nineteen tribunals set up in 1940 covered Wales, one for south Wales under Judge Frank Davies, one for the north under the chairmanship (until July 1941) of Judge Artemus-Jones. The latter, a former Liberal candidate of working-class background with service to the party in Merthyr in Keir Hardie's days, was relatively humane. Under Artemus-Jones's régime, only 9 per cent of applications for consideration as conscientious objectors (122 in all) were removed from the register. Jones also criticized local employers in north Wales who refused to give proper employment to objectors accepted as such by local tribunals.[76] Interestingly enough, his wife, Lady Mildred Artemus-Jones, was a

[72]Ibid., 25 February 1944.
[73]D. Lloyd George to Davies, 31 October 1940 (NLW, Davies papers, 1077).
[74]D. Lloyd George to Davies, 19 February 1943 (ibid., 1079).
[75]*National Service (Armed Forces) Act, 1939* (2 and 3 Geo. 6, ch. 81), section 5.
[76]*Peace News*, 24 January 1941. Also see Artemus-Jones's posthumous memoirs, *Without my Wig* (Liverpool, 1944), 184–5, where Principal D. Emrys Evans of Bangor hints that Jones's anxiety through wrestling with the moral problems posed by conscientious objectors may have shortened his life. 'Humanity was a prominent feature of his character', Evans wrote of Jones. Plaid Cymru objectors, however, were much more critical of Jones's role (private communication from Professor A. O. H. Jarman).

keen member of the Welsh pacifist movement. Artemus-Jones was succeeded in September 1941 by Judge Howel Walter Samuel, a former Labour MP and a much sterner figure. It was reported that no less than 54 per cent of applications (281 in all) were rejected under his aegis until March 1943, and the applicants removed from the register, some of them ending up in prison. This illustrated one major weakness of these tribunals as quasi-judicial bodies – their failure to observe uniform standards. Even so, the total number of conscientious objectors was small (even if proportionately larger than elsewhere in Britain). Only 2,920 in Wales were recorded in 1945, as opposed to 2,788 in Scotland and 26,589 in England.[78] Only a handful, too, were prosecuted under the defence regulations for failing to undertake industrial or other war work at home. The total imprisoned in Wales until 31 August 1944 was only forty-seven males and twenty females, and not all of them, perhaps, were political in motivation.[79]

However gentle the procedures of the tribunals may have seemed, that did not protect anti-war protesters from some of the old hazards. Some pacifist schoolteachers were dismissed by Cardiff Education Authority when registered as conscientious objectors, though George Thomas (a future speaker of the House of Commons) managed to escape punishment. The distinguished scholar and writer, Iorwerth Peate (registered unconditionally as a conscientious objector by the south Wales tribunal), was expelled from his post as keeper of the Folk Life department by the council of the National Museum of Wales in August 1941. Since criticism of him, by Lord Plymouth amongst others, related solely to his views as a member of the Welsh pacifist movement, this action can only appear as a senseless act of persecution. There followed a national campaign initiated by the editor of Y Llenor, Professor W. J. Gruffydd, and over two hundred motions to reinstate Dr Peate from cultural, educational, church and local authorities. Many letters were sent in from individuals prominent in political and academic life (including Lloyd George himself); the Welsh Parliamentary Party also intervened. The great majority of Welsh MPs

[77]Reply by Ernest Bevin, minister of labour, to Moelwyn Hughes MP, 30 June 1943 (Parl. Deb., 5th ser., Vol. 390, 1638–39). For a discussion of the way in which changes of the personnel on tribunals could influence their decisions, see Robert S. W. Pollard, 'Tribunals for conscientious objectors', in Pollard (ed.), Administrative Tribunals at Work (London, 1950), 70–1. Pollard's chapter is a useful summary of the activities and limitations of these tribunals between 1939 and 1945.

[78]Reply by Ness Edwards, Ministry of Labour, to Colonel Price-White MP, 23 October 1945 (Parl. Deb., 5th ser., Vol. 414, 1943).

[79]'Prosecutions under the Defence Regulations, 1941–6' (Public Record Office, LAB 16/80).

attended the annual meeting of the National Museum's court of governors (24 October 1941) where Aneurin Bevan had a memorable clash with Sir Cyril Fox and Lord Plymouth. Eventually, Dr Peate was restored to his post.[80] Ironically enough, after the war was over, he was appointed as curator of the new national Folk Museum at St Fagan's, in a manor house and grounds donated by the next Lord Plymouth. Again, some Welsh members of the Communist party were severely harassed by local police in 1939-40 in marked defiance of traditional safeguards for civil liberties. Notable among them was the veteran Revd Thomas E. Nicholas, Glais, who had given up the ministry for unlicensed dentistry. He was imprisoned in Swansea and then Brixton gaols in 1940 after some remarkably casual treatment by the Cardiganshire police. His *Prison Sonnets* originally in Welsh, later published in translation in 1948 with a foreword by Dr Iorwerth Peate, were a powerful riposte by 'No. 2740' to the injustices and coercions of prison life.[81] In addition, some conscientious objectors whose applications were endorsed by local tribunals met with hostile treatment from the local patriotic populace: those unpleasant incidents recorded in relation to Aberystwyth in the *Cambrian News* (where Nationalists were involved)[82] were not unique. In general, however, harassment of anti-war protesters is not a significant theme in Wales for the Second World War period since the sample of pacifists is so small and the sentiment in favour of war so overwhelming.

One important group of dissentients, however, can be categorized more precisely, since the war of 1939-45 did bring in a totally new ingredient to the anti-war movement. This was political objection to the war by Welsh Nationalists in Plaid Cymru, who refused to participate in what they regarded as an English war imposed unilaterally upon the Welsh people. Welsh nationalism not only upset the military authorities: it disturbed some of the pacifists as well. John Barclay of the Peace Pledge Union condemned in *Peace News* the excessive attachment of Welsh pacifists at Bangor to the use of the Welsh language; for this, he was fiercely attacked by Dewi Llwyd Jones of Plaid Cymru for 'arrogantly' assuming that all British pacifism must

---

[80]*Peace News*, 5 September 1941. There is material on Dr Peate's dismissal, not generally open to historians at present, in NLW, Thomas Jones papers, Class J, Vol. 20. Dr Peate discusses his case in *Rhwng Dau Fyd* (Denbigh, 1976), 122-9. (I am much indebted to Dr Peate for valuable information on this affair.)

[81]Personal copy from the author in the writer's possession. Especially effective is 'Stay Put', a comment on a Home Office circular read out by the prison chaplain after a service.

[82]Cited in Peter Madgwick and others, *The Politics of Rural Wales* (London, 1972), 60.

be English in origin and speech.[83] Some important new themes emerged here. Plaid Cymru had increasingly put forward the demand for a distinct Welsh foreign policy throughout the 1930s. The Penyberth episode in 1936 strengthened the mood of resistance to 'English' rearmament, even amongst writers like Kate Roberts and R. Williams Parry, hitherto relatively detached from politics. In May 1939, at the time of the passage of the National Service Act, party rallies at Caernarfon and Ystalyfera had attacked the concept of conscription variously on nationalist, religious and community grounds.[84] When world war broke out in September, the party's official stand was one of neutrality, with the assertion of the legal and moral right of Wales to formulate its own policy towards the European dictators. Saunders Lewis, the party's president until 1943, both in presidential addresses to party conferences and in his 'Cwrs y Byd' column in *Y Faner* elaborated the view that Wales was quite detached from the quarrels between England and Germany.[85] Strategic decisions such as the demand for a 'second front' in 1942 were ones upon which party members as committed Welsh Nationalists, simply need not pronounce.[86] This was the attitude adopted by Professor J. E. Daniel, K. E. Jones and other leading figures in the party.

However, Plaid Cymru was scrupulous in leaving decisions about participation in the war to the consciences of individual members.[87] Even Saunders Lewis himself made it clear that he was no doctrinaire absolutist pacifist. In his election address in the University of Wales by-election published in November 1942, he emphasized his view that a military balance ought to be achieved between the belligerent powers before peace terms were concluded. Therefore, he favoured a British victory in the Egyptian campaign to counter earlier military successes by the German army. 'I should not think it my duty in parliament to argue for peace at any price.'[88] Many Plaid members and sympathizers served in the armed forces. One of their most distinguished figures, Ambrose Bebb, a founder member of Plaid Cymru but also a passionate admirer of French culture, strongly endorsed the war and

[83]*Peace News*, 17, 31 October 1941. Barclay was later dismissed as an official of the Peace Pledge Union in June 1942 (Ceadel, op. cit., 312).

[84]J. E. Jones, *Tros Gymru* (Swansea, 1970), 213.

[85]*Western Mail*, 5 August 1940.

[86]Ibid., 8 December 1942.

[87]There is an excellent treatment of this theme in A. O. H. Jarman, 'Plaid Cymru in the Second World War', *Planet* (May 1979), 21–30. I am much indebted to Professor Jarman, to Dr John Davies and to Mr Gwynfor Evans for valuable information and advice on this topic.

[88]Saunders Lewis's election address (21 November 1942), p.2.

severed contact with the party for a time.[89] Other Plaid Cymru members were treated by military tribunals as pacifists on religious rather than political grounds, and were granted exemption from military service on that basis, as in the cases of Gwynfor Evans and the architect, Dewi Prys Thomas. In addition, the party focused attention on the impact of war in eroding Welsh culture as much as on the war itself, notably in the vain attempt to rescue 40,000 acres of upland farming land in the Epynt range in Breconshire from the operations of the Royal Artillery.

It was, however, in a different context that Plaid Cymru made its most striking impact on the anti-war movement. Several party members came before the north or south Wales tribunals specifically and solely as political objectors to this 'English' war. In some ways, they faced a machinery congenial to them. The establishment of separate tribunals for north and south Wales was some kind of renewed recognition of the identity of Wales, as was the Welsh appeals tribunal (paralleling one in Scotland and four in England). So, too, was the established procedure for having evidence given before these tribunals in the Welsh language – a practice upheld in the 1942 Welsh Courts Act.[90] Even so, Plaid Cymru members who offered political objection to the war faced massive pressures. Although the local Welsh tribunals were distinctly more inclined to accept political, as opposed to religious or humanitarian, objection to the war than they had been in 1916, it was uncertain as to whether Welsh nationalism would be included in this category. Indeed, British tribunals varied widely in their definition of conscientious objection. In Serial No. 2 (9 December 1940) an English Appellate Tribunal formally recorded its view that Welsh nationalism was indeed a basis for conscientious objection within the meaning of the 1939 Act.[91] There followed some individual cases of Welsh Nationalists coming before tribunals in London and elsewhere in England and having their beliefs recognized as a valid basis for exemption. But the tribunals in Wales itself were significantly more severe. Both the north and south Wales tribunals consistently refused to recognize nationalism as a valid reason for exemption from military service. They were steadfastly upheld in this view by the appellate tribunal for Wales. Here, the dominant figure was the barrister, Rhys Hopkin Morris, a past and future Liberal MP, a

---

[89]However, Bebb re-emerged as Plaid Cymru candidate for Caernarfonshire in the 1945 general election.

[90]'Suggestion for a Welsh-speaking appellate tribunal for conscientious objectors in Wales, 1939-40', file M/4386 (PRO, LAB 6/125).

[91]Denis Hayes, *The Challenge of Conscience: The Story of the Conscientious Objectors, 1939-1945* (London, 1949), 376-7.

leading Welsh Independent with a high reputation for moral rectitude, but also a man whose legalism and patriotism in this instance overrode his humanitarianism. The Welsh appellate tribunal consistently accepted that only an objection to performing combatant duties or to military service in general, rather than specific opposition to this particular 'English war', could be upheld, even though the legal justification offered was not impressive.

There resulted a series of cases in which Welsh Nationalists went to prison after refusing to submit to a medical examination or accept other procedures of the National Service Act. The first was Gwyn Jones of Bwlch Gwyn, near Wrexham, who spent three months in gaol in early 1941. Some better-known figures followed, including the eminent Celtic scholar, A. O. H. Jarman, editor of the Plaid Cymru newspaper, *Y Ddraig Goch*. One intriguing case that led to much publicity was that of J. E. Jones, Plaid Cymru's organizing secretary. He came before the Caernarfon bench of magistrates in April 1942 for refusing to submit to a medical examination after being removed from the list of objectors by the north Wales tribunal, a decision that was confirmed on appeal. He managed to persuade the court that section 17 rather than section 3 of the National Service Act was relevant here, which meant that he escaped with a £5 fine rather than imprisonment.[92] This, indeed, was not the first time that the Caernarfon magistrates had taken this view: John G. Williams had been treated with the same leniency in August 1942.[93] Jones came before the magistrates a second time in October 1942, and again escaped with a £5 fine (paid by friends). A third time his case came up in Caernarfon, this time in February 1943, with W. Arthian Davies KC dispatched there to demand of the magistrates that they state a case for the High Court to consider to justify their refusal to imprison J. E. Jones. After some wrangling as to whether Davies should address the court in Welsh – and whether a Gwynedd court would understand his Cardiganshire Welsh – the magistrates adhered to their previous position and rejected both twelve months' imprisonment and a £50 fine in place of another token fine of £5.[94] The Ministry of Labour then gave up, and Jones remained a very rare case of a Plaid Cymru activist who successfully resisted prosecution for his beliefs. Meanwhile the Caernarfon magistrates continued to fine objectors of nationalist beliefs rather then imprison them.

[92]Ibid., 177–9; J. E. Jones, op. cit., 239–46. For some general comments, see *Baner ac Amserau Cymru*, 17 Chwefror 1943, p.4.

[93]*Peace News*, 21 August 1942.

[94]*Baner ac Amserau Cymru*, 10 Chwefror 1943; *Carnarvon and Denbigh Herald*, 13 February 1943.

The total of Plaid Cymru anti-war men and women who came before the courts as political objectors was small, perhaps only two dozen or so. The total was larger than the number imprisoned since the Ministry of Labour placed some names on the 'NFA' (No Further Action) register. Their later impact was indeed a significant one, though one open to different lines of interpretation. It could be argued that the party's attitude weakened its popular appeal by associating it with disloyal or even collaborationist attitudes. It encouraged wartime critics like Thomas Jones, in his address to the Cardiff Cymmrodorion entitled 'The Native Never Returns' (1942), and the Revd Gwilym Davies in *Y Traethodydd* to denounce the party (unfairly) as totalitarian or even proto-fascist.[95] Quotations of Saunders Lewis's past sympathy for Mussolini-type 'distributist' economics or for the nationalist ethic of Charles Maurras' *Action Française* could be freely unearthed. At the time, Lewis's own unbending stand on religious matters may have alienated other opponents of the war, as was seen in the support that W. J. Gruffydd obtained in the University of Wales by-election (when he defeated Lewis) even from a pacifist like Iorwerth Peate. In 1945, Plaid Cymru was still the small struggling fringe group it had always been. On the other hand, the party did maintain a perfectly intelligible and defensible line of policy during the war, one which stressed the identity and putative sovereignty of Wales without straying into the quisling-type collaborationism of many Breton Nationalists in France. The party's ideas were made more distinct through the international aspects being made that degree more precise. The party did not seem to lose support for its wartime attitudes. J. E. Jones has claimed that membership rose from 3,750 in 1939 to 6,050 in 1945.[96] By 1946 the party was, temporarily at least, a lively force in parliamentary by-elections. Above all, it was able to express in this context its insistence on the political, as well as the cultural, reality of Wales. As the wartime passions of 1945 died away, opposition to war became a more attractive theme for a party now under the presidency of that lifelong pacifist, one deeply involved with the Peace Pledge Union, the Fellowship of Reconciliation and *Heddychwyr Cymru*, Gwynfor Evans. Its opposition to war in 1939 may have restricted Plaid Cymru in the short run, but it may also have made it more credible in its long-term aspirations.

[95]Gwilym Davies, 'Cymru gyfan a'r Blaid Genedlaethol Gymreig', *Y Traethodydd*, Gorffennaf 1942, 97–111. J. E. Daniel and Saunders Lewis replied in *Plaid Cymru Gyfan* (Caernarfon, 1942). For another, more moderate, attack on Welsh nationalism at this period, see an article by the principal of the University College of North Wales, Bangor, D. Emrys Evans, 'Y rhyfel a'r dewis', *Y Llenor*, XX (2) (Haf 1941), 69–76.

[96]J. E. Jones, op. cit., 247. Plaid Cymru records in NLW support this claim.

The history of peace movements in modern Wales is a patchy one. It can hardly be argued that there has been a specific coherent tradition of opposition to war, other than demonstrations by individuals and minority groups. Until 1939, Welsh anti-war movements, like those in England, veered between pacifists who objected to violence on absolute grounds and 'pacificists' who took a more political and internationalist approach. The Peace Pledge Union and the Peace Ballot were totally distinct movements. After 1939, there was the added element of Welsh Nationalist protest, a theme almost unknown before 1918. In each period, one is discussing a small group of rebels. In the Boer War, despite the charisma of Lloyd George and Keir Hardie, the pro-Boers (Liberal or Labour), were for a long time a minority, and found it hard to swim against the imperialist tide. In the First World War, Liberal pacifists were almost swamped by the war passions of the time, as the persecution endured by a man like Thomas Rees indicates. Socialist objectors followed their own distinctive, often sectarian, policy, while the labour unrest against the war served to divide the peace movement through its class basis at the time rather than create anything resembling a untied national body. In 1939, Welsh Nationalist and other conscientious objectors were few in number, though often influential as individuals. Since 1945, anti-war movements in Wales have been hard to isolate. The theme of Welsh Nationalist protest continued to be heard: in January 1947, a Welsh Nationalist was successfully defended by Wynne Samuel before the 2nd London Division of the Appellate Tribunal and gained exemption from national service on political grounds. Individual pacifists continued to make their stand and proclaim their faith: perhaps the most celebrated was the Quaker poet, Waldo Williams, who twice went to prison for refusal to pay taxes which might finance the war machine, in 1960–1.[97] Anti-war sentiment may have fuelled some elements of the growth of Plaid Cymru from the later 1950s; while the Campaign for Nuclear Disarmament in 1958–62 had support in many parts of Wales, from Bangor to Ebbw Vale, with nationalist, socialist and religious passion strengthening its varied appeal.[98] But these movements have tended to wax and wane in response to wider movements in British and world politics. Always the pressures of centralized government, party politics, social conformity and growing affluence have served to dampen their enthusiasm. The sterner pacifists have

[97]See J. Nicholas (ed.), *Waldo – Cyfrol Deyrnged* (Cardiff, 1977).

[98]I am grateful for information from Professor Mansel Davies, former secretary of the Aberystwyth Nuclear Weapons Committee. Frank Parkin, *Middle Class Radicalism* (London, 1968), a sociological study of CND, has nothing on Wales. The revival of CND in 1979–81 proved ephemeral.

always found the going hard. The progress of Plaid Cymru and the Welsh Language Society in the later 1960s saw the main emphasis placed rather on 'non-violent resistance' through the sit-in and other methods, a coercive if non-physical form of protest far removed from the creed of the purer pacifists.[99] Symbolically, poor George Maitland Lloyd Davies, the saintly martyr of non-violent, Christian pacifism in two world wars, ended his days tragically, a voluntary patient at Denbigh mental hospital. On 14 December 1949, he hanged himself.

Yet the peace movements recorded here offer far more than a record of negativism or failure. On the contrary, their victories, often post-humous, played a crucial part in the political and cultural evolution of modern Wales. The pro-Boers had captured the public conscience by 1902 and helped promote a great radical upsurge in the years up to 1914 with the greatest pro-Boer of them all at the helm. The anti-war Liberals and journals like *Y Deyrnas* in 1914–18 generated a re-awakening of the radical conscience. They helped channel much of the old Liberal Nonconformist culture into the new Labour movement and to graft on to the socialist struggle against the capitalist system an older libertarian tradition of dissent and humane idealism. By the thirties, much of the cultural and intellectual vitality of an increasingly left-wing Wales was the product of the anti-war men of 1914–18 and their descendants. The Plaid Cymru victims of 1939–45 created their legacy, too, as has been seen.

Perhaps the ultimate effect may be seen in moral terms. On each occasion, opponents of war have emerged at critical phases of Welsh history to question the dominant consensus and prevent its hardening into sterile dogma. The pro-Boers of 1899 helped to transform an unthinking commitment to British imperialism and to reassert the radical dynamic that underlay the spirit of *Cymru Fydd*. The anti-war Liberals and socialists after 1914 revitalized an ossified and inert radicalism already showing signs of internal decay after fifty years of easy victories. The Plaid Cymru dissentients in 1939 helped ensure that after 1945 a world reconstruction would not totally ignore the claims of Wales as it had done in 1918. Indeed, the potential threat from the Nationalists was one factor in impelling the 1945–51 government towards the reluctant grant of more devolution to Wales, with the Welsh Office in 1964 and the abortive devolution proposals of

[99]For this, see Colin H. Williams, 'Non-violence and the development of the Welsh Language Society, 1962–*c.*1974', *Welsh History Review*, 8 (4) (1977), 426–55.

1976–8 as its indirect consequences.[100] In all their diversity, these incorrigible rebels helped to keep Welsh political culture alive if not intact. More generally, they reminded their countrymen anew of the indomitable force of the free human spirit against the pressures and the violence of a monolithic world.

1981

[100]See the *New Statesman and Nation*, 24 August, 14 September 1946, 4 December 1948. Also cf. Labour party archives, Walworth Road: Policy Committee minutes, 18 September 1946, for discussion of Huw T. Edwards's memorandum, 'The Problem of Wales'.

7

Socialism and Syndicalism:
The Welsh Miners' Debate, 1912

W. H. Mainwaring, part-author of *The Miners' Next Step* (1912) and tutor-organizer for the Central Labour College of south Wales was MP for Rhondda East from 1933 until his retirement in 1959. His papers shed a revealing light on aspects of the political, industrial and ideological development of the south Wales miners in the twentieth century.[1] They include some rare examples of socialist pamphlet literature, together with papers that bear upon the history of the coal-mining history industry in south Wales since the First World War. There are also materials relating to proposals for governmental devolution. The two most important items, however, stem from Mainwaring's career as a fiery Marxist ideologue, through the Unofficial Reform Committee and the Central Labour College tutorial classes, in the years immediately preceding the outbreak of war in 1914. One is the original manuscript of *The Miners' Next Step*, that classic landmark of industrial militancy published by the URC at Tonypandy in 1912, of which Mainwaring (along with Will Hay, Noah Ablett, C. L. Gibbons, Noah Rees and George Dolling) was part-author. The proof copy of this historic pamphlet has long been deposited in the National Library of Wales.

The other item of especial interest, and printed *in extenso* below, is the debate on the nationalization of the mines, held at Trealaw on 13 November 1912. It was a tense and critical period for the Welsh miners

[1]The Mainwaring papers were acquired in 1975 by the National Library of Wales, Aberystwyth, through the generosity of Mr Mainwaring's daughter, Mrs Joyce Tudge of Oxford. They have recently been listed for scholars.

and their union leaders. The bitterness surrounding the riots at Tonypandy, the lengthy Cambrian strike, and Churchill's dispatch of the 18th Hussars to the Welsh coalfield still rankled.[2] There had been a brief national stoppage in successful pursuit of a miners' minimum wage in April. More sinister, in the view of many commentators on the labour scene, there were powerful new pressures for transferring leadership of the South Wales Miners' Federation to the militant rank-and-file, and for forms of workers' control. The *Rhondda Socialist* (later renamed the *South Wales Worker*), founded in 1911 and soon to be edited by Will Hay, a prominent syndicalist sympathetic to the industrial unionism expounded by Tom Mann, preached a radical version of socialism attainable only through industrial action. In the summer of 1912 plans for a complete overhaul of the SWMF, involving much more decentralization in policy-making and trans-ferring far more power to local lodges, was narrowly defeated. Above all, the appeal of *The Miners' Next Step* for industrial unionism and the comprehensive destruction of the capitalist system through quasi-revolutionary methods, was a seductive one.[3] Not only were the capitalist system and the Liberal and Unionist parties now on trial. Even the Labour party founded as the supreme instrument for working-class emancipation seemed outmoded. Its programmes and its concept of parliamentary pressure seemed a species of collaboration with the capitalist enemy.

The 1912 debate on the relevance of nationalization of the mines (faithfully transcribed in Mainwaring's careful shorthand) is thus particularly fascinating to students of labour history. None of the local south Wales newspapers carry any report of it. The four speakers form an interesting group, each in his way a symbol of an important strand in the history of the Welsh miners. The advocate of the SWMF scheme for nationalization was George Barker. He was an Englishman like many other Welsh miners' leaders at this period (a native of Hanley in

[2] These episodes are best approached through the local newspaper press. Churchill's role in sending troops to Rhondda, played down by his various biographers, is described in Sir Nevil Macready, *Annals of an Active Life* (London, 1924) vol.I, 136–57. Among the more helpful secondary works are David Evans, *Labour Strife in the South Wales Coalfield* (Cardiff, 1911); Eric Wyn Evans, *The Miners of South Wales* (Cardiff, 1961); Kenneth O. Morgan, *Wales in British Politics, 1868–1922* (Cardiff, 1963; 2nd edn., 1970); R. Page Arnot, *South Wales Miners* (London, 1967). M. Woodhouse, 'Rank and File Movements in South Wales, 1910–26' (unpublished University of Oxford D.Phil. thesis, 1970) is a very informative survey. Recent issues of the *Welsh History Review* and of *Llafur* are well worth study.

[3] *The Miners' Next Step*, 27–9, spent time in discussing the unifying of the men and the eliminating of the employers through such tactics as the 'irritation strike' and 'ca-canny' methods.

Staffordshire) and had been agent for the Monmouthshire western valleys since 1908. His election to the SWMF executive in 1910, along with Vernon Hartshorn and C. B. Stanton, had been taken as the harbinger of the new industrial militancy advocated by a younger generation of agents, in contrast to the class harmony preached by Mabon and the older Lib–Labs. Certainly Barker was a forceful critic of D. A. Thomas – the 'czar' of Tonypandy – and the other coalowners. Even so, this debate shows, that like Hartshorn, Barker was sceptical of the nostrums of the industrial unionists. (It might be added that Barker, born in 1858, was hardly of the younger generation himself.) He adopted unhesitatingly the view, increasingly the orthodox one, that the solution for falling wages, inadequate safety provisions and other travails of the miners lay in public ownership.

His supporter in the debate was Edward Gill, until recently a prominent supporter of the Unofficial Reform Committee. With Noah Ablett, he had drawn up in early 1911 a manifesto which issued a clarion call to the Welsh rank-and-file miners. However, since the minimum-wage strike, Gill also had turned to favour more conventional policies of collective bargaining. There was also a profound strain of patriotism in his makeup, which made him suspicious of the alien panaceas peddled by a Sorel or a de Leon. It is notable that in this debate he tried to reconcile his earlier and his present positions by claiming that only through public ownership would 'the coercive powers of the state' be destroyed.

On the other side were a truly formidable pair. Noah Ablett, a Rhondda man, was already a Marxist firebrand of legendary reputation. Originally destined for the Nonconformist ministry, he had been a founder of the Plebs League in October 1908, and a leading participant in the strike at Ruskin College, Oxford, which led to the founding of the Central Labour College in 1909. 'More than any other man [Ablett] brought me fully into the working-class struggle', wrote Arthur Horner. Ablett's unequivocal Marxism and class war rhetoric, allied to an apocalyptic fervour that bore testimony to the imprint of the Welsh religious revival that swept the coalfield in 1904–5, made him the most forceful voice for industrial unionism (though not, perhaps, for syndicalism, strictly defined) in any British coalfield.[4] His supporter in the debate was Frank Hodges, another Ruskin College product and hero of the 'strike' of 1909, still in his mid-twenties. He was a Gloucestershire man, also much stirred by the 1904 religious revival, who had been miners' agent for the Garw valley since 1911.[5]

[4]See W. W. Craik, *The Central Labour College* (London, 1964), esp. 64–6; Arthur Horner, *Incorrigible Rebel* (London, 1960), 15.

[5]Frank Hodges, *My Adventures as a Labour Leader* (London, 1926), 18–22.

Hodges echoed Ablett's deep suspicion of the state as 'a capitalist trust'. Indeed, in this debate he adopted a more frankly syndicalist approach, using analogies from France and elsewhere. Like Ablett he urged that industrial power be vested in the workers themselves, instead of in a remote bureaucracy. Nationalization he totally rejected, since 'the state was the stronghold of capitalism' and no compromise with it was conceivable.

The debate at Trealaw, chaired by W. P. Nicholas, clerk to the local council and later solicitor to the SWMF, was vigorous. Both the state socialist and the industrial unionist positions were cogently argued, with the debating honours perhaps even. In practice, however, the tide was turning against the industrial radicals. By the summer of 1914, the Unofficial Reform Committee was at a low ebb.[6] Associated bodies like the Industrial Democracy League had virtually petered out in south Wales. Even a man like Ablett was the target of fierce onslaughts in the *South Wales Worker*. As a more aggressive strategy was adopted by the south Wales leaders, committed however ambiguously to the Triple Alliance, pressure for rank-and-file control died away, save perhaps in Rhondda. Men like Barker (later to be MP for Abertillery, 1920–9) were already committed to constitutionalism and traditional procedures of collective bargaining. The outbreak of war in August 1914 at first further weakened the position of the industrial radicals. Gill, like Barker, endorsed entry into war and took part in recruiting campaigns along with other miners' leaders, including Vernon Hartshorn, James Winstone, David Watts Morgan and the egregious quasi-fascist C. B. Stanton. Frank Hodges, the rising hope of the stern, unbending syndicalists before 1914, also rapidly shed all contact with Ablett and the apostles of direct action. By 1918, he was serving as secretary of the Miners' Federation of Great Britain, at the age of thirty-one. The next year he vigorously expounded the case for nationalization of the mines on the Sankey Commission. It was Hodges's misfortune to end up as Lloyd George's victim on 'Black Friday' in April 1921, accused of class betrayal by miners everywhere. Later still, he completed his apostasy by becoming the director of an investment company, and a member of the Central Electricity Board. For many socialists, he provided an industrial version of Ramsay MacDonald.

Only Noah Ablett survived as the unmuzzled voice of militancy, and even his tone was somewhat muted during the war years. After 1918, although miners' agent for Merthyr and a member of the MFGB executive, he gradually retreated from the forefront for political and

---

[6]William Brace, a notorious Lib–Lab, had been elected president of the SWMF in 1912, with Barker as runner-up (*Merthyr Express*, 15 June 1912).

personal reasons. Arthur Horner, Aneurin Bevan and others have added to the legends that surround his name,[7] until Ablett's reputation is now perhaps unduly inflated, at the expense of Noah Rees and other contemporaries. As for Will Mainwaring, the watchful observer of the Trealaw debate, he undoubtedly sympathized ardently with Ablett and Hodges in 1912, and served the Central Labour College as a tutor in economics for several years more. When, however, he was elected to parliament for Rhondda East in 1933, defeating first Arthur Horner and then Harry Pollitt in two famous electoral contests, Mainwaring had become a vigorous anti-Communist and a fluent exponent of the Barker-Gill arguments of 1912. The wheel had come full circle for him, too.

Like Mainwaring, the Welsh miners generally opted for the orthodox view after 1918 – a crusade for a socialist society through the Labour party, with nationalization of the mines as a major panacea for economic depression and the class war. But the debate launched at Trealaw in 1912 still goes on. Pressure for rank-and-file control was resumed through the Minority Movement after 1923, through the success of Communists in capturing key posts in the Welsh Miners' Federation in the 1930s, and through the redefined militancy of the early 1970s. Further, from the general strike down to the productivity ballot in 1974, from the age of A. J. Cook to that of Dai Francis, the Welsh coalfield retained its own particularisms and loyalties. Labour historians who ignore its Welshness, the Nonconformity and the nationalism that helped to mould its society and culture, do so at their peril. The arguments in south Wales for and against centralization have not been stilled by the passage of public ownership. In many ways, the revived fortunes of the British coal industry in the 1970s give them added relevance. The great debate on industrial democracy, enshrined in the papers of Will Mainwaring, is still far from ended.

★ ★ ★

[7]Arthur Horner, op. cit., 15ff.; Michael Foot, *Aneurin Bevan* vol. 1 (London, 1962), 28–9.

TRANSCRIPT OF SHORTHAND NOTE OF DEBATE AT THE JUDGE'S HALL TREALAW 13 NOVEMBER 1912

THE NATIONALIZATION OF MINES. IS THIS IN THE BEST INTEREST OF THE WORKERS?

Affirmative	Negative
Mr George Barker,	Mr Noah Ablett,
Miners' Agent	Mardy
Seconded by Edward Gill,	Mr Frank Hodges,
Abertillery	Miners' Agent, Tondu
SWMF Executive Council	

Independent Chairman: W. P. Nicholas, The Garth, Trealaw

The chairman having remarked his pleasure in accepting the invitation to preside and to hold the balance between the debators, explained that Mr Barker would open the case for the affirmative. Then Mr Ablett would follow for the negative. After that Mr Gill, junior counsel to Mr Barker, would follow. Then Mr Frank Hodges, junior counsel to Mr Ablett, would follow. Finally Mr Ablett and Mr Barker would sum up their respective cases.

The chairman then called upon Mr Barker to open.

Mr Barker:

I have very much pleasure tonight in standing here to affirm that the nationalization of mines is in the best interest of the workers.

First of all, I should like to define what is meant by the nationalization of the mines. To nationalize the mines means to make the mines and the minerals of the United Kingdom the property of the nation, instead of being the properties of individuals or companies, as at present. It seems to me, looking at it as an elementary proposition, that it must meet with universal assent. The principle has been advocated by labour organizations for the last 25 years, and Trades Union Congresses and Miners' Conferences have affirmed and reaffirmed the principle of the nationalization of the mines of the country. It is, in my opinion, the first step out of what Mr Belloc has termed the servile state. At the present time you are very well aware that every man – every worker at any rate – is subject to someone else for his means of livelihood. He is in a servile state. He has to be hired by someone, and if he fails to get hired then one of two or three circumstances is the result. If he fails to get hired be becomes straight away a pauper. He either becomes that or a criminal, or else he has to perish for lack of subsistence. That is what has been termed by Mr Belloc and others as the servile state.

Nationalization of mines presupposes – and perhaps I shall be going out of my subject here – that all other industries also will be nationalized and eventually by getting the state to hold and control the whole of the industries of the country the workers will be emancipated from their present servile state. Now the question naturally arises; if the mines be nationalized, how are they to be nationalized? And it will be my duty tonight to show how this is to be brought about.

I have in my hand the bill which provides first of all that the mines are to be obtained by purchase. There are two ways of getting hold of the mines of the country, one by purchasing them, the other by confiscation. I think anyone who understands anything about the temperament of the British people will agree with me that to propose to obtain the mines by such a revolutionary method as confiscation is too remote to be realized by this or even the next generation, therefore the only feasible way to obtain the mines – and I wish to emphasize this – is to obtain them by purchase. This bill has been drawn up by a barrister who is acting for the Labour Party. It provides on pages four and five a method of valuation by which the approximate price can be fixed for obtaining the mines. I may say that this bill is based on legislation that has been enacted in the British colonies and other parts of the civilized world. It states that when 100,000 tons or less have been raised per annum during the five preceding years, that the value of the mine should be assessed at 12s. per ton; where more than 100,000 tons have been raised on the average, then 10s. a ton shall be the purchase price. Depreciation, development, and the probable duration of the life of the mine shall be taken into consideration by those who are ascertaining the value of the mine. For the purpose of paying the purchase price it is provided that the Treasury shall issue guaranteed 3% coalmine stock. We know the government had no difficulty in raising £100,000,000 or £200,000,000 in a very few hours during the time of the Boer war, and those who know anything about it say that the surplus uninvested capital in this country at the present time yields much lower interest than 3%; so there would be no difficulty in the government obtaining this money. Provision is made for redeeming this stock out of profits as will be shown later.

The case for nationalization will depend very largely upon the practicability of the financial proposals. We have made a calculation here based on the bill, and have made it even more liberal. It has been estimated by more than one authority that the value of the mines of the United Kingdom is about £120,000,000. I am prepared, for the sake of argument and for the sake of putting this case beyond cavil and dispute, to assume that the capital value of the mines is no less than £150,000,000. Now, the profits today out of the mining industry are, according to the statement of Mr Chiozza Money,[8] and also according to the value returned by the owners themselves and assessed for income tax, no less than £25,000,000 a year. This £25,000,000 today goes into the pockets of the idle shareholders. It is out of this money that the financial proposals are based for the acquisition of the mines of the United Kingdom. First of all, we propose that the state purchases these mines on these lines. I may say in passing that there were 3,298 mines in the UK in 1907, employing 1,014,998 men. To acquire this vast wealth for the nation it is proposed to pay some £150,000,000; it is proposed to redeem that £150,000,000 in something like the following manner. First of all, we have the interest fixed at 3%, as I stated a moment or two ago, but to make the position absolutely certain we have fixed the interest at $3\frac{1}{2}$%. This will take £5,250,000. The redemption of principal has been fixed at £5,000,000 per annum. To redeem £150,000,000 at this rate would, as you will see, take 30 years, but during these years the interest would decrease by £183,250 every year. Then for depreciation and development of new mines we have allocated £5,000,000 a year. Even supposing we give the workers, not the minimum wage as at present under the various awards, but the rates of wages asked for in the schedules and refused by this capitalistic government, we have ample to do that, and have allowed £5,000,000 per annum. Then there is the great question of safety in the mines, the greatest of all questions and the greatest of all reasons why the mines of the kingdom should be nationalized. In the interests of safety, we have allowed £1,250,000 to be added to the cost of production to make the lives of the workers more safe and healthy than they are now. Then distribution has not been left out, because the bill not only provides for the nationalization of the mines and minerals, but for the nationalization of the distribution of the minerals, and by that means wipes out at once the plunderer we describe as the middleman. For the reduction of the price of coal to the consumer we have allowed £3,500,000. Adding up all these amounts we have absorbed exactly the £25,000,000 profits made out of the mines of the United Kingdom.

Nationalization would unify the management of the mines, and this would dispense with many directors who are now getting fat salaries, to economize in the management and further increase the profits made

[8]Leo Chiozza Money (1870–1944): Liberal MP 1906–18; later joined the Labour party. Author of *Riches and Poverty* (1905) and other socio-economic works.

at present; and out of this new profit benefits would come to the workers in increased wages and better conditions, and also into the pockets of the community. And instead of being employed by men or combines who employ you merely for the purpose of making profit, you would be employed by the state, who would have to be responsible to the whole community for your safety. The number of lives lost in the mines is simply appalling, and I would remind my friends who are here to try to destroy my case, that if they do so they will become themselves in a measure indirectly responsible for the blood-guiltiness. The number killed in the mines of the United Kingdom in 1910 reached the appalling total of 1,769, while the number disabled for more than seven days amounted to no less than 153,000. To defer the proposals made in this bill means to continue this slaughter. The present system is one of producing for profit, and can anyone for a moment imagine that the conscience of the nation would allow lives to be lost in this way if the mines were nationalized? It is out of all reason to imagine such a thing and an insult to the nation to make such an allegation.

I have only a few minutes left. The benefits, and they are considerable, will be increased safety to all who work in the mines, curtailment of waste in the method of production. At the present time, owing to a wasteful system of production, millions and millions of tons of valuable mineral are left in the mines (hear, hear). But the quantity of mineral is strictly limited; it cannot be increased by a single ounce. This buried treasure is irrevocably lost and can never be recovered. Yet these patriotic mineowners are sacrificing millions of tons because they wish to produce 'large coal', instead of producing by natural means.

Nationalization of the coal mines will be followed by the cheapening of coal to the public, the abolition of royalties, the reduction of profits, and the elimination of the capitalists altogether from the mining industry of the country. I say these benefits are hardly measurable, and I challenge my opponents to furnish any practical alternative. It is no good to give us fanciful and utopian ideas. No doubt they wish to give you revolutionary methods instead of this practical one, to give you something which cannot be obtained in this generation or the next. The ideas in this bill are eminently practicable. There are mines today that have been nationalized.

I have in my hand a book compiled by Mr Bruce Glaisher,[9] who has gathered some valuable facts. In New Zealand, they have already nationalized several mines, and as a result have been able to reduce the cost of coal to the consumer from 35s. to 28s. per ton. The average

---

[9]*Sic.* Presumably J. Bruce Glasier (1859–1920), friend of Keir Hardie, chairman of the ILP 1900–3, editor of the *Labour Leader* 1905–10. The reference may be to his *Socialism and Strikes*.

wages of men and boys at the time the figures were compiled in the beginning of the year was no less than 17s. per eight-hour shift. This is the result of nationalization. If they can do this in New Zealand, what can we do in this the greatest mining country in the world? Our proposals are eminently practicable; you can enjoy them now and not have to wait for some subsequent generation. If the workers say they will no longer produce for exploiters, and if they stand by that as loyally as they did in the national strike, there is nothing that can prevent the nationalization of the mines.

In conclusion, I appeal to you to throw all your energies into this proposal – the greatest proposal the labour world has ever yet evolved. I ask you all, especially those of you who are employed in the mining industries, to concentrate all your efforts, not for a paltry advance in wages or for a paltry reduction in hours of labour, but for the things that are essential – to get the mines for yourselves (applause), as workers and citizens of a free nation.

The chairman then called upon Mr Ablett, who said:

Mr Barker has given you an impassioned appeal. He has prophesied that this side will put forth a position consisting of utopian dreams. It is for Mr Hodges and myself to show that Mr Barker's prophecies have no greater value than his arguments for the nationalization of mines. And those, when analysed, are simply a little bundle of 'supposes' and 'ifs'. If for the moment we grant his suppositions, and his ideals are realized, what then have we got? We have the state comprising on the one hand, Citizen D. A. Thomas and on the other Geo. Barker, with other harmonious elements mixed up into a cooperative society to govern a happy little family! We on this side are here tonight, not on behalf of the 'community' as at present organized; not on behalf of 'our' country; not even for the sake of the nation; not for any of these, but we are here in the interests of the working-class militant, and it is from their point of view alone will we judge this bill. I say this, because Mr Barker has used so many vague terms about the 'people', the nation, etc, and above all has claimed that the bill is going to free us from the servile state; on the contrary, Mr Barker, you would simply place an important section of the working class in the hands of a state servile to capitalists' interests, who would use their opportunity to increase the servility we now equally abhor. The state, as well as the unenlightened section of the workers who still support their masters, are more responsive to the suggestions, aye, and to the purse, power, and influence of D. A. Thomas than Mr Barker seems to think. He has told me – to my surprise – that any suggestion to confiscate the mines is utopian. But surely the scheme supported by Mr Barker is far more utopian than any confiscation scheme. For in that scheme it appears that the mines will be paid for by pieces of paper.

It is a wonderful plan the MFGB executive has evolved, if – but they, and Mr Barker is one, seem entirely to have forgotten that the only terms on which the mines will be nationalized will be those dictated by a Liberal or Tory government, whose sympathies with labour are so well known. Our friends sitting in the inviting atmosphere of the Westminster Palace Hotel seem entirely to have ignored this little obstacle. 'If' says Mr Barker, if the government were to take over the mines, and 'if' there were £25,000,000 of profits – with many other 'ifs' and 'supposes', then we could get not only the present minimum wage, but the whole of the schedules, and a five days per week. Really? Let me ask Mr Barker what reason has he to suppose that even 'if' the government could exploit us to the tune of £25,000,000 what reason has he to suppose that they will give it back in increased wages? What reason have you fellow-workmen to suppose such a thing? Is that the proverbial attitude of the government towards you, that the suggestion can be so readily supposed? Let us see. Do the postal workers subscribe to this idea? Are their wages increased in proportion to the increase of revenue from their labours? Recently they put in force proposals purporting to look after our health. In support of that scheme we are asked, nay, it is enforced, to pay 4d per week, while the poor employers only pay 3d. It is a very wrong assumption to assume that, if money goes from our labour to the state, there is the slightest reason to suppose it is coming back to us, as the government is not that kind of employer at all.

Mr Barker has passionately referred to the blood-stained hands we shall have if we oppose this bill. I went yesterday to see a friend who is dying from consumption through working under the insanitary and nerve-destroying conditions of a post office workshop. Let me give a few more pertinent reasons why Mr Barker and his supporters need to carefully examine their hands. Under nationalization of mines, as suggested in this bill, every proposal for the safety of the miners that will mean money cost will have the effect of delaying the day when the state will be the actual owner. Thus the safety of the workmen – not to speak of their wages – and the enthusiasm of Mr Barker's supporters (with their clean hands) to hasten the final act of nationalization run exactly counter to each other. The more safety the longer will the mines be privately owned; the less safety, the sooner will Mr Barker's ideals be realized, and the same thing applies to wages. Every increase of wages is bound to lower the profits in the same proportion as the increase, and it is from this fund the mines are to be bought. Hence the lower the fund the longer will it take to pay for the mines, and so from the financial standpoint we are strictly justified in saying that if the bill becomes law on the terms of a Liberal or Tory government, then Mr Barker and his colleagues will either have to abate their enthusiasm for state ownership, or become opposed to increases in wages and improvements for safety – in other words, from their own point of view, they will have to be reactionary in order to maintain their positions and promote the progress of the workers. The proposal is to first take over the mines on a cooperative community basis, and then afterwards to split up your community into state versus miner, and the miner must become a reactionary from his own ideals in order to improve his position.

Mr Hodges will tell you how the principle operates in this and other countries, and I will leave that side of the question to be developed by him.

You will have to face another thing after nationalization. In all future strikes and organization, you will be faced with a far more formidable organization of capitalists than the Cambrian Combine of the Coalowners Association of Great Britain. You will be faced by the state, and you know how much force and power is behind that to force through any matter they may desire. If you want another strike, you must strike against practically the whole of society, against the state. That is a much bigger job than striking against the coalowners. There will be no need for them to keep the ring; they will be the ring itself, and be inside the colliery gate itself. You are fighting the whole force of the police and military to back them up. You men of Tonypandy know by now what sort of sympathy you can expect when you are after a thing of that sort. If the government give way to any demand for an improvement in conditions to the nationalized miners they are only going to increase the agitation and unrest of workers in other industries.

If the mines are nationalized, the industry and its struggles will be transferred from the miners' organizations and the employers, to the state. All questions relating to increased wages or shorter hours will be debated on the floor of the House. They will be bitterly opposed by Liberals and Tories representing other employers of labour, whether they are for a shorter day, a minimum wage or improved conditions. As miners, we already have some of these things, and for many years to come must take a back seat until workers in other industries come up to us. We cannot very well ask for them from the state, when we consider the very low wages paid in other industries. As far as nationalization is concerned the miners must stand still for years to come before they get an advance in wages, whereas today we can get what we can enforce by our organized might from the body of owners.

We have some other internal difficulties when we come to consider questions of the practicability of the proposal from the financial side. It is proposed first of all to create stock consisting of 'perpetual annuities' and those persons who can claim a title to the mines can claim a title to the stock issued by the government. The MFGB executive place the dividend on these annuities – these perpetual annuities – at 3%. Of course we must not take them seriously. But whatever the figure, the point I wish to make is that the wages of the workmen must come from the surplus of the profits after payment to the national shareholders. They are the first charge and have the security of the nation behind them. Good shareholder? Good perpetual annuity? Excellent MFGB executive? But what of the workmen? What of the men of the Forest of Dean and Somerset and Bristol, what we may well call the sweated portion of the mining industry? On account of geological differences, the industry there cannot develop to give the same profits and pay the same wages as other coalfields. Their wages will have to be made up to the same level as better paying coalfields. Where is the money to come from? It must come from the returns of the whole industry or a separate tax must be placed on the community. In any case, it must be a subsidy to a sweated industry. What will the free traders say to that? Then again there are other proposals, all of which must delay nationalization if they are to be achieved, and if they are not what will Mr Barker's efforts in these directions mean? It means that they will negate each other. The more he supports nationalization, the less can he support those things for which he has always stood. I refer to the proposal for a five days per week; that the six turns for five for the night men shall be general; and that the organization of those employed in and around the mining industry shall be one big union. We read in the bill that the proposals are as follows (clause 16):

The Minister for Mines may from time to time make such regulations as he thinks necessary for any of the following purposes:

(a) The management of the coalmines under this act:

(b) The function, duties and powers of all persons acting in the management of coalmines under this act:

(c) The form of the accounts to be kept and the balance sheet to be prepared in respect of coalmines under this act:

(d) The mode in which the sinking funds and other funds connected with coalmines under this act shall be held and administered:

(e) Generally any other purpose for which, in the opinion of the Minister for Mines, regulations are contemplated or required.

All this proposed that the management shall be given into the hands of the Minister for Mines, who may be a hireling of the stock-owning owners, and there will be the financial proposal that the mines must pay the interest on the stock and repay the capital in so many years. He would be faced with a proposal which will operate against giving us any benefits, and any proposal to give us an increase of wages, a five days week, six turns for five or to organize the workers into one big union – will be met by resistance. They will not as the state allow us or want us to organize in a powerful union. The state has never so far allowed its workers to organize so freely as other workers can, and the workers have to recognize this. It is all very well to put in a clause humbly asking that although you are now the servants of His Majesty you may yet be allowed to organize (clause 15). You would be asking your consolidated enemies to allow you to do this? Is it likely that they will give you this power? Have they ever done so in the history of the world? They have never done so and there is no reason to suppose they will give it to you now. They will fight all Mr Barker's practical proposals. You will have a different enemy in the state. Let Mr Barker and the other nationalizers come down to questions of earth. We have increased our power to fight the coalowners, to remedy the surfacemen's grievance, to secure a five days working week, and to get the six turns for five. Let us democratize our forces and set a foundation stone for citizenship of an industrial republic.

I am going to read from a man I think every member of this audience will respect and admire as one of the great pioneers who have made the labour movement.

> The state then did not exist from all eternity. There have been societies without it, that had no idea of any state or public owner. At a certain stage of economic development, which was of necessity accompanied by a division of society into classes, the state became the inevitable result of this division. We are now rapidly approaching a stage of evolution in production, in which the existence of classes has not only ceased to be a necessity, but becomes a positive fetter on production. Hence these classes must fall as inevitably as they once arose. The state must irrevocably fall with them. The society that is to reorganize production on the basis of free and equal association of the producer will transfer the machinery of state where it will then belong, into the Museum of Antiquities by the side of the spinning wheel and bronze axe.
>
> FREDERICK ENGELS, *Origin of Family* pp.211–12

And to that museum Mr Barker would bring our organization if his nationalization ideals could be realized. But unfortunately the future does not lie in the direction of bureaucracy. The roadway to emancipation lies in a different direction than the offices of a Minister of Mines. It lies in the democratic organization, and eventually control, of the industries by the workers themselves in their organized capacity as trustees for a working-class world. No Minister of Mines will lead us to our emancipation. That must be the work of the workers themselves from the bottom upward, and not from the top downward, which latter means the servile state.(Applause)

Mr Gill then spoke as Mr Barker's seconder. He said:

I am inclined to think that Mr Ablett has become parochial in his outlook. First, he said he stood for the working class and not the nation, then after a short time we discovered that he stood for the miners. Then, seeing that he stood in Mid-Rhondda, we discovered that he stood in particular for the Mid-Rhondda miners. Of course, his appeal is an appeal to prejudice. Why should you men, who by some accident happen to be situated in the richest portion in this coalshed where national wealth has been concentrated, give out of your abundance to the miners of the Forest of Dean? How parochial we become. Mr Ablett is greatly concerned with Mr Barker's position, but after some stumbling he was gracious enough to assume that it might be possible to nationalize these mines and to have state ownership; but having got state ownership there might have to be put forward the plea that we want increased safety and better conditions in the mines of this country, and any proportion of the profits devoted to this would put off the day when you completely buy out these people to somewhere in the remote future. And in the same breath, I believe he said they were out as an alternative policy to get more wages and better conditions in the mines. Surely he should be satisfied if that is so. As far as the state is concerned he wants you in Tonypandy to remember your painful experiences with the state. If I understand those experiences aright, they arose out of the fact that a hundred and one boards of directors were possessed with an insane desire to get the greatest profit out of the mines, and a set of conditions was set up which eventually resulted in a few men throwing stones. Then they got in conflict with the police, and the state sent the military to assist the police. We come before you and say here is a practical proposal which will show you how a better state of things can be brought about. The conditions referred to will be done away with and the innumerable directors will also disappear. With their salaries we will give the men better wages and better homes. It is in the endeavour to get away from conditions that made the Mid-Rhondda scenes possible that we stand tonight advocating this bill. Mr Ablett turned to the Property Defence League for arguments. 'Look at the Post Office in this country,' he said. Now workers in the interests of socialism have always had to answer this bogy. Bad as the conditions of postmen are under a capitalist government, we have yet heard of postmen meeting and asking to be transferred to the tender mercies of private ownership (Hear! Hear!). The great difference is this from the political standpoint. In Tonypandy you have perhaps half a dozen postmen and half a dozen sprinkled here and there over the country. Apart from great causes, their influence in the political world to secure better conditions is practically infinitesimal, but as far as the miners are concerned they are concentrated in industrial centres, their vote practically determining the makeup of parties in the state; or at least they could do so. If we had nationalization – even brought about by a capitalist government – they could have such an influence in the political world that no government could do many of the things which Mr Ablett has assumed they would do. Many of us want to go a long way with Mr Ablett. The difference between us is that we do not look at it from the parochial point of view as he does. As a miner, I do not want to look merely at the miner. As far as this great wealth is concerned, I have to consider other kinds of labour as well as that of the miner (applause). You can persuade the man, with a little sophistry, who cut the coal, 'That is all mine', but there is the man who puts it in the tram, there is the latchboy, the labourer, the timberman, the cutters, rippers, and every grade of man and labour in the mine interested in cutting that ton of coal; firemen, overmen, mining engineers, colliery clerks, weighers etc. There is the railwayman, who transports the product to the dock; you must acknowledge that he is interested in that tram of coal, you must recognize that the docker, sailor, and others have to some extent had a hand in producing that ton of coal. You must also recognize that as far as we are concerned we have not had any opportunity of making the choice of the conditions which exist today. There are miners working in the less remunerative concerns, and for some time, from your own point of view, if you have no interest in their wages and conditions, you have to watch the conditions of these people in Somerset and the Forest of Dean in so far as they affect your own. You may say, if the pits do not allow good wages to be paid, close them up. Yes, close them, and let the workers come here to compete with you – a fair field and no favour! You may think no system of nationalization making it possible to pool profits in the interests of these workers would pay you. I appeal to you Mid-Rhondda miners to consider if it might not pay you to, even in your own interest, subsidise these men for some time until they can be absorbed in better paying places, thus preventing them overstocking more favoured places, with all the dire consequences the latter involves.

Mr Ablett objects to Mr Barker's position, because if he proposes to nationalize the mines, and for some time pay a restricted dividend, for that is what it amounts to, you will have state ownership. But you have not got rid of exploitation. I contend we must arrive at the stage when we will have state ownership as far as development of capital is concerned. In the end, the technical means of production, whether we like it or not, will be in the hands of the state. And if the state is all that Mr Ablett has painted it and I will go all the way with him in its coercive function – is it not better to have the naked issue before you, and not to have that issue obscured? Is it not better to have that straight fight with the state with the strength of industrial organization behind you? If the workers will become more solid in their organization, will it not be possible in the straight fight for the organized industries to pass through that stage? Will it not be possible for the workers, not only the miners, but the railwaymen and other workers, to pass safely through this stage? Mr Ablett quoted Engels in support of his contention that the state was not the 'means'. I mention the name of Kautsky as a supporter of the opposite point of view. It is for the workers with industrial emancipation in view to use political registration as a means to an end, viz., the destruction of the coercive powers of the state in order to usher in a more democratic state where men would be more concerned in the art of administration than in governing one another. I say that is the proper and natural development. Under nationalization, we could get better results than we have been able to get under the present system with all our so-called militant methods. I believe, in view of what has been done in New Zealand, that we could do at least as well here, and that is another reason why I am here to affirm that the bill, as drafted for the MFGB executive, is in the best interests not only of the miners, but of all the workers in this country.

Mr Frank Hodges, seconding Mr Ablett, followed; he said:

So far, what I have been able to glean has come in bursts of oratory, appeals to local or national sentiment, and direct appeals to the audience to give their support to a particular point of view. Mr Gill made a last point – about the only real point that has not already been answered – with reference to New Zealand. Mr Barker states that the New Zealand miner is in receipt of an average wage of 17s. per day. That is a stupendous wage from the point of view of hard cash. But when you compare the wages with the price of commodities in a new country, the real value of the 17s. is considerably decreased, even down to the level of the English minimum wage. Then we have on our hands, as Mr Barker has intimated in wholesale figures, a large quantity of blood. Mr Barker has put forward a very strong argument that nationalization of the mines must necessarily mean a reduction in the number of fatal accidents in the mines. He failed to give a single instance where that has actually occurred where state-owned mines exist. Will you permit me to quote for a moment from a speech by Herr Elphas, a representative of Holland at the International Miners Conference – the only country, except New Zealand, where the mines are under state control. I will read what he says with regard to the figures for fatal accidents. He said at the conference in Holland:

> As you have heard this morning we are in a fair way of getting a state monopoly. At the present time the state mines were very bad as far as safety is concerned. In one mine accidents resulted in six deaths and 431 injured out of 1,500 employed. He urged that to secure the safety of the hands this should be left in the hands of the men and not left in the hands of private capitalists.

That is a sufficient answer to the argument that state control must necessarily mean a reduction in fatal accidents, because in the only country where there is practically a complete national monopoly, we have a tremendous number of fatal accidents – much higher in comparison than Germany or Belgium. The whole point of this bill is just here – and I think Mr Ablett has very well elaborated its economic side – the whole business has to be transferred to the Minister of Mines, to a government department. Mr Gill imagines that under national control foremen, overmen, managers and agents would be elected to their posts in exactly the same way as if they were appointed by the men themselves. The absurdity of this is at once apparent, because, when the bill becomes law, it is suggested that these government employees be appointed and controlled by the self-same Minister of Mines, who will issue his instructions from Whitehall or some other place in the United Kingdom. Mr Gill will admit that government appointments do not always bear the hallmark of efficiency. If you have your mines controlled by a department in London, it is folly to think for one moment that you will have them better controlled than by boards of directors in Cardiff.

We have only to look around us and understand the development of the state during the last 50 years, to discover the real character of state institutions. In France, in 1910, they had one of the greatest strikes that has yet existed against the government in the history of the 19th and 20th centuries. You had the whole of the French railway workers striking against the French government, and the French government, immediately the strike broke out, by the operation of another statute, compelled all those railway workers who were conscripts to work on the railways, and if they refused they were shot for treason against the state. That was in 1910. With reference to the Post Office and the report about turning to the Property Defence League for arguments, let me just give you an idea of what actually exists in the governing of the Post Office in England. The government, by the systematic operation of the principle of pensions, makes it almost impossible for a real fighting organization to exist among government employees. The very threat of what may happen if the employees disobey instructions is sufficient to destroy any attempt to fight.

There is one other point which should be taken into consideration. In France, the teachers some few months ago formed themselves into a syndicate for the purpose of getting advances in wages from the government, their employers. The government forthwith disbanded them, and said there should be no syndicates in the teaching profession. It is just because the executive council of the Miners Federation has not yet distinguished what is the real function of the state that they are pressing forward this bill at the present time. Mr Gill calls Kautsky to his rescue to prove that state ownership is inevitable; then why does the Miners Federation take upon itself the responsibility of bringing something into existence which is inevitable in the evolution of the capitalist system? We all used to believe we were bound to evolve through capitalism into its highest sense, that is national monopoly. First, there was the individual employer; then the company; then a joint stock company; and afterwards the national monopoly. Thus we looked upon it in extreme youth when we were all utopians. Now we look upon the state as something which amounts to an anomaly in our social life. The state to the French nobility once meant the king, themselves, and the Clergy; afterwards the state became the merchant class of France; that is the state today in France, the government in power at any historical moment is the state. Are the working classes the governing power? If not, they cannot in reason call themselves the state. When there is nothing to govern there is no state. We know the state as described by Paul Lafargue:

> We believe that the state is the stronghold of capitalism; if the capitalist class had not its soldiers, its police, no magistrates, its gaolers to protect it, and being so few in numbers, it would suffice for the working class to rise up and cause it to disappear.[10]

If you help to transfer the present capitalistic form of production to the state, you are only helping the capitalist to destroy what the most far-seeing ones amongst (them) recognize must be destroyed; viz., that little external competition which still threatens the existence of many capitalists. The whole point of monopoly is to get rid of external competition. You have competition between combines at the present time, and soon these people who rule you will realize that their

[10]Paul Lafargue (1843–1911): French Marxist, Marx's son-in-law.

industries must become national. Are wages to go up under this national monopoly? Are conditions to be improved? You have to pay this interest out of your wages or at least out of your surplus value. You are going to buy the mines at £150,000,000, which Mr Barker says in 30 years will be repaid. But the prospect is that for 30 years the amount which is the difference between your real value and your wages will have to be paid over – if it is ever paid – and until it is, you will not get any substantial benefits in advances in wages. You may think the most important thing to you is advances in wages, and to you it is the only thing. At a certain point your advances in wages outstrip advances in profits, and as wages advance you automatically reduce the rate of profit, and where you do that you can step in with your added experience, newer ideas, and say 'Now we are going to make the last step and take over the collieries ourselves.' This does not say that you are going to exploit the mines to the detriment of the transport worker, railway workers and all other workers. Do we not propose to organize all workers into one great industrial union for communal purposes? If you nationalize the mines it will be more difficult, but if you increase your industrial solidarity now by that very means, systematically and almost directly form that industrial democracy, each part of which in its turn is to take over and administer its own industry. It is all very well to say that the docker in some South American state has something to do with producing the coal, but we say if that docker in South America is a necessary part of the coalmining industry, he will function in the future through his trade union as a transporter so that he will get his proportionate part in the social wealth.

I have pointed out to you that fact that you will have to pay out of your surplus value the interest upon this £150,000,000, and you know as a matter of fact that the government bondholders will get their pound of flesh on government investments. It is all very well to say you are going to give $3\frac{1}{2}$%, but these very people who get $3\frac{1}{2}$% and their capital redeemed will still exist as capitalists. Where are they going to put their capital? If the mines become a national monopoly, is it not possible for them to put their capital into the government bonds and receive again interest upon their investments in government stock? I am of definite opinion that the great function of the working class is to abolish profit, interest and rent, and the most systematic and practical way to do that is to go along with your industrial organization stage by stage, and wring from the employers advances in wages. If you have nationalization you will still have the police, you will still have the military. In short, you would have no control of the state. You will be fighting the state, the mighty state, and they would say: 'We will keep you down; we will put the police and the military, that is, government employees, to shoot the other government employees down.' Your function is to get rid of wages altogether. Under state control, you perpetuate wages because you must do so to meet capital charges. It is all very well to go into flights of oratory, but it is the real fact behind that matters. If it is clear to you that your real function as at last, is to get rid of profits because you mean to get rid of the wage principle, then it must be clear to you that any national action, such as that proposed in this bill, is of no use to you, because it fossilizes that principle. Under the bill that principle must go on for 30 years. That is the federation limit for you. For 30 years from the passing of this act your children will be ushered into the millenium. But to put an estimate on the period when the miners will have emancipated themselves is to pervert and to misconstrue the real historical facts that the workers have to proceed upon. If the miners with their friends, the transport workers, the dockers, and other workers, conceive that they are the exploited class producing all the wealth, the means of emancipation are in their own hands by consolidated effort. That is the point I want to put before you. You have not won much yet by solidarity but you have witnessed what can be done. Your weak point is that these people are not linked up with you; and you know as a matter of fact from your own historical experiences, that if the miners had taken up with the railway workers and the dockers, you would have won. That is the proper course in your development. You can have the government and the state! The government or state is always the power which is supreme at any historical moment, and at a time when a capitalist state is supreme you propose to make coal mining a state industry! I say, ours is the practical proposal. We have to tell you our best way. Mr Barker's best way is in the bill; he tells you that in 30 years you will be emancipated. We say the best way is to go on with our industrial solidarity, and so get the advances in wages which means a reduction in profits and we can gradually work ourselves to industrial emancipation. We will have automatically dissolved private ownership because we will have abolished private profit.

Mr Ablett, replying, followed Mr Hodges; he said:

In summing up the debate from this side – and I should like Mr Barker to reply directly to this summary – I will endeavour to enumerate the points we have demonstrated:

I.   It has been shown that where there are state workers, theirs is a servile condition; consequently we can expect some of this to apply to the miners under nationalization. We know more about the continent than elsewhere. We know that in France, where there are state railways, the most servile and helpless section of the workers are the state employees. This also applies to Germany.

II.   We have shown that state employees are used to defeat the other workers in their strikes.

III.   It is practically impossible to have trade unionism under nationalization, as governments are too strong, and will not allow their employees to organize. Desperate indeed is the condition of state workers engaged in an attempt to improve their conditions.

IV.   It has been shown that any improvement in safety or wages is immensely more difficult under the proposed bill than at present, as the enemy is so much stronger, and the contradiction between the voter, who is at the same time a miner, works to his disadvantage.

V.   It has been abundantly demonstrated that the MFGB executive's scheme is hopelessly behind the times. We don't know any day when an inventor, perhaps here in Tonypandy, will discover a process that will make the coalmine and the miner an obsolete, or at least, a decaying figure.

VI.   It has been shown that the other side want to improve our conditions by uniting our enemies.

VII.   It is clear that the bill will put off all constructive proposals for at least 30 years.

VIII.   The position of the other side is bureaucracy, of this side is democracy.

The most important thing to us as miners, is not whether the employer is Mr D. A. Thomas or the state, but whether our pay will grow. Which is it best to fight, a divided enemy which has points of weakness where we could attack it, or an enemy that is united, that has all the forces and the protection of society behind it? Which is it best to fight? Personally I think from the workmen's point of view, that it is better to fight the divided army than one of the most powerful governments. There is much to look forward to. With the increased cost of living we cannot afford to put our burning question off for 30 years. No delusive proposal shall stop us securing the best thing. We will know if their scheme is a sound one, and if it will rebound to the betterment of the mineowners, and consequently to the detriment of the miners. Does Mr Barker consider the reason for the recent disturbances in Ulster which arose over a little question? Let him consider whether the mineowner, having more to fight for, is going peacefully to let you vote him out of existence. I recommend him to see what transpired in Ireland, and to consider whether our fight against the state under nationalization would be the same. The difference between us is this: Mr Hodges and myself stand for industrial democracy; Mr Barker and Mr Gill stand for industrial autocracy, for 30 years at least. They are willing to let ignorance in Whitehall sit in judgement on knowledge in the Rhondda, to let the man who does not know govern the men who do. Meanwhile we can pray to our member of Parliament while we are putting our vote into the ballot box. The force and might of the workers should be organized now. We beat them the other day and we have a chance to beat them again, but if we take matters to Whitehall we shall find ourselves far removed from getting any redress. 'We only wish to capture the state to abolish it' said Mr Gill. It is not the way to conquer your enemy by giving him funds. Surely that is a bad policy and if you wish to do this thing, do not do something today that you will have to undo tomorrow. We stand for the industrial democracy, and if that is so, are we not compelled to use every effort in our power to prevent the idea of industrial autocracy from growing in the minds of the people? Mr Barker and Mr Gill are going to confiscate all above $3\frac{1}{2}\%$. We are going to confiscate the lot. They want us to lend our power into the owner's hands; we wish to take it out of their hands. Mr Gill says our proposals involve the selfish miner; we say that no proposal that is going to hurt the miner by keeping wages down can help the working class. I say it is best to keep as far as possible from the enemy's hands rather than to give your power into his hands. It is false reasoning to suggest that we should subsidise those miners who are worse paid than we are. We must bring them up to us.

To summarise, nationalization leads in the wrong direction for emancipation. Emancipation has another way. Servility and restriction lie in this way, not in the freedom and industrial development of the workers. Nationalization puts the power which exists in your own hands into the hands of Parliament. That is the wrong way. The road to industrial democracy lies our way. We claim to have made a case and we ask you to support our argument, which is in line with economic development. We stand here tonight in the interests of the coming democracy, and not only their bread and butter interests, but also for the development of those conditions favourable to the growth of the organized working class on the lines of self-development, where knowledge, discipline, solidarity, are all blended and harmonized to make possible the capture of society and the emancipation of the working class. (Applause)

Mr Barker then concluded the debate; he said:

It is exactly as I expected when I sat down. (Laughs). Our friends
have put nothing at all feasible or practical before you. They have
pictured the state as a big monster that devours its own children. If the
state is the monster they have depicted to you, can you do anything
better than go and get hold of the throat of that monster? The very
measure of opposition which this bill receives from the capitalist class
is the measure of the benefit it will confer on you. Why are the
capitalists opposing this bill if it is the enthronement and protection of
capitalism? How is it the capitalist is so deadly opposed to it? How is it
that the capitalist tries to fool you and buy you off at every election? It
is because he has found the state his refuge and wants to keep you
from getting into that refuge. The day is coming when the democracy
will take it from his grasp. 'If you keep the worker alternating between
various theories, the result will be that he will finish exactly where he
began.' You have been 25 years getting the workers educated to this
ideal and now just as you are getting public opinion ripe the workers
are sidetracking and going after another illusion. They have mocked
this period of 30 years. It will take a thousand theories to get the mines
by this confiscation. Mr Hodges said we were going to hand over our
industries to the state. Have we got any industries? What have we got?
We are absolutely disinherited. We stand in a so-called free country as
hirelings, depending on the capitalists to hire us. The measure of the
intelligence of the people is their power to organize. The state has been
pictured as a great monster. What is the state? We are told it is the
government. Who elects the government? The people. What is the use
of telling intelligent men that the government consists of men put in
Parliament by votes put in ballot boxes? Who puts the votes in the
ballot boxes? If this Minister of Mines is going to control the mines,
the Commons will control him and the workers will control the
Commons. Our friends have indicated the very principles of democracy. Representative government is the root principle of democracy.
The principle they have advocated is not industrial democracy but
industrial anarchy. We come back to where we started from. The very
fact that the capitalist is strongly opposing this measure is the measure
of the benefit it will confer upon the workers. We remember something
about a place called Featherstone, and a place called Llanelly. These
are the atrocities of capitalism. We want to destroy private interest in
the wealth of this nation. We have been taunted about perpetuating this
thing. But what did Mr Heppell tell the Conciliation Board three years
ago? 'Ten per cent is no good to us.' Does not the Cambrian Combine
pay not $3\frac{1}{2}$% but 20% to the shareholders? We propose to buy the
capitalist out of his own profits. The figures I gave you have never been

challenged. The profits today are £25,000,000 a year, and we propose to put £5,000,000 a year of that on one side to buy him out, and to use the remainder in the way I apportioned it. The whole argument of our friends is that the state is a monster which can throttle her children. You are the state. You have ten times more voting power than the capitalist, and therefore ten times more responsibility in creating this monster. I claim we have put before you a feasible proposal for obtaining the mines of this country, based on a business proposition. In opposition to that our friends have put some revolutionary proposal, which they call an industrial democracy based on confiscation. Is there any man with a knowledge of the democracy of this country who believes in the possibility of getting such a revolution to take place? I challenge our friends to produce that revolution. (Laughs). It is no good bringing German theories from books here. Is there any possibility of any man going out and persuading the people to take possession of the mines? No! He would be laughed at as a lunatic. We affirm again and again that the Nationalization of Mines Bill is in the best interests of the workers, aye, and of the nation.

1975

8

The Campaign
for Welsh Disestablishment

On a sunny June morning in 1920, on the palace lawn of St Asaph cathedral, in the presence of the prime minister, three archbishops and Welshmen of all denominations, Bishop Alfred George Edwards of St Asaph was solemnly presented as the first archbishop of the new ecclesiastical province of Wales. A century of bitter animosity between church and chapel had drawn to its close. Mr Justice Bankes expressed the hope that the Church that had now been disestablished by Parliament would be re-established in the hearts of the people of Wales. Throughout the land, there seemed to be a new mood of unity and of peace. Only a few voices re-echoed the old sterile bitterness. A few Nonconformists, led by the veteran Llewelyn Williams, attacked the disendowment provisions of the new Welsh Church Act of 1919 as a betrayal of the fundamental principle that there should be no endowment of religion by the state. Conversely, a few churchmen still resented the role played by Lloyd George in negotiating the final settlement, and vented their spleen on the Baptist premier for receiving Holy Communion during the enthronement ceremony, in defiance of the rubric of the Book of Common Prayer. But the vast majority of Welsh men and women, of all denominations, refused to prolong the old bitterness of the past century. They looked forward to a new era of denominational co-operation in keeping with the ideals of a world newly emancipated from the horrors of total war, and in general their views have prevailed.

Since 1920, therefore, the old conflicts over the 'alien church' or 'religious equality' seem to have receded into a scarcely intelligible past. New generations of Welsh people have been born to whom the sectarian passions that stirred the daily lives of their grandparents seem barely comprehensible. The social and political controversies of the days before 1914, when Bishops A. G. Edwards and John Owen on the one side, and Lloyd George and Revd Evan Jones on the other, could stir the passions of vast audiences with denunciations of 'Nonconformist agitators' or 'alien bishops' – those days appear utterly remote and forgotten. The bearded champions of that period seem as distant to us as did the United States of the Gilded Age to Thomas Wolfe, when he speculated whether Presidents Grant, Hayes or Garfield had not been born full-bearded and clad in the blue uniform of the Federal armies. Yet for almost a hundred years prior to the settlement of the disestablishment controversy in 1920, the position of the Church in Wales had been a major theme in Welsh life. At times, it had formed an explosive public issue in the politics of Britain as a whole. It had assisted in the rise of statesmen and in the downfall of governments. For decades, the Disestablishment Campaign Committee, the Liberation Society and similar organizations had absorbed much of the energy of the Nonconformist denominations, while Anglicans in Wales had devoted themselves to the needs of 'Church Defence'. In the later decades of the nineteenth century, the conflict over disestablishment had seemed to symbolize the role of Wales in public life, and to characterize the basic quality of Welsh society. John Morley could write in 1890 that 'Home Rule is not more essentially the Irish national question than disestablishment and disendowment are the Welsh national question'. Every major figure in Welsh radical politics, Lloyd George, Tom Ellis, D. A. Thomas, Samuel Evans and Ellis Griffith, established his reputation upon the scarred battlefield of disestablishment. If the issue of the Welsh Church now seems closed and uncontroversial, they might have regarded this as one of their major political legacies. To look back on the history of the campaign for disestablishment, therefore, is no mere antiquarian exercise. It is a theme that illuminates the innermost substance of the Welsh nation and its culture, in all its unity and in all its diversity. It helps to make intelligible the Wales of today.

The rise of the demand for the disestablishment of the Church in Wales was a product of a new society. The economic upheaval, with the coming of industry, and the surge of ideas released by the revolution in France in 1789, disrupted the pattern of life throughout Europe and the Americas. There was a new age of world-wide revolution and ferment, and Wales as elsewhere was profoundly affected. Until the last decades of the eighteenth century, Wales had seemed a static society, comfortably controlled by the Anglican gentry who had dominated life since the days of the Tudors. The scattered minority of dissenters,

mainly Baptist and Independent, were respectable and quiescent. Then
the new revolutionary ferment brought with it a period of change
unprecedented in its speed and in its impact. It extended in the course
of time to almost every aspect of social activity, and inevitably the
pattern of religious life was profoundly influenced. The demand for
disestablishment was one consequence of this transformation, in which
economic and social change proceeded side by side.

The advent of industrialization from the 1780s meant a revolution
in the social order, the rapid growth of heavy industry in the mining
valleys of Glamorgan and Monmouthshire, and a massive wave of
immigration into the coalfield. It produced new strains in the rural
areas also, since it was here in the countryside that the population
explosion seems first to have occurred; until the 1880s the migration
into the south Wales valleys came overwhelmingly from the over-
populated rural hinterland. These social upheavals led to unprecedented pressures upon the traditional institutions of society, and
chief among these was the Church of England in Wales. From the
outset, the coming of industry and the population explosion brought
new strains for the ancient, parochial structure of the Church.
Throughout the eighteenth century, it had been under fire for
pluralism, nepotism and other evils; the new impact of social change in
an industrial setting made its organization and social doctrine appear
equally out of date.

The transformation of the other religious communities was no less
dramatic. From the beginning of the nineteenth century, the
Nonconformist sects increased rapidly in numbers. Thousands of
migrants from the countryside brought with them the values and the
institutions of the chapel, and transplanted them in the growing
centres of industry. In thriving industrial areas like Merthyr and
Aberdare, the chapels provided a framework of social stability for the
new rootless proletariat of the coalfield. The high degree of initiative
shown by their lay members was in marked contrast to the relative
absence of participation by the laity in the denominational affairs of
the Anglican Church. Even in anglicized towns like Cardiff and
Newport, Welsh Zions, Calfarias and Bethesdas began to be
established. The Independent and Baptist denominations linked with
their brethren in England, expanded rapidly in numbers, especially in
southern and eastern parts of Wales. But in the mainly rural areas of
the north and west, it was the new Calvinistic Methodist Church,
founded through the inspiration of Thomas Charles of Bala in 1811,
which provided the major impetus for dissent. Initially a movement
within the established Church itself, and committed to the Thirty-
Nine Articles, the Calvinistic Methodist Church rapidly joined forces
with the older dissenters of the south. It began to emulate their more

settled pastorate in place of its own itinerant ministry. In turn, its own methods of organization and evangelization coloured their ideas and approach. The expansion of Nonconformity, then, was a product of the new industrial society. When Horace Mann's famous religious census was taken in 1851, it was found that roughly 80 per cent of worshipping Welshmen were adherents of the chapel; less than a fifth could be claimed as communicants of the established Church itself. Even if Nonconformist statistics had been inflated by the 'cholera revival' of 1849, the fundamental change in the pattern of religious affiliation in Wales was beyond dispute.

How far this Nonconformist influence extended within society is hard to determine. In Wales and in England, it seemed that most of the poorer strata of the working population remained unaffected by the ministration of any church. Even in the 1851 census, almost half of the population of Wales remained unaccounted for by the churches, Nonconformist or Anglican. Working-class chapel-goers tended to belong to the floating class of 'adherents' or 'hearers' rather than to the hard core of membership. More and more as the century proceeded, the 'big seats' of chapels would be composed of middle-class representatives, colliery managers, tradesmen or solicitors, rather than miners or ironworkers. The alienation of working men from the churches is very far from being a new phenomenon in the twentieth century: it is coterminous with the industrial age. Nor did the expansion of Nonconformity proceed at a constant pace. The excitement of revivals, such as those of 1836, 1849 or 1859, tended to be followed by periods of stagnation. Nevertheless, the influence of the chapels was fundamental in the shaping of the culture of the new Wales of the nineteenth century. In every major centre of population, it was the chapels which provided increasingly the major stimulus in the creation of social opinion. Voluntary cultural activity of all kinds – *eisteddfodau*, *cyrddau mawr*, the *cymanfaoedd canu*, and above all the Sunday schools – bore the indelible imprint of the chapel. The thriving popular press, in rural and industrial areas alike, was overwhelmingly Nonconformist in its origin and in its attitudes. All these elements testified to the force of the description of Wales as 'a nation of Nonconformists'. By the mid nineteenth century, this transformation was almost complete.

It could only be a matter of time before this social and religious revolution came to affect political life also. The older dissent of the pre-industrial age had been politically quiescent. Even the new ideological ferment of the French Revolution seems to have met with little response; Welsh radicals of Jacobin sympathies, such as Morgan John Rhys, who urged the severance of the ties between church and state, met with scant support. But in the years after 1815, a new

radicalism began to permeate Welsh political life, and increasingly it
was Nonconformists who were shaping its course. Beneath demands
for parliamentary and municipal reform lay the conviction that
Nonconformists represented an underprivileged minority of the
community, deprived unjustly of civic status and social power. The
repeal, in 1828, of the antiquated Test and Corporations Acts, a relic of
the reign of Charles II, was but a prelude to further pressure; petitions
had flooded in from Welsh Nonconformists and they had played their
part in the triumphant passage of repeal. After the passage of the 1832
Reform Act, there was a further impetus for civil equality on the part
of Nonconformists everywhere. The pressure that Sir John Guest faced
from the radical 'shopocracy' of Merthyr and Aberdare between 1832
and 1837 was but a part of a far wider pattern of protest. The burial
and marriage laws, and imposition of parochial tithe and of church
rates – these were merely the formal grievances of dissenters. Beneath
them lay a whole fabric of social injustices bitterly resented by an
emergent Nonconformist middle class, a residuum of class inferiority,
a feeling that at the pinnacle of social authority 'Nonconformists need
not apply'. These barriers were resented with particular keenness in
Wales where religious differences were reinforced by those of social
status and of race. As the Church in Wales seemed increasingly
threatened by the growth of mass Nonconformity, its character seemed
to become more and more defensive. It became stereotyped as the
church of the English-speaking squirearchy, cut off from the bulk of
the community by the various barriers of language, religion, and soon
of politics. As the Nonconformist protest became more and more
political in character, religious and social grievances merged into a
common campaign. In a dynamic world of rapid change, the
established Church could be all too easily portrayed as a static survival
from the past, outstripped by events.

By the 1840s, therefore, the Nonconformist protest was becoming
increasingly Welsh in character. Publicists like Samuel Roberts of
Llanbrynmair, while they used the standard rhetoric of English
dissent, were addressing a specifically native audience, and in their
native tongue. They clashed fiercely with Anglican champions like
David Owen (Brutus). As yet, however, the various campaigns of
Nonconformity remained unformed and imprecise, a series of sporadic
and ill-planned initiatives on behalf of specific grievances, such as the
abolition of church rates, rather than a co-ordinated effort. They
resembled, and contributed towards, other forces of ferment in Welsh
society in the years after 1832, the period of Chartism and of the
Rebecca riots. As the social agitation of the early 1840s died away with
the improvement of economic conditions, many observers thought that
Nonconformist radicalism would also prove to be a temporary

phenomenon. What gave form and direction to the new radicalism was the growth of a supreme national cause, which was to overshadow politics in Wales as had the single issue of Catholic emancipation in Ireland a decade earlier. This was the emergence of the cry for the disestablishment of the Church of England in Wales. Into this single theme, all the various grievances, real and imaginary, felt by Nonconformists everywhere were absorbed. For the next three generations, it was thought to symbolize their pressure for equality and for a more democratic pattern of society within Wales.

The separation of church and state had been, formally, a basic premise for dissenters everywhere since the seventeenth century. There had been active agitation by their pressure-groups in England and Wales throughout the eighteenth century – a period characterized by some historians as one of 'political inertia' – notably by the Protestant Dissenting Deputies. This organization had combined a theoretical attachment to the principle of disestablishment with action on behalf of such specific causes as the repeal of the hated Test and Corporations Acts. But until the 1830s the demand for disestablishment in England or in Wales was not very vocal. Indeed, the wave of conservatism that had swept the country in the aftermath of the French Revolution had tended to equate disestablishment with republicanism and Jacobinism – a correlation which might have been acceptable to Tom Paine or to Richard Price, but which smacked far too directly of rebellion to the cautious spokesman of dissent. Even in the 1830s, such Nonconformist polemicists as David Rees in *Y Diwygiwr*, who fulminated against the privilege implicit in the maintenance of established churches, made little headway amongst their more wary brethren. The Calvinistic Methodists, in particular, reacted strongly against the idea of disestablishment. After all, the pioneers of the Methodist revival, Howel Harris, Daniel Rowland, William Williams Pantycelyn, had remained faithful to the Church, *yr hen fam* (the old mother), who had tended to her children since the dawn of the middle ages. At the Bala *sasiwn* in 1834, John Elias and 500 Calvinistic Methodist divines passed a motion which strongly deprecated the actions of those who were trying to sever the ties of church and state.

If a starting-point is to be sought for the growth of disestablishment as a coherent campaign, it must be the foundation of the Liberation Society in 1844. This body, which sought to lend a new impetus to Nonconformist radicalism at a time when older bodies such as the Dissenting Deputies were in decay, was openly committed to liberating churches everywhere from state control. From the outset it made remarkable headway in Wales. For many years it seemed to Welsh people to be an alien foundation, the work of men such as Miall and

Sturge who formed the spearhead of English provincial urban dissent. Their main Welsh activists were men such as Henry Richard and Carvell Williams who had spent most of their careers in England. However, after 1844 the Liberation Society expanded considerably in Wales, until by 1868 it claimed at least fifty-five contributing branches in different parts of the country. It was a period of continuing popular tension, upheaval in the countryside in the aftermath of the Rebecca disturbances, rapid expansion in the industrial south as more and more valleys were being exploited for their deposits of coal. An increasingly literate public opinion was receptive to the message of such Nonconformist periodicals as *Yr Amserau* and *Seren Gomer*. The rise of a new breed of Nonconformist journalists like William Rees (Gwilym Hiraethog) suggested that the older dissent was shedding its former caution and uninhibitedly espousing the cause of reform. At a crucial moment came the publication of the notorious 'Blue Books' of the educational commissioners in 1847, which condemned Welsh cultural and social life in almost all its aspects. While many of the criticisms of the commissioners were fully justified, especially of the lack of educational provision, their lack of sympathy with, or understanding for, the ideals of Nonconformity made the chapels the spearhead of the national protest that followed. One fundamental effect that the commissioners unwittingly achieved was the radicalizing of the Methodists. In the face of the shame of the 'Blue Books', Methodists threw in their lot with their more political brethren of the Baptist, Congregational and Unitarian churches. It was Methodist publicists such as Thomas Gee (soon to found *Baner ac Amserau Cymru* in 1859) who were to voice Nonconformists' complaints over elementary education, the burial law, tithe and a host of other issues. And one overriding theme lent unity to their campaigns on the platform and in the press – that disestablishment was the supreme need of the Welsh people if they were ever to attain their self-respect.

To an ever-increasing extent, it was the Liberation Society which provided the machinery of protest. In the 1840s and 1850s it formed cells within a host of small urban centres throughout Wales; it was in the small country towns of the land that political awareness was most intense. Then, in 1862, the Society formed a national organization throughout the country, and another important stage of the disestablishment campaign was reached. The occasion was a massive meeting at Swansea called to commemorate the 'martyrs' expelled under the Clarendon Code in 1662. Miall and other English dissenting leaders were prominent; but the major impact of the meeting was made by speakers who were at least Welsh by nationality, even if many of them had spent their active careers mainly in England. Notable among them were Henry Richard, internationally renowned as secretary of the Peace Society, and John Carvell Williams, the secretary of the Liberation Society. Lewis Llewelyn Dillwyn, the radical member for Swansea District, an Anglican, undertook to sponsor the cause of disestablishment in Parliament. Not until 1862 could the crusade for Welsh disestablishment be described in any sense as a national Welsh movement, and it is significant that even then it was from England that the first inspiration was to come. In the next few years, the Society made extensive efforts to campaign throughout south Wales, and from 1866 in the north as well. In the 1865 election, Liberationist candidatures were threatened by Henry Richard and Dr Thomas Price of Aberdare, in Cardiganshire and Merthyr Tydfil respectively, though the lack of response to their efforts showed the limitations of the political understanding of Nonconformists at this time. In a county like Cardiganshire, Henry Richard's candidature in 1865 could founder in the face of the disapproval of the Pryse family of Gogerddan.

Confronted by this threat, the Church responded with new efforts at reorganization and self-examination. Under Bishops Burgess and Thirlwall in St David's diocese, and Bishop Ollivant in Llandaff, much of the apathy of the past had been cast aside. Ollivant in particular provided a new impetus when he succeeded Bishop Copleston in 1849. Through his Diocesan Church Extension Society, he helped to direct a massive programme of church building to cope with the needs of an industrial society in the mining valleys of Llandaff diocese. In St David's, there was a vast extension of National schools to provide the rudiments of an elementary education system. The number of communicants increased steadily until they numbered over 81,000 by 1886. A more serious effort was made, also, to appoint incumbents in sympathy with Welsh culture and with the Welsh language; there were good precedents for this policy since, earlier in the century, Anglican clergymen had played a major part in promoting the eisteddfod and in sustaining traditions of Welsh scholarship. Henry Thomas Edwards, vicar of Caernarfon from 1869 and later dean of Bangor, a High Churchman who nevertheless enjoyed a considerable reputation among many Welsh Nonconformists for his work on behalf of education and other national causes, was a symbol of the change in policy. In addition, since 1840 the Ecclesiastical Commission had had a profound effect on the administration of the Welsh dioceses. It had reorganized diocesan boundaries and succeeded in eliminating the remnants of pluralism, non-residence and other abuses. It was this consciousness of a new activity within the established Church itself that lent a new determination and momentum to Welsh Non-conformity, now in its most vigorous phase of growth. It introduced a new bitterness to the growing conflict over disestablishment.

The outcome was seen in the famous general election of 1868, perhaps
the first democratic election in Welsh history. It followed directly upon
the 1867 Reform Act which greatly expanded the electorate in urban
areas. In Merthyr Tydfil (which was now made a two-member
division), the electorate rose to over 14,500, an increase of over 1,000
per cent. The 'great election' in 1868 has been remembered in history
and legend for its dramatic Liberal gains, for Henry Richard's triumph
in Merthyr and Osborne Morgan's in Denbighshire, and for the
political evictions that followed. It is easy to forget that, in the main,
the pattern of Welsh politics revealed by the election results was
profoundly traditional. Parliamentary representation was still
overwhelmingly dominated by the gentry, while thirty of the thirty-
three Welsh members returned were Anglican by religion. Even the
other two Nonconformist candidates (apart from Henry Richard),
Richard Davies, successful in Anglesey, and Evan Matthew Richards in
Cardiganshire, owed much to the patronage of local Anglican gentry.
Nevertheless, there was a new tone to Welsh politics after this period,
and it is not inappropriate to date the democratic phase of political
development in Wales from this election. However, Welsh disestablishment, contrary to many later Nonconformist accounts, was hardly a
major question in the 1868 election, though by implication it was
prominent in some contests. In Denbigh District, Watkin Williams, a
radical lawyer returned over a Conservative opponent, linked
disestablishment of the Church in Ireland (which Gladstone now
advocated) with a similar measure for Wales. Osborne Morgan in
Denbighshire, although the son of a vicar, stressed his affiliation to the
Liberation Society, while E. M. Richards and other Liberals were
anxious to disavow it. Henry Richard in Merthyr, the most democratic
constituency in Wales and perhaps in the British Isles, owed much to
Nonconformist organizers such as Dr Thomas Price. For 1868 was a
triumph for English Gladstonian Liberalism, not for Welsh Nonconformist radicalism.

But the years after the election saw the pressure for Welsh
disestablishment becoming more intense. Within Wales, the Liberation
Society renewed its efforts to create a new network of agents and sub-
agents throughout the land. It flooded the countryside with pamphlets
and tracts which argued that church establishments everywhere were
unjust and unscriptural. Henry Richard urged that the established
Church was a relic of 'feudalism' in Wales, from which the people had
been newly emancipated in the glorious Liberal dawn of 1868. In
particular, the success achieved in passing disestablishment in Ireland
in 1869 encouraged Liberationists to turn to Wales as the next weak
link in the Anglican structure. Here, it was urged, was a similar
situation to that in Ireland, a small and unrepresentative Anglican

establishment being imposed on an alienated majority against its will. On 24 May 1870, then, came the first of the long series of Welsh disestablishment motions that were to occupy the attention of the House of Commons. It was moved by Watkin Williams (Denbigh District) and proposed to divert the endowments of the Church to educational purposes. But the motion mustered a mere forty-five votes, including only seven of the Welsh members. The Liberal prime minister, Gladstone, spoke strongly of the impossibility of distinguishing between the Church in Wales and in England. He denied that there was any analogy with Ireland: there, the establishment was an alien measure imposed as recently as 1800, whereas in Wales the Church was a part of a continuous national tradition that had endured as long as Wales itself. More interest attached to the discussions among Welsh Liberals and Nonconformists themselves over Watkin Williams's motion. Men like Henry Richard, weaned in the circles of the Liberation Society, were reluctant to distinguish between disestablishment in Wales and the cause of disestablishment in the United Kingdom generally. The establishment should be attacked as a whole, and not on quasi-nationalist grounds. But Thomas Gee and the younger generation of Welsh Noncon-formists were coming to argue strongly on national lines that because Nonconformists in Wales appeared to represent the overwhelming majority of the Welsh people, their wishes should be respected. The argument implicit was that Wales should claim a separate political personality, distinct from that of England. This tension was to have major repercussions in the near future.

Despite the feeble support shown for Watkin Williams in the House, the Church rightly took the threat of disestablishment in Wales very seriously. More and more, it was being forced to reassess its position and to question the complacency of the clerical and lay leaders of the Anglican community. It was not enough to point with self-satisfaction to the growing numbers of Easter communicants, to the baptisms and marriages that took place under the auspices of the Church, to the increase in pupils at National schools. Not all these developments were stimulated by affection for the Church and its message. At a period of unprecedented population increase, it was clear that the 'national' Church was in a realistic sense national no longer. It represented now only a small fragment of the population, perhaps less than 10 per cent. The fact that the most favourable statistics given by the Nonconformists showed their own proportion to be no more than 25 per cent was hardly any consolation. The Church, strong on the border fringe, in Radnorshire, Breconshire and eastern Monmouthshire, and in the anglicized and squirearchical Vale of Glamorgan, was palpably weak in the most Welsh area of Wales, rural and industrial. The

educational calibre of the Welsh clergy was a national cause of
concern. The Revd C. W. Sandford wrote to Gladstone on 7 March
1870: 'From all accounts, I fear that the Welsh Clergy are not models
of Pastoral propriety. They appear to be in many cases more fond of
hard drinking than of hard work.' Lord Aberdare despaired of the
'indigenous, home-educated clergy of Wales' ever producing a 'Welsh
Wilberforce or Temple'. Fresh efforts were therefore made to generate
a new vitality in the Church, and they began at the summit, with a new
attitude to the episcopate. The Revd Henry Thomas Edwards, in his
pamphlet *Church of the Cymry* in 1870, strenuously denounced the
tendency to appoint 'English bishops' to Welsh sees since the days of
Queen Anne. For Queen Anne was dead, and this relic of her reign
should be also. Edwards deplored the death of the Methodist preacher,
Henry Rees, an outstanding figure in Welsh life who would have been a
great ornament to the Church. Symbolic of the new mood was the
response of Gladstone later in the year, when he appointed a Welsh-
speaking Welshman to the see of St Asaph. This appointment won
praise from most Welshmen, Anglican and Nonconformist. Yet the
immense difficulty experienced in finding a suitable candidate from
amongst the native Welsh clergy was a disturbing sign. The Anglo-
Catholic *Church Times* (on 3 June 1870) blamed 'Whig Protestantism'
for the ills of the Welsh dioceses; it complained that 'priests in these
Protestant-ridden places are in the position of sheep among wolves'.
The successful candidate, the Revd Joshua Hughes, vicar of
Llandovery, was an indifferent scholar and a poor administrator; he
was not even a university graduate, but a B.D. of Lampeter, 'the curse
of Wales and the slaughter-house of literature', as it was described by
the chancellor of St David's, Sir Erasmus Williams. However, the
moral impact of appointing a native Welshman was considerable. It
was given prominence in a remarkable address given to the 1879
Church Congress at Swansea by the Revd Henry Thomas Edwards,
now dean of Bangor, in which he claimed quite uninhibitedly that the
Church had become estranged from the main currents of Welsh life.
The further appointment of Basil Jones to St David's by Disraeli in
1874 and Richard Lewis to Llandaff by Gladstone in 1882 were
further signs of a new attitude to the Welsh episcopacy. Churchmen
were showing a new sensitivity to growing Nonconformist allegations
that their Church was in reality an 'alien church', *Eglwys Loegr*, the
Church of England in Wales.

Despite this new sympathy of the Church for Welsh national
sensibilities, the Liberationist tide was building up irresistibly within
Wales. In the election in 1880, the Liberals again swept the country,
winning twenty-nine of the thirty-three Welsh seats. Further, there
were now eight Welsh Nonconformists in Parliament. The campaign

reached a climax in the years 1884–5, perhaps the nearest point ever attained in British history to achieving a total disestablishment of the Church. Joseph Chamberlain had now become the main apostle of the causes of Nonconformist radicals; 'disestablishment all round' figured prominently on his 'Unauthorized Programme' of radical reform. In October 1884, on the invitation of Thomas Gee, he visited north Wales and his stirring speeches at Newtown and Denbigh marked a new climax in the campaign for disestablishment.

Chamberlain was appealing to a Welsh democracy that had now been given new voice through the passage of further parliamentary reform. The Reform Act of 1884 and the attendant redistribution of constituencies greatly strengthened the political representation of Welsh Nonconformity, rural and urban. Henceforth, the ascendancy of the Anglican gentry in the parliamentary representation of Wales was utterly doomed. At the following general election in November 1885, Liberationist radicals were returned in great numbers: the Liberation Society claimed that 171 members now favoured 'disestablishment all round'. In Wales, the results were dramatic, Liberals capturing thirty of the thirty-four Welsh seats, and all but one of them pledged to Welsh disestablishment. Here, far more than 1868, was the *annus mirabilis* of Welsh radicalism, the true breach with the older 'politics of deference'. Half of the thirty Welsh members, indeed, were Nonconformist, including such notable new members as Alfred Thomas and Bryn Roberts. Early in the next session, this new pressure was felt directly in Westminster. The motion moved by Dillwyn on 9 March 1886 showed how far opinion had been transformed since the days of Watkin Williams's motion in 1870. From the forty-five votes of that time, the supporters of Welsh disestablishment now numbered 229, and Dillwyn and Richard, the veteran sponsors of the motion, found a wide range of support. Even Gladstone himself was equivocal on the issue, and was fast retreating from the abject hostility he had shown in 1870. Dillwyn's motion came within twelve votes of being passed (241 against 229), and it could now be claimed that Welsh disestablishment was a real political issue of some substance. In 1886, therefore, the Welsh Church emerged as a major question in the political context of Britain as a whole, and so it remained for a decade or more.

In the years following the political crisis of 1886, the campaign took a very different turn. The major reason for this lay in the transformation of the political scene that followed the Liberal split over Gladstone's Irish Home Rule Bill. The loss of almost all the Whigs and of the Birmingham radicals cost the Liberal party its majority in England. Only in 1906 would it again carry a majority of English constituencies. As a result, the 'Celtic fringe' gained a far greater influence in the counsels of the party. A new mood became apparent in the character of Liberalism in Wales itself; new, younger leaders rose to prominence, Tom Ellis in Merioneth, D. A. Thomas in Merthyr Tydfil, Samuel T. Evans in Mid-Glamorgan and David Lloyd George in Caernarfon Boroughs, all of them more militantly nationalist in their attitude and less content with servile obedience to the Liberal party leadership. As a result, the whole emphasis of the arguments over disestablishment, on the part of churchmen and Nonconformists alike, now changed very substantially. Until 1886, the usual Liberal line of attack had been to condemn established churches in general, and to use Wales, in the words of the Liberation Society, 'as a means of attacking the establishment in a special way'. But after 1886 the main emphasis was to be laid on the fact that Wales was a nation, that the Church had for many centuries been alienated from national life, and that the democratically-expressed wishes of the Welsh electorate for disestablishment should therefore be heeded at Westminster. Churchmen also were forced to change their standpoint to some extent. Hitherto, one of the main forms of defence had been the argument that the Welsh Church was indistinguishable from the English, and that furthermore, any suggestion of legislation for Wales alone was unconstitutional – it would encourage further schism and disunion on the Irish pattern. After 1886, this kind of defence seemed increasingly unwise in the face of the growing recognition of the political existence of Wales. The Anglo-Catholic *Church Times* and *Guardian* were especially vehement on this point. Instead, Churchmen urged that, far from being an 'alien Church', the Church in Wales had been a major force in sustaining Welsh culture, in promoting the Welsh vernacular translation of the Bible and in many other ways. Tithe and other ancient endowments underlined the traditional attachment of the Welsh people to 'the old mother'; to alienate Church property and turn it to secular purposes would be both illegal and sacrilegious.

This growing emphasis on the essence of Welsh nationality led both sides to much use and abuse of history. Nonconformists spent much antiquarian ingenuity in suggesting that the Church had been cut off from Welsh national life in the past. Great attention was paid to early Celtic Christianity by partisans of both sides. Nonconformists sought to emphasize the isolation of British Christianity from continental Christendom, and to suggest that the Synod of Whitby in 663 had imposed a new Roman authority over the Celtic Church. Churchmen, conversely, maintained that there was an essential continuity throughout the pre-Conquest period and minimized the differences between British and continental Christianity. Nonconformists, secondly, tended to suggest that it was with the Norman Conquest that the true process of alienation came, with the appointment of

26 April 1894 Asquith introduced the first-ever Welsh Disestablishment Bill. The provisions of this measure foreshadowed in its main
outlines the later proposals that were to pass on to the statute book.
New vested interests and appointments to benefices would be
terminated from 1 January 1895. The Welsh bishops would be
excluded from the House of Lords and the Welsh clergy from
Convocation. Most complicated were the proposals for disendowment.
The Church would keep only its endowments granted since 1703 –
this date being chosen on the assumption that it was only after this
year that its character was beyond dispute. Bishops' palaces, chapels of
ease, graveyards, glebe and tithe vested in the Church before 1703
would be taken away, while the four Welsh cathedrals would become
national monuments. The income from these endowments, a total of
£233,000 out of a gross total of £279,000, would be handed over to
the new county councils for the creation of a national museum and
library and other secular purposes. It was by the standards of the day a
severe measure; in some respects it was more rigorous than the Irish
Disestablishment Bill of 1869, which had included the commutation
of life interests and compensation for curates. Inevitably the bill
inspired a massive Church Defence campaign throughout the land.
Not until the bill was withdrawn by the government in July, having
gone no further than the first reading, did the agitation of Welsh
churchmen subside.

Not all Welsh churchmen, however, reacted so strongly against the
measure. Five clergymen put forward the so-called 'Bangor scheme' in
January 1895. This measure, which proposed a compromise over
disendowment, was in part the suggestion of a group of Anglo-
Catholics of nationalist persuasion, notable among them J. Arthur
Price. They believed that disestablishment would help to restore the
independence of the medieval Catholic church and would pave the
way towards a form of Welsh Home Rule. Among the people
implicated in the drawing up of this scheme was David Lloyd George,
now caught up in the toils of the *Cymru Fydd* campaign. However, the
'Bangor scheme', similar in many ways to the settlement eventually
agreed upon in 1919, failed to satisfy the extremists of either side.

In the 1895 session, amid growing signs of ministerial feebleness,
the Rosebery government brought forward a second Welsh Disestablishment Bill, on lines very similar to that of 1894. On this occasion,
after a four-day debate, it passed its second reading by forty-four votes
on 1 April, Joseph Chamberlain voting for it to the scandal of his
Anglican allies in the Unionist party. How much interest the bill
evoked in the country as a whole is very doubtful, but in Wales it was
obviously a topic of burning concern. But, not for the first time, Welsh
radicals were far from united over the terms of the government's bill.

One particularly significant cause of dissension lay in the deadlock between D. A. Thomas and some other south Wales Liberals on the one hand, and most of the north Wales radicals on the other, over the proposed allocation of the secularized tithe. Thomas argued strongly that to allocate endowments on a parochial basis and not on the basis of population would be monstrously unjust to the industrial countries of south Wales. Cardiff, instead of receiving the £2,000 which was her due, would obtain only a paltry few hundreds, while Glamorgan would receive only £26,000 annually instead of £97,000 to which she was entitled. Anglesey would receive twelve times per head of population compared with that of Glamorgan. This disagreement, which foreshadowed the future disintegration of *Cymru Fydd*, was to play a major part in bringing the government down, as Thomas tried to solicit support from Liberal leaders. Lloyd George was another divisive factor. Absorbed in the *Cymru Fydd* movement, an attempt to rebuild Welsh Liberalism upon the programme of Welsh Home Rule, he argued that tithe should be turned over to a nationally-elected Welsh council, an embryo parliament. As the Welsh Bill lurched its erratic way through committee, the free-lance tactics of Thomas and Lloyd George gravely prejudiced its course. On 20 May, on an amendment by Lloyd George, the government's majority fell to ten and on 18 June an amendment by Thomas to vest Church property in a national Council saw it slump to eighteen. Finally, on 20 June, Thomas's amendment that tithe should be reallocated nationally on a population basis provoked the ultimate crisis, the majority declining to a mere seven. The next day, the shattered government resigned after a snap defeat on a vote concerning cordite supplies, and there were many to argue subsequently that Lloyd George and Thomas had seriously contributed to the government's downfall. Certainly, Asquith developed from this time onwards a deep distrust of Lloyd George that never wholly left him thereafter.

The subsequent general election saw the first major setback that the disestablishment campaign had experienced since 1868. Not only did the Liberals lose heavily in Britain as a whole, but even in radical Wales six seats were lost, including Cardiff and Swansea. In several other seats, the Liberal majorities fell alarmingly, though Lloyd George, to the dismay of his critics, was among the survivors. The Church Defence Committee, sustained by the resources of wealthy landowners such as the Duke of Westminster, had campaigned hard against Liberal candidates, though the deepening trade depression seems also to have played a major part in the Unionist successes. A seat like Carmarthen Boroughs turned mainly on the impact of the McKinley tariff in the United States (which produced heavy unemployment in the tinplate industry), not on the terms of the Welsh Disestablishment

Bill: indeed, the victorious Unionist candidate here, Sir John Jones Jenkins (later Lord Glantawe), was himself a past supporter of Welsh disestablishment. Whatever the causes, however, the Liberal party suffered a heavy defeat from which it would take years to recover. For a considerable period, therefore, Welsh disestablishment receded from the forefront of the political stage.

In the years after 1895, the Welsh disestablishment movement was in the doldrums. The Liberals remained out of office, divided over the leadership and over basic policy issues, especially over imperialism. In Wales, it seemed that for the first time since 1868 Liberalism had lost much of its impetus. The fiasco of the break-up of the *Cymru Fydd* movement promoted widespread disunity and distrust. In Parliament, the Welsh Party, under the quiescent leadership of Sir Alfred Thomas, was but a shadow of what it had been in the days of Rendel's leadership. The premature death of Tom Ellis in 1899 was another discouraging portent. Two further disestablishment motions, indeed, were moved during this period – in 1897 and 1902 – but neither made much impact. Indeed, there are many signs of a decline in the self-confidence of Welsh Nonconformists at this period. For the first time for a century, their own statistics seemed to show that they were static at best, if not indeed in decline. In the period 1893–1903, when the population of Wales soared, with a massive rate of immigration into the southern coalfield, the total of Nonconformist members rose only from 397,250 to 465,794. In the years 1900 and 1901, three of the four main denominations, the Independents, Baptists and Wesleyans, actually had to report a drop in numbers. The outer fringe of 'adherents', mainly working class, showed an even more ominous decline. The weakening hold of the Welsh language further undermined the influence of the chapels in industrial areas. The mounting total of debts testified to the gross over-building of chapels in the past, as a result of uncontrolled local enthusiasm. On the other hand, the established Church was evidently maintaining the momentum of the past few decades. The figures for Easter communicants and for Sunday school pupils all showed an encouraging advance. Even if much of this progress was being gained amongst the English or anglicized sections of the population, the policy of adapting the Church to the national characteristics of Wales was being continued apace. Symbolic of the new mood was the appointment to the see of St David's in 1897 of Bishop John Owen, the son of a Llŷn weaver, a more conciliatory personality than Bishop Edwards of St Asaph and unmistakably Welsh in accent and in attitude. When William Jones (Liberal, Arfon) moved his Welsh disestablishment motion in February 1902, he freely admitted that the Church was showing every sign of

regeneration. His main argument was therefore based on the somewhat lame premise that disestablishment would be a means of
ensuring that this revival would continue.

More generally, these years seemed to show a revulsion against the
older sectarian politics of the past. The new concern with social and
economic issues in the 1880s and 1890s was now having its impact on
Wales. A Nonconformist writer in *Y Geninen* (April, 1907) could argue
that, in comparison with such burning injustices as unemployment and
malnutrition in the industrial areas, the disestablishment of the
Church seemed almost trivial. In the mining valleys of south Wales,
this feeling was growing more intense. The great coal stoppage of 1898
kindled a new mood of class bitterness; the older generation of miners'
leaders, men like Mabon and David Morgan, products of the chapel-
dominated society of the past, were increasingly under fire. As new,
younger men migrated into the eastern valleys of the coalfield from
England, the value of Welsh Nonconformity seemed irrelevant, even
an anachronism. The emerging Independent Labour Party seemed to
regard the Nonconformist minister more as a class enemy than a
popular champion. Keir Hardie's return for Merthyr Tydfil in the 1900
election, in particular, represented a decisive breach with a generation
of political activity in Wales. The issues that he pronounced in his
campaign were secular and nationwide, not sectarian and Welsh. The
improvement of working conditions and living standards for the
working proletariat, the injustices and exploitation of the Boer War
formed the substance of his programme. His rhetoric carried marked
overtones of the old evangelical politics – 'my cause is the cause of
labour, the cause of humanity, the cause of God'. Socialism and
Christianity were synonymous, he claimed, and the programme of the
ILP was little more than an extension of the Sermon on the Mount
and the message of the carpenter's son who died on Calvary. 'Who was
their Saviour but a Labour man?' Hardie himself supported Welsh
disestablishment on general democratic grounds. But his arguments
were very different in emphasis from those of the older generation of
Liberals. He condemned the establishment of a class of 'state priests';
first, he alleged, the proletariat was lowered to depths of poverty and
misery, and then a priest was paid by state funds to urge them to
remain content with their condition. He welcomed the disendowment
of the Church as a preliminary to the disendowment of landlords and
a general revolution in the ownership of property. These were hardly
the orthodox Liberal arguments; they could be turned with almost
equal ease against the Nonconformist ministers themselves, while in
any case Hardie showed little sign of regarding disestablishment as a
major political priority. It was a traditional grievance which should be
rapidly dealt with, so that governments could turn to the real problems

of the time. Hardie's attitude found more and more response in the industrial valleys. As relations between capital and labour became more bitter, the chapels seemed left behind by the course of the class war. Their message, fundamentalist and unphilosophical, a crusade against materialism and intemperance, essentially otherworldly in emphasis, had little to contribute to social and economic debate. As the challenge of the Church seemed less imminent, the Nonconformist bodies found themselves faced by new and graver challenges that confounded their dogmas and their experience.

At this period of disillusion and apparent decline, Welsh Nonconformists suddenly found new impetus. In part, at least, they wrought their own salvation. The reaction against Balfour's Education Act of 1902, universally condemned by Nonconformists as a concession to clericalism which would put 'Rome on the rates', gave a revived stimulus to political dissent. In Wales, for three years the county councils, under the skilled direction of Lloyd George, conducted a campaign to frustrate the working of the act. While the 'Welsh revolt' against Balfour's Act was only indirectly concerned with the question of disestablishment, it clearly emphasized the minority position of the Church in Wales. The county council elections of February 1904, which saw sweeping Liberal gains in all Welsh counties, seemed to give new substance to the traditional view of Wales as 'a nation of Nonconformists'. Further, the chapels were given a fortuitous impetus by the sudden torrent of the 1904–5 religious revival. In the next two years, chapel membership soared upwards everywhere under the inspiration of young Evan Roberts and his revivalist disciples. The total of communicants for the four major Nonconformist churches increased by nearly 100,000 in the period 1904–6 and the ascendancy of the chapels in Welsh society seemed dramatically confirmed. Many leading Nonconformist ministers found that the revival impelled them to a new concern with social issues, often along the lines of R. J. Campbell's quasi-socialist 'new theology'. Lloyd George and other Liberal advocates of disestablishment proclaimed with heavy emphasis that the new vitality of the chapels would lead to a political revival also, and so it proved.

In the year 1906, the year of the famous Liberal landslide victory, established churches everywhere seemed to be on the defensive. The trend in many countries in Europe and the Americas appeared to be towards disestablishment. Ferry in France and Crispi in Italy had drastically curtailed clerical privileges in education. On the eve of the election, the final attainment of disestablishment in France by the Combes radicals, gave new inspiration to all who believed in the separation of church and state. This played its part in the 1906 election results. In their landslide triumph, the Liberals captured every one of the thirty-four Welsh seats, save for Hardie's constituency at Merthyr Tydfil. All the Welsh members were pledged to disestablishment – and indeed twenty-five of them were claimed as Nonconformists. How prominent Welsh disestablishment was as an election issue is arguable – in Wales the 1902 Education Act received much more attention – but at least the new flood of Nonconformist Liberationists into the Commons seemed a guarantee of immediate action. The new Liberal government, with David Lloyd George himself a member of the Cabinet, seemed certain to introduce a measure that would at last satisfy Nonconformist aspirations after nearly a century of effort.

In fact, there followed four years of sad disappointment. Part of this was the result of the effect of obstruction by the House of Lords which so disrupted the legislative programme of the government. But there were more specific causes relating to Wales. The new government introduced in May 1906 not a Disestablishment Bill but a Royal Commission, which would acquire definite information about the various religious bodies in Wales. The news was very popular with Welsh churchmen, who saw it as a means of postponing still further the passage of disestablishment. Nonconformists, however, generally received the Commission with dismay: it recalled too much the religious census which they had always resisted in the belief that it would unduly favour the state Church. In any case, the Commission was unnecessary: in the words of D. A. Thomas, it was taking evidence when the verdict had already been given. The Commission, it was thought, would quietly shelve an awkward problem while the government turned to more pressing questions of policy. In fact, the Commission was largely the idea of David Lloyd George, president of the Board of Trade. He had persuaded the archbishop of Canterbury, Randall Davidson, to agree to it in the hope that a compromise measure would be passed which would leave to the Church most of her endowments. Like some of his co-religionists, Lloyd George now regarded the Welsh disestablishment issue as a tedious legacy from the past which should be rapidly eliminated. In the event, the course of the Commission from 1906 to 1910 confirmed the worst fears of Welsh Nonconformists. There was constant deadlock between the free church and Anglican members of the body, while its chairman, Lord Justice Vaughan Williams, gravely aggravated matters by his cantankerous behaviour. Much of the disagreement centred on the terms of reference of the Commission. The Nonconformists tended to urge that the work of the religious bodies should include their role in Welsh society and culture more generally; this would illuminate more fully the activity of the chapels. After nearly a year of frustration, three Nonconformist members of the body resigned in April 1907. Their successors included such disputatious figures as J. H. Davies and the Revd J. Morgan Gibbon; this ensured that the Commission would continue to lurch along its stormy way.

The failure of the government to introduce a full-blooded measure of disestablishment led to further protests in Wales, as in 1894. These reached a crescendo in the summer of 1907 with a massive protest meeting in Wood Street chapel, Cardiff. However, Lloyd George was able skilfully to draw the sting of the protest here by appealing to his own long record of agitation on behalf of Welsh Nonconformity. The revolt collapsed and the Welsh free churches remained quiet for the next few years. In any case, it was quite obvious that Welsh disestablishment and every other government measure would remain a dead letter until the problem of the House of Lords was finally dealt with. Until their veto was removed, it would block the way towards all the objectives of Welsh and English radicals.

In the years 1909–11, the road to Welsh disestablishment was at last cleared. Lloyd George's 'people's budget' of 1909, which the Lords rashly rejected, led ultimately to the passage of the 1911 Parliament Act. This measure made it possible for the government to force through any legislation which had passed through three sessions of Parliament, whatever the attitude of the Lords. Welsh disestablishment would clearly be one of the issues directly affected, and so it proved. Even before the two general elections of 1910, the government had briefly introduced another Welsh Disestablishment Bill on 26 April 1909, as an earnest of its good faith. It was brought in by the prime minister, Asquith, who still retained that concern for ecclesiastical politics he had shown in his youthful appearances on behalf of the Liberation Society. His bill was largely based on the abortive measure of 1895, with the terms of disendowment made more generous to the Church. There were some changes, however. The year 1662 was now used as the date after which the Church could retain its own property, instead of 1703. Cathedrals and burial grounds were no longer to be secularized. The new representative body should pay incumbents as much life compensation annuity as was proportionate to the annual value of the emolument transferred to them: in the 1895 measure the whole had been reinvested in the Welsh commissioners by the representative body during the life of the incumbent. The most notable change, however, lay in the fact that the commissioners were now to be only temporarily in control. A new national Council would be set up to administer the secularized tithe and other property; in this way, Lloyd George's notorious amendment to the 1895 bill received retrospective sanction. However, with Lloyd George's budget now consuming almost all the time of the House, it was clear that the bill could proceed no further than the first reading.

In the two elections of January and December 1910, the usual Liberal pluralities were piled up in Wales. Welsh disestablishment was given some prominence, though it was clear that it was the budget in January and the Parliament Bill in December that were the major issues before the electorate. Once the Parliament Act became law in August 1911, however, the government had no longer any valid excuse for failing to redeem its pledges to Welsh Liberals. One excuse for delay had been removed when the notorious Church Commission had finally succeeded in issuing its findings in 1910. Amid a bewildering array of majority and minority reports, memoranda and counter-memoranda, some firm information did manage to emerge. Some statistical basis was provided for the numerical claims of Non-conformists; their total membership (in 1906) was given as 550,280, as against 193,081 communicants for the established Church. The evidence presented before the Church commissioners, with all its limitations, provided the most valuable of sources for assessing the condition of the churches at the beginning of the twentieth century. While church spokesmen expressed general satisfaction with the recent progress of the established Church, the Nonconformist bodies seemed aware of an acute sense of crisis. Many Nonconformist spokesmen noted with concern that the impetus of the 1904 revival was already petering out and that the chapels were again losing their hold over the industrial valleys. The original doctrinal issues that had divided the free churches were becoming irrelevant, and few now adhered to the old rigidity of predestinarian Calvinism. The organizational methods of the chapels were also being re-examined, and the Calvinistic Methodists were tending to favour the more settled pastorate of the Independents and Wesleyans. What was perhaps most depressing of all, however, was that the gulf between the Church and the chapels was as profound as ever. Seldom was there interdenominational co-operation; on all sides the old suspicion and hostility prevailed. Nonconformist objections to the 'wanton proselytizing' of the Church were paralleled by Anglican attacks on 'the chapel screw'. Neither side, it seemed, sought for compromise; over disestablishment and many other issues, it was to be a fight to the finish. This was also the view of the Liberal government. Ellis Griffith, leader of the Welsh Party and an ardent Calvinistic Methodist, was appointed under-secretary to the Home Office early in 1912 to help prepare the Welsh Disestablishment Bill. His colleague, the home secretary, Reginald McKenna, was himself a Welsh member (for North Monmouthshire). So on 23 April 1912, McKenna introduced the third Welsh Disestablishment Bill. The stage was set for the final clash of wills. The last act of the long story of the disestablishment campaign was now to be played out.

In the next two and a half years, the Welsh Disestablishment Bill, like the Irish Home Rule Bill, dragged its weary way through the parliamentary ritual prescribed by the Parliament Act. It passed the Commons in January 1913, but was promptly thrown out by the House of Lords. A second time it passed the Commons, in July 1913, but in the Lords it again had short shrift, mustering only forty-eight supporters. Yet a third time it ground its way through the Commons in the summer of 1914, assisted by the frequent use of the 'guillotine'. On this occasion, the Lords blocked its passage by appointing petitions in Wales against the bill. McKenna's measure resembled its predecessors in its main provisions. Of the income from endowments, £260,000 in all, £173,000 from ancient sources before 1662 would be secularized – an arrangement which, churchmen claimed, would leave the Church only 1s. 5½d. in the pound, but which McKenna asserted was more like 6s. 8d. in the pound. On the 1894 pattern, Welsh Church commissioners were to be appointed, who would transfer cathedrals, churches, palaces, deaneries, parsonages and glebe from modern sources to a new representative body of the Church. The national council of 1909 would not now be set up, but parochial endowments would be handed over to the county councils for them to administer. The old and familiar arguments for and against the measure were deployed on the platform, in the Commons and in the usual flood of pamphlet literature issued by the Church Defence Committee, the Liberation Society and similar organizations. The advocates of Church Defence launched themselves into a last desperate stand, including a monster demonstration in Hyde Park on 12 June, addressed by the archbishop of Canterbury and York, the bishop of St Asaph, the duke of Devonshire and Bonar Law, the Unionist leader. Most of their fire was trained upon the disendowment clauses of McKenna's bill which were claimed to be 'the robbery of God'. However, disestablishment was also condemned, although less unequivocally. It was asserted that it undermined the religious basis of the state; as F. E. Smith put it, during the second reading debate in the Commons, in one of his more sententious moments, 'it would offend the souls of Christian people everywhere', a view which Chesterton mercilessly satirized in his poem 'Anti-Christ'. On the Liberal side, the simple argument reiterated time and again was that Wales was a nation, and that the wishes of its people, as demonstrated at elections since 1868, should be allowed to prevail. As before, there was much delving into past history, especially on the origins of tithe and the other endowments of the Church. McKenna propounded the theory that tithe was a tax, a legal impost first exacted in the twelfth century, which Welshmen had always resisted. In reply, Bishop John Owen, ridiculing this 'freak theory of tithe', asserted that tithe was the inalienable property of the Church, the voluntary donation of 'pious ancestors' which dated from the pre-conquest Celtic 'Gwestfa'.

The denominational divisions, however, were not as clear-cut as in the past. There were some prominent churchmen who advocated disestablishment, among them Bishops Gore of Oxford and Hicks of Lincoln. Gore, like many Anglo-Catholics, held that the state connection inhibited the Anglican community and prevented its ministering to the poor in the same way as the Roman Catholics and the Salvation Army. This point of view was also expressed in the Commons by Liberals such as Hobhouse and C. F. G. Masterman, and in Wales by the Revd A. W. Wade Evans in his *Papers for Thinking Welshmen*. On the Liberal side, there were also dissentients, some of them vocal in the Commons. Under pressure from a group of Liberal Church back-benchers, led by W. G. C. Gladstone, grandson of the former premier, the government was forced to make a number of concessions over the terms of endowment. On 18 December 1912, the Church was conceded the income from Queen Anne's Bounty and parliamentary grants since 1800. The following month, a scheme for the commutation of life interests was also included by Asquith and McKenna. There were major back-bench revolts against the government on amendments to leave glebe to the Church and to allow for the compensation of curates (the latter an issue that attracted the sympathy of several Labour members including Keir Hardie). Many leading Nonconformists – the Revd F. B. Meyer of the Free Church Council, Sir Henry Lunn, C. P. Scott, the editor of the *Manchester Guardian* – all called for moderation over the disendowment provisions, as though conscious of their own weakening political position. At least one prominent Congregationalist minister, the Revd J. Fovargue Bradley, came out entirely against the bill, and proved one of the most effective of Church pamphleteers. But the intransigence of the Anglican side made compromise impossible. At a time of increasing party animosity, they fought the bill line by line and clause by clause in the House. Neither side would yield; neither would raise its sights beyond total victory or total surrender.

In fact, there is much evidence that there was declining interest in the bill. In the world of Tonypandy and the Dreadnoughts, of the suffragettes, the National Insurance Bill and the Curragh crisis, the time-worn issue of Welsh disestablishment seemed little more than an irrelevance. In England, the bills of 1912–14 aroused scant concern. The Church Congresses and Free Church Councils of these years lacked their old vehemence. Even in Wales itself, the old fervour was absent. Large public meetings addressed by Lloyd George, Ellis Griffith, the Revd J. Towyn Jones and others in the heart of radical Wales failed to rouse much enthusiasm. The Welsh press, *Y Genedl, Y Tyst* and the rest, instead of showing the old militancy, lapsed into gloomy dismay about the concessions made by the government during the passage of the bill. Over 100,000 Nonconformists in Wales signed petitions against the bill – some on the grounds that to remove the Anglican establishment would greatly enhance the position of the Church of Rome. In the key by-election at Flint District in January 1913, the Liberals deliberately played the issue down in the hope that their vote would be sustained by other political questions. Nor is it transparent that churchmen regarded the bills with as much dismay as Unionists claimed in the Commons; the process of the secularization of public life had proceeded so far in the past fifty years that the additional passage of disestablishment would hardly bring about any significant change.

Nevertheless, Liberals and Unionists plodded on with the ritual of debating the bill from 1912 to 1914, calling in the authorities of Stubbs, Freeman, Maitland and other historians to lend their arguments a flavour of factual authenticity. Then the outbreak of the world war in August 1914 made an immediate settlement a matter of urgency. As a result of negotiations with Bonar Law and the Unionist leaders, the Lords were prevailed upon to pass both Irish Home Rule and Welsh disestablishment on 18 September 1914, on condition that they were suspended in their operation until after the war. Sir David Brynmor Jones and other Welshmen sang the Welsh national anthem in the lobby of the Commons, but their mood was hardly one of jubilation. However, at least some progress was allowed with the passage of Welsh disestablishment, unlike that of Irish Home Rule. The commissioners were appointed and proceeded with their work of administering the endowments of the Church during the war years. In this unsatisfactory state of suspended animation, the Welsh disestablishment problem was shelved until the end of the war.

For the next few years, the position of the Welsh Church was most unsettled. Churchmen bitterly resented being left in a limbo of uncertainty, and there was even talk of passive resistance by the Welsh clergy (on the model of Nonconformists after 1902) to frustrate the working of the Church commissioners. On the Liberal side, there was a flurry of excitement in March 1915 when the government suddenly proposed a Postponement Bill which would have delayed the operation of Welsh disestablishment until six months after the end of the war. In an unexpectedly effective gesture of defiance, the Welsh members protested that this was a breach of faith, and even Lloyd George failed to placate them. In view of the precarious balance of opinion in the wartime Commons, the government agreed to withdraw the bill. In the mean time, the Welsh Church was at last coming face to face with the inevitable, and viewing its position realistically. In October 1917, in a convention of churchmen at Cardiff, the fact of disestablishment was recognized at last. Lords Justice Atkin and Bankes drafted a new constitution for the ecclesiastical province of Wales. A new governing body and a representative body were set up, the latter under the secretaryship of the Oxford don, Frank Morgan of Keble College. Negotiations were also begun for the settlement of the financial terms of disendowment, especially in relation to the commutation of life interests. But all would depend on the attitude of the new prime minister, David Lloyd George, in the past one of the bitterest partisans of Welsh Nonconformity.

The ending of the war and the signing of the peace at Versailles brought on all sides an ardent wish for the settling of the old time-worn controversy over disestablishment. Action was suspended while Lloyd George was abroad in the Paris peace conference, but on his return in the middle of July events moved rapidly. A bewildering series of negotiations was conducted by him single-handed with Bishops Edwards and Owen, reminiscent in style of the 'secret diplomacy' that had aroused the protests of radicals at Versailles. The mood was one of unity and goodwill; the terms of the settlement, however, were kept deliberately vague. The entire manoeuvres bore all the hallmarks of Lloyd George's usual political methods as he skilfully exploited the tension between the two Welsh bishops. The home secretary, Shortt, a Coalition Liberal, had only vague ideas about the measure he was supposed to introduce on 6 August. It mattered little. Lloyd George was at the zenith of his power and any settlement that he had personally sponsored would be passed in the summer of 1919. In two weeks the new Welsh Church Temporalities Act was the law of the land, and the disestablishment controversy was at last brought peacefully to its close.

After the passage of the Act of 1919, the Welsh Church was formed into a new ecclesiastical province and totally severed from the Convocation of Canterbury. However, the financial terms of disendowment were greatly modified to take account of the inflation of the war years. The Welsh Church had benefited from the war, contrary to the allegations of many churchmen. The value of tithe (only £77 per £100 in 1914) had risen to £136, while interest on the capitalized value of tithe-rent-charge had inflated to over 5 per cent. The main need was for government assistance to help the Church Commissioners to pay the Church for the redeemed tithe and other property. They had to find the huge total of £3,400,000. They had security to raise £2,150,000 by way of loans, while a further £250,000 would come from a remission of rates charged upon tithe vested in the commissioners. That left a balance of £1,000,000 and this would be met by a direct grant from the Treasury. The county councils, which would receive the alienated tithe and other disendowed property, would by 1950 be in possession of an income of £212,000 per year to be donated to 'national purposes'. There were a few protests from unrepentant churchmen, like the brothers Lord Hugh and Robert Cecil, who claimed that Lloyd George had deceived the Welsh bishops into surrendering. Also some Nonconformist Liberals, notably Llewelyn Williams and David Davies of Llandinam, complained that the terms of disendowment were far too generous to the 'greedy prelates'. The Church had already benefited from the inflation of the interest upon the capitalized value of life interests; now it would benefit from the enhanced value of tithe and from stipends paid out to clergy during the war. The Church, they argued, stood to make a net profit of at least £1,000,000. The hard-faced men who had done well out of war had, it appeared, episcopal accomplices. But these protests were largely ignored in the interests of a rapid settlement.

In June 1920, the disestablishment provisions came into effect, and henceforth the new ecclesiastical province of Wales was in being. Its new freedom of organization was at once seen in the creation of new dioceses, Swansea and Brecon, and Monmouth, in the next two years. The terms of disendowment brought no hardship – on the contrary. By 1935 the second archbishop of Wales, C. A. H. Green, could report that the initial loss had been more than made good, partly by wise investment of the capital sum remitted for the life interests of pre-1914 incumbents, partly by a voluntary appeal which by 1934 had brought in over £700,000. As a result, schemes had been introduced to pay pensions to incumbents, and to look after their widows and children; a minimum stipend of £250 was guaranteed. In a more general sense, the Church also greatly progressed in the years after disestablishment. It seemed to be far more democratic in structure and more in harmony with the native culture and aspirations of the people of Wales. It could act on a national, and not merely a diocesan, basis. Since 1920, indeed, it has been the Nonconformist churches which have faced a serious reappraisal. Their organization and even more their moral values have come under severe challenge in a world where the spirit of puritanism seems less and less relevant. The final irony remains that, while few churchmen would now wish to return to the old days before 1914, Nonconformists look back nostalgically at the dynamic years half a century ago when they were chafing under the burdens and restraints of the state establishment.

In surveying the literature of the disestablishment controversy on both sides, it is all too easy to assume that the question was the major theme of Welsh public life for almost a century. In fact, the period when it was a dominant issue was relatively brief. Even in 1868, it was not a

question that aroused mass enthusiasm or interest in Wales; many
Nonconformists were more aware of the links that bound them to the
Anglican Church than of the elements that estranged them. Thousands
of Nonconformists in Wales still used the parish church for their
marriages and burials; the foundation of Anglican 'National' schools
owed much to the voluntary contributions of ordinary Methodists,
Baptists and Congregationalists. Only in the 1880s and 1890s did the
question clearly come to dominate political and social discussion in
Wales, and then as part of a wider ferment of national consciousness at
a time of economic crisis. The early 1890s, perhaps, mark the
climacteric of Welsh disestablishment as a political movement. After
the 1890s, the question declined in importance, as imperialism and
other foreign and domestic questions attracted growing attention.
When the Liberals were returned in the 1906 election, again the Welsh
Church issue came to the fore and was much debated, and the
Nonconformist radicals who agitated for disestablishment clearly
spoke for a narrower and narrower segment of public opinion. Even in
Wales, general social and economic issues were the main topic of
concern by 1914. It was only in the 1880s and 1890s, moreover, that
the Welsh Church question made any great impact on opinion outside
Wales, and then as part of a more general ferment of Liberationism
and political dissent. After 1900, most English observers regarded it
with indifference. It is easy, therefore, to be misled by the constant
barrage of newspaper agitation and the torrent of pamphlet and other
ephemeral literature into thinking that disestablishment was for years a
critical issue. The extent to which it ever had mass support is, indeed,
uncertain. By the 1890s, it was an older generation of radicals, men
like Thomas Gee, Dr John Thomas of Liverpool, and Revd Evan Jones
of Caernarfon, who took the lead in free church demonstrations.
Indeed, it was notorious that some of these Nonconformist publicists,
Gee for instance, seldom if ever appeared at denominational
assemblies. The younger ministers who succeeded them from the
1890s, men like Dr 'Gomer' Lewis and, later on, Silyn Roberts and Dr
D. Miall Edwards, were less perturbed by the symbolic status issue of
disestablishment. They were far more concerned with the failure of
their own churches to cope with the problems of ministering to a
rapidly increasing population in a much-changed climate of ideas. As
one of the most distinguished of the new theologians, Dr J. Cynddylan
Jones, wrote to Gee in March 1887, 'If the Church has been a failure
in relation to the education of the masses, the Nonconformity of today
is not much of a success . . . Nonconformity ridden by committees and
conclaves to death, has not much to boast of compared to the
Church'. At the Calvinistic Methodist assembly of 1908, Cynddylan
Jones condemned his brethren for their failure to attend to social

problems; he confessed that he himself had been voting Labour for many years.

Indeed, for much of the time, disestablishment roused relatively little concern for itself alone. It entailed few direct and obvious injustices. As the Montgomeryshire Liberal, A. C. Humphreys-Owen, wrote in 1891, there were few tangible cases of hardship that could be proved where the Church was concerned: 'one must keep hammering on at generalities'. Many of the younger Welsh Liberals, Tom Ellis and Lloyd George especially, were notorious for regarding disestablishment as a stalking-horse for other objectives such as land reform and Home Rule. It was hard to claim that the position of the bishops in the House of Lords or any of the other appendages of the establishment imposed any physical injustice; even the imposition of tithe, which clearly added to the burdens of the rural community at a time of agricultural depression, was hardly a major hardship, while in any case Liberals were not proposing to abolish it, but rather to divert it to the use of county councils. Disestablishment was, in fact, for most of its advocates largely a symbol, a token of the social equality of the articulate majority of the political nation. But long before disestablishment was finally attained in 1919, that equality was in substance a reality. Nonconformists had long gained admission to universities and to grammar schools; church rates had been abolished and tithe commuted; the burial and marriage laws no longer offended the sensibilities of the Nonconformist community. The ascendancy of democratically-elected county councils in place of the old Anglican gentry after 1888 was an index of the social revolution of the past thirty years, in which Nonconformists had attained full rights of citizenship at last.

By 1914, indeed, much of the rhetoric of the supporters of disestablishment was undeniably nostalgic in tone, harking back to the distant days of the tithe riots of the 1880s or the evictions of the 1860s. Much of the social content of their campaign had evaporated. The actual merits or de-merits of the act of disestablishment were largely lost sight of. Instead, the issue had become merged in a far wider crusade for national recognition for Wales as a separate entity, part of the many-sided pressures for Welsh separatism during the past half-century. But in fact disestablishment was an unsatisfactory symbol for a national crusade, on the lines of Irish nationalism. After all, the Church in Wales was undeniably Welsh in its character, as the presence of men like Bishop John Owen of St David's testified. There was nothing 'alien' about the weaver's son of Ysguborwen. This became more and more apparent in the years after 1900. As Liberalism lost much of its national content in the period after the break-up of *Cymru Fydd* in 1896, so the disestablishment campaign lost much of its momentum too. By 1914 the movement seemed in some ways outdated, based on national injustices and oppression that had real substance in the days of the 'Blue Books', but which a generation or more of democratic achievement had made a thing of the past.

It is easy also to exaggerate the monolithic quality of the disestablishment campaign. Perhaps it had such a character in the early years down to the 1868 election, when it was given a new sense of purpose by the Liberation Society. But as the Society lost its momentum in the 1870s and 1880s, the disestablishment campaign became more and more fragmented, in keeping with the fissiparous nature of Welsh Nonconformity in general. It had become a series of sporadic initiatives by a host of independent committees and organizations. Even the Disestablishment Campaign Committee had to compete for authority with the *Cymru Fydd* League, the North and South Wales Liberal Federations, and a mass of purely denominational bodies. By the 1890s the campaign for religious equality was degenerating into a struggle for power between the rival supporters of Stuart Rendel, Thomas Gee, Tom Ellis and Lloyd George, and others within the coalition that made up Welsh radicalism. In the end, all came to depend on the activities of the Welsh members of Parliament, but time was to prove them an unreliable guide. They totally lacked the self-discipline and clarity of purpose of the Irish Nationalists under Parnell. By 1914, the Welsh Party was totally under the spell of David Lloyd George, and so was the disestablishment movement. Welsh disestablishment had become a facet of Lloyd George's kaleidoscopic career, and its strengths and weaknesses both stemmed from this fact.

If Welsh Nonconformity proved unexpectedly fragile during the disestablishment campaign, Welsh churchmen cannot look back on it with a great deal of satisfaction. For much of the time, until the 1890s, the favourite argument used to rebut Liberationist critics was that England and Wales were indissoluble, that Wales was, in the phrase of the misguided Bishop Basil Jones of St David's, 'a geographical expression'. The Church in Wales was coterminous with the Church in England, as England and Wales themselves were part of a common entity. By the 1890s, this attitude was being made to seem increasingly outmoded: institutions such as the national federal University of Wales, created in 1893, were testimony to the reality of Wales as a nation, and to the growing recognition of that fact. Thereafter, churchmen had to change their ground. Even then, they were undecided over their premises, especially as to whether disestablishment or disendowment was the greater evil. Conclusions varied on this point, but churchmen usually plumped for disendowment as the worse calamity – to the ribald joy of their radical opponents who lampooned them, not entirely without justification, for their concern with the 'loaves and fishes' of their faith. Disendowment in fact was rebutted all too often by a view of the sanctity of property that would have seemed obsolete in 1800, let along 1900. Churchmen refused to concede that the passage of time could make a significant difference to the title of their property, or that the religious pattern of Wales had been permanently transformed in the past two centuries. In the long debates on the origin of tithe, the basis of Queen Anne's Bounty and a host of other learned topics, churchmen were usually historically more accurate than their Liberal opponents. But if they had history and logic on their side, common sense was too frequently neglected.

The campaign over disestablishment was a lengthy one. It was prolonged unduly because on the Church side, as well as on the part of the Nonconformists, the extremist mentality gained control. Compromise was regarded as unthinkable, and vested with a biblical rhetoric that made it seem even sacrilegious. Ecclesiastical statesmen such as Bishop Gore, who tried to elevate sectarian controversy to a higher place of argument, were denounced for their treachery. The settlement so speedily reached in the post-war atmosphere of 1919 seems in ironic contrast to all this. Both churchmen and Nonconformists took an apocalyptic view of the struggle in which they were engaged, and this made a practical settlement hard to attain. In the event, it may well be doubted how much either side gained from its acrimonious campaigns. Certainly, the issue prevented common action on behalf of other Welsh causes. The conflict of the religious bodies delayed for years the fulfilment of a national system of education, while the movement for Welsh Home Rule that Tom Ellis tried to kindle in 1890 was stifled by denominational antipathy. At least, it is urged, the religious life of Wales has been revitalized since 1920. The fact of disestablishment has indeed resulted in the Church in Wales becoming far more Welsh and more democratic in its ethos; no longer is it dominated by a reactionary landed class in social and economic decline. For Nonconformists it has at least provided a symbolic statement of their place in Welsh society since the advent of industrialism; it has given them positive objectives, in place of a negative campaign against the Church. Neither side, however, has been able to halt the onrush of the forces of secularism and indifference. The outcome today is that in Wales, a disestablished Wales, there are fewer and fewer religious adherents. On all sides, the symbols of the evangelical traditions of the Victorian age are being torn down, and puritanism and sabbatarianism on the pre-1914 pattern are in full retreat. Whether they welcome these changes, or whether they attempt to hold them back, the churches seem inevitably to be among the victims, and their role in society more vulnerable year by year.

Perhaps, however, the historian is unreasonable to wish that there might have been a more reasoned approach shown during the disestablishment conflict. Political issues are not resolved so simply; they are not conducted in the hothouse atmosphere of the laboratory or the university seminar. They are the products of a whole, confusing culture in all its complexity, all its passions and all its prejudices. The historian himself is inextricably involved in them – to pretend that he is somehow above them, 'a V.I.P. on the saluting base' in E. H. Carr's phrase, is to distort his craft. It may well be that religious deadlock in the nineteenth century, like racial discrimination in the twentieth, could be resolved only through conflict and stress. Only thus, perhaps, could a true rationality emerge. May it be that in Wales a recollection of the bitter acrimony of the days of the disestablishment campaign will turn the churches to those issues that unite them rather than those that divide.

1966

9

Post-war Reconstruction in Wales, 1918 and 1945

In twentieth-century Wales, as in Britain as a whole, the experience of total war has been powerful in shaping the political, social, economic and intellectual development of the nation. But, for Wales, as for Britain generally, the emphasis by historians has too often centred, somewhat misleadingly, upon the actual years of wartime themselves. In many respects, this is inappropriate. Developments during 1914–18 and 1939–45 respectively had often only an indirect effect on subsequent history. They generated some false or abortive starts, as in the apparatus of wartime controls introduced in 1914–16, or gave transient and misleading prominence to temporary prophets (for example, Milner in 1916 and Beaverbrook in 1941) whose influence promptly diminished sharply as soon as peace returned. Lloyd George, so transcendent a figure as Wales's national hero in 1916, was a supreme war casualty in 1922. In any case, to concentrate upon the events of wartime seems peculiarly inappropriate for a radical nation such as Wales, where peace movements, whether Liberal, socialist or nationalist, have been so powerful in the present century, as the present writer has argued elsewhere.[1]

It is the post-war years, the periods immediately after 1918 and 1945, that were the real crucibles of modern Wales, both for the ways in which they continued or rejected innovations of the war years and for the new themes thrown up as soon as peace was restored. The continuities and contrasts between the two Welsh post-war

---

[1]K. O. Morgan, 'Peace movements in Wales, 1899–1945', *Welsh History Review*, 10 (3) (1983), 398–430 (published in this volume, 84–116).

experiences, especially during the years 1918–22 and 1945–51, are crucial to the understanding of the nation's evolution. In fact, the two post-war phases are usually seen in stark contrast with one another, as in Britain generally. The period of the Lloyd George coalition of 1918–22 is seen as a time of betrayal when pledges given during the war of building up a land fit for heroes were wantonly neglected. Conversely, the years of the Attlee government of 1945–51 are viewed as a period of fulfilment when faith was kept with the working-class electors who had returned Labour to power with such a massive landslide majority. The contrast seems stark indeed between Black Friday in 1921 and the Miners' Charter in 1946, between the Geddes 'axe' and the National Health Service, between deflation after one war and full employment after another, between the treatment of Ireland in 1920 and of India in 1947.

This view was popularized, for Welsh and other readers, in Aneurin Bevan's powerful tract *Why not Trust the Tories?* It was published under the pseudonym 'Celticus' in 1944 and in many ways is his most effective political publication – certainly more so than *In Place of Fear* (1952), a compilation of fragmentary writings, many of them brilliant, but put together at different times and with no dominant theme. In *Why not Trust the Tories?* Bevan linked modern social democracy with an ancient libertarian socialist tradition in Britain, going back to the Levellers and Tom Paine. But the main thrust of the argument underlines the contrast between the consequences of 1918, the legacy of deceit and betrayal left by a Tory-dominated coalition in 1918–22, and the politics of hope opening up as the Second World War came to its close. Bevan spelt out, with furious passion, the record of mass unemployment, housing failures and disastrous labour relations that had been the miserable outcome of pledges in 1918 to build a 'land fit for heroes'. In Bevan's view, the conclusion to be drawn was the basic incompatibility between the Tory ethic and political democracy itself.[2] He ended with a call to all electors and especially to the working class to make certain that in the post-war election shortly to follow in 1945 or 1946 no such betrayal of popular aspirations occurred again. After six years of Labour government ending in 1951, Bevan continued to insist that faith had indeed been kept. Despite the bitterness that was to surround his resignation from the government in April 1951 over charges on the NHS and the wider scale of rearmament during the Korean war, despite the internecine quarrelling associated with the rise of 'Bevanism' between 1951 and 1955, Bevan, like his Gaitskellite opponents, continued to emphasize that the contrast between post-war Britain after 1918 and after 1945 was overwhelming and complete.

[2]A. Bevan, *Why Not Trust the Tories?* (London, 1944), 79ff.

Whatever dissensions marked the later period of the Attlee government, the general record of the administration in which Bevan himself had served for almost six years stood in total contrast to the years of 'Tory rule' after 1918.

How far is this picture correct? And, in particular, how accurate an account does it provide of the experience of Bevan's native Wales? Is Bevan's account of capitalist reaction after one world war and of progressive social revolution after another to be dismissed as the over-simplified version of the facts provided by an angry, embittered partisan? Does a more sober historical reflection upon the two post-war periods suggest continuities as well as contrasts? These are the questions that I now propose to examine in greater detail.

In some ways, in fact, there were broad similarities between the two post-war periods in Wales, between the régime of Lloyd George's coalition and the society presided over by Attlee's peaceful revolutionaries. Certainly, both post-war phases in Wales were marked by dramatic and convulsive change. In each case, the established social order was radically transformed and the values associated with it emphatically overturned. After 1918, Wales experienced a pronounced change of mood. The remnants of the old ascendancy of both the Anglican Church and the squirearchy, against which radicals had crusaded since the 1840s, were swept aside. There was disestablishment of the Church in 1920, and a more subtle disestablishment of the gentry, too, as many great estates were dissolved for ever. Conversely, the old Liberal quasi-nationalist Nonconformist ethic, which had dominated Welsh life at least since the general election of 1868, proved to be a casualty of total war. The position of the chapels, and the puritanical sabbatarian ethic that they embodied, was henceforth to be in steady decline. There was a persistent loss of membership, and a wider diminution of influence, of which the erosion of the 1881 Welsh Sunday Closing Act in successive local polls from 1961 onwards was one landmark. The vibrant Welsh culture associated with the heyday of such writers and scholars as Sir John Morris-Jones and Sir Owen M. Edwards before the war was henceforth defensive. A new sense of the vulnerability of Welsh culture in the face of new pressures promoting Anglicization was widespread from the early 1920s. It did not help that literary patriots like Morris-Jones and Edwards had somewhat tarnished their reputations in radical circles with their rampant jingoism in Welsh-language journals such as *Y Beirniad* and *Cymru* in 1914–16.[3] The new and heightened nationalism associated with

[3] See particularly, J. Morris in *Y Beirniad*, Oct. 1914, 217–24 and Oct. 1915, 191–205; O. M. Edwards, *Cymru*, Feb. 1915 and editorial notes in that journal, from November 1914 onwards.

Saunders Lewis and the founding of Plaid Genedlaethol Cymru in 1925 was a very different force from the national movement of the pre-war era, though manifestly the creed of a minority.

After 1945, too, there were mighty changes. The surviving heirs of private capitalism, the position of mining capitalists such as Sir Evan Williams and Sir David Llewellyn and the traditional policies of treasury finance as maintained during the 'special areas' programme of the 1930s could not survive the massive state intervention in the economy and the new regional policies instituted during the wartime years. New developments such as the steelworks and hot strip-mill to be located at Port Talbot, announced by Hugh Dalton while a member in the Churchill government in early 1945, together with the combination of steel firms that led to the formation of the Steel Company of Wales in 1947, owed everything to state intervention. Conversely, the trade unions, pariahs in the social order that prevailed after 1918, were vital to the new planning policies operating under Labour after 1945. Arthur Horner, the tribune of Maerdy, 'little Moscow', who was imprisoned in 1919 for refusal to serve in the armed forces, was, as secretary of the National Union of Miners, a major architect of post-war economic recovery and the dramatic surge of industrial production after 1945. The old Welsh poacher narrowly avoided turning gamekeeper, since he seriously considered appointment to the National Coal Board after nationalization,[4] truly a sign of the times.

Just as Wales showed some common features in the social, economic and intellectual changes that engulfed it after each world war, so, too, its governmental structures were not necessarily as divergent as popular left-wing legend would have us believe. Both after 1918 and after 1945, the land was governed by what appeared at first to be the most progressive reforming administration that was available at the time. Both post-war governments, that of Lloyd George in 1918 and that of Attlee in 1945, drew inspiration from the sweeping new social blueprints drawn up during wartime. There were the programmes of the Ministry of Reconstruction in 1917–18 and of the Beveridge, Uthwatt and other reports that emerged between 1940 and 1945. Nor was there as great a disparity between the general elections that followed each world war as has often been claimed. Lloyd George in the 'coupon election' of November to December 1918, like Attlee and his Labour colleagues in June to July 1945, campaigned largely as a social reformer.[5] Housing, health, insurance, pensions, agriculture and industrial relations were more characteristic themes in the rhetoric of coalition ministers in 1918, even Tory ones, than chauvinistic cries for

---

[4] A. Horner, *Incorrigible Rebel* (London, 1960), 182–3.
[5] K. O. Morgan, *Consensus and Disunity* (Oxford, 1979), 39–41.

'hanging the Kaiser' or squeezing the Germans until the pips squeaked, for all Keynes's subsequent avowals to the contrary.

And yet, it is evident that there was, in the immediate aftermath of war a crucial contrast between the two periods, especially in Wales. Indeed, in some ways, the post-war phases illustrate yet again (1910–14 is another example) the ways in which Wales has tended to diverge from the English experience at critical times in our political and economic history. A case could be made out for there being many similarities in the policy pursued by the Lloyd George coalition and by the Attlee government in industrial policy, in finance, in colonial policy and in foreign affairs. But the case cannot be reasonably sustained in Wales. In his native land above all, Bevan's diagnosis, however extreme or exaggerated in its language, is broadly correct. After 1945, in Wales as in other older industrial areas, the social and economic reforms of wartime became permanently enshrined in the new social order that was created. There was no hint of betrayal now. Indeed, the Attlee government was very much aware of the way in which popular disillusionment had been created after the previous world war. In the 1945–51 Cabinet, to remind them of these past events, there was the septuagenarian Lord Addison, who had resigned from Lloyd George's government in 1921 in disgust at the betrayal of his housing programme then. In Wales, the 1920s brought disillusion, despair and the crushing weight of mass unemployment and stagnation as the legacy of wartime. The later 1940s, by contrast, brought a clear sense of renewal, of economic growth unknown since 1918 and of community pride. By the mid 1920s, association with the Lloyd George coalition was a badge of shame for many in Wales, especially the remnants of his old Coalition Liberals, even in such rural areas as Cardiganshire where the Wee Frees gained ultimate revenge. E. W. Evans, publisher of *Y Cymro* weekly newspaper, wrote to Sir Herbert Lewis, MP for the University of Wales, that 'the Labour Party is going to sweep the board. A great number of our ministers are silently joining the Labour Party, not because they like it, but because it is the best choice they can make'.[6]

The Attlee government's reputation, on the other hand, was further enhanced even after the government itself fell from power in October 1951. Indeed, it has been plausibly argued[7] that Attlee initiated a new social consensus that broadly dictated British domestic policy until the advent of the Thatcher government, committed as it was to

[6]In the 1922 general election, R. Hopkin Morris (Independent Liberal) defeated Ernest Evans (National Liberal), formerly Lloyd George's private secretary, in Cardiganshire: E. W. Evans to J. Herbert Lewis, 13 January 1920, Herbert Lewis papers (National Library of Wales).

[7]P. Addison, *The Road to 1945* (London, 1975), 270–8.

monetarism and a reversal of Keynesian-style management, in 1979. Welsh politics for three decades after 1945 tended to be a commentary upon the consequences, and the active Keynesian-style regional policies, of the 1945 Labour government.

In three areas, then, the divergence between the post-war experiences of Wales after 1918 and 1945 is transcendently clear – in party politics, in social policy and, above all, in the handling of organized labour. In the sphere of post-war politics in each case, the differences between the two periods is very marked indeed. As has been noted above, the Lloyd George coalition so triumphantly elected in 1918 (its 'couponed' supporters carried twenty-five Welsh seats out of thirty-six) did not seem necessarily illiberal. All Labour MPs elected for Welsh constituencies – William Brace in Abertillery, Mabon in Rhondda West, John Williams in Gower and even Vernon Hartshorn in Ogmore – claimed to be supporters of the domestic and foreign policies of the coalition government. John Williams, in the confusion typical of the time, even claimed to be a possessor of the precious 'coupon' himself![8] The charisma of Lloyd George, hero in peace and war, 'the greatest Welshman yet born', surrounded by a kind of Welsh Mafia in Downing Street, was more potent than ever. But nemesis came very rapidly. By the summer of 1919 the fundamental characteristics of the government were coming through, and meeting with a powerful popular reaction.

The revulsion against the government was more evident in Wales than in any other region of Britain, with Lloyd George's Coalition Liberals the usual victims of it. In 1919 Labour gained control of the county councils of Glamorgan and Monmouth, which apart from a brief interlude in the 1920s were to remain continuously in Labour hands until the counties were abolished and transformed into 'Gwent' and other novelties in 1973. Urban district councils in Aberdare, Maesteg and Llanelli followed this pattern. By-elections in south Wales showed a massive shift towards the Labour party, beginning with Swansea East in July 1919 which the Coalition Liberals narrowly retained at the height of the furore surrounding the Sankey Commission on the coal industry. There were further swings to Labour in other by-elections in Welsh mining seats, such as Abertillery (December 1920), Caerphilly (August 1921), where Morgan Jones, imprisoned during the war as a conscientious objector (and therefore unable to vote), was victorious; and in Gower and Pontypridd in July 1922, in both of which Labour gained seats from a Lloyd George

[8]*Labour Voice*, 7 Dec. 1918. In this speech at Treboeth, Williams urged that Germany should pay the maximum in war indemnities. V. Hartshorn, ibid., 29 December 1918, expresses his strong support for Lloyd George's coalition.

Liberal. In the 1922 general election, the revulsion against both the outgoing Lloyd George coalition and its leader was very pronounced in Wales. Only the rural constituencies of the west and north, and not all of them, stayed faithful to him. There were eight further Labour gains, six in the south Wales coalfield, one in Wrexham, another industrial seat, in the north-east, and, most startling of all, one in Caernarfonshire. Here, in Lloyd George's own bailiwick, the secretary of the North Wales Quarrymen's Union, R. T. Jones, was returned.[9] In Aberdare, there was a symbolic defeat for C. B. Stanton, the very embodiment of the bellicose jingoism of wartime, at the hands of the miners' agent, George Hall. For the proto-fascist Stanton, the war was finally over. Dick Wallhead, another wartime conscientious objector and an old lieutenant of Keir Hardie, captured Merthyr Tydfil from the Coalition Liberals. With Labour now holding eighteen Welsh seats, half the total, it was clear that the 'khaki election' of 1918, with its patriotic euphoria, had been totally unrepresentative of the underlying changes in Welsh political culture.

On the other hand, Welsh politics after 1945, if anything, merely confirmed the election results. At the polls, Labour had made seven gains and now held twenty-five seats out of thirty-six. But the leftward tide continued to flow strongly, in local government elections in 1945–6, and in by-elections at Ogmore, Aberdare and Pontypool, where only Plaid Cymru mounted any sort of challenge. Labour remained buoyant and expansionist during the Attlee years in Wales. The period from 1945 saw it making new inroads in north and mid Wales as well, both traditional Liberal territory. The statistics are evocative of the change. In 1945, Labour won twenty-five seats, with 58 per cent of the vote. In 1950, after the redistribution of constituencies, it claimed twenty-seven seats, and 58.1 per cent of the vote. In 1951, the election that saw the downfall of Labour in government, the Labour party retained twenty-seven Welsh seats, with gains in Anglesey and Merioneth in the far north to compensate for losses at Barry and Conway. Labour's percentage of the poll, 60.5 per cent, was the highest ever, higher even than in the *annus mirabilis* in 1945, while the very high turn-out of well over 80 per cent in most Welsh constituencies confirmed the enthusiasm that the Labour government aroused amongst its natural supporters despite the Bevanite controversies. All the evidence points to continuing enthusiasm in Wales for the Attlee administration's policies, for nationalization, social welfare, 'fair shares', colonial freedom and above all full employment through vigorous regional policies. In 1951 in

[9]R. Merfyn Jones, *The North Wales Quarrymen, 1874–1922* (Cardiff, 1981), 320–1.

Wales, as in Britain generally, Labour gained the highest poll ever obtained by a British political party. Converts continued: the famous Liberal name of Lloyd George appeared as a Labour MP in 1957. The pattern endured until 1966 when Labour reached its high-water mark of achievement with thirty-two seats out of thirty-six.

Apart from these somewhat mundane statistics of electoral performance, one can detect more subtle changes in the intellectual bases of politics if one compares the two post-war periods. After 1922, Welsh intellectuals moved sharply to the left, to socialism or even to pacifism. The victory of George Maitland Lloyd Davies in the 1923 general election for the University of Wales seat, even if it owed much to a split between two Liberal candidates, spoke volumes for the changing mood in the Welsh intelligentsia in this old stronghold of *Cymru Fydd*. A literary journal like *Y Llenor*, founded by W. J. Gruffydd in 1922, owed much of its impetus and distinction to anti-war or neo-pacifist writers.[10] It afforded a platform, too, for the new kind of nationalists such as Saunders Lewis or Ambrose Bebb, who were destined to form the tiny Plaid Cymru in 1925. Beyond the cloistered world of the Welsh-language *literati*, the Central Labour College in Regent's Park, London, provided a powerful stimulus to socialist activists. Young students at the college between 1918 and 1926 like Aneurin Bevan, James Griffiths, Morgan Phillips and Ness Edwards, all miners, were to create a new generation of political and industrial leaders for the Welsh labour movement.[11] The intellectual energy of Wales was as Labour (or sometimes nationalist) in character after 1922 as it had been overwhelmingly Liberal before 1914. In total contrast though, the intellectual developments within Wales after 1945 confirmed the electoral victory of the Labour party at the polls. From then onwards, perhaps until the 1970s, all the major debates leading up to the arguments over governmental devolution during the Crowther Commission, were in large measure debates within the Labour ranks. Until Plaid Cymru experienced a resurgence in 1966 and thereafter, there was no significant challenge to the political and intellectual dominance of Labour, the product of the war years and their aftermath. The difference from the experience of Lloyd George and his contemporaries after 1918 was overwhelmingly apparent.

A second area in which a clear contrast can be noted is the realm of social policy and administration. The Lloyd George government in

---

[10]Notable among them were the poet, Thomas Parry-Williams, whose academic preferment at Aberystwyth in 1920 had been endangered because of his wartime pacifism, and the literary critic, G. J. Williams. Gruffydd himself was staunchly anti-militarist: see his *Hen Atgofion* (Aberystwyth, 1936).

[11]W. W. Craik, *The Central Labour College* (London, 1964), 112–25.

1918–19 began with a blaze of reformist activity. It looked as if the new Liberalism of pre-war was being re-enacted, notably by such Liberal ministers as Addison at the new Ministry of Health.[12] There were new state-subsidized council houses, new schools, a new provision for public health, increased pensions and a comprehensive system for unemployment insurance. The Addison housing programme, above all, largely carried out the main lines advocated by the Tudor Walters committee at the end of the war. But these measures were limited in scope: the Addison Housing Acts, for instance, gave only limited assistance to working-class occupants and made little impact on the massive housing shortage in industrial areas. It tended instead to favour well-planned open estates and semi-detached cottages in suburban districts such as Rhiwbina in Cardiff, Townhill in Swansea, Barry garden suburb or the' Acton Park estate in Wrexham, originally intended for miners from the Gresford colliery. The entire social programme of the government was in any event being fatally undermined by the treasury. Austen Chamberlain, the chancellor, and his successor, Robert Horne, were reinforced by Warren Fisher within the bureaucracy long before the downfall of the government. The deflation that presaged a return to the gold standard made matters worse by inflicting high interest rates on local authorities trying to launch public housing programmes. The housing drive was completely wound up after Addison's resignation in 1921, while much of the rest of the social policy, including education, in spite of Fisher's strenuous resistance at the Ministry, was undermined by the Geddes 'axe' in 1922. The Welsh elementary and 'county' schools, proud creations of the national movement before 1914, were struggling throughout the 1920s. The 'anti-waste' business tycoons, over whom Eric Geddes presided, reduced Lloyd George's social programme to shreds. In any case, it could be argued that some of the government's legislation had been aimed at social control rather than social improvement, and had been counter to the interest of the working class in Wales. The revised National Health Insurance scheme, for instance, had curbed the miners' own union-sponsored medical schemes and had helped whittle away voluntary provision.[13] By the mid-1920s, as Bevan angrily wrote, the social prospectus of the coalition government of 1918 was a mockery.[14] Accounts of the state of housing and health in the 1930s, notably the annual reports of the Welsh Housing and Development Association prepared by Edgar

[12]Morgan, *Consensus and Disunity*, chapter 4.
[13]R. Earwicker, 'Miners' medical services before the First World War: the south Wales coalfield', *Llafur*, 3 (2) (1981), 39–52.
[14]Bevan, *Why not Trust the Tories?*, 24–6.

Chappell and others, gave alarming details of the extent of slum housing and urban and environmental decay in Wales. The parliamentary committee on the anti-tuberculosis services, chaired by Clement Davies, painted a quite appalling picture of the extent of the 'white scourge' of TB in rural and urban Wales alike, largely because of damp, insanitary housing and other social inadequacies.[15]

The findings of that committee also illustrated a significant divergence between industrial and rural Wales by the 1930s. Cost-conscious local authorities in north and mid Wales were far less anxious to expend money raised by the rates on health, housing and other social services than were Labour authorities in Carmarthenshire, Glamorgan and Monmouthshire in the south and Wrexham in the north-east. In short, it is clear that by the 1930s, the wartime pledges of sweeping social reforms, betrayed by central government from 1920 onwards, were only being honoured, if at all, by the local endeavours of county and municipal councils under Labour control. In the 1930s, in the worst years of depression and unemployment, Labour local authorities kept up public spending in south Wales on social services as best they could. Local resources were remarkably fully deployed on behalf of slum clearance, health provision, free midday meals and free school milk for children, parks, libraries, baths and other public amenities. The Labour local authorities were also most active in such places as Newport, Cardiff, Aberdare, Rhondda, Llanelli and Swansea in campaigning against the means test and attempts by the central government to curb local social expenditure. Particularly strong resistance was mustered against both restrictions upon unemployment assistance, and Circular 170 of September 1932, which sought to cut down the number of free places in secondary schools and to impose a new means test on fee payments.[16] In addition, many local authorities were remarkably enterprising in trying to enlist aid from the Nuffield Trust and other bodies in order to introduce new industries into the depressed mining valleys. In short, social policy in Wales from the mid-1920s onwards is largely a tale of the Labour-run local councils (and also the trade unions, notably through the Miners' Welfare Fund, set up in 1920, and the miners' own medical aid provision)[17] trying to repair the damage wrought by the abdication of responsibility by central government.

After 1945 it was all very different. Central and local government

[15]Ministry of Health, *Report of the Committee of Inquiry into the Anti-Tuberculosis Services in Wales and Monmouthshire* (1939).

[16]See E. Jones, 'A Study of the Influence of Central Institutions on the Development of Secondary Education in Wales, 1944–49' (University of Wales, University College of Swansea Ph.D. thesis, 1979).

[17]D. Smith and H. Francis, *The Fed* (London, 1980), 429–30.

were largely united in the creation of the welfare state. Labour-run local authorities now played a less conspicuous role. In many respects, indeed, the social programme now enacted went distinctly beyond the blueprints of the wartime years. Certainly it is an error to see the Attlee government as merely reproducing the schemes of planners such as Beveridge. James Griffiths's National Insurance Act of 1946 was more comprehensive and included more generous scales of payment than Beveridge's report had proposed. This was partly the result of intervention by backbenchers such as Sidney Silverman. Aneurin Bevan's National Health Service was more radical than Willink's wartime compromise scheme, especially in the nationalization of the hospitals and the abolition of the sale of private practices. Throughout the post-war years, the impact of the new welfare measures on the social and economic fabric of Wales, as on that of many older industrial areas, was immense. Indeed, the popularity of such literary works as *How Green was my Valley* and A. J. Cronin's *The Citadel* during the war years had helped to make south Wales a key point of reference in the entire debate about launching a welfare state. From 1940 onwards, there were rising standards of health, housing and nutrition amongst children and old people. Bevan's housing programmes, so often criticized (frequently without regard to the wider economic picture or to such technical problems as the shortage of imported soft wood for building), had a powerful effect in many Welsh towns. Swansea, ravaged by the blitz, engaged in a programme of building 6,000 council houses between 1946 and 1952.[18] Elsewhere, in mid and north Wales, such towns as Aberystwyth, Caernarfon, Newtown and Holyhead were much revived by a progressive policy of public housing aided by low interest rates. The NHS was from the start very popular in Wales where such diseases as tuberculosis and silicosis had been scourges in the recent past. Environmental conditions in long-depressed areas like the slate-quarrying districts of Caernarfon and Merioneth were revolutionized. *Lancet* reports indicated a greater enthusiasm for the NHS amongst general practitioners in Wales than in other parts of Britain. Aneurin Bevan's own personal experience of health provision in the mining communities, such as in his own Tredegar Medical Aid Society, also played its part in launching the new service. Nor was this simply a case of action by central government alone. Voluntary activity also played its part, notably in Arthur Horner's prolonged campaign against lung disease among miners, and in the National Union of Mineworkers' efforts on behalf of the rehabilitation of disabled mineworkers.

---

[18]W. G. V. Balchin (ed.), *Swansea and its Region* (Swansea, 1971), 188. These developments were largely in the Penlan area.

The outstanding difference in the social history of Wales after 1945, compared with the years after 1918, was that the momentum of wartime was kept up. This time the Treasury maintained a generally benevolent attitude towards social spending. This was obviously so under Dalton, but also during the more austere régime of Cripps in 1947–50 when a high level of welfare expenditure was maintained despite balance of payments difficulties. Even during the balance of payments troubles of 1949 that led to devaluation, there was no hint of a Geddes 'axe'. It is ironic that a conflict over welfare expenditure led to the resignation of Aneurin Bevan from the Attlee government in April 1951. In the end, a gap of only £13 million was all that divided Bevan from the politically less experienced and unnecessarily rigid Gaitskell in the Cabinet debates on the 1951 budget. Cripps, with his long and close personal relationship with Bevan since the 1930s, had avoided a clash over the 1950 budget by imposing a general ceiling on public health expenditure rather than impose charges; Gaitskell was less adroit. Despite this episode, it is clear that the pledges of both wartime and the polls were generally honoured after 1945, and that Wales, like other regions, experienced a buoyancy unknown for thirty years as a result. The contrast is most clearly demonstrated by the records of the two major social reformers within the two post-war governments. Addison became an outcast in 1921, driven out of Lloyd George's government in disgust at the emasculation of his housing schemes. His reputation as a minister suffered (quite unfairly) as a result. Bevan, in contrast, gained immensely in public stature through the creation of the welfare state, and of the NHS in particular; his eventual resignation did not affect the achievement. The careers of Addison and Bevan, Cabinet colleagues between 1945 and 1951, point the distinction in Wales and other areas in social provision after two world wars.

The greatest difference of all in the two post-war experiences in Wales is to be found in industrial relations, an area which Dr Pelling has made so very much his own. The starting-point in each case is not so very different. Both the Lloyd George coalition in 1918 and the Attlee Labour administration in 1945 aimed at first to maintain the easy access to the trade union leadership that had obtained during the war. Both established 'emergency powers' provisions to deal with industrial disturbances. Both used them several times, Lloyd George in putting down what were, in fact, official strikes of the railwaymen in September 1919 and the miners in April 1921, and Attlee in countering local strikes by London dockers and power workers between 1947 and 1950.

The Lloyd George government made some show of maintaining the wartime consensus with both sides of industry: the National Industrial

Conference called in April 1919 embodied the industrial harmony of the war years. But it soon emerged that this façade of conciliation was superficial. The National Industrial Conference yielded nothing, and broke down amidst much recrimination.[19] Above all, public dialogue with the miners was the most disastrous of failures, one which coloured the relations of the trade unions generally with central government until 1926 and beyond. The failure of the Sankey Commission to get the government to accept nationalization of the mines in August 1919; the chain of events leading to 'decontrol' of the mines that began in the autumn of 1920; and above all the calamitous breakdown of negotiations that produced the miners' lockout between April and July 1921, all testified to the disastrous record of the government, and of Lloyd George in particular. The pretence that he enjoyed a special relationship with the trade unions, nurtured since Board of Trade days in 1905–8, lay in ruins. Horne, a conciliatory minister of labour in 1919, was now a most intransigent chancellor. Points can be put on the other side, of course. The miners, pressing for a 30 per cent wage advance in 1919, were aggressive and hopelessly optimistic in the aftermath of the wartime boom. The handling of the miners' case by Smillie, Smith and the Miners' Federation of Great Britain (MFGB) executive before the Sankey inquiry was the reverse of adroit; they were not politicians, whatever their skill as industrial negotiators. The extent to which the miners were interested in nationalization, as opposed to some kind of wage advance and a pooled system for wages, is very doubtful. For all that, the government manifestly mishandled the course of negotiations throughout the Sankey hearings, while its abject surrender in 1920–1 to the private coalowners, hated as they were, inevitably caused massive resentment throughout the mining communities.

South Wales reacted the most vehemently of all the mining districts. Indeed, the promise that the post-war period would inaugurate a new era in labour relations here had always been distinctly hollow. Throughout the war years, the Welsh coalfield had been identified as a unique problem area. The Commission on Industrial Unrest in 1917 had reported in ominous terms on the explosive nature of relations between miners and coalowners. Since at least the Cambrian miners' strike and the turbulence at Tonypandy in 1910, south Wales had been officially regarded as a haven for every variant of extreme socialist ideology. Scotland Yard co-operated with the government in 1919 in dispatching secret reports to the Ministry of Labour on the alleged subversive activities of Bolsheviks and others in the Welsh valleys. It

[19]R. Lowe, 'The failure of consensus in Britain: the National Industrial Conference, 1919–1921', *Historical Journal*, XXI (3) (1978), 649–76.

was entirely predictable that south Wales should react the most vehemently of all the British mining districts after the breakdown of negotiations following the Sankey inquiry. The Welsh miners balloted strongly for strike action in September 1920 (141,721 to 40,047). When a national strike was actually called by the Miners' Federation a few weeks later, they voted against a return to work (98,052 to 51,647);[20] moreover, they were foremost in the struggle in April to July 1921 when the mines were returned to the hands of the capitalists and the government subsidy came to an end. Even a man like Vernon Hartshorn, who was always a moderate, was driven into desperate defiance when he succeeded to the presidency of the South Wales Miners' Federation, on the death of James Winstone, in 1922. In a famous phrase, Hartshorn had declared that the miners were 'deceived, betrayed, duped' over Sankey.[21] In the local press, he had vividly described how the Welsh miners were becoming 'serfs, demoralised and half-starved'[22] as severe wage cuts were imposed by the coalowners when international recession took its toll in 1921. In any event, the Welsh mining community was moving rapidly to the left, in confrontation not merely with the government but possibly with the executive of the miners' union itself. There was a revival of the 'unofficial' movements of pre-war days among rank-and-file miners. Soon they were to issue forth, under communist leadership, in the minority movement within the SWMF.[23] Left-wing figures such as S. O. Davies and Noah Ablett were powerful upon the South Wales Miners' executive. Arthur Cook, backed up faithfully by Arthur Horner in the Rhondda No. 1 District, was becoming the dominant figure in the Welsh miners' union. In 1924, he was to succeed another product of the Welsh mining valleys, Frank Hodges, as secretary of the Miners' Federation of Great Britain.

From this time onwards, the Welsh mining community was in embittered revolt, evolving its own alternative radical culture and its own rival structure of leadership. During the General Strike and miners' lock-out in 1926, the whole community was mobilized;

[20]*The Times*, 1 September 1920; *South Wales Daily News*, 1 September 1920, 4 November 1920. South Wales was the only major district to vote against a return to work in November 1920.

[21]*House of Commons Debates (Hansard)*, 5th ser., CXIX, 18 Aug. 1919, col. 2096.

[22]See *South Wales Daily News*, 31 Dec. 1921 for V. Hartshorn's article 'The coming storm in the coal trade'. Also see P. Stead, 'Vernon Hartshorn: miners' agent and Cabinet minister', in S. Williams (ed.), *Glamorgan Historian*, VI (1969), 83–94.

[23]M. G. Woodhouse, 'Rank and File Movements among the Miners of South Wales, 1910–1926' (unpublished University of Oxford D.Phil. thesis, 1970).

schoolteachers, shopkeepers and Nonconformist ministers all lined up in support. The return to pre-war ascendancy by coalowners and managers such as the Hann family of Powell Duffryn had a disastrous impact upon labour relations in south Wales. The resultant amalgamation of colliery concerns led to vast profits for the few and mass redundancies for the many. The failure of the government to provide any protection against the scourge of mass unemployment drove all the miners' leaders from Hartshorn to Cook into furious antagonism. Worse still, there was a calculated campaign by many coalowners to break the power of the 'Fed', the miners' union. Non-unionism, on the pattern of American company unionism, was encouraged in Bedwas and many other collieries. By the end of 1922, a variety of pressures had resulted in SWMF membership falling sharply from a peak of 197,000 in 1920 to 87,000 by the end of 1922. Membership continued to fall, especially after the trauma of the General Strike in 1926. Not until 1935, after a revival of the union leadership under newer, moderate leaders such as James Griffiths and a successful campaign against non-unionism (culminating in the dramatic 'stay-down' stoppages at Nine-Mile-Point colliery), did the tide begin to turn.[24] Only in the mid-1930s did MFGB membership revive and its funds significantly increase. Until that time, the unions and the miners were in implacable opposition to what they regarded as the Tory front that Lloyd George, their one-time hero, had first imposed on them.

After 1945, how different was the mood! The Attlee government had, of course, a most intimate relationship with the Trades Union Congress, as the presence of Bevin and ex-miners such as Bevan, Griffiths, Shinwell, Hall and Lawson within the administration symbolized. At all levels of the party – the party conference, the national executive, grass-roots constituency bodies – the association between the Labour party and the trade union movement was exceptionally close, probably closer than at any period in the history of the Labour movement. The career of Morgan Phillips, an ex-miner from Aberdare, as Labour's general secretary from 1944, reflected this happy symbiosis. The policies of the Attlee government followed the 1945 manifesto, and this in turn was closely geared to the demands of the unions. The repeal of the 1927 Trades Disputes Act, nationalization of the mines and other industries and services, the maintenance of full employment, the operation of a vigorous regional policy by the

[24]D. Smith, 'The struggle against company unionism in the south Wales coalfield, 1926–1939', *Welsh History Review*, 6 (3) (1973), 354–78. For an excellent study of one community, see R. L. Williams, 'Aberdare in 1926' (University of Wales, University College of Swansea MA thesis, 1981).

Board of Trade, the building up of trading estates and the use of the powers of the Distribution of Industry Act, 1945, were all dear to the heart of the Welsh working-class community. So, too, was the implementation of the National Union of Mineworkers' (NUM) Miners' Charter, as agreed by Shinwell at the Ministry of Fuel and Power, with the extension of the 'day wage' system, the five-day week and other much needed reforms. The responsiveness of the government to pressure from Wales for economic assistance was notable throughout. In July 1946, when unemployment again seemed to be reaching alarming levels in the mining valleys, Attlee, Cripps and Isaacs were solicitous in the face of protests from the Welsh Labour MPs.[25]

In return, there was a degree of co-operation from the unions in Wales quite unknown after 1918. In the interests of boosting the production record of the Labour government, items agreed in the Miners' Charter, including the five-day week, were relaxed. Whatever the difficulties of labour relations in the new nationalized industries, the industrial atmosphere was immensely more cordial than it had ever been in the 1920s. Major strikes in the south Wales pits virtually disappeared. There was nothing comparable to the prolonged dispute at Grimethorpe and other collieries in southern Yorkshire in August to September 1947. Government decisions such as the implementation of the wage freeze in 1948 or the devaluation of sterling in 1949, which added somewhat to the miners' cost of living, were loyally accepted. Even Arthur Horner, a critic of a 'wage-freeze' policy, accepted it in the cause of labour solidarity. No such concession could have been made over Churchill's return to gold in 1925. The mood in the mining communities by 1950 was remarkably changed. Maerdy, an embittered, besieged community in the 1920s, was by 1950 the beneficiary of a new £5 million investment 'horizon' mining project to connect the upper Rhondda with the Bwllfa colliery in the Aberdare valley. The links that bound the Labour ministers to their own native communities were exemplified by men such as Bevan, Griffiths and Ness Edwards. The new mood continued after 1951 despite a rash of minor stoppages and 'go-slows' that cost 276,000 tons in output in that year.[26] In the thirteen subsequent years of Conservative government, which saw the beginning of a rigorous policy of colliery closures, the unions were

[25]Parliamentary Deputation on Unemployment in Wales, 1946, PREM 8/272 (Public Record Office, London). Unemployment in Wales, which had been only 15,000 in June 1945 had risen to 66,300 (9 per cent of the insured labour force) by June 1946. Thereafter the government's advance building programme trading estates and other measures had a positive effect.

[26]National Coal Board: Annual Report, 1951, Parliamentary Papers, 1951–2, VIII, (190), p. 95.

never so isolated again. Will Paynter, another Welsh communist who became secretary of the NUM after Horner, enjoyed amiable relations with ministers. There was nothing resembling the period of victimization which followed the miners' strikes of 1921 and 1926. The Bourbon restoration after 1920 found no similar echo; the communal life of the valleys and other regions of Wales was the healthier for it.

It has been seen therefore that, whatever the elements of continuity in Wales in two post-war phases, there was a marked change of mood in the crucial areas of political conflict, social policy and labour relations. There is, however, one final point that the Welsh historian must consider, namely, what, if anything, the post-war periods added to, or subtracted from, the sense of Welshness. Was the awareness of national identity, with the institutions and social groups that sustained it, significantly altered by the aftermath of war?

As far as the First World War is concerned, it has already been suggested that the old kind of semi-nationalism, with which the prime minister, Lloyd George, was so intimately associated, largely passed away. The reaction against it in 1922 was almost as pronounced in Cardiganshire, Caernarfonshire and Flintshire as in the mining valleys of the south. Old cries such as land reform, temperance and governmental devolution aroused little interest. Disestablishment, the national objective for two generations past and the old prize striven for by Samuel Roberts, Henry Richard, Thomas Gee and other radicals in former years, was achieved in 1920 amidst monumental indifference. Indeed, the Nonconformist chapels were henceforth far more apprehensive of the future, once their ambition had been attained, than was a newly-liberated and invigorated Church, whose communicant members in Wales rose steadily in number. Plaid Cymru, formed in 1925, embodied a nationalism of a very different style from that of men like O. M. Edwards before 1914. Some of its key personalities were sympathetic to Roman Catholicism. The party was far more detached in outlook from the English and imperial governmental and social system than the pre-war nationalists had ever been. Plaid Cymru, in short, was almost entirely the vehicle for the Welsh-speaking minority. That minority itself was becoming increasingly desperate as linguistic censuses in 1921 and 1931 showed incontestable evidence of the decline of the language. The 'Anglo-Welsh' school of writing, heralded by the sardonic short stories of Caradoc Evans, illustrated one kind of reaction. Conversely, the unemployment and economic recession of the interwar period reinforced a sense of class solidarity in the valleys at the expense of either the appeal of community or Welshness. The involvement of some young Welshmen, miners and others, in the International Brigade in Spain in 1936–9 added a new kind of outward-looking dimension to this mood.[27] The post-war years after 1918, therefore, marked the effective end of one lengthy phase of Welsh national achievement, even though such symbols as the University of Wales survived to shape major aspects of the outlook of succeeding generations.

The impact of the Second World War was not so clear-cut. After 1945, there was a general mood in favour of centralization and planning initiated at the centre of economic decision-making. The hopes expressed in the Welsh Reconstruction Advisory Council in 1943 that Wales might become a distinct economic planning unit, a view advanced with especial fervour by James Griffiths, led nowhere.[28] Pressure by Welsh MPs both during and after the war for a secretary of state for Wales was strongly resisted by the government. Herbert Morrison argued that a secretary of state for Wales would lead to both bad government and a negation of efficient central planning in the principality. In any case, there would not be enough competent Welsh civil servants available to staff a new Welsh Office.[29] He rebutted James Griffiths's protests when the nationalized electricity services for Wales were divided into two in 1946, so that north and mid Wales became linked with Merseyside.[30] In the Cabinet, Aneurin Bevan, a stern enemy of both particularism and anything that resembled Welsh devolution, had a more powerful voice in the Cabinet Home Services Committee. So the Attlee government made only the most perfunctory gestures towards Welsh national sentiment, a response strongly endorsed by Morgan Phillips in Transport House. Morrison very reluctantly set up the Council for Wales in 1949. His aim was, in part, to combat the Ministry for Welsh Affairs that the Conservatives proposed to create when they returned to power. But for the next seventeen years of a somewhat ghostly existence, the Council, as a purely advisory and non-elective body, was largely the ineffective talking-shop that Morrison himself had prophesied.[31]

Even so, something did survive the centralization and hostility to

[27]H. Francis, 'Welsh miners and the Spanish Civil War', *Journal of Contemporary History*, 5 (3) (1970).

[28]*First Interim Report of Welsh Advisory Council* (1943), pp. 111ff and materials in James Griffiths papers, C1/2.

[29]Report by Morrison, 23 January 1946, 'The Administration of Wales and Monmouthshire', CP (46) 21, CAB 129/6 (Public Record Office, London) (hereafter PRO CAB); correspondence between Morrison and Griffiths, October 1946, Griffiths papers, C/2/6–11.

[30]Note by Griffiths on 'The Area Boards covering Wales under the Electricity Bill', 17 December 1946, CP (46), 462, PRO CAB 129/15.

[31]Cabinet conclusions 15 October 1948, PRO CAB/13; E. L. Gibson, 'A Study of the Council for Wales and Monmouthshire' (University of Wales, University College of Wales, Aberystwyth MA thesis, 1968).

nationalism of the Attlee years. Within the Labour party machinery itself, the Welsh Council of Labour was formed in early 1947. The South Wales Regional Council, directed by Cliff Prothero, was merged with eight scattered bodies existing in north Wales and loosely linked with the trade unions there. The central party gave the sum of £100 to facilitate the merger. It was a belated reluctant recognition by the Transport House *apparatchiki* that Wales was a nation rather than a mere region. A battle waged since Arthur Henderson's administrative reforms within the party in 1917–18 was finally won.[32]

The pressure for a secretary of state went on, despite the government's overall hostility. D. R. Grenfell and W. H. Mainwaring attempted to pressurize Attlee over a Welsh secretaryship but, predictably, got nowhere.[33] When Labour finally did commit itself to setting up a secretary of state for Wales in its 1959 party manifesto, even Aneurin Bevan endorsed it, although admittedly with great reluctance. However weak the Welsh Office was when it was launched in 1964, its tenure by the veteran James Griffiths inaugurated a new chapter in Labour's attitude towards the Welsh national identity. From 1966 onwards, spurred on by the revival of Plaid Cymru, the Welsh Labour party was even committed to some form of Welsh devolution, although the eventual outcome, the humiliating defeat of the scheme in Wales in March 1979, suggests that backing for it amongst Labour party supporters was skin-deep only. At least, though, it can be argued that some viable notion of Welshness was handed on during the post-war phase after 1945. Unlike the exclusive, sectarian nationalism of the kind favoured by the embryo Plaid Cymru in the 1920s, it was a kind of vision that could appeal to the English-speaking majority in Wales as well. As the formation of the Welsh TUC in 1973 suggests, it was relevant to a modern, industrial, technologically-advanced society, and not merely to rural uplands nostalgic for the sentimental idylls of *Cymru Fydd* and an arcadian past. It was, too, an idea of Welshness that could be related to a contemporary secular world instead of the chapel-bred, 'eisteddfodic' introverted nationalism that flourished before the First World War.[34] Such a sentiment could generate a kind

[32]Meeting of Organization Sub-committee of National Executive Committee (NEC), 15 January 1947, Labour party NEC Minutes, 22 January 1947 (Labour party archives, Walworth Road). Cf. R. I. McKibbin, *The Evolution of the Labour Party, 1910–1924* (Oxford, 1976), 167–70.

[33]Correspondence between Attlee and Welsh Labour MPs, 1946, Morgan Phillips papers, GS/9/2 (Labour party archives). Also see Attlee to Goronwy Roberts, 31 July 1946, ibid, GS/9. (I am indebted to Henry Pelling for the latter reference.)

[34]For some intemperate and ill-informed comments which argue the contrary view, see L. Abse, *Spectator*, 29 May 1981.

of nationhood that could provide a more unified society rather than one embittered, ingrown and riven by linguistic and sectarian divisions.

Here again, therefore, in the supreme area of national consciousness, the experience of the two post-war phases is in contrast. More generally, as has been seen, the differences are transcendent in political, social and industrial life. Aneurin Bevan was a prophet, a propagandist but not a philosopher. His diagnosis is inflammatory, rhetorical and often exaggerated. The cautious academic would hedge his verdicts with all manner of qualifications. Nevertheless, in broad outline the views expounded in *Why not Trust the Tories?* are unquestionably correct. As far as Bevan's own nation is concerned, the Wales of post-1945 is part of a living, usable past; the Wales that emerged after 1918 is a world well lost.[35]

1984

[35]I am grateful to Peter Stead for some helpful comments on this article.

10

Welsh Nationalism:
The Historical Background

'For Wales – see England.' This notorious directive in the early editions of the *Encyclopaedia Britannica* crystallizes all the emotion, the humiliation, and the patronizing indifference which helped to launch the national movement in modern Wales. Welsh nationalism forms a major theme in the evolution of British democracy over the past hundred years, but one which observers of the political scene have long chosen to ignore. However, after the astonishingly high polls of Plaid Cymru at Carmarthen, Rhondda West, and Caerphilly between July 1966 and July 1968, the Celts have come in from the fringe. Welsh nationalism has become academically respectable and commercially marketable. Political commentators have been compelled to reassess the basic diversity of the United Kingdom. Whether Plaid Cymru's recent progress really heralds the dawn of a new era of separatism in Wales still seems most unlikely; in the 1970 general election all thirty-six Plaid candidates were defeated, twenty-five of them losing their deposits. What, however, is beyond dispute is that these by-election results are only the latest manifestation of a national struggle that goes back for at least a century. It is a struggle that in the ultimate sense may still seem incomplete. There may be a Welsh nation, but there is not yet a Welsh state. Yet it may be that the limits of the achievement reflect accurately the limits of the aspiration. What surely requires equal emphasis is the way in which public attitudes have been transformed. No longer can Wales be relegated to the status of a mere region. Still less can it be dismissed, as it was by Bishop Basil Jones of St David's in 1886, as just a 'geographical expression'.[1] Welsh

---

[1] J. Vyrnwy Morgan (ed.), *Welsh Political and Educational Leaders in the Nineteenth Century* (London, 1908), 153–4; W. Watkin Davies, *Lloyd George 1863–1914* (London, 1939), 116.

nationalism, like other nationalisms during the past hundred years, has been something of a rearguard action, but not an unsuccessful one. Its outcome has been that, by the mid twentieth century, the nationhood of Wales is no longer seriously in dispute.

A sense of nationality is as old as the Welsh themselves. Bede commented on the sense of difference between the Welsh and the Anglo-Saxons at the time of the coming of Augustine in 597. It provided a constant theme for Welsh poetry and prose throughout the middle ages. Giraldus Cambrensis, in his efforts to ward off the encroachment of Norman centralization upon the Welsh church in the twelfth century, gave it eloquent expression, and there were echoes of it at times in the Glyndŵr rising in the early fifteenth century. But this awareness of an identity of language, culture, and race lacked any institutional focus. The fragmentation of Welsh political development was completed when the last independent princedoms were subjugated by Edward I in 1283. Under Henry VIII the process of conquest was carried further when Wales was wholly assimilated into the English governmental system. Only a few distinct Welsh institutions survived the Union, such as the Courts of Great Sessions (eventually abolished in 1830 amid much local protest). Subsequently, the natural leaders of Welsh society, the landed gentry, adopted the speech and customs of their English counterparts, as they had been doing for two centuries past, and became increasingly isolated from the great mass of a peasant population.[2] Wales continued to be widely regarded as a remote tribal backwater, economically backward, obstinately adhering to its antique language in the face of 'the march of intellect'. It was a picture that even a sympathetic observer like George Borrow in his *Wild Wales*, first published in 1862, was substantially to confirm.

For formal purposes, the United Kingdom down to the mid nineteenth century was regarded as being composed of three countries rather than of four. Ireland's distinct nationhood was a familiar and unhappy feature of British government over the centuries. Its Act of Union dated only from 1800, while generations of Irish leaders from Grattan to de Valera served as eloquent witnesses to the reality of 'the Irish question'. Scotland's national identity was equally clear. It had been united with England as recently as 1707, while distinct Scottish institutions survived the Union, in the Kirk, the legal system, and a separate structure of education. The Scottish aristocracy were themselves the most articulate exponents of Scottish nationality, while in the early nineteenth century the romantic writings of Sir Walter

---

[2] See Glyn Roberts, 'Wales and England: antipathy and sympathy, 1282–1485', *Welsh History Review*, 1 (4) (1963), 375–96.

Scott gave Scottish history and culture a new popular currency. The public attitude to Wales, however, was totally different. There was simply no 'Welsh question', any more than there was a 'Cornish question'. Despite the vigorous survival of the Welsh language, despite the perpetuation of a distinct Welsh society based mainly on small farms of the peasant type, the official mind still saw Wales and England as inseparable. Or, in the reiterated litany of Westminster politicians, 'there was no such place as Wales'.

Then in the early nineteenth century the position was dramatically transformed. Two new forces arose which were to permeate every aspect of Welsh society and to form the basis for a new national movement. The first was the growth of industry.[3] From the expansion of the ironworks around Merthyr and Dowlais in the 1780s, perched on the rim of the coalfield, the advance of industrialization throughout Monmouth, Glamorgan, and eastern Carmarthenshire was spectacular and inexorable. By 1914 the Welsh coalfield was one of the mainsprings of the British economy. More important, for the first time Wales contained major towns – Cardiff, Newport, Swansea, Merthyr Tydfil – with ethnically diverse populations. The effect of industrialization has sometimes been seen as a retarding factor upon Welsh national consciousness by emphasizing anew the economic ties binding Wales and England. The towns of Wales have been held to be 'outposts of English influence'. This is surely most misleading. The growth of industry meant that there was now a vital safety-valve in Wales itself for the surplus population of the impoverished countryside. Unlike the peasants of rural Ireland, the farmers and labourers of rural Wales found opportunity in their own land – often in collieries owned and managed by Welshmen – instead of having to migrate to England or the United States. Furthermore, it was in the towns of Wales, the industrial conurbations of the south, expanding market towns of the north and west, that many of the main instruments of late nineteenth-century national feeling were to thrive – the immense array of new chapels, the Welsh-language newspaper press, local eisteddfodau and choral festivals. In many ways it was the growth of towns, and the new bourgeoisie that they produced, that made modern Welsh nationalism possible. If there was one outstanding cradle of the Welsh national revival, it can be found not in the agrarian hinterland, so beloved of many apostles of 'peasant culture', but amid the blast furnaces and winding-shafts of the working-class metropolis of Merthyr Tydfil.[4]

[3] For a challenging treatment of this theme, see Brinley Thomas, 'Wales and the Atlantic economy', *Scottish Journal of Political Economy*, November 1959.

[4] See Glanmor Williams (ed.), *Merthyr Politics: The Making of a Working-Class Tradition* (Cardiff, 1966).

The other great change that revolutionized Welsh life in the early nineteenth century was the explosive rise of Nonconformity.[5] Sparked off by the Methodist revival, finding a new buoyancy in the 'older dissent' of the Baptists and the Independents, Nonconformity gave a new unity to Wales. Migrants from the countryside brought the institutions and the ethos of the chapels with them into the new industrial communities, and shaped their character in fundamental respects. The exact nature and extent of the growth of Nonconformity is still hard to determine. There was always a large floating population of 'adherents' only loosely attached to the chapels. The expansion of Nonconformity did not proceed at an even pace. The excitement of revivals such as those of 1836 or 1859 tended to be followed by periods of quiescence. Even so, the religious census of 1851 showed beyond question that almost four-fifths of those attending places of worship in Wales were to be found in the chapels, rather than in the Anglican church. It could indeed be claimed, as Gladstone was to assert in 1891, that 'the nonconformists of Wales are the people of Wales'.[6]

At first the attitudes of the pioneers of Welsh Nonconformity were hard to distinguish from those English dissenters. They revered the same puritan heroes. They adhered to the same intellectual and theological tradition. They battled against the same obstacles – the Test Acts, the tithe and burial laws, the church rates – as did Non-conformists everywhere. Even so, it was becoming transparently clear by the end of the 1840s that Welsh Nonconformity was developing a culture and a momentum of its own. Publicists like Samuel Roberts of Llanbrynmair ('S.R.') or William Rees (Gwilym Hiraethog), the editor of the journal, *Yr Amserau* (The Times), irrespective of denomination, were addressing a specifically Welsh audience and in its own tongue. One episode which had an exceptionally powerful effect in underlining the Welshness of Welsh Nonconformity was the report of the commissioners inquiring into the state of Welsh education in 1847. This document became known in popular tradition as 'the treachery of the blue books' (*Brad y Llyfrau Gleision*).[7] While including some well-merited criticisms of the feeble state of Welsh schools, the report also made some free-ranging and uncomprehending attacks upon the religious, social, and moral habits of the Welsh. Nonconformists like

[5]An excellent discussion of aspects of the growth of Nonconformity is to be found in E. T. Davies, *Religion in the Industrial Revolution in South Wales* (Cardiff, 1965), chaps. 1 and 2. For the rural areas, see David Williams, *The Rebecca Riots* (Cardiff, 1955), chap. 5.

[6]Hansard, 20 February 1891, 1265.

[7]*Reports of the Commissioners of Inquiry into the State of Education in Wales* (Accounts and Papers, 1847, vol. 27).

'S.R.' were in the van of the uproar that followed. Welsh nationalism and Welsh Nonconformity were now united in a crusade for national self-respect. In some ways this was a paradoxical development, since it had been Anglicans like Lady Llanover and 'literary clergy' like Walter Davies (Gwallter Mechain) who had hitherto supported much of the consciously national culture of early nineteenth-century Wales. They had pioneered literary and antiquarian studies and patronized the revival of local eisteddfodau.[8] But now these enthusiasts were being overtaken by political events. For the rest of the century, the Welsh national causes were to be promoted by a Nonconformist intelligentsia. The national movement in Wales was to be cradled in the chapels, while the Anglican church was to appear isolated from it, and even to be its enemy.

These changes gave a new direction to national emotion in Wales. Above all, they provided it with one overriding objective which was to dominate Welsh political life for three generations. This was the position of the established Church, the 'alien Church' so-called, the Church of an exclusive minority which symbolized more clearly than any other institution the domination of an anglicized squirearchy over Welsh society, rural and urban.[9] Welsh radicals were united by this disestablishment issue, whereas Scottish radicals were to be divided by it. Thus it was that in the years down to 1914 Welsh national feeling tended to focus not on Home Rule but on the disestablishment of *Eglwys Loegr*, the Church of England in Wales. With all its limitations, Welsh disestablishment became the ultimate symbol of national equality, and the pressures for social and religious equality which were bound up with it.

What gave momentum to the Welsh national movement was political power.[10] A disparate series of radical movements in the 1850s and 1860s, expressed in bodies like the Liberation Society, was transformed by the franchise reforms of 1867 and 1884. In the words of the radical Henry Richard, they marked the death of 'feudalism' in Wales.[11] For now the Welsh *pays réel*, the Welsh-speaking Nonconformist majority, could participate directly in political life. The route to national liberation seemed to lie through the ballot box. The effect was a political revolution which, more than in any other part of the United

[8]See Bedwyr Lewis Jones, *Yr Hen Bersoniaid Llengar* (Penarth, 1963).

[9]For the disestablishment campaign, see P. M. H. Bell, *Disestablishment in Ireland and Wales* (London, 1969); Kenneth O. Morgan, *Freedom and Sacrilege?* (Penarth, 1966), (published in this volume, 142–76).

[10]For a more extended discussion of what follows, see Kenneth O. Morgan, *Wales in British Politics, 1868–1922*, 2nd edn. (Cardiff, 1971).

[11]Cf. Henry Richard, *Letters and Essays on Wales* (London, 1884), 119–24.

Kingdom, transformed the entire pattern of authority in Wales, and which also made Wales for the first time a significant element in the wider British scene. During these exciting years, Wales, no less than Ireland, developed a political style of its own, reflecting in the main the radical Nonconformist wing of the Liberal party which came to dominate its politics between 1868 and 1922. By the later 1880s, the first generation of Liberal leaders, whiggish Gladstonians like Sir George Osborne Morgan, cosmopolitan Manchester-school radicals like Henry Richard, even home-grown heroes like 'S.R.', were becoming out-of-date. They were yielding to a generation of new leaders, much younger, more militant, and more intensely nationalist. These new men reflect the enormous social and intellectual diversity of the Welsh national movement at the summit of its influence. Tom Ellis, the son of a Merioneth tenant farmer, was a product both of Aberystwyth college and of Jowett's Oxford, with its new urge towards social reconstruction; he was to become Liberal chief whip in 1894.[12] Llewelyn Williams, another farmer's son, was also an Oxford graduate, a passionate Nonconformist who revered the cultural inheritance of sixteenth-century Welsh recusant Catholicism. D. A. Thomas, later Lord Rhondda, was an industrial tycoon whose career showed that the mercantile bourgeoisie of the Cardiff chamber of commerce could be as nationally conscious as could tenant farmers from the rural heartland.[13] And, most striking of all, there was the young radical Cricieth solicitor, David Lloyd George, democrat and dictator in equal measure, who for thirty years was to serve as perhaps the decisive catalyst for change in Welsh political life.

The programme that these ambitious young middle-class nationalists advocated – and partially achieved – tells much of the character of the Welsh national movement in its *fin-de-siècle* phase. Their supreme objective was Welsh disestablishment. Its attainment, of course, depended wholly upon the return of a Liberal government and on the exact degree of priority that Gladstone and other Liberal leaders would give it. However, disestablishment and disendowment bills were introduced in 1894, 1895, 1909, and 1912–14. The last was on the point of becoming law when war broke out, and it finally took effect in 1920. The other Welsh demands made more chequered progress. The 'tithe war' of the mid-1880s resulted in tithe being paid by the owner rather than by the occupier of land, but the financial burden on the tenant was the same. The contentious issue of Church

[12]See T. I. Ellis, *Cofiant Thomas Edward Ellis*, 2 vols. (Liverpool, 1944–8).

[13]See Viscountess Rhondda (ed.), *D. A. Thomas, Viscount Rhondda* (London, 1921); Kenneth O. Morgan, 'D. A. Thomas: the industrialist as politician', *Glamorgan Historian* (Barry, 1966), 33–51 (published in this volume, 419–34).

schools set off a mighty explosion after 1902, when Lloyd George marshalled the Welsh county councils in a united protest against the enforcement of Balfour's Education Act. But this also ultimately petered out, though a Welsh department of the Board of Education was created in 1907. Nor did Nonconformist pressure for temperance reform have much to show either – apart from the notable achievement of the Welsh Sunday Closing Act of 1881, a striking recognition that Wales could or should receive distinct legislative treatment separate from England. Perhaps the most profound change of all in these years lay elsewhere. The Local Government Act of 1888 brought about a social revolution, when Nonconformist-dominated county councils were elected to supplant those Tory and Whig squires who had ruled the countryside for centuries past as justices of the peace.[14] The Welsh gentry, whose 'rise' many historians have lovingly chronicled, were now visibly in decline, if not in decay. The Nonconformist majority was no longer in any real sense a second-class citizenry. It was the heir of the new Wales it had largely created.

The Welsh national movement, however, had other goals beyond merely furthering the ambitions and interests of the Nonconformists. To a limited extent it had economic objectives. While Wales produced nothing comparable to the bitter conflict of the land war in Ireland, there was profound tension in the Welsh countryside, paralysed by depression from the late 1870s. The Welsh Land Commission which Gladstone appointed in 1893 provided a useful forum for the grievances of tenant farmers. Some writers, indeed, have compared the Welsh national movement with the populist agrarian radicalism of the western and southern United States at the same period.[15] Like the populists, the Welsh radicals seemed able to unite farm and factory in a common cause, to appeal alike to the aspirations of industrial workers and of tenant farmers. However, the analogy between the Welsh movement and populism is not a complete one. For the land question was only an intermittent theme of national protest in Wales, and social rather than economic in emphasis. In practice, conditions on the land showed some improvement after the turn of the century, especially with impoverished farm labourers now able to migrate to the thriving coalfield of south Wales. In any event, governments, Liberal and

[14]For the effects in one county, see Kenneth O. Morgan, 'Cardiganshire politics; the Liberal ascendancy, 1885–1923', *Ceredigion*, 1967, 330–1 (published in this volume, 216–50). In this county, only three major landowners were returned in a council of forty-seven.

[15]This is suggested by Gwyn A. Williams in a brilliant and stimulating argument, 'Twf hanesyddol y syniad o genedl yng Nghymru', *Efrydiau Athronyddol*, XXIV (1961), 29. Cf. Norman Pollack, *The Populist Response to Industrial America* (Cambridge, Mass., 1962).

Unionist alike, were shrewd enough to see that Welsh nationalism, unlike Irish, in its economic aspect could indeed 'be killed by kindness'.

A much more important facet of the Welsh national movement was the crusade for higher education. One academic leader, J. Viriamu Jones, the first principal of the University College at Cardiff, could even claim in 1896 that 'the history of Wales in the past twenty-five years has been the history of its educational progress'.[16] Certainly many Anglicans were much involved in the education movement – men like Dean H. T. Edwards of Bangor, for instance. But here again the leadership was provided mainly by Nonconformist Liberals. In this field, they had indeed much to show for their efforts. The Welsh Intermediate Education Act of 1889 was a great achievement. It created a distinct network of Welsh 'county schools' which were to form a unique source of social mobility in Wales in succeeding decades. To crown the edifice, there was the University of Wales, created deliberately on a federal basis in 1893 so that the separate colleges of Bangor, Cardiff, and Aberystwyth could be fused into a national whole. The University was in some respects the supreme achievement of nineteenth-century national consciousness, one in which the whole population shared. The subscriptions given by countless Welsh working men on the 'University Sunday' to finance the struggling Welsh colleges stirred the public imagination. As time went on, there were patriots who complained that a university created to serve the 'needs of Wales' was becoming excessively international in its outlook. Certainly, educational pioneers like Sir Hugh Owen had been much more concerned with creating a new class of technically-trained specialists on the European model than with promoting the cause of nationalism.[17] Even so, there was real justification for the heady rhetoric of the official historians of the University of Wales who saw 'the history of learning in Wales is the history of the nation itself'.[18] It is not surprising that one of the more effective national protests in Wales in the early 1960s was in response to a misguided attempt to defederate the University of Wales.[19]

By 1914 then, Welsh Liberals could look back on a remarkable half-century of progress. New institutions like the University had been

[16]J. Viriamu Jones, 'The University of Wales', *Wales*, January 1896, 6.

[17]Gwyn A. Williams, 'Hugh Owen', *Pioneers of Welsh Education* (Swansea, 1964), 72.

[18]W. Cadwaladr Davies and W. Lewis Jones, *The University of Wales* (London, 1905), xi.

[19]There is much illuminating evidence on this in Alwyn D. Rees (ed.), *The University of Wales Review* (Summer 1964).

created; old ones, like the Anglican Church, had been rejuvenated to harmonize with the new mood in Welsh life. But how far can all these movements be described as truly nationalist? Certainly they aroused the alarm of English Unionists. Wales seemed to be succumbing to the same contagion of separatism as was Ireland. Politicians like R. C. Raikes cited the classical tag, *Proximus ardet Ucalegon* – a kind of Virgilian domino theory – to imply that the immediate disintegration of the empire was close at hand.[20] Visits by an Irish Nationalist like Michael Davitt to the quarrying areas of north Wales in 1886 and 1898 added fuel to these fears.[21]

What can be said is that a Nonconformist campaign for social equality, directed at quite narrow and specific objectives, tended to merge with a far broader movement. The imaginative and periodical literature of the decades down to 1914 does show a new concern with the roots of national culture, drawing at times on the so-called 'unhistoric' nationalism of the Balkans and central Europe, especially that of Hungary.[22] In journals like *Young Wales*, *Wales*, and *Welsh Outlook*, patriots dilated upon the precise aspects of the Celtic genius displayed by Welsh businessmen, musicians, or rugby players, often with the fashionable Darwinian emphasis. Poets found new inspiration in Celtic folklore, as in T. Gwynn Jones's poem on 'The Passing of Arthur', while John Morris-Jones conversely extolled the virtues 'not of the Wales that is past but of the Wales that is to be' (*Nid Cymru fu ond Cymru fydd*). Owen M. Edwards, an Oxford history don who later resigned his fellowship to become inspector of schools in Wales, tried to kindle a new faith in the organic culture of his people through the journal *Cymru*; while the historian, John Edward Lloyd, brought to his academic studies of Welsh history before the Edwardian conquest the passionate glow of patriotic devotion. Some observers feared that the movement might become too dominated by political Nonconformity and insufficiently aware of the need to regenerate Welsh culture and especially the Welsh language. The young Llewelyn Williams, later a fiercely sectarian Liberal MP, warned in 1894 of the dangers of the Welsh members following the arid nationalism of Parnell's followers, rather than the idealism of Thomas Davis's 'Young Ireland'.[23] The formulation of the term 'Young Wales' (*Cymru Fydd*) was intended to

---

[20]Hansard, 7 March 1888, 487. The reference is to the burning of Troy described in Virgil's *Aeneid*, Book II, 311.

[21]T. E. Ellis to D. R. Daniel, 17 February 1886; H. W. Massingham to D. R. Daniel, 15 May 1898 (NLW, D. R. Daniel papers, 302, 2010).

[22]See Marian Henry Jones, 'Wales and Hungary', *Transactions of the Honourable Society of Cymmrodorion*, 1968, 1, 7–27.

[23]Llewelyn Williams to J. E. Lloyd, 21 September 1894 (Bangor University Library, Lloyd papers, MSS. 314, no. 592).

evoke this mood. This line was followed by several of the Welshmen prominent in Cymdeithas Dafydd ap Gwilym, a society of Welsh undergraduates at Oxford, for whom Mazzini was a major prophet.[24] A different strain was introduced by J. Arthur Price, a High Church Tory, who called for a new nationalist spirit that would restore to Welsh culture the richness it had lost since the Protestant Reformation and the arid puritanism that had followed it.[25]

Cultural nationalists like these helped to bring new standards of scholarship and new creative insights to literary and historical studies. Yet in politics theirs were lone voices. The conclusion is irresistible that the Welsh national movement before 1914 was nationalist only to a very limited degree. Its philosophy was static rather than dynamic. Whatever their reverence for Welsh culture, the philosophy of these men was moulded by the English world around them. It was the liberalism, not the nationalism of Mazzini that inspired them, while there were no Welsh prophets of the Celtic *Volksgeist*. This conclusion holds even for a sensitive patriot like Tom Ellis, the admirer of 'the work and memory of Joseph Mazzini',[26] but far more important, the close associate of Asquith, Sidney Webb, and the London 'Co-efficients', and the disciple of the imperialism of Cecil Rhodes. Lloyd George, who flirted with Home Rule in the mid-1890s as a means of by-passing Nonconformist clericalism, had little interest in the native culture, beyond the rhetoric of the pulpit; he soon turned to contemplate the wider horizons of a reviving British Liberalism after the disunity of the South African War (though he retained many of the instincts and assumptions of a Welsh radical all his life).[27] The Welsh Liberals might orate on Kossuth and Mazzini. They might cite some of Matthew Arnold's more meaningless passages on the spiritual qualities of the Celt. They might even write optimistically of the reclamation of 'Cambria Irridenta' on the Welsh Marches.[28] But it was Cobden and J. S. Mill, Gladstone and Joseph Chamberlain, who provided them with their framework for action. For the supreme object of these Welsh

[24]See T. I. Ellis, *Thomas Edward Ellis*, I, chap. 5, in which he describes the 'A.C.C.', a forerunner of the Dafydd ap Gwilym Society; also David Williams, *Thomas Francis Roberts* (Cardiff, 1961), 13–19.

[25]J. Arthur Price to T. E. Ellis, 21 October and 22 November 1891 (NLW, Ellis papers, 1698, 1699). Price wrote a good deal in this vein in the 1920s in journals like *Welsh Outlook* and *Y Ddraig Goch*.

[26]T. I. Ellis, *Thomas Edward Ellis*, II, 91, citing a visit by T. E. Ellis to Italy in the summer of 1889.

[27]This is argued in Kenneth O. Morgan, *David Lloyd George: Welsh Radical as World Statesman*, 2nd edn. (Cardiff, 1964).

[28]J. E. Lloyd, 'The geographical limits of Welsh Home Rule', *Welsh Outlook*, November 1921, 247–8, and letter by E. Lloyd Owen, ibid., January 1922, 28.

national leaders was essentially equality within the United Kingdom and an expanding empire, not severance from it. Welsh and Irish nationalism were fundamentally different. Despite all the efforts of ingenious journalists to invent one, there was simply no 'Parnell of Wales'.

As a result, the demand for Welsh Home Rule was a relatively minor feature of Welsh politics down to 1918. As Tom Ellis wrote in 1890, this movement was still only in 'the educational stage'.[29] Those who called for separation from England were a very small minority. Their most notable voice was the Revd Michael Daniel Jones, an Independent minister with a bitter hatred of all things English. He eventually played a major part in founding a settlement in the remote wastes of Patagonia as a means of preserving a Welsh cultural community free from English contamination.[30] This community, *Y Wladfa*, survives to the present day, but its impact on events in Wales itself has been negligible.

In Wales, campaigns for political separatism made little headway. Pressure for a secretary of state for Wales or a Welsh educational council had nothing to show. Only one openly nationalist movement did achieve significant strength. This was the *Cymru Fydd* League, originally a cultural movement which began, significantly enough, with Welsh exiles in London and Liverpool in the mid-1880s, and later spread to Wales itself. In 1895 it merged with the North Wales Liberal Federation and, if the south Wales Liberals also were to come in, it seemed highly probable that the entire corpus of Welsh Liberalism would be subsumed in a united nationalist movement. In fact, the South Wales Liberal Federation, under its belligerent president, D. A. Thomas, categorically refused to merge with this organization, led as it was by Lloyd George, already a highly controversial figure. At a fateful meeting of the SWLF at Newport in January 1896 Lloyd George had the rare experience of being howled down, and the *Cymru Fydd* movement at once collapsed.[31] Its disappearance seemed to confirm the new division between the more cosmopolitan coalfield (or rather the mercantile ports on its southern fringe) and the Welsh hinterland. Giraldus Cambrensis had lamented centuries before, 'If we were inseparable, we should be insuperable'. But disunity between north

---

[29]T. E. Ellis to W. J. Parry, 25 May 1890 (Bangor University Library, Coetmor MSS., 1B).

[30]See R. Bryn Williams, *Y Wladfa* (Cardiff, 1962); Alun Davies, 'Michael D. Jones a'r Wladfa', *Transactions of the Honourable Society of Cymmrodorion*, 1966, I, 73–87.

[31]*South Wales Daily News*, 17 January 1896. The background is sketched briefly in Kenneth O. Morgan, 'D. A. Thomas', art. cit., 41–4, and in William George, *Cymru Fydd* (Liverpool, 1945).

and south Wales, reinforced by clashes of personality, are too simple an
explanation for the collapse of *Cymru Fydd*. It had always been
something of a paper organization with few firm roots among rank-
and-file Liberals. It was in large measure a bid for power by Lloyd
George, an attempt to redirect and redefine Welsh Liberalism now that
the Liberal government had been swept from office, and now that his
own private negotiations with the Welsh clergy for a self-governing
Church within a self-governing Wales had led nowhere. It was always a
narrowly political movement, one which Tom Ellis, for instance,
viewed with the utmost suspicion. After *Cymru Fydd*, no prominent
Welsh Liberal talked the language of separatism. There was an abortive
revival after 1910 in a campaign led by E. T. John, an ironmaster from
Middlesbrough who later joined the Labour party, and the journalist,
Beriah Gwynfe Evans. They were supported after 1914 by *Welsh
Outlook*, a new periodical founded by Thomas Jones, soon to be lost to
view as deputy-secretary to the Cabinet. E. T. John even introduced a
Welsh Home Rule Bill before Parliament in 1914 but it aroused no
interest.[32] The reason was clear. The entire Welsh national movement
had been a campaign for national equality. It sought the recognition by
the English government and by English opinion of the needs and
national status of 'neglected Wales'. Why, then, should Welshmen wish
to return to the impotence of isolation?

In the years before 1914 many Welshmen sensed that the national
movement was beginning to lose its momentum. Many of the old
objectives had now been attained; even the historic goal of disestablishment seemed less beguiling than it had done thirty years earlier and
the issue was clearly losing its appeal. Instead, as the Cardiganshire
Liberal J. M. Howell complained, Welsh life was being poisoned by the
'self-seeking, hypocrisy and cant' of religious sectarianism.[33] The
chapels were beginning to lose their ascendancy, especially in the
coalfield. The relative decline of the Welsh language, the falling
population in the rural areas, the growing challenges to the ethic of
puritanism and sabbatarianism – all these were playing their part in
producing a subtle erosion of the religious pattern of Wales.
    Far mightier than these forces, however, was the rise of Labour. The
industrial working class had lent general support to the old nationally-
minded Liberalism down to the 1890s; in particular, the movement for
higher education had aroused wide enthusiasm among miners,

[32]Hansard, 11 March 1914, 1235–8.
[33]J. M. Howell to Thomas Jones, 11 April 1899 (NLW, Howell collection 27).
The writer, a Calvinistic Methodist, was writing in a mood of despondency
induced by attending Tom Ellis's funeral.

dockers, and quarrymen. But the years of class conflict that followed the coal stoppage of 1898, which threw 100,000 Welsh miners out of work for six months, produced a growing cleavage between capital and labour. By 1914 the old harmony between master and man was a thing of the past; it had perished at Taff Vale and Tonypandy. Often the employers against whom the workers were contending were Welsh Nonconformist Liberals – men like D. A. Thomas, once revered as a radical 'pro-Boer', but now the 'tsar' of the coalfield, the hated owner of the collieries of the Cambrian Combine at Tonypandy. Inexorably, then, the rise of Labour and of socialist movements like the Independent Labour Party meant a loosening of the ties that bound men like Thomas with their employees in a united national movement. In some ways, certainly, the Labour movement here retained its Welsh features. Keir Hardie, who sat for Merthyr Tydfil from 1900 until his death in 1915, admired the national characteristics of the Welsh – 'Like all Celts, they are socialists by instinct.'[34] He was an advocate of Welsh Home Rule. The growth of syndicalism in south Wales before 1914 was in some sense a separatist movement, a romantic gesture in favour of industrial devolution in place of the bureaucracy and centralization of capitalist industry. The syndicalists were often led by intensely Welsh leaders like Noah Ablett, perhaps the one original thinker that Wales has produced in the past hundred years, a Marxist whose social conscience had been awakened by the religious revival of 1904.[35] Industrial militancy was not confined to the younger English immigrants of the eastern valleys, but flourished also in the profoundly Welsh atmosphere of the anthracite valleys of west Wales, where the radical journal *Llais Llafur* (Voice of Labour) circulated. Causes like Jim Connolly's 'Citizen Army', which sought to unite revolutionary socialism with Irish nationalism, caught the imagination of many Welsh workers.[36] Even so, the ultimate effect of the Labour advance was to make the old radical programme – Welsh disestablishment, educational, land, and temperance reform – seem almost ludicrously irrelevant to a proletariat passionately involved with industrial causes such as the crusade for a living wage. More and more by 1914, Welsh miners were making common cause with their English and Scottish comrades in the trade union Triple Alliance, and with the aspirations of the working class all over the world. The appeal of class was undermining the call of community.

The First World War really marks the end of the first great national movement in Wales. Ever since, Welsh nationalism has shown a more

[34]*Labour Leader*, 9 July 1898.
[35]W. W. Craik, *The Central Labour College* (London, 1964), 64ff.
[36]See Arthur Horner, *Incorrigible Rebel* (London, 1960), 25–6.

fragmentary character. The war brought the effective demise of the Liberal party, and the steady erosion of the Nonconformist chapels which gave it life. The disestablishment of the church was indeed accomplished in 1920 amid monumental indifference. The domination of the bishops over Welsh society was now a thing of the past, as was the ascendancy of the squire, now reeling under the financial hammer-blows of the post-war years. The national movement of the years before 1914, girding against the 'unholy Trinity' of the bishop, the brewer, and the squire, seemed to reflect a temporary phase of Welsh society, one that a half-century of democratic achievement and social change had whittled away. Instead, Wales after 1918 was dominated by the Labour party, thriving amid the economic depression of the inter-war period. Labour was now unmistakably committed to the 'internationalist' position. Socialists like Aneurin Bevan could argue that Welsh nationalism was a bourgeois illusion, irrelevant to the struggles of the working class.[37] Not until after 1945, when Labour MPs were returned for the first time for rural, Welsh-speaking counties like Merioneth, Anglesey, and Cardiganshire,[38] and when some of them were involved in the 'parliament for Wales' campaign of the early 1950s, did any significant section of the Welsh Labour party move towards a quasi-nationalist position. It was a trend that resulted in the Labour government setting up the Welsh secretaryship of state in 1964.

Nationalism in Wales after 1918, then, became increasingly attenuated. However, as is often the case, it became more shrill in emphasis. While some young Welshmen turned after the horrors of total war to a complete rejection of the national ideals of their fathers before 1914, others were stimulated by a new and heightened nationalism. They noted that the 'little five-foot-five nations' on whose behalf Lloyd George said the war had been fought, conspicuously did not include Wales – certainly not at Versailles. In consequence, there was formed Plaid Cymru (the Welsh Nationalist party), in 1925.[39]

[37]See Bevan's speech in the House, Hansard, 17 October 1944, 2311–14. Cf. James Griffiths, *Pages from Memory* (London, 1969), 162.

[38]An unofficial 'Labour' candidate, General Sir Owen Thomas, who later turned Independent, sat for Anglesey, 1918–23; the Labour party, through R. T. Jones, briefly held Caernarfonshire, 1922–3.

[39]There is as yet no adequate scholarly treatment of the origins of Plaid Cymru: A. Butt-Philip is providing one. For a brief outline, see *The Historical Basis of Welsh Nationalism* (Cardiff, 1950), chap. 5 (written by Gwynfor Evans). There is a lucid exposition of the main bases of Plaid Cymru's programme by Gwynfor Evans and Ioan Bowen Rees in *Celtic Nationalism* (London, 1968), 252–96. Two helpful surveys of Welsh national movements in recent times are Sir Frederick Rees, *The Problem of Wales and Other Essays* (Cardiff, 1963), chap. 1; and Glanmor Williams, 'The idea of nationality in Wales', *Cambridge Journal*, (1953), 145–58.

Some of its members were veterans of the old Nonconformist nationalism of pre-1914. In particular, the pacifist instincts of many Welsh Nonconformists were newly aroused by Plaid Cymru's opposition to 'English' rearmament before (and after) 1939. Other members of Plaid Cymru however, like its first president, Saunders Lewis, a converted Roman Catholic, regarded their party as a complete reaction against the bogus nationalism of the days of *Cymru Fydd*, and, indeed, several Catholic intellectuals occupied key positions in the party. Plaid Cymru's programme was totally different from that advocated by any significant group before 1914. It demanded dominion status for Wales, an almost complete severance from the political and economic fabric of England. But, significantly enough, the party made little headway for forty years. Even as late as the general election of 1966, its twenty-two candidates polled disappointingly, saving only two deposits. Certainly, by-elections between 1966 and 1968 saw an astonishing nationalist resurgence, crowned by the return of Gwynfor Evans for Carmarthen, Plaid Cymru's first MP. But these results were in large measure a protest against the economic policies of the Labour government rather than a positive vote for separatism. In the 1970 election, in which it contested every seat in Wales for the first time, Plaid Cymru significantly failed to maintain the momentum shown in by-elections. Its candidates polled remarkably well in a few areas; in seven constituencies, they gained over 20 per cent of the votes, and in three of these, over 30 per cent. However, no seats were captured, Gwynfor Evans being conclusively defeated in Carmarthen, and the results suggested that even a rejuvenated Plaid Cymru might not succeed in holding back the ebbing tide of political nationalism in Wales.[40]

A much more significant feature of Welsh nationalism since 1918 has been the cultural campaign. In practice, this has meant quite specifically a struggle to protect and encourage the Welsh language. Curiously enough, the language issue played only a minor part in the national movement before 1914. Its revival since then has been in part a symbol of retreat from the nationalist politics of twentieth-century Europe, with its totalitarian implications (although it might be noted that the urge to preserve the language was the overriding motive that brought many scholars, writers, and intellectuals into Plaid Cymru in

For a more general treatment, see Reginald Coupland, *Welsh and Scottish Nationalism* (London, 1954), chaps. VIII and X.

[40]In the 1970 general election, the thirty-six Plaid Cymru candidates polled 175,016 votes (11.5 per cent of the total in Wales). Deposits were saved in eleven seats.

the 1920s).[41] As a rule, Welsh Liberals before 1914 had been concerned that Nonconformists should be christened, married, and buried, should vote and be elected, as Nonconformists. They were much less preoccupied by which language they used for the purpose. The achievement by the Welsh Language Society of the 1880s of the teaching of Welsh in elementary schools aroused relatively slight interest, while the new county schools did little to foster the language. It has even been argued that these anglicized schools helped to kill the Welsh-language popular culture of the Victorian period. The first lecturer in Welsh appointed to a Welsh university college, John Morris Jones at Bangor, was required to teach his subject through the medium of English.[42] The comparative lack of interest among Welsh radicals before 1914 in the language issue is something of a puzzle. Perhaps they simply assumed that acquiring a sound knowledge of English would pose no threat to their native tongue. They were relatively oblivious to the consequences of the massive migration of English people into urban and industrial Wales in numbers too large to be assimilated in the two decades before 1914. However, the years since the First World War have resulted in Welsh visibly losing ground. In the 1961 census, not much more than a fifth of the adult population was recorded as being able to speak the language, and in many parts of industrial Wales and along the English border it has almost entirely died out. Efforts to perpetuate it have accordingly become more and more intense. Much has been achieved. Organizations like *Urdd Gobaith Cymru*, a youth movement initiated by Owen M. Edwards's son, have had considerable influence. Welsh is now generally taught in primary schools, and there are all-Welsh primary and secondary schools. Radio and television programmes provide considerable coverage in Welsh, especially on the BBC, while the Hughes-Parry Committee in 1965 successfully called for Welsh to have 'equal validity' with English in government business and in the courts. Even so, the Welsh-language world has been steadily contracting and becoming more ingrown. The Welsh-language newspapers and period-icals are but shadows of their former selves, while the eisteddfod, on its cultural side, has lost much of its impact. In these depressing circumstances, it is not surprising that the youthful partisans of the modern Welsh Language Society should become increasingly desperate and turn their energies to 'direct action' against physical symbols of Anglicization. In this sense, cultural nationalism in Wales

---

[41]For example Professor G. J. Williams or the novelist, Kate Roberts.

[42]J. E. Caerwyn Williams, 'Sir John Morris-Jones: y cefndir a'r cyfnod cynnar. Rhan II', *Transactions of the Honourable Society of Cymmrodorion*, 1966, I, 56ff. At first this hardly mattered, as Morris-Jones had no students to teach. He acquired pupils (and a hyphen) later in life.

seems basically conservative, a crusade not only against the dominance of English but even against the twentieth century itself, and the inexorable encroachments of an alien, Anglo-Saxon world.

The Welsh national movement, in all its many aspects, is an important part of the making of modern Britain. It has clearly owed a little to nationalisms elsewhere, to Hungarian nationalism and most of all to Irish. But in large measure it has been dictated by circumstances peculiar to the British political and cultural scene, and to Wales itself. Its cultural side remains very much alive; indeed, in some sense, Welsh nationalism, like Flemish, is now essentially linguistic. Welsh nationalists have returned to Fichte in seeing language as the essential test of nationality, and in regarding a nation deprived of its language as being bereft of its humanity also.[43] Political nationalism, however, presents a less clear picture. Even Plaid Cymru pleads basically for the British government to remedy its neglect of Wales and to rejuvenate its economy, rather than for Wales to be left separatist and alone. In this respect, it is indeed the heir to the pre-1914 nationalism that it has rejected. The national movement of these earlier years still dominates much of the life of Wales today. It gave Wales a disestablished church and a disestablished gentry; its own university, national library and museum; its own distinct system of higher education; its own legislation and departmental autonomy. Wales by 1914 had achieved recognition as a nation, not as a mere duplicate of Kent or Yorkshire. Ultimately, though, Welsh nationalism was a crusade against indifference, and here, even after the careers of Lloyd George and Aneurin Bevan, this battle is still far from won. Perhaps it never will be. Perhaps the Welsh will be left, like the Serbs after Kossovo, to sing of their defeats. But as long as the sense of struggle endures, so long will Welsh nationality remain vigorous and alive. So long will Welsh nationalism have its ultimate vindication.

1971

---

[43] J. G. Fichte, 'Addresses to the German nation', *Sämtliche Werke*, VII (Berlin, 1846), 259ff. For a valuable conspectus of literary and cultural movements in nineteenth- and twentieth-century Wales, see H. Idris Bell's translation of Thomas Parry, *History of Welsh Literature* (Oxford, 1955). Wyn Griffith, *The Welsh* (Cardiff, new edn., 1964) is a useful introduction.

II

Places

Cardiganshire Politics:
The Liberal Ascendancy, 1885–1923

'There is a spirit of vassalage among the tillers of the soil, begotten by the tyranny of the past. The shadows of the oppression and evictions of 1868 have not lifted from among the people.'[1] This evidence, given before the Welsh Land commissioners at Aberaeron in April 1894, evokes the spirit of the modern phase of Cardiganshire politics – the politics of nostalgia. It found a fitting spokesman in 1894 – John Morgan Howell, ironmonger, of Portland House, Aberaeron; alderman on the new county council (and soon to be its chairman for 1895–6); prominent Calvinistic Methodist and Oddfellow; and, above all, active Liberal politician. Howell and many others like him were the residuary legatees of this political nostalgia that characterized their native county. They had come to form a new ruling élite, progressive in political ideals, yet essentially drawing on the memories of the *gorthrymedigion*, the martyrs of Liberalism evicted for having voted according to their convictions at the great election of 1868. For men like Howell, indeed (he was born in 1855), the events of 1868 constituted the dominant impression of their formative years. It was memories such as these, kept vivid by the oral tradition of the countryside, which served to make Cardiganshire subsequently the most impregnable of all Liberal strongholds in Wales. In 1909, in one of those truisms that only he could make arresting, Lloyd George declared that if all constituencies were like Cardiganshire, there would not be a single Tory surviving on the Opposition benches in the House of Commons.[2]

---

[1]*Royal Commission on Land in Wales and Monmouthshire, Evidence*, Vol. III (*P.P.*, 1895, XL), qu. 47,489 (J. M. Howell).
[2]*Cambrian News*, 31 December 1909.

At first sight, Cardiganshire politics in this period appear uneventful, featureless, as placid and unchanging as the beautiful Cardiganshire countryside. The county produced no major political figure, none with the charismatic appeal of an Ellis, a Lloyd George, or a Keir Hardie. Its life went on undisturbed by any profound clash of ideologies, or by conflict between capital and labour. Its parliamentary representation seemed to follow an inexorable and predetermined course. The country seat went Liberal at the election of 1880, and the Liberals easily maintained their ascendancy for the next three generations, until final defeat at the hands of Labour in 1966. And yet this appearance of outward calm is utterly deceptive. On two crucial occasions, first in the years 1885–6, and again, a generation later, in 1921–3, Cardiganshire was the scene of intensely bitter political controversy, a battleground for the Liberal conscience and the Liberal soul. During these periods of crisis, the politics of the county were marked not by consensus but by conflict. The causes for this are profound, and extend far into the social fabric of the county. For there are important reasons why these conflicts should have taken place at those precise occasions, and why Cardiganshire, rather than other counties in rural Wales, should have been the arena in which they were fought out to the end.

These two periods of crisis, indeed, provide the focal points of the political history of Cardiganshire in its modern, democratic phase. They implied separately, and in conjunction, an upheaval even more momentous and sweeping than the 'cracking of the ice'[3] that was heralded by the election of 1868 and the evictions that followed. These two crises, in 1885–6 and 1921–3, have, indeed, many points of resemblance. Both were essentially civil wars between rival Liberal factions. Both were dominated by an overpowering national personality – Gladstone in 1885, Lloyd George in 1921. Both essentially posed the conflict between prescription and patronage on the one hand and local independence on the other. Taken together, these two crises lend to Cardiganshire politics in the period a unity all its own. In 1885–6, the character of the Liberal ascendancy in the county was firmly established. In 1921–3, its values were redefined. As a result of that later reappraisal, Liberalism in Cardiganshire gained a new vitality which enabled it to prosper for almost half a century more. At a time when, in rural and industrial areas alike, observers detected irrefutable evidence of 'the strange death of Liberal Wales', these crises, and the new energy that was released by them, were to give the

---

[3] Ieuan Gwynedd Jones, 'Cardiganshire politics in the mid-nineteenth century', *Ceredigion*, V (1964), 15.

Liberal ascendancy in Cardiganshire a life and a momentum of its own.

In the early 1880s, the political structure of Cardiganshire was being transformed by a dynamism and an excitement that had not been known for centuries. The immediate cause of this lay in the effects of the process of franchise reform. The Reform Act of 1867, concerned mainly with extending household suffrage in the boroughs, had had only a relatively modest effect on a rural county such as Cardiganshire.[4] However, Gladstone's new Reform Act in 1884, together with the Redistribution Act passed a year later, introduced a radically different kind of politics into the county. The 1884 Reform Act added between five and six thousand new voters to the register by extending household suffrage to the counties. There is not much doubt as to who these new voters were: tenant farmers, some more substantial agricultural labourers, householders in small towns such as Tregaron, Aberaeron, Tal-y-bont, or Borth, which had not been part of the old Cardigan Boroughs constituency. Equally crucial was the Redistribution Act of 1885. It abolished the Boroughs seat and merged the four contributory boroughs, Aberystwyth, Cardigan, Lampeter, and Adpar, with over 2,500 voters, into the county division.[5] Thus the more static politics of the county were injected with the more complex tensions and the more radical passions of urban voters. The joint effect of these two measures was that Cardiganshire's registered electorate rose from 5,026 in 1883 to 12,308 by 1886, an increase of almost 150 per cent.[6]

Even in such a socially static county as Cardiganshire had been, this revolution in the location of political power could not fail to have a dramatic effect. It meant, first of all, a much larger electorate, more geographically dispersed and harder to control. Indeed, there had been complaints by Morgan Lloyd (Liberal, Beaumaris District), while the Reform Bill was before the Commons, that the Cardiganshire elector-

---

[4] The main effect of the 1867 Act on the county franchise was the enfranchisement of the £12 occupation voter, this being based on the rateable value.

[5] 'Return showing County and County Borough Constituencies and Constituencies as constituted by the "Redistribution of Seats Act, 1885"' (P.P., 1884-5, LXII, 271). Cardiganshire had sent two representatives to Westminster, one for the County and one for the Boroughs, since the Act of Union in 1536. The Boroughs constituency formerly consisted of five contributory boroughs, Aberystwyth, Cardigan, Lampeter, Adpar, and Tregaron, but Tregaron was disfranchised in 1730. Adpar had been disfranchised also in 1742, but its privilege was restored by the Reform Act of 1832.

[6] Electoral statistics given in P.P., 1883, LIV, 369; and in P.P., 1888, LXXIX, 919. In 1888, the ownership voters numbered 2,516 and the occupation voters 9,786.

ate was now too large, and that, with only one member representing 73,000 people, the county was the victim of unfair discrimination.[7] The average for Welsh county seats as a whole, indeed, was one member per 58,000 people.[8] The electorate was not only larger, it was also far more secure. It was protected, not only by the secret ballot (which had been on the statute book since 1872) but by the Corrupt Practices Act of 1883. In many ways, this was a measure of even greater significance, with its drastic limits upon campaign expenditure and more effective curbs upon bribery.[9] As a result, Cardiganshire passed quite suddenly from the politics of deference to the politics of democracy, with consequences that were to determine almost every facet of its future development. Even in 1868, Cardiganshire politics had been essentially deferential in tone. Evan Matthew Richards, the victorious Liberal candidate in the county seat, had owed his return in large measure to the patronage of the Pryses of Gogerddan.[10] In the Boroughs, the member returned here was Sir Thomas Lloyd of Bronwydd, a Whig landowner, who owned over 2,000 acres in the county and over 5,700 in neighbouring counties.[11] Such inroads as democracy made in 1868 seemed to be transient ones. Cardiganshire politics were still, in the vivid phrases of Henry Richard, 'feudal' politics, a system in which 'clansmen struggled for their chieftains'.[12] In the next general election, that of 1874, the Tory squirearchy was powerful enough to exact revenge for the defeat of 1868. Pressure was widespread, and E. M. Richards met defeat at the hands of T. E. Lloyd of Coedmore, the last Conservative returned for the county. But the franchise reforms of 1884–5 totally transformed this pattern. Henceforth, the old style of politics, based on the subtle permeations of 'influence' and 'interest', and on implicit Burkeian assumptions about the organic unity of rural society, would be unrecognizable. Seldom would anything resembling them ever be seen again.

The political upheavals of Cardiganshire in the 1880s had their

[7]Parl. Deb., 3rd ser., CCXCIV, 1953ff.

[8]P.P., 1884–5, LXII, 271.

[9]For the best discussion of this question see Cornelius O'Leary, The Elimination of Corrupt Practices in British Elections, 1868–1911 (Oxford, 1962). On this, as on all aspects of the politics of the period, H. J. Hanham, Elections and Party Management (London, 1959) is an admirable guide. The same theme is discussed in Henry Pelling's valuable Social Geography of British Elections, 1895–1910 (London, 1967), 11–13, 429–30.

[10]For a magisterial discussion of this point see Ieuan Gwynedd Jones, op. cit., 31–6.

[11]John Bateman, The Great Landowners of Great Britain and Ireland (4th edn., 1883), s.n. 'Lloyd'.

[12]Henry Richard, Letters on the Social and Political Condition of Wales (London, 1867), 80.

roots, however, in forces more profound even than the legislative enactment of electoral reform, important though that was. In a far wider context, they reflected the economic depression that deeply affected every segment of society. In the early 1880s, Cardiganshire, like every other county in rural Wales, was in the grip of a prolonged recession. This was intensified by the collapse in the price of foodstuffs that afflicted the farming community from 1879 onwards as the effects of American and Russian competition came to be felt. But its roots really went far deeper. Indeed, in some respects, the impact of the agricultural depression on such a county as Cardiganshire can be exaggerated. Stock and dairy farmers in the Welsh hills suffered far less from foreign imports than did wheat-growing farmers in the south and east of England. In some ways, pastoral farmers even benefited from the depression, for instance in the fall in the price of animal feeding stuffs, which reduced production costs. The economic decline of Cardiganshire was far more deep-seated in origin than a mere downturn in the level of prices.[13]

The most obvious index of this decline was to be seen in mass emigration from the county; even in the 1880s rural depopulation was already the most fundamental of all the social and economic problems confronting Cardiganshire, and mid Wales in general. Between 1881 and 1891, the registration county of Cardiganshire showed a fall in its population of 9.2 per cent. Only Montgomeryshire of all the Welsh counties showed a more sweeping decline in that decade.[14] Indeed, over a much longer time-span, the population of Cardiganshire fell persistently, from over 73,000 in 1871 to only 59,000 in 1911. This process continued, more gradually, after the First World War, with the result that in 1967 there were 20,000 fewer people living in this county than there had been a hundred years earlier. A steady stream of emigration more than nullified the spectacularly high rate of natural increase. The reasons for this are transparently clear. There was little enough to retain able-bodied young men in the county, especially at a time of economic boom elsewhere. Old hopes, kindled anew by the election of E. M. Richards, a Swansea industrialist, in 1868, that Cardiganshire's destiny lay in an expansion of its industry, had by the 1880s been proved to be hopelessly illusory. In the face of powerful competition elsewhere, and a sharp decline in the price of lead, those small communities set up to extract the lead and silver ores from the

[13]For a discussion of the agricultural depression see F. M. L. Thompson, *English Landed Society in the Nineteenth Century* (London, 1963), 308ff. The effect on Cardiganshire is discussed by many of the witnesses before the Welsh Land commissioners in April 1894 (*Land Commission, Evidence,* Vol. III, *P.P.,* 1895, XL, 338–752).

[14]*Census of England and Wales,* 1891: *General Report* (*P.P.,* 1893–4, CVI, 642).

hills of the southern and eastern fringes of the county were in rapid decay. Overcapitalization in company mining and inefficient management practices accelerated this decline. The 1881 census recorded only 1,824 leadminers, male and female, in the county; a decade later, the total had fallen to a mere 781, and communities such as Ysbyty Ystwyth were on the way to becoming ghost villages.[15] The election of a mining agent, Captain Brown, to represent Cwm-rheidol on the new county council in 1889 was only a faint echo of the glowing hopes of industrial prosperity that had so recently been entertained. Mining and manufacturing industry, therefore, figures only in a minor way in the occupational statistics recorded in the census returns of these years. A more revealing fact shown in the 1881 census was that 489 blacksmiths were resident in Cardiganshire – one being a woman (and another the present writer's great-grandfather). Cardiganshire in the 1880s may hardly have witnessed a halcyon period for mortal man, but, as Dr Richard Phillips has reminded the members of the Antiquarian Society, it was indeed 'the golden age of the horse'.[16]

Given the collapse of leadmining and other industry, the great mass of the population was, of course, engaged directly or indirectly in the pursuit of agriculture. Indeed, with almost 20 per cent of its adult population engaged directly on the land, as farmers or as labourers, Cardiganshire had in 1891 the fifth highest proportion in England and Wales.[17] Furthermore, it was agriculture of a notoriously precarious kind. The most numerous class in the social hierarchy consisted of those small tenant farmers whose holdings ranged in size between one and a hundred acres; Bateman recorded over 1,500 of them in 1883, farming 61,290 acres between them.[18] This precarious and depressed class was the subject of immense economic pressures in the 1880s. In part, this was the chain-reaction released by the agricultural depression, which led to the vacation of many holdings in the marginal uplands areas. More crucial, though, was the powerful counter-attraction of the expanding coalfield of south Wales, where the mines of Rhondda and elsewhere were approaching their peak in the production of sale-coal. This inspired a vast emigration from counties like Cardiganshire, especially of agricultural labourers of whom there was a large surplus. This movement, already considerable, was stimulated anew when the railway was extended to Llandysul in the south of the county, which made the Glamorgan coalfield far more accessible to

[15]*Census of England and Wales*, 1881 (*P.P.*, 1883, LXXX, 511); ibid., 1891 (*P.P.*, 1893–4, CVI, 303). The definitive study of the leadmining industry is W. J. Lewis, *Leadmining in Wales* (Cardiff, 1967); see particularly 170–201.

[16]Richard Phillips, 'Oes aur y ceffylau', *Ceredigion*, V (1965), 125ff.

[17]*Census*, 1891: *General Report* (*P.P.*, 1893–4, CVI, 677).

[18]Bateman, op. cit., 512.

migrants from the rural hinterland. The Welsh Land commissioners in 1894 were to be treated to a chorus of complaints about the effects of this constant migration of young men to the coalfield, and the consequences of this in a shortage of labour and other respects. Thomas Davies, building contractor of Aberaeron, combining inaccuracy with racial prejudice, complained that the flight of young Welshmen opened up Cardiganshire to 'the scum of England and Ireland', the 'Smiths and O'Briens'.[19] The results of this emigration can be traced precisely. While the population of Cardiganshire fell so alarmingly in the eighties, the 1891 census also recorded that in the Rhondda valleys the population now included nearly 6,000 men born in Cardiganshire.[20] Other young 'Cardis' had ventured still further afield; some were beginning to establish that stranglehold over the milk distributive and retail trade of London which has become such a familiar feature since.

On all sides, therefore, Cardiganshire manifested the grim symbols of a depressed area – the loss of young males, the high prevalence of idiocy and deaf-mutes in the county, the preponderance in its age-structure of the 45–65 and over-65 age groups, and a truly staggering surplus of unmarried females. The proportion of females to males was the highest in England and Wales recorded in six successive censuses: in 1891, there were 1,274 females for every 1,000 males. The census commissioners quaintly attributed this phenomenon to the difficulty that monoglot Welsh women from Cardiganshire found in gaining employment in domestic service outside the county.[21] It is clear, however, that this, like so much else in the demographic structure of Cardiganshire, really rested in the long-term pressures of economic decline. Even matrimony followed the census returns.

The influence of this decline on the social character of the county was profound. In particular, it had a shattering effect on the fortunes of the landed gentry, who had ruled over the countryside for three centuries and more. Of the three major families in the county, all of whom owned estates comprising more than 20,000 acres, the Lisburne family of Trawscoed, and Pryses of Gogerddan, and the Powells of Nanteos, all were in severe financial difficulties by the 1880s. All three were deep in debt, partly as a result of their own extravagance and mismanagement, but more from the effect of severe terms for mortgages and marriage annuities with which all three estates were encumbered. All were seriously affected, in addition, by the drastic loss of income that resulted from the closing down of the lead mines, the

[19]*Land Commission, Evidence,* Vol. III (*P.P.,* 1895, XL), qu. 47,822.
[20]E. D. Lewis, *The Rhondda Valleys* (London, 1959), 236. This figure refers to the Ystradyfodwg Sanitary District.
[21]*Census,* 1891: *General Report* (*P.P.,* 1893–4, CVI, 661).

failure of mineral leases, and the loss of royalties on production. Mr John Howells has shown, for instance, that the output of the lead mines on the Trawscoed estate fell in value from £32,339 in 1871 to only £3,249 in 1891.[22] These large estates also suffered from the fall in the level of rents that accompanied the agricultural depression after 1879, although rents on Welsh estates had generally been kept below an economic level for decades on grounds of custom.[23] Throughout the 1880s, landowners, great and small, decided to cut their losses and to sell off outlying holdings. They resolved to concentrate on the home demesne, even at the cost of breaking up the unity of their estate. Thus in 1887, at a time when the land market in England was stagnant, the *Estates Gazette* could report activity in land sales in Wales, thousands of holdings being sold, many of them to the sitting tenants for as much as thirty years' purchase.[24]

All these factors tended to depress the fortunes of the great land-owners of Cardiganshire. However, the statistics of the fortunes of an estate do not tell the whole story. They conceal the way in which purely personal or fortuitous factors could assist in undermining the position of landed families. Statistics, for instance, cannot make explicit the effect of extravagance at race-meetings of the fifth and sixth earls upon the Lisburne estate, or the preoccupation of Sir Pryse Pryse with the Gogerddan hunt at Bow Street, or with female companionship on the French Riviera.[25] The fortunes of Nanteos never really recovered from the eccentric career of George Edward Powell, who inherited the estate in 1878. Powell was bored by the minutiae of estate management, and turned instead for solace to the poet Swinburne, who visited him frequently. Edmund Gosse sentimentally describes Powell and Swinburne 'gazing over the bay of Cardigan to the tender west'. This is a geographical impossibility at Nanteos and, in any event, it appears that a more regular form of entertainment for the

[22]J. M. Howells, 'The Crosswood Estate and its Growth and Economic Development, 1547–1899' (University of Wales unpublished MA thesis, 1956). This thesis is in all respects an admirable survey of its subject.

[23]See H. A. Rhee, *The Rent of Agricultural Land in England and Wales, 1870–1943* (London, 1949). This bases its findings largely on Schedule A assessments of income tax (on income arising from the ownership of land). I have benefited from conversation with Mr David Howell, of the London School of Economics, whose researches into Welsh land problems in the nineteenth century will undoubtedly prove to be of fundamental importance.

[24]F. M. L. Thompson, op. cit., 318, citing *Estates Gazette*, 7 January 1888.

[25]For the Lisburnes, see J. M. Howells, op. cit. On the Pryses, see David Jenkins, 'The Pryse family of Gogerddan', *National Library of Wales Journal*, III (1953–4). There is an engaging and informative account in H. M. Vaughan, *The South Wales Squires* (London, 1926). Also helpful is Francis Jones, 'The old families of south-west Wales', *Ceredigion*, IV (1960), 1ff.

two old Oxford friends consisted of visits to dubious taverns in Aberystwyth, to enjoy the Rabelaisian conversation of the barmaids.[26] This factor alone would assist materially in explaining why the 'influence' of Nanteos, so powerful down to the 1865 election, was quite negligible in Cardiganshire politics from the 1880s onwards. Throughout the county, indeed, the landed gentry were in full retreat. The only signs of a more hopeful future on the land were to be found in the fertile country in the vale of Aeron and parts of southern Cardiganshire, with their more mixed farming and profitable by-products such as butter and cheese. It is not, perhaps, accidental that the most politically active landowner between 1880 and 1914 resided in this area. This was J. C. Harford, of Falcondale near Lampeter, who had married into the powerful Conservative family of Raikes and who was to contest the seat in 1895 and 1900.[27] For the rest, throughout the county, the gentry, whose 'rise' had been so absorbing a passion for Welsh and English historians for many years past, were firmly and irretrievably in decline.

The social pattern of Cardiganshire in the 1880s, however, was not entirely one of decline and depression. There was some real compensation in the rise of new urban centres; especially was this true of Aberystwyth, whose population rose steadily, if slowly, and almost doubled between 1871 and 1921, reaching over 11,000 by the latter date. Here was a more complex society, with a far more varied range of social relationships, and marked by a less respectful and instinctive attitude towards the traditional bases of authority. Ieuan Gwynedd Jones has brilliantly analysed the distinction between 'the closed society of the rural areas and the relatively open society of the towns'.[28] In the 1880s, the countryside was to become increasingly 'open' also, but it was the towns which largely provided the stimulus. In particular, Aberystwyth, and to a lesser extent Cardigan, was experiencing the rise of a powerful new force within its society, namely, the emergence of an urban and commercial middle class. Its spokesmen were men like Peter Jones, coal merchant, D. C. Roberts, timber merchant, C. M. Williams, draper (all from Aberystwyth), and J. M. Howell, the Aberaeron ironmonger to whom reference has already been made.[29]

Associated with them were influential Nonconformist ministers such

[26]Edmund Gosse, *Algernon Charles Swinburne* (London, 1917), 158. Also see H. M. Vaughan, op. cit., 82ff. There are some restricted, but unremarkable, letters from Swinburne in the Nanteos papers, National Library of Wales.

[27]J. C. Harford (1860–1934) married the second daughter of the Rt. Hon. H. C. Raikes in 1893. Bateman gives Harford's holdings as 5,782 acres, making him the fourth biggest landowner in the county.

[28]Ieuan Gwynedd Jones, op. cit., 22.

[29]All are included in *Who's Who in Wales*, 1920. Further details may be found in

as the Revd Job Miles and the Revd Thomas Levi. These were in a real sense new men, newly emancipated. Those fables of the rise of *y werin* in Wales are (or ought to be) largely the story of their ascent to social power, and that of many others like them. They were men with their own values and their own institutions – commercial institutions like the Aberystwyth Chamber of Trade, and, above all, their own religious institutions in the Nonconformist chapels. They were almost invariably Nonconformists: Peter Jones, Roberts, and Howell were Calvinistic Methodists, C. M. Williams an Independent. In 1905, the Welsh Church commissioners were to find that the Methodist and Independent denominations claimed over 24,000 members in Cardiganshire between them, as contrasted with a mere 9,169 for the Anglican Church.[30] These new men had also their own organs of communication. The most influential of these was the Aberystwyth *Cambrian News*, edited by the Lancastrian John Gibson, whose vitriolic attacks on privilege and vested interests chimed in with the mood of the urban bourgeoisie.[31] Finally, these were men with their own, self-generating channels of opportunity. No section of the community benefited more from the expansion of elementary education after the Forster Act of 1870, particularly from the non-denominational Board Schools; among the most notable of these was T. H. Kemp's famous school at Tal-y-bont, founded by an Englishman who learnt Welsh and left an indelible mark on a small community. These men were to benefit still further from the six 'county' schools set up under the Welsh Intermediate Education Act of 1889, a great charter of freedom for Welsh boys and girls, especially in rural areas with a traditionally low rate of upward mobility. These men felt, then, a sense of optimism and of dawning hope. In a county so largely paralysed by economic backwardness and shackled by the depressing legacy of the past, they felt that the future belonged to them.

Now the political consequences of these social changes were many and profound. They served to colour the pattern of Cardiganshire politics for the next fifty years. First, and perhaps most crucial, they meant the

the local press, especially the *Cambrian News* and the *Welsh Gazette*. For Howell, the J. M. Howell collection in NLW contains some political material.

[30]*Royal Commission on the Church and other Religious Bodies: Nonconformist Statistics* (*P.P.*, 1910, XIX, 9, 18). The Methodist membership is given as 13,014, and that of the Independents as 11,465.

[31]There is no good account of John Gibson and few letters from him have survived. There is much useful material in *Cambrian News: Jubilee Supplement 1880–1930*, 16 January 1931. I am also grateful for the loan of the papers of J. H. Richards, a *Cambrian News* journalist, from Mrs Haslett, Aberystwyth. The other major Liberal organ, *Welsh Gazette*, first appeared in 1899.

capitulation of the gentry as, in any real sense, political leaders. The impact of the economic depression, added to the political blows undergone since 1872, proved decisive in their effects on the influence of the landed families, great and small. The very concept of 'influence' in this period requires a more sensitive and many-sided gauge than that provided by the formal statistics of acreage and rental returns. It does not lend itself to precise quantitative assessment. The façade of influence survived, but its significance was essentially symbolic, a ritual deference, which masked a profound decline in real authority. Among the Liberals, the old Whig landlords ceased to play any major part in the councils of their traditional party after 1886. In that year, the Pryses of Gogerddan were rebuffed, along with David Davies of Llandinam, and not until a dramatic re-emergence by Sir Loveden Pryse in the 1921 by-election did the Pryses play more than a passive role in political affairs.[32] On the Conservative side, the effect on the party of 'church and squire' was even more profound. The misfortunes of Trawscoed and Nanteos left them largely leaderless. It was significant that in 1885 they had to turn for direction to such a minor and (before his marriage) impoverished squireen as Matthew Vaughan Davies. (The 'new Domesday Book' of 1873 showed that his Tan-y-bwlch estate of 3,674 acres yielded a mere £974 in rental.) Writing to Lord Salisbury immediately after the election, Vaughan Davies rightly drew the prime minister's attention to his own gallant labours:

> We have no Leader, being all 'esquires' with the exception of Lord Lisburne who will do nothing. He does not even subscribe to the Registration Fund, which at great trouble and expense I do my best to keep going.[33]

Salisbury was further reminded of the feeble condition of the Tory gentry in Cardiganshire in June 1888, when a vacancy occurred in the lord-lieutenancy of the county on the death of Colonel Pryse. The prime minister was in a quandary, and Viscount Emlyn, writing from Golden Grove in Carmarthenshire, gave him gloomy advice:

---

[32]In 1886, Colonel Pryse was rejected by the Liberal Association because of his opposition to Gladstone's Irish Home Rule programme (*Cambrian News*, 2 July 1886). The family supported David Davies in the election but continued to regard themselves as Liberal. Lewis Pugh-Pugh of Abermâd, the Whig who sat as Liberal member for the county from 1880 to 1885, turned Unionist and campaigned for Davies in 1886 and William Jones in 1892.

[33]M. Vaughan Davies to Lord Salisbury, 11 February 1886 (Christ Church Library, Oxford, Salisbury papers, class E; I am grateful to the 5th Marquess of Salisbury for permission to quote from these papers).

There are very few men of marked light and leading [*sic*] there. Lord Lisburne is the only peer. He is young, and, I am told, a nice fellow, but his father had one dreadful failing and I am not sure the son is entirely free from it. His appointment would be a great risk . . . Sir Pryse Pryse does not attend to public business at all, is abroad a great deal and gives himself no trouble about anything . . . Sir Marteine Lloyd I should say was quite out of the question.[34]

It was a significant commentary on the situation that Salisbury had to choose Herbert Davies-Evans of Highmead, near Llanybydder, whose estate lay almost entirely in Carmarthenshire. Emlyn had said that 'Davies-Evans has done more for the Conservative cause in Cardiganshire and Carmarthenshire than any one I know'.[35]

Cardiganshire, indeed, provides an interesting case study in the history of Conservatism in modern Wales, still largely unwritten. Even though the Conservative party could poll over 10,000 votes there in such a catastrophic year as 1906, its fortunes have been largely ignored by Welsh historians hitherto. It is interesting to speculate on the causes of this neglect. Perhaps it reflects the mountains of manuscript material left by Liberal politicians, many of whom were notably archivally-minded. Perhaps it is because so many professional historians in Wales, even the medievalists, tend to be men of the left. Wherever the truth may lie, there are some crucial themes here still awaiting examination – the tension between gentry and clergy over such issues as the tithe-rent-charge (the gentry wanting a quiet life, the clergy demanding their rights); the political consequences of the growing Anglicization of Wales; the implications for Welsh Conservatism of such phenomena as the growth of suburbia in Swansea, Newport and Cardiff. On all these questions research has scarcely begun. In the rural areas, Cardiganshire presents a contrast with almost every other county. Elsewhere, Conservatives could rally round a leader, a dominant family still strong enough to provide patronage and inspiration: the Cawdors in Carmarthenshire, the Powis family in Montgomeryshire, the Penrhyn family in Caernarfonshire, and, of course, the Wynns in so much of north and mid Wales. Elsewhere there was a focus of command. In Cardiganshire, there was none. Deprived of support from their natural patrons, the squires were in full and disorganized retreat. They left behind them a social and political vacuum which had the most profound of consequences.

[34]Viscount Emlyn to Lord Salisbury, 1 June 1888 (Salisbury papers, class E) 'Private'. Emlyn's father, the second earl of Cawdor, wrote to Salisbury in similar vein (31 May 1888).

[35]Viscount Emlyn to Lord Salisbury, 1 June 1888. Davies-Evans, vice-chairman of the Carmarthenshire Quarter Sessions in 1888, owned no land in Cardiganshire at all.

Secondly, the new urban middle class formed a powerful élite poised to fill that vacuum. These men, shopkeepers, tradesmen, solicitors, ministers, doctors, were anxious for position and status – for magistracies and for other local honours. They resented the fact that (in 1893) 105 magistrates in Cardiganshire were Conservatives, and only seventeen Liberals. They hastened to fill the gap left by the retreating gentry. So also did wealthier tenant farmers: it is worth noting that in 1880 over 20 per cent of the land in Cardiganshire was owned by occupying freeholders and that, in the first instance at least, they were able to raise the purchase capital.[36] These men found their voice in John Gibson of the *Cambrian News*. Truly a self-made man, Gibson's own dramatic Odyssey from being a poor paper-boy on the streets of Lancashire cotton towns, through journalism in Shrewsbury and Oswestry, to become editor of the *Cambrian News* in 1873 (and chief proprietor in 1880) symbolized the aspirations of the new middle class. In some ways, perhaps, Gibson was an unlikely champion for them. He was an Englishman. He was not a chapel-goer, having left the Baptists in his youth. He was outstandingly ignorant of the Welsh language; he once apologized to E. W. Evans of *Y Goleuad*: 'I know a little girl whose name is Mefanwy [*sic*], so I thought Goronwy must be also.'[37] Gibson was a prickly and intractable individual who found friendships hard to sustain. And yet, his fearless attacks on tradition and his committed radicalism captured the mood of the emergent class for whom he spoke. Along Cardigan Bay and in mid Wales no voice was more influential than that of John Gibson; Lloyd George continued to pay it heed even when he became chancellor of the Exchequer. By the beginning of 1904, the weekly circulation of his *Cambrian News* had risen to over 7,000.[38] Significantly also, the Conservative newspaper in Aberystwyth, the *Aberystwyth Observer*, which lasted until 1914, was far less squirearchical in tone than was usually the case with Tory journals in Wales. Its editor, John Morgan, was an ardent disciple of Joseph Chamberlain, and openly advocated Welsh disestablishment and disendowment.[39] In the face of the challenge of these aggressive and self-confident men, the gentry in large measure subsided without a fight.

[36]*Royal Commission on Land in Wales, Report (P.P.*, 1896, XXXIII, 277).

[37]John Gibson to E. W. Evans, 13 March 1907 (NLW, Frondirion MSS., 10,851B).

[38]John Gibson to Lord Rendel, 8 January 1904 (NLW Rendel MSS., 195). This followed a reduction of the journal's price to 1*d*.

[39]*Royal Commission on Land in Wales, Evidence*, Vol. III (*P.P.*, 1895, XL), qu. 9,493 (John Morgan's evidence). Morgan came under fire in 1895 for supporting Joseph Chamberlain's view that Unionists should concede disestablishment in Wales; see his letter to *The Times*, 1 March 1895, and *Liberal Magazine*, March

There is one further point that needs to be made about the effect of social and economic change upon Cardiganshire politics. Obvious though it may seem, it is often forgotten. It is that the very lack of economic growth in the county made the pattern established in the 1880s a permanent one. There was a classic picture of economic stagnation – steady emigration out of the county; the isolation of geography reinforced by the preponderance of a monoglot Welsh-speaking population (over 70 per cent in 1891 when the first language census was taken); an ageing population, over 90 per cent of whom were born in the county.[40] Finally, and of crucial importance, there was no major immigrant group to introduce a clash of values as occurred in the south Wales coalfield; the Irish population, for instance, totalled a mere 103 in 1881, and only ninety-eight a decade later.[41] In the absence of any fundamental disturbance in the social and economic structure, the pattern imposed by the changes of the 1880s upon the form of Cardiganshire politics was to endure, and to dominate the collective memory and experience of the county for generations to come.

The subsequent course of politics in Cardiganshire can be seen as being shaped in three distinct periods. The first was that of 1885–6, when the Liberal ascendancy was established and its character laid down. The member first returned for the newly-enlarged county division in the 1885 general election was David Davies of Llandinam, who had been member for the old Cardigan Boroughs seat from 1874. He triumphed over the Conservative, Vaughan Davies, by over 2,000 votes. David Davies, the railway king of Wales, pioneer of the Rhondda coal-miners and shortly of Barry Docks, seemed the prototype, almost the parody, of the self-made man.[42] He never ceased to glory in his origins in egotistic public speeches; Disraeli once sarcastically remarked in the Commons that 'it was good to hear the honourable member praising his creator'. Davies was an ineffective and incoherent public speaker, but his support in Cardiganshire was immense. Not least was this because he had been a generous patron of local causes,

1895. For an exposition of Morgan's views at more length, see *Aberystwyth Observer*, 18 October 1900, in which he stressed the need for more self-government in the Church and for a limited measure of disendowment.

[40]These figures are taken from the 1891 census. In the registration district, out of a population of 86,383 (deducting infants), 61,624 were Welsh monoglot, and a further 17,111 bilingual. In the age structure, 177 per 1,000 were in the 45–65 age group and 88 per 1,000 over 65. Both these figures were the highest in Wales.

[41]*Census of England and Wales*, 1881 and 1891.

[42]There is an excellent biography of David Davies in Ivor Thomas, *Top Sawyer* (London, 1938). See particularly chapters XX–XXII.

notably the college on the sea-front at Aberystwyth. But his main asset was not his money (which was largely invested outside the country) but his Methodism; with over 13,000 members, the Methodists were clearly the most numerous and influential denomination in the county. In the 1885 election Davies drew support from many sources, including the Pryses of Gogerddan, but the basis of his triumph lay indisputably in the chapels.

Closely linked with them was the newly-formed Liberal Association, whose activity in 1885 demonstrated in the clearest possible way how the style of politics had changed since 1868. Under the Liberal registration agent, H. C. Fryer, an Aberystwyth solicitor who was later to become the first clerk to the county council, the Association maintained a complex and sophisticated machinery to register voters and bring them to the poll on time.[43] Excursion trains were arranged to bring *émigré* voters back from Merthyr Tydfil to vote for 'David Davies, the working man's friend'[44] – an instance of one of the loopholes in the Corrupt Practices Act. Careful attention was paid to the special characteristics of individual areas; 'Lampeter, being a collegiate town, is not to be considered an ordinary place. Consequently some special efforts ought to be made to send a professional Welsh spouter there.'[45] The campaign was also notable for the varied apprehensions expressed by Liberal party workers at the alleged machinations of their opponents. Landlord pressure and intimidation were a general fear, particularly in the Tregaron area 'which has been a very conservative one owing to the influence of the late Powells of Nanteos had [*sic*] over their tenants'.[46] Among the other stratagems of which Conservatives were accused were tampering with the register and polling under-age or dead voters, while Tory interference with the mail was suspected by one angry partisan in Devil's Bridge.[47] More formidably, H. Tobit Evans (at that time a Liberal organizer in the Aberaeron region) reported: '*Very quiet* ladies are out with the Tories and are very busy.'[48] However, the electors were proof against all these blandishments or menaces, real or imaginary, and the Tory challenge

[43]This account of the 1885 election is based mainly on the *Cambrian News*, *Aberystwyth Observer* and *South Wales Daily News*. There is important material in NLW MS. 19,643B, the papers of H. C. Fryer, dealing with the 1885 election.

[44]NLW MS. 19,643B.

[45]D. J. Jones to H. C. Fryer, 'Wednesday noon' (NLW, ibid.).

[46]J. Davies to H. C. Fryer, 20 October 1885 (NLW, ibid.).

[47]E. Thomas to H. C. Fryer, 23 November 1885 (NLW, ibid.).

[48]H. Tobit Evans to H. C. Fryer, 18 November 1885 (NLW, ibid.). Another Liberal suspected, however, that Evans's efforts on behalf of David Davies were at best equivocal (NLW, Davies of Llandinam papers, 301: D. J. Jones to Edward Davies, 6 March 1886).

proved a weak one. Vaughan Davies had stood mainly in the hope of receiving a baronetcy from the Conservative patronage secretary, Akers-Douglas.[49] He had the backing of none of the leading county families in his campaign, his meetings were badly reported, and he was heavily defeated.

However, doubts soon began to multiply about the victor of the election. David Davies was increasingly coming under fire as an unsuitable representative for a self-styled radical constituency like Cardiganshire. Tom Ellis, writing to his friend D. R. Daniel, probably spoke for many nationally-minded young Welshmen when he condemned Davies for 'buying landed estates and sinking deeper into Whiggism after each transaction'.[50] The main charge against Davies, indeed, was that he was a Whig, a social conservative, for all his Methodism and his alleged sympathy with the working man. It was noted that when Henry Broadhurst had introduced the first of many leasehold enfranchisement bills in 1884, Davies failed to support it, or even to attend the debate.[51] In towns such as New Quay and Aberaeron, leasehold reform was even then a critical issue, though over eighty years more were to elapse before the grievances of leaseholders were redressed. Again, when Jesse Collings threw out the Conservative government on his 'three acres and a cow' amendment in February 1886, Davies actually voted against it. More and more in early 1886 he was under fire from constituents; on 11 March he felt constrained to intervene in debate in the Commons to explain that his reason for sitting on the Tory benches was the shortage of accommodation on the government side.[52] Davies was, in fact, a reversion to an older type of Liberal member, the self-made industrial patron who entered politics as a reflection of his industrial or commercial position, in the mould of Guest in the 1830s or Fothergill in the 1860s. In the new political context, dominated by political parties rather than by economic 'interests', Davies was simply out of date. Suspicions of his conservatism reached a climax when he joined six other Welsh Liberals in voting against the second reading of Gladstone's Irish Home Rule Bill in June 1886. Davies enlisted in the 'Loyal and Patriotic Union', a body dedicated to maintaining the integrity of the empire against

[49]Sir Stafford Northcote to M. Vaughan Davies, 23 April 1885 (copy); M. Vaughan Davies to A. Akers-Douglas, 14 October 1885 (copy); M. Vaughan Davies to Lord Salisbury, 11 February 1886 (Salisbury papers, class E).

[50]T. E. Ellis to D. R. Daniel, cited in T. I. Ellis, Cofiant Thomas Edward Ellis (Liverpool, 1944), Vol. I, 194.

[51]Parl. Deb., 3rd ser., CCLXXXVI, 212ff. Leaseholders (Facilities of Purchase of Fee Simple) Bill. Also Thomas Evans to Edward Davies, 28 June 1886 (NLW Davies of Llandinam papers, 302).

[52]Parl. Deb., 3rd ser., CCCIII, 516.

Celtic separatism, and, after some confusion, announced his intention of standing as a Liberal Unionist candidate at the next election.[53]

The result was a campaign fought with fierce intensity. Davies was backed by almost all the squires of both parties. He also received the support of several prominent Liberals, especially from his own Methodist church. One notable supporter was the eminent preacher and theologian, the Revd J. Cynddylan Jones; when he preached a sermon on the hymn 'Dewch hen ac ieuainc, dewch' during the campaign, he was attacked for introducing politics into the pulpit – as though that were a novelty.[54] But the great mass of Cardiganshire Liberals stayed faithful to Gladstone, whom they regarded as the symbol of their claim to civil and national equality. C. R. M. Talbot, another Liberal Unionist, writing to Sir Hussey Vivian, wrote scornfully of the 'infatuation' of the Welsh for the Grand Old Man;[55] by comparison, the issue of Irish Home Rule was for them a secondary issue. That formidable Gladstonian, John Gibson, came out strongly against David Davies in the *Cambrian News*.[56] So, too, did most of the Nonconformist ministry. After the poll, one of Davies's supporters, D. J. Jones of Lampeter, was to reflect:

> I never thought that the 'bugeiliaid Methodistiaid' would have been guilty of such base conduct. To see Williams the bugail at Lampeter, in conjunction with the Independent Ministers, on the same platform with Michael Davitt, was what I did not expect would ever take place.[57]

He complained that the people of Lampeter were 'Gladstonians to the core'.[58]

The Liberal candidate, W. Bowen Rowlands, a lawyer from Haverfordwest, was almost unknown in the county. His knowledge of Welsh was negligible. Far from being a Nonconformist, he was actually a high Anglican who was shortly to become a prominent Roman Catholic. He made little effort to conceal his sympathy for the Irish cause; Michael Davitt came to speak on his behalf at Lampeter and

[53]*Cambrian News*, 9 July 1886. Davies decided to stand when the Liberal Association turned down Col. Pryse.

[54]Ivor Thomas, op. cit., 249n. ('Come, young and old, come')

[55]C. R. M. Talbot to Sir H. Hussey Vivian, 18 June 1886 (NLW, Vivian papers). For a discussion of Welsh attitudes to Irish Home Rule, see Kenneth O. Morgan, *Wales in British Politics, 1868–1922* (Cardiff, 1963), 68–75.

[56]Although Gibson seems to have remained on cordial personal terms with the Davies family. See Gibson to Edward Davies, 1 and 7 May 1886 (NLW, Davies of Llandinam papers, 303).

[57]D. J. Jones to Edward Davies, 14 September 1886 (NLW, ibid.).

[58]D. J. Jones to Edward Davies, 'Sunday Noon' (NLW, ibid.).

Aberystwyth, having already established contact with Welsh electors among the quarrymen of Ffestiniog.[59] His opponent, David Davies, conducted a vigorous and resourceful campaign; electors were even brought up from Rhondda to vote for him (although Davies's son was later told that in fact they nearly all voted for Rowlands).[60] Even so, despite all the apparent disadvantages he faced, Bowen Rowlands scored a remarkable triumph over the money and the Methodism of David Davies by the margin of just nine votes. The *Aberystwyth Observer* rightly attributed the result to the influence of the Nonconformist ministers over their congregations.[61] For David Davies, disappearing from politics after serving in three Parliaments, the result was hard to bear, and harder to understand. Characteristically, he retaliated by withdrawing his support from the college at Aberystwyth. He deeply resented the failure of Principal Thomas Charles Edwards of Aberystwyth to vote for (or, indeed, against) him, while he had been the victim of hooligan behaviour in the town. 'I cannot therefore support a College in a place where I cannot go to see it.'[62]

Narrow though Bowen Rowlands's triumph had been, it was decisive. Patronage, even hyphenated patronage in the form of 'Liberal-Unionism', had been rejected, and Cardiganshire Liberalism stayed firmly committed to the values of the Nonconformist middle class. Liberal Unionism was henceforth redundant, as it was to be in Britain as a whole, once hopes of a reunion faded in 1887. This was emphatically confirmed at the next general election, in July 1892. Joseph Chamberlain ran a string of Nonconformist Unionist candidates in several Welsh constituencies, with the aim of appealing to local prejudice against Irish Catholicism. In Cardiganshire, his nominee was William Jones, a Birmingham draper who hailed from the county and a Welsh-speaking Methodist.[63] Jones campaigned vigorously against Irish aspirations. He spent the large sum of £1,258 8s. 0d., almost twice that of Rowlands; each of Jones's votes cost 7s. 8d., compared with 2s. 8d. for each of his opponent's. To prove his true Liberal antecedents, he produced a farmer evicted after the 1868

[59]*Cambrian News*, 9 July 1886; *Aberystwyth Observer*, 10 July 1886. For a sketch of Bowen Rowlands see T. R. Roberts, *Eminent Welshmen* (Cardiff, 1908).

[60]T. Davies to Edward Davies, 16 July 1886 (NLW, Davies of Llandinam papers, 302).

[61]*Aberystwyth Observer*, 17 July 1886.

[62]David Davies to Lewis Edwards, 19 October 1886 (T. I. Ellis, ed., *Letters of Thomas Charles Edwards* [Aberystwyth, 1953], 261–2).

[63]*Cambrian News*, 3 June 1892. Jones's nomination brought many protests from orthodox Conservatives: see letter by C. Marshall Griffith in *The Times*, 26 August 1892.

election, James Jones of Tŷllwyd, on his platforms.[64] Even so, Jones
lost overwhelmingly by almost 2,000 votes. Whatever his religion or his
origins, Jones's association with the gentry and the eternal memories
of past oppression ensured a heavy defeat.

The second period, from the mid-1880s down to the end of the First
World War, was a period of consolidation for the Liberal ascendancy.
The pattern of parliamentary representation in this period was
uneventful. Bowen Rowlands seldom visited his constituency, despite
his victories at the polls, and it was little surprise when he gave up his
seat for an impending county court judgeship in 1895. Some interest,
however, attaches to the nomination of his successor. The candidate
eventually selected by the Liberal Association was none other than
Matthew Vaughan Davies of Tan-y-bwlch, just south of Aberystwyth,
who, as has been seen, actually fought the seat as a Conservative in
1885.
    Vaughan Davies seemed in all respects to be an extraordinary
choice.[65] He had long been a pillar of Conservatism in the county, and
remained prominent in Unionist circles until his marriage to Mrs
Mary Jenkins, a wealthy widow from Swansea, in 1889.[66] She was a
pronounced Liberal (shortly to be elected president of the Aberystwyth Women's Liberal Association)[67] and the effect on Vaughan
Davies's political principles was marvellous to behold. His first public
emergence as a Liberal came in the 1892 election when he lent his
carriage to Bowen Rowlands's supporters.[68] Thereafter, it became
known that he was ambitious for the Liberal nomination. Chairman of
the Llanilar bench and master of foxhounds, Vaughan Davies seemed
the very archetype of those small backwoods squires who sustained the
tattered flag of Welsh Toryism in successive disasters – ill-educated
(though he claimed to be a Harrovian on the basis of having spent a
year in that eminent school), uncultured, ill-informed. His political
views were unsophisticated to the point of absurdity; he once

[64]*Aberystwyth Observer*, 16 June 1892. This meeting (at Aberystwyth) was
largely disrupted by organized Liberal heckling.
    [65]No papers of Vaughan Davies survive. For character sketches of him see Ivor
Thomas, op. cit., 231–2, 251–2, and Thomas Richards, *Atgofion Cardi*
(Aberystwyth, 1960), ch. 6.
    [66]Vaughan Davies attended the Welsh Union of Conservative Associations on
29 July 1887 (W. H. Meredyth to Lord Salisbury, 2 August 1887, Salisbury
papers, class E).
    [67]NLW MS. 19,658C (Minutes of Aberystwyth Women's Liberal Association).
Mrs Vaughan Davies was elected its first president in 1893. It put pressure on her
husband to vote for women's suffrage (which he did).
    [68]*Aberystwyth Observer*, 21 July 1892.

explained that he was in favour of women's suffrage, but for widows and spinsters only![69] He spoke no Welsh, and was an Anglican, the patron to a living in Llanychaearn. He appeared before the Welsh Land commissioners in 1894 as a spokesman for the local farmers, to uphold their demand for a Land Court to provide fair rents and security of tenure. Unfortunately, the sittings of the Commission brought to light his own malpractices as a landlord towards his own tenants, one of whom he had deceived over repairs to property on his holding. The Commission, when its report was eventually published in 1896, roundly censured him on these points.[70]

When it became known early in 1895 that Vaughan Davies was seeking to follow Bowen Rowlands as Liberal member, many local Liberals were up in arms. Gibson thundered away in the *Cambrian News*: 'Mr. Vaughan Davies has changed not only in his political opinions, but in his views as to honesty and dishonesty.' 'His candidature is being urged on the low and demoralising ground that money can be got out of him.'[71] He sourly wrote to D. A. Thomas that the one benefit to emerge from the inquiries of the Land Commission was that it had ruined Vaughan Davies's chances of the nomination.[72] J. M. Howell urged: 'We want a Welsh speaking man and better still a Welsh patriot. Vaughan Davies is an apostate, and flexile [sic], feeble and flabby.'[73]

Nevertheless, Vaughan Davies's chances were by no means hopeless. There was no overwhelmingly strong opponent. Llewelyn Williams, the apostle of *Cymru Fydd* nationalism, was backed by J. H. Davies of Cwrtmawr; but he was little known in the county (since he was born in Llansadwrn, a full twelve miles from the Cardiganshire border) and retired at an early stage.[74] Not until 1921, near the end of his life, did Williams intervene decisively in the politics of Cardiganshire. Another outside candidate was J. Wynford Philipps, another Pembrokeshire barrister, who had sat in the Commons as member for mid-Lanark from 1888 to 1894 (defeating Keir Hardie in the famous 1888 by-

[69]*Cambrian News*, 24 October 1885, reporting a speech at Zoar Chapel, Borth (though cf. note 67 above).

[70]*Land Commission, Report* (*P.P.*, 1896, XXXIII, 307). See Vaughan Davies's evidence before the Land commissioners, *Evidence*, Vol. III, qu. 47,068ff. and qu. 49,006ff.

[71]*Cambrian News*, 15 February, 24 May 1895.

[72]John Gibson to D. A. Thomas, 3 April 1894 (NLW, D. A. Thomas papers). This must be an error for 3 May as the Land Commission did not reach Cardiganshire until 23 April.

[73]J. M. Howell to J. H. Davies, 31 January 1895 (NLW, Cwrtmawr collection).

[74]J. H. Davies to J. M. Howell, 4 February 1895 (NLW, ibid.); *Cambrian News*, 5 April 1895.

election); but he proved a half-hearted campaigner.[75] Some favoured the youthful squire of Cwrtmawr, J. H. Davies, one of the very few Nonconformist squires in the county. Davies was later to demonstrate in full his prowess in electoral intrigue, but as a young man of barely twenty-four was still, at this stage, an unknown quantity.[76] More remarkable was the fact that many local Liberals actually backed Vaughan Davies, despite his Tory antecedents. Many farmers favoured a landowner who could at least express their own standpoint.[77] In the southern parts of the county, tenant farmers and occupying freeholders rebelled at having an outsider foisted on them by the 'shopocracy' of Aberystwyth – a sentiment that was to re-emerge in 1921 when the nomination came up again. Vaughan Davies in this sense had some positive virtues. He was unquestionably a local man, a nephew of Colonel Morris Davies of Penpompren, Tal-y-bont, and of the Revd Charles Davies of Ynys-hir, Glandyfi. His very roughness of manner, his dedication to the foxhounds, his crude, even profane, language (which led a heckler at Tal-y-bont, Dafydd Edwards of Felin-fach, to ask him whether he would favour an act of parliament to prevent swearing in public places)[77] – these qualities probably endeared him to those earthy electors who resented the social climbing of the Aberystwyth bourgeoisie. In the event, when the Liberal delegates met at Lampeter on 4 July, Wynford Philipps withdrew his name, amid allegations that Unionists had been attempting to sway district associations, and Vaughan Davies was nominated unopposed. The *Cambrian News* commented: 'The Old Liberal Gang, considered to be identified with Aberystwyth, has been annihilated.'[79] Vaughan Davies now had to win the seat – no easy task against the lively challenge of J. C. Harford, the young squire of Falcondale. In that year of disaster for Liberalism all over the country, Vaughan Davies's majority fell by over 800 votes, compared with 1892. Even so, his position was obviously beyond challenge. Although he was nearly fifty-five years of age, he was to retain his seat comfortably enough for over a quarter of a century more. Even when he departed from Parliament, it was Lloyd George rather than his Creator who was responsible. Vaughan Davies eventually died in 1935 at a vigorous and profane ninety-four. His house at Tan-y-bwlch, appropriately, was turned into a convalescent home.

[75]*Cambrian News*, 24 May 1895. Philipps was created Viscount St Davids in 1908.

[76]There is a useful biography of Davies in T. I. Ellis, *John Humphreys Davies* (Liverpool, 1963).

[77]J. M. Howell to J. H. Davies, 9 February 1895 (NLW, Cwrtmawr collection).

[78]Thomas Richards, *Atgofion Cardi*, 56.

[79]*Cambrian News*, 5, 12 July 1895.

With Vaughan Davies in the House, a silent back-bencher, interest in parliamentary politics in Cardiganshire was largely suppressed for a generation. At the next general election, the 'khaki election' held during the South African War in the autumn of 1900, Vaughan Davies had again a hard battle against Harford's eager challenge. Handicapped by weak organization and a partially deserved reputation for a 'pro-Boer' voting record in the House, Vaughan Davies's majority slumped to a mere 781, the worst Liberal performance against a Conservative in the entire period 1880–1966.[80] However, in later contests the Liberal majority soared upwards once again. In 1906, the *annus mirabilis* of the Liberal party, Vaughan Davies scored a record majority of 2,869 over C. Morgan-Richardson, a Cardigan solicitor who had once been a Liberal.[81] In the next general election, in January 1910, Vaughan Davies achieved a further record majority – 3,405 this time – and gained over 70 per cent of the poll. His opponent in this contest, dominated by Lloyd George's 'people's budget', was G. Fossett Roberts, an able young Aberystwyth man with connections with the brewing trade. The *Cambrian News* assailed 'the peer, the priest and the publican' with immense gusto. Towards Vaughan Davies, however, Gibson was unforgiving: 'We do not think the people will presume that Mr Vaughan Davies won any considerable portion of his majority by his individual attraction and influence . . . If anything, Mr. Vaughan Davies's personality would lose him votes.'[82] At the next contest, in December 1910, fought on the issue of the Parliament Bill, as again in the 'coupon election' of December 1918 after the war, Vaughan Davies was returned unopposed.

During these years Cardiganshire Liberalism fell into steady decay. A *Cambrian News* correspondent lamented that 'the most enervating torpor has seized the Liberal Party from Cardigan to Ynyslas. The enemy blustered about, but the Liberals only snoozed'.[83] Once-vigorous bodies such as the Aberystwyth Women's Association and the Junior Radical Club in that town fell into decline in the later 1890s, and their purpose seems to have become largely social (though

[80]*Aberystwyth Observer*, 18 October 1900.

[81]*Cambrian News*, 26 January 1906. Morgan-Richardson was treasurer of the Welsh Liberal Unionist Association. Rather surprisingly, he supported Joseph Chamberlain's proposals for tariff reform.

[82]*Cambrian News*, 4 February 1910. The *Welsh Gazette* announced that the contest was one of 'beer against bread'.

[83]*Cambrian News*, 19 October 1900; a comment by 'our Aberayron Correspondent' (? J. M. Howell).

teetotal).[84] Above all, the Cardiganshire Liberal Association, so vigorous a decade earlier, had by the later 1890s become something of a national scandal. At the annual meetings of 1897 and 1898, it was found that most of the local districts were totally moribund, registration had been ignored by the agent, and debts had accumulated. The total reserves in the Association's account stood at £11 2s. 6d. There was further criticism when Vaughan Davies, as treasurer, personally assumed responsibility for the Association's debts – a generous offer, but an exercise of patronage by the local member that many found hard to accept.[85] The vitality of the great days of *Cymru Fydd* seemed to have drained away; the Cardiganshire Liberal Association wasted away like the South Wales Liberal Federation to which it was nominally affiliated. Many Cardiganshire men indeed deplored the enervated condition of their party and their nation. J. M. Howell, writing in a mood of depression induced by attending Tom Ellis's funeral at Bala in April 1899, wrote: 'Wales is paltry, petty and mean; with its little sectisms [*sic*] like vermin eating into its vitals and consuming its sap and vigour. Our political and religious and even our commercial interests are blasted by self-seeking, hypocrisy and cant.'[86]

This decay of politics, indeed, reflected the mood of the time. The fierce social conflicts of the past were dying away and old issues losing their relevance. There were some echoes of the old bitterness in the early 1890s. There were violent incidents at tithe-distraint sales in Cardiganshire, notably at the 'Plevna' of Penllwyn.[87] Again, the scheme introduced for the county's intermediate education system, under the Act of 1889, provoked some predictable clerical opposition from St David's College, Lampeter. The county scheme, in fact, was voted down by the House of Lords, on a motion by Bishop Jayne of Chester, but the Rosebery government decided to ignore it.[88] Thereafter, the tensions of the past seemed increasingly out of date. Disestablishment of the Church seemed by the turn of the century to have lost its urgency; it now aroused the interest mainly of an older generation of ministers and publicists, weaned on the sectarian

[84]NLW MS. 19,658C; NLW MSS. 5425A and 5426C (Minute book of the Aberystwyth Junior Radical Club). Its chairman in 1888–9 was D. C. Roberts, and one of its leading members, J. Hugh Edwards, a student at the time and later to be MP for Mid-Glamorgan, 1910–22, and biographer of David Lloyd George.

[85]*South Wales Daily News*, 8 January 1897; 10, 13 June 1898.

[86]J. M. Howell to Thomas Jones, 11 April 1899 (NLW, Howell collection, 27).

[87]NLW MS. 15,321 (Reminiscences of the Revd Robert Lewis, tithe collector in southern Cardiganshire and northern Carmarthenshire).

[88]*Parl Deb.*, 4th ser., XVI, 1841ff. The protest concerned the failure to provide a 'county' school in the Lampeter area.

passions of 'S.R.', and Thomas Gee.[89] The land question also aroused far less controversy than before. The very publication of the Land Commission's report in 1896, even though it was not implemented, had a therapeutic effect on the countryside. In fact, the Cardiganshire landowners, so long the hapless victims of radical abuse, came comparatively well out of the Commission's findings. The charge of political intimidation or eviction was shown to be obsolete; the only instances brought up before the Commission related to 1869 and earlier. Neither was the charge of extorting excessive rental sustained by Liberal spokesmen in any very convincing way. Cardiganshire landlords, backed by their ever-vigilant lawyer, J. E. Vincent, were able to produce clear documentary evidence of abatements or reductions in rental during the past ten years.[90] In any event, rents had been kept below an economic level for decades on customary grounds, or simply to avert discontent, and not until the 1870s was any general effort made to raise them. The case of the tenant farmers, as advocated before the Commission, seemed somewhat less plausible when subjected to critical scrutiny. The panacea of a Land Court was less convincing when even a businessman like J. M. Howell could not offer any suggestion as to how it might arrive at a definition of a 'fair rent'.[91] Many of the complaints brought forward turned out to be unsubstantiated gossip.

There was undoubtedly poverty on the land, but the Commission seemed to suggest that many popular diagnoses were based on faulty premises. The real problem lay less in ownership than in capital. One aspect of the Cardiganshire land question vividly underlined in the report in 1896 was the financial hardship of many small freeholders, having to mortgage their holdings at crippling rates of interest.[92] They were hardly a promising model for the kind of peasant proprietorship that Tom Ellis and other Liberals wished to create. Meanwhile, the immediate crisis on the land passed away from the mid-1890s onwards; prices of farm products improved, and capital became more freely available. Indeed, the flight from the land was temporarily checked, and in the decade 1901–11 the agricultural population actually rose in rural Wales, the only increase recorded in the century from 1851 to 1951. Cardiganshire landlords took the opportunity to sell up more and more of their outlying holdings, while some estates

[89]For a more extended discussion of this point see Kenneth O. Morgan, *Freedom or Sacrilege?* (Penarth, 1966), 20ff. (published in this volume, 142–76).

[90]*Land Commission, Evidence,* Vol. III, *passim.* See also J. E. Vincent, *The Land Question in South Wales* (1897).

[91]*Land Commission, Evidence,* Vol. III, qu. 47,579–47,588.

[92]*Land Commission, Report,* 54–5.

(for instance Alltyrodyn and Llaethlliw) were sold up completely. Much of the old social division had disappeared, as the nomination of Vaughan Davies in 1895 indicated. A radical like J. M. Howell could support the claims of Herbert Davies-Evans, the lord-lieutenant, for a baronetcy or a peerage in the Jubilee honours list in 1897.[93] The gentry, responding to the changing structure of rural society, attempted to integrate themselves more intimately in the community – for example, by helping to found the Cardiganshire Antiquarian Society in 1909.[94] An interesting phenomenon was the rise of a small class of Nonconformist gentry, such as J. H. Davies, the young squire of Cwrtmawr. His election in 1919 as principal of the University College of Wales, in the face of the dominant influence of Lord Davies of Llandinam on behalf of Thomas Jones, was a remarkable testimony to the success of the Liberals of Cardiganshire in attaining social equality and social power.[95]

Even during this period of quiescence, however, the ascendancy of Liberalism was fully maintained. The most dramatic evidence of this was provided by the election of the first county council in January 1889.[96] The Liberals triumphed by thirty-seven to ten, while the squires were humiliated. Against only three major landowners to be returned (Lord Lisburne, Colonel Davies-Evans, and Major Lewes of Tŷ-glyn Aeron) there were thirteen tenant farmers, eleven small businessmen (ironmongers, drapers, and so on), and four Nonconformist ministers. Peter Jones, a Methodist coal merchant from Aberystwyth, was elected first chairman of the county council, over the head of Lord Lisburne. There were some impressive indications of the revolution that had taken place – Sir Marteine Lloyd of Bronwydd losing to an unknown farmer at Troed-yr-aur; Henry Bonsall of Cwm, Clarach, beaten by William Morgan, coal merchant (and grandfather of the first Labour member for Cardiganshire, Elystan Morgan) at Bow Street; T. J. Waddingham of Hafod meeting defeat at the hands of the local postmaster at Devil's Bridge. Despite some half-hearted protests by the *Cambrian News* that the elections ought to be 'non-political', the political implications of the new Liberal majority were made very plain from the outset. In its early years, the council passed

[93]J. M. Howell to Viscount Emlyn, 28 April 1897; Viscount Emlyn to Lord Salisbury, 6 June 1897 (Salisbury papers, class E). The appeal failed.

[94]See E. G. Bowen, 'From antiquarianism to archaeology, 1909–1959', *Ceredigion*, III (1959), especially 260–1.

[95]On this controversial election see. T. I. Ellis, *John Humphreys Davies*, 127–31, and Thomas Jones, *Welsh Broth* (London, 1951), 156–61. When the Thomas Jones papers in NLW are consulted by historians they will be seen to contain some intriguing information on this episode.

[96]*Cambrian News*, 25 January 1889. See also H. M. Vaughan, op. cit., 172.

overtly political resolutions, in favour of disestablishment of the Church, or affiliation to the *Cymru Fydd* league.[97] Its Liberal members caucused to secure aldermanships, coronerships, and chairmanships of committees for themselves: thus Morgan Evans of Oakford, Aber-aeron, was appointed chairman of the council for 1892–3.[98] The revolution in local government in 1889 illustrated vividly the extent of the advance of democracy in rural Cardiganshire. No longer would the gentry reign over the countryside from the eminence of the quarter sessions; like the Church, the justices of the peace were to be disestab-lished too. By comparison, the events of 1868, in reality though not in mythology, were, as Ieuan Gwynedd Jones has explained, merely 'the cracking of the ice'.[99] But 1889 was the year of the flood.

The third and final phase of Cardiganshire's Liberal years came with the period between the end of the First World War in 1918 and the general election of 1923. This was a period of redefinition and of renewed conflict. Cardiganshire, like other rural areas, was profoundly affected by the advent of total war. The war brought new prosperity to the farming community through such measures as the Corn Production Act of 1917.[100] Indeed, the population of Cardiganshire actually rose slightly, from 59,000 in 1911 to 61,000 in 1921, due largely to an increase in the Aberystwyth district.[101] More profoundly, the war brought about a crisis of values. Amid the pressures of world war, the old certainty attaching to Nonconformist Liberalism was severely shaken. Episodes such as the persecution of Dr Hermann Ethé, the eminent Aberystwyth linguist, on purely racialist grounds made some wonder what had happened to the old humane, civilized principles of the radical tradition.[102] Young Cardiganshire men back from the front, after surviving the slaughter in the trenches or Allenby's campaigns in Palestine, returned with a more detached and critical attitude towards the society from which they had sprung. The young Caradoc Evans of Rhydlewis, indeed, rebelled totally against the

[97]NLW, Cardiganshire County Council Minute Book, 1889–1902.

[98]NLW, Howell collection: Minute Book of Liberal caucus on Cardiganshire County Council, 1892–4.

[99]Ieuan Gwynedd Jones, op. cit., 15.

[100]Arthur Marwick, *The Deluge* (London, 1965), 248.

[101]*Census of England and Wales*, 1921: *Preliminary Report* (*P.P.*, 1921, XVI, 315–16). Aberystwyth municipal borough's population rose from 8,794 to 11,220 during these years.

[102]For this episode see David Williams, *Thomas Francis Roberts* (Cardiff, 1960), 44–5. Several prominent Aberystwyth academics took an anti-war position in journals such as *Y Wawr* and *Y Deyrnas*.

hypocrisy and cant he saw permeating 'my people'.[103] Old institutions and values were now under fire, and in this atmosphere the Liberal ascendancy could not hope to escape.

Even in the uncontested 'coupon' election of December 1918 there was criticism of Vaughan Davies for supporting the coalition government of Lloyd George, and accepting the 'coupon' in return. Professor T. A. Levi spoke out belligerently to this effect at the adoption meeting on 21 November. Vaughan Davies, indeed, had been listed as a recipient of the 'coupon' as early as 20 July.[104] The following year, the local Liberal Association, with J. M. Howell presiding, welcomed Asquith to Aberystwyth.[105] A new element was also heard for the first time, the Cardiganshire Labour party. Its most prominent spokesman was John Davies of Llangeitho, organizer of the Agricultural Labourers' Union, a man uprooted from his background who had been profoundly stirred by the dual impact of the 1898 coal stoppage in south Wales and the religious revival of 1904.[106] Labour did not fight the seat in 1918, although there was some scope for its energies in Aberystwyth in the candidature of Mrs Millicent Mackenzie for the newly-created University of Wales seat. The rise of Labour in rural Wales, in an election which saw the party gain striking success in Anglesey and Caernarfonshire, was a major portent for the future.

The growing mood of dissatisfaction with the time-worn Liberal ascendancy resulted in the startling outcome of the by-election of February 1921. Its prologue came in January when it was suddenly announced that Vaughan Davies had been given a peerage.[107] It was an announcement that greatly embarrassed Sir George Younger, the Coalition Unionist chief whip, since it complicated the agreement between the two main government parties about the lists of

[103]Evans's best-known works are *My People* (1915), *Capel Sion* (1917), and *My Neighbours* (1920). He eventually settled down in Aberystwyth.

[104]*Cambrian News*, 29 November 1918; F. E. Guest to David Lloyd George, 20 July 1918 (Beaverbrook Library, Lloyd George papers, F/21/2/56: I am indebted to Mr A. J. P. Taylor and the Beaverbrook Foundation for permission to work on these papers).

[105]H. H. Asquith to J. M. Howell, 14 November 1919 (NLW, Howell collection, 29). I have discussed Welsh politics at this period at greater length in 'Twilight of Welsh Liberalism: Lloyd George and the Wee Frees' (*Bulletin of the Board of Celtic Studies*, XXII, IV (1968), 389–405.

[106]*John Davies* (Gregynog Press, privately printed, n.d. [1937]). From 1920 to his death he was secretary of the South Wales WEA.

[107]*Cambrian News*, 7 January 1921. Vaughan Davies had latterly been chairman of the Welsh Parliamentary Party.

honours.[108] After an unsuccessful effort to obtain the title of Lord Ceredigion (his photograph actually appeared in the *Cambrian News* bearing this title), Vaughan Davies went to the Lords as Baron Ystwyth: 'he sought a county but had to be content with a river.' It soon became clear that this was a device by Lloyd George to leave the seat open for his private secretary, Captain Ernest Evans, an Aberystwyth man. However, the local Liberal Association seethed with resentment at being made a 'hand-maiden' for a government composed largely of Unionists and already tainted with the atrocities of the 'Black and Tans' in Ireland.[109] Efforts were made to get either J. M. Howell or D. C. Roberts to stand, but it transpired that they both supported Lloyd George. Finally, at an immensely stormy meeting of the Liberal Association at Lampeter on 25 January, in which charges of corruption were hurled by both sides and Vaughan Davies was shouted down, Evans was rejected. By 206 votes to 127 the Association chose instead the recorder of Cardiff, Llewelyn Williams, a veteran radical, now a leading Asquithian and a violent opponent of Lloyd George ever since the introduction of conscription in 1916.[110] Evans then announced, at a rival convention, his intention of standing as a coalition Liberal, and the succeeding contest between him and Llewelyn Williams, the 'Independent Liberal', ushered in a new crisis of conscience for Cardiganshire Liberals which caught the attention of the whole political world.

Llewelyn Williams and Ernest Evans were an interestingly matched pair. They were respectively symbols of first- and second-generation Liberalism in Wales. Williams, born in 1867, the son of a Carmarthenshire tenant farmer, was a survivor of the national emotions of the great years of *Cymru Fydd* in the 1880s and early 1890s.[111] In 1885, the year that Ernest Evans was born, Llewelyn Williams was assisting in founding the Dafydd ap Gwilym Society at Oxford, with important consequences for the Welsh national movement. Williams dealt mainly with the issues of the past, so far as he concentrated on issues at all: the 'betrayal' over the disendowment settlement in 1919, the killing of the Welsh Licensing Bill in 1920, the failure to grant Welsh Home Rule after the Speakers' Conference. His appeal was essentially nostalgic. Ernest Evans represented a younger generation. Born in 1885, he also

[108] Sir George Younger to Bonar Law, 2 January 1921, quoted in Lord Beaverbrook, *Decline and Fall of Lloyd George* (London, 1963), 241.

[109] J. Puleston Jones to J. M. Howell, 3 February 1921 (NLW, Howell collection, 27).

[110] *Welsh Gazette*, 27 January 1921; Kenneth O. Morgan, *Wales in British Politics*, 277, 295.

[111] There is, as yet, no satisfactory study of Llewelyn Williams. For instances of his earlier nationalist fervour see Kenneth O. Morgan, ibid., 70, 105–6, 110.

came from impeccable Liberal antecedents. Like Llewelyn Williams, he was a pupil at Llandovery College; he also was a barrister. A Calvinistic Methodist where Williams was an Independent, Evans was well known in Aberystwyth as son to the clerk of the county council; he was a member of Tabernacl church, the minister of which was the formidable Revd R. J. Rees. However, to one of Evans's age group, the national emotions of *Cymru Fydd*, of the *jeunesse dorée* of Tom Ellis, were remote from his experience.[112] Evans was a Liberal of the silver age. The difference between him and Llewelyn Williams lay not in their philosophies but in the generations they represented.

The by-election revealed immense latent tensions which had lain dormant for years. Llewelyn Williams was able to exploit residual tensions between the upland areas of the south and east, and the middle class of the seaside towns. Here, in the rural heartland, in places like Tregaron, Lampeter, Llandysul, Llangeitho, and Tal-y-bont, Williams found his main political base.[113] The religious composition of his support also reflected a wider sociological cleavage; behind him were the Independents and Baptists of the 'older dissent' and the Unitarians of the Teifi valley.[114] Other groups also flocked to the Independent Liberal banner. Several prominent University figures campaigned hard for Williams, notably the controversial professor of law, Thomas Arthur Levi, whose father had fought side by side with Bowen Rowlands in 1886.[115] Williams also gained the implicit, though not, as he had hoped, the explicit support of the Labour party. On the other extreme, the blue ribbon of the Pryses of Gogerddan was again paraded before the radical voters of Bow Street, Llandre, and Dol-y-bont for the first time since 1886. Indeed, Sir Lewes Loveden Pryse had himself threatened to come out as an 'Independent Liberal' candidate on the anti-waste programme popular in the period before the Geddes 'axe' descended.[116]

Ernest Evans's supporters were more concentrated. They lay essentially in the coastal towns – Cardigan, New Quay, Aberystwyth,

[112]For the past few years Ernest Evans had served as one of Lloyd George's private secretaries in the 'Garden Suburb'.
[113]For an analysis of local district associations, see *Welsh Gazette*, 20 January 1921. Also NLW, Herbert Lewis papers, Lewis's diary *sub* 18 February 1921.
[114]The account that follows is based largely on *Cambrian News, Welsh Gazette, South Wales News, Liverpool Daily Post, Manchester Guardian, The Times, Western Mail.* There is scattered MS. material in NLW in the Herbert Lewis papers and the J. M. Howell collection, and in the Lloyd George papers in the House of Lords Record Office.
[115]*Welsh Gazette*, 3, 10 February 1921.
[116]*Cambrian News*, 7 January 1921. Sir Lewes Pryse announced his withdrawal on 1 February (*Welsh Gazette*, 3 February 1921); thereafter he campaigned for Llewelyn Williams.

and Borth, places with middle classes, seaside landladies, and golf-courses, some of the last-named admittedly only of nine holes.[117] Evans had the vehement support of the *Cambrian News* (though the other local Liberal journal, the *Welsh Gazette*, was very hostile to him). Many leading members of his own Methodist denomination were behind Evans, notably the Revd R. J. Rees, though other prominent Methodists (for instance, Levi) came out for Williams. Finally, and crucially, Evans had the scarcely-veiled support of Cardiganshire Conservatives (estimated to number at least 7,000), and as the campaign went on it was clear that it was on these that he had increasingly to rely. For over three weeks, in glorious, spring-like weather, the campaign was fought out with tremendous bitterness. Families and churches were divided, and there were occasions of physical violence. Windows were broken, posters mutilated, car tyres slashed. Llewelyn Williams added to the general acrimony by personal abuse of Lloyd George, the 'tawdry rhetorician' of Downing Street.[118] Much debated was the issue of whether Lloyd George or Asquith was the true author of old age pensions back in 1908.[119] Ernest Evans had a rough handling in Llandysul; Puleston Jones, the blind preacher, was shouted down by Coalitionists in New Quay; while Sir John Simon, speaking for Williams, failed even to gain a hearing from the angry voters of Borth.[120] Many outside celebrities were brought in. The Asquithians, scenting perhaps their most hopeful contest since Asquith's own triumph at Paisley, brought in Simon, Runciman, Maclean, Wedgwood Benn, and Lady Violet Bonham-Carter, among others. Williams received messages of support from such varied sources as the veteran Dr Clifford, T. P. O'Connor, A. G. Gardiner, and Mrs Jones-Davies, sister of the late Tom Ellis. The last-named proclaimed that Cardiganshire, having yielded to military conscription, would never submit to political conscription by Lloyd George. The coalition Liberals relied mainly on Welsh political eminences such as Sir Herbert Lewis, Sir Edgar Jones, and J. Hugh Edwards. The outcome, indeed, was hard to predict. Few local observers shared the confidence of Lord Reading who forecast an easy victory for Evans.[121] The 1918 Representation of the People Act had increased the electorate from 13,000 to over 32,000 and there had been no contest

[117]Ibid., 11 February 1921.
[118]Kenneth O. Morgan, ibid., 295.
[119]The answer is both.
[120]*Cambrian News*, 18 February 1921; *Welsh Gazette*, 17 February 1921; *South Wales News*, February 1921 *passim*.
[121]Marquess of Reading to David Lloyd George, 13 February 1921 (Lloyd George papers, F/43/1/57).

in 1918 to test feeling.[122] Over 14,000 of the electors now were women, and a shrewd move by the coalition Liberals was to bring in Mrs Lloyd George. In a fortnight she delivered fifty-eight speeches, and her appeals of loyalty to Cardiganshire women to vote for *Dafydd yr Hwsmon* won much acclaim. Her husband, a connoisseur of such matters, said 'that Mrs. L.G. had displayed remarkable skill, and had said some very shrewd things, particularly on the drink question.'[123] In a record poll of over 78 per cent, Ernest Evans triumphed by 14,111 to 10,521, a majority of a little over 3,500 votes. It was clear, however, that the bulk of Liberal votes had gone to his opponent. Evans had got home with the aid of Tory votes and of over 250 Tory-owned motor cars. The night was lit up by flaming beacons on hilltops from Aberystwyth to Cardigan, the work of joyful Coalitionists. The overjoyed prime minister responded in more characteristic fashion: 'He warmly embraced Mrs. L.G. bestowing several hearty kisses upon her and telling her that she had won the election.' But for the Independents, in the words of a saddened *Welsh Gazette* columnist, Lilian Winstanley, a university lecturer, 'it was a victory for material power over spiritual power'.[124]

However, 'spiritual power', in the persons of the Asquithians, kept up the fight in the general election which followed the downfall of the Lloyd George coalition government in October 1922. One of the conspicuous weaknesses of Lloyd George's Liberals was their lack of effective local organization. In Cardiganshire, as in many other constituencies, the Independent 'Wee Frees' maintained firm control of the party machine. Llewelyn Williams had died early in 1922, after despatching a pathetic letter to Lloyd George from his deathbed.[125] At the general election Ernest Evans was opposed now by Rhys Hopkin Morris, another barrister, and the son of an Independent minister from Maesteg. In some ways Morris was a more positive candidate than Llewelyn Williams had been. Instead of harping on the past, his speeches dealt with the whole range of domestic issues, as well as with problems of international reconstruction in Europe. He probably attracted a greater share of the Labour vote.[126] Evans now faced the

---

[122]The electorate in 1919 was 30,751 (17,075 men and 13,676 women): *P.P.*, 1919, XL, 797.

[123]*Cambrian News*, 18 February 1921 ('David the Husbandman'); Lord Riddell, *Intimate Diary of the Peace Conference and After, 1918–23* (London, 1933), 279.

[124]*Welsh Gazette*, 24 February 1921; Lord Riddell, ibid., 279.

[125]Lord Riddell, ibid., 373.

[126]This account of the 1922 general election is based on the *Cambrian News* and *Welsh Gazette*. The papers of Rhys Hopkin Morris in NLW contain nothing on Cardiganshire politics.

erosion of further Liberal support, now that Lloyd George was out of office, and his majority over Hopkin Morris (who added nearly 2,000 to Llewelyn Williams's poll) fell to a mere 515. Without Tory support, Evans would never have been returned at all. Trevor Wilson's verdict on coalition Liberalism in this election is particularly apposite in Cardiganshire: 'they survived, where they survived at all, as a kept party.'[127]

The internecine warfare between the two Liberal factions went on remorselessly in 1923. Yet another general election was held in December of that year. This was occasioned by Baldwin's speech at Plymouth (25 October) which, by calling for the return of protection, openly challenged the old Liberal shibboleth of free trade. Faced with this threat, Asquith and Lloyd George arranged an immediate reunion. All over the country their supporters forsook their past differences and agreed on a common candidate. In only two constituencies in the British Isles, indeed, was harmony not restored in the Liberal ranks. One was Camborne in Cornwall, where the Welsh Asquithian, Leif Jones, was to fight, and defeat, the coalitionist, Captain Moreing, who was backed by Cornish Conservatives.[128] The other was Cardiganshire. The Liberal Association here totally refused all offers from London to come up to Abingdon Street and patch up differences, and so the battle of 1922 was fought again.[129] However, this time the Conservatives felt emboldened to intervene. The earl of Lisburne came out as the first candidate of his party in the county since January 1910; his programme was strongly protectionist. In the event, he was to poll over 6,000 votes, and this doomed whatever chance Ernest Evans may have had. Again there was intense personal bitterness throughout. Evans denounced the 'Mussolinis of North Parade' (a reference to the existence of two Liberal clubs in Aberystwyth) and the Asquithians replied in kind.[130] It was noticeable, however, that even in his old strongholds, such as New Quay and Borth, Evans had a less enthusiastic reception than before. The outcome was preordained. Hopkin Morris triumphed easily by over 5,000 while Evans only narrowly beat Lisburne for second place. Evans's brief and unhappy tenure of the seat had come to its end, and in the following year he had to seek refuge in the presumably more tranquil atmosphere of the University of Wales.

[127]Trevor Wilson, *The Downfall of the Liberal Party, 1914–35* (London, 1965), 237.

[128]*The Times*, 23 November 1923, includes Captain Moreing among the Unionist candidates.

[129]*Cambrian News*, 23 November 1923. Evans was technically the 'official Liberal' candidate and exploited the fact in his election literature.

[130]*Cambrian News*, 30 November 1923.

The crisis years 1921–3 were crucial for the Liberal ascendancy. The values of Cardiganshire Liberalism, its rigid independence, its contempt for patronage, whether stemming from the gentry or from the party whips, had been confirmed. Hopkin Morris's victory in 1923 served to revitalize the Liberal ascendancy and to restore some of the crusading idealism that it had lost. It helped to keep the middle-class élite of the coastal towns firm to the old cause; 1923 was, above all, a victory for the countryside, for the 'older dissent', and for the most Welsh parts of the county. The wheel had indeed come full circle since the days of 1868 when these areas were the most static and quiescent. The 1921–3 crisis served to underline the continuity of tradition in Cardiganshire politics; active in these campaigns were men like Peter Jones, J. M. Howell, D. C. Roberts (all Coalitionists), and C. M. Williams and Sir John Williams (both Asquithians), veterans of 1886, and, in some cases, of the earlier evictions of 1868, memories of which they frequently invoked.[131] However, the victory of 1923 had implications for the future also. In lending new life to Liberalism in the county, it helped to delay the rise of Labour. While Labour polled strongly in many Welsh rural constituencies in 1922 and 1923, in Cardiganshire no Labour candidate was to appear until the 'doctors' mandate' election of 1931 – when John Lloyd-Jones (Labour) lost to Hopkin Morris by over 13,000 votes. The Liberal ascendancy was preserved by the two following members, both Nonconformist barristers, D. Owen Evans (1932–45) and E. Roderic Bowen (1945–66). Not until Bowen's majority shrank alarmingly at the 1964 election did it appear that Labour might repeat in Cardiganshire the success it had gained in so much of the rest of Wales.[132]

In some ways, the Liberal ascendancy in Cardiganshire might be seen as a negative, backward-looking movement. Certainly it was in large measure the product of a society that was largely passing away. After 1920, the old tirades against the bishop and the squire had little meaning. Once disestablishment was attained, political Nonconformity lost much of its impetus, and became increasingly enervated. The rule of the gentry was also now a thing of the past. After the end of the First World War, with the new buoyancy in the land market induced by heavier death duties and inflated land values, the sale of estates went on apace. After 1945, even the great houses of Trawscoed and

[131]See speeches of Peter Jones (for the Coalitionists) and T. A. Levi (for the Independents).

[132]Labour eventually captured the seat in 1966 on a 3 per cent swing. A major factor in this victory seems to have been the record of Elystan Morgan as a former member (and vice-president) of Plaid Cymru. He continued to take a strongly nationalistic position in the Commons on such issues as an elected council for Wales and the status of the Welsh language.

Gogerddan were to pass out of the hands of those families which had maintained them for so many centuries. In 1967, it was announced that Nanteos was to be sold also.[133] A new generation of tenant farmers, newly settled in their freeholds, found themselves, in the inter-war years, far more oppressed by the banks and high interest rates than they had been by the rents of private landowners in the years before 1914. The price of social emancipation had been financial distress, and not until the Agriculture Act of 1947 did more stable conditions return for the farming community. The announcement by the Labour government in May 1967 that they would apply for membership of the European Common Market threatened hill farmers with the possibility of a return to the old insecurity.

In some respects, then, the victories won by Cardiganshire Liberals after 1885 proved to be somewhat empty ones – but that is often the way of victories. The forces against which the Liberals girded, though intangible, were not unreal. The Liberal ascendancy in Cardiganshire was part of an infinitely more complex process in British society, the ramifications of which were to prove ever more extensive. It was part of a changing attitude towards authority, a release from the old deference towards prescriptive rights and ancient tradition, an awareness that authority and power were things that were created rather than revealed. It was part of a process which brought new mobility to a poor, remote county, and new opportunities to the poorest of its people. The Liberal ascendancy in Cardiganshire was thus the spearhead of a far wider social revolution. It was symbolized, in an institution, by the new county council elected in 1889, and, in an individual, by the life of Dr Tom Richards, as shown in his incomparable *Atgofion Cardi* which traces the progress of a poor farmer's boy to the heights of scholarly distinction. Through the revolution in which Tom Richards and many others of his generation shared, the 'spirit of vassalage', the 'feudal' spirit of 1868, had finally been exorcised. The people of Cardiganshire today are the heirs to that revolution. We can pay tribute to its architects, to our parents and grandparents, that they forced it through, and that they bequeathed to us a more secure, a more satisfying, and a more hopeful future.

1967

---

[133]Gogerddan was taken over by the University College of Wales's Welsh Plant Breeding Station and Trawscoed by the Ministry of Agriculture. In April 1967 it was announced that Nanteos would have to be sold (*Cambrian News*, 21 April 1967).

Appendix: Cardiganshire Election Results, 1885–1923*

1885	(Popn. 70,270; reg. electorate 10,123)	David Davies (Lib.)	5,967
		M. Vaughan Davies (Con.)	3,644
1886	(Popn. 70,270; reg. electorate 12,308)	W. Bowen Rowlands (Lib.)	4,252
		David Davies (Lib. Un.)	4,243
1892	(Popn. 62,596; reg. electorate 13,155)	W. Bowen Rowlands (Lib.)	5,233
		William Jones (Lib. Un.)	3,270
†1893	By-election: (July)	W. Bowen Rowlands (Lib.) unopposed	
1895	(Popn. 62,630; reg. electorate 12,994)	M. Vaughan Davies (Lib.)	4,927
		J. C. Harford (Un.)	3,748
1900	(Popn. 62,630; reg. electorate 13,300)	M. Vaughan Davies (Lib.)	4,568
		J. C. Harford (Un.)	3,787
1906	(Popn. 60,240; reg. electorate 13,215)	M. Vaughan Davies (Lib.)	5,829
		C. Morgan Richardson (Un.)	2,960
1910	(Jan.)(Popn.60,240; reg. electorate 13,333)	M. Vaughan Davies (Lib.)	6,348
		G. F. Roberts (Un.)	2,943
1910	(Dec.)	M. Vaughan Davies (Lib.) unopposed	
1918	(Popn. 59,578; reg. electorate 30,368	M. Vaughan Davies (Lib.) unopposed	
1921	By-election: (21 Feb.)	Capt. Ernest Evans (Co. Lib.)	14,111
		W. Llewelyn Williams (Ind. Lib.)	10,521
1922	(Popn. 61,292; reg. electorate 32,695)	Capt. Ernest Evans (Co. Lib.)	12,825
		R. Hopkin Morris (Ind. Lib.)	12,310
1923	(Popn. 61,292; reg. electorate 32,881)	R. Hopkin Morris (Ind. Lib.)	12,469
		Capt. Ernest Evans (Lib.)	7,391
		Lord Lisburne (Con.)	6,776

* *Sources: The Times* surveys of elections; *Dod's Parliamentary Companion; Cambrian News.*

† By-election necessary on Bowen Rowlands being appointed recorder of Swansea.

12

Montgomeryshire's Liberal Century: Rendel to Hooson, 1880–1979

The title of this chapter requires some qualification. There is, of course, the arithmetical point that the period 1880 to 1979 does not quite add up to a century. There is the more important factor that, down to the 1918 general election, Montgomeryshire consisted of two constituencies, the county and the old Montgomery District seat, comprising the contributory boroughs of Welshpool, Newtown, Llanfyllin, Llanidloes and Machynlleth, whose electorate in December 1910 was a mere 7,928. This small borough constituency was, in fact, in Unionist (Conservative) hands between 1892 and 1906, and again from December 1910 to 1918, alongside and in contradistinction to the consistent Liberalism of the county representation. Its Tory members from 1892 to 1906 were first the famous Newtown woollen entrepreneur and mail-order pioneer, Sir Pryce Pryce-Jones, then his son, Colonel Edward. And, finally, Montgomeryshire's Liberalism did not, of course, come to its close in 1979. On the contrary, Alex Carlile recaptured the seat in 1983 and has retained it into the mid 1990s.

Nevertheless, there is a kind of thematic unity in the period under discussion. Montgomeryshire between 1880 and the 1970s was central to Liberal Wales – its rise, its overwhelming hegemonic ascendancy down to the First World War, its slow decline thereafter, though with still a powerful legacy remaining in institutions such as the University of Wales, the BBC or the world of the quangos. Its story is colourful, even dramatic. The essence and variety of Montgomeryshire Liberalism are best captured, perhaps, in the five remarkable politicians who provided its parliamentary representatives in this period – Stuart Rendel (1880–94), Arthur Humphreys-Owen (1894–1905), David

Davies (1906–29), Clement Davies (1929–62) and Emlyn Hooson (1962–79), and it is upon them that this article will largely focus.

It was extraordinary that Stuart Rendel should represent a place like Montgomeryshire at all. To this overwhelmingly rural, heavily Nonconformist and Welsh-speaking county there came an Englishman, a High Anglican, a product of Eton and Oriel College, Oxford, where he proved to be one of the less distinguished scholars of that historic establishment.[1] He was immensely rich with several country and town houses in England and on the French Riviera. He pursued active business contacts with China, Korea and the Far East generally. Most incongruous of all, he was an armaments manufacturer, an expert on heavy artillery, a partner in Armstrongs, the important ordnance firm at Elswick near Newcastle-upon-Tyne. A 'merchant of death' was indeed a most unlikely political spokesman in the land of Henry Richard, Wales's 'apostle of peace'. Yet Stuart Rendel impressed himself on Welsh political, social and educational life to a remarkable, indeed unique, degree. He became the embodiment of at least some aspects of Welsh Liberalism and the leading honorary Welshman of his time.

He first visited Montgomeryshire in 1877 when he campaigned in the Montgomery District by-election. In this, the Hon. Frederick Hanbury-Tracy of Gregynog Hall, a frivolous Whig, defeated Lord Castlereagh, the son of the marquis of Londonderry, in an expensive contest. Here Rendel met some notable local personalities: the Llanbrynmair antiquarian, Richard Williams (who was to become his election agent later), the Revd Josiah Jones, Machynlleth, and above all, the Cambridge-trained landowner of Glansevern near Berriew, Arthur Humphreys (recently converted into Humphreys-Owen in order to acquire Glansevern), who was to become his successor and lifelong friend.

Early in 1878 Rendel accepted the nomination to become the Liberal candidate for Montgomeryshire. This meant that he would take on the Wynn interest, which had held the seat, largely unopposed, since 1799. More than most counties, Montgomeryshire was 'feudal' in Henry Richard's sense,[2] and of course its county franchise had not

---

[1]It is extraordinary that, despite the vast collection of Rendel papers in the National Library of Wales, Aberystwyth (NLW), he has inspired neither a biography nor a thesis. His name does not appear in the *Dictionary of National Biography*. The best introduction is still F. E. Hamer (ed.), *The Personal Papers of Lord Rendel* (London, 1931); Hamer was a former Welsh editor of the *Manchester Guardian* who later joined the Labour party.

[2]Henry Richard, *Letters on the Social and Political Condition of Wales* (London, 1867), 80.

been seriously altered since the Reform Act of 1832. In the general election of 1880, which took place with the Beaconsfield government embroiled in colonial wars in South Africa and Afghanistan, Rendel faced massive landlord pressure upon the voters – from Wynnstay (144,500 acres) and Powis Castle (60,559 acres) in the east of the county; Plas Machynlleth (7,399 acres in the county), the marquis of Londonderry's seat, in the west. The county, then as later, revealed an historic socio-cultural divide. The eastern areas, along the Severn valley and bordering Shropshire, were more anglicized in speech and Anglican in religion, with Welshpool the 'Tory headquarters' for Wales. With perhaps a third of all worshipping Christians, the Church was far more vigorous here than in neighbouring Merioneth or Cardiganshire. On the other hand, the more western areas of the county beyond Newtown were strongly Liberal, Welsh-speaking and Nonconformist (especially Methodist). This division in the county, paralleled in some ways by Pembrokeshire in the south-west of Wales, remained noticeable and influential down to and beyond the Second World War.

Rendel's election in 1880 was a tumultuous affair. There were several violent episodes. Riots broke out at a Liberal meeting in Welshpool, where David Davies, MP, the coalowning magnate of Llandinam, had his hat damaged, and George Osborne Morgan, another Liberal MP, lost his altogether. 'The whole affair casts a stigma which can never be effaced from the name of Welshpool', commented the Aberystwyth *Cambrian News* censoriously. It might be noted that the forty-two hotels of the town (forty of them being Tory) ran free drinks for all that evening.[3] Tory activists were attacked with stones in Newtown; elsewhere there were mutterings about the heritage of socialism, no less, in Llanidloes dating from the era of Robert Owen and the Chartists in the 1830s. There was much money spent on both sides in this final election before the passage of the 1883 Corrupt Practices Act, Rendel spending £12,000 and Wynn £20,000 (so it was estimated).[4]

It was in every sense a passionate and epoch-making campaign. Rendel fought for Welsh disestablishment and the rights of tenant farmers; he turned his fire on Beaconsfield's 'bastard imperialism'. While Rendel's support included a few Liberal landowners such as Lord Sudeley, Wynn had behind him the historic influence of Wynnstay which owned 70,559 acres, half of its entire holdings, in eastern Montgomeryshire. In the end, it was announced that Rendel had overthrown the Wynn ascendancy by 2,232 votes to Wynn's 2,041,

[3]*Cambrian News*, 11 April 1880.
[4]J. M. Robertson to Mrs Peter Hughes Griffiths, 16 June 1912 (NLW, Daniel papers, 34).

a majority of 191 or 4.4 per cent. Rendel was carried in triumph shoulder-high by his supporters to the Owain Glyn Dwr Hotel in Machynlleth. 'It was long before Machynlleth resumed its usual aspect', the local press commented.[5]

Rendel retained his seat with some difficulty thereafter: it remained comparatively marginal. He raised his majority to 655 in 1885, held the seat by 579 in the Irish Home Rule election of 1886 and improved his margin to 815 (12.6 per cent) in 1892. In each case, he focused his campaign on the west of the county: 'We need the solid vote of the Welsh districts to beat down the English vote', he wrote in 1885.[6] His wider career has been traced by the present writer elsewhere and can be largely passed over here.[7] He was a far-seeing politician whose impact on Wales at this crucial period was profound. He devised a new comprehensive Welsh political programme, headed by Church disestablishment. He created a new national party structure, with the establishment of the North Wales and the South Wales Liberal Federations in the winter of 1886–7. He was elected first leader of the so-called 'Welsh Parliamentary Party' in 1888. More important still, he became a close personal friend of Gladstone himself and used his influence with skill and sensitivity to advance the political causes of Liberal Wales. Gladstone's fourth ministry in July 1892 was formed at Rendel's London home, No. 1 Carlton Gardens. Rendel's second daughter, Maud, married Gladstone's third son Henry. Symbolically, Rendel was a pallbearer at Gladstone's funeral.

Stuart Rendel was especially active on behalf of Welsh education. He played a major role in the passage of the Welsh Intermediate Education Act of 1889 which set up the 'county' schools, and also took up with special fervour the cause of the 'college by the sea' at Aberystwyth. He persuaded the Salisbury government to restore the annual £4,000 government grant to the college.[8] In due course, he became the president of the University College of Wales and a major benefactor both in direct financial terms and the purchase of land. His name is commemorated at the college still in the Rendel chair of English and the hall of residence, Neuadd Rendel.

By the 1890s, however, Rendel felt himself becoming politically somewhat isolated. The agrarian radicalism, and even more the political nationalism, of much younger MPs like Tom Ellis and David

[5]*Cambrian News*, 16 April 1880.

[6]Rendel to the Revd Josiah Jones, 9 December 1885 (NLW MS. 6411B).

[7]Kenneth O. Morgan, '"The Member for Wales": Stuart Rendel (1834–1913)', *Transactions of the Honourable Society of Cymmrodorion*, 1984, 149–71 (published in this volume, 339–59).

[8]Rendel to Thomas Charles Edwards, 25 August 1885, T. I. Ellis (ed.), *The Letters of Thomas Charles Edwards* (Aberystwyth, 1953), 251.

Lloyd George alarmed him greatly.[9] Both, he felt, drew unwise parallels between the grievances of Wales and those of Ireland. The anti-tithe campaign seemed a portent of this, with its analogies with the Irish land war. In March 1894, when Gladstone finally retired as prime minister, Rendel took the opportunity to resign his seat and to move on to the House of Lords. He wrote in some disillusionment to Thomas Gee at this time of how he felt he was 'an Englishman standing between the Welsh and Englishmen', a kind of second-hand representative.[10] But he soon recovered his spirits. He became a vigorous supporter of Lloyd George, both during the South African War and in the campaign for the 1909 'people's budget'. He died in 1913, a committed radical to the end. Undoubtedly, he was a major figure in making Wales a democracy, and it was in the county of Montgomeryshire that he made his base.

Arthur Humphreys-Owen is a much less well-known figure. Born plain Arthur Humphreys, he was a Cambridge-educated barrister who inherited the 4,482 acres of the Glansevern estate, along the River Severn between Garthmyl and Berriew, in 1876. He became a notable local patron and personality. He served as chairman of the quarter sessions and first chairman of the new Montgomeryshire County Council in 1889. Like his close friend, Rendel, he was especially zealous in educational causes, as an active member of the council of the University College of Wales, Aberystwyth, and the first chairman of the Central Welsh Board in 1896, with Principal J. Viriamu Jones of Cardiff as vice-chairman. Education became very much his main priority in public life. The journalist, T. Marchant Williams, commented how, with his long beard and tiny narrow-focus spectacles, Arthur Humphreys-Owen looked like some kind of German professor of philosophy. But he was not as dull as he seemed. He also, we are told, sported 'a gorgeous fur-lined coat', a 'wonderful little French hat worn at Llanbrynmair fair', and gaiters which 'he puts on but never wears'.[11] How this conspicuous consumption went down with the plain farmers of Maldwyn is open to speculation.

Humphreys-Owen, a thoughtful, donnish figure, had powerful political ambitions as a dedicated follower of Mr Gladstone. He was indeed turned down for four north Wales constituencies in succession in 1888–91 by local Liberals who perhaps felt that a hyphenated, non-Welsh-speaking Anglican was not to their taste. One of these

[9]For example, Rendel to Humphreys-Owen, 28, 29 May 1892 (NLW, Glansevern papers, 596, 597).

[10]Rendel to Thomas Gee, 22 March 1894 (NLW, Gee papers, 8308C, 282); cf. Rendel to the Revd Josiah Jones, 17 April 1893 (NLW MS. 6411B).

[11]T. Marchant Williams, *The Welsh Members of Parliament* (Cardiff, 1894), 15.

constituencies was Caernarfon Boroughs, which preferred the astonishingly youthful 25-year-old David Lloyd George, 'a second-rate country attorney', thought Humphreys-Owen in one of the more memorable misjudgements of modern history. In return, Lloyd George was to attack Humphreys-Owen later on for his lack of sympathy with Welsh Home Rule. 'He is the quintessence of complaisant self-assurance.'[12] Humphreys-Owen was the natural successor to the Montgomeryshire seat in April 1894. But, as has been seen, it was anything but a safe Liberal citadel. It was a very hard contest for Humphreys-Owen in the by-election, with Gladstone having resigned and the unpopular Rosebery's Liberal government losing support fast in the country and apparently close to its demise. Humphreys-Owen eventually clung on by only 225, a fall of 600 in the Liberal majority, in the by-election. One of those who spoke on his behalf, incidentally, was Lloyd George who may, or may not, during that campaign have formed a misalliance with Mrs Catherine Edwards, the wife of a doctor from Cemmaes Road.[13] In the difficult election of 1895, in which the Liberal government was heavily defeated and swept from office, Humphreys-Owen held on by a fractional majority of only twenty-seven over yet another Wynn representative (0.4 per cent).

Humphreys-Owen was not a particularly charismatic member for Montgomeryshire. His main concern, as has been noted, was education; on land reform, as a wealthy landowner, he was cautious, although he dutifully spoke on behalf of the rights of Welsh tenant farmers in the Commons. He supported the Liberals' mass 'revolt' against the Balfour Education Act of 1902 but became alarmed when civil disobedience threatened and when the Montgomeryshire County Council, with its thirty-eight to nineteen Liberal majority went into default after refusing to operate the act.[14] He criticized Lloyd George's headstrong tactics in leading the Welsh councils into illegality: 'Having had no literary education himself, he is unable to realize the needs of the education system. He regards it simply as a political scaffolding.'[15] Yet he retained his staunch Liberalism to the end. Not for nothing was he a nephew of that humane reformer, Judge Arthur Johnes. He

[12]Humphreys-Owen to Rendel, 19 August 1888 (NLW, Rendel papers, XIV, 496); Lloyd George to Alfred Thomas, 30 November 1897 (Glamorgan Archive Service, Pontypridd papers).

[13]John Grigg, The Young Lloyd George (London, 1973), 233ff.

[14]See Gareth Elwyn Jones, 'The "Welsh Revolt" revisited: Merioneth and Montgomeryshire in default', Welsh History Review, 14 (3) (1989), especially 428ff. Only the schools in the Welshpool area, where Col. Pryce-Jones was a manager, remained fully in operation.

[15]Humphreys-Owen to Rendel, 19 June 1905 (NLW, Rendel papers, XIV, 704a).

remained an Irish home ruler, and never a Liberal or any other kind of Unionist. During the South African War, he was, along with Lloyd George, Herbert Lewis and Frank Edwards, one of the four consistent 'pro-Boers' in the Welsh Parliamentary Party. He stood up bravely to the jingo fever in his own county. In the 1900 election, when his majority struggled up to 264, he declared that Wales would 'not bend the knee to the khaki idol' and launched vigorous rhetorical onslaughts on Joseph Chamberlain.[16] His friend, Rendel, backed him strongly and spoke contemptuously of backsliding Liberal imperialists in Wales – 'the Salem chapel jingo' and the 'imperial Perks element'.[17] Humphreys-Owen remained to the end a Gladstonian radical and a socially-minded philanthropist. The thousands of his letters in the Glansevern collection in the National Library of Wales cry out for a proper biography.[18] He died in December 1905, just before the dissolution of Parliament and on the eve, as it happened, of the greatest-ever electoral triumph of Welsh Liberalism.

In 1906, after twenty-five years of bitter partisanship, Montgomeryshire Liberals turned the clock back to an earlier era of patronage and 'influence'. They nominated David Davies, the 25-year-old heir to the Llandinam fortunes, grandson of 'top Sawyer' himself, the pioneer of the Welsh railway system, the coal-mines of Rhondda and the founding of Barry Docks. The younger David Davies was indeed a multiple millionaire. His family had become Unionist in 1886, with both his grandfather and his father, Edward, turning Liberal Unionist.[19] He himself evidently diverged from the official Liberal line on many, if not most issues. He was flatly opposed to Irish Home Rule; he favoured tariff reform on the lines advocated by Joseph Chamberlain, with perhaps the taxing of imported food; he was lukewarm on Church disendowment; he had opposed the education 'revolt' of 1902 and campaigned against Richard Jones, one of his own tenants, and on behalf of a churchman, in the 1904 county council elections in Llandinam.[20] His main claims to Liberal sympathies were his devoted,

[16]*South Wales Daily News*, 13 October 1900, for a survey of the campaign in Montgomeryshire. His Unionist opponent was a representative of the Wynn interest.

[17]Rendel to Humphreys-Owen, 29 March 1901 (NLW, Glansevern papers, 704).

[18]There is an inadequate entry on Humphreys-Owen in the *Dictionary of Welsh Biography*. There is a rather better one in J. V. Morgan (ed.), *Welsh Political and Educational Leaders in the Victorian Era* (London, 1908), by F. E. Hamer.

[19]Cf. David Davies to Edward Davies, 27 January 1886 (NLW, Davies of Llandinam papers, 301).

[20]*South Wales Daily News*, 5 December 1905.

even fanatical, commitment to Calvinistic Methodism and to the cause of temperance. Many local Tories felt he might well rejoin them in years to come. In 1906, so Herbert Gladstone, the outgoing Liberal whip, reported to Campbell-Bannerman, the prime minister, Davies was actually nominated by both parties[21] and returned unopposed like some eighteenth-century landowner.

After this, Montgomeryshire local politics went into genteel decay. The Liberal Association entered a deep slumber. There was no electoral contest there in either of the 1910 elections, nor in 1918, 1922 and 1923. In 1924 Davies had to fight the county's first ever Labour candidate, Arthur Davies, a trade unionist, whom he trounced by 10,558 (a majority of 54.6 per cent) in a straight fight. It was truly the politics of patronage, administered by an erratic and imperious leader.

Davies followed very much his own course in politics: he voted against the land clauses of Lloyd George's 'people's budget' in 1909, for instance. The following year he pronounced against Irish Home Rule.[22] He was a generally inactive member of Parliament, and was indeed much more concerned with wider public campaigns. Much the most notable of these was the National Memorial Association, with its crusade to set up medical institutions to deal with the scourge of tuberculosis: it was this that began a memorable connection with the youthful Thomas Jones, who became the Memorial Association's secretary.[23] Davies also became the major benefactor of Welsh education, especially of the University College of Wales, Aberystwyth, whose president he became in 1926. He endowed there, in particular, the first chair of 'international' politics in the world, the Woodrow Wilson chair held first by Sir Alfred Zimmern in 1919. The Gregynog trust, later on, endowed geography, music, Welsh and extra-mural studies at the College, while the family made Gregynog Hall, near Newtown, a unique centre of cultural and intellectual activity.[24] After the war, Davies's main passion was the campaign for collective security and world peace. He was part-founder of the League of Nations Union and campaigned for a world police force and equity tribunal to deter international aggression through military sanctions. He also founded the New Commonwealth Society in 1932 to promote the idea of a tribunal to deal with disputes outside the purview of the Permanent

[21]Cf. ibid., 15 December 1905.

[22]See his election addresses in the January 1910 and December 1910 general elections.

[23]See material in Thomas Jones papers, NLW, H/1/37–57.

[24]Glyn Tegai Hughes et al., Gregynog (Cardiff, 1977), 59–60. Davies's Gregynog Estates Limited Company owned Gregynog Hall from March 1914.

Court of Justice at The Hague. Throughout the 1930s, he took a vigorous part in the debates over appeasement and endorsed such non-party, anti-government candidates as Vernon Bartlett and the duchess of Atholl after the Munich settlement.[25]

The main disruptions in his erratic parliamentary career came through his relationship with Lloyd George during and after the First World War. As a prominent pro-government Liberal, he was enlisted into the prime minister's 'Garden Suburb' of private advisers in December 1916, with a special responsibility for the drink trade and its possible state purchase. But his role as self-appointed candid friend soon antagonized the prime minister and other members of the government as well. Davies was reduced to self-parody as 'a harmless sort of lunatic – always grousing and criticising'.[26] Lloyd George dismissed him from his secretariat with some savagery and Davies had to enlist in the army instead. He and the prime minister were at daggers drawn thereafter. In the 1918 general election, Davies disclaimed the 'coupon' letter of support from Lloyd George and Bonar Law as a coalition-sponsored candidate, but he received it nevertheless. 'I did not want that letter but there it is.'[27] In the period of the peacetime coalition government he was frequently opposed to the policies of the Lloyd George administration, including the basis for its settlement of the disendowment of the Welsh Church. However, he warmed to the prime minister after the conclusion of the Irish treaty in December 1921 which he strongly backed. 'He has gone off the rails in the past but he is on the right track now', was Davies's verdict on the premier.[28] He actually offered £1,500,000 to purchase *The Times* as a pro-Lloyd George newspaper on Northcliffe's death in the summer of 1922, but in vain.[29] (One scenario was that the prime minister should actually become editor of the newspaper, a unique episode in news-

[25]See Lord Davies of Llandinam papers, NLW, A/13/15; also cf. Goronwy J. Jones, *Wales and the Quest for Peace* (Cardiff, 1970).

[26]Davies to Lloyd George, 27 May 1917 (Lloyd George of Dwyfor papers, House of Lords Record Office, F/83/10/5); John Turner, *Lloyd George's Secretariat* (Cambridge, 1908), 15–19, 180–4. Davies, along with Dr Christopher Addison, played a notable part in enlisting Liberal support for Lloyd George against Asquith in November–December 1916, and in the creation of the 'Garden Suburb'.

[27]Davies's address to Montgomeryshire Liberals at Newtown, 26 November 1918 (Lord Davies of Llandinam papers, A/13/1).

[28]Davies to Thomas Jones, 7 December 1921 (ibid., A/13/2). For a good account of Davies's activities in the 1920s, see J. Graham Jones, 'Montgomeryshire politics, Lloyd George, David Davies and the Green Book', *Montgomeryshire Collections*, (1984), 79–98. I am indebted to Mr Jones for advice on sources for this period.

[29]*History of the Times, 1912–1948*, part II (London, 1952), 688ff.

paper history.) Thereafter he became strongly alienated by Lloyd
George's renewed radicalism as the Liberals tried to reunite their
forces from 1923 onwards. In particular, Davies strongly opposed
Lloyd George's proposals for a kind of land nationalization,
'cultivating tenure', which were contained in the Green Book, *The
Land and the Nation*, in 1925,[30] a document which saw another Welsh
MP, Sir Alfred Mond, cross the floor and join the Tories. The land
programme seemed to him rank socialism. Davies told another
Liberal, F. H. Lambert, 'It appears to me that so long as Lloyd George
remains in control of the Liberal Party there cannot possibly be very
much hope for it.'[31]

In 1926 it came as little surprise when Montgomeryshire Liberals
were told that Davies would not stand for Parliament at the next
election. But still it caused a major local crisis. After all, Davies was
president of the local party and donated £300 out of an annual party
income of £351.[32] In typically imperious fashion, he tried to nominate
his own successor, W. Alford Jehu of Llanfair Caereinion, with an offer
to pay all his expenses. But the local Liberals, headed by Richard
Jones, rebelled at such patronage; in any case, Jehu, for all the
momentum implied in his name, lacked charisma. Other names were
mentioned, including that of Herbert Samuel. In the end, the
respected barrister, Clement Davies of Llanfyllin, spoken of as a
possible Liberal member since 1910, was nominated by the party 'by
an overwhelming majority' in November 1927.[33] He was a strong
supporter of Lloyd George at this stage, thus guaranteeing David
Davies's opposition.

Like his grandfather before him, David Davies had an extraordinary
impact on the public life of Wales and, increasingly, of Britain through
the League of Nations Union. But his impact on Montgomeryshire
Liberalism was largely negative and sterile. He might have pushed for
powerful causes, such as the Welsh devolution preached by his
periodical *Welsh Outlook*, with which Thomas Jones was also closely
associated, but he did not press the issue home. Davies was a creative,
dynamic figure, but he displayed these qualities largely outside the
confines of Montgomeryshire politics.

Clement Davies, a Cambridge-trained barrister and QC, former
lecturer at Aberystwyth, was a man of immense legal ability whose

[30]Material in Davies of Llandinam papers, A/13/2.

[31]Davies to F. H. Lambert, 15 March 1927 (ibid.).

[32]Montgomeryshire Liberal Association minute books, entry of 30 November
1926 (NLW).

[33]Ibid., 19 November 1927. It is recorded that Clement Davies defeated Jehu
'by an overwhelming majority': *Montgomeryshire Express*, 22 November 1926.

progress at the bar had been swift indeed.[34] In the general election in
June 1929, he was returned over Conservative and Labour opposition
by a majority of 2,128, despite a vigorous challenge from the Conservative, J. M. Naylor of Llanfair Caereinion. But thereafter Davies,
elected with such high hopes, proved to be a distinctly eccentric MP.
He was lucratively involved with Lever Brothers as a director of the
firm, which financed his business trips to West Africa, and his political
work suffered. He also fell out with Lloyd George and in 1930, after
less than a year in the House, announced to the dumbfounded local
Liberals that he would not stand next time.[35] They promptly
nominated instead C. P. Williams, formerly Liberal member for
Wrexham, while Davies compounded his offence by joining the pro-
Conservative 'National Liberals', led by Sir John Simon. Then, in the
political turmoil that surrounded the founding of the National
government in September 1931, Davies suddenly declared he would
stand again after all, because the local Conservatives had promised
that they would not oppose him at the polls.[36] With astonishing self-
effacement, C. P. Williams promptly withdrew. Labour were unable to
field a candidate, and Davies was thus elected unopposed as a Liberal
National.

Throughout the dramas of the 1930s, Clement Davies remained a
National Liberal supporter of the government. He was strongly
attacked for his stance by many Montgomeryshire Liberals, including
their president, the previous MP now elevated to the title of Lord
Davies, for defending Neville Chamberlain's policy of appeasement
and the settlement at Munich in 1938.[37] G. F. Hamer, a notable local
Liberal, claimed that Clement Davies was 'well on the way to the Tory
Party'.[38] Lord Davies was engaged in a constituency manoeuvre in
December 1938, at a time when the MP was working for Lever
Brothers in West Africa, to force him to resign, to affiliate the local
Association to the independent Liberal party and perhaps to impose
David Davies, Lord Davies's son, on the constituency as its Liberal
member.[39] Clement Davies resisted this with some belligerence and

[34]The best general account to date is D. M. Roberts, 'Clement Davies and the
Liberal Party, 1929-56' (University College of Wales, Aberystwyth, unpublished
MA thesis, 1975). Also see J. Graham Jones, 'Montgomeryshire politics, Clement
Davies and the National government', *Montgomeryshire Collections*, 73 (1985),
96–115. Clement Davies's substantial papers make a proper biography essential.
[35]Montgomeryshire Liberal Association minute books, entry of 23 September
1930.
[36]Ibid., 13 October 1931.
[37]Material in Davies of Llandinam papers, NLW, A/13/5.
[38]J. Graham Jones, op. cit.
[39]Material in Davies of Llandinam papers, NLW, A/13/5.

the crisis blew over. But, in another twist, he turned vehemently against the Chamberlain government after the start of the war in September 1939, and on 14 December resigned as a Liberal National to emerge again as a supporter of the official Liberal party, now led by Sir Archibald Sinclair. As an earlier article in this journal by D. M. Roberts has shown, Clement Davies played a leading role in the fall of Chamberlain in May 1940, through his connections with Lloyd George, with independent Conservatives like Robert Boothby, and with Labour leaders such as Attlee and Greenwood. William Jowitt, a future Labour lord chancellor, christened Davies 'Warwick the Kingmaker' for his role in the crisis, but Churchill, no doubt mindful of Davies's role at the time of Munich, refused to give him a post thereafter. He had to content himself with a role as a somewhat embittered back-bencher within the dwindling ranks of British Liberalism.[40]

From that time on, Davies, an erratic member of Parliament hitherto, became increasingly involved with the wellbeing of his county. The process was assisted by his resigning as a director of Unilever in 1941. He had already massively increased his reputation by heading a pioneering inquiry into the resources available to combat tuberculosis in Wales; its report, published in 1939, drew a grim picture of poor housing and inadequate health services throughout the principality.[41] It could soon be said of Davies, like Rendel before him, that he was indeed 'the member for Montgomeryshire'.

From 1945 onwards, Davies became chairman of the parliamentary Liberal party, which indeed numbered only twelve members after the election. It was a most difficult time for the new leader. Originally a strong supporter of many of the measures introduced by the Labour government, such as the National Health Service, he now became plausibly accused by Megan Lloyd George, Emrys Roberts and other radicals of a 'drift to the right'. Dingle Foot wrote ironically to Lady Megan Lloyd George in 1949 of how

> Clem intends to sound the clarion call next month to blood, toil, tears and sweat. But the quantity of the blood, the nature of the toil, the number of the tears and the precise purpose of the sweat are still undecided.

[40]D. M. Roberts, 'Clement Davies and the fall of Neville Chamberlain, 1939–40', *Welsh History Review*, 8 (2) (1976), 188ff. For harsh views of Davies, see Ben Pimlott (ed.), *The Second World War Diary of Hugh Dalton* (London, 1986), e.g. entry of 14 May 1941 (p. 204), when he sees Davies as 'sour, self-important and intriguing'.

[41]*Report of the Committee on the Anti-tuberculosis Service in Wales and Monmouthshire* (HMSO, 1939).

Emrys Roberts, Liberal member for Merioneth, believed that Davies wanted the Tories back in office.[42] On the other side, Lady Violet Bonham-Carter and some right-wingers advocated a formal anti-socialist electoral pact with the Conservatives.[43] In the 1951 election (in a local variant of such a pact which also applied to Roderic Bowen in Cardiganshire), Davies was not opposed by a Conservative; neither was he in 1955. He was apparently offered a government post 'of Cabinet rank', perhaps concerned with education, by Churchill in 1951, but party pressure forced him into refusal.[44] Nationally, it was an unhappy time for him, with the Liberal ranks reduced to only nine members in 1951 and doing no better four years later. In 1956, just before the Suez crisis, he gave up the party leadership in favour of the younger, more dynamic figure of Jo Grimond, though he remained in the House of Commons.

Locally, however, his career was to confirm strongly the Liberalism of Montgomeryshire. Labour could make little impact, while Plaid Cymru did not even stand in the county. He defeated Conservative and Labour opposition with some ease in 1959. By this time, there were fears that the Boundary Commission might actually abolish the Montgomeryshire seat altogether, perhaps merging it with Merioneth.[45] He died in 1962. All in all, Clement Davies had an odd career with his talents largely unfulfilled. He left behind him a considerable reputation for ability and acumen in the opinion of many shrewd observers. The report on anti-tuberculosis services was a major social document. But it is a paradox that someone who was for so long a political maverick became so powerfully identified with the harmonies and historic continuities of Montgomeryshire Liberalism.

The final member of this notable quintet of Liberal members was Emlyn Hooson.[46] He was another gifted barrister, a QC at a young age, a product of the law department of the University College of Wales, Aberystwyth. Much public attention focused on the by-election

[42]Dingle Foot to Lady Megan Lloyd George, 15 August 1949 (Lady Megan Lloyd George papers, NLW, 20475C, MS. 3174); Mervyn Jones, *A Radical Life* (London, 1991), 213.

[43]Lady Violet Bonham-Carter to Clement Davies, 23 September 1950, 27 October 1950 (Clement Davies papers, NLW, J/3/40, J/3/43); Davies to Bonham-Carter, 15 November 1950 (ibid., J/3/45).

[44]See D. M. Roberts, 'Clement Davies', on these matters.

[45]Montgomeryshire Liberal Association minute book, 1920–60.

[46]Lord Hooson's papers have been deposited in the National Library of Wales but are not presently available to researchers. I have benefited from discussions with Lord Hooson on his career. There is material in an article by J. Graham Jones, 'The Liberal party and Wales after 1945', *Welsh History Review*, 16(3) (1993), 326–55.

in May 1962 since it followed closely on the Liberals' extraordinary triumph at Orpington, and there was a large influx of MPs of all parties into the constituency. Liberal organization in Montgomeryshire was still haphazard, with resources of only £50 in the bank a few years earlier,[47] but Hooson had at least a most able agent, Mrs Garbett-Edwards. Plaid Cymru contested the seat for the first time, in the person of the novelist, Islwyn Ffowc Elis, but he made no impact and lost his deposit. With the Conservatives on the defensive, and Labour feeble, Hooson swelled the Liberal majority to the comfortable margin of 7,549, and held the seat with some ease thereafter in 1964, 1966, 1970, and both elections in 1974. In October 1974, for instance, his majority over the Conservative, the highly traditional figure of W. R. C. Williams-Wynn, an Eton-educated chartered surveyor of squire-archical pedigree, was nearly 4,000 (17.3 per cent). He stood unsuccessfully against Jeremy Thorpe for the party leadership in 1967.

In this period, Montgomeryshire Liberal politics still retained traditional aspects. Prominent roles were still played by long-established local families – the Hamers of Llanidloes (who included Mrs Hooson) and even the Davies family of Llandinam. The Honourable Edward Davies was still president of the local party in the late 1960s. But Hooson took this traditional-looking party into uncharted waters. He was far more strongly committed to Welsh devolution than his predecessors had ever been. He became president in 1967 of a new organization called 'the Welsh Liberal Party', though some in the local Liberal Association expressed their unease.[48] He was interested also in international affairs, and was active as a parliamentary delegate to NATO.[49] On the other hand, he was a rare Liberal critic of the European Community, mainly on economic grounds such as the harm that would be done to Welsh hill farmers, although he also objected to the loss of sovereignty. He was the one Liberal MP to vote against entry into the Common Market in 1972.

Even in the 1960s and early 1970s, the historic socio-cultural divide in Montgomeryshire politics was still in evidence. The further away from the border with England, the better Hooson's vote held up. He was most secure in the most strongly Welsh-speaking parts of the county, in the rural uplands and in market towns like Machynlleth, Llanfyllin, Llanbrynmair and Llanidloes. Newtown was balanced in its sympathies, with Welshpool tilting towards the Conservatives. (By the early 1990s, however, the balance seemed to have shifted considerably,

[47]Montgomeryshire Liberal Association minute book, 4 October 1952.

[48]Ibid., 12 December 1968. On 1 December 1969, Emlyn Thomas, secretary of the WLF, complained to the Executive Association that Montgomeryshire Liberals 'had not really participated in his scheme'.

[49]Cf. Emlyn Hooson, 'In defence of U.N.O.', *Liberal News*, 26 November 1970.

with Alex Carlile finding more support in Welshpool and areas such as Four Crosses and Llandrinio than his predecessors from Rendel onwards had done.) Hooson always benefited from a strong affinity with the farming industry, as a part-time farmer himself in Llanidloes. In 1974 Montgomeryshire was noted as still one of the most intensely agricultural constituencies in Britain with 40 per cent of local children going to work in farms or rural trades closely connected with agriculture. With a population of 45,000 people, the constituency contained about 7,000 farms of one acre or more.[50]

However, the social and demographic character of Montgomeryshire could not remain ossified for ever. There were now signs of change and industrial growth, above all the prospect of a major new conurbation in the constituency. Discussions on a mid Wales town to revive the economy of rural Wales were lively in the mid-1960s. Hooson himself was part-author of a major Liberal scheme in 1965 for mid-Wales rural development, *The Heartland*, written in conjunction with the social anthropologist, Geraint Jenkins.[51] It recalled Lloyd George's 'Yellow Book' of the 1920s. Among their proposals was a considerable expansion of the town of Aberystwyth to reach perhaps a population of 60,000 by the end of the century. The Mid-Wales Development Association, of which the secretary was Peter Garbett-Edwards, the husband of Hooson's election agent, was targeted for a major growth and to be turned into a Rural Development Corporation. The new secretary of state for Wales, James Griffiths, however, had a different kind of development in mind, namely, one large 'new town' in Montgomeryshire itself, in the region of Caersŵs, with a projected population of up to 100,000.[52] The Welsh Office had already approved the draft of such a scheme. But it brought immense local foreboding with rumours of the population of this new town, perhaps citizens of darker hue, coming from Birmingham overspill. In the end, Cledwyn Hughes, the new secretary of state for Wales, in succession to Griffiths, vetoed the plan for a new town in 1967. Among other considerations, such a scheme would conflict with the new town already growing up nearby at Telford in Shropshire.[53] Instead, there came the idea of a Mid-Wales Development Corporation to build up local industry around Newtown. Already by 1974 there were more than 2,000 new voters in the area, as local light

[50]Conservative party constituency material, October 1974 general election, in the author's own archive. I am much indebted to Alex Carlile MP for advice on the nature of Montgomeryshire Liberalism in the 1980s.

[51]Emlyn Hooson and Geraint Jenkins, *The Heartland: A Plan for Mid-Wales* (Welsh Radical Group Publications, 1965).

[52]James Griffiths, *Pages from Memory* (London, 1969), 177–9.

[53]Information from Lord Cledwyn.

industries developed, while there was further suburban growth around Welshpool in the neighbourhood of Guilsfield. Clearly the social admixture of the county was being transformed and historic Welsh Liberalism would have to adapt to it and to the viewpoints of new immigrant voters, many of whom had no background of voting Liberal.

In the general election of May 1979, social change resulting from population increase (the electorate rose by 2,200 between October 1974 and 1979) was only one of Hooson's problems. His own vocal support for Welsh devolution was not popular in what was now a relatively anglicized constituency. Of 888 new families living in housing estates built by the Newtown corporation, 435 had come from England. It is also worth noting that Powys had voted very heavily 'no' in the devolution referendum of 1 March, indeed at 82 per cent almost more heavily than any other Welsh county. The 'Lib–Lab' pact with the Callaghan government in 1977–8 (in which Hooson, as Liberal home affairs spokesman, collaborated happily with Merlyn Rees, Labour's home secretary) also provoked criticism, while there were *sub rosa* murmurs (fanned by Conservative canvassers) about the scandals, ranging from homosexuality to attempted murder, surrounding the former Liberal leader, Jeremy Thorpe. In these difficult circumstances, Hooson was defeated by Delwyn Williams, a Conservative lawyer and farmer from the Welshpool area – and also, like Hooson, a law graduate of the University College, Aberystwyth.[54] In a year which saw the Welsh voters reject the notion of devolution by a majority of three to one, an historic phase of Welsh identity had, it seemed, come to its close. Many surmised that Liberalism would now survive in Montgomeryshire as only an historic remnant. Remarkably, somewhat against the electoral tide in the 1983 election which the Thatcher government won handsomely, Alex Carlile reclaimed Maldwyn for the old cause, and a new chapter began.

Throughout these hundred years, Montgomeryshire politics were always *sui generis*. The county was never a secure Liberal stronghold in the same sense as Cardiganshire over most of that period. Nor was it as radical in its instincts as, say, Merioneth or Caernarfon. Lloyd George's writ never ran with the same force in a border county where the squirearchical politics of Shropshire were not far away. Anti-socialism was always a strong factor: as noted, the pact with Labour in 1977 was unpopular. Until the 1920s, Montgomeryshire was a relatively marginal seat where the Conservatives always felt they had a chance. Its historic socio-cultural divisions between east and west

[54]*Western Mail*, 4 May 1979.

added to its unpredictability. On the one hand, nationalism, and its vehicle, Plaid Cymru, were always weak as they tended to be along the line of Offa's Dyke generally. Classic rural, small-town Liberalism survived in the ascendant down to the 1980s. Again, despite the romantic heritage of Robert Owen's co-operative socialism and of Llanidloes Chartism in former times, there was never any prospect of Labour making an impact and winning the seat as it did variously in Anglesey, Caernarfon, Conwy, Merioneth, Cardiganshire and Carmarthenshire between 1951 and 1966.

In this Liberal century, Montgomeryshire boasted five talented and significant representatives. Each of them added his own perspective and priorities. Stuart Rendel helped to create a wider Welsh outlook and strategy, with immense long-term consequences. Humphreys-Owen added a specialist concern with local government and education at all levels. David Davies, a backwards-looking figure in many ways, nevertheless linked the county with wider crusades such as health and world peace. Clement Davies identified it with national leadership and the themes of warfare and welfare. Emlyn Hooson offered an international Atlanticist dimension, along with New Deal-style regional planning (one of his political allies was Representative, later Mayor, John Lindsay of New York). Each of them made Montgomeryshire, to some degree, a crucible for change. The point needs a wider emphasis. Welsh political historiography has, perhaps, been unduly coloured by the experiences of industrial Wales and of the radical 'matrix' of Merthyr Tydfil, in particular. It is worth recalling here that in the green hills and tranquil valleys of mid Wales profound transformations were also in train, which coloured the Welsh political identity.

As an appendix, it may be added that there was one institutional connection which linked all five Montgomeryshire members discussed here. All were closely identified with the University College of Wales, Aberystwyth. Rendel and Lord Davies became its presidents and generous benefactors. Humphreys-Owen was a highly influential council member there. Clement Davies and Emlyn Hooson were distinguished figures from its law department. The fortunes of Montgomeryshire's Liberal century were thus, from first to last, inextricably bound up with the fortunes of the 'college by the sea'. This is perhaps a conclusion with which another distinguished old student, the late June Gruffydd, in whose memory these thoughts were originally compiled, would have readily concurred.

1992

13

The Merthyr of
Keir Hardie

Keir Hardie's election as member of Parliament for Merthyr Tydfil is part of the saga of the British Labour movement. Long before his death in 1915, Hardie had assumed a kind of heroic stature in his constituency. His portrait had replaced those of the Queen or Mr Gladstone upon the walls of many a humble miner's cottage. After his death, interpretations of Hardie's career became increasingly mystical; he was depicted as a messianic figure, a Moses who led the children of Labour out of bondage. Fifty years later, the inspiration of Hardie's leadership survives in full: the merest mention of his name can reduce the Labour Party Conference or the Trade Union Congress to ecstasies of enthusiasm and unity. No Labour leader since, not even George Lansbury, has inspired quite the same devotion. For the British working class, Hardie will always be revered as one of the saints who for their labours rest.

However, his position in Merthyr and in the Labour party as a whole becomes much more intelligible if it is set against the background of his time. It was a facet of the radicalization of the political structure within the Merthyr Boroughs, the consequences of which set up a chain reaction far beyond the confines of the constituency. It lent new impetus to the growing democratization of society in the south Wales coalfield as a whole. This process of radicalization and democratization had been under way long before Hardie's election to Parliament in 1900. It was to build up with mounting intensity after his death. For several years after 1915 the political situation in south Wales remained highly fluid and uncertain. Not until the triumph of the Labour party at the 1922 election did a new political order crystallize. Only then did Labour finally emerge from its pioneering phase. Only then did the age of Keir Hardie come to an end.

For two generations before 1900, Merthyr Tydfil had been notorious as the major storm-centre of Welsh politics. The Merthyr Boroughs, consisting primarily of Merthyr and Aberdare, with Mountain Ash, Dowlais and Penydarren, had been a cockpit of political and social upheaval since the violent riots of 1831. In the latter decades of the nineteenth century, this tradition of radical militancy was to acquire a new rhetoric and new significance.

In the years following the famous election of 1868, the politics of Merthyr were largely determined by a complex of factors which were unique in Wales. In the first place, Merthyr Tydfil was unquestionably the most democratic constituency in the principality, perhaps in Britain as a whole. Ever since the 1867 Reform Act had increased the electorate by over 1,000 per cent and granted the Boroughs a second member, Merthyr politics had been characterized by a degree of popular participation of a peculiarly intense kind. The 1868 election provided a dramatic commentary upon this, with the return of the radical Henry Richard, easily at the head of the poll. In part, Richard owed his triumph to the influence of political Nonconformity, as exploited by local middle-class politicians such as Dr Thomas Price of Aberdare. In addition, Richard drew upon the legacy of working-class agitation in Merthyr and Aberdare which dated from Dic Penderyn and the Chartists. For many years the area had pioneered new forms of working-class institutions: in 1860, the first Co-operative Society in Wales had been founded at Cwmbach, near Aberdare. The later extensions of democracy after 1868 – the Ballot Act of 1872 and the Reform and Redistribution Acts of 1884–5 – greatly strengthened these elements in the radical tradition of Merthyr. In particular, Labour remained an important factor in Merthyr politics to a quite unusual degree. In the 1874 general election, Thomas Halliday, the secretary of the short-lived Amalgamated Association of Miners which had recently swept through the mining valleys, polled nearly 5,000 votes. Although Halliday may have owed something to the mischievous support given him by the marquess of Bute and local Conservatives, his poll was remarkable at a time when Labour was in the doldrums as a political force in Britain generally. But as yet the Labour vote was still a dormant giant, and Halliday failed to be returned. Henry Richard survived until his death in 1888, being joined in the 1880 election by another Liberationist radical, C. H. James. Between them, Richard, Congregational minister, cosmopolitan radical with wide contacts in the Anti-Slavery and Peace Societies, and James, a Unitarian solicitor and a scion of the local 'shopocracy,' symbolized the power of political dissent in Merthyr, ecumenical and parochial at the same time.

The politics of Merthyr were also radically shaped by the social and economic character of the Boroughs. Merthyr Tydfil itself was a town in social and economic upheaval. In 1815 it had been easily the biggest town in Wales, with a population of over 50,000. While it remained an important urban centre (in 1908 it was to attain borough status), after 1870 it seemed comparatively static at a period when south Wales as a whole was exploding with new life. Throughout the period after 1870, the population of Merthyr was sluggish in growth: in the 1870s its registration district actually showed a decline of over 2.6 per cent, and long before the turn of the century it had been outstripped by Cardiff and Swansea. Merthyr seemed to be a static outpost on the rim of the coalfield, at a time when the valleys generally were in the throes of dynamic expansion. The increase in the population of the Merthyr Boroughs between 1871 and 1911 was due mainly to Aberdare, which by 1914 claimed over half the electorate. In addition, the quality of Merthyr's population was greatly changing. It had long been the most cosmopolitan town in south Wales. Now more and more immigrants poured into the area from beyond the confines of Wales. Irishmen, Spaniards and Italians added picturesque variety, and new tensions, to the population of Merthyr and Aberdare. The Merthyr Irish were particularly prominent, not least in politics. By the 1880s, the Irish population of Merthyr outstripped that of Swansea, and five Catholic priests were active in the town.

Underlying these variations in the social structure was a radical transformation of the economy. Down to the 1850s, Merthyr had been in the forefront of the advance of new industry. Its economy was dominated by the four mighty iron works of Cyfarthfa, Dowlais, Penydarren and Plymouth, monuments to the English entrepreneurs who had pioneered the exploitation of Welsh iron ore from the 1780s. But, by 1870, the Penydarren and Plymouth works had closed their doors for ever, while the other two works were in severe difficulty. Throughout the last thirty years of the century, the iron industry continued in severe and irreversible decline, as competition from Germany and the United States mounted in intensity. In 1891, the bulk of the Dowlais works was transferred to Cardiff. All this meant a major social upheaval in the town of Merthyr. No longer was its labour force dominated by ironworkers: they numbered only 3,315 in 1871 and only 2,436 in 1891 (out of a total population of 59,000). As some compensation for the disintegration of the iron industry, the coal industry was expanding dramatically, especially in the Aberdare valley. By 1906, over 43 per cent of the electorate of Merthyr Boroughs was classified as miners. But the economic weaknesses of the area remained, and they were in part reflected by the later political success of Keir Hardie. Long before 1914, Labour in Merthyr had been characterized as the depression party, the residuary legatee of unemployment, industrial recession and human misery. In the grim decades after the end of the First World War, this sombre reputation was to be amply sustained.

Since 1868, Merthyr's politics had been determined by its record as one of the safest Liberal strongholds in the British Isles. Time and again, unfortunate Conservative candidates were swamped at election time; in 1892 the two Liberals received majorities of over 9,000, the largest in the country. Most of the local institutions of Merthyr society and culture were dominated by Liberal Nonconformity. Newspapers such as the *Merthyr Express* and *Tarian y Gweithiwr* (the miners' organ published in Aberdare) were firmly Liberal, and vented their scorn and their scurrility on Tory opponents. Social life was in large measure dominated by the chapels; the 1851 religious census had shown that already sixty-five chapels were flourishing throughout Merthyr and Aberdare, the great bulk of them Baptist and Welsh Independent. As the Church revived after 1870, especially in Aberdare, their militancy was intensified. As a result, the usual Nonconformist and Liberal demands for social equality found a ready echo in the Merthyr division. The necessity for disestablishment of the Church, reform of the tithe system and a popular, undenominational educational structure was expounded from scores of platforms and pulpits. And yet the pattern of local politics was far more complex than the superficial picture of unquestioned Liberal ascendancy might suggest. There was the long tradition of internecine rivalry between Merthyr and Aberdare. More important, there were social cross-currents beneath the surface which were to play, indirectly, a major part in assisting the rise of Keir Hardie and the Labour movement.

These complex cross-currents were clearly illustrated by the two important by-elections that occurred in Merthyr in 1888. They mark, as clearly as any other episodes, the period of transition from the Merthyr of Henry Richard to that of Keir Hardie. At the first by-election, in March 1888, there was returned unopposed D. A. Thomas, later Viscount Rhondda. Thomas was to sit for the constituency for the next twenty-two years; like Richard Fothergill in 1868, his position shows how the local influence of a mighty industrialist could sway even as democratic a constituency as Merthyr. Already Thomas had inherited the Cambrian Collieries from his father; in the next quarter-century, he was to build them up into the massive Cambrian Combine and to create a huge industrial empire of dynastic character. Throughout this period he exercised a remarkable personal dominance over Merthyr politics from his dignified estate in Llanwern Park. In politics, as in industry, his methods were entirely his own. He maintained his own private election machinery, his agent being for a time J. M. Berry, father of the newspaper barons, Lords Kemsley and Camrose. Time and again, he finished comfortably at the head of the poll with the minimum of effort. But Merthyr Liberalism as a collective entity suffered in consequence. In the Commons, Thomas proved himself an original mind but an impetuous tactician. He became an ardent spokesman for Welsh national sentiment, but solely from the standpoint of the mercantile bourgeoisie of the coalfield, and of Cardiff in particular, where he was for years president of the Chamber of Commerce. Indeed, the quality of his Liberalism reflected the cosmopolitan business interests of the shippers and exporters of Cardiff rather than the inner-directed aspirations of the popular democracy of Merthyr. He agitated violently for south Wales interests during the *Cymru Fydd* ('Young Wales') controversy of 1895–6; this led to a bitter feud with Lloyd George and the Liberals of north Wales which lasted for almost twenty years. On the whole, Thomas's party political career was a failure. His free-lance methods, more appropriate to the age of Peel or Palmerston, were out of date. His erratic individualism, so fitted for the ruthless Darwinian world of industry and commerce, proved unsuited to the discipline of party politics where rebellions proved increasingly fatal. As a result, not until the Lloyd George Coalition ministry during the First World War in 1916 were his talents used in government, when he was appointed successively president of the Local Government Board and food controller. As far as Merthyr politics were concerned, the very extent of Thomas's personal ascendancy helped to undermine the organization and the morale of Liberalism in the constituency. Without realizing it, this prototype of the industrial tycoon had helped to make possible the awakening of Labour as a political force.

At the second by-election, in October 1888, there was returned W. Pritchard Morgan, the itinerant son of a Wesleyan minister from Usk, whose search for wealth and fortune had taken him as far afield as Australia and Korea. To *Tarian y Gweithiwr* (which detested him) he was *yr aelod dros China* ('the member for China'). His return in 1888 led to the complete disintegration of the Merthyr Liberal Association, which had been built up laboriously under the presidency of the much-respected Thomas Williams of Gwaelod-y-Garth. The Association had promised to nominate a working man as candidate when Henry Richard died, but had gone back on this pledge. At once there was a flood of protest from Labour, as there had been three years earlier when the Rhondda Liberal Association turned down the miners' leader, Mabon (William Abraham). The intervention of

Pritchard Morgan in the Merthyr by-election was an unexpected development: with some show of plausibility, he claimed to be the Labour candidate. Morgan was opposed by a galaxy of political talent, by D. A. Thomas and by Mabon, by Tom Ellis and the nationalistic *Cymru Fydd* element, and by most of the press. All these supported Morgan's Liberal opponent, Ffoulkes Griffiths, a Baptist barrister from London who had been hurriedly nominated. But, after being alone in the field for two months, his campaign ably directed by the solicitor, John Vaughan, Morgan easily beat off Griffith's challenge, and won by 7,149 votes to 4,956. He benefited from Conservative backing, but also from some Labour support, particularly in Aberdare where the Merthyr Liberal Association was distrusted as a middle-class clique. Morgan's campaign cost him nearly £1,100, but it was money well spent. The result of this by-election was that Merthyr Liberalism remained divided down to 1900. The Merthyr Liberal Association disappeared completely and did not re-emerge until 1909. Until then, Merthyr was one of the most ill-organized constituencies in Wales. The only formal survival of Liberal organization was the existence of Liberal Clubs at Merthyr and Aberdare, the latter being enhanced by a bar and, perhaps for that reason, the more flourishing of the two. Otherwise, only a very few local bodies, such as the Brecon Road Liberal Association, provided a framework of organization for the Liberal party.

The next few years, however, seemed to demonstrate that organization was irrelevant to so overwhelmingly a Liberal stronghold. At the 1892 and 1895 elections, Thomas and Morgan crushed a variety of opponents with ease. And yet, beneath the surface, the fabric of the party was much weakened, and new tensions were complicating the political structure. They were symbolized by the bitter animosity between the two Liberal members. D. A. Thomas continued his erratic way in Parliament; he co-operated with Lloyd George in the 'revolt' over the 1894 Disestablishment Bill, then broke with him fatally over *Cymru Fydd* in 1896. For years after, he remained sourly isolated from most of his Welsh colleagues. Meanwhile, Pritchard Morgan extended his search for El Dorado from the mountains of Merioneth to the distant wastes of Korea, where he spent much of his time after 1895. In the 1890s, indeed, many observers felt that Merthyr Liberalism was becoming increasingly moribund, far less vital than in the heady days of 1868, a survival from the past fighting battles of long ago that had already been won.

The first real challenge to Merthyr Liberalism came not from the somnolent forces of local Toryism, which remained in genteel repose, but from the upsurge of Labour. Hardie's candidature and return in

1900, which seemed later on fortuitous, even miraculous, were in reality the culmination of years of development. In the 1890s, working-class politics in Merthyr had become increasingly assertive, and the first echoes of the creed of socialism were being heard in the coalfield. An Independent Labour Party branch had been formed at Merthyr in 1895 which claimed 278 members by 1898. Satellite branches at Aberdare, Merthyr Vale, Penydarren and Troedyrhiw also showed a rising membership of over one hundred each. In 1895, also, had been formed the Aberdare Socialist Society. Its first secretary was the flamboyant Charles Butt Stanton, who combined the appearance of an Oscar Wilde with the rhetoric of a Mussolini, and who had made his first violent mark in Labour politics by firing a revolver in a revolutionary demonstration.

All these local bodies, however, would have remained weak and fragmentary had it not been for the growing deterioration of the economy throughout the area. Wales had hitherto played only a minor and peripheral role in the political or industrial growth of the Labour movement. It was the depression of the 1890s that galvanized the Welsh working-class into new life and unity. One index of this was the growth of the so-called 'new unionism'; not only did it provide a stimulus to unskilled workers such as labourers and construction workers, but it lent new vitality to older skilled unions such as the Amalgamated Society of Railway Servants (which had a powerful branch in Aberdare). One product of this 'new unionism' was the formation of new Trades Councils, usually under the direction of committed socialists. This was the case with the Aberdare Trades Council, formed in 1899 largely under the leadership of ILP militants such as John Prowle and Edmund Stonelake. The Merthyr Trades Council was founded the following year.

These new bodies were born at a time of growing economic dislocation. Throughout the coalfield, the paralysis of depression could be felt; demand was sluggish, wages were falling, and trade disputes were frequent. A growing militancy from labour was paralleled by a new intransigence among the coalowners, headed by the notorious W. T. Lewis (later Lord Merthyr), 'the last of the industrial barons'. The outcome of this collapse in industrial relations was the immense coal stoppage of 1898 – a strike to the owners, a lock-out to the men. During six terrible months, almost 100,000 men were thrown out of work in south Wales; there was immense hardship in the Merthyr and Aberdare valleys as elsewhere. Gifts of cocoa and tea by philanthropic observers, such·as George Cadbury and Sir Thomas Lipton, barely alleviated the starvation and despair widespread throughout the coalfield. The stoppage came to an end in September 1898 with complete defeat for the men. The wage rate was not raised, the hated 'sliding scale' was retained, and 'Mabon's Day,' the monthly holiday, was abolished, a crushing humiliation for the miners' leader whose name it bore. The defeat of 1898 proved a traumatic experience for both the political and industrial sides of the Labour movement. Industrially, the scattered mining unions welded themselves into the unity of the South Wales Miners' Federation: in Merthyr at least, effective mining unionism had been virtually unknown. Politically, the stoppage gave an immense impetus to the ILP. During the months of unemployment and hardship, ILP organizers such as Willie Wright of Mexborough had toured the Welsh valleys. *Clarion* vans had conveyed Blatchford's gospel to the mining villages. Above all, for the first time Keir Hardie had become personally known in the coalfield. He had spent several weeks there during the stoppage of 1898; his compassionate articles in the *Labour Leader* made known the facts of industrial distress in south Wales to a wider public. For some years, Hardie had enjoyed considerable esteem amongst the Welsh miners, ever since he had startled delegates at the Swansea TUC by a fierce attack on the eminent 'Lib–Lab', Henry Broadhurst. Hardie was, of course, nationally celebrated as leader of the ILP and former member of Parliament (1892–5) for West Ham South. In 1894, he had protested in the Commons that the honourable members seemed more anxious to utter platitudes in celebration of a royal baby (the future Edward VIII, in fact), than to express their sympathies with the dependants of 260 miners in Wales who had lost their lives in the Albion Colliery disaster. However, it was in 1898 that Hardie the man became generally known in south Wales for the first time.

It is clear that his personal impact upon the coalfield was electric from the start. Meetings he held at Penydarren and Troedyrhiw resembled the evangelical gatherings of the chapels in their revivalist intensity. Hardie appealed simply to a common sense of humanity and compassion: 'my programme is the programme of Labour. My cause is Labour's cause – the cause of Humanity – the cause of God . . . I first learnt my Socialism in the New Testament where I still find my chief inspiration.' His appeal to Welsh miners lay in his being able to translate socialist ethics into the imagery of popular Nonconformity. This, he claimed, was 'real religion', the creed of Robert Burns, of the Ten Commandments and the Sermon on the Mount, not of pharisaical ministers and their bourgeois congregations of self-satisfied men of property. Hardie himself seemed to symbolize the simplicity, even the saintliness, of his own message. In the words of W. J. Edwards, 'the man and his gospel were indivisible'.

However, Hardie would never have been elected for Merthyr Boroughs had he not possessed qualities more mundane than those of the saint in politics. Like Gandhi, he was also an extremely shrewd politician, with a profound appreciation of the art of the possible. He showed this in outmanoeuvring Bernard Shaw and the Fabians at the London conference of February 1900 when the Labour Representation Committee was founded. His political skills now enabled him to create a political base in Merthyr that he was able to retain until his death.

After the South African War broke out in 1899, new radical currents began to surge through the Merthyr constituency, notably in the new Trades Councils. Among the miners, a new era dawned when in 1899 C. B. Stanton succeeded the venerable David Morgan ('Dai o'r Nant') as agent for Aberdare. Stanton was nominated as the fiery socialist he professed to be. From him and from others was heard the cry for a Labour candidate for Merthyr in the coming general election to replace Pritchard Morgan. This flamboyant speculator, mainly concerned to obtain government aid for his derelict gold mines in Dolgellau, seemed to be an incongruous representative for the working class of Merthyr. In any case it was widely believed that his activities in China to discover new coal deposits would result in unfavourable competition for Welsh coal in world markets.

The consequence was the nomination of Keir Hardie. However, there was nothing inevitable about it. Indeed, Hardie's sponsorship was the result of a good deal of local intrigue and rivalry. The miners of Penrhiwceiber and Mountain Ash wanted William Brace, vice-president of the SWMF, while others urged the claims of Tom Richards, treasurer of that body and also well known in the area. Aberdare Trades Council tended to favour the militant Marxist, Tom Mann. In the face of these various challenges, Hardie's ILP supporters, such as Stanton, Stonelake and Archer, had to prepare their ground carefully. At the decisive meeting of the Merthyr and Aberdare Trades Council at Aberaman on 22 September 1900, there were angry exchanges between the rival factions. Brace's supporters challenged the voting procedure and alleged that the meeting had been rigged. Eventually they left in disgust, and in their absence Hardie was nominated by thirty-two votes to seven for Richards. From this unpromising beginning, his campaign was to be launched.

From the start, there were the gravest difficulties facing Hardie's candidature. The war years had provoked the same kind of jingoistic hysteria in Wales as elsewhere: the evidence is overwhelming that support for imperialism was widespread throughout rural and industrial Wales. Pritchard Morgan was its raucous spokesman. The *Aberdare Times* was ecstatic over the relief of Mafeking; Baden-Powell's somewhat diluted Welsh blood provoked fervent accounts of 'what Wales has done in the war'. Hardie's uncompromising stand against the South African War was therefore provocative and dangerous: 'vote against D. A. Thomas and Keir Hardie, both pro-Boers' was the slogan of Pritchard Morgan's supporters. The ILP offices in Aberdare were stoned, and Hardie's election workers physically attacked. Hardie faced particularly severe opposition from Nonconformist ministers. They had been somewhat apathetic in the 1895 Merthyr election, but now almost to a man they rallied to denounce Hardie's socialist creed as tantamount to atheism and republicanism. Pritchard Morgan was later to trade on this uninhibitedly: 'socialism means sedition, anarchy, no government, no King, no God – absolute impenetrable darkness!' Allied to this was the charge that Hardie was a Scottish outsider, out of sympathy with the language and customs of Wales. But the major obstacle in the way of Hardie's campaign was the fact that he had so little contact with the constituency. He was also candidate for Preston and, indeed, considered his prospects much more hopeful there. Only when he was defeated in Preston did he travel down to Merthyr. He held only three meetings, and claimed later that he had spent only 'eleven waking hours' in the constituency. In the circumstances, his campaign was a remarkable tribute to his supporters in Merthyr, who had produced 'Hamlet' for so long in the unavoidable absence of the Prince of Denmark.

On the other hand, other factors worked in Hardie's favour. One considerable asset was the animosity between Pritchard Morgan and D. A. Thomas. This had come to a climax during the South African War, of which Thomas was a severe critic. Thomas's attitude towards Hardie was at least one of benevolent neutrality; he knew as well as any man the potential of the Labour vote, and it did not frighten him. Indeed, he was himself an advocate of reforms such as a minimum wage, and urged a planned control of production in the coalfield instead of the primitive anarchy of *laissez-faire* which had produced the disaster of 1898. Hardie clearly benefited by appearing in some sense as Thomas's running mate, however incongruous the partnership might appear on the surface. Again, if imperialism was a powerful influence in Merthyr, with the new affluence brought about by the advent of war, so too was anti-imperialism. The pacifist tradition of Henry Richard was still abroad in the land, and many Welsh people felt disengaged in a war waged by English generals and capitalists of unidentifiable race in a remote country. Some Welsh publicists argued that there was a kinship between the Welsh and the Boers, also a small, predominantly pastoral God-fearing people of Calvinist stock. The Irish of Merthyr went further in their anti-imperialism: they wanted England to lose the war, and they flocked to Hardie's banner.

Finally, the working-class co-operative tradition of the Merthyr community, a constant thread from the Chartist period down to the days of Richard and Halliday, was still very much alive. It had been greatly stimulated by the disastrous outcome of the 1898 stoppage. In the event, these factors turned the scale. While Thomas easily headed the poll, Hardie gained 5,745 votes to Morgan's 4,004, and was thus returned as the second member for Merthyr. The great mass of his votes – 4,437 of them according to the local press – had been cast jointly for himself and for D. A. Thomas. Few 'plumped' for Hardie at this stage. Nevertheless, Hardie had gained a permanent base which was never to desert him. He had been returned not as a miners' representative or any kind of 'Lib–Lab', but as an unequivocal socialist and a nominee of the new Labour Representation Committee. As such his personality was to serve as the decisive catalyst in the politics of Merthyr for years to come.

For the next few years, Hardie spent much time in building up his position in Welsh politics. He joined the Welsh Parliamentary Party when the new House met in December. He combined with his Liberal colleagues in Wales in denouncing the 1902 Education Bill as a surrender to clericalism, and in warding off the threat of Tariff Reform. He pressed for Welsh disestablishment, although his arguments for it were somewhat eccentric, since he welcomed it as a preliminary to a more general disendowment of all vested interests, landlords and capitalists included. He claimed to be a Welsh nationalist, though on socialist grounds: as a socialist he wished the land of Wales to become the property of the people of Wales. He scorned the spurious nationalism of Liberal capitalists such as Sir Alfred Mond: 'the Nationalist Party I have in mind is this – the people of Wales fighting to recover possession of the land in Wales . . . that is the kind of Nationalism that will be emblazoned on the red flag of Socialism.' He poured contempt on the ceremonial that attended the investiture of the Prince of Wales at Caernarfon in 1911, under the stage management of Lloyd George: 'Wales is to have an "Investiture" as a reminder that an English King and his robber barons strove for ages to destroy the Welsh people, and finally succeeded in robbing them of their lands, driving them into the mountain fastnesses of their native land like hunted beasts, and then had his son "invested" in their midst.' Hardie was genuine enough in his sympathy for the Welsh people; like Tom Ellis and Michael Davitt, he considered the Celts were socialists by instinct, with their traditional sense of comradeship and co-operation. Hardie even learnt a modicum of Welsh, sufficient at least to sing the Welsh national anthem. He found new friendships in the theological colleges of rural Wales, in whose secluded shelter a growing number of young Christian socialists were to be found.

However, Hardie was also becoming in many ways a figure more and more remote from Wales, as his fame in the British and international socialist movement increased. In 1906 he was elected the first chairman of the Parliamentary Labour Party. He frequently attended European socialist gatherings, and the congresses of the Second International. He preserved links with Debs, Gompers and other Labour leaders in the United States, and visited that country three times in all. In 1907 he went on a much-publicized journey round the world, to India, Australia, New Zealand, Japan and South Africa; he helped to fan the nationalist passions of the Congress movement in Bengal. All this, inevitably, led to some neglect of his constituency, and Hardie kept only indirect control over his local political machine. True, he was quick to respond to local hardship. Largely single-handed, he managed to settle a serious labour dispute in the Dowlais foundry in 1911. He wrote a famous open letter to King George V on working conditions in the iron works of Guest, Keen and Nettlefolds. But he had to face the fact that the political position of the Labour party was still precarious, and that even in Merthyr his own standing was not wholly secure.

But, gradually, Labour strength was building up at the local level in Merthyr, the essential preliminary to any future expansion. The missionary campaigns of visiting socialist celebrities, such as Bruce Glasier and Philip Snowden, were reaping their harvest. Labour representatives were now being elected to a variety of local bodies in Merthyr: R. J. Wilson and T. Weale to the Board of Guardians, C. E. G. Simmons to the Urban District Council. Most remarkable of all was the success of all twelve Labour candidates (nearly all miners) in the 1905 municipal elections, and Enoch Morrell, a Welsh-speaking checkweighman later to become a member of Parliament, was elected the first Labour mayor of Merthyr. Industrially, also, Labour was becoming a more coherent force. The hated 'sliding scale' had disappeared in 1902 and this heralded a further expansion of strength by the SWMF. By 1906 a majority of the Welsh miners were voting for affiliation to the Labour party. In any case, the threat to trade unionism embodied in the Taff Vale verdict of 1901, which left unions liable to meet the costs incurred in industrial disputes, spurred on more and more smaller unions to affiliate. All this reinforced Hardie's position. He now even had his own periodical, the *Merthyr Pioneer*: a bilingual production, itself a pioneer in the chequered history of socialist journalism.

It was generally assumed that Hardie would have a clear run in Merthyr in the general election of January 1906. All over the country, pacts had come into being between local Liberal parties and the struggling Labour Representation Committee. At the last minute, however, there was unexpected Liberal opposition in the person of Henry Radcliffe, a prominent Welsh Methodist and a Cardiff shipowner who had once been president of the Cardiff shipping association. Radcliffe's candidature demonstrated in the clearest way the suspicion that Nonconformist Liberals still entertained towards Hardie; many local ministers, such as the Revd J. Morgan Jones, campaigned hard for Radcliffe, and Hardie had to fight to retain his seat. His assisting speakers were a bewildering miscellany: Michael Davitt (who was to die in the following May) to appeal to the Irish vote, Annie Kenney (of the Women's Social and Political Union), and the Revd George Neighbour, a Baptist minister from Mountain Ash. Hardie's platform was uncompromisingly radical, including a reduction in arms expenditure, nationalization of basic industries, old age pensions, women's suffrage, abolition of the House of Lords, and Home Rule all round, with Ireland having priority. In the event, he won fairly comfortably over Radcliffe (10,187 to 7,776) on an 85 per cent poll, the 1906 election generally being marked by a huge Liberal landslide. D. A. Thomas, however, still outstripped Hardie at the polls by nearly 4,000 votes. Liberalism and Labour were therefore *de facto* still running in double harness.

For the next few years, the uneasy truce between Liberals and Labour in Merthyr endured. But the growing social unrest of the years up to 1914 made it increasingly unworkable. As each year went by, the strain of maintaining the partnership became more and more intense.

One cause of this was the revival, artificial though it was, of official Liberalism in the constituency. This was largely a result of the removal of the massive influence of D. A. Thomas. It became known at the end of 1909 that he had accepted the nomination for Cardiff, a far less secure Liberal seat which perhaps only he could win (and did). As a result, a new Liberal Association was formed in Merthyr in November 1909, after twenty years of hibernation. Its president was Alderman D. W. Jones, once D. A. Thomas's agent. After a good deal of the usual animosity between Merthyr and Aberdare, a new constitution was drafted, with seven ward associations each in Aberdare and Merthyr. The leaders of this renaissance were W. Rees Edmunds, a local solicitor and deacon of Calfaria Baptist chapel, D. M. Richards, registration agent for Aberdare, and the Revd J. Morgan Jones, former editor of *Tarian y Gweithiwr*. Their implied purpose was clearly to fight Keir Hardie. In succession to D. A. Thomas, they nominated Edgar Jones, a schoolmaster and a prominent Baptist, in January 1910. Later in the year, they appointed a full-time agent, O. T. Hopkins of the Ynyshir and Wattstown Co-operative Society. The breach with Labour became more and more clear-cut, until in 1914 a second Liberal candidate was nominated, the eminent barrister (later a judge) Thomas Artemus Jones. Had the general election come in 1915, he would have opposed Hardie at the polls.

In addition, these years were marked by growing militancy within the Labour movement. The ILP branches at Merthyr and Aberdare continued to expand; in 1912 the annual conference of the party met in Merthyr, a dedication service being held in Tabernacle Baptist chapel, Aberdare, with the Revd Rowland Jones officiating. However, it was industrial Labour that most clearly demonstrated the new passions, the ILP seeming almost staid by comparison. Throughout the coalfield there was a growing revulsion against the constitutional method and bourgeois politics in general. This had a striking effect upon Merthyr itself. No longer was it an isolated radical outpost remote from the mainstream of south Wales Labour; increasingly its politics were indistinguishable from those of the coalfield as a whole. In 1908 and 1909 a wave of violent strikes broke out, beginning with major stoppages by the Powell-Duffryn men in the Aberdare valley. Stanton seemed increasingly in the ascendant, urging older miners' leaders such as Mabon, with the maximum of emphasis, to 'move on or move out', and threatening forms of industrial violence. Finally, there were the frightening eruptions of November 1910 during the year-long Cambrian stoppage. The riots at Tonypandy were paralleled by equally wild disturbances in the Merthyr and Aberdare area where almost 26,000 men were out on strike. In the first week of November, there were violent riots around the Powell-Duffryn washery, after a march to Cwmaman led by the inflammatory Stanton. He threatened the owners with a 'fighting brigade' of miners 'to give the police a taste of what they have given our people'. A miner, Samuel Rays, lost his life, and hundreds of special constables and mounted hussars, despatched by the home secretary, Churchill, patrolled the coalfield. A few months later, two workers were shot and killed during a railway strike in Llanelli. The most violent excesses of industrial America, of the Homestead and Pullman strikes, seemed to have been transplanted to the peaceful Welsh valleys, and Aberdare ranked second only to Rhondda as a centre of turbulent unrest.

This turbulence continued for several years more. The Cambrian Combine strike of 1910–11 was followed by a second mighty explosion over the minimum wage in 1912. Merthyr was in the van in this second stoppage: indeed, the Merthyr district of the SWMF was the only one to vote against a resumption of work in May 1912. New militant ideas were surging through the mining valleys, syndicalism, anarchism and other philosophies of 'direct action' imported from France or the United States. Especially influential was the Labour College movement, the product of the breakaway of young Marxist students from Ruskin College in 1909 to found the Central Labour College in London. Through its tutorial classes in south Wales, Marxist sociology and economics became widely familiar throughout the eastern coalfield. This was no mere abstract speculation. The Unofficial Reform Committee, controlled by Noah Ablett and other young Marxists, was a practical machinery for putting the ideas of the Labour College movement into reality, and for supplanting the moderate executive of the SWMF who were accused of class betrayal. It was Ablett and his colleagues who published the revolutionary *The Miners' Next Step* at Tonypandy in 1912. The whole of the mining community seemed to be seething with violent rebellion of apocalyptic fury. It seemed significant that many of the young leaders most influenced by the new ideologies had been profoundly stirred by the religious revival of 1904. This was common to Noah Ablett, Frank Hodges, A. J. Cook and Arthur Horner; some, such as Ablett, had even served as lay preachers. They had now long since left the chapels behind, but the evangelical fervour of the revival, its impatience with earthly disciplines, its search for a new pattern of human relationships within society, left its unmistakable imprint upon them. On the messianism of the religious revival, they superimposed the Marxist dialectic. It served to make the class war in south Wales all the more naked and complete.

Where was Keir Hardie, the apostle of peace, during this wave of violent eruption? He could not fail to be deeply moved by the protest of the miners. In the Commons he passionately denounced police brutality at Tonypandy and Aberaman, in many cases quite unprovoked, and in vain sought government redress. However, he was basically in a dilemma. He was firmly committed to the parliamentary method, and basically an empiricist in tactics. He fought off the challenge from the extremist element in the ILP led by Victor Grayson. For Hardie, the socialist revolution must come through consent, not through violence. The inflammatory approach of a Stanton or some of the syndicalists offended his gentle character, as much as it did his code of ethics, based as it was on Robert Burns and the Old Testament. Even so, his political position in Merthyr had become by now impregnable. In January 1910, one of his opponents was none other than the itinerant Pritchard Morgan, back in the fold and running as an alleged 'Independent' with the support of the Anti-Socialist Union, of Conservatives and of the *Merthyr Express*, never a lover of Keir Hardie. Hardie, backed by the usual exotic collection of speakers that included Bernard Shaw, Arthur Henderson and Mrs Cobden Sanderson (the daughter of Richard Cobden), won the day easily. Despite Morgan's scurrilous campaign, which accused Labour, among other things, of atheism, assassination and the advocacy of free love, Hardie's poll increased by over 3,000 votes.

In the second election of 1910, in December, fought mainly on the

House of Lords issue, Hardie again won comfortably, this time defeating a so-called 'Liberal Unionist', J. H. Watts. Each time, however, the Liberal Edgar Jones headed the poll; later he was to claim, probably correctly, that his vote amongst the miners was larger than that of Hardie himself, though it should be added that Hardie's total of 'plumpers' was five times larger. In each election in 1910, a striking feature was the new attitude of the Nonconformist ministry. In 1900 the chapels had been almost universally hostile to socialism; they had recently vented all their venom upon Vernon Hartshorn in the Mid-Glamorgan by-election. But Hardie's candidature in Merthyr seemed to be in a different category. One phenomenon stimulated in large measure by the 1904 religious revival was that of 'social Christianity', a movement that worked within the religious bodies themselves, in contrast to the Marxist messianism of Ablett and the syndicalists. The social gospel of R. J. Campbell, which aimed to give Christianity a social rather than an individualistic code of ethics, was widely discussed; the minutes of Aberdare Socialist Society in these years show discussion of such themes as 'Socialism and the Ten Commandments' and 'The Sermon on the Mount'. A new generation of Nonconformist ministers was arising, who rejected the exclusive political sectarianism of the days of Thomas Gee. They were preoccupied with the failure of the chapels to adapt themselves to the problems of an industrial society, and their inability to communicate with the proletariat in urban areas. In 'darkest Cardiff' or 'darkest Merthyr', the denominational refinements of Baptist, Methodist, Independent or Unitarian seemed painfully irrelevant. For these ministers, Hardie served as a living symbol of the validity of the 'new theology'. His election platforms were graced in 1910 by several young ministers, notably the Revd Rhondda Williams (Union Church, Brighton), the Revd D. G. Rees (Bridgend), the Revd Cynnog Williams (Aberdare), the Revd James Nicholas (Moriah, Tonypandy) and the Revd Thomas Nicholas (Seion, Glais). Several of these were Baptists, this denomination being particularly stirred by the impact of the 1904 revival. They flocked to Hardie's banner, uninhibitedly sporting his colours, red (Labour in revolt), green (nature and nationalism), and white (purity and strength). Political dissent, in a very different context, provided impetus for Keir Hardie in 1910 as it had for Henry Richard a generation earlier.

The outbreak of the First World War saw the beginning of the end of the age of Keir Hardie. Hardie, like Jaurès and Bernstein but unlike many socialists, was unequivocal and honest in his attitude to the war. He spoke courageously at a peace meeting at Aberdare on 6 August 1914, denouncing the war as an outrage, the ugly offspring of capitalism and militarism. He was howled down, the meeting broken up by an angry and sadistic mob, and he had to flee for his life. He remarked at the home of a Merthyr friend that evening that he now understood as well as any man the sufferings of Christ at Gethsemane. Behind the mobs which broke up his meeting was none other than C. B. Stanton, miners' agent and Mussolini combined, whose unstable mind turned easily from industrial unionism to bellicose patriotism. The Labour organization in Merthyr was henceforth fatally divided between those who agreed with the official Labour leadership in supporting the war, and the pacifist supporters of Hardie and the ILP who stood out against the passions of the time.

These last months were sad ones for Hardie. He was racked by ill-health, while he faced now the same kind of hysterical jingoism that had confronted him during the Boer War fourteen years earlier. His colleague, Edgar Jones, denounced him in the House for stirring up sedition. In September 1915 Hardie died, old before his time (he was only fifty-nine), and the divisions in the Labour movement in Merthyr at once reasserted themselves. The by-election saw two Labour candidates in the field. The official candidate was the miners' agent, James Winstone, a Baptist lay preacher, and a prominent recruiting speaker. But Winstone was a member of the ILP and, while no pacifist himself (he had a son serving at the front), he unwisely brought down anti-war speakers such as Ramsay MacDonald and Fred Jowett. C. B. Stanton, also a self-styled 'Labour' candidate, came out against Winstone, with the scarcely-veiled backing of local Liberals and Conservatives. Stanton's tirades against 'the brutal butchers of Berlin' suited the mood of the hour, and he trounced Winstone by over 4,000 votes.

Was Hardie's work then in vain? Had he been merely the beneficiary of Liberal charity? Was his status as an 'independent Labour' member merely an illusion? The position of Labour in the Merthyr Boroughs remained highly ambiguous. The social tensions of the war years made the position even more complex. The political weakness of Labour was underlined in the 'coupon election' of December 1918. Merthyr Boroughs had now been divided into two separate constituencies under the 1918 Representation of the People Act. In the Merthyr Tydfil seat, Sir Edgar Jones (as he now was, as a reward for his wartime business activities) defeated the unfortunate Winstone. In the Aberdare division, the irresponsible Stanton, howling for vengeance against the 'filthy murderous Huns', swamped the ILP candidate, the Revd Thomas E. Nicholas, a pacifist, by over 16,000. Nicholas, a former contributor to Hardie's *Merthyr Pioneer* and an eisteddfodic bard of great distinction, found himself in danger of his life, not least from newly-enfranchised women electors crazed with the lust for revenge. The electoral weakness of Labour seemed to be amply confirmed.

Only after 1918 did it become clear that the war, far from undermining the Labour position, had brought it immense strength. Politically, it had spelt the doom of the Liberals, and Labour now succeeded them as the leading party of the left. Industrially, trade unions were far more powerful, and movements such as the shop stewards made them far more aggressive. Ideologically, there was the growing mood of revolutionary fervour launched by the new Bolshevik regime in Russia; workers' soviets were formed in several Welsh mining valleys. As before, Merthyr reflected this national trend. The new militancy was shown by the election of S. O. Davies (now member for Merthyr) as miners' agent for Dowlais, and of Noah Ablett, pioneer of Welsh syndicalism, as agent for Merthyr, in succession to John Williams. The industrial passions of the immediate post-war years, the resentment at the betrayal of 'Black Friday' and the non-implementation of the Sankey Report recommendations (which included a demand for nationalization of the mines) all lent new fervour to the Labour cause in Merthyr. This was finally confirmed in the 1922 election when Labour captured both seats. George Hall won comfortably enough in Aberdare; R. C. Wallhead of the ILP (who had been imprisoned during the war as a conscientious objector) got home by a narrow margin of less than 2,000 in Merthyr against Sir R. C. Mathias, a Liberal. In fact, however, both Merthyr and Aberdare were to remain Labour strongholds henceforth, even during the disasters of the crisis of 1931. They had passed through the pioneering phase; the age of Keir Hardie, therefore, may be considered to have come to an end.

The general characteristics of Merthyr politics in the age of Keir Hardie are difficult to delineate, so many cross-currents complicate the picture. Nevertheless, two general conclusions stand out. One is the surprising resilience of the Liberal tradition down to 1918; the dominance of D. A. Thomas and, less decisively, of Edgar Jones, over the working-class electors of Merthyr is a tribute to this. Thomas's role shows that Merthyr had yet to transcend the politics of deference for the politics of democracy. The second conclusion is the remarkable disorganization of Labour down to 1914. Indeed, to postulate a unified 'Labour movement' at all is in many ways to create a myth. 'Labour', that over-simple concept, in reality consisted of a series of different initiatives and pressures from a variety of different bodies, some political, some industrial, some religious or cultural. There was immense uncertainty about means and ends, about the relationship between the techniques of democracy and the doctrine of socialism, about the primacy of the political method. Not until the General Strike of 1926 underlined the futility of direct industrial action did the

Labour movement attain a final coherence, in Merthyr as in Britain as a whole.

In these circumstances, the achievement of Keir Hardie was immense. With disorganized supporters and a powerful opposition, he provided leadership and inspiration for a whole class. He was to lead Merthyr politics from the individualistic 'radicalism' of the nineteenth century, based largely on Merthyr itself, to the social democracy of our own day, in which Merthyr people feel a sense of kinship with the working-class movement throughout the world. He was able to introduce new English or Scottish ideas and assumptions, and to adapt them for a Welsh setting. In this process, his faithful supporters at Merthyr played an honoured part. Hardie himself recognized this towards the end of his life, when he paid tribute to the Merthyr electors in 1900 and to 'the disciples of Henry Richard who were then uncorrupted'. Perhaps today we can similarly venerate the disciples of Keir Hardie who also remained uncorrupted, and the man himself, the embodiment of political incorruptibility, of the dignity of labour and the brotherhood of man.

1967

14

Rhondda West*

1964		1966	
32,401 electors 80.7% voting		*31,189 electors 80.3% voting*	
I. R. Thomas (Lab.)	20,713 (*79.3%*)	I. R. Thomas (Lab.)	19,060 (*76.1%*)
N. Lloyd-Edwards (Con.)	2,754 (*10.5%*)	V. Davies (Plaid Cymru)	2,172 (*8.7%*)
V. Davies (Plaid Cymru)	2,668 (*10.2%*)	B. Sandford-Hill (Con.)	1,955 (*7.8%*)
		A. C. True (Comm.)	1,853 (*7.4%*)
Lab. maj. over Con.	17,959 (*68.8%*)	Lab. maj. over P.C.	16,888 (*67.4%*)

'North of Pontypridd, they've just stopped thinking', a disconsolate Conservative agent complained. He probably had Rhondda West in mind. Not since 1931 had the Conservatives saved their deposit there. In 1966 their candidate polled a mere 7.8 per cent of the votes, and finished third, just above the Communist. The Labour candidate, I. R. Thomas, gained over 76 per cent, confirming Rhondda West as just about the safest Labour seat in the British Isles.

Rhondda West consisted mainly of the more westerly of the two Rhondda valleys, some twenty miles north-west of Cardiff. Its six wards comprised a series of small mining townships, winding along the bleak sides of the valley, from Tonypandy up to Treorchy. It formed the very heart of the south Wales coalfield, and symbolized the bitter passions of two generations of industrial conflict. The Tonypandy riots took place here, around the Cambrian colliery and in Pandy Square, back in 1910. In the 1920s, there were violent strikes and protest

*Co-authored with Peter Stead.

marches; the red flag flew at pit-heads. In the 1930s came crushing unemployment; there were 24,352 on the dole in Rhondda in 1932. After the war, nationalization brought a new deal for the Rhondda miner, but it also speeded up pit closures. There were now only 4,000 miners in the constituency, as compared with 20,000 fifty years earlier. The Rhondda West electorate had fallen by 1,200 since the 1964 election.

Gwyn Thomas has written of 'the psychoses of poverty and dread' in the Rhondda of his youth. Since 1945, they had largely disappeared. Nearly thirty standard factories had been introduced, notably a clothing factory which employed over 1,500. People still lived in the drab, terraced houses of the last century, but everywhere there were symbols of a new and unfamiliar prosperity. In particular, there was an immense array of social clubs of all kinds, monuments to eighty years of Sunday closing. As one disillusioned socialist veteran reflected, 'We were out to build the new Jerusalem, and all we've got is a fairground.'

The politics of Rhondda West had always been dominated by the miners. Since Rhondda first returned an MP in 1885, the area had only three members, William Abraham (1885–1920), Will John (1920–50), and now I. R. Thomas, all miners. The sitting member, 'Iorrie' Thomas, had represented the division since 1950. He was a 70-year-old veteran of strikes and lock-outs, who had spent some months in gaol in the 1920s. He was sponsored by the National Union of Miners who paid 80 per cent of his election expenses. But by 1966 only a few of the local Labour party executive were miners; unions like the Amalgamated Engineering Union and the Tailors and Garment Workers were increasingly active in the local organization. Mr Thomas therefore presided over a constituency socially much more complex than ever before.

Labour was all-powerful in the politics of Rhondda. Thirty of the borough council of thirty-two were Labour members, even though in so highly unionized an area individual party membership was traditionally low. The changing industrial pattern had made little difference to Labour's overwhelming dominance. Rhondda people moving up the social scale preserved their old political loyalties.

By comparison, the other parties were mere splinter groups. The Conservatives barely existed in their own right. Their main organizational base lay in the seven Conservative clubs in the division. However, the stimulation sought was evidently liquid rather than political, since their membership was many times greater than the total Conservative vote. Only a glamorous club at Treorchy even tried to make party loyalty a test of membership, and, as one member ambiguously remarked, 'It's going the way of all flesh like the rest.' The Conservative candidate, Dr Sandford-Hill, a 31-year-old doctor, was imported from Cardiff, like his agent and many of his helpers, just before the campaign began.

The Communists were fighting Rhondda West for the first time since 1931. However, they had a base from which to build, since many lodges had a long Marxist tradition, and often elected Communist agents. In neighbouring Rhondda East, the Communists had always maintained a high poll, since Harry Pollitt's campaigns in the 1930s. Like Plaid Cymru, they regarded the election as a recruiting drive for future municipal contests. Their candidate was Arthur True, a 45-year-old ETU official and ex-miner.

The Welsh Nationalist party, Plaid Cymru, had fought the seat before; in 1959 it had gained 17 per cent of the poll. It relied traditionally on an older Liberal chapel vote, but claimed new support from schoolteachers and students. Its candidate, Victor Davies, was backed by three local branches of his party. A local lecturer and a former AEU shop steward, he was clearly trying to broaden Plaid Cymru's support among trade unionists disillusioned with the Labour government. In addition, his party regarded Thomas as a marked man, since he was a caustic and frequent critic of the nationalist spirit in Wales.

There was a brief, abortive threat of a fifth candidate, D. T. Davies of Chalfont St Peter, who had fought Smethwick on an anti-immigration platform in 1964. He claimed to stand as a 'Welsh Progressive Labour' candidate on the issue of pit closures, and promised to donate his parliamentary salary to the miners. Thomas dismissed him as a 'political adventurer' and urged him to 'take his thirty pieces of silver' elsewhere. After this harsh criticism, Davies did not in fact contest the seat.

The campaign followed the time-honoured pattern. Labour held no meetings and conducted no canvass. The election addresses were delivered by hand so that the free postage was not used. Thomas spent his evenings visiting social clubs and giving a brief invocation to the faithful before the evening's bingo and dancing began. There were twenty such visits, and all candidates testified to their value. During the day, he toured the constituency by car, equipped with loudspeaker and tape-recorded speeches. These set addresses were occasionally interrupted by live 'greetings' to passers-by and irreverent children. The main feature of Labour's campaign, in fact, was the help given to neighbouring marginal seats. Many Rhondda party workers went to Cardiff North, where the Conservative, Donald Box, was a well-known critic of trade unionists, and the Labour candidate, Edward Rowlands, an ex-resident of Rhondda. They had the satisfaction of seeing Box ousted on a 4.4 per cent swing.

The other candidates in Rhondda West followed much the same

approach. The Conservative made nine club visits, and also placed prominent advertisements in the local journal, the *Rhondda Leader*. The Communists alone held meetings. All these were badly attended, save for one addressed by John Gollan, but the Communists' club visits aroused more discussion than those of other candidates. The Communists attributed this interest in their policies to the impact of Gollan's television broadcast. For Plaid Cymru, Victor Davies took only one day off from lecturing and concentrated on leaflets and loudspeaker work. His young supporters were severely handicapped by the proximity of school examinations.

Thomas fought solely on the Labour government's record. 'A vote for I. R. Thomas is a vote for Harold Wilson.' Many houses and even shops displayed Harold Wilson posters. The other three candidates fought on local issues. The Conservatives ignored Edward Heath; they stressed the need for more doctors in the Rhondda valleys. As their candidate was a doctor, he laid himself open to the obvious retort that it would help if he came to live there himself. The Communist and Plaid Cymru candidates, both of whom advocated Welsh Home Rule, emphasized the industrial future of Rhondda. The main issue here was obviously that of pit closures. The largest colliery in the division, the Parc and Dare, had closed in December 1965, and there was great uncertainty about the future. Davies and True both demanded an end to closures and a national fuel policy. But Thomas was well armed with pre-recorded replies: he pointed out that the Labour government had written off £415 million of the National Coal Board's debt.

As polling day approached, Harold Wilson's record seemed virtually the only theme. The Conservatives appeared almost an irrelevance. There had been some Labour concern at the possible size of the Communist vote, which some forecast might be as high as 3,000. In fact, however, Arthur True took only 1,853 from Iorrie Thomas's crushing majority. These votes presumably came mainly from miners or ex-miners disillusioned with Labour, and from those who felt Thomas ought to retire. There was the traditionally high poll of over 80 per cent; psephological purists could note a 0.3 per cent swing against Labour. Once again, the Conservatives found they had no hope of any progress in this area; they contested the seat presumably to swell their national vote and to curb the flow of Labour workers into more marginal seats. Plaid Cymru – as the Carmarthen by-election was to show in July 1966 – continued to form a useful refuge for older Liberals and for young romantic idealists, disillusioned with one-party government. Labour, however, remained utterly impregnable in an old mining area where to vote Labour was less a political act than a pledge of loyalty to your own community, its memories, its values and its way of life.   *1966*

15

Swansea West

	1959		1964

	58,045 electors 82.2% voting		59,091 electors 81.4% voting

1959		1964	
J.E.H. Rees (Con.)	24,043 (50.4%)	Alan Williams (Lab.)	23,019 (47.9%)
Percy Morris (Lab.)	23,640 (49.6%)	J.E.H. Rees (Con.)	20,382 (42.4%)
		O.G. Williams (Lib.)	4,627 (9.7%)
Conservative majority	403 (0.88%)	Labour majority	2,637 (5.5%)

Swansea West was the most marginal seat in south Wales. First formed in 1918, it had returned on different occasions Liberal, National Liberal, Conservative and Labour members. In 1959 it was the only seat in Wales to change hands, Hugh Rees winning it for the Conservatives from Percy Morris, the Labour member since 1945. But Rees's majority was only 403 and Labour would recapture the seat with a swing of under 0.5 per cent. Early in 1964 both major parties brought their leaders to Swansea. Sir Alec Douglas-Home opened his pre-election campaign in the Brangwyn Hall on 20 January, and Harold Wilson followed a few days later. In May, George Brown addressed local party workers.

The constituency formed part of a prosperous town, whose economy had been largely transformed since the war. Light manufacturing industries, partly based on a trading estate in the north, had replaced the old metallurgical works, while the need to restore bomb damage had contributed to a substantial building boom. The docks continued to thrive, especially on the import of oil. Work for women could be found in the expanding professional and shopping services. Thousands of Swansea men, however, found employment outside the town and commuted to work; the massive steel works at Margam employed 2,000 men and the new Trostre and Velindre tinplate works a further 1,000. In early 1964 the dispute which closed down the Margam works seriously affected Swansea's working population. More ominous still, in May the closure of the Prestcold refrigerator factory threw 1,500 men out of work. But in general the town bore an unmistakable air of affluence and satisfaction. During August an enormously successful National Eisteddfod in Singleton Park coincided with the Glamorgan cricket team's first-ever victory over the touring Australians at St Helen's.

For an urban division, Swansea West was unusually scattered. Set in the narrow coastal plain along the curve of Swansea Bay, it extended from the docks in central Swansea to Mumbles Head five miles away. It covered an area of nearly 10,000 acres and, with many open green spaces, seemed less like a community than a network of urban villages. All three parties found difficulty in assessing its basic character. Nevertheless, the social division between east and west had become increasingly marked since the war. East of the docks and the River Tawe, Swansea survived as an old Welsh industrial settlement; in the west, the growth of private suburban housing accompanied the rise of a very different type of society. It was in Swansea West that most of the symbols of the new expansion could be seen, notably the University College with over 2,300 students. For forty years Swansea's population had tended to move westwards, as families migrated from their old neighbourhoods to the more desirable areas along Mumbles Road and towards the Gower peninsula. In many ways, the difference in class structure and outlook between Swansea East and West symbolized the great divide between two generations in south Wales.

This social division was faithfully reflected in politics. Swansea East was an impregnable Labour fortress; at a by-election in 1963 the Conservative candidate finished fourth and lost her deposit. But in Swansea West the political balance was finely poised. Of its eight wards, three – Brynmelin, Townhill and Fforestfach – voted overwhelmingly Labour and returned Labour candidates to the borough council; all were typical Welsh industrial communities. A fourth, Victoria, returned Independent councillors but voted predominantly Labour at parliamentary elections. The other wards – St Helen's, Ffynnone, Mumbles and Sketty – mostly returned Ratepayer councillors and the Conservatives had had little success in challenging them despite the wards' middle-class character. In practice, the party conflict in Swansea West took the form of a clash between the old industrial centre and the expanding residential fringe. Prior to the election, Labour supporters noted anxiously that their own solid wards were losing population, much of it to council estates in Swansea East; Sketty, by contrast, swelled in population after 1959 from 7,000 to 10,000. But these changes were less unfavourable to Labour than at first appeared. The increase in Sketty included a massive sky-scraper council estate, one of the first municipal projects in the constituency for many years.

Labour had dominated the Swansea council for a generation or more. By 1964 it was Labour that had to contend with the feeling that 'it was time for a change'. The council's housing and comprehensive school programme both came under heavy fire. In both divisions, Labour's affairs were managed by the executive of the Swansea Labour Association, whose offices, next door to a cinema near the High Street railway station, were reminiscent of the old cloth-cap days of the movement. Two full-time agents were maintained: in the East, J. G. Davies, a remarkable patriarchal figure who had acted as secretary of the Association since 1916; in the West, Peggy England Jones, an experienced and able campaigner who had served in Swansea East from 1950 to 1959. Active branches or 'ward councils' existed in all eight wards in Swansea West, and it was their relative autonomy which had partly led to the defeat of 1959. Until then Labour's organization had had the edge, but in 1959 the 'grass-roots' methods used in the strongest Labour areas broke down under the impact of rehousing. Few postal votes went to Labour, and at some polling stations in Labour wards turnout was under 60 per cent. Since then immense efforts had been made to rectify the faults. Although financially the party still relied heavily on voluntary activities and contributions (the candidate was unsponsored by a trade union), paid canvassers were imported from Neath and Aberavon during the summer of 1964. Postal votes were processed (more than 500 by the end), removals traced, and new efforts made to persuade all ward councils to prepare marked registers. By polling day there had undoubtedly been an improvement since 1959.

The Conservatives had steadily improved their organization during the 1950s. They had gradually cut adrift from the Ratepayers' Association and Independents, the breach being almost complete after 1959. Conservative branches operated in each ward, along with fourteen women's branches and three of the Young Conservatives. The women mainly staffed committee rooms; the Young Conservatives predominated as canvassers and stewards (though they seemed less conspicuous than in 1959 when Mr Rees's youth and bachelor status inspired eager feminine assistance, and a profusion of 'Hugh for me' rosettes). The Conservative agent, F. C. Jones, active in the constituency since 1953, hid force and tenacity beneath a genial exterior. Largely through his efforts, 1,200 of the 2,000 postal vote applications in 1964 had been processed in the Conservative offices. The premises themselves were new, while their structural repairs led visitors to joke incessantly about 'modernization'.

Administratively the association was linked with the area office in Cardiff, which provided specialist services such as speakers' panels. Financially it was self-sufficient, though the Swansea West Association's victory in 1959 had caused its quota payable to Central Office to rise from £100 to £300. With their own surveys in the summers of 1963 and 1964 confirming the national trend towards the government (and also indicating a Liberal decline), the Conservatives looked forward with some confidence to the coming battle.

The Liberals were a new element. As the 'Mecca of Nonconformity' (it still contained 142 chapels in 1964), Swansea had once been a Liberal stronghold, but no Liberal had fought Swansea West since 1929 and the local party had disappeared in the National Liberal split of 1931. A new association, however, was formed in 1961 and by 1964 it had over 150 members. Some were older chapel-goers who had once cheered Lloyd George and voted for Sir Alfred Mond; other were younger suburban Liberals of the Orpington school. The local executive of eighteen, headed by a university economics professor, had an average age of thirty-five. Although in the 1963 local elections the Liberals polled over 800 votes in the Labour ward of Townhill, the party concentrated its canvassing efforts mainly in the Conservative wards of St Helen's, Ffynnone and Sketty. They gave the impression throughout of conducting a predominantly anti-Conservative campaign. The Conservatives complained bitterly that the Liberals were fighting Swansea West only because the Conservatives had decided to fight Carmarthen, a seat where the Liberals hoped to do well. The Liberals retorted that they would get between 5,000 and 7,000 votes in Swansea West. From the outset, the Liberals appeared amateurish, short of workers and short of funds, but their enthusiasm was infectious. It was personified by the agent, Robert Morgan, a vigorous young works manager in a timber firm who had himself been a local government candidate in Ffynnone.

No Plaid Cymru candidate came forward. The party had decided to fight more seats than ever before – twenty-three, out of the thirty-six in Wales – and membership of Swansea West branch had risen to 120 under the leadership of two university lecturers. But a fight in the constituency was apparently never contemplated, and local members helped instead the Plaid Cymru candidates in Gower and Swansea

East (the latter being the cousin of Hugh Rees). The Western division contained only a small fraction of the 27,000 Welsh-speaking inhabitants of Swansea, and the town as a whole was becoming increasingly anglicized: the Welsh bookshop and Welsh chapels in the centre of Swansea seemed almost incongruous in so un-Welsh a community. In fact, Plaid Cymru in Swansea West dissociated itself from all three parties, though its members may have leant towards the Liberal candidate, who was most obviously Welsh in his sympathies.[1]

The Conservative, Labour and Liberal candidates were all able young Welshmen. Hugh Rees, the sitting Conservative, was 36 years old; he had been born in Swansea and educated partly at a local grammar school, and was by profession a chartered surveyor in the town. Much was made of his local connections during the campaign, and in his speeches he referred naturally to local places and issues. A diligent constituency member, he had suffered somewhat since 1962 from the silence imposed on him as a junior whip. He spoke easily without notes, in an attractive Swansea accent, and proved the most accomplished platform performer of the three. Only at question time did he tend to become a little belligerent.

Alan Williams, the Labour candidate, was even younger, the 33-year-old son of a Caerphilly miner, a graduate of London and Oxford universities, and now lecturer in economics at the Welsh College of Advanced Technology, Cardiff. He had fought Poole in 1959. Despite frequent television and radio appearances, he was less well known in Swansea than Rees, though this may have had its advantages since Percy Morris in 1959 was believed to have suffered from being a prominent figure on the local council. Williams spoke less fluently than his Conservative opponent but gained confidence as the campaign went on; he seemed most comfortable answering questions, which he did with friendliness and good humour.

Owain Glyn Williams, 41, the Liberal, was fighting his first

---

[1]Plaid Cymru decided to fight on a wide front in 1964 largely to maintain the impression of nation-wide strength created five years earlier, when twenty seats had been fought. In the event, this led to a disastrous dispersal of effort. Twenty-one deposits were lost and only in Merioneth and Caernarfon, two rural, Welsh-speaking constituencies of declining population, was a substantial poll gained. Plaid Cymru's failure in 1964 may be partly explained by Labour's attractive new policy for Wales. More generally, Plaid Cymru discovered again that there was little sense of purely national grievance in Wales – nor had there been since the Church in Wales was disestablished in 1920. For a century, the trend in Welsh politics had been towards national equality rather than national separatism. After the election, Plaid Cymru began to re-examine its basic strategy, with no evidence of progress, until the dramatic boost given by Gwynfor Evans's victory in the Carmarthen by-election in July 1966 and two later by-elections in 1967–8.

campaign. An Ammanford solicitor and law graduate of the University College, Aberystwyth, he was the most identifiably Welsh of the three candidates; he spoke Welsh fluently, his accent still betraying his native Merioneth. Like his Labour namesake, he was little known despite several television appearances. During his campaign, he sought publicity in the local press with aggressive letters which insisted that the truly 'wasted' votes would be the ones for the Conservative candidate. His platform appearances made up in evident sincerity what they sometimes lacked in precision; his great personal charm showed itself at question time. Throughout, he displayed energy and resourcefulness.

With the election date announced, all three parties swung immediately into action. The Liberals adopted Owain Williams on 16 September, dubbing him 'the rose between two thorns'. Their flamboyant headquarters in Walter Road (only four doors from that of the Conservatives) owed much to the inspiration of a former member of the Rank organization. The Conservatives set out to overwhelm the opposition with a well-advertised adoption meeting in the Dragon Hotel, eye-catching press advertisement, and innumerable posters, window bills and car stickers. A poster which earlier in the year had advised the startled Swansea citizens to 'take a Greater London pride with the Conservatives' had been removed. Labour moved quietly at first, but with a more purposeful air than in 1959. Close supervision of the constituency was maintained by the regional office in Cardiff. Canvassers were numerous and better distributed than five years before, and the number of car stickers was much higher. Thirty thousand copies of 'Points from Labour's Plan' were issued from the Labour Association offices, together with literature on issues such as pensions and leasehold reform. None of the three election addresses was outstanding; only the Liberals listed proposals specifically for Swansea itself.

The strategy of each candidate soon became obvious. Rees sought to turn Labour's flank by attacking the Swansea Corporation. He criticized their failure to repair corporation housing and to permit leasehold enfranchisement of council property, and their decision to abolish the 11-plus examination. He praised the government's financial 'good housekeeping' and its success in transforming the industrial pattern of south Wales. In general, he dwelt more on Welsh issues than did either of his opponents. Some of his best speeches came late in the campaign, when he ranged far and wide over both domestic and foreign questions. He was especially effective on housing, where he could exploit his professional knowledge as a surveyor. Like Keith Flynn in Cardiff West, however, Rees ran into some difficulty over leasehold reform; in the last week, the

Conservatives published 'Swansea Election News', a newsletter which pointed out that he had introduced a Leasehold Tenure Bill in 1962, though without receiving government support. Attendance at the seventeen Conservative meetings exceeded the totals of either or the other parties; about 2,000 people turned up in all. Mr Rees alone addressed fourteen meetings, being joined for the other three by Sir Keith Joseph, Lord Brecon and Selwyn Lloyd. The last named met with persistent heckling from university students, not all of them intoxicated by Selwyn Lloyd's eloquence alone.

For Labour, Alan Williams declined to be drawn into local controversies. He derided Hugh Rees for appearing to campaign for the local council instead of for parliament, and accused him of 'looking around for a parish pump handle to shake'. In his thirteen meetings, and in two joint meetings with the Liberals, Williams dwelt almost exclusively on domestic issues, notably pensions, housing, leasehold reform, and education. Although an economist, he devoted less time to analysing the country's economic weaknesses than to explaining how newly-created wealth should be shared throughout society. He seldom used local analogies, illustrating the evils of the Rent Act, for instance, with examples drawn from London. Mr Williams alone thought it worth while to address the University College students; they rewarded him on polling day when student canvassers abounded. At his meetings, he usually spoke for about twenty-five minutes, and his speeches varied little from ward to ward; his average audience numbered around seventy. The main outside speakers were Douglas Jay, who drew about two hundred to a large cinema in the centre of town, and Sir Frank Soskice, who addressed a smaller audience in a Sketty grammar school.

Owain Glyn Williams relied less on meetings, holding only seven. He deplored the other parties' ties to vested interests, and depicted the Liberals as the only force for new ideas in British politics. Like his Labour opponent, he dwelt almost wholly on domestic issues. On leasehold, he quoted Lloyd George's 'Yellow Book' to support the claim that the Liberals had the best record. He looked forward to a Welsh Parliament, but generally paid less attention to Welsh affairs than might have been expected. Although he attacked the other parties with equal enthusiasm, Owain Williams gave the impression of regarding the Tories as his main target. No doubt, this was partly because a Conservative held the seat; but also the Swansea Liberals believed their long-term destiny lay in ousting the Conservatives as the main opposition to Labour. The impression of an anti-Tory front was reinforced by the holding of two lively Liberal-Labour meetings. Hugh Rees declined to appear at either, and his written replies to questions were greeted with some derision.

Questions at meetings almost all concerned domestic affairs, especially housing, the cost of living and social security. Defence, foreign policy and nationalization were hardly mentioned. The issue that caused all three candidates most trouble was old age pensions. Hugh Rees had to explain the government's inability to raise pensions to higher levels, and to explain away the prime minister's 'donation' remark (this being one of the few instances when the national campaign impinged on Swansea). Alan Williams was pressed on Labour's refusal to promise to abolish the earnings' rule, and also on why Labour's pensions plan would take so long to implement. A lady in her seventies taxed Owain Glyn Williams's ingenuity by pointing out, with chapter and verse, that the highest pension the Liberals promised her would still not cover her rent and food and fuel bills. Among the questioners were a few hardy regulars: the earnest lady preoccupied with the underdeveloped countries, the student with incessant queries on Ferranti, the avuncular stalwart of the Socialist Party of Great Britain whose class-war rhetoric seemed somehow out of character.

All parties complained of posters defaced or removed, but for the most part of the election passed off quietly. Rees displayed some anger when he alleged that his opponents were making common cause behind his back and were guilty of 'innuendo and personal smear'. In a television confrontation, he and Alan Williams had a few icy exchanges. But otherwise feeling was amicable, and all three parties seemed to enjoy sharing the limelight. The local newspaper, the *South Wales Evening Post*, contributed to the calm atmosphere by reporting the campaign with Solon-like impartiality; only three meetings of each candidate and the two joint meetings were covered, while although the three candidates were allowed to make personal statements, no press conferences took place. The Cardiff *Western Mail* was more partisan, reporting Rees's pronouncements almost exclusively; earlier the *Mail* had been attacked by local Conservatives for failing to print his speeches in its Swansea editions. Neither paper covered the campaign in detail, since both had extensive circulations outside Swansea.

By the eve of the poll, the Conservatives and Labour had both conducted virtually complete canvasses. The Conservative returns showed roughly 22,500 for each of the main parties, with less than 4,000 for Liberal. Labour claimed 24,500 votes and a majority of over 2,500. The Liberals hoped for 7,000 votes but their canvass was sketchy. The Conservatives and Liberals agreed that Owain Glyn Williams would probably take votes equally from the other parties. Only on the new housing estate of Killay, in north Sketty, did the major parties' canvass returns conflict sharply; Labour claimed half of the young owner-occupiers on the estate, the Conservatives 60 per cent, with the Liberal canvass tending to confirm Labour's findings. Conscious that the result would be close, all three candidates, although visibly tired, finished strongly. Hugh Rees wound up with what was probably his best performance before three hundred people in Sketty, Alan Williams was enthusiastically received by a solid Labour audience in Brynmelin, while Owain Glyn Williams addressed a quieter meeting, also in Sketty. Then there was nothing more but to wait.

On 15 October, it was clear from early morning that the poll would be heavy. In some polling districts, one elector in four had voted long before mid-day, and by 5 p.m. the Conservatives estimated that 70 per cent of their supporters had turned out. The day began fine, but heavy showers after tea caused momentary anxiety to Labour. By 6 p.m., however, Labour's forecasts of their victory margin were edging upwards. Both major parties used fully marked registers everywhere, and all their committee rooms appeared fully staffed. The Conservatives had as many cars as they could use; Labour, with nearly a hundred, had never had more. Transport presented a particular problem to Labour, so many of whose supporters had moved within the town; in the Labour Association offices, a transport officer worked all day regulating vehicles. No help, however, was received from the Swansea East Labour organization, now cruising home to a 23,000 majority. The Liberals, though hampered by a shortage of workers, managed to run fifteen committee rooms at least part-time; the drivers of cars, however, were sometimes wastefully used. Quite unexpectedly, all three parties had occasion to complain of the local returning officer's organization. In Dunvant and Brynmelin, nearly 1,500 voters were directed to the wrong polling stations; in Brynmelin they were told to go to a building which had been torn down four years before. Elsewhere a polling-station officer persistently refused to admit 'Y' voters. The count, by contrast, was conducted with exemplary efficiency and dispatch.

Shortly after midnight, the result was declared. It had been awaited with considerable anxiety, not least by Harold Wilson who had personally enquired of Swansea West from Cliff Prothero, the party's Welsh regional organizer, during the day. But any Labour fears proved groundless. On an 81.7 per cent poll, Alan Williams gained the seat from Hugh Rees with a majority of 2,637. Owain Glyn Williams, with 4,672 votes, lost his deposit. Turnout could not be blamed for the result – it had apparently been between 75 per cent and 85 per cent in every polling district – and local Conservatives were inclined to blame Liberal intervention for their defeat. Certainly, Liberal votes seemed to have come overwhelmingly from the Conservative wards of Sketty, St Helen's and Ffynnone. But for Liberal intervention to have cost the Conservatives the seat, Owain Glyn Williams would have had to take more than four votes from Rees for every one from Alan Williams, an extraordinarily high ratio. Moreover, the swing from Conservative to Labour in Swansea West was 3.2 per cent. If Liberal votes were coming disproportionately from the Conservatives, the Swansea West swing should have been higher than in comparable south Wales constituencies where no Liberal was standing. In fact, it was lower; the pro-Labour swing in Newport was 4.4 per cent, in Barry 5.3 per cent. Of course, Alan Williams's majority might have been greater if his namesake had stood down, but, as Hugh Rees sportingly conceded, 2,637 was 'a good, proper majority', the largest in the division since 1950.

Did Swansea West in 1964 afford any evidence of the particularity of Welsh politics as a whole? The most distinctive feature of political activity in Wales for the past century had been the built-in radical tradition, or, to put it negatively, an instinctive hostility to the Conservative party, more pronounced than in any other part of the United Kingdom. Since the 1867 Reform Act, Wales had been the overwhelming preserve of the political left. Until after the First World War, it was the Liberal party that was invariably predominant, appealing especially to the chapel vote. After 1922, Labour, thriving on memories of the depression years, had been equally dominant. Since 1945 Wales had been one of the few areas where Labour had actually improved its position: its tally of Welsh seats had risen from twenty-five to twenty-eight, and its advance in rural Wales was still sufficiently recent for the party to retain there some of its early crusading zeal.

The 1964 election emphasized that in no part of the British Isles had the Conservative party made less permanent headway than in Wales. Indeed, in the years since the 1884 Reform Act it had made virtually no progress at all. Never had it obtained more than nine Welsh seats (this was in 1895) while in the Liberal landslide of 1906 it failed to win even one. In 1964, the political strength of the Conservatives in Wales was still largely based on the same pockets of support it had enjoyed about 1890. Then, their strength had lain in suburban Cardiff and Swansea, in the eastern border fringe of Monmouthshire, Radnorshire, and parts of Flintshire, and in few other areas such as the Vale of Glamorgan and the coastal strip of Caernarfonshire from Bangor to Conway. To an astonishing extent, the pattern still asserted itself in 1964; Cardiff North, Barry, Monmouth, West Flint, Conway and Denbigh were the only seats claimed after nearly a century of effort. In most of the rest of Wales Conservatism still had no real political base. This was hardly remarkable in industrial south Wales; the lost Conservative deposits in Rhondda East and West in 1964 came as no surprise. But even in rural Cardiganshire,

Carmarthen and Merioneth, the party trailed a poor third or fourth. In 1964, deposits were lost in the last two of these, in marked contrast to the traditional strength of Conservatism in rural England and much of lowland Scotland. The old populist radicalism of the days of Lloyd George still exerted an almost mystical influence in rural and industrial Wales alike. The Conservative party seemed in some sense the enemy of the Welsh nation.

There were, however, exceptions to this pattern, and Conservatives hoped that Swansea West might be one of them. In the thriving coastal fringe between Swansea and Newport, where many of the new industries of south Wales were located, the growing professional and managerial population of the suburbs felt less identification with the radical or socialist traditions of the past. Here, it seemed, anglicization and Conservatism went hand in hand. Since these areas formed the growth points of the Welsh economy, and since there was a 'pull to the south-east' within Wales as well as in England, the political implications could be significant. It might be that in these suburban constituencies the Conservatives were finding a new core of strength after the decades of failure that followed the collapse of the old Tory gentry at the end of the last century. The 1964 election, however, did not appear to confirm these hopes. Throughout this area, in Monmouth, Newport, Barry and the three Cardiff seats, Labour markedly improved its position. In Swansea West, the pro-Labour swing of 3.2 per cent was close to the national average. Here and elsewhere, Labour showed that it could diversify its appeal to the varied constituents of what were still untypical Welsh seats, finding new middle-class support to build on the old closely-knit Labour communities of the past. Clearly, however, Swansea West remained a highly marginal seat. The succeeding months or years of Labour government would probably determine whether it would change its allegiance yet again and become once more a solitary Conservative outpost on the periphery of the radical heartland of Wales.

1965

16

The City of Swansea:
The Challenges of Democracy

Swansea has played an unusual, distinctive part in the politics of south Wales, and of the United Kingdom as a whole. Like almost all constituencies in industrial Wales, it has in general been a stronghold of the British left, ever since it first received the right to return a member of Parliament on its own in 1832. At the same time, as a port rather than a valleys constituency, as a centre of trade rather than of extractive or manufacturing industry, as a comparatively anglicized outpost against a hinterland with a more distinctly Welsh culture, it has often gone against the prevailing trend. At various times, it has offered a gleam of hope for Welsh Conservatives. Yet it has provided an early and important base for Welsh socialism and labour politics, too. Its perspective towards some of the wider themes of modern Wales, its industrial radicalism and overtones of nationalism, has been all its own. In its politics, therefore, as in so much else, Swansea is no ordinary town.

Its political identity first crystallized with the surging growth of industry and the attendant explosion of population in the immediate hinterland, and increasingly in the mining and tinplate towns and villages of the Swansea valley, in the nineteenth century. At the time of the passage of the 1832 Reform Act, Swansea was the chief seaport and urban metropolis of South Wales, far more so than was Cardiff. Its growing status and commercial importance were duly recognized in the 1832 Act, with Swansea District being granted a member of Parliament on its own, along with 'contributory boroughs' of Aberavon, Kenfig, Loughor and Neath. At first, Swansea's politics, like the Guest regime in Merthyr, were a model of industrial deference and paternalism. The first local MP, who held the seat unopposed until 1855, was John Henry Vivian, from the copper-smelting dynasty originally hailing from Cornwall. Secure in his neo-Gothic fastness of Singleton Abbey, the former 'Marino' on the shores of Swansea Bay (and now the University College), Vivian was a ceremonial MP whose presence at Westminster masked the dynamic growth and social reformation of Swansea as a borough, an urban market and a centre of trade.

But, beneath the surface, Swansea's politics, like those of other urban communities in England and Wales, were being revolutionized. The causes lay in the growth of assertive middle-class pressure-groups from the world of business and industry, and especially in the massive expansion of the Nonconformist chapels from Morriston to Dunvant. By the 1860s, Swansea was popularly known as 'the Mecca of Nonconformity', and its politics soon reflected the fact. The town's political life moved out of 'prehistory' in 1855 with the election of Lewis Llewelyn Dillwyn, son of the notable botanist and antiquarian, Lewis Weston Dillwyn of Sketty Hall. Although L. Ll. Dillwyn owed his initial election to his being a representative of industrial and commercial interests, his greater prominence came from being a radical of the (relatively) far left, in mid-Victorian terms at least. He was a resolute champion of parliamentary reform, and took a major part in the back-bench parliamentary manoeuvres that led to the passage of the Reform Act of 1867. He was also a strong opponent of Victorian imperialism and of war, as befitted a man with Quaker antecedents. With Henry Richard, he led the call for international disarmament. Above all, although an Anglican by formal religion, Dillwyn was a passionate advocate of the disestablishment of the Church of England, including in Wales, and an active member of the Liberation Society devoted to this end. He was one of the seven Welsh Liberals who voted for Welsh disestablishment in the first-ever Commons vote on the subject in 1870, thereby incurring the wrath of Gladstone himself. Dillwyn was to remain MP for Swansea, first for the old District seat, then for Swansea Town from 1885 until his death in 1892. By then he was somewhat out of date, a relic from the mid-Victorian world of Cobden and Bright, out of touch with the new politics of young Welshmen like Tom Ellis and David Lloyd George. But Dillwyn, nevertheless, was the prophet of democratic politics in modern Swansea, a parliamentarian of courage, independence of mind, and distinction. He deserves to be remembered.

Swansea's politics took a massive step forward with Gladstone's Reform and Redistribution Acts of 1884–5. The town now gained an additional parliamentary seat. The Swansea Town constituency included the docks, the business centre and the residential suburbs extending westwards towards Mumbles. Swansea District included the older industrial areas east of the River Tawe, with all their environmental pollution, along with substantial parts of neighbouring tinplate and coal-mining communities. In addition, Gower or West Glamorgan, one of the five constituencies into which the county of Glamorgan was carved, gave representation to the industrial workers of the Swansea valley almost as far north as Ystradgynlais. The results were considerable. In 1880, Swansea's voters had numbered only 13,631, a minute fraction of the town's population. In 1885, with Swansea Town's electorate of 7,597, Swansea District's tally of 16,072 and a further 10,562 enfranchised in Gower, the dawn of a more democratic system of politics (or at least of male politics) was now visible. It is from 1885 that democracy, as any kind of meaningful description of Swansea politics, can be dated.

From 1885 down to the end of the First World War, Swansea's politics were dominated by the hegemony of the Liberal party. This period spanned the later phase of Gladstone's leadership and the Edwardian ascendancy of Asquith and Lloyd George. Swansea District, with its plethora of tinplate and steel works, along with other metallurgical industries and anthracite pits, was a natural Liberal stronghold. Its MP down to 1893 (when he took the title of Lord Swansea) was the senior, influential figure of Sir Henry Hussey Vivian, of the famous local industrial dynasty of Singleton Abbey. He had briefly defected to the Liberal Unionist camp in protest against Gladstone's first Irish Home Rule Bill of 1886, but soon returned to the fold as a respected elder statesman. As will be seen, he acted as host to Gladstone on the famous visitation of 1887. Vivian was followed in a by-election in 1893 by William Williams, a Morriston tinplate owner, and then in 1895 by David (later Sir David) Brynmor Jones QC. He was the very quintessence of the upwardly mobile Liberal lawyer, almost unbearably respectable, something of an historian and the son of a famous Congregational minister, the Revd Thomas Jones of Walter Road Chapel. Brynmor Jones embodied the ethos of 'the great and the good'. If quangos had been invented, he would have chaired plenty of them. His election was no triumph of social radicalism but it did mark the strength of Welsh-language Nonconformity in Morriston and other parts of Swansea District, even though Jones's own proficiency in the native language was not strong. He served down to 1914 as the very model of 'official Liberalism', the élite ascendancy which had ruled the social and political life of Wales since the 1870s.

Swansea Town was much more uncertain in its allegiance. Indeed, with the strong business community around the docks and growing suburban fringe towards the Gower peninsula in such areas as Sketty, it was one of the relatively few seats where the Conservatives could challenge with some hope of victory. After Dillwyn's death in 1892, the seat was retained for the Liberals by R. D. Burnie, an Englishman who owned a local wagon works, but with a majority of only 722 over Sir John Dillwyn-Llewelyn of Penlle'r-gaer, a cousin of L. Ll. Dillwyn. In the 1895 general election, which saw the Liberal party swamped nationally and several Tory (or Unionist) gains in Wales, Swansea was indeed narrowly won for the Conservatives by Dillwyn-Llewelyn. The marginal St Helen's ward seems to have swung in his favour.

Thereafter, having experimented with Burnie who proved too radical for some tastes, the local Liberal Association played safe and chose a series of very wealthy businessmen intended to appeal to mercantile and financial concerns. In 1900, the Liberals recaptured the seat through Sir George Newnes, the millionaire newspaper and magazine proprietor, owner of *Titbits, Strand Magazine* and other organs, the unflamboyant Robert Maxwell of his day. Heavy emphasis was placed in Newnes's nomination on his having provided a free library for Putney and a town hall, a cliff railway and a pier for Lynton – 'that was the stamp of man they had in their midst!' Newnes stayed on until January 1910, a largely inarticulate MP intent on his business interests; then he was succeeded by Sir Alfred Mond of the huge chemical combine, Brunner-Mond, the Mond nickel works at Clydach and much else besides. Conservatives seized the opportunity to pillory a Viennese Jew who represented the dissenters of Swansea and proclaimed his undying belief in Welsh disestablishment. 'Vales for the Velsh' was the unashamedly racist and anti-semitic Tory election cry. But, as a Liberal capitalist who directly employed many of the Swansea population (and, indeed, as a highly capable politician who served in Lloyd George's Cabinet as minister of health after 1918), Mond's position also seemed comparatively secure.

Likewise in the Gower constituency, Liberals retained this overwhelmingly industrial and largely Welsh-speaking seat with some ease at first, F. A. Yeo being the MP from 1885 and David Randell from 1888, although, as will be seen, it was in Gower that the first major cracks came in the Liberals' position with a powerful, and shortly triumphant, challenge from Labour.

The most notable feature of the period was a broad Liberal culture that dominated Swansea life in its commercial and industrial heyday to 1918. It was a broad, many-sided coalition, straddling organized labour and capitalist shipowners and merchants, the worlds of finance and of industry, the Nonconformists of the older industrial villages and the Irish community in its ghetto in Greenhill. Swansea's local authority remained under solid Liberal control until the First World

War. Its Liberalism was much more than a matter of formal organization or political machines. Indeed, the Swansea Liberal Association tended to become an increasingly exclusive body of businessmen, while the Gower Liberal Association was a largely dormant, if not obsolescent, body which only came to fitful life at election time.

It was rather that the ethos of Liberalism intersected at all points with the urban and business life of a thriving mercantile community. With its docks, shipping interests and neighbouring tinplate plants, spelter works and anthracite pits, Swansea was a natural citadel for free trade. Thus, Brynmor Jones was returned unopposed in Swansea District in 1900, 1906, 1910 (twice) and (in a by-election) in 1914 on this basis. Swansea's Liberalism also related to its vibrant life as a centre of the Nonconformist chapels, the Baptists and Congregationalists above all. It boasted some of the most eminent Welsh preachers of the day. It responded to the galvanizing effect of the 1904 religious revival, which began in nearby Loughor. The town also took a lively part in the Welsh Nonconformist 'revolt' against the 1902 Education Act which put Church and Catholic schools on the rates. The Swansea local authority fell foul of both King's Bench and the House of Lords in a famous high court case. *The Board of Education v. Rice and others*, after the council had refused to raise the salaries of teachers in Oxford Street Church of England elementary school. The local press had also a strong Liberal bias, with the old *Cambria Daily Leader* keeping the banner aloft as in generations past. Liberal business and professional interests were prominent in such civic landmarks as the founding of Swansea rugby football club (though its first two presidents, the earl of Jersey and Sir J. T. Dillwyn-Llewelyn, were both Tories). This found new celebrity in the triumphs of the Welsh rugby team in the early years of the twentieth century, with local heroes such as the famous half-backs, Dickie Owen and Dickie Jones, 'the dancing Dicks', well to the fore.

Swansea Liberalism in its pre-war heyday was relatively unadventurous, as the nomination of men like Newnes and Brynmor Jones might indicate. Rebels who might rock the boat were generally turned aside. Thus, R. D. Burnie, the defeated candidate in 1895, was turned down as candidate by the Swansea Five Hundred early in 1900, after having denounced the Boer War as 'imperialist claptrap' in letters to the press. Swansea, like Cardiff, was a strongly imperialist town and many key Liberals, including Brynmor Jones, were emphatic 'Lib. Imps.'. On the other hand, Swansea was also a proud centre of civic Liberalism which the national leaders of the party had to take seriously. One ceremonial episode of much importance occurred in June 1887 when Gladstone stayed with Sir Hussey Vivian in Singleton

Abbey and received a march past of perhaps 50,000 Welsh supporters over a period of four and a half hours. Sixty special trains brought them; they included 300 ministers, the flower of Nonconformity. It was a kind of public benediction of Swansea Liberalism by its chosen pope. Equally, it was in Swansea venues such as the Albert Hall and the Elysium that Lloyd George and others came to make ringing declarations to denounce the bishops, the brewers, the peers, the landlords and other proven enemies of mankind, and to proclaim the old, imperishable creed of economic freedom and civic and religious equality. It was in Swansea also, in October 1908, that Lloyd George spelt out the basic premises of his 'new Liberalism' of social welfare and economic reform. Down to the holocaust of 1914–18, therefore, when Wales like much of the rest of the world was turned upside down, Swansea was a major centre of urban vitality, whose Liberalism chimed with an era of commercial expansion, cultural vigour and civic pride unique in the history of the town.

By 1914, however, the Liberal ascendancy was already entering a darker and more difficult phase. It was as early as the 1880s that the first stirrings came of a challenge far more persistent and fundamental than the paternalist Tory values of Sir John Dillwyn-Llewelyn, the squire of Penlle'r-gaer. This was the upsurge of Labour. Swansea became a centre of the militant 'new unionism' among unskilled workers in the 1880s and early 1890s, amongst the dockers, general workers, gasworkers and others. A new Workers' Union, organized by Matt Giles of the Independent Labour Party, originally an employee of Fry's Cocoa, struck roots in Swansea, while militant socialists like Ben Tillett and Tom Mann visited the town. There were strikes by dockers and others in the early 1890s. For all the rooted strength of the Liberal hegemony, this would surely soon have political implications, and so it proved.

By the turn of the century, there were five Labour members on Swansea town council, and the Labour presence in local government on boards of guardians, the school board and elsewhere continued to grow. Apart from politically active trade unionists, within individual unions and on the trades council, there was also a growing socialist thrust with the local expansion of the Independent Labour Party in such nearby places as the steel town of Briton Ferry, a few miles across the bay.

It was not, however, in Swansea but in the neighbouring Gower constituency that Labour made a breakthrough. Here, not only were the unions growing in size and in militancy but there were also major branches of the ILP, especially in Ystalyfera which in 1897 had produced the first Welsh-language socialist newspaper, *Llais Llafur*, the

Voice of Labour, founded by Ebenezer Rees. In the 1900 'khaki election', held at the height of the frenzied jingoism of the Boer War, the Liberal domination was seriously challenged by a Labour candidate. This was no particular surprise, in fact. The previous Liberal MP, David Randell, member for Gower from 1888 to 1900, owed his initial nomination to the support of the Tinplate Workers' Union in the Gower constituency and was thought, initially at least, to be a friend of the working man. In 1900, the Liberal, an anodyne local tinplate employer and former mayor of Swansea, J. Aeron Thomas, was challenged by an outsider, John Hodge, an Englishman and secretary of the Steel Smelters' Union. Hodge had much union support locally and was well received in such tinplate communities as Morriston, Pontardawe and Ystalyfera. He poured effective scorn on Aeron Thomas as an alleged supporter of temperance reform, pointing out that he owned shares in Swansea United Breweries. In the end, the obstacles to Hodge's success were just too great. The chapels rallied strongly to the Liberal cause, as did some local labour leaders, including the miners' agent for the area. Even so, Hodge polled 3,583 votes to Aeron Thomas's 4,276. It was a close-run thing and an extraordinary achievement for an outsider like Hodge, almost as remarkable as Keir Hardie's contemporary victory at Merthyr Tydfil.

The rise of Labour as a serious force in the Swansea valley continued apace in the years after 1900. Another strong Labour challenge was inevitable in Gower when the next election came in January 1906, after Balfour's Unionist government resigned. This time the workers' candidate was an authentic local man, a Welsh-speaking miners' agent of impeccable Liberal and Nonconformist background, John Williams. He was a well-known lay preacher. His prospects were much stronger than those of Hodge. There were now Labour Representation Committee and ILP branches throughout the valley, while Williams had the inestimable benefit of having his campaign expenses met by the South Wales Miners' Federation which sponsored him. He also won some notable support from local Nonconformist patriarchs, in particular, the Revd J. Gomer Lewis of Capel Gomer, Swansea. Lewis, a Baptist like the Labour candidate, adopted an emotional social-Christian approach. 'Who was their Saviour but a Labour man?' he asked rhetorically of the voters of Gorseinon, who seemed disposed to agree. He also ridiculed the capitalist 'with his rubber-tyred brougham' with much effect. John Williams defeated the Liberal candidate, a local tinplate owner, T. J. Williams (chosen after much confusion by the Gower Liberal Association), by 4,841 votes to 4,522, with the Tory a poor third and 85 per cent of the electors registering their votes. Gower had become a Labour stronghold and it has remained so to the present day.

But Labour's political progress among the relatively homogenous workers of the tinplate and mining communities of the valley was much harder to achieve in the heterogeneous and fragmented population of the port of Swansea, despite successes in local government. In urban centres, the franchise registration regulations (for instance, those relating to lodgers) told against potential Labour voters. The Swansea Labour Association was formed in 1906 at the Working Men's Club, Alexandra Road, with John Beynon, a schoolmaster, as its first president. But squabbles with the trades council caused early difficulties. In the January 1910 election, for the first time Labour fought Swansea Town, in the person of the famous dockers' leader, Ben Tillett. But it was a divisive and unhappy campaign, and in any case Tillett was no politician. He finished well down at the bottom of the poll with 1,451 votes, only 12 per cent of those cast. Thereafter, Labour focused its efforts on strengthening its position on the local council in such areas as the Alexandra and Brynmelin wards, in St Thomas and Landore. It also pressed strong Labour issues on the watch committee, such as attacking the anti-strike tactics adopted by local employers, including the use of non-union 'free' labour and the use of the military in industrial disputes.

The war years, however, saw a notable impetus to the strength of Labour in Swansea, as elsewhere. Among other factors, the crisis of war severely undermined the organization and morale of the local Liberals. This was intensified in a famous by-election in Swansea in early 1915, when T. J. Williams was elected unopposed for the Liberals after severe local divisions involved with an attempt by Lloyd George to find a seat for the displaced government minister, C. F. G. Masterman. In addition, Labour became more articulate and aggressive in Swansea, partly through the rapid spread of wartime trade unionism, partly through a new and heightened radicalism variously fostered by the revolution in Russia, by resentment towards conscription and by weariness at the sufferings and inequalities of the war. One celebrated and brutal episode that roused much left-wing opposition was a meeting of soldiers' and workers' delegates at the Elysium in Swansea in July 1917 to denounce the war and call for a negotiated peace. It was broken up with extreme violence by local pro-war thugs, with serious injuries inflicted on Arthur Horner and other courageous socialists prominent at the Elysium meeting. It only served to make the Swansea Labour Association and its members the more effective as the voice of anti-war protest, social radicalism, civic equality and industrial reform.

At the general election in December 1918, although the coalition Liberals who backed Lloyd George as premier retained both Swansea constituencies, there was a new temper of industrial revolt to be detected. The old Liberal cries of free trade, land reform, temperance and (especially) Church disestablishment were rapidly becoming out of date in the face of the growing militancy of Labour. In the newly created constituencies of Swansea West (held by Mond) and Swansea East, a vastly larger electorate of 27,185 and 31,884 respectively was based on residence, not on property qualifications, and it also included women over thirty. There was a genuinely democratic impetus as never before. A particular hazard for Sir Alfred Mond in 1918 was that local Conservatives were reluctant to back him under the coalition 'coupon' arrangements. Local Tories, racialist to the last, anxious to 'hang the Kaiser', complained to Bonar Law of having to support 'a pure bred German who has not one drop of British blood in his veins'. No doubt the Star of David was in their minds, too.

The 1920s saw the onset of serious economic depression in the Swansea area, as in other south Wales constituencies. Labour was the inevitable beneficiary. In Gower, Dai Grenfell, another miners' agent, succeeded as Labour member in a by-election in 1922 notable for some degree of support for his party from the chapels, and he was to hold the seat until he retired, by then Father of the House, in 1959. In the 1922 general election, Swansea East (roughly based on the old Swansea District seat to the east of the Tawe) was captured for Labour by David Williams, who held the seat until his death in 1940. It has been an impregnable Labour stronghold ever since. At the same time, David Williams, a JP, Sunday school teacher and temperance crusader as well as a boiler-makers' leader and long-serving local councillor, in many ways was a symbol of the values of the old Liberal heritage rather than the harbinger of any kind of socialist millennium. Like most of his comrades, Dai Williams was no class warrior.

Swansea West was far more unpredictable. Sir Alfred Mond found himself in increasing difficulty after 1918 as local Liberals dissolved in acrimony during the Liberal schisms that marked the peacetime Lloyd George Coalition government of 1918–22. William Jenkins of Swansea gave the prime minister a lucid analysis of the disintegration of Swansea Liberalism, via Mond, in August 1922. He described how miners, tinplaters and other workers were moving towards Labour in the western valleys, while the town Liberals lacked organization, public relations flair or perhaps even belief in themselves. Mond himself, who had reversed the bold housing programme of the post-war coalition government and was unfairly identified with the Geddes 'axe' of social services, was an unpopular figure with the left, a rich Jewish capitalist suspected of flirtation with Torysim. Indeed, he did join the Conservatives in the mid-1920s. He clung on to his seat in 1922 but in 1923 was defeated by a Labour man, Walter Samuel, a barrister and future recorder of Merthyr Tydfil.

In the next general election, in October 1924 after the downfall of the first Labour government of Ramsay MacDonald and held during the 'red scare' of the Zinoviev letter, Samuel was himself beaten by the Liberal ex-minister, Walter Runciman, from a famous shipping family in Newcastle upon Tyne. He was now a distinctly right-wing figure and shortly left Wales to represent St Ives. Again Labour won the seat back in 1929, through Walter Samuel, with a narrow majority of 643 (2 per cent) over a Liberal; but in the next election, fought in October 1931, Samuel lost a second time, to a 'National Liberal' who supported the so-called National government of Ramsay MacDonald. Samuel's defeat by 6,000 votes reflected the mood of hysteria at that time, following the downfall of the second Labour government, the run on the pound, the Invergordon 'mutiny' in the Navy and Britain's decision to devalue sterling and go off the gold standard. At the same time, Samuel's opponent, who held the seat for fourteen years, was a considerable local figure. This was an Ammanford man, Lewis (later Sir Lewis) Jones, secretary of the South Wales Siemens Steel Association and a notable patron of the recently founded University College of Swansea, whose vice-president he later became. Jones held Swansea West with some ease in 1935, and remained in the Commons as a 'National Liberal' down to the war, a vigorous back-bench supporter of Neville Chamberlain's foreign policy of appeasement.

During the period from the turn of the century to 1945, the Swansea political scene became increasingly dominated, therefore, by the impact of Labour and the attempt to find an anti-socialist alternative to it, at least in Swansea West. At a local level, Labour captured twenty-one council seats out of forty-five in 1918, and won overall control in 1927. The council remained continuously in Labour hands from 1933 onwards. During the years of depression and unemployment, Labour in Swansea took up the usual themes. It denounced unemployment, and the government's policy of imposing the 'means test' in assessing the need for social benefit. It pressed for housing reforms, for maintaining levels of spending on education and school meals, for new initiatives to create employment. It was commended for its efforts by the 1939 Clement Davies Committee on measures to combat tuberculosis in Wales, whereas penny-pinching Tory or 'Independent' councils stood condemned for their parsimony. Labour in Swansea also attacked the brutality with which demonstrations by unemployed workers and hunger marchers were put down by local police chiefs. They particularly condemned the bellicose approach of Captain Lionel Lindsay, chief constable of Glamorgan for over forty years, who had won his spurs in suppressing the *fellaheen* of Egypt under Sir Garnet Wolseley.

At the same time, Labour in inter-war Swansea did somewhat

diverge from the norm. After all, Swansea as a port fared less badly during the 1930s than did the mining valleys to the north and east. The anthracite coalfield continued to find markets while the steam-coal industry was eroded, and the port of Swansea found new vitality from the refining of oil for BP at Llandarcy. The civic life of Swansea was certainly not at a total standstill in the 1930s – witness the thriving theatres, cinemas and music-halls, suburban house building and the creation of Sir Percy Thomas's civic centre and Guildhall. The 'ugly, lovely town' in which Dylan Thomas grew up may suggest many things, but surely not stagnation or sterility. Thomas satirized its 'snug-suburbed' lower-middle-class gentility. The truth, perhaps, is that Labour in its turn took over the old Liberal mantle of being the custodian of civic independence and municipal pride. Labour councillors, in the depression of the 1930s, like their Liberal predecessors in the prosperity and growth of the Edwardian high noon, took their stand as champions of a distinctive local community rather than as spokesmen for a class or an ideology. During the suffering of the wartime blitz, in which Swansea suffered severe damage and 387 civilians were killed, this role was further sustained.

In Swansea, as elsewhere, the Second World War brought a shift to the left. This was demonstrated in Labour's electoral triumph in 1945. In Swansea East, the steel worker, Dai Mort, who had won the seat in a by-election in 1940 after the death of David Williams, won by a landslide. In Swansea West, with its more delicately balanced political structure, Labour won, this time much more solidly than in the 1920s. Its new champion was Percy Morris of the Railway Clerks' Union, a moderate, a Congregationalist lay preacher and a fanatic for temperance, who held the seat until 1959. At the same time, the new tribe of psephologists had identified Swansea West as a marginal seat: after all, Morris's majority in 1955 was a mere 1,021 (2.4 per cent) and Wales had precious few marginal seats compared with the rest of Britain. Much attention, therefore, focused on the 1959 election which saw the Conservatives, in the person of Hugh Rees, a local estate agent, win Swansea by a narrow majority of 493 (0.8 per cent), broadly reflecting the national swing which confirmed Harold Macmillan in his tenure of 10 Downing Street.

In the early 1960s, British politics went through much volatility as the façade of apparently impregnable Conservative rule crumbled. A variety of factors, ranging from 'Orpington Man' amongst suburban Liberals to the excitements of the Profumo affair, led to a slump in the Conservatives' popularity. Swansea West was inevitably targeted by Nuffield College analysts as a seat likely to change hands, and so it proved. On a personal level, Hugh Rees had been somewhat handicapped by the silence imposed on him as a junior government whip. It was, however, largely traditional factors that dictated the outcome in 1964. Labour relied heavily on mobilizing its strength in the old working-class core of Swansea West, around the Vetch football field in the centre of the town, in Victoria and Brynmelin wards, in the Townhill council estate, and in Fforestfach to the north of the constituency. The Conservative, led by an active agent, F. C. Jones, sought to fight back in middle-class St Helen's and Ffynnone, and in Sketty and Mumbles on the bourgeoisified western fringe of the town. To some degree, it was a fight between the classic Labour core and the suburban Conservative periphery, as it had been back in 1895. Although the Liberals also fought Swansea West, they made little impact. Orpington Man was evidently not a phenomenon widely known amongst Welsh voters. Young, married mortgage-holders on the Killay and West Cross housing estates tended to back Labour. The outcome, in a hard-fought campaign, was victory for Labour by a majority of 2,637 (5.5 per cent).

Labour's campaign seemed in many ways traditional in form. Its election campaign organizers (notably, their able agent, Peggy England Jones) maintained a base in peeling and dingy rooms at the back of the Elysium cinema, the scene of the famous brutal assault on the peace protesters in 1917. But it was also a different, somewhat updated, Labour campaign which chimed with the image of modernity that Harold Wilson attempted to create for Labour in 1964. Labour stressed economic growth, house ownership and education. Many students and lecturers of the nearby University College were prominent in Labour's campaign. The new Labour MP, Alan Williams, was a lecturer in economics at the College of Advanced Technology, Cardiff, a symbol of the new appeal of Labour to the educated, professional classes. What was clear was that Williams would have some difficulty in holding his heterogeneous, distinctly bourgeois constituency, and indeed his majority was to fall to as low as 401 in 1979. However, he was somewhat assisted by boundary redistribution in 1983, when parts of the residential areas on the west of the constituency were siphoned off into Gower (where Labour's majority notably slumped as a result). Labour thus held Swansea West in both 1983 and 1987, and Alan Williams has remained Swansea West's MP for over a quarter of a century, with a period of office in the Wilson and Callaghan governments in the 1970s thrown in.

Swansea East had, meanwhile, continued its even tenor with Labour majorities of well over 20,000. Dai Mort was succeeded after his death in 1963 by another trade unionist, the Scotsman, Neil McBride. After his death in mid-1974, he was replaced by Donald Anderson. The latter, however, again represented the increasingly modern and middle-class face of Welsh Labour. A Swansea boy and a distinguished product of the local schools and University College, he went on to serve in the Foreign Office and to become in turn a university lecturer in politics at Swansea, before being briefly Labour MP for Monmouth and then a barrister. Anderson's presence in so traditional and unionized a constituency as Swansea East is evidence of a profound tide of social mobility and structural change. Even in Wales, the old representatives of heavy staple industry, men like David Williams, Grenfell and Mort in the past, are in rapid retreat.

Swansea at the local level remained in Labour hands. For the most part, it was well governed and economically thriving. However, it was on Swansea particularly that accusations fastened to allege that permanent, monolithic one-party rule had its dangers. This theme was originally voiced by novelists like the Rhondda-born Rhys Davies (1903–78). It was now taken up by the crusading newspaper, *Rebecca*, and its editor, Paddy French. He alleged that the darker side of one-party rule in south Wales, as in T. Dan Smith's Tyneside, was corruption and malpractice on a huge scale. There were exciting tales of local councillors and officials being in receipt of a range of attractions, from tickets for the England–Wales rugby match at Twickenham to trips to the 'red light' district of Amsterdam. In the end, a case did come to court in 1977 and the result was the conviction of the housing director and of Gerald Murphy, former Labour council leader, on a variety of corruption charges. It was also established that improper inducements had been offered by the Everwarm central-heating firm to obtain contracts in Swansea's publicly-financed housing. As a result, Everwarm, which later went into liquidation, won £2.2 million in contracts to the cost of local ratepayers. The *Sunday Times* gleefully reported on 'how greed ate its way into Labour's heartland', with further cases reported from Merthyr Tydfil, Port Talbot and Glamorgan County Council. Labour's position in Swansea slumped heavily in the 1976 local election.

At the same time, too much should not be made of these cases, serious though each individual one was. In general, Labour dominated Swansea's local government not because it was corrupt but because it was committed, and able to provide a range of social and public services increasingly denied the electors by central government, especially after 1979. Democratic machine-run politics in Swansea may have had their price at times, but they also had genuine social rewards and achievements. Many of the same points may be made here as of the machine politics of New York, which filled a social vacuum and fulfilled community needs, albeit in a fashion that employed graft and sometimes terror. In Swansea, it may also be added that the rebuilding and replanning of the city after the desperate ravages of the blitz, the initial success of its comprehensive schools programme, public spending on libraries, parks and the Glynn Vivian Art Gallery, suggest a more positive and creative view of the city fathers than the temporary *frisson* of the corruption trials of the 1970s.

It remains to assess what kind of general themes emerge from this account of Swansea's political evolution between the passage of the 1832 Reform Bill and the party conflicts of the present. In some ways, for all its location in Welsh life, Swansea's political development may not differ too sharply from the urban politics of other middle-sized industrial and commercial towns in modern Britain.

One conclusion is that its politics in general have been those of moderation. Only the somewhat eccentric figure of Lewis Llewelyn Dillwyn, Liberationist, little Englander and passionate radical, emerges as a figure on the leftwards fringe of his own time – and, in any case, his comfortable industrial background suggested other, less disturbing values. Otherwise, the Liberal ascendancy down to the 1920s threw up, in the main, moderate or positively right-wing figures, appropriate for the leadership of business or industry, like Newnes, Mond or Runciman, or a well-heeled representative like Brynmor Jones. A rare left-winger like R. D. Burnie, whose anti-war views during the conflict in South Africa in 1900 rocked the boat, was rapidly cast aside. Left-wing Liberals of Lloyd Georgite or other hue were repeatedly spurned.

Labour representatives have also, in general, been anything but extremists. In the pre-war industrial turmoil, a left-wing spokesman like Ben Tillett made little headway. Instead, all the Labour MPs for Swansea, from David Williams and Walter Samuel in the 1920s to Alan Williams and Donald Anderson in 1995, have been of the moderate persuasion. The Swansea Labour party and its management committee have also tended to follow a mainstream or centre-right alignment, and to ignore fringe movements such as the neo-syndicalism of Rhondda around 1910–14 and the Unity Front campaign of the 1930s. Divisions over CND and the bomb were shelved by 1964. The Communists have never made much headway in Swansea, while a brief efflorescence by Militant Tendency in Swansea West in the early 1980s appears to have been suppressed. Swansea has in the main been anything but a hotbed of extremism; its communal corporate identity has kept it firm to the centre, moderate ground of the liberal-left.

Swansea has also been a town with a fairly consistent pattern of two-party confrontation somewhat on the lines of Gilbert and Sullivan's *Iolanthe*. Before 1914 it was usually a conflict between Liberals and Conservatives in Swansea; even in Gower, the victorious Labour man, John Williams, was distinctly a Lib–Lab, committed to Victorian values. As the Liberals gradually disintegrated after 1918, this partisan polarization gave way to a contest between Labour and the Conservatives and their allies. Since the 1920s, the Liberals have never threatened to echo in Swansea, or elsewhere in south Wales, the kind of revival they have intermittently managed in the west of England, suburban fringes of Greater London and lowland Scotland. The Communists, as noted, have never been political challengers in Swansea, though occasionally active in some of the local unions and the trades council. In the early 1930s there was a brief proto-fascist upsurge, led by a right-wing Tory, W. T. Mainwaring Hughes. This led to a public meeting addressed by Oswald Mosley at the Plaza cinema in July 1934 and to a rare political outburst by Dylan Thomas directed against Hughes's open racism. The poet's Marxist friend, Bert Trick, was active in an anti-fascist Democratic League. But this crisis fortunately very soon passed by.

Nor has Welsh nationalism made any impact of significance in Swansea politics. The Welsh language, still widely used in the valley, in eastern parts of Swansea such as Morriston and Llansamlet, and frequently heard at St Helen's rugby ground (though, significantly, seldom at the Vetch Field soccer ground), has nevertheless been the language of a small, declining minority for some decades. A Welsh bookshop in the town, some Welsh chapels, Welsh-language playgroups and primary schools, a Welsh department of much distinction in the University College, have ensured a vigorous Welsh-language foothold. National eisteddfodau held in Singleton Park have been immensely successful. But neither socially nor culturally have Welsh Nationalists found much joy in Swansea. In the early 1960s, perhaps symbolically, two local intellectuals prominent in Plaid Cymru circles, both connected with the University College, were respectively an Austrian who had taught in Puerto Rico, and a Pole. Apart from a by-election in Swansea East in 1963, the party has never made much impact: even then it managed only 5 per cent of the vote.

In its wider horizons, Swansea's politics have always had the aspect of being the public expression not just of a town – a city since 1969 – but of a region. In the Edwardian heyday before 1914, Swansea's city fathers, when pronouncing on free trade or industrial progress, always had the sense of speaking on behalf of 'west Wales', a somewhat amorphous entity which might extend anywhere from Haverfordwest to Port Talbot, but was at least juxtaposed against the quite divergent interests of Barry, Cardiff, Penarth and Newport in the south-east. In the hard years of the 1930s, and especially in the economic renewal of south Wales from the 1940s to the late 1970s, Swansea's claims to represent the needs and political weight of a region, and not simply of one town, became more and more explicit. From the time of the opening of the Severn Bridge and the extension of the M4 motorway only as far as the eastern approaches of Swansea at the end of the 1960s, Swansea politicians were vocal in protesting against the attempt to siphon all the economic activity in south Wales – perhaps in Wales as a whole – to the greater Cardiff area. On the one hand, there were the symbols of Swansea's lessening status in contrast to Cardiff: its smaller transport and commercial infrastructure; its difficulty in attracting more than branch factories of major concerns; the closure of Swansea airport in the 1960s while Rhoose airport near Cardiff flourished; the much greater involvement of the Welsh Office in the Cardiff/Newport area than in south-west Wales; the rapid expansion of the University College and UWIST in Cardiff. Swansea had no Julian Hodge. On the other hand, economic geographers defined the emergence of 'Swansea Bay City', somewhat on transatlantic lines, a huge industrial conurbation extending from Port Talbot in the east to Llanelli in the west (and taking in many of the major Welsh rugby teams *en route*). This factor alone has given Swansea politics much more than a purely parochial significance and made its political spokesmen, local and parliamentary, the voices for a widely-ranging, diversified and expanding regional economy. The relative decline of Swansea Docks in the period since the 1960s has not minimized the importance of these wider perspectives.

And yet, while Swansea's politics have had their regional, synoptic aspect, they have to only a limited degree been Welsh politics. As far as some of the major themes of contemporary Wales are concerned, or at least in terms of the definition of a distinctive Welsh identity, Swansea's role has been a semi-detached one. Like Winston Churchill's famous description of his own view of the Church of England, Swansea has propped up Welsh national politics like a flying buttress: it has given support but only from the outside.

Certainly, Swansea could never be claimed to be any kind of stronghold of Welsh nationalism. From the early nineteenth century, when it arose as a notable entrepôt and centre of commerce, and thus of wider contact with an anglicizing wider world, Swansea was unlikely to sympathize with nationalist sentiment or emotive cries of 'Wales for the Welsh'. In the early 1890s, when for the first time a significant movement for Welsh Home Rule arose, the so-called *Cymru Fydd* or Young Wales movement spurred on by Lloyd George and other young Liberals, Swansea stood aloof. The Welsh-speaking nationalist, Llewelyn Williams, who took over the editorship of the Swansea *Daily Post* in 1894, wrote to a Cardiff Liberal, Edward Thomas (Cochfarf), of how 'anti-Welsh the Liberals of the place are'. He deplored what he called 'the howling wilderness of Swansea philistinism'. In disgust, Williams moved elsewhere in south Wales to try to kindle the nationalist spark amongst his fellow countrymen in the valleys.

This reluctance of Swansea's social and political leaders to involve themselves seriously in movements of a nationalistic hue has been a consistent theme from that time on. As late as the controversy over Welsh devolution in the 1970s, two of the three local MPs, Donald Anderson (Swansea East) and, more surprisingly, the Welsh-speaking Ifor Davies (Gower), came out against their own government's proposals, while the third local member, Alan Williams (Swansea West), though a government minister, appeared little more than lukewarm. The poll on 1 March 1979 showed resoundingly that this reflected the view of the voters in Swansea, too.

One after another, Swansea in the present century has tended to reject the badges of Welshness as variously identified. The Sabbatarian ethic of the Welsh chapels, and the closing of cinemas and other places of entertainment on Sundays, have been rejected by the voters in the one-time 'Mecca of Nonconformity'. So, too, in 1961 was the Welsh Sunday Closing Act of 1881, whose operation in the Swansea area was voted down by a huge majority in the local option polls held in that year. No doubt other factors than simple Welsh sentiment were involved here – a Welsh Nonconformist minister in Morriston lamented how 'Swansea had bowed the knee to Bacchus'. But it is clear that any effort (for instance, that made by a neighbouring MP, James Griffiths, in Llanelli) to claim that the Tory government was deliberately rejecting a legislative token of Welshness and fragmenting Wales with local option polls found scant support in Swansea. The Welsh Language Society had few members here, too, even in the University College with its bilingual notices such as 'Acwariwm'. When the defederalization of the University of Wales was under debate in 1964, it was noted that the principal of the University College of Swansea, an English historian who shortly migrated to Harvard, supported Cardiff in urging a splitting up of the national university. On the other hand, as a sign of changing times perhaps, in 1989 the University College of Swansea and its major officers, including the president, Lord Callaghan, supported the Goronwy Daniel Committee's proposals for strengthening the University and its federal planning structure. In general, though, the Swansea ethos, common to Liberals, Conservatives and Labour over the years, has tended to reinforce the dichotomy in Welsh life between a hinterland with some commitment to Welsh sentiment and the native language, and a coastal fringe, extending from the mouth of the Severn to Mumbles Head, anglicized and anti-separatist in its attitude.

Throughout the years, however, the vibrancy of Swansea politics has remained an expression of civic identity, cultural vigour and social compassion. It has made Swansea's history a relatively peaceful and civilized one, and enabled Irish, Arab, Chinese and other immigrants to be peacefully absorbed in this cosmopolitan Welsh town. The anti-semitic disturbances in Tredegar in 1911 or the alarming race riots around Cardiff's Tiger Bay in 1919 were never paralleled in Swansea. There are many other indices of the historic dynamism of Swansea as a community – its industrial and commercial growth, its active literary and musical life, its sporting achievements. Many of them are celebrated elsewhere in other volumes. But the political record of the town in its modest way is a hymn of praise to the kind of controlled adjustments that a tolerant and sophisticated people have been able to make, using political power to create a decent and durable community, and build to last.

1990

III
People

17

Liberals, Nationalists and
Mr Gladstone[1]

It is difficult to convey in contemporary terms the extent to which Gladstone's massive personality dominated political life in Britain for at least the last thirty years of his active career. In a period when party discipline and composition were far more loosely constructed than they are today, Gladstone's supporters in Parliament and in the country as a whole were united less by ideology or economic identity than by personal adherence and devotion to their leader: it was more of a personal connection in the mould of the Canningites or the Peelites, both great influences on Gladstone's political outlook, than an integrated party in the modern sense. In time, the Conservative newspapers were to describe the Liberal party, with perfect accuracy in my view, as the Gladstonians. General elections turned to a great extent, not on long-term class attitudes as they are today, but on what Gladstone's latest campaign happened to be – Gladstone's plan for Irish disestablishment, Gladstone's denunciation of the 'unspeakable Turk', Gladstone's proposal for Irish Home Rule. The dominance of Gladstone's overshadowing personality was still more apparent after the severe Liberal division over Irish Home Rule in 1886. Both Sir Robert Peel, Gladstone's master, and David Lloyd George, his unorthodox disciple, destroyed their parties and their own political prospects, ending their days as the lonely leaders of isolated and ever-diminishing splinter groups. Gladstone alone survived the upheaval he had let loose with an effective political instrument in the National

---

[1]An address delivered before the Honourable Society of Cymmrodorion in London, 9 January 1959. Chairman: C. A. Gladstone, Esq., MA.

Liberal Federation and a substantial measure of popular support in the country. Even after his death, Gladstone's memory was powerful enough to rally the disintegrating Liberal factions. Liberal imperialist and Little Englander, industrial capitalist and trade unionist, Welsh disestablisher and Liberal Churchman – all could reassemble in apparent harmony beneath the banner of Gladstonian economics, and advance to the immense election triumph of 1906.

The very diversity of Gladstone's support during his lifetime, however, has served somewhat to impair his later reputation. Each section, each pressure-group, has represented a different Gladstone, a Gladstone created in its own image. Nowhere is this more apparent than in his reputation in Wales. During his career, Gladstone's position was more secure in Wales than in any other part of the United Kingdom, yet scarcely anywhere has he received a worse press since his death. I believe that this is due, in large measure, to the fact that Gladstone's last years coincided with the rise of the nationalist movement generally known as *Cymru Fydd*. For *Cymru Fydd*, even though its history as an effective political force covered barely three years, has had nevertheless a profound impact on the influential Welsh journalists, publicists, and historians of the twentieth century. Many of them were intimately associated with the leading personalities of the movement at Aberystwyth and elsewhere, and the type of nostalgic nationalism in which they specialize has helped to determine their attitude towards Gladstone – and, through them, the attitude of their many readers. The picture has been built up of an ageing, conservative High Churchman, rooted in the past, as a permanent obstacle to what are believed to have been the united, dynamic, national demands of the rebellious young spokesmen of Nonconformist Wales. I see that William George, in his very interesting recollections of his brother's career, refers to Gladstone as a 'drag on the wheel'.[2]

It is something of a curiosity that in this, if in nothing else, both Nonconformist Liberals and Anglican Conservatives seem to agree. Churchmen, such as A. G. Edwards, the first archbishop of Wales, have seen in Gladstone a respectable old man who allowed himself to be bullied into one reluctant concession after another by the Welsh extremists on his flanks and coerced into acquiescing in the destruction of the great institutions which provided the substructure of society. So far as Gladstone is concerned, Welsh nationalists and Nonconformists (the terms are virtually synonymous) agree with this view. Both sides find it puzzling, if not inexplicable, that in 1886 Calvinist Wales should prefer Gladstone's policy of Home Rule for Catholic Ireland to the strident programme of radical reform offered

[2]William George, *My Brother and I* (London, 1958), 176.

by Joseph Chamberlain. How can one account for this? How can one analyse a view that unites Archbishop Edwards with Beriah Gwynfe Evans? Was it that Gladstone in his later years become so out-of-date, as radicals believed, or so unscrupulous, as Tories maintained, that he would submit to any blackmail, and make any concessions, however extreme, as long as he could keep his supporters united on behalf of Irish Home Rule? Was he fundamentally out of sympathy with the Welsh national movement, and with the Nonconformist radicalism, which was its political expression? Or is the truth rather that Gladstone was both an idealist and an extremely shrewd politician, whose intentions baffled contemporaries and have often misled his successors?

For Gladstone's later reputation is in strange contrast with the enthusiasm, the reverence, the devotion that he enjoyed in Wales during his lifetime. The use of quasi-religious terms is deliberate. After all, Thomas Gee, the militant publicist of Welsh Nonconformity, once described the Welsh people as Gladstone's 'political worshippers'.[3] Gladstone's occasional journeys from Hawarden to the Eisteddfod or to other Welsh ceremonies assumed the atmosphere of a pilgrimage. The reception of Queen Victoria, when she visited Wales in 1889, was quite undemonstrative by comparison. A national mythology grew up around occasions such as that in June, 1887, when Gladstone stood on the steps of the building that is now the University College of Swansea, and received the wild acclamation of 60,000 Welshmen thronging Singleton Park below him. The speeches that Gladstone made on that visit to south Wales are not entirely exhilarating to read today. For example, speaking of the demand for Welsh Home Rule, he said, in terms of characteristic Delphic obscurity, that 'there was ground for recognizing it as a fact, and endeavouring to give to the demand for information that is not unnaturally entertained whatever satisfaction the question may permit'.[4] We can hardly visualize such words arousing a tumult of enthusiasm. But Gladstone did, in addition, speak warmly of the value of Welsh culture and of Welsh nationality, and robustly refuted the recent view of Bishop Basil Jones that Wales was merely a 'geographical expression'. This was not all an isolated statement, designed to flatter his audience – it is fully consistent with his policy and outlook, and is, I believe, the key to his relations with the Welsh people. To a nation still smarting from the contemptuous censure of the *Llyfrau Gleision*, Gladstone brought a practical recognition of the separate and distinct claims of Wales, in a number of different directions. More than any other statesman of the

[3]Gee to Gladstone, 23 February 1891. (BL Add. MS. 44512, f. 121.)
[4]*The Times*, 6 June 1887.

time, he showed an intuitive appreciation of the desire of the Welsh to be recognized, as Scotland and Ireland were recognized, as a distinct and equal nationality and not merely a haphazard agglomeration of a dozen westerly counties of England. When Gladstone died in May 1898, it was felt, in the press and in the pulpit, that Wales particularly had suffered a grievous loss. In the magazine *Young Wales*, Tom Ellis praised the personal sympathy Gladstone had always shown towards the spiritual basis of the national movement. 'He was', Ellis wrote, 'more Celtic than the Celts, more Cymric than the Welsh themselves.'[5]

The Welsh problem that increasingly forced itself upon the attention of statesmen in the later years of the nineteenth century had many complicated aspects, political, economic, religious, and cultural factors being intertwined and working one upon the other. It expressed itself in terms of class, in a revolt against the traditional leadership of Welsh society by the squires and parsons who were increasingly marked off from the mass of the people by the barriers of class, religion, politics, and language. The spokesmen of the revolt – sometimes rather inappropriately termed *y werin* – were middle-class men, farmers, commercial men, lawyers, journalists, ministers, but their common denominator was Nonconformity. The Welsh lawyer, unlike the Scottish lawyer, had to win his spurs on English circuits; the Welsh businessman was constantly dealing with English firms and companies; the Welsh farmer was the prey of the same economic fluctuations as his English counterpart. The Nonconformist chapels alone provided an indigenous and largely exclusive native Welsh institution, with a trained and experienced leadership in the ministers of each denomination, and three dozen or more Welsh-language newspapers and periodicals to express their propaganda. The objects of the movement were social rather than economic – it was a struggle for equality. Anglican parsons, usually harmless and peaceable men, were made the scapegoats for a system which compelled Nonconformist children to learn the catechism in Church schools and Nonconformist parents to pay tithe for their upkeep. With Nonconformity able to bridge the gap between rural and industrial Wales, and providing a ready instrument for the aspirations of working-class people, the campaign for disestablishment could unite Welshmen in a way that Welsh Home Rule was never able to do. Methodist, Independent, and Baptist could reconcile their rivalry. Great industrialists like Richard Fothergill or D. A. Thomas could, without incongruity, represent the Nonconformist democracy of Merthyr Tydfil. Sectional differences could be submerged in the campaign against the Unholy Trinity of the squire, the brewer and the bishop. It

[5] *Young Wales*, June 1898.

is a phenomenon that resembles more the radical movements of the United States, associated with Andrew Jackson or William Jennings Bryan, rather than any parallel development in English history.

The cultural question, though distinct, is related to these politico-religious considerations. Latent nationalism in Wales had been stung by the shame of the wholesale condemnation of Welsh society, culture, religion and morals, given in the Education Blue Books, the notorious *Brad y Llyfrau Gleision* of 1847. It was not a very happy starting-point for a national movement – not as effective as Cromwell's massacres in Ireland, for example, or even Lord North's actions in North America. Henceforth, the Welsh people were fighting against nothing more vicious than contempt. Nevertheless, it was this that provided the inspiration for the national movement with which Gladstone and others had to contend. It assisted in identifying the grievances of Nonconformists with the national grievances of Wales. The prejudice it implied took long to disappear: in 1866, *The Times* confidently asserted that 'The Welsh language is the curse of Wales' – a view that still persists in some quarters apparently. Underlying the many aspects of the movement, the campaign against the Established Church, the movement for educational and land reform, the fight for the recognition of the Welsh language – underlying these was the desire for national self-respect.

I have spent some time in analysing what appear to be the main aspects of the Welsh question, because it is fundamental, I believe, to understanding Gladstone's attitude. Because it was in appreciating this desire for national self-respect that Gladstone showed most understanding and sympathy. He was himself a Celt, purely Scottish in blood, Highland as well as Lowland, and he seemed able to enter into a personal communion with the audiences in Wales, as with his fellow-countrymen at Midlothian. Again, there was, in spite of his High Church views, a profound hereditary strain of Calvinism in Gladstone's make-up. He believed himself to be the personal instrument of a predestined divine purpose, whether he were deflating Disraeli or rescuing prostitutes in the West End, and this Calvinist trait deepened his understanding of the character of Welsh life. And finally, he had close personal ties with Wales. His wife, Catherine Glynne, came from a famous north Wales family, and from the late 1840s Gladstone came to set up residence at Hawarden in Flintshire.

Two of his most intimate friends – in so far as Gladstone achieved intimacy with anyone – were closely associated with Welsh affairs. The first was Henry Austen Bruce, first Lord Aberdare, who was home secretary in Gladstone's first ministry. He played an active part in the creation of a University of Wales and was often consulted by Gladstone on Welsh questions. Bruce, however, was too anglicized and too much the Whig patrician to be a wholly reliable guide to Welsh opinion: it was this that had caused his defeat at the Merthyr Tydfil election of 1868, at the hands of the famous Congregationalist minister, Henry Richard.

Gladstone's other informant about Wales was more influential. I refer to Stuart Rendel, Lord Rendel, as he later became, who was first drawn to Gladstone's notice when he won a sensational victory over the Wynn representative at the Montgomeryshire election of 1880. Rendel, an engineer and manufacturer, never attained office of any kind, yet although generally a silent back-bencher, he achieved a warm personal friendship with Gladstone. When Gladstone retired, Rendel also retired from active life: he was a pall-bearer at Gladstone's funeral. Rendel was not a man of profound mind: at Oxford, he graduated from Oriel with a fourth class. His letters are marked by dogged earnestness rather than by acute penetration. But he had other, perhaps more important qualities – self-effacing loyalty, personal charm, and immense tact. Gladstone found in Rendel, as he found in Lord Granville, a quiet refuge to whom he could retreat from the turbulent ambitions of his more brilliant colleagues. Rendel was almost unique among Gladstone's intimates in being a genuine radical – although he lacked the eloquence and the temperamental restlessness to make his radicalism articulate. In his later years he vigorously opposed the Boer War and Balfour's Education Act, and later still warmly supported Lloyd George's 'people's budget' and Insurance Act. But above all, although an Englishman, Rendel was a fervent advocate of the causes of Wales, particularly disestablishment and education, and became the first chairman of the so-called 'Welsh Party', comprising the Welsh Liberal members of Parliament. With great skill, Rendel used his many points of contact with Gladstone, both at his residences on the French Riviera and at No. 1, Carlton Gardens, to instruct him in the grievances of Wales and to elicit his active co-operation. Although often under attack from the Young Wales section, led by Tom Ellis and Lloyd George, Rendel's cautious Fabian tactics were amply justified by the practical results he achieved in winning Gladstone's active support.

The record of the relations of Gladstone, the politician, with the Welsh people is divided sharply by the year 1886 when the first Irish Home Rule Bill irretrievably split the Liberal party. Before that date, Gladstone turned only occasionally to the affairs of Wales. But the Welsh national movement was at this stage halting and ineffective. The great victories at the election of 1868 were Liberal rather than nationalist – they indicated the great expansion of the electorate after the Reform Bill of 1867. It was the subsequent evictions of many tenants who had voted Liberal, particularly in Cardiganshire and

Carmarthenshire, which made such an impression on popular recollection. Even in this earlier period, however, Gladstone showed his sympathy with Welsh national feelings in many ways. He said later that the series of articles which Henry Richard wrote in the *Morning and Evening Star* in 1866 had first opened his eyes to the neglect of Welsh affairs.[6]

It was, characteristically, over the question of the Welsh Church that Gladstone made his first impact on opinion in Wales, when in 1870 he appointed the Revd Joshua Hughes to the see of St Asaph, the first Welsh-speaking Welshman appointed since the reign of Queen Anne. This is by no means a matter of narrowly ecclesiastical interest – Nonconformists such as Thomas Gee and Henry Richard were just as interested in Gladstone's eventual choice as Churchmen were. Cabinet ministers nowadays are inclined to complain that the pressure of work upon them is almost unbearable: no doubt there is something in this. But it is salutary to note that in January and February, 1870, when his attention was already distracted by a host of questions at home and abroad, Gladstone was writing scores of letters about the St Asaph vacancy – and writing copies of most of them. It was a bewildering episode. Over a dozen candidates were proposed, all with enthusiastic admirers, most with severe critics. Gladstone wrote in despair to Bruce, his home secretary: 'If you read in the papers some morning that I have been carried to Bedlam and that a straight-waistcoat is considered necessary, please to remember it will be entirely owing to the vacancy in the see of St. Asaph.'[7] The truth seems to be that the comparatively inferior quality of the native Welsh clergy made a choice difficult. The eventual choice, Joshua Hughes, was far from ideal: he was a man of few obvious gifts and a few obvious defects. The squires objected to his middle-class origins. But he was a Welsh-speaking Welshman, and Gladstone's appointment had thus a profound influence on the growing nationalism of Wales. Gladstone had appreciated the importance of this despite the gloomy prophecies of Bruce and many others. In one letter he stated that he considered the St Asaph vacancy the most urgent matter requiring attention since he had taken office.[8]

During Gladstone's second ministry, the same situation recurred, when the see of Llandaff fell vacant in December 1882. Again the same protracted negotiations took place between Gladstone and prominent Welshmen. Gladstone, already harassed by Egypt, Ireland,

[6]Speech at Mold Eisteddfod. (*The Times*, 20 August 1873.)

[7]Gladstone to H. A. Bruce, 18 February 1870. (BL Add. MS. 44086, f. 123.)

[8]Gladstone to archbishop of York, 12 January 1870. (BL Add. MS. 44424, f. 90.)

and the Transvaal, complained that 'a vacancy in a Welsh see costs me more trouble than six English vacancies'.[9] But again a Welsh-speaking Welshman was chosen, although again not a very distinguished one. A permanent precedent had been set, and the Church of England in Wales began slowly to recover lost ground.

Gladstone's motives seem to have been based partly on expediency, partly on sentiment. In part, it was a recognition of the simple fact which Henry Richard had stressed that clergymen unversed in even the rudiments of the Welsh language were unlikely to make much appeal to a population over half of whom had little or no acquaintance with English. But also it was the traditional aspect of Welsh nationality which appealed to Gladstone – the history of the old British Church, and its saints, the ancient Welsh devotional literature and the language, 'a venerable relic of the past', he called it. This same feeling served to make him at first suspicious and hostile to the campaign for Welsh disestablishment. When Watkin Williams, the member for Denbigh Boroughs, first brought up the question in the House of Commons,[10] Gladstone strongly opposed it, stating that the Welsh Church was an integral part of the Church of England. His uncompromising attitude has been held against him since. But Gladstone was a practical politician. At times doctrinaire to the point of obstinacy, he could also appreciate politics as the art of the possible. Just as he came to see that Home Rule in Ireland was inevitable so by 1884 he had come to acknowledge that the demand for Welsh disestablishment could not be resisted even if placed on no other ground than the right of small nations to determine their own affairs. In Ireland and in Wales, Gladstone showed himself to be adept at the strategic withdrawal. When Joseph Chamberlain campaigned with his Unauthorized Programme, hurling abuse at the House of Lords and demanding disestablishment all round, Gladstone's main concern was a tactical one – a fear that Chamberlain should disrupt the Liberal party by alienating its Anglican supporters.

Meanwhile, Gladstone had been showing his sympathy for Welsh sensibilities in many other ways. He spoke on behalf of higher education in Wales and appointed the famous Education Committee under Lord Aberdare,[11] which contrasted so favourably with the *Llyfrau Gleision*. He encouraged the new Welsh colleges in north and

[9]Gladstone to bishop of Durham, 28 December 1882. (BL Add. MS. 44478, f. 271.)

[10]9 May 1870. (*Parl. Deb.*, 3rd ser., CCI, 1274 ff.)

[11]Report of a Committee appointed to inquire into the condition of Intermediate and Higher Education in Wales, 1881.

south Wales,[12] although the jealousy of Bangor, Cardiff and half a dozen other Welsh towns nearly drove Gladstone and everyone else to distraction. He supported the private members bill for Sunday closing in Wales, which for the first time saw a separate act of Parliament involving a distinct principle, applying to Wales alone as a country distinct from England.[13] Again Gladstone attended the Eisteddfod at Mold, the first leading political figure to do so. It was a wet day, but Gladstone's warm support for Welsh nationality aroused great enthusiasm, although *The Times* considered it all rather revolutionary. Finally, Wales, with its permanent Nonconformist majority and its long tradition of opposition to war and imperialism, as expressed by Gwilym Hiraethog and others, reacted particularly warmly to the Midlothian campaign in the winter of 1879. It is not surprising, therefore, that these concessions to national feeling should inspire immense personal devotion in Wales to the Grand Old Man.

The Irish Home Rule Bill in 1886 completely transformed the political situation. As we have seen, many people have considered it puzzling that Nonconformist Wales should have followed Gladstone rather than the radicalism of Joseph Chamberlain. After all, Chamberlain did win over, temporarily, no less a person than Thomas Gee, and even the youthful Lloyd George, who might have become a Liberal Unionist, had he not muddled up the date of a meeting. But Chamberlain had done little for Wales. He advocated disestablishment and land reform in a general way: Chamberlain lost his appeal when he allied himself to the Selbornes, Derbys, and Cavendishes. Jack Cade turned into Cardinal Wolsey. Gladstone, on the other hand, had a far more profound appeal, and he swung over many Nonconformist votes in Wales. A remarkable example is in Cardiganshire, where Gladstone's candidate, Bowen Rowlands, a High Churchman who later became a Roman Catholic, turned out the sitting member, the wealthy and philanthropic Methodist, David Davies of Llandinam, in one of the violent elections for which Cardiganshire is deservedly famous.

The general election of 1886 destroyed the old Liberal party. Chamberlain often alleged that Wales had indefinitely postponed the reforms on which she had set her heart, by hitching her wagon to the star of Irish Home Rule. There can be little doubt, however, that the election in fact greatly helped on the Welsh national campaign. The Liberals had lost their majority in England and their hold on the big cities was growing weaker. Even Liberal Scotland had a strong element

---

[12]Stuart Rendel to A. C. Humphreys-Owen, 15 December 1883. (NLW, Glansevern MS. 132).

[13] Cf. Gladstone's speech on the second reading (*Parl. Deb.*, 3rd ser., CCLX, 1772.)

of Liberal Unionism. Liberalism, in fact, was being based on the Celtic fringe and the influence of Welsh Liberals in the party, at Westminster, and in the country increased correspondingly. In addition, these years saw the arrival of a new type of member, younger, more vigorous and more militantly nationalist, and their arrival coincided with a new attitude in Wales itself. Ireland was not the model. The same circumstances that paralysed Irish social life, the tyranny of a small landowning class over the mass of the peasantry, from whom they were divided by politics and religion, seemed to be reproduced in Wales.

There were new personalities, also. Foremost among them was Tom Ellis, returned triumphantly for Merioneth, after a campaign conducted largely in Welsh; the son of a tenant farmer, he was hailed as the 'Parnell of Wales'. This was a misunderstanding. Ellis could never have fulfilled this role, even had he wanted to. He worked within the patrician circle of the Liberal leadership – he is a personal symbol of the process that Welsh Liberalism underwent during his lifetime, the development from an intense, though vague, nationalism into professional, technical Liberalism, 'wearing its rue with a difference'. Ellis was a convincing rather than a compelling orator: he was the Cobden rather than the Bright of Welsh Liberalism. Asquith once called him 'Wales's greatest administrator'. He was more in sympathy with the constructive Fabianism of Rosebery or Cecil Rhodes, rather than the turbulent egalitarianism of his colleague, Lloyd George. Had he lived to see the South African War, he would have been a Liberal imperialist and not a Pro-Boer. Within these circumscribed limits, however, Ellis made a considerable impression on political life and on Gladstone. His impressive array of statistics, illustrating the hardship of the Welsh farmers, made a great impact on the Liberal leader. Ellis himself often recalled how Gladstone invited him to his room in the Commons to discuss the inland revenue returns relating to Welsh land.

But Ellis was only one of the most brilliant group of men ever to represent Wales at Westminster. There was D. A. Thomas, later Lord Rhondda, an erratic individualist who never found a happy niche in politics, and eventually retired to his coal-mines in disgust after twenty-two unrewarding years on the back-bench. Yet Thomas, difficult as he must have been as a colleague, had a most penetrating mind, with an original approach to the industrial questions of south Wales, on which Liberals were usually silent. There was Samuel Evans, later president of the Court of Probate, Divorce, and Admiralty, and a great judge. Although more of a barrister than a politician, in his early years Evans was one of the most militant Nonconformists in Parliament. There were to follow other prominent national leaders – also very young men – such as Herbert Lewis and Ellis Jones Griffith.

And, finally, there was the young Lloyd George, already gifted with the talents of the demagogue and of the flexible diplomat. Men such as these appealed to Gladstone from 1886 onwards. Like Parnell's Irishmen, they had a specific programme. They tended to sit together in the House in a distinct Welsh body. Wales, for so long the Cinderella among nations, attracted the attention of Parliament more and more. When it came to unpopular measures such as the Tithe Bills Lloyd George and his friends could be just as ingenious in time-wasting obstruction as Parnell himself.

Why did Gladstone give way to them so often? His opponents – and many of his supporters – had a simple explanation – 'log-rolling'. He was an 'old man in a hurry', who, like a Tammany Hall boss, would make any concessions, however extreme, to get his various incoherent factions into line. Even apart from the question-begging assumption that there was something inherently disastrous in the Welsh demands, this does not seem a very satisfactory explanation. Gladstone's attitude before and after the Home Rule split is sufficiently consistent. Even over the decisive question of disestablishment, he had been slowly changing his mind. His withdrawal was skilful, but a withdrawal it was. If it is said that Gladstone paid Wales *more* attention after 1886 because the Welsh members were in a position to put pressure on him – well, that is a simple fact of political life. I can see no moral objection to it. And Gladstone could be a most shrewd politician. I believe that here we have one of the major deficiencies in modern British historiography. Gladstone's personality we have had brilliantly depicted (most fully by Colin Matthew), but Gladstone the politician has not always been fully presented to us. As a result, we have this irritating stereotype of 'the old, wild and incomprehensible man of eighty-two and a half', without it being brought out how radical Gladstone became in his old age. The Newcastle Programme he intended to be a direct challenge to the House of Lords. Gladstone had little fear of Welsh radicalism. He did not want Wales to turn into another Ireland, but there was little danger that she would. The Welsh Land League resembled its more famous Irish counterpart in little except the name. The Welsh Party could never become independent: unlike the Irish Nationalists, it could put pressure only on the Liberal party. If the Welsh separated from it, their one hope of political advancement would disappear. Any danger of separatism was removed by the urbane presence of Stuart Rendel, chairman of the Welsh Party, who continued his self-effacing role as the *fidus Achates*, Gladstone's unobtrusive mentor on Welsh affairs.

Being in opposition gave the Welsh members freedom of manoeuvre, and in one way after another Gladstone intervened to sanction their claims. He was helpful in the passing of the Intermediate Education

Bill that set up the network of county schools which formed the structure of Welsh secondary education.[14] The campaign for land reform, or more specifically for a land court, was too uncomfortably similar to events in Ireland to gain Gladstone's unqualified approval. However, he was sufficiently impressed by Ellis's statistics to promise a 'dispassionate inquiry'.[15]

Above all, there was the grievance of the Established Church which had ceased to be a religious issue and was now in essence a nationalist campaign expressed in terms of the class struggle. The demand militated against one of Gladstone's most profound beliefs, the need for an established religious organization as a bastion against materialism and atheism. There can be little doubt that he was temperamentally opposed to upsetting the structure of the Church after nearly 1,000 years. There was, in strict ecclesiastical law, no Welsh Church: the diocesan boundaries made no distinction between Wales and England. The violence of the controversy must have alienated a churchman like Gladstone. He once wrote that he was sometimes more in agreement with his opponents than with his supporters.[16] He could hardly be expected to appreciate David Lloyd George accusing the Rhyl Church Congress of being floated on barrels of beer, or describing Bishop Edwards of St Asaph as a 'no-rate theologian and an irate priest'.

But Gladstone knew it was not a matter of legal technicalities any more than religious tests at Oxford and Cambridge had been. Disestablishment must be judged according to practical circumstances, as Gladstone himself had judged it in Ireland. Gladstone chose to work indirectly in a manner that infuriated his enemies and often exasperated his friends. The Liberal party committed itself to Welsh disestablishment in 1887, but Gladstone restricted his own pronouncements to the occasional vague half-sentence. When the Tithe Bills came up in Parliament, as a direct consequence of the riots in the Vale of Clwyd, Gladstone, harassed by Archbishop Benson on his right flank and Thomas Gee on his left, said nothing at all – an almost unique act of self-abnegation for him on an ecclesiastical subject. There were loud complaints in Wales, and murmurs of rebellion. Even the loyal Rendel had to admit that a more positive lead would be welcome. These criticisms are understandable from the Welsh point of view. Welsh disestablishment is a dead issue today: it was all settled many years ago. Elections no longer turn on denominational questions.

[14]Cf. Gladstone's speech on the second reading, 15 May 1889. (*Parl. Deb.*, 3rd ser., CCCXXXVI, 135.)

[15]*Parl. Deb.*, 4th ser., II, 985.

[16]Gladstone to Revd W. Morgan Jones, 17 September 1892. (BL Add. MS. 44549, f. 10.)

But in 1890 they were political dynamite. The threat of disestablishment inspired the parish clergy to great activity. Bishops, less
restrained than they are inclined to be today, pronounced freely on
political platforms, while church-going landlords had still ample
means of influencing dissenting tenants in the countryside, despite the
protection of the ballot. In the big cities, the brewers were very
influential. All this had little effect in Wales, but however popular
disestablishment might be there, in England it was likely to lose many
votes. English Nonconformity, at the zenith of its political power, felt
the grievances of Wales to be too remote to justify a major campaign.

After much equivocation, Gladstone made his position clear. He
spoke and voted for Welsh disestablishment, asserting that, as in
Ireland, the Church was the church of the few and the church of the
rich.[17] Disestablishment in Wales and Scotland took second place in
the Newcastle Programme only to Irish Home Rule. Gladstone and
disestablishment dominated the 1892 general election in Wales, as a
result of which thirty-one Liberals were returned out of thirty-four
seats. As the total Liberal majority in Britain was only forty (including
the Irish), the Welsh representatives had a unique chance to put their
independence to the test.

When Gladstone became prime minister for the fourth time, at the
age of eighty-two, Irish Home Rule again dominated the scene. But
Wales was certainly not ignored – in fact, this weak and brief government advanced the Welsh cause to a unique extent. Gladstone actually
completed the formation of his government in Rendel's house in
Carlton Gardens, and this afforded Rendel a rare opportunity to insert
the requirements of Wales.[18] The new government was given a spectacular introduction at the famous meeting at the foot of Snowdon, at
which Lloyd George, Tom Ellis, Bryn Roberts, and other Welsh leaders
spoke in Welsh, and Gladstone spoke more precisely than before on his
policy for Wales.[19]

Results soon followed. The University of Wales came into being,
Gladstone ignoring the opposition of the House of Lords to its
charter.[20] After a brief controversy[21] a Royal Commission on the Welsh

[17]*Parl. Deb.*, 3rd ser., CCCL, 1265.
[18]*Personal Papers of Lord Rendel* (London, 1931), 311.
[19]*The Times*, 14 September 1892.
[20]On 29 August 1893, the House of Lords carried by forty-one votes to thirty-
two the bishop of Chester's motion to withhold the Royal Assent from the
proposed University of Wales, owing to the exclusion of St David's College,
Lampeter. Gladstone ignored it.
[21]This dispute arose over Gladstone's decision, which Rendel supported, to
appoint the more limited mechanism of a select committee to inquire into the
Welsh land question, instead of a Royal Commission as had been generally

land question was appointed: it effectively shelved the matter, as Royal Commissions often do, but, by bringing the old animosity of landlords and tenants out into the open, it greatly cleared the atmosphere in the Welsh countryside. Another, earlier, decision of great interest to Wales, again owing its inspiration to Rendel, was the offer of junior office to Ellis. He decided to accept, becoming only the second Welsh Privy Counsellor of recent years (Osborne Morgan was the first). This acceptance by Ellis, is still, perhaps, slightly controversial, but I have no doubt that Ellis was fully justified in believing he could do far more within the charmed circle of government, where he could co-operate with his friends, Asquith and Acland, than by vague sharp-shooting on the flanks. Welsh history is littered with 'revolts', parliamentary and otherwise, that have never materialized.

Lastly, there was the Church. Here again, Gladstone's tactics had much to commend them. Ireland blocked the way, as far as Welsh disestablishment was concerned, but Gladstone instead introduced a bill to suspend the creation of new interests, as a preliminary. It annoyed the Queen, who accused Gladstone of threatening the Church of which she was the head.[22] When the bill came up for debate in the Commons, Gladstone replied to an attack by Lord Randolph Churchill with one of those bursts of almost superhuman energy that he could still produce at times, even at the age of eighty-three. 'Vote! Vote! Vote! for Irish Home Rule and Welsh Disestablishment', he roared, and for half an hour he set the Commons ablaze.[23]

After the defeat of the second Irish Home Rule Bill, Gladstone's radicalism continued to mount. He now seemed to have meditated an all-out attack on the Lords, in which Welsh disestablishment would play its part. Nonconformists in Wales were still very impatient, but, in fact, in the autumn of 1893 Gladstone and Asquith were preparing a Welsh Disestablishment Bill.[24] When Gladstone met opposition in the

anticipated. Ellis, together with Herbert Lewis and Lloyd George, enlisted the backing of Asquith, Harcourt, Morley, and Acland, and on 14 December 1892 the Cabinet agreed to a Commission instead. This episode indicated one of the lines of division within the Welsh Party, Rendel disagreeing with the emphasis put upon the land question by the 'Young Wales' section. Cf. Ellis to Asquith, 21 October to 28 November 1892 (Bodleian, Asquith papers, box 19); Harcourt to Gladstone, 23 November 1892 (BL Add. MS. 44202, f. 287); Gladstone to Rendel, 12 November 1892 (BL Add. MS. 44549, f. 39); Rendel to Gee, 30 October 1892 (NLW, Gee MSS. 8308C, 274); Rendel to Gee, 17 November 1892 (NLW, Gee MSS. 8308C, 276); correspondence of Ellis and Herbert Lewis, 7 November and 1 to 19 December 1892 (NLW, Ellis papers).

[22]Gladstone to Asquith, 26 February 1893. (BL Add. MS. 44549, f. 68.)

[23]*Parl. Deb.*, 4th ser., IX, 278.

[24]Cf. Asquith to Gladstone, 7 November 1893. (BL Add. MS. 44549, f. 299.)

Cabinet to his proposal for a dissolution of Parliament, and also over the naval estimates, he pleaded old age and resigned. As a result, Ellis became chief whip, a role in which he was not unduly happy, while Rendel retired to the obscurity of the House of Lords.

The story of Gladstone and Wales is not quite ended, however. He held aloof as Rosebery's ministry staggered from crisis to crisis, and Wales fell increasingly under the spell of Lloyd George and *Cymru Fydd*. Then, at the very end of the Liberal government, Gladstone emerged from retirement to announce that he had withdrawn his support for the Welsh Disestablishment Bill then in Committee, having passed its second reading, as there were some 'points of detail' with which he disagreed.[25] Does this mean that Gladstone was really hostile after all? I do not think so. Gladstone made it clear that he supported the principle of disestablishment, while believing that the treatment of Church property was too severe. He had often put forward this view and many other Liberals took the same line – including, later on, W. G. C. Gladstone, the premier's grandson and member for Kilmarnock.[26] It is easy to forget how revolutionary the bill of 1895 must have seemed – cathedrals secularized, churchyards handed over to the county councils, endowments of £279,000 a year alienated. The measure that became law in 1919 was far more moderate. As far as the principle of Welsh nationality was concerned, Gladstone was committed.

Gladstone's retirement marked the end of a remarkable era in Welsh history, when nationalism and social democracy seemed to progress together. The election of 1895 marked the beginning of ten years of Conservative government, while the Liberals indulged in recriminations in the wilderness. The disaster of Cymru Fydd gravely weakened Welsh nationalism, and Celtic separatism disappeared in the tidal wave of imperialism. The period from 1868 to 1895, therefore, seemed in the hazy retrospect of nostalgia, to be a kind of golden age. Welsh writers have understandably stressed the part played by Welsh leaders in this movement – Gee, Ellis, Lloyd George, and the others. Gladstone and other English politicians, by contrast, appear all too often as unsympathetic or obtuse, living incarnations of the notorious direction in the *Encyclopaedia Britannica* – 'for Wales, see England'. This, however, is a one-sided presentation. Without the active help of English statesmen, Welsh affairs would have remained the residual stirring in the undergrowth they had been for hundreds of years. No one did more than Gladstone himself. The Welsh national movement, as a political factor, was transitory. Wales was strong only when the

[25] *The Times*, 19 June 1895.
[26] Cf. speech of 13 December 1912. (*Parl. Deb.*, 5th ser., XLV, 973).

Liberal party was weak. The election of 1886, breaking up the Liberal 'Broad Church' of radicals and Whigs, closed one period. The election of 1906 introduced another, in which the rise of the Labour party indicated the political advance of the industrial proletariat, a period in which economic and industrial questions would gradually displace narrower political issues such as the Lords veto or Welsh disestablishment. In 1906, all the thirty-four Welsh members were Liberal or Labour, yet this election, in fact, destroyed the Welsh Party as a serious force in politics. Welsh Liberalism lost much of its national character: Lloyd George, Samuel Evans, and Herbert Lewis found the refusal of office too high a price to pay for concentration on the marginal grievances of Wales. In any case, many of these grievances had disappeared. Nonconformists were no longer an inferior caste. Nonconformist county councils had undermined the traditional dominance of the Tory squire. Religious sectarianism was being displaced by religious indifference. The Welsh bishop seemed harmless enough in comparison with the coalowners of Tonypandy and Aberdare, many of whom were Liberals. When E. T. John tried to revive the Welsh Home Rule movement shortly before the First World War, he found that the dynamic Welsh nationalism of Gladstone's day had disappeared for ever.

The reason for this must surely be that the battle had, in fact, been won, and the personal influence of Gladstone was one of the leading factors in this triumph. He taught sceptical Englishmen a new attitude to Welsh nationality, with Welsh schools and colleges, a Welsh University, a Welsh Land Commission, Welsh bishops, Welsh legislation and administrative departments, and Welsh disestablishment as its practical expressions. Monmouthshire was restored as part of Wales. Gladstone's influence was not confined to his own party: the Conservative party also slowly changed its attitude. In 1895 the Conservatives attacked the Welsh Disestablishment Bill on the grounds that any separate legislation for Wales was unconstitutional; in the debates of 1912–14, this criticism was never heard. Conservatives recognized, as British public opinion recognized, that Wales was something more than a region, another Yorkshire or Cornwall. Gladstone moved slowly, cautiously – too slowly for *Cymru Fydd* and its successors who have often seen Gladstone's gradualism as so gradual as almost to be moving backwards. He kept in the background, restricting his own pronouncements and leaving other to provide the misinterpretation of his actions. But his oblique approach was effective. The cultural and the political were subject to the same principles. Nothing could have been more appropriate than that in 1888 Gladstone should attend the Wrexham Liberal Association before lunch and the Wrexham National Eisteddfod after, although

The Times condemned him for attending either.[27] It is doubtful whether any of Gladstone's colleagues really troubled to understand the Welsh question – Morley and Asquith were remote, Harcourt frankly abusive. To Gladstone, however, the question of nationalism had a more serious significance – after all, he had been impelled towards Liberalism by the unification of Italy and towards radicalism by the oppression of the Bulgarians. As a Scotsman, Gladstone could understand that nationalism in Scotland and Wales was not separatist. Wales was not another Ireland, however much the Unionists might protest, however much enthusiasm Michael Davitt might excite from the quarrymen of Ffestiniog, and however forceful the propaganda of Lloyd George and the Home Rulers. The Welsh landlords were unpopular, but they were still Welsh. The earl of Powis and Mabon could appear cheerfully together on the same eisteddfod platform – it is difficult to imagine such harmony between, say, Parnell and the earl of Longford. Irish opinion wanted the maximum degree of separation – Parnell fought a desperate battle to restrain his own extremists. Where Ireland wanted exclusion, Wales wanted equality, 'a place in the sun', a distinct share in the expanding economic opportunities of the empire – which is why Ellis admired Cecil Rhodes. When the Boer War came, even the most ardent Welsh pacifists joined in praise of the courage of the Welsh troops in South Africa – an interesting example of conflicting loyalties. If was, if you will, sentimental, but at least Gladstone, above all others, was able to recognize the role that sentiment plays in politics. Gladstone once described the Welsh people, not unkindly, as 'a singularly susceptible population'.[28] But it was by playing on chords such as these that Gladstone was able to raise the Welsh people up from relative obscurity into a continuity and a tradition of their own.

1960

[27]*The Times*, 5 September 1888.
[28]Gladstone to bishop of St Davids, 12 January 1870. (BL Add. MS. 44424, f. 28.)

18

'The Member for Wales':
Stuart Rendel (1834–1913)

Stuart, Lord Rendel, MP for Montgomeryshire between 1880 and 1894, was a self-effacing, uncharismatic man. After a fourteen-year period at Westminster, he retired from the limelight for ever. He added to his invisibility by a somewhat gloomy, hypochondriac temperament and personality. He went to his grave largely convinced that Wales had failed to appreciate his lifelong efforts on her behalf. When he died, his title became extinct, since all his children were female. He did not appear in the pages of the *Dictionary of National Biography*. His career was largely ignored until the former Newtown journalist, F. E. Hamer, once Welsh editor of the *Manchester Guardian* under C. P. Scott, published Rendel's *Personal Papers* in 1931.[1]

Rendel, then, is today almost a forgotten man – and from a largely forgotten age, that great era of Liberal ascendancy in Welsh public life between 1868 and 1914. The current vogue amongst Welsh historians for Labour history (to which the present author has made some contribution) has become somewhat unbalanced in its effects. Liberalism in Wales is now considered, if at all, largely in terms of its division and decline in the years after 1918. But Rendel's career, by contrast, reintroduces us to that glowing period of Liberal achievement, political, social, economic and cultural, in later-Victorian and Edwardian Wales. It is an epoch that has been largely ignored by Welsh

---

[1] *The Personal Papers of Lord Rendel* (London, 1931). Hamer, the editor, was editor of the *Montgomeryshire Express*, 1888–93, and Welsh editor of the *Manchester Guardian*, 1893–1916. He was on the editorial staff of Benns, the publishers of his book, 1916–32. In the 1920s he was an active member of the Labour party.

historians since the mid-1960s – apart from a continuing sequence of biographies of the young Lloyd George – and it well deserves to be resurrected. So it is very pleasing to commemorate the 150th anniversary of the birth of Stuart Rendel. It recalls a dedicated, astute and remarkably successful public figure, who contributed immensely to Welsh political and educational life, and whose legacy is central to the understanding of the Wales of today.

Although Rendel was designated 'the member for Wales', it is well to remember that he was a man of far wider interests. He was a knowledgeable observer of both the British and the international political scene. He was the close confidant of Gladstone, Rosebery, Morley and many other leading Victorian politicians. His business activities took him, between 1865 and 1878, to St Petersburg, Vienna, Berlin, Madrid, Rome, Constantinople and Cairo. He became especially involved with the Far East, since his concern with the Chinese coolie traffic to South America in the early 1870s. He was caught up in peace negotiations between China and France after the Tonkin War in 1885, and in abortive secret peace discussions between China and Japan, to resolve their differences over Korea and the Liao Tung peninsula, in 1894.[2] His horizon was far from being circumscribed or parochial.

But his main historical significance undoubtedly lies in his relationship to Wales. He became the most important and influential figure in Welsh politics at a vital time, those dramatic years between 1880 and 1894. He guided Welsh Liberalism then to an unprecedented peak of influence and achievement. His very involvement in Wales at all is a most extraordinary story. Rendel was an Englishman, and a High Anglican. He was a product of Eton and Oriel College, Oxford (where he gained a fourth class degree). He was immensely rich, with several country and town houses, in England and on the French Riviera.[3] Most unexpected of all, he was an armaments manufacturer. Following his father, who was a noted civil engineer, Rendel became a partner in Armstrongs, a major ordnance firm at Elswick, near Newcastle-on-Tyne. For seventeen years he worked on the marketing of the latest forms of artillery and other advanced military technology. A 'merchant of death' was indeed a most unlikely figure to come to prominence in the land of 'S.R.' and Henry Richard! And yet this strange, brooding alien personality was to impose himself in Welsh life. He became, like A. H. D. Acland, one of those Englishmen who became so Celtic that they make the Welsh themselves seem slightly

---

[2]*Personal Papers*, 244–66.

[3]He rented a villa at Valescure on the French Riviera, and later bought the Chateau de Thorenc, near Cannes.

foreign. So it is as an honorary Welshman that Rendel deserves recognition from Welsh people today.

Rendel's significance for Welsh politics has four main components. First of all, he became the member for Montgomeryshire. More than that, he achieved a victory in that rural county, which reverberated throughout Wales for decades to come. He first visited Montgomeryshire in 1877 when he campaigned on behalf of the Honourable Frederick Hanbury Tracy of Gregynog Hall, the heir to Lord Sudeley.[4] Here, Rendel met some notable local personalities. In addition to Hanbury Tracy – himself an eccentric and somewhat frivolous appendage of the Gladstonian Liberal party – Rendel met up with the Llanbrynmair antiquarian, Richard Williams, who was to act, perhaps improbably, as his election agent in 1880, and fiery Nonconformist ministers like the Revd Josiah Jones. Above all, he first encountered Arthur Humphreys-Owen, the enlightened squire of the 4,400 acres of the Glansevern estate between Garthmyl and Berriew, and already an active figure in Welsh educational and political life.[5] Rendel and Humphreys-Owen struck up a great friendship which lasted for life. Indeed, the hundreds of letters on either side, contained in the Rendel and Glansevern collections in the National Library of Wales and covering the period 1877–1905, provide a most moving testament to selfless public activity by two dedicated individuals.

Rendel's victory in Montgomeryshire in the 1880 general election was a most spectacular one. He needed to defeat the mighty Wynn family of Wynnstay who had held the seat continuously since 1799.

[4]The complex relationship of Rendel with the Hanbury Tracy family is well covered in David W. Howell 'The estate and its owners, 1795 to 1920', in Glyn Tegai Hughes, Prys Morgan and J. Gareth Thomas (eds.), *Gregynog* (Cardiff, 1977), 52–8. Rendel and Lord Sudeley broke with each other in 1886 when Sudeley opposed Gladstone's Irish Home Rule Bill, though Rendel did manage a kind of reconciliation years later in 1902. Sudeley was an active Liberal Unionist from 1886 on: see Kenneth O. Morgan, 'The Liberal Unionists in Wales', *National Library of Wales Journal*, XVI (2) (1969), 163–9. Frederick Hanbury Tracy remained a Gladstonian Liberal after 1886, and split away from his father. But he was a quite impossible person and Rendel and Humphreys-Owen worked to ensure that his candidature for Montgomery Boroughs was not renewed after 1894 (Howell, op. cit., 56).

[5]There is a somewhat inadequate entry on Humphreys-Owen in the *Dictionary of Welsh Biography*, 398. A better one, by F. E. Hamer, appears in J. V. Morgan (ed.), *Welsh Political and Educational Leaders in the Victorian Era* (London, 1908). He also appears in T. Marchant Williams, *The Welsh Members of Parliament, 1894* (Western Mail, Cardiff, 1894), 15–16, where Humphreys-Owen is described, curiously, as 'too cool, too calculating for strong friendships'. With the riches of the Glansevern papers available in the National Library of Wales, it is surprising that no proper study of Humphreys-Owen's important career has ever been undertaken.

From the outset he had to face intense pressure from the 'prevailing interests' of Wynnstay and Powis Castle in the east of the county, and the Londonderry family of Plas Machynlleth in the far west. Land agents were active amongst a rural population only recently acquainted with the secret ballot. The eastern part of Montgomeryshire, adjacent to the English Marches, was difficult territory for Liberals while Welshpool was known to be 'the Tory headquarters' in the county. Conversely, the more intensely Welsh, Nonconformist areas of Montgomeryshire to the west of Newtown, and including places like Llanidloes, Cemmaes and Machynlleth, were known to be more sympathetic to Liberalism. 'We need the solid vote of the Welsh districts to beat down the English vote', Rendel wrote later.[6]

There was a good deal of disorder during the campaign. After a meeting in Tory Welshpool, there were physical attacks on David Davies MP (whose hat was damaged in the mêlée) and George Osborne Morgan MP (who lost his); Hanbury Tracy was assaulted with a stick at Welshpool station. 'The whole affair casts a stigma which can never be effaced from the name of Welshpool', declared the *Cambrian News*, a Liberal newspaper.[7] The Liberals responded with onslaughts on individual Tories in Newtown, who took refuge from a barrage of stones in the Elephant and Eagle hotels. Money was spent freely. Rendel, according to one later account, spent £12,000 and the Tories £20,000, in this, the last election held prior to the passage of the Corrupt Practices Act of 1883. 'Every lawyer got a retaining fee from one side or other and charged at 3 or 5 guineas a day for his services in canvassing. All the hotels in Welshpool (about forty Tory and two Liberal) ran free drinks as well on the night of the great Liberal meeting and riots there when they got soldiers down to protect us.'[8]

Rendel raised the political temperature by his highly radical campaign, which included attacks on Beaconsfield's 'bastard imperialism', demands for Church disestablishment and even women's suffrage, as well as local themes such as the plight of tenant farmers and the injustices of the Burials Act. In the end, Rendel defeated the Hon. Charles Wynn (Conservative) by just 191 votes. After the result was announced at Machynlleth town hall, bonfires were lit, and Rendel

[6]*Cambrian News*, 16 April 1880; Rendel to Revd Josiah Jones, 9 December 1885. (NLW, Jones MSS., 6411B).

[7]Ibid., 9 April 1880.

[8]J. M. Robertson to Mrs Peter Hughes Griffiths (the widow of Tom Ellis), 16 June 1912 (NLW, Daniel papers, 34).

carried in triumph to the Owen Glyndŵr hotel. 'It was long before Machynlleth resumed its usual aspect', the press observed.[9]

Rendel clung on to Montgomeryshire in three more close contests – with especial difficulty in 1886 when the local Liberals were sorely divided over Gladstone's bill for Irish Home Rule. His majority never reached 1,000, and indeed Montgomeryshire did not become a safe Liberal seat until the era of David Davies after 1918, when, among other things, Welshpool became belatedly Liberalized. Rendel inaugurated in the county a period of ninety-nine years of Liberal dominance lasting from 1880 to 1979 (and resumed in 1983). In that time, Montgomeryshire was represented by just five members, all of them distinguished – Rendel (1880–94), Humphreys-Owen (1894–1905), David Davies (1906–29), Clement Davies (1929–62) and Emlyn Hooson (1962–79). But, far beyond that county, Rendel's famous victory inaugurated a new phase of liberation from landlord rule in the Welsh countryside. It was a landmark in the winning of democracy in Wales.

Rendel's second contribution lay in his forming of a new programme and organizational structure for Welsh Liberalism. From his election in 1880 onwards, he was committed to making the Welsh politically effective. To this end, he drafted a new list of priorities, headed by the supreme issue of disestablishment of the Church of England in Wales. This, Rendel believed, provided 'a clear and effective issue with all Anglicizing influences in Wales and practical declaration of the case for Welsh Nationalization outside Wales'.[10] He brought that great disestablisher, Joseph Chamberlain, to address a major Liberal rally at Newtown in October 1884; for the first time, a Cabinet minister had pronounced in favour of Welsh disestablishment.[11] The Church question came rapidly to the fore thereafter. This process was much assisted by the deep Liberal schism over Irish Home Rule in 1886 which was to give new leverage to the Welsh and other minorities within the Gladstonian Liberal party. From now on, Welsh disestablishment was a leading question of the day.

[9]*Cambrian News*, 16 April 1880. Also see *Oswestry and Border Counties Advertiser*, 11 May 1892, for retrospective comment.

[10]*Personal Papers*, 306.

[11]Joseph Chamberlain to Stuart Rendel, 1, 26 September, 5 October 1884 (NLW, Additional Rendel MSS., 20571D, 221, 222, 224; Rendel to Sir Michael Grant Duff, 7 October 1884 (ibid., 20572D, 382). Rendel wrote to Grant Duff 'I doubt whether Nonconformity will keep solidly Liberal after all grievances are redressed, or even unless grievances are being redressed . . . The only great grievance left is the Establishment. Chamberlain will find Wales the best fulcrum for his Free Church programme and so I think he is the man to keep us [?] alive and to give us weight.'

But Liberalism needed an organizational base, as well as a programme, to weld together the notoriously fragmentary and parochial constituency associations of Wales. To this end, Rendel presided over the formation of the North Wales and South Wales Liberal Federations in 1886–7. In this, he worked in close harmony with Francis Schnadhorst, the secretary of the National Liberal Federation in London, who was anxious to see the Liberals recast on a new popular basis throughout Britain, and to secure the enlargement of local federations affiliated to the parent body.[12] What happened next is somewhat misrepresented by Rendel in his memoirs. Matters did not go at all according to plan. Rendel's objective was a tripartite division, with a Mid-Wales Liberal Federation to counterbalance those in the north and the south. 'Tell me of "North Wales" and I tell you of "Mid-Wales"', he wrote to Humphreys-Owen.[13] He feared that a North Wales Federation, based at Rhyl as desired by W. H. Tilston and other Clwyd Liberals, would be but a weak puppet of the Liberal Central Office. 'We cannot allow our teeth to be drawn and our claws pared.'[14] However, his opposition melted away after he was tactfully appointed president of the new North Wales Federation at a meeting held at Rhyl on 14 December 1886. Thereafter, a parallel South Wales Federation was founded in January 1887, and the two Liberal Federations finally came together in the so-called Welsh National Council, established at Newtown in October 1888 at a meeting attended by John Morley himself.[15]

At the time, these structural innovations caused much attention, and not a little anguish. Comparisons were drawn freely with the organizational base of the Nationalist party in Ireland. But it is clear that any parallel with events in Ireland was totally misleading. The Welsh National Council was only a loose affiliation of the two rival Federations of the north and the south. Its origin owed much to the rivalry that existed between Tilston and R. N. Hall, respective secretaries of the two local bodies. Far from serving as a spearhead for

[12]Schnadhorst's views as recorded in Rendel to Humphreys-Owen 18 December 1886 (NLW, Glansevern MSS., 290) and Schnadhorst to Gladstone, 24 September 1887 (British Library Add. MSS. 44295, f. 145). For a wider discussion of the growth of Liberal party machinery at this time, see Kenneth O. Morgan, *Wales in British Politics, 1868–1962* (Cardiff, new edn., 1980), 77ff.; Michael Barker, *Gladstone and Radicalism* (Hassocks, 1975), 117–28; G. V. Nelmes, 'Stuart Rendel and Welsh political organization in the late-nineteenth century', *Welsh History Review*, 9(4) (1979), 468–85, especially the last-named.

[13]Rendel to Humphreys-Owen, 24 November 1886 (NLW, Glansevern MSS., 274).

[14]Rendel to Humphreys-Owen, 6 December 1886 (ibid., 279).

[15]*South Wales Daily News*, 9–10 October 1888; *Baner ac Amserau Cymru*, 13 and 17 October 1888.

nationalism or separatism, the Welsh National Council was formed in large measure to frustrate the far more assertive nationalism of the younger Liberals of the *Cymru Fydd* school.[16] It never added up to much. But at least it could be said that, throughout Wales, north and south, there now existed a platform and an organization for proclaiming the national demands of Welsh Liberals which were, from their inception in 1887, organically linked to the Liberal party in Britain as a whole. The Scottish Liberal Federation, by contrast, was a totally separate body. Largely as a result of this structural distinction, the Liberals north of the border were to prove far less successful than the Welsh in promoting disestablishment and other national causes in political campaigns over the next thirty years.

Rendel's third political achievement, perhaps the most important of them all, was the creation of the Welsh Parliamentary Party in October 1888. From his entry into Parliament, he was anxious to make the Welsh MPs united, vocal and effective. For decades, he wrote, the Welsh had been ignored or derided as almost in 'an inferior category, a cheaper sort of member'.[17] The opportunity for transformation came after the schism over Ireland in 1886. There was the increased radicalization of what was left of the Liberal party. In Wales, older mid-Victorian figures such as Henry Richard, Fuller-Maitland and Lewis Llewelyn Dillwyn were passing from the scene. Almost unnoticed, Rendel was appointed first chairman of the Welsh Party in December 1888 at a poorly attended meeting in a committee room of the House of Commons, with two south Wales members, D. A. Thomas (Merthyr Tydfil) and A. J. Williams (South Glamorgan) as joint whips.[18]

It was indeed a modest step towards national consciousness. Rendel, who remained chairman of the Welsh Party until his retirement in March 1894 (when he was succeeded by Osborne Morgan), was anxious above all else to keep the Welsh loyal to the party whips. He was deeply upset by the fiery nationalism of Tom Ellis, Lloyd George and the zealots of 'Young Wales', and concerned in the 1892–4 period to smother any prospect of revolt or rebellion by the Welsh back-benchers.[19] Rendel's influence was a considerable one and so, then

[16]See Nelmes, op. cit., 470–9. The South Wales Liberals at the time were anxious to include representatives of the *Cymru Fydd* movement and the Welsh Land League in the Welsh National Council, but Rendel thwarted them.

[17]*Personal Papers*, 313.

[18]*South Wales Daily News*, 13 December 1888. Only about sixteen Welsh MPs attended, but there were only two dissentients, Bryn Roberts (Eifion) and William Rathbone (Arfon), both predictable.

[19]For example Rendel to Humphreys-Owen, 4 March, 1894 (NLW, Glansevern MSS., 649). Sir Edward Reed, member for Cardiff, was a particular *bête noire* of Rendel's at the time.

and later, there followed much disillusion about the false hopes kindled by the Welsh Party, the passivity of the 'Parnells of Wales' compared with the militant independence of the real Parnell across the Irish Sea.

And yet, cynicism with the Welsh Party, as it emerged in the 1890s, can go much too far. Without such a body, however docile, proposals for disestablishment, educational and land reform, or the extension of devolution would have got nowhere. Long before Rendel's death in 1913, the Welsh Party had become a respected, effective political force. It had its own whips, its own balloting arrangements, its own quietly influential methods for putting pressure on the political parties in a reasoned, constitutional manner, without the threat of violence or bloodshed. It was backed up by an extensive popular press, a renascent Nonconformity and an embattled mass democracy. In so far as the rebirth of Welsh nationhood between the 1880s and the present time assumed political form, the Welsh Party, and its architect, Stuart Rendel, are entitled to much of the credit.

Rendel's fourth and final contribution to Welsh politics was a private one – his great personal friendship with Gladstone and the use he made of it. He first met Gladstone soon after moving the address in the 1880 parliamentary session. He sat next to the prime minister at an official dinner shortly afterwards, during which they had a lengthy and intimate conversation on political and other topics.[20] An enduring friendship had been forged. Towards the veteran Liberal leader, Rendel was always tactful and sensitive in the extreme. He was an excellent listener and a considerate host. Gladstone repaid his courtesy with several visits to Rendel's various houses, including the Chateau de Thorenc on the French Riviera. Gladstone fully responded to Rendel's charm – and so, indeed did Mrs Gladstone. Rendel himself wryly noted that there might have been a matrimonial interest here, in view of his four eligible and wealthy daughters: indeed, the liaison bore fruit, in that Rendel's second daughter, Maud, duly married Gladstone's third son, Henry. It was symptomatic that Gladstone formed his fourth and final ministry while staying with Rendel at No. 1 Carlton Gardens (Lord Ripon's former London home) in August 1892.[21] Here, Rendel managed to get Gladstone to agree to all his major Welsh demands – a Welsh Church Suspensory Bill, a prelude to disestablishment; a charter for the University of Wales; an inquiry into the problem of Welsh land; and Tom Ellis to be appointed a junior whip. It is relevant to recall that the Welsh Party in 1892 numbered

[20]*Personal Papers*, 21–4.
[21]Ibid., 311–12; Rendel to Humphreys-Owen, 15 October 1892 (NLW, Glansevern MSS., 613).

thirty-one at a time when the new government's majority was only forty. The two men remained friendly right to the end; indeed Rendel was to act as pall-bearer at Gladstone's funeral in 1898.

More than any other politician, Rendel used his influence to turn Gladstone into a patron of Welsh Liberal and national causes. He persuaded the Oxford-bred, High Anglican squire of Hawarden, an 'out and out inequalitarian' as he called himself, that Nonconformist, popular Wales, like Italy and Bulgaria (and, indeed, Ireland) was also a nation rightly struggling to be free.[22] As a result, Gladstone spoke out boldly, in the Commons and elsewhere, on behalf of Welsh temperance, educational, cultural and literary causes. Addressing a mass rally on the slopes of Snowdon in 1892, he showed some sympathy for Welsh tenant farmers.[23] He was even persuaded to speak and vote on behalf of Welsh disestablishment in 1891 and to draw up a bill to effect Welsh disestablishment during his last few months in office in 1893–4. Rendel always regarded the winning over of Gladstone as a major achievement. In return, Gladstone became an immense national hero in Wales. Rendel himself was shrewd enough to recognize this. In the difficult election of 1886 he agreed that 'we must go to the country on the Gladstone ticket, and say as little as we can about Ireland . . .'[24]

Rendel's attitude towards Gladstone was emollient and diplomatic throughout. He was apprehensive that the Grand Old Man might be upset by the violent anti-clericalism shown by young hawks like Tom Ellis and Lloyd George during the debates on the Clerical Discipline Bill of 1892. He deplored the 'madness of Wales in slapping John Morley and Mr. Gladstone in the face'.[25] He urged Thomas Gee and others to give Gladstone the benefit of every doubt, and to place the most favourable construction on each of their leader's Delphic and serpentine pronouncements upon Welsh affairs.[26] As a result, these

[22]I have dealt with Gladstone's attitude towards Welsh affairs in 'Liberals, Nationalists and Mr Gladstone', *Transactions of the Honourable Society of Cymmrodorion* 1960, 36–52 (published in this volume, 322–38); and 'Gladstone and Wales', *Welsh History Review*, 1 (1960), 65–82. The phrase 'out-and-out inequalitarian' appears in John Vincent, *The Formation of the Liberal Party 1857–1868* (London, 1966), 212.

[23]*South Wales Daily News*, 14 September 1892. Rendel later considered this speech 'a somewhat unlucky impromptu': Rendel to Gee, 30 October 1892 (NLW, Gee MSS., 8308C, 274).

[24]Morgan, *Wales in British Politics*, 134–42; Humphreys-Owen to Rendel, 20 June 1886 (NLW, Rendel MSS., XIV, 293).

[25]Rendel to Humphreys-Owen, 28, 29 May 1892 (NLW, Glansevern MSS., 596, 597).

[26]For example Rendel to Gee, 30 October 1892 and 22 March 1894 (NLW, Gee MSS., 8308C, 274, 282).

Fabian tactics – the policy of 'Rendelism' – were roundly condemned by Lloyd George and others at the time.[27] But in political terms such methods were clearly successful in the long term. The entire Rendel-Gladstone relationship is a testimony not only to deep personal friendship but to a notably effective and successful political partnership. It was Gladstone's Boswell or *fidus Achates* who won the ultimate victory.

The main themes which preoccupied Rendel during these complex political manoeuvres on various levels followed the major priorities of radical Liberals of the time. As has been noted, the supreme national objective was always held to be Church disestablishment. It was, indeed, an extraordinary achievement for the Welsh Church question, very much a fringe concern in 1880, to be catapulted into joint second place on the Liberals' Newcastle Programme in 1891. Subsequently, Welsh disestablishment remained a lively issue in British politics. It passed its second reading in the Commons in 1895 and later completed its passage through both Houses of Parliament in September 1914. After being suspended in its operation during the war years, it finally took effect in 1920. Nowadays, the rhetoric and the jargon of the disestablishment campaign seem tedious and out-of-date. Clerical politics appear to bear no relation to our current socio-economic discontents. But at the time, in the late-Victorian period, it encapsulated for many Welshmen supreme principles of civic, religious and national equality.

Rendel himself showed immense skill throughout in directing the main lines of strategy. As a first task, it was essential to wrest the initiative from the Liberation Society which aimed at 'disestablishment all round' and saw no essential distinction between Wales and England. Rendel told Thomas Gee that Wales had for too long been the Liberationists' 'catspaw'.[28] By contrast, he placed the emphasis squarely on Welsh nationhood and separate legislation for Wales. After all, 'the nonconformists were the people of Wales'. Their wishes, as expressed in successive general elections from 1880 to 1910, were unambiguous. Rendel also displayed much skill and artifice in winning over a succession of Liberal leaders to endorse the cause – Morley, Rosebery, Trevelyan, Spencer, Harcourt and, of course, the supreme prize of Mr Gladstone himself. In this process, Rendel could tread the low road with as much aplomb as the high. He extracted a tortuous announcement from John Morley in October 1886 which endorsed Welsh disestablishment in principle. Characteristically, Morley

[27]Lloyd George to Tom Ellis, 27 November 1890. (NLW, Ellis papers.)
[28]Rendel to Gee, 18 March 1887 (NLW, Gee MSS., 8308C, 258).

confessed that he had 'private misgivings' about rousing yet another antagonistic vested interest. He later angrily rebuked Rendel for releasing a purely private communication to the London press.[29] But not for nothing was Morley renowned as 'the Grand Old Maid' of the Liberal party.[30] Like it or not, he was committed. When it came to pushing on the political demands of Wales, Rendel ran rings round him.

An equally enduring priority for Rendel was the many-sided crusade on behalf of Welsh education, intermediate and higher. After the shock waves launched by the Aberdare Committee report of 1881, with its fierce criticisms of the quality of educational provision in Wales, Rendel became a passionate and selfless advocate of the cause. His main achievement here was the piloting throughout the Commons of the Welsh Intermediate Education Act of 1889, a measure that applied to Wales alone and created a system of secondary education that anticipated by many years the structure created in England by the Balfour Act of 1902. There has been some scholarly dispute about who should gain the major credit for the passage of the Intermediate Education Act. Professor Webster has championed the cause of A. J. Mundella.[31] The Conservative ministers involved, Sir William Hart Dyke and W. H. Smith, also deserve their meed of praise for a sympathetic attitude unusual for their party at the time. Certainly, Rendel himself almost lost his nerve during the committee stage on occasion, notably over the threatened exclusion of Monmouthshire from the bill, and the creation of *ad hoc* local education committees to administer the new system in each county.[32] Among the Welsh MPs, Tom Ellis was an important calming influence throughout. But the precise allocation of credit is hardly a major concern for historians. Without question, Rendel, who introduced the bill and handled it throughout its passage, was responsible for the main strategic decisions at every turn. Even in the difficult crises of the committee stage, his nerve held. Not least of his services was the immense array of allies he managed to enlist – Gladstone himself, who made a powerful speech in the second reading debate; Tories like George Kenyon and Sir John Puleston; even the atheist, Charles Bradlaugh, whose frequent

[29]Morley to Rendel, 30 October 1886 (NLW, Rendel papers 544) and Morley to Rendel, 6 November 1886 (NLW, ibid., 545).

[30]Campbell-Bannerman termed him 'a petulant spinster': see Kenneth O. Morgan, 'John Morley and the crisis of Liberalism, 1894', *National Library of Wales Journal*, IV (4) (1968), 451ff.

[31]J. R. Webster, 'The Welsh Intermediate Education Act of 1889', *Welsh History Review*, 4 (3) (1969), 290. Mundella had drawn up the original bills of 1884 and 1885 on which Rendel's measure of 1889 was based.

[32]Morgan, *Wales in British Politics*, 100–2.

expulsions from the House had made him a rare expert on the intricacies of parliamentary procedure.[33] In the House of Lords, Rendel was content to let the bill be handled by the Conservative peers, another triumph of diplomacy.

The Welsh Intermediate Education Act survived, as a monument to late-Victorian Liberalism, until the Butler Act of 1944. As Gareth Elwyn Jones has explained in an important book,[34] its later history was marked by numerous crises, especially the prolonged civil war between the Central Welsh Board and the Welsh department of the Board of Education after 1907. Perhaps it never really fulfilled all the expectations of its architects back in 1889. And yet its effect on modern Wales was far-reaching, even revolutionary. Without the hundred-odd 'county' schools created right across Wales from Holyhead to Chepstow, between 1889 and 1914, the entire history of the nation, in terms of social mobility and social leadership, would have been totally different. Generations of working-class children would have been much the poorer. No part of Rendel's legacy to modern Wales glows more brightly in retrospect.

He also worked industriously and with determination on behalf of Welsh university education. In 1883 his great friend, Arthur Humphreys-Owen (now on the college council) persuaded him to take up the flagging cause of the 'college by the sea', the University College of Wales at Aberystwyth, founded in 1872. This institution, through whose portals many remarkable young students had already passed, was dying on its feet through lack of funds. Rendel, with his many allies in high Liberal places and his highly-developed sense of loyalty to mid Wales, was now persuaded, without difficulty, to champion the college in Parliament. In a notable debate in March 1884, he pointed out to the Commons that, while the government was prepared to subsidize new higher-education colleges at Bangor and Cardiff, the established mid Wales college of Aberystwyth was threatened with an early demise.[35] He gained the powerful support, amongst others, of the eminent Liberal historian and jurist, James Bryce, and Mundella and the Liberal government were clearly shaken.

Thereafter in 1884–5 Rendel used his unique reserves of tact and influence to persuade the recalcitrant Erskine Childers, at the Exchequer, to allow an annual grant of £2,500 to Aberystwyth.[36] In August 1885, the succeeding Conservative government under

[33]*Personal Papers*, 309.

[34]Gareth Elwyn Jones, *Controls and Conflicts in Welsh Secondary Education, 1889–1944* (Cardiff, 1982), especially ch. 1.

[35]*Parl. Deb.*, 3rd Ser., CCLXXX, 1589ff. (14 March 1884).

[36]Rendel to Humphreys-Owen, 15 December 1883 (NLW, Glansevern MSS., 132).

Salisbury agreed to raise this amount to £4,000, on the same basis as Bangor and Cardiff. Aberystwyth was therefore saved, and flourished ever after. The edifice was crowned in 1893 with the drawing up of the charter of a federal University of Wales, comprising all three colleges, with John Viriamu Jones, principal of Cardiff, as its first vice-chancellor. Again, Rendel was deeply involved. A university charter for Wales was prominent in the demands that he persuaded Gladstone to accept, when the fourth administration of that veteran leader was being constructed in Rendel's home in Carlton Gardens in August 1892. Rendel endorsed Arthur Acland's suggestion that the Oxford historian, Owen M. Edwards, be appointed as commissioner, prior to the drafting of a charter, and a teaching, and not merely examining, University of Wales was then created.[37] The protests of bishops and other Anglicans, dismayed at the exclusion of St David's College, Lampeter, were brushed aside.

But Rendel's involvement with Welsh higher education did not end there. In 1895, after he retired from the House of Commons, he agreed to serve as president of the University College of Aberystwyth, in succession to Lord Aberdare. As has been seen, 'Aber' had long held an important place in his affections and in his vision of a thriving progressive 'mid Wales'. Until his death in 1913 he proved to be a tirelessly active college president: certainly, he was anything but a figure-head, as Dr E. L. Ellis's admirable centenary history amply shows.[38] As president, Rendel was always a prey to manic-depressive bouts of melancholia and paranoid fears that he was insufficiently appreciated by the native Welsh. He needed tactful and sensitive handling by Principal T. F. Roberts. But this gentle, scholarly Merioneth academic (son of the policeman at Aberdyfi) proved admirable for the task. Rendel was to write to Roberts in 1909 of how 'your touch is the gentlest I have ever experienced, and a letter from you is always healing'.[39]

Fortified by Roberts's emollient approach, Rendel worked for Aberystwyth with powerful effect. Apart from shrewd conduct of administration and finance, he also proved himself a major benefactor of the college. Despite his fear of the 'megalomania' of extensive building projects, he bought up fourteen acres of the Grogythan estate, high up on Penglais hill, at a cost of £2,000. These were originally intended for college buildings; but later in 1905 Rendel was persuaded to allocate them for a future national library of Wales instead. This

[37]Morgan, *Wales in British Politics*, 130–1.

[38]E. L. Ellis, *The University College of Wales, Aberystwyth, 1872–1972* (Cardiff, 1972); cf. David Williams, *Thomas Francis Roberts* (Cardiff, 1961), 39.

[39]Rendel to T. F. Roberts, 3 September 1903 (quoted, Ellis, op. cit., 140).

episode was caught up in the rivalry with Cardiff, which claimed the national museum; but Rendel's benefaction helped secure the library for Aberystwyth – indeed, he purchased further land at Cae'r Gôg to assist with access to the putative national library. In addition, he was a major patron of the college in other directions; for instance, from 1901 onwards he donated annually £750 to help augment the miserable stipends of the university teaching staff. When he died in 1913, his will left a further £5,000 to the college, and the interest from his legacy was used to endow a new chair of English language and literature. The Rendel chair and the student hostel of Neuadd Rendel today commemorate a devoted and dedicated servant of the University College of Wales and of Welsh higher education in general.

On other issues, Rendel was far more hesitant. The Welsh land question, for instance, aroused a good deal of apprehension in his mind. Like Humphreys-Owen, the squire of Glansevern, he was anxious not to raise wild accusations against landlords, in relation to excessive rental or capricious evictions, charges which could not be substantiated. His caution has been echoed by modern economic historians who have tended to be far more charitable towards nineteenth-century Welsh landowners than was once the case – maybe we have now gone rather too far in this direction.[40] Even more important, Rendel was desperately concerned to minimize any resemblances between Wales and Ireland. The Welsh and Irish land problems, he maintained, were poles apart; there could be no justification for Wales emulating the violence, arson and intimidation of the Irish Plan of Campaign. As Humphreys-Owen put it, 'Welsh farmers cannot play the Irish game'. Rendel was very worried by the rise of the Welsh Land League under Thomas Gee, and the sporadic agrarian violence or rioting that punctuated the Welsh anti-tithe campaigns of the later 1880s.[41] This behaviour, among other things, would totally undermine his cautious, patient campaign on behalf of Welsh nationality.

But Rendel did recognize the deep-seated poverty, and economic and social harassment, faced by Welsh tenant farmers in the 1880s and 1890s during the depths of the late-Victorian agricultural depression. It was he who proposed to Gladstone in August 1892 some kind of far-ranging inquiry into the Welsh land problem – although his objective was a more limited select committee rather than the highly publicized

[40]Cf. Humphreys-Owen to Rendel, 15 June 1888 (NLW, Rendel MSS., XXIV, 433). For the economic background, see David W. Howell, *Land and People in Nineteenth-Century Wales* (London, 1977), especially 73–92.

[41]Humphreys-Owen to Rendel, 4 November 1887 (NLW, Rendel MSS., 396); Rendel to Humphreys-Owen, 27 November 1889 (NLW, Glansevern MSS., 474).

Royal Commission that Gladstone was eventually persuaded to set up.[42] The Welsh Land Commission of 1893–6 yielded virtually nothing, overtaken by events (and a return of a Tory government) long before it could report. At the very least, though, modern Welsh historians can benefit in tranquillity from its evidence and memoranda as a priceless source for the investigation of late-Victorian rural society!

On governmental devolution, Rendel was even more cautious. He argued consistently in such periodicals as the *Contemporary Review* and *Cymru Fydd* against any form of Welsh Home Rule.[43] He never favoured even the more moderate Chamberlain/Lloyd George version of 'home rule all round'. The future of Wales, and especially of Welsh Liberalism, lay firmly within the United Kingdom. The object of Wales was equality within that mighty system, and its imperial attachment, not exclusion from it. He argued firmly against Alfred Thomas (East Glamorgan) when he urged a campaign on behalf of a Welsh secretary of state, on the lines of that created for Scotland in 1885. 'A Welsh Secretary under a Tory Government was not my idea of helping the national cause of Wales', Rendel observed.[44] He was aghast at the rise of the quasi-separatist *Cymru Fydd* campaign, headed by Lloyd George in the 1894–6 period which seemed to threaten his life's work. He rejoiced in its eventual crushing defeat.[45]

What Rendel advocated was rather the maximizing of Welsh pressure within the framework of the United Kingdom. A supreme example of his approach lay in his persuading Gladstone to appoint the youthful Tom Ellis as a junior whip in August 1892.[46] It would, of course, help to keep the Welsh quiet, and silence their most powerful young spokesmen. But, in Rendel's consistent view, it would also substantially reinforce the voice of Wales at the centre of government. That, after all, was where decision-making took place, not in the drowned landscape of the Celtic fringe.

Stuart Rendel retired in March 1894, full of paranoid fears that his

[42]For more detail, see Morgan, *Wales in British Politics*, 124–6, and the footnote references from the Gladstone, Gee, Ellis, Herbert Lewis and Vincent Evans papers cited therein.

[43]See Rendel's articles in the *Contemporary Review* (December 1886) and *Cymru Fydd* (January 1888), 20–8. Also see his comments on 'A Welsh national policy', *Cymru Fydd* (October 1888), 621–2.

[44]Rendel to Humphreys-Owen, 27 August 1891 (NLW, Glansevern MSS., 555).

[45]For example Rendel to Humphreys-Owen, 12 October, 10 December 1895 (ibid., 666, 672).

[46]Rendel to Revd Josiah Jones, 17 November 1892 (NLW, Jones, MSS., 6411B).

life's work had come to nothing. A peerage from Gladstone when that great statesman withdrew from office was no consolation. Publicly, he released a letter to Humphreys-Owen announcing his immense satisfaction at the achievements of the past few years. He listed disestablishment, land reform, intermediate and higher education. As for the Welsh Party, nobody was 'more united, more capable and, for their numbers, more influential'.[47]

But privately, his soul was full of bitterness and cynicism. He told Humphreys-Owen of his feelings:

> I should not have retired had I felt I could put the least reliance upon the favourable construction of Wales. But in no question have I seen so much real gratitude as I hope to obtain *by going*. It is in fact want of political sobriety and wisdom. At much sacrifice and by real effort I carried the introduction of the Suspensory Bill. I got absolutely no support – no credit – rather reproach . . . What pains me is that while in all politics success follows mere shouting, in Welsh affairs there seems a conscious preference for unrealities.[48]

To Thomas Gee, he wrote in similar vein. 'I was no longer the unselfish champion of Welsh popular causes. I was an Englishman standing between the Welsh and Englishmen. You cannot realise how much the H. of C. dislikes 2nd hand representatives.'[49]

After his resignation, his disillusion was increased when, in the by-election that followed, his friend Humphreys-Owen saw the Liberal majority fall by 600 to a mere 225 votes, a five per cent swing against the government. (It was in this by-election, incidentally, that Lloyd George may, or may not, have become involved with Mrs Kitty Edwards and the station-master of Cemmaes Road.)[50] The egregious Hanbury Tracy had already lost Montgomery Boroughs in 1892 and it remained a Tory seat until 1906. The great triumphs of 1880 seemed to be evaporating.

However, the tide turned and Rendel's bitter mood did not last. As has been seen, he found happy and fulfilling work to do as president of the college at Aberystwyth. He remained actively interested in politics (including Chinese politics), and sometimes attended the House of Lords. Indeed, in his remaining years, his radicalism became more pronounced than before. During the Boer War, he followed Lloyd George, Humphreys-Owen and the 'pro-Boer' minority in denouncing

[47]Rendel to Humphreys-Owen, 28 February 1894 (NLW, Glansevern MSS., 648); similarly, Rendel to Herbert Lewis, 2 March 1894 (NLW, Penucha MSS.).
[48]Rendel to Humphreys-Owen, 4 March 1894 (ibid., 649).
[49]Rendel to Gee, 22 March 1894 (NLW, Gee MSS. 8308C, 282).
[50]See John Grigg, *The Young Lloyd George* (London, 1973), 228–39.

the war and Chamberlain's policy in provoking it. He fiercely attacked the 'imperial Perks element' currently rampant in the Liberal party.[51] 'The Salem chapel jingo is as monstrous as he is repulsive.' During the 'revolt' by the Welsh county councils against the 1902 Education Act, he contributed £500 to the support of Lloyd George's illegal campaign against operating this act in Wales.[52] Like Lloyd George, Rendel saw the act as basically a surrender to clericalism.

He was a staunch supporter of the 'people's budget' in 1909 and even defended Lloyd George's class-war rhetoric in his speech at Newcastle. 'There is more rowdyism in the Tory camp than ever there was in the Liberal host', he told Principal T. F. Roberts. 'If ever there was justification for a passionate appeal on behalf of the toilers it has of late been created by the outburst on the part of those that owe far more to toil than they can ever repay.'[53] Rendel also warmly backed the Parliament Bill to curb the powers of the Lords over finance and other legislation. Although he had differed sharply from Lloyd George in the past over *Cymru Fydd* and other separatist outbursts (he had considered the MP for Caernarfon Boroughs 'honest' but 'impulsive'),[54] he had the insight and generosity to see his political genius. Lloyd George stayed with Rendel at the Chateau de Thorenc on the French Riviera on several occasions and (writing to his wife) professed himself deeply shocked by the spectacle of the Cannes Casino.[55] In December 1907 Rendel tried to persuade the Liberal prime minister, Campbell-Bannerman, to assist Lloyd George's shaky personal finances with a grant from party funds, but Lloyd George robustly declined. He would not follow Tom Ellis in becoming 'the party's doormat'.[56]

By 1909 Rendel's admiration for Lloyd George was complete.

He is thought rude and vulgar, and held guilty of degrading his great office. No credit is given him for real chivalry and fairness to opponents. Think of Chamberlain or even Disraeli and their rancour

[51]Rendel to Humphreys-Owen, 29 March (NLW, Glansevern MSS., 704).

[52]Morgan, op. cit., 195; Rendel to Humphreys-Owen, 10 September 1904 (NLW, Glansevern MSS., 806).

[53]Rendel to Principal T. F. Roberts, 10 October 1909 (UCW, Aberystwyth, archives P (VB) 2).

[54]Rendel to Humphreys-Owen, 4 March 1894 (NLW, Glansevern MSS. 649).

[55]Lloyd George to Mrs Lloyd George, 6 January 1905, cited in Kenneth O. Morgan, ed., *Lloyd George Family Letters, 1885–1936* (Cardiff and Oxford, 1973), 142. Lloyd George describes the Casino as 'Uffern o le' (a hell of a place).

[56]Campbell-Bannerman to Rendel, 22 December 1907 (NLW, Rendel Additional MSS., 20571D 212); Lloyd George to Mrs Lloyd George, 10 January 1908 (loc. cit., 151). Lloyd George had once again been staying with Rendel at the Chateau de Thorenc, following the death of his daughter, Mair.

and bitterness! There is neither snobbishness nor uncharitableness in Lloyd George. And to me his total want of pose and pretension is a charm of character as well as manner that more than compensates for any occasion over freedom of expression.[57]

For his part, Lloyd George always treasured Rendel's ominous advice, as he recalled later on to Frances Stevenson – 'There is no friendship at the top.'[58]

Rendel's final appearances in the House of Lords in 1912–13 were in support of the Welsh Disestablishment Bill now being pushed forward by the Asquith government. At this late stage, he showed some inclination to compromise: he and the Liberal bishop of Hereford proposed a scheme for the commutation of life interests to ease the financial burden on the disendowed Welsh Church.[59] Gladstone's grandson, W. G. C. Gladstone, introduced it in the House of Commons during the Committee stage. But Rendel's adherence to the principle of disestablishment, on national grounds, was as firm now as it had been in 1880. He died in June 1913, just before the outbreak of that holocaust of war which put the principles of Liberals everywhere to the ultimate test. But it can reasonably be concluded that Rendel was a consistent and unremitting radical and man of the late-Victorian left, to the very end of his long and distinguished life.

In assessing the significance and validity of Rendel's ideas and activities, it is important not to proceed to eulogistic extremes. He was not a man of immense intellectual penetration; nor would he ever have claimed to have been an effective orator, either in the Commons or on the stump. He was never really a politician of the first rank, even if he walked at times with princes and prime ministers.

His outlook may be seen to have its limitations in a number of key respects. First of all, his philosophy – characteristic of his generation – had virtually no understanding of class issues in political or social life. In the Welsh countryside, he failed to see the socio-economic roots of the agrarian and tithe disturbances of the 1880s. Even there, he was liable to emphasize sectarian or civic themes such as disestablishment, temperance, the burials, legislation or secondary education rather than problems of economic policy. In relation to the industrial troubles of

[57]Rendel to Principal T. F. Roberts, Christmas Day 1909 (UCW, Aberystwyth, archives, P (VB) 2).

[58]A. J. P. Taylor (ed.), *Lloyd George: A Diary by Frances Stevenson* (London, 1972), 267. John Grigg, op. cit. 140, speculates that Rendel's comment was inspired by his own relationship with Gladstone.

[59]Morgan, *Wales in British Politics*, 269; Rendel's letter to *The Times*, 8 January 1913.

the *fin-de-siècle* period, as a capitalist employer he had virtually nothing to say. The aspirations of the organized working class, vocal in Wales from the six-month coal lock-out of 1898 onwards, were beyond his comprehension, which had not advanced beyond the 'Lib–Lab' shibboleths of 'harmony of interest'. The type of working-class politician he understood was a Nonconformist radical like Mabon, a man rapidly becoming dated in his own lifetime. Rendel lived long enough to see the socialism of Keir Hardie take root in Merthyr and the neo-syndicalism of *The Miners' Next Step* noised abroad by the Unofficial Reform Committee in Rhondda. But Rendel, an 'advanced radical' survivor from the Gladstonian heyday, had no comprehension of either of them. The world of Taff Vale and Tonypandy was an unknown territory.

Again, towards the main impulses of Welsh politics, Rendel's outlook was in many ways a limited one. He showed constant anxiety when popular upsurges in Wales, as during the anti-tithe campaign or the 'Rhyl resolution' passed by the North Wales Liberal Federation at the behest of the young Lloyd George in 1890, threatened the authority of the party leaders. He wanted no kind of 'Parnellite' secession.[60] In the journal *Cymru Fydd* in January 1888 he expressed his fear at the emergence of 'mere Welsh-based activity in Wales'. This unhappy phrase provoked a fierce correspondence with the first editor of *Cymru Fydd*, T. J. Hughes (Adfyr), a pungent journalist from Bridgend.[61] Rendel's attitude towards Welsh politics was in some ways colonial or paternalist. It was an outlook becoming dated even by 1894, and made to seem increasingly so ever since.

Again, his view of Welsh nationality was highly qualified. It was basically political and social. It contained scant insight into the cultural roots of nationality as expounded by *Cymru Fydd* or, later, Sinn Fein in Ireland. Rendel, too, showed little enough interest in the future of the Welsh language, which, though an Englishman immersed in Wales for so long, he never troubled to acquire. His vision of nationalism was far removed from the romantic folk-consciousness of the European *volksgeist*. If anything, it approximated to the civic principles of Mazzini's Italian version of the liberal idea (without its religiosity), a crusade for self-determination on behalf of a small, distinct people, suffering from definable injustices under alien rule. Rendel's constant insistence that Church disestablishment, rather than any kind of Home

[60]*Fourth Annual Report of the North Wales Liberal Federation, 1890*, 5–7; Michael Barker, op. cit., 124–5; Rendel to Humphreys-Owen, 19 June 1890, 15 October 1892 (NLW, Glansevern MSS., 491, 613); Humphreys-Owen to Rendel, 4 May 1890 (NLW, Rendel MSS., 536).

[61]For the correspondence in January 1888 between Rendel and 'Adfyr', see Glansevern MSS., 8433–5).

Rule or political independence, was the supreme objective, is symptomatic of his limitations.

Even in narrowly territorial terms, his nationalism was distinctly limited. At times, it seemed, he thought less in terms of 'Wales' as a coherent entity than of 'mid Wales', a vague, amorphous region stretching from the hills of the Marcher lands of Powys to the little fishing ports of Cardigan Bay. In promoting the cause of the college at Aberystwyth in 1883–4, and again in pushing for a Mid-Wales Liberal Federation in 1886–7, it was the vision of 'mid Wales' that seemed to spur Rendel on. Now certainly, mid Wales is a term that still has some currency – not least for the present author, whose father came from the south shore of the Dyfi estuary and whose mother hails from the northern edge of that glorious waterway! Mid Wales is a concept enshrined in such varied institutions as the mid Wales economic development board, the surviving post-Beeching transport artery of the mid Wales railway line, or the mid Wales football league which takes in teams stretching from Aberystwyth to Welshpool. But clearly 'mid Wales' as an entity lacks any economic, social or cultural homogeneity. It is a useful working hypothesis but basically an artificial construct. Like patriotism, mid Wales is not enough.

So Rendel, like the rest of us, had his intellectual and political limitations perhaps. But it would surely be quite wrong to accuse him of failure to grapple satisfactorily with themes of socialism or nationalism which have baffled generations of Welshmen since his death. Indeed, the débâcle of the collapse of *Cymru Fydd* in 1896, and even the outcome of the referendum on Welsh devolution in 1979, might be taken to confirm Rendel's scepticism about the validity of political separatism. Most Welsh political leaders, from Lloyd George to Neil Kinnock, appear to have agreed with him.

In his own time and circumstances, Rendel's work on behalf of political and social democracy, and educational progress in Wales was unique and priceless. The democratic Wales of the twentieth century, that land of county councils and county schools which raised up three generations of Liberal and Labour politicians to influence and eminence was as much the work of the Englishman, Stuart Rendel, as it was of more charismatic native figures such as Tom Ellis or Lloyd George. More than anyone else in the 1880s and 1890s, he gave the Welsh people a sense of direction and a sense of purpose. He gave their awareness of their national identity, their faith in their history and destiny, a new resonance and meaning. Further, as he wrote of himself, 'My conversion was an object lesson for my English friends.'[62] The indifference, ignorance or neglect with which Englishmen had

[62]Rendel to Revd Josiah Jones, 17 April 1893 (NLW, Jones MSS., 6411B).

treated Welsh affairs over the centuries rapidly disappeared. The glories of Edwardian Wales before the deluge in 1914 were in many ways his personal achievement.

In his apologia as 'member for Wales', Rendel wrote his own epitaph: 'while I cannot be proud enough of my attachment to Wales, I cannot be so humbled as by Welsh praise'.[63] This provides an appropriate verdict on a remarkable career.

1984

[63] *Personal Papers*, 314.

19

Tom Ellis versus Lloyd George: The Fractured Consciousness of Fin-de-siècle Wales

The contrasting roles of Tom Ellis and Lloyd George dominate any serious consideration of Welsh public life in the era after 1868. These two symbolize, of course, the high noon of Liberal Wales. It is an era seldom studied these days, when so much attention is focused on the decline of Liberalism after 1918, the rise of Labour, and the ordeal of the industrial societies of the coalfield. Much recent research, often of great insight and brilliance, has focused on a Wales in decline. Ellis and Lloyd George, conversely, represent a glorious, if deceptive and brief, era of national awakening, one to which they themselves mightily contributed. It was a period which saw a dramatic cultural, and especially literary, renaissance, with scholars and poets like John Morris-Jones, Owen M. Edwards and T. Gwynn Jones in pivotal roles. It was a time of quite spectacular industrial and commercial expansion in the Welsh coalfield, and the great ports and entrepôts of the south-east. The coalfield provided an irresistible magnet for young migrants from the rural hinterland; in time the countryside too began to share, however modestly, in the new prosperity. Politically, it was a moment of reawakening and rediscovery. Between 1868 and 1914, Wales experienced the heady advent of mass democracy, both at national and local level. In that process, two towering figures, Tom Ellis of Cynlas in Merioneth and David Lloyd George of Llanystumdwy in Eifionydd, were powerful catalysts. They created much of the national rhetoric; they participated in many of the national achievements. They are key exhibits of Welsh national politics and self-awareness in the *fin-de-siècle* period.

In their very different ways, the two young men created a romantic image of themselves. Two 'cottage-bred boys' (or so it was claimed), they launched a new Welsh hagiography. Years later, this was most powerfully conveyed in W. Hughes Jones's book of 1937, *Wales Drops the Pilots*, where they appear as the spurned leaders of an unhistoric nation, 'prophets without honour', 'men of vision finding their countrymen blind'.[1] Tom Ellis was venerated as the archetypal 'lost leader', a rare charismatic force, 'burning with a peculiar intensity'.[2] His early death from bronchial illness in 1899, at the tragically early age of forty, merely added to the affectionate legend. He was Wales's refugee from the magic mountain, waiting for a Celtic Thomas Mann to rediscover him. Ellis's latest biographer, Wyn Jones, observes of him that 'no man ever loved his country more deeply and expended himself more selflessly on her behalf'. Ellis, we are told was seen as a 'political Moses' poised to lead his people towards a promised land of equality and freedom.[3]

The young Lloyd George, in somewhat different fashion, also kindled a new myth. His rise to the chancellorship of the Exchequer in 1908 was depicted by early biographers like Beriah Gwynfe Evans and John Hugh Edwards, both Liberal journalists, as a veritable 'life romance'. It was a saga of the simple country boy who trod the primrose path from Llanystumdwy to Downing Street.[4] By 1914 the Welsh national movement, at least in political terms, was largely identified with him and his programme. At election time at the end of the First World War, he could be hailed as 'the greatest Welshman yet born',[5] though admittedly this hyperbole was soon to dissolve in the harsh realities of the post-war world.

Yet the same time, Tom Ellis and Lloyd George also embody the frustration, as well as the triumphalism, of the national politics of post-1868 Wales. For all its achievement, the national movement of this period was overlaid with a tragic sense of incompleteness and lack of fulfilment. Nationalism in Wales, unlike the case of Ireland, had not implied separatism or any form of self-government. Wales had by 1914 become more and more firmly bound to England, to the English constitution, the English class system, English capitalism. Several prized achievements appeared by 1914 to be turning somewhat sour –

---

[1] W. Hughes Jones, *Wales Drops the Pilots* (Liverpool, 1937); John Lloyd in the *Western Mail*, 29 October 1960. See also Hughes Jones, *A Challenge to Wales* (Liverpool, 1938), written under the pseudonym 'Elidir Sais'.

[2] J. A. Spender, *Sir Robert Hudson: A Memoir* (London, 1930), 24.

[3] W. Jones, *Thomas Edward Ellis, 1859–1899* (Cardiff, 1986), 87, 89.

[4] J. H. Edwards, *From Village Green to Downing Street: The Life of David Lloyd George* (London, 1909); B. G. Evans, *The Life Romance of David Lloyd George* (London, n.d. [1915]).

[5] *Welsh Outlook*, 6 (1919), 6.

witness the growing disenchantment with the Welsh educational system and the democratic glories of the 'county schools', as the quarrels between Owen M. Edwards and the Central Welsh Board bore witness.[6] Sometimes, these discontents were linked, personally and directly, with Ellis and Lloyd George. Ellis was attacked, even by a friend and admirer like the High Church nationalist, J. Arthur Price, for his decision to take the whipship in July 1892, thereby betraying his principles, in the view of some patriots, for the loaves and fishes of office. It was noted by Tory opponents that Ellis's will revealed that the champion of the poor Merioneth farmers had left his heirs the considerable sum of over £11,000. Lloyd George, in time, was to be even more fiercely condemned for his neglect of Welsh interests when in office, and especially when prime minister in 1916–22. Wales was conspicuously not one of the 'little five-foot-five nations' supposedly liberated after years of war by the byzantine deliberations of the Paris peace conference. Llewelyn Williams, an old *Cymru Fydd* comrade of Lloyd George's in the 1890s, angrily condemned him as the prisoner of the Tories and a man who had betrayed his country. Assailed both by Labour and the Conservatives, bereft of much of his old Welsh Liberal constituency, Lloyd George had by the late 1920s become a kind of universal scapegoat, the only true begetter of the strange, sudden death of Liberal Wales.

But all these judgements, both eulogistic and hostile, beg many important questions. They fail to explore the essential nature of the Welsh national movement of the later nineteenth century. Even more, they tend to assume an inherent congruence of outlook between Ellis and Lloyd George, at least in fundamental principles. They were, we have been sentimentally told, 'at all times like David and Jonathan'.[7] At times, Cain and Abel might have been a more suitable Biblical analogy. At all events, a more searching analysis of *fin-de-siècle* politics might lead one to emphasize the differences rather than the similarities between these two remarkably gifted young Liberals. The contrast between them provides, at least in some respects, a key to the story of modern Wales, and to the political consequences of the historical themes analysed by Ieuan Gwynedd Jones.

The origins of Ellis and Lloyd George show important differences from the outset. Tom Ellis was manifestly a leader of a new kind, the first to thrill the national emotions in overtly political terms. He was born and brought up on a farm at Cynlas, near Bala in north-east

---

[6]For an authoritative discussion of these matters, see G. E. Jones, *Controls and Conflicts in Welsh Secondary Education, 1889–1944* (Cardiff, 1982), esp. chap. 1.
[7]Hughes Jones, *Wales Drops the Pilots*, 36 (citing W. Llewelyn Williams).

Merioneth, that cradle of revivalist Nonconformity. In 1859, the year of Ellis's birth, a massive religious revival galvanized the chapels. In the same year, following the victory at the general election of David Williams, a Liberal landowner from Penrhyndeudraeth, several local tenant farmers were evicted from their holdings on straight political grounds.[8] Among them were four relatives of Tom Ellis himself. A generation later he told the Land commissioners how these grave events had sent a 'thrill of horror' throughout the countryside.[9] At Bala, too, Ellis came early under the spell of the radical nationalist and Independent minister, Michael Daniel Jones, the very embodiment of the folk consciousness of *y werin*, and a guru for the politically alert younger generation.

Ellis then went on to study at the new 'college by the sea' at Aberystwyth, even then increasingly caught up in intense national ferment. Here, he met gifted young fellow nationalists like the future Liberal MPs, Ellis Griffith and Samuel T. Evans, and the great historian, John Edward Lloyd. Here Ellis first conceived a new vision of organic nationalism within Wales, not so much political as fired by the stimulus of continental folk-culture, of literature, music and decorative art, and by the cult of the countryside as the custodian of the essential national virtues. He was, then and later, very much an agrarian politician. His vision of Young Wales was primarily cultural, literary, philosophical, spiritual. So it was to remain throughout his life. It is highly indicative that in the mid-1890s, when he was Liberal chief whip and a major parliamentary figure at Westminster, Ellis should devote himself to studying the works of that mystical seventeenth-century Puritan, Morgan Llwyd.

Yet the young Tom Ellis was not just an inbred, parochial figure. He was, above all, a man who moved out. To be precise, he moved out to New College, Oxford, in 1880; after graduating there (without great distinction) in 1884, he moved on to London to serve as the private secretary of the radical Liberal millionaire MP, Sir John Brunner. Both at Oxford and in London, Ellis added new dimensions to his nationalist creed. At the former, he absorbed the moral ethic of Ruskin, the educational passion of Matthew Arnold (without the freezing fog of the 'Celtic twilight'), and especially the social compassion of the tragic figure of the young Arnold Toynbee, a penetrating critic of the new industrial order and its injustices. Many new themes thus emerged, all to be absorbed somehow in Ellis's nationalist credo. He responded to the social philosophy of the Fabians and their intense

---

[8]For this election, see I. G. Jones, *Explorations and Explanations* (Llandysul, 1981), 83–165.

[9]*Evidence to the Welsh Land Commission*, I (P.P. [1894] C.7439), qu. 16,912.

commitment to local government and popular participation. He was deeply influenced by the dawning New Liberalism, professed by the neo-Hegelian and Darwinian disciples of T. H. Green, with a more positive attitude towards the state and citizenship. Ellis warmed, too, to the heady vision of that social imperialism increasingly influential in Oxford in the early 1880s. This applied not only to Benjamin Jowett's Balliol, but also to Ellis's own New College, where the proconsular Alfred Milner was a recent fellow. No fewer than nine of the eleven founder members of Milner's 'kindergarten' in South Africa were New College men, including Brand, Kerr and Curtis. Empire thus became another key to Tom Ellis's idea of Welsh nationality, indeed its culmination and fulfilment. It was this complex, eclectic philosophy that he brought with him to late-Victorian Welsh politics when elected MP for Merioneth in the election of June 1886.[10]

David Lloyd George, by contrast, was neither aesthete nor intellectual. He experienced a more obviously political and partisan upbringing. Born in 1863 and soon to lose his schoolmaster father, his earliest memories were of the great Welsh Liberal election victories in the *annus mirabilis* of 1868. His childhood and early manhood were caught up in disputes with local clergymen, magistrates and land-owners; even in his little Anglican primary school in Llanystumdwy, Lloyd George was a strike-leader and rebel. He went on to become a solicitor in Porthmadog, the very prototype of the self-made, small-town, middle-class politician so central to the Wales of the 1880s. In such episodes as the famous Llanfrothen burial dispute, he became the embattled young champion of the Nonconformist tenantry against an outworn social ascendancy. Even within the fragmented world of Welsh Nonconformity, he was an outsider, since he was brought up by his shoemaker uncle as a Campbellite Baptist, a radical offshoot of the old Dissent; in this and other respects, he matched the Quaker Bright and the Unitarian Chamberlain within the Nonconformist firmament. In the late 1880s, though still only in his mid-twenties, Lloyd George rose very rapidly to political prominence. He was active in the anti-tithe campaign in south Caernarfonshire. He took part in local journalism and tried with some friends to found a new quasi-socialist newspaper, *Udgorn Rhyddid*, the trumpet of freedom.[11] He served as the 'boy alderman' on the first county council elected for Caernarfonshire in January 1889, as part of a huge Liberal majority.

[10]There is an excellent, highly subtle analysis of Ellis's intellectual development in N. Masterman, *The Forerunner* (Llandybïe, 1972); a useful work is R. Symonds, *Oxford and Empire* (Oxford, 1986).

[11]See R. E. Price, 'Newyddiadur cyntaf David Lloyd George', *Journal of the Welsh Bibliographical Society*, II (1976), 207–15; NLW, D. R. Daniel papers, 2744, Lloyd George to Daniel, 12 December 1887.

Within the North Wales Liberal Federation, Lloyd George represented the most militant of tendencies, threatening national rebellion unless Gladstone and the party leadership paid far more heed to the just claims of Nonconformist Wales.[12] While Ellis had imbibed the social and imperial ideologies of élitist Oxford, Lloyd George was evolving his own particular *Zeitgeist* at home, on the political platforms, in the chapel vestries and county courts of rural Wales. He was elected to Parliament for Caernarfon Boroughs in April 1890 – it was a Liberal by-election 'gain' and very far from being a safe seat. At the age of twenty-seven, he was already a controversial and colourful politician and stump orator, feared and admired as few were in Welsh public life.

Following on from these highly distinct backgrounds, it soon emerged that Ellis and Lloyd George had markedly different political outlooks. A mutual friend like their endlessly loyal colleague, D. R. Daniel of Llandderfel, came to appreciate their differences, eventually with painful results in his later life.[13] In a variety of ways, Ellis and Lloyd George, as they made their way through Welsh and British politics, were political animals of contrasting species.

Ellis, for example, was a quintessentially agrarian radical. From Bala to the South African veld, the pure, uncorrupted qualities of rural, farming society were his touchstone of nationality, indeed of a morally wholesome society. For Ellis it was 'in the soil of the country areas, and the slope of the hills, in the remote valleys, that the best sources of a nation's life are to be found. It is there that the cradle of a worthwhile humanity exists' to bring balm and succour to 'the casualties of the unmerciful struggle of the cities'.[14] It might have been William Jennings Bryan, of 'cross of gold' fame, speaking. Lloyd George, on the other hand, was representative not of the farming community but of the emergent professional bourgeoisie of the small towns, of which Cricieth and Porthmadog were prototypes. He was never that much at ease with farmers pure and simple. His father was a schoolteacher, Uncle Lloyd an artisan. Lloyd George's differences with his prospective father-in-law, Richard Owen, a substantial Methodist farmer, added to the myriad social and sexual complications of his courtship of Maggie Owen of Mynydd Ednyfed.[15]

In denominational terms, Ellis was always a loyal Calvinistic

---

[12]NLW, Minutes of the North Wales Liberal Federation, esp. for September–December 1889.

[13]K. W. Jones-Roberts, 'D. R. Daniel', *Journal of the Merioneth Historical and Record Society*, 5 (1965), 58–78, is a useful discussion of this forgotten patriot. His extensive papers in the National Library of Wales are a most valuable source for both Ellis and Lloyd George.

[14]Jones, *Ellis*, 37.

[15]See K. O. Morgan (ed.), *Lloyd George Family Letters, c. 1886–1936* (Oxford and

Methodist. He was a devout chapel-goer if never a bigot, with some sympathy for the aesthetic and cultural vision of High Anglicans like Arthur Price. Ellis's religious convictions and affiliations were beyond dispute. Lloyd George, by contrast, viewed with scorn and contempt the petty jealousies and social pretensions of the chapels, especially the 'glorified grocers' of the *sêt fawr*, or philistine 'beatified drapers' like D. H. Evans.[16] Although popularly seen as the epitome of the Nonconformist conscience in politics, Lloyd George was in religious terms a critic of the chapels; his creed, *pace* W. R. P. George, was that of at best a deist, perhaps even a free thinker.[17] In personal life, unlike the respectable aesthete Ellis, Lloyd George was emphatically no puritan. As most of his biographers have pointed out (usually to a vastly excessive extent), he prefigured the so-called permissive society.

Again, as has been seen, Ellis was always deeply involved with the cultural and literary aspects of Welsh nationality. In this he followed his early model, the youthful Protestant prophet of Young Ireland in the 1840s, Thomas Davis (who also died young, as it happened).[18] Ellis's vision of Welsh nationality always had an essentially literary base, as did that of Llewelyn Williams, as he grappled with the anglicized, philistine, 'howling wilderness' of Swansea and Barry.[19] Ellis frequently addressed Welsh colleges and the Honourable Society of Cymmrodorion on the need to sustain the Welsh language, foster its literature and scholarship, to encourage Cymric traditions in the visual arts, and build them up in architecture and design.[20] In the 1890s he campaigned vigorously (and successfully) for public support for the scholar Gwenogvryn Evans in his work of editing manuscripts of

Cardiff, 1973), 19–22. Lloyd George mused in his diary on 30 August 1887 that Maggie deserved 'something better than a farmer'.

[16]Ibid., 28 (Lloyd George to Margaret Lloyd George, 10 June 1890). The phrase 'glorified grocers' (in connection with a proposed reform of the composition of the House of Lords in 1910) appears in L. Masterman, *C. F. G. Masterman* (London, 1939), 200.

[17]See W. R. P. George, *The Making of Lloyd George* (London, 1975), 107ff, for a contrary view. Also see B. B. Gilbert, *David Lloyd George, a Political Life: The Architect of Change 1863–1912* (London, 1987), 35–7.

[18]T. W. Moody, 'Thomas Davis and the Irish Nation', *Hermathena*, 103 (Dublin, 1966), 5–31.

[19]NLW, Ellis papers, 2134, W. Llewelyn Williams to Ellis, 19 February 1892; Cardiff Public Library, Cochfarf papers, W. Llewelyn Williams to Edward Thomas, 'Cochfarf'.

[20]See T. E. Ellis, *Speeches and Addresses* (Wrexham, 1912), a posthumous publication sponsored by his wife, Mrs Annie Ellis (later Mrs Peter Hughes Griffiths). Particularly relevant are Chapters 2, 3, and 6, on 'Domestic and decorative art in Wales', 'A plea for a Welsh School of Architecture' and 'The duty of the Guild towards the literature and records of Wales'.

medieval poetry.[21] He pressed for a Welsh Historical Manuscripts Commission, a national library and museum; he urged the University Guild of Graduates to help set these enterprises in motion. Ellis's intellectual powers had their limitations, certainly, but the range of his intellectual interests and ambitions was almost of Gladstonian proportions. they provided the *fons et origo* of his belief in Welsh nationhood. Lloyd George, conversely, although a fluent Welsh-speaker, had relatively little interest in Welsh culture, literary or musical, other than the populistic implications of hymn-singing. Unlike Ellis, he very seldom read Welsh (or any other) poetry or literary criticism for pleasure; his awe before the architectural splendours of Rome or Florence did not get much beyond the casual window-gazing of the tourist. Lloyd George's preferred reading matter was inspirational social texts such as Dickens or Hugo's *Les Misérables*, together with romantic novels of the wild west.[22] He acquired knowledge, not through bookish learning, but through personal contact and conversation. His methods of self-education were instinctive, intuitive, inspirational; his favoured companions were 'responsive personalities' of a similar outlook. In this at least, L.G. was the very model of the impressionable Celtic spirit as Matthew Arnold had misidentified it.

It followed from this that the two young Welsh Liberals contrasted sharply in their response to the contemporary pressure for Irish Home Rule. Ellis, the disciple of Davis and Mazzini, saw Irish nationalism in almost religious terms as a mass movement for social and cultural liberation. He mingled harmoniously with Irish MPs on the backbenches during the so-called 'union of hearts' phase from 1886 down to the Parnell/O'Shea divorce scandal in 1890. He was present, along with Labouchere and William O'Brien, at the meeting in Mitchelstown, County Cork, in September 1887 where the authorities opened fire on a crowd of peaceful Irish farmers, killing three of them.[23] On Irish Home Rule, Ellis was a fundamentalist, a Sinn Feiner out of his time. Lloyd George, on the other hand, was initially strongly opposed to Irish Home Rule in 1886. He came within an ace (or, according to one version by J. Hugh Edwards, a misread railway timetable) of joining Chamberlain's Radical Union in that year.[24] Protestant hostility to Rome Rule in Ireland, rather than sectional sympathy for

---

[21]Ibid., 149–50.

[22]It should be added that Lloyd George also read a certain amount of history during his boyhood, including the work of Gibbon, Macaulay and J. R. Green, though not much later.

[23]Masterman, *Forerunner*, 62–3.

[24]For a discussion of this question, see J. Grigg, *The Young Lloyd George* (London, 1973), 51, n.2. He rightly points out that Edwards suppressed the point in his later versions of Lloyd George's career.

the Orangemen of Ulster, seems to have been the decisive factor for Lloyd George. It is true that by 1890 he was committed to Irish Home Rule on Gladstonian lines. He was to make at least one good friend among the Irish MPs, 'Tay Pay' O'Connor, significantly enough a prominent London journalist and editor. Even so, from the 1880s down to the 'troubles' of the 'Black and Tans' in 1919–20, Lloyd George was never an unambiguous supporter of Irish Home Rule as Gladstonian Liberals understood the concept. Many of his biographers have misrepresented his views on this very point. He was advocating the separate status of Ulster within the government in 1913–14 and again in June to July 1916; in 1918 he stood firm against its 'coercion'. The basic divergence between him and the Mazzini-like Ellis in the 1880s cast its massive, baleful shadow over British policy towards the Irish nation from 1886 down to the Free State treaty concluded with Griffith and Collins in December 1921. The roots of the Anglo-Irish war of 1919–21 and of the Irish civil war that followed in 1922–3 lay, in some sense, in the complexities of Welsh politics in the 1880s. [25]

Above all, as has already been observed, Lloyd George, unlike Ellis, simply did not move out of Wales at a formative stage of his career. He never went to Oxford as a student, or indeed to any institution of higher education at all. In 1890 his outlook was the more truly local, even provincial. Far more than Ellis could ever be, Lloyd George remained, in his erratic way, essentially Welsh, a political outsider in a manner that Ellis, the confidant of Liberal imperialists and neo-Fabians like Haldane, Asquith, Buxton and Grey, could never be. There was a personal and philosophical detachment about Ellis's political ideas that contrasted sharply with the inbred enthusiasms of the youthful Lloyd George. The fissure that resulted ran deep through the national consciousness of *fin-de-siècle* Wales.

The political priorities of the two also show significant divergences. Of course, as part of the new wave of young, radical, largely Nonconformist MPs elected between 1886 and 1892, Ellis and Lloyd George symbolized a massive generational change in Welsh politics, as dramatic as that when Parnell and his followers supplanted Isaac Butt in Ireland a decade earlier. [26] Along with D. A. Thomas, David Randell, Samuel T. Evans, J. Herbert Lewis, and Frank Edwards, Ellis and Lloyd George represented a younger, more aggressively nationalist movement. They left far behind in their wake, not only veterans like

[25] I have discussed Lloyd George's attitude towards Ireland and the Irish more fully in a paper published jointly by the British and Irish Academies, *Ireland after the Union* (1989), 83–103.

[26] For fuller discussion of this theme, see K. O. Morgan, *Wales in British Politics, 1868–1922* (Cardiff, 3rd edn., 1980), chap. 3.

Lewis Llewelyn Dillwyn, Henry Richard and Sir Hussey Vivian, but even heroes of 1868 like Sir George Osborne Morgan. This was truly a new breed of Welsh representatives that dominated the recently-formed Welsh Parliamentary Party, somewhat cautiously led by the Englishman, Stuart Rendel, from 1888 onwards. In this context, Ellis and Lloyd George worked closely together. They were an effective pair of free-lance snipers, alarming to Gladstone and Morley as well as to the Conservative government on such matters as the 1892 Clergy Discipline Bill. They appear to have got on well personally. Ellis took his younger Caernarfon colleague on a tour of the more colourful London cafés, and there were theatre excursions as well, with suitable female company. Ellis was a bachelor; Lloyd George's wife chose to remain moored in Cricieth. Ellis was effusive in his praise of Lloyd George's maiden speech in June 1890; the latter responded that Ellis was 'a good sort' and pleasant company despite his already uncertain health.[27]

Yet the main priorities of the time were seen in significantly different lights by the two men. This comes across clearly if the major themes of Welsh land, local government, education and, above all, governmental devolution are examined in turn.

As regards Welsh land, Ellis took a very broad view of the question. He had a Fabian passion for the statistics for rent returns, and the details of easy credit arrangements for freeholders.[28] But the land question, in Wales as in Ireland, was to him above all a crucial facet of emergent nationhood. Land, indeed, included the labour question as well – 'Nationality and labour are our two main principles', he wrote to his Flintshire colleague, Herbert Lewis.[29] The system of landed tenure comprehended the Church establishment, tithe, the very structure of the social order and of the national ethic. A remodelled Welsh land system, on the basis of a small-scale freeholding proprietorship would be the very basis of that peasant democracy from which the new Wales would arise. Lloyd George, however, saw land reform in more dialectical terms, as a form of disestablishment of the landlords, and levelling the gross social inequalities of Welsh rural society. For him, as for many others, the essence of Welsh land was social rather than economic. He was less interested in ideals of freehold tenure and of diffused peasant proprietorship than in taxing the unearned increment on land, urban as well as rural, as advocated by Pan Jones of Mostyn in

[27]Morgan, *Family Letters*, 47, David Lloyd George to Margaret Lloyd George, 5 April 1892, in which Ellis compares, for Lloyd George's benefit, an Egyptian restaurant and 'cyclorama' in London with the real Egypt.

[28]See particularly Ellis's speech in the Commons, 29 June 1888 (*Parl. Deb.*, 3rd. ser., 337, 1792ff.), when introducing a resolution on agricultural tenancy in Wales.

[29]NLW, Ellis papers, 2890, Ellis to Herbert Lewis, 31 October 1891.

Y Celt, perhaps even with land nationalization as an objective.[30] Significantly, his main hero amongst the Irish members was not the aloof Protestant landowner, Parnell, but the quasi-socialist land nationalizer and friend of Keir Hardie, Michael Davitt.[31] Lloyd George was more attracted to the single-tax theories of the American, Henry George, than Ellis could ever be. The 1909 Budget with its multiple taxation on the landowner, along with the semi-nationalization of the 'Green Book', *The Land and the Nation*, in 1925, were proposals that could only have come from Lloyd George, never from Tom Ellis.[32]

As regards local government, Ellis saw it as the instrument of populism. He cited Tocqueville's view that local assemblies of citizens 'constituted the strength of free nations'.[33] He took a keen interest in the provisions of the 1888 Local Government Act, which he thought could be developed in the localities so that the Welsh county councils could combine to provide something like a functional Welsh assembly. He was equally excited by the potentialities of the 1894 Parish Councils Act, passed by the Rosebery government while he was chief whip. The measure would provide civic training; it would enable local communities to secure and retain their hold over the land; it would offer a forum for the public debate of local issues; it would provide an essential machinery for energizing and elevating the national spirit.[34] The Welsh, Ellis believed, had a natural capacity for local collective association. Theirs was a land of *cyfraith, cyfar, cyfnawdd, cymorthau* and *cymanfaoedd*, all of them concepts which embodied the co-operative ethic.[35] By extension, Ellis took a keen interest during his various travels in the growth of similar self-governing rural communities, such as the Swiss cantons (a famous late-Victorian obsession), the Austrian Tyrol, and the Boer republics in South Africa. His concern with local government was subtle and refined and voiced with a religious passion.

Lloyd George's view of local government by contrast, was relatively simple, at least at the conceptual level. He had no specialist interest in

[30]P. Jones-Evans, 'Evan Pan Jones – land reformer', *Welsh History Review*, 4 (1968–9), 143–59.

[31]Lloyd George noted in the early 1880s that Michael Davitt was his 'most admired character in real life' (George, *Making of Lloyd George*, 113).

[32]The 1909 budget included a 20 per cent tax on the 'unearned increment', payable when land was sold and when it changed hands after death. The 'Green Book' included a form of quasi-nationalization, 'cultivating tenure', for all land deemed to be productive.

[33]Ellis, *Speeches and Addresses*, 167.

[34]Ibid., 165ff.

[35]Ibid., 22.

the mechanics of local government as the germ of a wider devolution of power. He took no part in the debates on the 1894 Parish Councils Act. Nearer home, his membership of Carnarfonshire County Council was conspicuous for a poor attendance record; he did not share Ellis's Fabian enthusiasm for highways, allotments and drains. Unlike many other men of the left, Liberal and socialist, from Joseph Chamberlain to Herbert Morrison, Lloyd George did not develop his administrative skills at the local level at all. He became interested in local government only when it could be used as a political lever. Hence his extremely shrewd decision in December 1902 to transfer the powers of the Welsh local authorities under the 1889 Intermediate Education Act to the new local authorities constituted under Balfour's new Education Act – a vital move in welding together the 'revolt' of the Welsh county councils against the Balfour Act.[36] Lloyd George henceforth found himself at the head of a nation-wide rebellion by all the Welsh local authorities (with a handful of backsliders) in 1903–5, and threatened with mandamus writs by central government. But here his concern with the potentialities of local government was far narrower in concept and more purely partisan than was ever the case with Ellis.

It followed that much the same could be said about education, another of Ellis's abiding passions. A product of Aberystwyth and Oxford, as has been noted, he was a major architect of the Welsh Intermediate Education Act of 1889. The precise degree of credit to be allocated to Ellis, Stuart Rendel, A. J. Mundella, the Tory education minister, William Hart-Dyke, and others, has been subject of some historical debate,[37] but perhaps this is of secondary importance. There is no doubt that Ellis was enormously interested in the Act and the social potentialities of the secondary education system it created. He saw the new 'county schools', which by 1914 numbered well over a hundred in all Welsh counties (including Monmouthshire for this purpose), as the creators of a new educated élite, intellectually superior, but instinctively in tune with the new democracy. Liberal littérateurs like Morris-Jones he saw as paradigms of the new kind of social and intellectual leadership that would emerge. Ellis was zealous in turning the funds of Welsh educational charities to good purpose; he was active in rescuing such famous old local academies as the grammar school at Botwnnog.[38] Equally, he was deeply involved, first

---

[36]NLW, Herbert Lewis papers, Herbert Lewis's diary, 11 November 1902.

[37]See J. R. Webster, 'The Welsh Intermediate Education Act of 1889', *Welsh History Review*, 4 (1969–70), 290–1; K. O. Morgan, '"The Member for Wales": Stuart Rendel (1894–1913)', *Transactions of the Honourable Society of the Cymmrodorion*, 1984, 160–1 (published in this volume, 339–59).

[38]NLW, Daniel papers, Ellis to Daniel, 24 August 1891.

in reinforcing the new fledgling college at Aberystwyth, and then, in 1893, in encouraging the drafting of the charter for the federal University of Wales, which was then composed of the colleges at Bangor, Aberystwyth and Cardiff. The clerical delaying tactics from the Anglicans of St David's College, Lampeter, were dismissed with some ruthlessness. Ellis was intimately connected with the work of his friend, Arthur Acland, a resident in Caernarfonshire, the minister for education under Gladstone in 1892–4, in this and other contexts. When the Aberystwyth Old Students' Association came into being in 1892, Ellis was its natural first president, as he was later for the new University of Wales Guild of Graduates. Both of them he saw as active pressure-groups for scholarship and the arts. Here was a politician of no ordinary kind, one who saw higher education as the key to a wider, participatory view of democracy, a Welsh Greece to England's Rome.

Lloyd George, on the other hand, was unusually detached from the movement for higher education, on which so much of the national endeavour of *fin-de-siècle* Wales was expended. Arthur Humphreys-Owen, another Liberal MP closely connected with Welsh education, noted that Lloyd George, having had no formal literary education himself, was 'unable to see the needs of the educational system. He regards it simply as a political scaffolding'.[39] Lloyd George stood largely outside the Welsh higher education crusade of the 1890s, the campaign for the intermediate schools, the creation of a Central Welsh Board and inspectorate, the founding of a University of Wales, all with their class-collaborationist and consensual overtones. He became decisively involved with Welsh education only in the purely political context of the 'revolt' against the 1902 Balfour Education Act which has just been described, and in subsequent unsuccessful attempts to build on that movement by creating some kind of Welsh council of education.[40] It is certainly the case that, later on, Haldane, amongst other Cabinet colleagues, managed to broaden Lloyd George's interest in education in the 1910–14 period, and that education, including technical instruction, was one of the prospective beneficiaries, along with health and housing, of his abortive budget of 1914.[41] The Fisher Education Act 1918 was given every encouragement by the prime minister, who himself saw the historian, H. A. L. Fisher, as another

[39]NLW, 79466C, no 704a (Rendel papers), A. C. Humphreys-Owen to Lord Rendel, 18 June 1905.

[40]Morgan, *Wales in British Politics*, 198, 223–6; L. Wynne Evans, 'The Welsh National Council for Education', *Welsh History Review*, 6 (1972–3), 49–88.

[41]E. Ashby and M. Anderson, *Portrait of Haldane at Work on Education* (London, 1975), 116–19.

Guizot or Morley.[42] Nevertheless, it remains true that Lloyd George's lifelong attitude to education as a social and political priority was less ardent than that of Tom Ellis. As late as the Cabinet discussions on the cuts proposed by the Geddes Committee in 1921, the prime minister was zealous to economize by raising the age of school entry and cutting back on further education, including the day continuation schools.[43] He had received little formal education himself, and it had not done him any harm. His stance was that of the self-made, self-taught man, to be contrasted with the arid abstract learning of the schoolmen. In this sense, Lloyd George differed, not merely from Ellis but also from Herbert Lewis, Humphreys-Owen, Samuel Evans, Ellis Griffith, Llewelyn Williams and most other major figures in *fin-de-siècle* Welsh Liberalism. Even the coal-mining tycoon, D. A. Thomas, himself a Cambridge graduate with a decent degree in mathematics, championed the need for technical education. In his philistinism, Lloyd George stood almost alone.

Finally, there was the supreme political priority of Welsh Home Rule. As an MP from 1886 onwards, Ellis moved steadily towards the need for Welsh self-government, as a political, perhaps spiritual, necessity. His mystical experiences beside the temple at Luxor in Egypt merely deepened his commitment. His speech at Bala on 18 September 1890 was a passionate statement of the need, not merely for wider recognition of Wales in political, religious and cultural terms, but for a Welsh assembly, elected on a broad democratic basis by all adult Welsh men and (be it noted) women as well.[44] His involvement with the current movement for Irish self-government gave his concern for Welsh Home Rule additional overtones. A subsequent visit to South Africa in 1891, during which he talked with personalities as varied as Cecil Rhodes and Olive Schreiner (though, apparently, with no black people), no less than his reveries beside the Nile, merely strengthened a passionate affirmation of the need for self-determination. For Ellis, an elected assembly would 'form the highest embodiment of the national unity and the main instrument for fulfilling the national will and purpose of Wales'.[45]

Lloyd George's early Welsh nationalism was no less genuine and determined. It dominated his election address in the by-election for

[42]BL Add. MS. 50905, f. 211, C. P. Scott's diary, 30 November–1 December 1919.
[43]PRO, CAB 27/165. Report, Proceedings and Memoranda of the Cabinet Committee appointed to examine Parts I and II of the first interim report of the Committee on National Expenditure: proceedings of 26 January 1922.
[44]*Baner ac Amserau Cymru*, 24 September 1890.
[45]Ellis, *Speeches and Addresses*, 184.

Caernarfon Boroughs in April 1890. At the same time, Lloyd George's outlook was markedly free from Ellis's commitment to cultural nationalism (including the sacred cause of the Welsh language). Lloyd George became deeply involved with the *Cymru Fydd* movement only in 1894–6, when he saw it primarily as a political instrument for uniting Welsh constituency parties and thereby putting pressure on the Liberal party leadership and the London-based party machine.[46] The self-governing Wales that Lloyd George ardently championed from 1894 onwards had highly political objectives – disestablishment, land reform, temperance and somewhat vaguely-conceived labour policies among them. It flowed from his inability to persuade his parliamentary colleagues to support him in his attempted 'revolt' against the Liberal party leadership in April to May 1894, when four Welsh Liberals announced their independence from the party whip owing to the delays in introducing a disestablishment bill. On the other hand, Lloyd George's courage in championing *Cymru Fydd* in the 1894–6 period is beyond dispute; he came far closer to entering the political wilderness than Ellis ever did. It can also be argued that Lloyd George's campaign for some kind of national assembly was more realistic and practical in form than Ellis's inspiring oratory. Lloyd George worked specifically within the hierarchies and power structures of Liberal Wales, north and south. Conversely, his tactics could also embrace a wide range of allies, including some High Church disestablishers in early 1895.[47] They might help get disestablishment (more specifically disendowment) out of the way, to leave the way clear for Welsh Home Rule. The future coalitionist and architect of new forms of inter-party liaison from 1910 onwards can certainly be discerned in Welsh politics in 1895. In this sense, and some others, Ellis was far the purer – though not necessarily the more effective – Liberal of the two.

For both Ellis and Lloyd George, the events of July 1892 marked a turning-point. Welsh members, with disestablishment and other major demands heading their programme, were in a rare position to put pressure on Gladstone and the new Liberal government. After all, the Welsh numbered thirty-one while the government's majority was barely forty. There was also the offer of the position of junior whip to Tom Ellis. This was a crisis not only for him personally but for his

---

[46]For the *Cymru Fydd* crisis, see Morgan, *Family Letters*, 77–95; W. George, *Cymru Fydd: Hanes y Mudiad Cenedlaethol Cyntaf* (Liverpool, 1945); and Gilbert, *David Lloyd George*, 120ff.

[47]This refers to Lloyd George's indirect involvement in the so-called 'Bangor scheme' of January 1895, in which J. Arthur Price and four other Welsh High Churchmen advocated a compromise settlement over Church endowments for the sake of Welsh Home Rule: see E. E. Owen, *The Early Life of Bishop Owen* (Llandysul, 1958), 179–81.

friends also, and for the Welsh national movement as a whole. Ellis, as we have noticed already, was attacked by J. Arthur Price, then and later, for 'grasping the Saxon gold',[48] but he took his prime loyalty to the Liberal party for granted. He pointed to the Welsh disestablishment measures of 1894–5, the University of Wales charter, and the Royal Commission on Welsh Land as evidence of his effectiveness within the charmed circle of government. Lloyd George was not so sure: later on, he was to speak of the party making Ellis its 'doormat' (long before Arthur Henderson commandeered the term!).[49] The example of the Irish Nationalists was a beguiling one, showing how resolute independence could be made to serve the national cause. Lloyd George seems initially to have endorsed Ellis's decision to accept the whipship in July 1892, as a way of securing greater political pressure on behalf of Welsh causes. It would also ensure that a somewhat aged government, headed by an octogenarian, had some new radical blood.[50] Equally, he endorsed Ellis's succession to Marjoribanks as chief whip in March 1894. But Lloyd George himself proved to be a persistent rebel against the whips, Ellis included, in the 1892–5 Parliament. This included the highly contentious circumstances in which the Rosebery government fell from office on 20–21 June 1895; in this episode, Ellis's later loyal defence of Lloyd George's role was more ardent than Asquith and others felt was justified by the facts.[51]

Overall, the effect of Tom Ellis's becoming a whip in July 1892 marked a clear rift between him and his old political comrade-in-arms, David Lloyd George. The latter emerged all the more strongly as a Welsh free-lance, a *mauvais coucheur* and a permanent headache for the party leadership. Ellis was a loyalist now, essentially a Welsh-speaking but London-based politician. His main friends were Englishmen like Acland, Buxton and Robert Hudson. This most essentially Welsh of politicians was imperceptibly drifting from the Wales of his own day, with its harsh internecine and interreligious conflicts, and clashes of interests. He was becoming something of a stranger in his own honoured land.

[48]UCNW, Bangor Library, Lloyd papers, 314, 449, Price to J. E. Lloyd, 14 October 1892. This view is curiously echoed in H. Spender, *The Prime Minister* (London, 1920), 54, no doubt reproducing Lloyd George's own views.
[49]Morgan, *Family Letters*, 151, Lloyd George to Margaret Lloyd George, 10 January 1908. The more celebrated 'door-mat', of course, was Arthur Henderson in August 1917.
[50]NLW, Ellis Griffith papers, 385, Ellis to Ellis Griffith, 25 August 1892.
[51]BL, Herbert Gladstone papers Add. MS. 46022, f. 94, Lloyd George to Ellis, ?April 1894; NLW, Ellis papers, 74, 'private', Asquith to Ellis, 30 November 1895.

The gulf that had now opened up between Ellis and Lloyd George became very apparent during the *Cymru Fydd* crisis of 1894–6. Ellis, like Llewelyn Williams, saw *Cymru Fydd* as the institutional agent of a wider cultural movement. He was distant from the movement in 1894–5 to unite the Liberalism of north and south Wales and sub-ordinate both to the Welsh Home Rule cause. This was not simply because he was chief whip, but because he saw *Cymru Fydd* under Lloyd George's aegis as a narrowing, pedestrian, even philistine kind of national self-expression. It was a caricature of the ideal of *Cymru'n Un*. Ellis would have agreed with Llewelyn Williams in seeing it as the kind of limited, stereotyped creed that Parnell/Redmond nationalism had become in Ireland, far removed from the cultural idealism of Young Ireland in the 1840s (or, indeed, of Sinn Fein a few years later).[52] Ellis was much upset by the free-lance tactics that Lloyd George adopted against his own party comrades in the later months of 1895. He regarded the collapse of the *Cymru Fydd* League after the fiasco at Newport in January 1896 without emotion.[53]

Lloyd George, by contrast, saw *Cymru Fydd*, as it spread throughout Wales, as an instrument of power and control. He managed to capture the North Wales Liberal Federation as part of the base for his new all-Wales movement. The Liberals of south Wales, however, were far more resistant, partly on linguistic grounds. The Newport meeting saw their mercantile, English-speaking spokesmen howl Lloyd George down. The essential conflict between Liberalism and nationalism was starkly revealed. In a narrow sense, *Cymru Fydd* under Lloyd George failed because of the social and linguistic divisions between rural and industrial Wales. Wales was not a unity in 1896 any more than it had been in the Age of the Princes centuries earlier. Perhaps it never could be. But in reality, the fragility of *Cymru Fydd*, as a basis for Welsh self-government, had emerged clearly in every single Liberal association and club throughout the land. Ellis, the idealist, continued to hope that the vision of *Cymru Fydd*, for all its practical difficulties, could provide the stimulus for a wider nationalist upsurge, as in so many continental countries. If there could be Pan-Slavism, why not Pan-Celticism? Lloyd George, the clear-headed realist, had no such illusions. He knew that the cause of Welsh separatism was lost, at least for his generation. After a mild resurgence of the cause in 1897–8,[54] he withdrew from the Welsh Home Rule campaign almost as rapidly as he

[52]UCNW, Bangor Library, Lloyd papers, 314, 592, Llewelyn Williams to J. E. Lloyd, 21 September 1894.

[53]For a discussion of this point, see T. I. Ellis, *Thomas Edward Ellis: Cofiant*, 2 (Liverpool, 1948), 260–1. Also see T. E. Ellis's speech at Aberdyfi, *South Wales Daily News*, 4 February 1896.

[54]Morgan, *Wales in British Politics*, 170–1.

men like Herbert Lewis and C. P. Scott of the *Manchester Guardian* bore witness over the years.[56]) Whether Tom Ellis, if he had lived, would have held major office in the Liberal governments of 1906–14 is a nice question for counter-factual debate. On balance, after a quarter-century of reflection the present writer is now inclined to feel that, warts and all, the more realistic figure of Lloyd George may have been rather more appropriate for tensions and fractured sensibilities endemic in the divided, schizophrenic Wales of his day. Further, he had the ambition and drive to harness them, on behalf not of personal ambition alone, but also of wider social and international objectives. In a hard, brutalizing world, Lloyd George, the disenchanted man of action, rather than Ellis, the noble man of vision, might have been what Welsh Liberalism and the nation as a whole required.

But it is perhaps wrong to try to choose between them in so arbitrary a fashion. Really, Wales needed them both. Each was central to the national renaissance of the *fin-de-siècle*. Ellis and Lloyd George were, above all, great democrats who applied their very different talents, temperaments and philosophies to promoting national equality for their countrymen. They did so without stirring up class war, without revolution, without the violence and bloodshed that continue to scar the national experience of Ireland. They redefined the national identity with permanent results. They contributed mightily to what the present writer, in a literary conceit, once termed Wales's Antonine Age.[57] Together and separately, Ellis and Lloyd George grasped many of the opportunities first elaborated in the mid-century. They enabled their Wales to come to terms with its past, and to contemplate a more fulfilling and creative future.

1988

[56]The Herbert Lewis papers in the NLW and the Scott papers in the BL are a valuable corrective to many wild criticisms by later writers.

[57]K. O. Morgan, *Rebirth of a Nation: Wales, 1880–1980* (Oxford and Cardiff, 1981), 123, referring to the 1900–14 period.

20

Lloyd George and
the Historians

It would be presumptuous and arrogant to try to offer here any ultimate thesis on Lloyd George as a political phenomenon. Indeed, we have it on the authority of the late Lord Keynes that this simply cannot be done by anyone who did not encounter Lloyd George personally, and experience his unique personal magnetism at first hand. 'Who shall paint the chameleon, who can tether a broomstick?' as Keynes asked rhetorically and pessimistically.[1] What I would like to try to do is more oblique and indirect – to try to study Lloyd George by studying those who have written about him, and may do so in the future. I would like to pursue two main themes. First to look at the way in which the judgements of Lloyd George's biographers and historians have evolved over the past sixty years, and to try to see why they have gone through so many bewildering reversals. Secondly, to look at the state of historical understanding now, and to suggest some of the basic questions that present-day and future historians might ask about this great Welshman.

For over sixty years, historians, journalists and political commentators have found Lloyd George an irresistibly fascinating topic – witness the fact that there are already fifty biographies of him in print. For years, he has provided the parched lips of authors with 'rare and refreshing fruit'. Even now, he has a unique capacity to inspire or to enrage. I see

---

[1] J. M. Keynes, *Essays in Biography* (London, 1961), 32–3.

that Lord Annan has written of him, in a notable issue of the *New York Review of Books*, 'he had no principles, no scruples and no heart'.[2]

It is not hard to see why Lloyd George still arouses such violent emotions. First of all, his career was chequered with bitter conflicts – the struggle over *Cymru Fydd*, the clashes with the House of Lords, the battles with the generals during the First World War, the internecine struggles within the Liberal party after that war. In all these, he played a uniquely belligerent role. He was, indeed, a very combative man: one is struck by the frequent appearance in his private correspondence of the verb 'to smash', long before it was appropriated by student demonstrators. Again, Lloyd George's political career went through many extraordinary reversals. He was at various times, an anti-militarist and a jingo; a little Englander and an imperialist; an extreme partisan and an advocate of coalitions. He was the unpuritanical, permissive champion of the Nonconformist conscience. All this makes it remarkably difficult to see his career whole. Again, his personality was an elusive one. It was not just that he was a Welsh Baptist outsider, thrusting his way through a hostile Anglo-Saxon world – though this is an important element. Beyond this, he was a singularly complex, many-sided man. Many contemporaries believed him to be totally devoid of fixed principle. In Keynes's view, he was 'rooted in nothing' (though this did not prevent Keynes from working fruitfully with him a few years after writing these bitter words). The point was put more kindly in 1917 by the American ambassador, Walter Hines Page (actually a great admirer of Lloyd George) when greeting a Scottish friend: 'Oh, he's truthful, perfectly truthful. But a Scotsman's truth is a straight line. A Welshman's is more or less a curve.'[3]

And finally, Lloyd George's career is inextricably linked with a great tragic theme – the death of the old Gladstonian Liberal party. Many have held him to be largely responsible for this, and for the decline of the liberal ethic widely associated with it, with that decline in the belief of progress and in the certainty of moral values which the conflicts and the ambiguities of the years since 1914 have steadily promoted. Lloyd George has been popularly regarded as both a catalyst and a scapegoat for the wider travails of British society in this recent period and all this, too, has been reflected in historians' treatment of him.

[2]*New York Review of Books*, 12 February 1972. To be fair, Lord Annan offered a very different verdict on Lloyd George in later correspondence in the same journal on 23 March 1972. Here he described Lloyd George as 'the most gifted man and possibly the greatest, ever to have become Prime Minister in this century'. The 1918–22 government he termed 'a great administration'.

[3]Burton J. Hendricks (ed.), *Life and Letters of Walter H. Page*, Vol. III (London, 1925), 371.

This treatment by historians has gone through three main phases. The first takes us through the years of greatness down to his fall from power in October 1922. This is the period of Lloyd George seen as populist folk-hero, an era of heroic, even hagiographical treatment. Most of those who wrote about him were Liberals intimately associated with the radical crusades that he led, and many of them were Welshmen. These early authors are symbolized by the title of the first biography of Lloyd George to be published: *From Village Green to Downing Street*, written by J. Hugh Edwards in 1908 to coincide with his hero's becoming chancellor of the Exchequer. Edwards (1869–1945), an Independent minister, a prominent radical journalist who had edited the periodical *Young Wales* (1895–1904), and from 1910 Liberal MP for Mid-Glamorgan, described Lloyd George's life here as a 'striking and fascinating romance'.[4] He depicts, in a book which is still of much value for the historian of Lloyd George's early career, the triumph of the 'cottage-bred boy' who grappled with the 'unholy Trinity' of the bishop, the brewer and the squire, and emerged as the champion of Wales and the Messiah of the underprivileged. It is a Caernarfonshire version of the Horatio Alger story of the 'log-cabin to president' kind, popular in the United States at the same period. A later biographer, Beriah Gwynfe Evans (1848–1927), formerly editor of *Y Genedl Gymreig* but then a free-lance journalist, was somewhat more measured in a new biography published in early 1916. After all, Evans had had somewhat strained relations with Lloyd George since the failure of the *Cymru Fydd* League (of which Evans was secretary) in 1896.[5] Also Evans was uncertain of the probable direction of Lloyd George's post-war career. Evans was writing during the political struggles brewing over military conscription, and he noted the growing estrangement from most of his Liberal colleagues that this crisis brought about for Lloyd George.[6] Even so, Evans called his informative biography *The Life Romance of Lloyd George*, and looked forward to his subject's presiding over a vast new post-war imperial confederation.[7] (Evans himself was always something of an imperialist.) English writers on Lloyd George during this same period

[4] J. Hugh Edwards and Spencer Leigh Hughes, *From Village Green to Downing Street: The Life of the Rt. Hon. D. Lloyd George, M.P.* (London, 1908), 145. Edwards wrote virtually all of this book. In later life, he produced four- and two-volume biographies of Lloyd George.

[5] Cf. Beriah Evans to Lloyd George, 25 May 1905 (Beaverbrook Library, Lloyd George papers, A/1/5/2).

[6] Beriah Gwynfe Evans, *The Life Romance of Lloyd George* (London, n.d. [1916]), 221.

[7] Ibid., 234ff. There is a shrewd portrait of Evans in E. Morgan Humphreys, *Gwŷr Enwog Gynt: Yr Ail Gyfres* (Aberystwyth, 1953), 120–31.

– the barrister, Herbert du Parcq in 1912; the journalists, Harold Spender in 1920 and E. T. Raymond in 1922 – were also highly sympathetic.[8] Spender, an ally of long standing, wrote of the prime minister's 'vision of a State deliberately consenting to sink faction in the cause of a larger purpose',[9] although the details of this vision remained understandably vague.

The second phase in Lloyd George historiography was heralded by the fall from power in October 1922. The tone was set by Stanley Baldwin at the famous meeting of the Unionist MPs at the Carlton Club on 19 October. Here he described Lloyd George as 'a dynamic force' – and 'a dynamic force', Baldwin characteristically added, 'is a very terrible thing'.[10] The major assaults on the fallen Welsh prime minister, however, came now from disillusioned Asquithian Liberals, embittered beyond measure by the schism in their party since the 'coupon election' in 1918. Writers like J. A. Spender and A. G. Gardiner lost few opportunities in the 1920s to decry Lloyd George and all his works, even after the somewhat fragile Liberal reunion in November 1923. By contrast, the coalition Liberals (H. A. L. Fisher for instance) remained largely silent: after all, a good many of them, including Churchill, had now joined the Conservatives. In a notably hostile biography in 1930, Charles Mallet (1862–1947), a Liberal MP in 1906–10 and later an Asquithian Liberal candidate in 1922 and 1923, attacked Lloyd George as morally corrupt.[11] In a volume of 313 pages, he dismissed his subject's record before 1914 in the first forty-two. The emphasis is heavily on the period after 1918 in which the author was an active 'Wee Free' partisan: characteristically, fourteen pages are spent in describing the activities of the 'Black and Tans' in Ireland, but only one in discussing the peace settlement with Sinn Fein in December 1921. Mallet attacked Lloyd George's penchant for 'programmes'. Elections, he argued, were not won on the basis of programmes: the Orange Book and the other policies in 1929 were 'mere manipulative figures'. 'Excessive expenditure and excessive taxation lie at the root of our economic troubles today', declared Mallet with impressive irrelevance. He called for the Liberal party in 1930 to return 'to the moral power of Mr. Gladstone'.[12] This hostile view was greatly reinforced by the publication of J. M. Keynes's bitter 'essay in

[8]Herbert du Parcq, *Life of David Lloyd George*, 4 vols. (London, 1912); Harold Spender, *The Prime Minister* (London, 1920); E. T. Raymond, *Mr Lloyd George* (London, 1922).

[9]Harold Spender, op. cit., 337–8.

[10]G. M. Young, *Stanley Baldwin* (London, 1952), 41–2.

[11]Sir Charles Mallet, *Mr Lloyd George: A Study* (London, 1930).

[12]Ibid., 207, 267, 298, 312.

biography' in 1933, originally omitted from *The Economic Consequences of the Peace* in 1919. In this he described Lloyd George, among other things, as 'half-human' and 'a vampire and a medium in one'.[13]

During these years, even writers who sought to be sympathetic to Lloyd George tended to confirm this hostile view. Thus Watkin Davies, the son of the Revd Gwynoro Davies of Barmouth, one of Lloyd George's foremost Welsh allies, pointedly stopped short at 1914: this excellent volume provided by far the best account in print to date of Lloyd George's early years. After 1914, Davies felt, Lloyd George's career was 'purposeless': he sees the death of 'Uncle Lloyd' in 1917 as a great divide, when the foundations of Lloyd George's 'old life at Criccieth' were finally sapped. The prime minister was henceforth 'left to his own devices and seconded by charlatans whose grip of political principles was even weaker than his own'.[14] (Davies, a staunch apostle of the League of Nations Union and formerly editor of the high-minded periodical *Welsh Outlook*, seemed to have had Lord Riddell particularly in mind.) Again, Lord Beaverbrook's remarkable accounts of politics between 1914 and 1922, intended, I believe, to be sympathetic to Lloyd George as well as to Bonar Law, tended nevertheless to show the Welshman as eager only for power, anxious only for sole occupation of 'the driver's seat', careless of the direction in which the vehicle was going.[15]

The wave of denigration continued to mount after Lloyd George's earldom (which was much resented in Wales) and his death (26 March 1945). Successive biographies by Sir Alfred Davies, George Malcolm Thomson and Frank Owen among others failed to stem the tide.[16] Even Thomas Jones's biography in 1951, by far the best one-volume study of Lloyd George to date, was rather too impersonal and detached.[17] Jones (1870–1955) was inclined to give the view of the man from Whitehall, as befitted the former assistant secretary to the Cabinet from 1916 to 1930. His biography concentrated largely on the period 1914–22, though it should be made clear that this was by no means the author's fault. At the behest of the official readers for his

[13]Keynes, op. cit., 35, 36.
[14]Watkin Davies, *Lloyd George, 1863–1914* (London, 1939), 279–81, 289.
[15]Lord Beaverbrook, *Politicians and the War 1914–1916* (London, 2 vols., 1928 and 1932); *Men and Power, 1917–1918* (London, 1956); *The Decline and Fall of Lloyd George* (London, 1963). The reference to 'the driver's seat' appears in *The Decline and Fall*, 11.
[16]Sir Alfred T. Davies, *The Lloyd George I knew* (London, 1948); Malcolm Thomson, *David Lloyd George: The Official Biography* (London, 1948); Frank Owen, *Tempestuous Journey* (London, 1954). This last volume has some valuable source-material.
[17]Thomas Jones, *Lloyd George* (Oxford, 1951).

American publishers, Harvard University Press, much of the early Welsh material was deleted: an entire chapter on the campaign for Welsh disestablishment from 1886 to 1914 was compressed into one brief paragraph.[18] Also the sections covering the years after 1922 on which Thomas Jones was knowledgeable were severely abbreviated at the request of the Press. Its reader, a distinguished historian of early nineteenth-century Britain with, perhaps, scant interest in the twentieth, suggested that Americans were 'not much excited by the long-drawnout demise of the Liberal Party and Lloyd George's part in it'.[19] Today we can only deplore this loss. Other biographers tended to emphasize Lloyd George's personal characteristics, again much to his disadvantage. A. J. Sylvester, Lloyd George's former private secretary, writing in 1947, revealed his master as a soured, autocratic and peevish old man.[20] The biography by Lloyd George's eldest son, the second earl, in 1960, gave a consistently hostile view of his father's personal and, to some extent, political behaviour.[21] Finally, Donald McCormick, in a most readable work, *The Mask of Merlin*, published in 1963, laid stress on 'the sultry smouldering evangelism of the Welsh valleys with its undertones of sexual obsession', 'with Nonconformity and lust stalking hand in hand',[22] a theme he described quite literally in loving detail. The wheel, it seemed, had come full circle. Llanystumdwy had been transformed into Llareggub. The 'cottage-bred boy' had turned into 'No-good Boyo'.

Serious academic historians of the period also tended to reflect this consistently critical view.[23] A. J. P. Taylor, in his fascinating volume, *English History 1914–1945* (1965), appeared to combine admiration for Lloyd George as a political operator (a judgement foreshadowed

[18]Thomas Jones papers A, Vol. III (final typescript of *Lloyd George*), 50; and Vol. IV (the working proof). Consulted by kind permission of Lady White.

[19]David Owen to T. J. Wilson (of Harvard University Press), 18 August 1948 (ibid., Vol. I, f. 80).

[20]A. J. Sylvester, *The Real Lloyd George* (London, 1947), for example 293. Mr Sylvester's private diaries were published in 1975, edited by Colin Cross.

[21]Richard Lloyd George, *Lloyd George* (London, 1960). The author was anxious to uphold the memory of Dame Margaret: see his *Dame Margaret* (London, 1947), written under the name of Viscount Gwynedd.

[22]Donald McCormick, *The Mask of Merlin* (London, 1963), 17, 28. The author, a journalist, has also written studies of Maundy Gregory, Victor Grayson and Jack the Ripper.

[23]One exception was the present writer's *David Lloyd George: Welsh Radical as World Statesman* (Cardiff, 1963, new edn. 1982). This was treated with kindly indulgence by the critics, but they seem mostly to have regarded it as a youthful *jeu d'esprit*. Another biography at the same period sympathetic to Lloyd George was Charles Mowat's 'Clarendon Biography', *Lloyd George* (Oxford, 1964), a perceptive work intended mainly for schools.

earlier in a most stimulating Leslie Stephens lecture in 1961)[24] with
distaste for him as a person. 'He had no friends and did not deserve
any', Mr Taylor declared.[25] Trevor Wilson, in his superb study, *The
Downfall of the Liberal Party 1914–1935* (1966), compared Lloyd
George with 'the Machiavel of the Elizabethan stage', purposeless and
'revelling in intrigue for its own sake'. He strove to explain how an
upright and honest man like C. P. Scott of the *Manchester Guardian*
(whose papers Dr Wilson has since brilliantly edited) could be
attracted to Lloyd George at all.[26] Lloyd George's reputation in 1966,
therefore, was at its lowest ebb.

But since 1966 a third phase in interpretation has begun. Almost every
major work of scholarship since then has tended to take a much more
sympathetic, or at least more detached view of Lloyd George's career
and objectives. This is very apparent in recent major works by Martin
Gilbert, Cameron Hazlehurst, Robert Skidelsky and Peter Clarke, and
in the various authors of the *Lloyd George Essays* edited by Mr Taylor
and based on papers delivered at the Beaverbrook Library seminars.[27]
It is fruitful to speculate, therefore, why this remarkable change has
occurred in recent years.

It may be partly the result of new sources. Since 1967 we have had
released the magnificent collection of Lloyd George papers housed in
the Beaverbrook Library, an archive which comprehensively covers the
period from December 1916. We have also had Mr Taylor's valuable
edition of the diary of Frances, Countess Lloyd-George, which begins
in September 1914.[28] And now there are available to historians the two
thousand or more Lloyd George letters in the National Library of
Wales at Aberystwyth, which the present author has been editing,[29]

[24]A. J. P. Taylor, *Lloyd George: Rise and Fall* (Cambridge, 1961). Here Mr Taylor
observes of Lloyd George's 1918–22 administration: 'there was hardly a problem
where he did not leave success behind him' (33).

[25]A. J. P. Taylor, *English History, 1914–1945* (Oxford, 1965), 74.

[26]Trevor Wilson, *The Downfall of the Liberal Party, 1914–1935* (London, 1966),
387. Cf. idem, *The Political Diaries of C. P. Scott, 1911–1928* (London, 1970), 24–9.

[27]Martin Gilbert (ed.), *Lloyd George* (New Jersey, 1968); Cameron Hazlehurst,
Politicians at War, July 1914 to May 1915 (London, 1971); Robert Skidelsky,
Politicians and the Slump (London, 1968); P. F. Clarke, *Lancashire and the New
Liberalism* (Cambridge, 1971); A. J. P. Taylor (ed.), *Lloyd George: Twelve Essays*
(London, 1971); Mr Gilbert's magisterial *Winston S. Churchill*, Vol. III (London,
1971) is also notably just in its treatment of Churchill's Welsh contemporary and
ally.

[28]A. J. P. Taylor (ed.), *Lloyd George: A Diary by Frances Stevenson* (London, 1971).

[29]Kenneth O. Morgan (ed.), *Lloyd George: Family Letters, 1885–1936* (Oxford
and Cardiff, 1973).

and which trace Lloyd George's career in great detail from 1885 to 1936. There was previously little enough evidence for this earlier period, and in some ways Lloyd George's case tended to go by default.

The new revisionism may also be partly the product of generational change. Younger historians, remote from the old controversies surrounding the Maurice debate, the 'coupon election' or the 'honours scandal', may be prepared to look at Lloyd George freer from the lumber of ancient prejudice. Perhaps younger historians, too, products of the 1960s and 1970s and their changing *mores*, are less shocked by one who was above all else a great critic of society and of institutions, and a great rebel against convention. Lloyd George certainly seems, in my experience as a university teacher, a much more congenial figure to students and to the young generally. They see him as one who met with the constant and implacable hostility of the establishment from George V downwards, and this naturally enhances his appeal. To them also he appears to be a more contemporary and relevant figure than, for instance, Churchill, whose views on empire or on the working class make him already a curiously dated figure. It may be then, that an objective assessment of Lloyd George, in which he will emerge neither as superman nor as a scapegoat, is becoming possible for the first time. We are moving from pre-history into history.

In the light of these recent changes, what kind of fundamental questions about Lloyd George ought historians now to be asking? I would like to suggest four or five major areas of research in the remainder of this chapter.

First of all, there is Lloyd George's attitude to social reform. It is often blandly assumed that he was a dedicated and consistent social reformer from his earliest years in politics. This is commonly thought to be the joint result of the impact of novels such as Hugo's *Les Misérables* upon his youthful imagination, and of the documented surveys of urban poverty conducted by Booth, Seebohm Rowntree and other social scientists in the 1890s and 1900s.[30] In fact, down to his entry into the Cabinet in December 1905, Lloyd George was basically an 'Old Liberal', caught up with disestablishment of the Church, sectarian education, temperance, land reform, and other traditional issues. He was essentially a rural radical, with scant understanding of industrial problems. We find him telling the railwaymen and quarrymen of Bethesda in October 1892 that there was no need for them to form a Labour party: 'The land question, the temperance

[30]For example Thomas Jones, op. cit., 33–4. For a good discussion of Lloyd George's approach to social reform, see Asa Briggs, *Seebohm Rowntree* (London, 1961), 62ff.

question and the question of disestablishment were equally of interest to labourers as was an Eight Hours' Bill.'[31] Even after the mighty strikes at the Penrhyn quarries in his own Caernarfonshire between 1896 and 1903, he still showed no clear grasp of labour questions. In the Cabinet as president of the Board Trade (December 1905–April 1908), his diagnosis of social and industrial problems was superficial. In a speech to the Welsh National Liberal Council in October 1906, he identified the causes of poverty as 'drink and the land question'. He told his fellow Welsh Liberals: 'If they tackled the landlords, and the brewers and the peers, as they had faced the parsons and delivered the nation from the pernicious control of the monopolists, then the Independent Labour Party would call in vain upon the working men of Britain.'[32]

A turning-point in his career came in the summer of 1908 with his famous visit to Germany to examine pensions and insurance schemes in that country. This is a crucial episode for his emerging concern with foreign affairs as well as social questions: he floated the idea of an Anglo-German agreement on naval reductions, and had a lengthy though unsuccessful conversation with Bethmann Hollwegg. Yet the evidence for it is tantalizingly sparse apart from a brief account in the autobiography of the journalist, Harold Spender, who accompanied him.[33] After his return from Germany, Lloyd George was a Liberal transformed, a vehement champion of the New Liberalism of social reform. At Cricieth he explained the principles of compulsory health and unemployment insurance to the newly married Winston Churchill in what the latter subsequently (in September 1912) termed 'two days very memorable to me'.[34] His speech to the Welsh Liberals in Swansea in October 1908 was totally different from his address at Cardiff two years earlier. At Swansea he called for a radical attack on the roots of poverty and unemployment, for pensions, labour exchanges and health and unemployment insurance.[35] Henceforth his whole outlook was totally different. He introduced the 'people's budget' in 1909, a financial base for a long-term programme of social welfare. There was the historic National Insurance Bill of 1911, a great landmark in the growth of a welfare state. There was the land campaign of 1913–14 which directed concern towards housing and urban renewal. And there was the budget of 1914, in some ways more sweeping than that of

[31]*North Wales Observer and Express*, 28 October 1892.
[32]South Wales Daily News, 12 October 1906.
[33]Harold Spender, *The Fire of Life* (London, n.d. [1926]), ch. XVII, 161–6. Also see Bentley Gilbert, *The Evolution of National Insurance in Great Britain* (London, 1966), 291–3.
[34]I owe this interesting point to Dr Henry Pelling.
[35]*South Wales Daily News*, 2 October 1906.

1909 with a new super-tax and a new graduated income tax upon earned incomes. Throughout this period, Lloyd George led an expanding concern of Liberalism with urban and industrial problems, in England and to a lesser extent in Wales.[36]

But why did this change occur? Was it simply the result of Lloyd George's going to the Treasury, and at last being able to implement long-held ideas? This seemed unlikely as previous chancellors had not been conspicuous as champions of expenditure on social welfare. Was it the forceful influence of Winston Churchill, president of the Board of Trade in 1908–10, pointing towards the 'untrodden field in politics', the field of social reform?[37] Was it alarm at successive Liberal by-election defeats? Was it the cathartic effect of the death of Lloyd George's beloved eldest daughter, Mair, in October 1907 which left him prostrated by grief?[38] Certainly he was the only consistent advocate of social reform in the great Liberal government of 1908–14, but the roots of his concern are still in many respects unclear.

A second area that merits more research is Lloyd George's rise to the premiership in December 1916. This is an episode which has already been explored with the pedantic precision of the medieval schoolmen. We have been told that a week in politics is a long time. The first week of December 1916 seems to some of us a veritable eternity! The events of those dramatic December days have done Lloyd George's reputation immense harm. Charles Mallet and many others have taken it as axiomatic that he became prime minister after 'a well-organized and carefully-engineered conspiracy'. Many historians have tended to follow this view, even to some extent Dr Trevor Wilson.[39] It has been taken as a sinister intrigue in which Asquith, the noblest Roman of them all, was stabbed in the back by an envious Casca from Cricieth. But some facts can now be established, and asserted without serious dispute.

[36]I shall be discussing the comparatively limited impact of the New Liberalism in Wales in 'The New Liberalism and the challenge of Labour, 1885–1929', *Welsh History Review*, 6 (3) (1973) (published in this volume, 59–83).

[37]Winston Churchill, 'The Untrodden Field in Politics', *The Nation*, 7 March 1908, 812–13.

[38]David Lloyd George to Mrs Lloyd George, 4 December 1907 (NLW, Lloyd George MSS., 20,429C, f. 1303). In this letter, Lloyd George states his belief that the cruel blow of the loss of his daughter may lead him to relieve the 'misery and sorrow' of the masses.

[39]Mallet, op. cit., 87; Wilson, *Downfall of the Liberal Party*, 90ff. Wilson argues that Lloyd George's becoming premier was 'the unexpressed, and perhaps unacknowledged object for which Lloyd George and Bonar Law were working'. He adds, 'There is little point in criticising Asquith for declining proposals apparently designed to secure rejection'.

First, Asquith was kept fully informed of the conversations between Lloyd George, Bonar Law and Edward Carson from 20 November 1916 onwards. Secondly, there is no basis whatsoever for the view that Lloyd George, either directly or through lieutenants like Addison, Kellaway and David Davies, was building up an anti-Asquith faction in the Liberal party. The Liberal War Committee, for instance, had virtually dissolved since April, while Lloyd George had had little apparent contact with its leaders. Thirdly, Asquith accepted the revised scheme prepared later on that day by Hankey, Edwin Montagu and Bonham-Carter, Asquith's secretary. Fourthly, it was Asquith who threw the scheme over the following morning, 4 December, for reasons which are hard to discern. Certainly the explanation that Asquith himself gave, that he was upset by an apparently inspired leading article in *The Times* that morning (actually written by Geoffrey Dawson), does not seem to make much sense.[40] It remains a great mystery. And fifth, it was only after that breach that Lloyd George was able to think of becoming prime minister, or to garner all-party support within the Unionist and the Labour parties. Until the morning of 4 December he was politically a very isolated figure.

In the light of these points, historians could well reflect on what, if anything, remains of the 'conspiracy theory'. There is no record of any long-term difficulty between Asquith and Lloyd George until the forming of the first coalition in May 1915. Historians might also consider what other means existed of removing a prime minister, with manifestly failing powers, saddened by private grief, palpably unable to cope with the strains of total war.

Third, historians might look again at the post-war premiership as Dr Maurice Cowling has now done in a very fascinating book.[41] Lloyd George's peacetime administration from 1918 to 1922 has been a prime target for his critics. It occupies about two-thirds of the space in Charles Mallett's hostile biography of 1930. Lloyd George's premiership, perhaps, has been attacked partly on grounds of political style. His post-war administration after 1918 was highly unorthodox by any

---

[40]Asquith to Lloyd George, 4 December 1916 (David Lloyd George, *War Memoirs*, London, new edn., 1938, Vol. I, 590–1). Lord Beaverbrook very fairly observes on this point: 'It wrongs Asquith to suppose him capable of changing his whole policy at the crucial moment of his life because of a leading article in a newspaper' (*Politicians and the War*, 477). Also cf. S. D. Waley, *Edwin Montagu* (Bombay, 1964), 108–9. There is an excellent discussion of the crisis in Robert Blake, *The Unknown Prime Minister* (London, 1955) 291–341; and in Roy Jenkins, *Asquith* (London, 1964), 421–63.

[41]Maurice Cowling, *The Impact of Labour, 1920–1924* (Cambridge, 1971).

standards. He was a prime minister without a party in the recognized sense. He developed a method of quasi-presidential 'prime ministerial government': this has led some to compare him with Harold Wilson, a political leader to whom I believe Lloyd George bears virtually no resemblance. Lloyd George's expansion of the central executive was believed by *The Times* to be undermining the constitution: its editor, Wickham Steed, quoted Dunning's resolution in 1780 in alleging that this tendency 'had increased, was increasing and ought to be diminished'.[42] Lloyd George was indeed in every way a most unusual prime minister. It was unconventional to have a 'garden suburb' of private advisers domiciled in the grounds of No. 10 Downing Street. It was unconventional for the Cabinet to meet in Inverness Town Hall.[43] It was unconventional for a prime minister to indulge so freely and so unapologetically in the sale of honours for political services rendered (though it might be noted that the scandalized Unionists were not above sharing in 50 per cent of the proceeds).[44]

Yet, whatever its defects of style, Lloyd George's post-war government was not just a government of reactionaries, of 'hard-faced men who looked as if they had done very well out of the war', to quote Baldwin via Keynes. Nor was Lloyd George the passive prisoner of Tory diehards: most of them felt that they were his prisoner. The picture presented by Keynes in *The Economic Consequences of the Peace* is fundamentally misleading.[45] In reality, the government of 1918–22 was a moderate one for most of its course. It pursued conciliation in foreign affairs. Lloyd George, rather than Woodrow Wilson, was the major agent working for moderation at the Paris peace conference in 1919. This was especially evident in the Fontainebleau memorandum of March 1919, worked out by Lloyd George, Philip Kerr, Sir Maurice Hankey and Field Marshal Sir Henry Wilson, perhaps the first document to argue in favour of the 'appeasement' of Germany (in the non-pejorative sense) with regard to frontiers and to financial indemnities.[46] It was Lloyd George also who fought for national self-determination for Upper Silesia: against President Wilson's opposition,

[42] *The Times*, 29 and 30 March 1921.

[43] On 7 September 1921. Here, the Cabinet drafted its invitation to de Valera and the other Sinn Fein leaders to a conference to settle the Irish issue.

[44] See Sir George Younger to Bonar Law, 2 January 1921 (Lord Beaverbrook, *The Decline and Fall of Lloyd George*, 241–3). Younger was afraid that Freddy Guest, the coalition Liberal whip, was 'nobbling our men'.

[45] Op. cit., 127–33.

[46] For an interesting discussion of this point, see Martin Gilbert, *The Roots of Appeasement* (London, 1966), 43ff. Lloyd George's views are given in Lloyd George to Bonar Law, 31 March 1919 (Lloyd George papers, F/30/3/40), 'Confidential', which covers Reparations, Danzig and the Rhineland.

he managed to secure a plebiscite which ensured that Germany retained about two-thirds of the territory in dispute. For three years thereafter, with limited assistance from his foreign secretary, Curzon, Lloyd George strove to bring Germany into the comity of nations; to wind up the Allied invasion of Soviet Russia, and to change its pariah status; to restore European trade, credit and monetary stability. In all these respects, the failure of the Genoa conference in April–May 1922 – an inevitable failure after the Rapallo pact between the Soviet Union and the Weimar republic – was a disaster for Europe. It was ironic that the Chanak crisis in the Dardanelles in October 1922, when the British government undoubtedly did pursue a belligerently pro-Greek policy against the Turks in Asia Minor, brought about the downfall of the coalition government, since this was very much at variance with the general spirit of its foreign policy.

There was a moderate tone to other aspects of the government's policies. It was an administration which pursued disarmament, at countless international conferences and in the 1922 Washington naval agreement on capital ship construction. It pursued peace in India: General Dyer was dismissed after the massacre at Amritsar. It eventually pursued peace in Ireland, where, after the disastrous retaliatory policies of the 'Black and Tans' (perhaps the saddest episode in his entire career), Lloyd George achieved a remarkable (and, I believe, still defensible) settlement with the Sinn Fein leaders in December 1921.[47] At home, it was a government of social reform. Its leader was anxious to repel the die-hards and to beat off the challenge of 'Bolshevism' by constructive and progressive policies. So there followed Addison's housing schemes (admittedly financially unsound), Fisher's Education Act, general unemployment insurance in 1920, increased old age pensions, the new Ministry of Health in 1919, new quasi-Keynesian policies to promote trade and employment.[48] Certainly, many of these reforms owed more to the coalition Liberals in the government – men like Addison, Montagu, Fisher and Mond – than to Lloyd George himself, who was mainly preoccupied with foreign affairs.[49] Admittedly also, the swinging of the Geddes axe in 1922 savaged all these schemes, and set back a coherent social policy for the next two decades. Still, Lloyd George with some justice defended his government's record to C. P. Scott in December 1922 as

[47]The best account is still in Frank Pakenham, *Peace by Ordeal* (London, new edn., 1962). Also see K. Middlemas (ed.), *Thomas Jones: Whitehall Diary*, Vol. III (Oxford, 1971), 119–83.

[48]There is a helpful account of some of these measures in Bentley Gilbert, *British Social Policy, 1914–1939* (London, 1970), especially chapters II and III.

[49]I have discussed the role of the coalition Liberals in 'Lloyd George's stage army', Taylor (ed.), *Lloyd George: Twelve Essays*, 225–54.

a liberal (and Liberal) one. 'I cannot accept the part often proposed to me as a traitor to Liberalism who can only be taken back as a penitent.'[50] The government's record on the social front, especially, compares favourably with the timid generalities uttered by the Asquithians at the same period, apprehensive as they were of rising government spending and zealous for 'anti-waste'. In 1918–22, the New Liberalism made its last heroic stand.

Yet Lloyd George's post-war government clearly was a failure. It failed in part because it had no meaningful party political base. The failure to achieve a 'fusion' of the coalition Liberal and Unionist parties was a significant one.[51] The coalition government was not to be underpinned by a 'National' party, and its leader had now no clear long-term future. There was also something more fundamental. In 1919–22 Lloyd George destroyed his 'special relationship' with organized labour, which had been a vital thread in his career ever since his triumphs as an industrial conciliator while at the Board of Trade in 1905–8. His handling of the 1919 Sankey Commission on the coalmines; his undermining of the Triple Alliance on 'Black Friday' in 1921; his mindless attacks on 'Bolshevists and Pacifists' in the labour movement, leading him even to compare Arthur Henderson and J. R. Clynes with Lenin and Trotsky[52] – all this meant that for large sections of the working-class electorate Lloyd George could no longer be regarded as a credible leader of the British left.

Fourthly, Lloyd George's career in the inter-war period between 1922 and 1939 needs far more study. Often it has been wrongly regarded as 'a long diminuendo'. In 1939, Professor Gwyn Jones (reviewing Watkin Davies's biography) referred to Lloyd George as 'the sarcophagus of Radical Liberalism, not its symbol'.[53] In fact, Lloyd George was clearly a dominant and uniquely creative figure throughout this period: if Churchill isolated himself in the thirties by his conservatism, Lloyd George did so, in part, by his radicalism. In some ways he overshadowed British politics in the 1920s: Baldwin and MacDonald both represented reactions against his premiership. *We Can Conquer Unemployment*, in which Lloyd George and Keynes outlined new 'pump-priming' schemes to combat economic recession,

[50]C. P. Scott's diary, 16 December 1922 (British Library Add. MSS., 50906, ff. 207–8).

[51]Cf. 'Lloyd George's stage army', loc. cit., 246–8.

[52]*The Times, Manchester Guardian*, 19 March 1920. Lady Violet Bonham-Carter countered: 'When I think of Mr. Clynes and Mr. Henderson, my flesh positively refuses to creep.'

[53]*Welsh Review*, I (3) (April 1939). The writer adds: 'It is plain fact that for men and women of the reviewer's age, Mr. Lloyd George has counted for next to nothing in public life.' Professor Jones was born in 1907.

dominated the 1929 general election: unfortunately, the electors voted for 'safety first' with MacDonald, Baldwin and the big battalions. As C. F. G. Masterman truly wrote to his wife in 1926: 'When Lloyd George came back to the Party, ideas came back to the Party.'[54] In 1935 Lloyd George's 'Council of Action for Peace and Reconstruction' (produced when he was seventy-two) was taken sufficiently seriously for him almost to enter the government in April–May 1935; but the hostility of Baldwin and Chamberlain was implacable.[55] In the later 1930s, Lloyd George was a major critic both of the domestic and of the foreign policies of the National government. He was the protagonist of a British 'New Deal' on the American model, and an inspiration to younger men like Robert Boothby and Dingle Foot.[56] His credibility, without doubt, was much weakened by his gullible attitude towards Hitler in the mid-thirties. His famous visit to Germany in the summer of 1936, when he met Hitler at Berchtesgaden, and investigated public works schemes, in many ways contrasts sharply with the famous earlier visit in 1908. After his return he inadvisedly referred to Hitler in the *Sunday Express* as the 'George Washington of Germany'.[57] This euphoric tribute (which Lloyd George came to regret) may well have been the product of his despair at western democracy in the 1930s which could allow itself to be led by men like Neville Chamberlain (such a pale imitation of his father, the hero of Lloyd George's youth). 'Not a bad mayor of Birmingham in a lean year'. Even so, Lloyd George's pronouncements on foreign affairs in the 1938–40 period had a profound effect. He attacked the Munich agreements. He was a trenchant critic of the guarantee to Poland in March 1939 which, he showed, was meaningless without agreement with the Soviet Union.[58] He played his part in the downfall of Chamberlain in May 1940. He might well have entered Churchill's War Cabinet in June; alternatively he might have become ambassador to Washington in succession to his old friend, Lord Lothian, the following December.[59] Undoubtedly, we need a thorough historical study of Lloyd George's overall role in the politics of the inter-war period. There are some fascinating hints here in Thomas Jones's published diaries, while his private papers in Aberystwyth show that

[54]Lucy Masterman, *C. F. G. Mastermann* (London, 1939), 345–6.

[55]K. Middlemas and John Barnes, *Baldwin* (London, 1969), 808–10; *Lloyd George: A Diary by Frances Stevenson*, 305–11.

[56]Cf. Robert Boothby, *I Fight to Live* (London, 1947), 26–33.

[57]*Sunday Express*, 17 September 1936.

[58]*Parl. Deb.*, 5th ser., 345, 2505–11 (3 April 1939).

[59]Paul Addison, 'Lloyd George and compromise peace in the Second World War', *Lloyd George: Twelve Essays*, 372–5. This chapter is an excellent analysis of Lloyd George's attitudes to foreign policy issues in the 1936–44 period.

much of the post-1922 material in his biography of Lloyd George was excised to satisfy the demands of his publishers.[60]

Finally, historians should look again at Lloyd George's Welsh background and its influence upon his career. It is surely untrue that he was 'rooted in nothing' as Keynes alleged. Rather was he rooted in a world Keynes never knew, the populist radicalism of rural Wales in the late nineteenth century. Wales is a consistent thread in his career – the land question, the Nonconformist chapels, the popular press were all constant influences. Yet the nature of this Welsh background has too often been misunderstood. He is often taken as a highly typical product of late nineteenth-century Welsh radicalism. After all, he was brought up in an Anglican school; he took a leading role in the Llanfrothen burial case; he was a democratic and anti-clerical back-bencher; he was, unlike many other Welshmen, an ardent pro-Boer; he spearheaded the Welsh county councils' 'revolt' against Balfour's Education Act of 1902. His career seems to be a kind of parable of the Welsh national movement as a whole.

Yet in reality Lloyd George was a very untypical Welsh radical. Just as he was a great outsider in British politics, so in many ways he was a great outsider in Welsh society and politics also. His background was unusual. Almost every other leading Welsh Liberal of the period – Tom Ellis (Aberystwyth and New College, Oxford), Ellis Griffith (Aberystwyth and Downing, Cambridge), Samuel Evans (Aberystwyth), Herbert Lewis (McGill and Exeter, Oxford), Llewelyn Williams (Brasenose, Oxford), Frank Edwards (Jesus, Oxford), D. A. Thomas (Gonville and Caius, Cambridge) – was university-educated. Lloyd George, by contrast, had virtually no higher education: he was self-educated and self-made, with a natural bias in favour of the common sense of the common man. This gave him a unique independent perspective of his own. Again, he was often critical of the Welsh Nonconformist chapels, even though ministers such as the Revd John Williams, Brynsiencyn, and Dr Thomas Charles Williams, were close friends. In August 1890 Lloyd George tells his young wife of his dislike of 'being cramped in a suffocating, malodorous chapel, listening to some superstitions I had heard thousands of times before'.[61] His correspondence reveals his contempt for the arid puritanism of the chapels, and the petty snobberies of the 'glorified grocers' on the *sêt*

---

[60]Donald C. McKay to Thomas J. Wilson, 6 August 1948 (NLW, Thomas Jones papers, A, Vol. I, f. 79).
    [61]David Lloyd George to Mrs Lloyd George, 13 August 1890 (NLW, Lloyd George papers, 20,407C, f. 126).

fawr.[62] He was anxious that *Cymru Fydd* should be a totally secular movement, and free from domination by Nonconformist clericalism. Again, he was unmoved by many other aspects of Welsh life at the time. He had no real interest in Welsh culture or its literature. His appearances at the eisteddfod were ceremonial and quasi-political: indeed, he was a supremely political man with scant concern for the arts. Nor was Lloyd George much involved in those great Welsh campaigns in the 1880s and 1890s for higher education. He had little to say on this in the House, apart from using it as an occasional weapon to belabour the Church of England. Arthur Humphreys-Owen, MP, a great ally of the University of Wales, wrote not unfairly to Lord Rendel in 1905: 'Having had no literary education himself, [Lloyd George] is unable to realise the needs of the education system. He regards it simply as a political scaffolding.'[63]

And yet, as Frances Lloyd-George's diary makes transparently clear,[64] Lloyd George was passionately and consistently caught up in Welsh affairs, even as prime minister. In particular, more than any other leading Welsh Liberal of the day, he had sympathy with political nationalism. After all, he was in part a disciple of Michael Daniel Jones.[65] Lloyd George assumed command of the *Cymru Fydd* movement in 1894 and tried to turn it into an avowedly separatist direction. He sought to divert the education 'revolt' in 1903–5 into a devolutionist movement for a national Education Council for Wales. There were echoes of the earlier nationalism in the 1920s, as when he tried to persuade Sir Francis Edwards in 1926 to revive the old 'Welsh Party' of the 1890s.[66] Sir Alfred Davies described him at this period as 'a narrow Welsh nationalist'.[67] Lloyd George reacted furiously to the transference to London of the case of Saunders Lewis and his two

[62]Cf. David Lloyd George to Mrs Lloyd George, 10 June 1890 (NLW, ibid., 20,406C, f. 98). For the term 'glorified grocers', see Lucy Masterman, op. cit., 200: Lloyd George tells Balfour in 1911, 'I know that our glorified grocers will be more hostile to social reform than your Backwoodsmen'.

[63]A. C. Humphreys-Owen to Lord Rendel, 18 June 1905 (NLW, Rendel papers, XIV, f. 704a).

[64]Op. cit., 15, 288–9 and *passim*.

[65]Beriah Gwynfe Evans, op. cit., 19; J. Hugh Edwards, *Life of Lloyd George* (London, 1913), Vol. II, 132–3. For the famous meeting at Blaenau Ffestiniog when Michael D. Jones, Michael Davitt and the young Lloyd George spoke, see *Y Celt*, 19 February 1886.

[66]David Lloyd George to Sir Francis Edwards, 11 March 1926 (H. of L. Record Office, Lloyd George papers, G/6/11/13). I have published this letter (of which the copyright is owned by the Beaverbrook Foundation) in full in 'Twilight of Welsh Liberalism, 1918–1935' *Bulletin of the Board of Celtic Studies*, XXXII (IV) (1968), 404.

[67]*The Lloyd George I Knew*, 124.

Plaid Cymru colleagues in 1936. 'This is the first government that has tried Wales at the Old Bailey.' It flinched before Mussolini but was prepared to bully 'gallant little Wales'.[68] Lloyd George's shade, one surmises, might not have been wholly displeased with the result of the Carmarthenshire by-election in July 1966, which saw the end of the Lloyd George tradition in Welsh politics!

Now one would not argue that he could be categorized in a fundamental sense as a Welsh nationalist: that would be somewhat absurd for one who became prime minister of Britain for six years, and who very much wanted to become premier again. But, unlike, for instance, Tom Ellis, the friend of the Webbs, the high-minded 'Co-efficients' and the Liberal Imperialist patricians, Lloyd George was not sufficiently an admirer of English or of imperial institutions to think that national equality for Wales within the United Kingdom was sufficient. He was a persistent and irreverent critic of Parliament, of the parties, of the court,[69] of the civil service, of the chiefs of staff, with basic roots in the warm populism of his Criccieth home. Dame Margaret was undoubtedly an important influence here, keeping him true to the old values. Welsh sentiment was, I would argue, a vehicle for Lloyd George's deep discontent with the political and social structure of *fin-de-siècle* Britain. Perhaps this made his downfall all the more inevitable in 1922. But it also made his outlook in many ways far more truly radical than that of the Labour party, which has been generally very conservative in its attitude towards British institutions. Certainly, one can see what Bonar Law had in mind when he described Lloyd George (for whose leadership he had immense admiration) as 'the most dangerous little man who ever lived'.

The interpretation of Lloyd George's extraordinary career is a never-ending process. There is a need both to explore individual episodes (such as the events of 1–7 December 1916) in minute detail, and also to try to view his career as a whole – to see how and why, for instance, the leader of *Cymru Fydd* in the 1890s turned into the champion of the Council of Action in the 1930s. Lord Boothby has noted Lloyd

[68]David Lloyd George to Megan Lloyd George, 1 December 1936 (NLW, Lloyd George papers, 20,475C, f. 3151). Lloyd George was writing at the time from Montego Bay, Jamaica.

[69]Cf. David Lloyd George to Mrs Lloyd George, 16 September 1911 (NLW, ibid., 20,430C, f. 1385). Here Lloyd George, writing from Balmoral, complained that 'the whole atmosphere reeks with Toryism. I can breathe it and it depresses and sickens me'. However he seems to have got on well personally at this time with the king and queen. But during the First World War, George V's open sympathy for Haig and Robertson (which was freely confided to President Wilson via Colonel House) caused very strained relations between the prime minister and the court.

George's mutability about persons but his immutability about things and objectives.[70] It may well be that an extended survey will reveal a deep inner consistency about Lloyd George's career.

Perhaps two final thoughts will assist towards an understanding of him. First of all, he was unusual in being a radical who could use power. Unlike, for example, Keir Hardie or William Jennings Bryan, he was not just a prophet or an instrument of popular protest. He was an artist in the uses of power, as effective in government as in opposition. As in the case of the National Insurance Bill in 1911, his crusades were never merely destructive or denunciatory, but were linked to broad long-term social objectives and were harnessed to immense executive ability.

And secondly, Lloyd George might with advantage be assessed in future in extra-British or international terms. Many of his critics were essentially 'Little Englanders' (even those of them who came from Wales), convinced of the ultimate rightness of Englishness and of English values. Witness Watkin Davies stressing in 1939 'the great ideals which uphold the British Commonwealth':[71] someone from my more disillusioned, post-war generation can only marvel at his certainty. Perhaps we ought to view Lloyd George in a far wider, international context, and see him as one of the great mass leaders of the modern world. Like Eric Hoffer's *True Believer*, like Lincoln, Gandhi or Roosevelt, he could 'harness men's hungers and fears . . . in the service of a holy cause'.[72] Lloyd George, certainly, would have been immediately intelligible in the context of American politics. He could combine the democratic passion of the agrarian Populists in the south and west with the use of 'broad executive power' by the urban Progressives of the east. He was William Jennings Bryan and Theodore Roosevelt rolled into one, a prairie radical and a 'New Nationalist'. At the same time, he was conspicuously free from much of Bryan's provincialism or from 'T.R.'s' more strident racism. Possibly the analogy

[70]Robert Boothby, op. cit., 29, citing Lord d'Abernon.

[71]*Lloyd George, 1863–1914*, 18–19. It must be said that, in this passage, the author compares Lloyd George favourably with Owen M. Edwards whom he accuses of 'narrow nationalism'. Davies was an active lecturer for the League of Nations Union in the 1920s.

[72]Cited in T. Harry Williams, *Huey Long* (New York, 1970), 436–7. I am indebted to Professor Williams for drawing my attention to Hoffer's penetrating monograph. In conversations with Professor Williams, we have both been struck by certain similarities between Huey Long's brand of agrarian radicalism and some of the techniques and ideals of Lloyd George. I would not, however, claim Lloyd George to be the 'Kingfish' of Wales!

between Franklin D. Roosevelt in the thirties and Lloyd George's quasi-presidential techniques provides a better comparison still.[73]

Perhaps historians over the next thirty years – years when presumably our membership of the European Community will, for good or for ill, have made further inroads into our insularity – may find Lloyd George less puzzling and more intelligible. Perhaps they may be able to arrive at a fuller and fairer appreciation of how and why he carried Britain kicking and screaming into the twentieth century. But, perhaps, even then an ultimate understanding of David Lloyd George, and his restless creative genius, will be only just beginning.

1972

[73] I am indebted to Mr Roy Jenkins for this comparison. In my view, Lloyd George particularly admired Franklin Roosevelt's New Deal in so far as it appeared to be the heir of Theodore Roosevelt's New Nationalism of 1912. Lloyd George greatly respected Theodore Roosevelt (whom he met twice) both for his vigorous nationalism and for his assertion of executive power. In particular, the concept of using non-partisan commissions to look scientifically at such issues as tariffs and trusts greatly appealed to Lloyd George. He advocated something similar himself in his coalition proposals for national reorganization in the summer of 1910. On the other hand, he criticized Theodore Roosevelt after his defeat in the 1912 presidential election: 'he ought not to have quarrelled with the machine' (Harold Spender, op. cit., 359). In the years after 1918 Lloyd George might well have remembered the fate of the 'Bull Moosers' in the United States. Lloyd George applied the term 'New Deal' to his own 'Council of Action' proposals in early 1935. But a study of his specific schemes suggests that they were largely based on his own plans of the late 1920s, rather than a direct borrowing from Roosevelt's New Deal about which Lloyd George was relatively ill-informed. But certainly in his quasi-presidential methods, in his use of 'brains trusts' and of the media of mass communication Lloyd George resembles both Roosevelts.

21

Lloyd George
and Welsh Liberalism

No political figure more comprehensively justifies a conference being devoted to studying his career and outlook than does David Lloyd George. As Churchill rightly declared to the Commons at the time of his old ally's death in March, 1945,[1] Lloyd George was the central personality in early twentieth-century British history, and indeed one of the great mass leaders of the modern age. Hitherto he has inspired over a hundred biographical works, along with thousands of other monographs and studies. This is, indeed, the second volume devoted uniquely to a series of Lloyd George studies: the first, edited by Mr A. J. P. Taylor (to which the present writer also contributed) was published in 1971.[2] And yet the mystery of his career, the controversies and enigmas of his outlook, style and personality remain. Historians are not that much nearer 'painting the chameleon' or 'tethering the broomstick' than when Keynes first wrote his brilliant, if highly misleading, 'essay in biography' shortly after the Treaty of Versailles in 1919.[3]

This article will concentrate on at least one feature of Lloyd George which is generally acknowledged even if the interpretations of it vary enormously – namely the centrality to his career of this association with Wales. He was, without question, the most important and influential Welsh politician who has ever lived. He is the only Welshman who has been prime minister. As a party politician in time

---

[1] *Parl. Deb.*, 5th ser., 409, 1335.
[2] A. J. P. Taylor (ed.), *Lloyd George: Twelve Essays* (London, 1971).
[3] J. M. Keynes, *Essays in Biography* (London, 1961), 32–3.

of peace and of war, as chancellor, minister of munitions and supremely as prime minister his impact on domestic politics and on social policy was immense. For a time, perhaps between the summer of 1919 and the late autumn of 1921, he was the most important politician in the world. In the Soviet Union, in Ireland, in India, in the founding of Palestine, in the Middle East, his legacy is still direct and powerful. The crisis surrounding Iraq's occupation of Kuwait in the summer of 1990 was yet another political consequence of Lloyd George, since it flowed from his original definition of the boundaries of Mesopotamia, made up of the *vilayets* of Basra, Baghdad and Mosul, in 1921. His mighty shadow looms over Saddam Hussein.

Yet, throughout all these great events, he was transcendently associated with Wales. He created, single-handed, much of its national rhetoric and sense of identity. More than anyone else in Welsh life between the 1860s and 1914, he symbolized the revolutionary impact of democracy, national and local. He came to transcend normal partisan and class differences since his admirers ranged from the Communist preacher/agitator/bard, the Revd Thomas Nicholas, Glais, to the serpentine Bishop A. G. Edwards, first archbishop of Wales.

He was closely identified with the political advance of Wales in highly personal terms. Long before the outbreak of war in 1914, there was a veritable cult of Lloyd George, almost resembling the cult of Hawarden in Gladstone's later years. There was the annual triumphal visitation to the Eisteddfod on 'Lloyd George's Day'; the family association with Castle Street Baptist church; fond boyhood tales of climbing, swimming in the Dwyfor, and (implicitly) poaching. There was indeed a good deal of romanticism in the way the Lloyd George legend was projected by early biographers such as J. Hugh Edwards or Beriah Gwynfe Evans.[4] Before 1914, his very identification with Wales, indeed, was a source of strength, the personification of grass-roots populism, in the saga of the 'cottage-bred boy' who trod the primrose path from Llanystumdwy to Downing Street. He took on the 'unholy Trinity' of the bishops, the brewers, and the squires (afforced by the backwoodsmen of the House of Lords) and laid them low as that earlier David had slain the Philistines.

Yet after the First World War, Lloyd George's identification with Wales became increasingly a source of weakness. His methods as prime minister, his un-English disregard for institutional propriety, his contempt for the honours system, made him increasingly suspect.[5]

[4] J. Hugh Edwards, *From the Village Green to Downing Street: The Life of the Rt. Hon. D. Lloyd George* (London, 1908); Beriah Gwynfe Evans, *The Life Romance of Lloyd George* (London: n.d. [1916]).

[5] See especially G. R. Searle, *Corruption in British Politics, 1895–1930* (Oxford, Clarendon Press, 1987), 350ff.

After all, Taffy was supreme among thieves, while T. H. W. Crosland (not to mention Caradoc Evans) currently expounded the theme of the 'unspeakable Celt'. Lloyd George's very virtues as a Welsh outsider, now came to be widely seen as defects. With his unorthodox private life as well, he was made a personal scapegoat for the wider decline of Welsh and British Liberalism, perhaps the decline of Britain itself since 1918. This theme became fashionable even amongst his fellow Welsh Liberals. In 1937 there appeared *Wales Drops the Pilots* by the literary critic, W. Hughes Jones, 'Elidir Sais'. He dwelt lovingly on the nationalist crusade waged by Tom Ellis and the young Lloyd George back in 1890s. But the book was really an implicit attack on Lloyd George himself for neglecting the ideals of his own youth, the ideals of *Cymru Fydd* and the Wales that was to be.[6] Even more was it an attack on the Welsh of their generation for failure to respond to their youthful champions.

In his emergence as a politician, Lloyd George was intimately caught up in that immense Welsh political resurgence that took place between the general election of 1868 and that of 1906, which saw the land of Wales left with no Tory member at all, and only Keir Hardie in Merthyr interrupting the solid mass of Liberals. Lloyd George was deeply caught up in this Liberal ascendancy. Far from being 'rooted in nothing' as Keynes falsely claimed,[7] he was rooted in a political culture far removed from the acquaintance of 'the Apostles' and a fellow of King's. Lloyd George was certainly more intimately enmeshed with Welsh politics and society in the later nineteenth century than was Tom Ellis, who went to New College, Oxford, and served as the adviser of Liberal politicians in London.[8] The comparison applied all the more strongly to the leader of the Welsh Liberals at the time of Lloyd George's first election to Parliament in April 1890, Stuart Rendel, an Englishman, and Anglican and, amazingly, an arms manufacturer.[9]

Lloyd George was a politician from the age of five. His first memory was of the great Liberal victory in Caernarfonshire in 1868, when he was carried on Uncle Lloyd's shoulder to election meetings. He referred to this at the time of the fight for the 'people's budget' in

---

[6]W. Hughes Jones, *Wales Drops the Pilots* (London, 1937), especially 88–90.

[7]Keynes, op. cit., 36.

[8]See Kenneth O. Morgan, 'Tom Ellis versus Lloyd George: the fractured consciousness of *fin-de-siècle* Wales', in Geraint H. Jenkins and J. Beverley Smith (eds.), *Politics and Society in Wales* (Cardiff, 1988), 91ff. (published in this volume, 360–79.

[9]Kenneth O. Morgan, 'The member for Wales: Stuart Rendel (1834–1913)', *Transactions of the Honourable Society of Cymmrodorion* (1984), 105ff (published in this volume, 339–59).

1910.[10] As a young schoolboy at Llanystumdwy National School he came into conflict with the Anglican authorities, not least in organizing a kind of strike amongst the pupils as a protest against reciting the Creed – in effect against clerical and squirearchical control. He became articled as a solicitor in Portmadoc, an admirable base for a career in late nineteenth-century politics, and was later active in political protest movements like the anti-tithe campaign in southern Llŷn. He participated in local journalism and briefly founded a new radical newspaper, *Udgorn Rhyddid*, the 'Trumpet of Freedom', with his friend, D. R. Daniel.[11] He entered local government as the 'boy alderman' on the first Caernarfonshire county council in 1889. In the North Wales Liberal Federation, he represented a kind of militant tendency, denouncing his own party's leadership for failing to devote sufficient attention and priority to disestablishment and the other demands of Wales.[12] He was elected to Parliament in the famous by-election at Caernarfon Boroughs in April 1890 on a strongly national-istic programme, including Church disestablishment, and land, temperance, and education reform.[13] He appeared to be, therefore, the most typical product of Welsh Liberalism at its most buoyant and determined.

Yet it is crucial to the understanding of Lloyd George as a Welsh Liberal to see that, even in these very early years (and, after all, he was only twenty-seven when he entered Parliament for all his frenetic activity), he was a maverick and an outsider, even in Wales.

In the first place, he was an outsider even in the world of Welsh Nonconformity. He was, after all, a Campbellite Baptist, a minority within a minority, a fringe sect of strongly radical persuasion. Further he viewed with scorn the social pretensions and petty jealousies of chapel life – the 'glorified grocers' and 'beatified drapers' of the big seat.[14] He complained to his young wife of 'being cramped up in a

[10]Speech at Queen's Hall, 23 March 1910, quoted in *Better Times* (London, 1910). 'It woke the spirit of the mountains, the genius of freedom that fought the might of the Normans . . . The political power of landlordism in Wales was shattered as effectively as the power of the Druids.'

[11]Lloyd George to D. R. Daniel, 12 December 1887 (National Library of Wales, Aberystwyth, Daniel papers, 2744); Emyr Price, 'Newyddiadur cyntaf David Lloyd George', *Journal of the Welsh Bibliographical Society*, XI (1975), 207ff.

[12]North Wales Liberal Federation minute-book, 1887–92 (NLW).

[13]See Emyr Price, 'Lloyd George and the Caernarvon Boroughs Election of 1890', *Transactions of the Caernarvonshire Historical Society*, XXXVI (1975).

[14]D. Lloyd George to Mrs Lloyd George, 10 June 1890 (NLW, Lloyd George papers, 20, 406, f.98), for 'beatified drapers'. For 'glorified grocers', see Lucy Masterman, *C. F. G. Masterman*, repr. (London, 1968), 200: Lloyd George told Balfour in 1911, 'I know that our glorified grocers will be more hostile to social reform than your Backwoodsmen'.

suffocating, malodorous chapel listening to some superstitions I had heard thousands of times before'.[15]. He had some tension with his father-in-law, his wife, and his brother, William, on this point. Truly Lloyd George was no puritan. His daughter, Lady Olwen, was to observe much later that her father really only went through the motions as far as religious observance was concerned.[16] He was a free-thinker in religion, as in finance.

Secondly, although the leader of a rural radicalism, a kind of British version of American mid-west or southern populism, David Lloyd George was never truly an agrarian figure. He knew little directly of farming – another point of tension with his father-in-law. Only in his old age did he go in for market gardening and small-scale horticultural production in Churt. Far from being a typically rural figure, on the model of Tom Ellis, he represented rather the aspirations and ambitions of the small-town bourgeoisie.

Again, he had only a scant interest in the cultural or literary aspects of the Welsh nationalism of his youth. He was very different in spirit from Tom Ellis or Llewelyn Williams, both of them of scholarly inclination and deeply versed in Welsh antiquities, history, and poetry. Lloyd George had relatively scant concern with Welsh literary or musical culture, other than the lusty singing of Welsh hymns. Nor did he have any particular involvement with moves to protect the Welsh language – although it should be said that Lloyd George in this respect was typical of virtually every Liberal of his time since there was not the same anxiety about 'the fate of the language' of the kind that emerged in the inter-war period.[17] Lloyd George's approach to Welsh culture was genuine enough, but it was the result of knowledge gained by upbringing, personal contact and conversation. It was instinctive and intuitive, rather than intellectual. At times, it was plain sentimental.

And finally, he was a maverick even in the world of Welsh politics. From his earliest rebellious entry into Parliament, he was a member of what used to be called in the army 'the awkward squad'. When Rosebery's government appeared slow in taking up the cause of disestablishment, he briefly resigned the party whip, along with Herbert Lewis, Frank Edwards, and D. A. Thomas, in April 1894.[18] He failed to support his party in key divisions on the Welsh

[15]David Lloyd George to Mrs Lloyd George, 13 August 1890 (NLW, Lloyd George papers, 20,407C, f. 126).

[16]Lady Olwen Carey-Evans, *Lloyd George was my Father* (Llandysul, 1985).

[17]There was a useful pressure-group, *Cymdeithas yr Iaith Gymraeg*, 'The Society for the Utilization of the Welsh Language', with Beriah Gwynfe Evans as secretary, but it was a body of scholars and educationalists in the main.

[18]Kenneth O. Morgan, *Wales in British Politics, 1868–1922* (3rd edn., Cardiff, 1980), 144–5.

Disestablishment Bill committee stage in June 1895 – when the Liberals had a majority in the house of only two![19] He was always liable to engage in covert negotiations with Bishop A. G. Edwards or other clerical enemies, as in 1895 or in 1903.[20] Like his hero, Theodore Roosevelt,[21] he was not at all a 'party regular'.

From the time of his entry into Parliament in 1890, he promoted all the main national themes, and took up all the main points on the Welsh Liberal agenda. But he did so in a manner distinctly his own. On most of the key issues of the time, he supplied his own nuances and twists. More than almost any other key Liberal of the time, he related the major issues on the Welsh national programme to aspects of social class, the maldistribution of property, and of political and economic power. Thus he placed his own stamp on a succession of key issues.

On the central issue of Welsh land, he took a distinctly different view from fellow Liberals such as Tom Ellis, Llewelyn Williams, or Ellis Griffiths. They focused on tenurial aspects, on landlord-tenant relations within a relatively static rural class structure. Lloyd George was rather anxious for the disestablishment of the landlords, no less than of the Church. He followed with enthusiasm the campaign of the Revd E. Pan Jones of Mostyn for land nationalization in the columns of Y Celt.[22] It was the agrarian socialism, as much as the Irish nationalism of Michael Davitt, with whom he shared a famous platform at Ffestiniog in February 1886, that appealed to him.[23] In his 'people's budget' in 1909 he took up the theme of land taxation, and attempted, though in vain, to tax the 'unearned increment' acquired by landlords as a result of general urban development. In his even more remarkable budget of 1914, one deflected by procedural and other problems in the House, he tried for the first time to make land taxation an integral feature of the fiscal system,[24] mainly through the taxing of site value. For modern readers, it might be added that one option which he totally rejected as impracticable and socially regressive was that of a poll-tax, even if disguised under the soubriquet of 'community charge'.[25]

---

[19]Ibid., 152–3.

[20]Eluned E. Owen, *The Life of Bishop Owen* (Llandysul, 1961), 179–81; J. Arthur Price to Tom Ellis, 21 January 1895 (NLW, Ellis papers, 1701).

[21]See D. Lloyd George, *The Truth about the Peace Treaties, II* (London 1938), 232 for his reaction to Roosevelt's death and Wilson's cold response in 1919.

[22]See Peris Jones Evans, 'Evan Pan Jones – land reformer', *Welsh History Review*, 4 (2) (1968), 143ff.

[23]W. R. P. George, *The Making of Lloyd George* (London, 1976), 129–30.

[24]Budget speech of 4 May 1914.

[25]See Bruce K. Murray, 'Lloyd George, the Navy estimates and the inclusion of

Another theme in which he took his own course was that of
education. He largely stood outside the great inter-party movement for
secondary and higher education, which absorbed so many Welsh
Liberals at the time – Rendel, Ellis, Herbert Lewis, Arthur
Humphreys-Owen to name but a few. It was a movement which
yielded great results – the 1889 Intermediate Education Act, which
created the famous 'county schools', the Central Welsh Board, the
Welsh university colleges at Aberystwyth and later at Bangor and
Cardiff, the national and federal University of Wales in 1893.
Although a schoolmaster's son, Lloyd George saw education more as a
political weapon, and kept aloof from these educational campaigns.
Humphreys-Owen was to complain during the county councils 'revolt'
against the Balfour Education Act of 1902: 'Having no literary
education himself he is unable to realize the needs of the education
system.'[26] Not until around 1914, when Haldane worked on him and
persuaded him to create the basis of the University Grants Committee,
did Lloyd George involve himself more fully in public education for its
own sake.[27] Even then, his earlier background continued to assert
itself. During the discussions on economies in educational and other
public expenditure on the Geddes committee in 1921, when he was
prime minister, Lloyd George was still cavalier about such matters as
the school entry age and the size of classes.[28] 'He was sure that the
brighter children would learn just as quickly and readily in a class of
seventy as they would in a much smaller class.' He would continue to
uphold the common sense of the self-taught common man, rather than
arid learning, or scholarship – though that did not prevent his winning
the devotion of great scholars such as the historian, Herbert Fisher,
and the philosopher, Sir Henry Jones.

Much of the same applied to another shibboleth of many Welsh
Liberals – local government. An idealist like Tom Ellis saw the county
councils created in 1889 as the instruments of populism. He compared
them to small autonomous communities like the Tyrol, the Swiss
cantons – or the Boer republics. Other Liberals like Herbert Lewis or
Arthur Humphreys-Owen had detailed and expert first-hand know-

rating relief in the 1914 budget', *Welsh History Review*, 15 (1) (1990).

[26]A. C. Humphreys-Owen to Stuart, Lord Rendel, 18 June 1905 (NLW, Rendel
papers, xiv. 704a).

[27]Eric Ashby and Mary Anderson, *Portrait of Haldane at Work on Education*,
(London, 1974), 114–18. Lloyd George and Haldane had earlier clashed on
educational policy: 'Land not education was the next great subject to be taken up
by the government' (ibid., 115).

[28]*Report, Proceedings and Memoranda of the Cabinet Committee . . . on Public
Expenditure*, 22 Jan. 1922 (Public Record Office, CAB 27/165).

ledge of how local government really worked and its potentialities.[29] Lloyd George did not. He played little part in the Caernarfonshire county council to which he was elected an alderman in 1899, and was only indirectly involved with the expansion of the Welsh local government, rural or urban, in the 1890s. Then, in the rebellion against the 1902 Balfour Education Act, in the period 1903–5, he emerged as the leader of the Welsh county councils, all of them with a Liberal majority from February 1904.[30] But this was because of their political potential in undermining the Tory government and frustrating its educational reforms. Again, he developed his interests more fully in mid-career. His 'people's budget' of 1909 was in part designed to relieve the pressing burdens of local government finance, with the enormous pressures impinging on local authorities as their welfare and other responsibilities expanded.[31] But here again was a key issue in the Welsh Liberal agenda where Lloyd George followed his own line.

Again, on the dominant issue of Welsh Home Rule, Lloyd George's vision of *Cymru Fydd* in the 1890s was again distinctive. It had none of Tom Ellis's cultural/imperial overtones, with its adoration of the mystical nationalism of Giuseppe Mazzini or Thomas Davis.[32] The Irishman that most impressed Lloyd George was the agrarian radical Michael Davitt, not the philosopher, Thomas Davis. To him, *Cymru Fydd* was far from being the embodiment of a cultural or quasi-mystical ideal. Rather was it a totally realistic method of putting pressure on the Liberal party machine and on Liberal headquarters in London on behalf of the various Welsh national causes. Lloyd George saw the 'revolt' of 1894–6, the attempt to merge the Liberal Federations of North and South Wales within a 'Welsh National Federation' in strictly political terms. It was thus a narrowly conceived movement – and hence its downfall, in much acrimony. It collapsed after the ignominious South Wales Liberal Federation meeting at Newport in January 1896 when Lloyd George was howled down by the anglicized mercantile Liberals of the south Wales ports.[33] But the causes lay in wider factors than merely the regional rift between north and south Wales. Rather was there a fatal ambiguity, implicit in Lloyd George's vision of *Cymru Fydd*, between liberalism and nationalism. It

---

[29]See K. Idwal Jones (gol.) *Syr Herbert Lewis*, 1858–1933 (Caerdydd, 1959), 79ff., and, for Humphreys-Owen, the Glansevern papers, NLW, *passim*.

[30]Morgan, *Wales in British Politics*, 187–98; Gareth Elwyn Jones, 'The Welsh revolt revisited: Merioneth and Montgomeryshire in default', *Welsh History Review*, 14 (3) (1989), 417ff.

[31]See Bruce K. Murray, 'Lloyd George and the land' in J. A. Beynon *et al.* (eds.), *Studies in Local History* (Oxford, 1976), 37ff.

[32]See Neville Masterman, *The Forerunner* (Llandybïe, 1971), esp. 17–18.

[33]*South Wales Daily News*, 17 January 1896.

emerged that Welsh Liberalism was, in general, far from separatist. As a result, separatism, in however modest form, was not a major force in Welsh politics for the next seventy years, not until the devolution measures for Scotland and Wales put forward by the Callaghan government in the later 1970s. Lloyd George's version of Welsh self-government had dissolved. On the other hand, so had that of everybody else. Perhaps what Lloyd George's abortive *Cymru Fydd* campaign really achieved was to show that pressure for self-government in Wales was limited and largely sentimental. The defeat of devolution in 1979 was to confirm the point. *Cymru Fydd's* collapse thus demonstrated vividly to the world that Wales was not Ireland.

A final area where Lloyd George took his own course is perhaps more unfamiliar – the theme of empire. Contrary to what legend has sometimes maintained, the Welsh Liberals were in the main highly attracted to the appeal of empire.[34] In the 1890s they saw the expansion of the British empire as intimately linked with the progress of Wales out of poverty and neglect. This especially applied to 'imperial south Wales' where trade, industry and urban growth boomed in the wake of the transatlantic and imperial economy.[35] But it applied to much of Liberalism in north and mid Wales, also. Most Welsh Liberals emphatically supported the war against the Boer republics, the Orange Free State and the Transvaal, in 1899; men like Ellis Griffith or David Brynmor Jones were as imperialist as were Asquith or Rosebery. Lloyd George took quite the reverse view. He had been prepared to defend the expansion of British interests in Africa in the 1890s, though reluctant to oppose France in the Fashoda in the Sudan in 1898.[36] He was no 'little Englander' and indeed later in his career was the close associate of imperialist evangelists such as Philip Kerr or Lord Milner. He regarded the Boer War, though, as unjustified and unjust, the product of incompetent diplomacy, corrupt finance, and vainglorious jingoism. He withstood with passion and courage the hostility and violence of imperialist mobs, not only in Chamberlain's Birmingham but even in his own constituency. In the cathedral city of Bangor he had to flee from the frenzy of a jingo mob. He wrote to Herbert Lewis of how 'the mob were seized of a drunken madness and the police were helpless'.[37] It was indeed a distinctly minority position to be a 'pro-Boer' in Liberal Wales in 1990. By the end of the war in May 1902, the

[34]On this theme, see Kenneth O. Morgan, 'Wales and the Boer war – a reply', *Welsh History Review*, 4 (4) (1969), 367ff. (published in this volume, 46–58).

[35]For a brilliant discussion, see Gwyn A. Williams, *When was Wales?* (London, 1985), 221ff.

[36]Harold Spender, *The Fire of Life* (London, n.d. [1920]), 53 but cf. John Grigg, *The Young Lloyd George* (London, 1973), 223 for a different view.

[37]Lloyd George to Herbert Lewis, 13 April 1990 (NLW, Penucha MSS.)

sympathy aroused by the Boer 'guerrillas' and the distaste resulting from the death of women and children in Kitchener's concentration camps showed that the tide of opinion was turning in Lloyd George's favour. But at the time of Mafeking, in the face of the overwhelming imperialist passion of the Welsh press and politicians, it required courage indeed to stand up against the storm. It is truly amongst the most glorious passages in Lloyd George's career.

Lloyd George's heyday in Wales was the Edwardian period, if we may extend the period to continue down to 1914. It was for the Welsh nation a unique time of prosperity, influence, self-awareness and national pride.[38] Welsh industry reached new heights of productive growth, symbolized by the domination of Welsh steam coal in the world's export trade, and the colossal expansion of the ports of Cardiff and Barry in particular. Cardiff became a new metropolis, the bastion of 'King Coal'.[39] In Welsh cultural life, it was a period of extraordinary literary renaissance, of poets like T. Gwynn Jones and the young Parry-Williams, of scholars like Sir John Morris-Jones and Sir John Lloyd, of popular evangelists for the Welsh language like Sir Owen M. Edwards. In religion, Welsh Nonconformity reached its high noon, with the 'big guns' of the pulpit blazing away, and chapel membership inflated to unprecedented levels by the 1904–5 religious revival.

In politics, this national resurgence was perhaps the most dramatic of all, with Liberals virtually sweeping the board at the 1906 general election, and Welshmen prominent in the Liberal government. Lloyd George, president of the Board of Trade from December 1905, chancellor of the Exchequer from April, 1908, the most dynamic and charismatic politician of the day, symbolized all of this and more. In the later words of one excited Welsh journalist, he was 'the greatest Welshman yet born'.[40] With old age pensions, the people's budget, the Parliament Act, then National Health Insurance, triumph followed upon triumph.

Lloyd George's role, indeed, indicates that profound difference between England and Wales as political cultures in the early twentieth century. In Edwardian England, he was a deeply controversial and divisive figure. His onslaughts on the peers, land, and vested interests generally drew upon him the virulent opposition of Conservatives in general, from up-country squires to King George V. A *Punch* cartoon depicted him in the guise of John Knox, denouncing 'motorists, golfers

---

[38]See, generally, Kenneth O. Morgan, *Rebirth of a Nation: Wales, 1880–1980* (Oxford and Cardiff, 1981), ch. 5.

[39]M. J. Daunton, *Coal Metropolis: Cardiff 1870–1914* (Leicester, 1977).

[40]See generally *Wales*, 1911–14 edited by Lloyd George's biographer, J. Hugh Edwards, MP.

and all those miserable sinners who happen to own anything'.[41]
During the Marconi affair of 1912–13, when it emerged that the
chancellor had bought (and sold at a loss) some shares from the
Marconi company, which was shortly to be contracted to the British
government, his opponents came close to driving Lloyd George out of
public life for ever.[42]

By contrast, in his own Wales, Lloyd George was increasingly a
unifying force, a reflection in part of the almost blanket domination of
Welsh political and cultural life by the Liberal party. His prestige was
far from being confined to Gwynedd or to the rural areas; on the
contrary, while president of the Board of Trade, he was approached
about the Liberal candidacy for the metropolis and seaport of
Cardiff.[43] His nation-wide leadership in the promotion of social
reform added to his supra-party appeal, as the Welsh belatedly took an
interest in the New Liberalism that had long been exciting journalists
and politicians in London.[44] No episode better illustrated how
transcendent Lloyd George had become within Wales, even amongst
Conservative/Anglican opponents, than his role in orchestrating (and,
indeed part inventing) the ceremonial and ritual that attended the
investiture of the young Edward as Prince of Wales at Caernarfon
Castle in 1911. Lloyd George's ally in this enterprise was his old
sparring partner, Alfred George Edwards, bishop of St Asaph.[45] In
return, Lloyd George rewarded his nation with much assistance from
the public purse. As chancellor he was able to approve grants of
£1,500 to the National Museum, £2,500 to the National Library at
Aberystwyth, £15,000 to the Welsh University Colleges in the course
of an eventful twenty-four hours in February 1909. As he gaily told
Herbert Lewis, 'What's the use of being a Welsh Chancellor of the
Exchequer if one can do nothing in Wales?'[46] Even the triumphs of the
Welsh rugby football team in that golden era were adroitly turned to
advantage by a man who had once condemned the unresponsive
colliers of the south Wales coalfield for their 'morbid footballism'.[47]

Yet there were signs, even before August 1914, that his position in

[41]*Punch*, 26 October 1910.

[42]Frances Donaldson, *The Marconi Case* (London, 1962).

[43]Lloyd George to Mrs Lloyd George, 31 July 1907, Kenneth O. Morgan (ed.),
Lloyd George: Family Letters, c. 1885–1936 (Oxford and Cardiff, 1973), 147.

[44]Kenneth O. Morgan, 'The New Liberalism and the challenge of Labour: the
Welsh experience, 1885–1929' in K. D. Brown (ed.), *Essays in Anti-Labour History*,
(London, 1974), 159ff.

[45]Archbishop A. G. Edwards, *Memories* (London, 1927), 141ff.

[46]John Grigg, *Lloyd George and Wales* (Aberystwyth, National Library of Wales,
1988), 9.

[47]Lloyd George to Mrs Lloyd George, 19 November 1895 (*Family Letters*, 91).

Wales, like that of Liberalism in general, was becoming less secure. There were clear indications that the man who in 1910 proposed a cross-party coalition to grapple with the mighty themes of social welfare and national defence[48] was becoming impatient, if not positively bored with the old Welsh causes. Welsh land reforms receded as the volumes of the 1896 Royal Commission on Welsh Land mouldered away on library shelves, unread except by ardent history research students. Temperance had stalled, while the chancellor took little interest in the worthy efforts by E. T. John, Liberal member for East Denbighshire, to promote the cause of Welsh devolution, perhaps on the basis of 'home rule all round'.[49] As regards the transcendent issues of Welsh disestablishment, while Lloyd George made aggressive speeches during the Commons debate in 1912–13 (Lord Hugh Cecil's family was accused of having 'hands dripping with the fat of sacrilege'),[50] behind the scenes the chancellor was anxious to bury the issues. Back in 1906 he had told Randall Davidson, the archbishop of Canterbury, that he hoped that appointing a royal commission on the Welsh churches would lead to 'a moderate bill' being framed, with concessions on disendowment to speed on the rapid passage of a measure that would resolve a century-old and increasingly irrelevant question for ever.[51] Compared with health, housing, and child malnutrition, the Welsh Church hardly loomed in the forefront of the public agenda.

Apart from Lloyd George's own inclinations, there were signs, too, that Wales in general was beginning to drift away from him and the old Liberal inheritance. This was most emphatically true in the mining valleys of south Wales. By 1914, there were five Labour MPs there, a myriad of Labour-controlled councils and an increasingly powerful socialist movement mostly focused on the spread of the Independent Labour Party. More ominous still were the new quasi-revolutionary currents surging through the South Wales Miners' Federation.[52] Although 'Lib–Labism' in the mould of Mabon and William Brace remained powerful throughout the coalfield down to 1914, the new movements associated with the Unofficial Reform Committee and the Plebs League, the Marxist tutorial classes of the Central Labour College and quasi-syndicalist *The Miner's Next Step* published at Tonypandy, heralded a quite new era of industrial politics. Industrial south Wales, which had thrilled to the oratory of Lloyd George in the

[48]John D. Fair, *British Interparty Conferences* (Oxford, 1980), 91ff.

[49]J. Graham Jones, 'E. T. John and Welsh Home Rule, 1910–1914', *Welsh History Review*, 13 (4) (1987), 453ff.

[50]*Parl. Deb.*, 5th ser., 37, 1278 (25 April 1912).

[51]G. K. A. Bell, *The Life of Archbishop Davidson* (London, 1935), 504.

[52]See Hywel Francis and Dai Smith, *The Fed* (London, 1980), ch. I.

immediate past, seemed now almost the cockpit of the class war. Welsh Liberalism truly had many mansions. But it was quite unable, socially or ideologically, to accommodate the labour movement, not only fringe radicals like Noah Ablett or Will Hay but even more mainstream miners' agents like James Winstone, Enoch Morrell, and Vernon Hartshorn.

Lloyd George's decline from political eminence after 1918 is, of course, part of the wider decline of Liberalism in Britain as a whole in the post-war period. It had deep-seated socio-economic causes – the erosion of Nonconformity, the weakening of the rural communities and of agrarian radicalism, the collapse of the old free-trade staple industries of coal, shipping and textiles, all of them important adjuncts of the Liberal party across the land. But, in Lloyd George's case there were more specifically Welsh and personal causes as well. Of course, he remained down to the Second World War a politician of immense national and international authority, the only one of the three 'peace-makers' at Versailles to survive as a significant force into the 1930s. He was a fount of new economic ideas in the late twenties, the first major politician to see the political implications of the ideas of Maynard Keynes. He generated new discussion of both domestic and international issues in the thirties, and his Council of Action for Peace and Reconstruction in 1935 made a notable impact, with even some suggestion that Lloyd George might join the National government under his old adversaries MacDonald and Baldwin.[53] In May 1940, at the age of seventy-seven, he was still an effective force in helping to remove Neville Chamberlain from Downing Street, and was subsequently offered a government office by Churchill.[54]

For all that, the later phase of Lloyd George's career is clearly one of waning influence, and, amidst all the other factors bearing on the question, there are some important features relating to Liberalism in Wales. In particular, it can be argued that he failed adequately to engage with newer currents of thought in Welsh life. This applies especially to the three major themes of socialism, nationalism, and militarism.

As regards socialism, there was no obvious social reason why Lloyd George should not have become a socialist or at least joined the Labour party. After all, the Labour government included some far more improbable figures who did, upper-class figures like Attlee, Dalton or Cripps. Quite apart from his astonishing achievements as a

[53]Keith Middlemas and John Barnes, *Baldwin* (London, 1969), 808–10.

[54]See David M. Roberts, 'Clement Davies and the fall of Neville Chamberlain, 1939–40', *Welsh History Review*, 8 (2) (1976), 208–11. Harold Nicolson actually records that a Lloyd George government was thought to be imminent in May 1940.

social reformer, Lloyd George was well-known for his special relationship with the labour movement before 1914, and for his rare skill in settling contentious issues with trade union leaders. He showed this facility during the settlement of a threatened national railway strike in the autumn of 1907 and, even more dramatically, in ending the national miners' strike on behalf of a minimum wage in 1912. [55] In the Treasury agreement concluded with the TUC in March 1915 to prevent wartime strikes he showed himself yet again a patron and an ally of organized labour, and one deeply sympathetic to the needs of the ordinary working man.

Yet he was, by background and understanding, remote from the sense of class identity and the roots of social conflict that characterized the British industrial working class. As Keir Hardie had rightly observed in the *Labour Leader* in 1905, Lloyd George, a man with whom radical socialists could collaborate over anti-imperialism, the rights of women or world peace, 'had no settled opinions on social questions'.[56] Lloyd George's imagination could cope with local issues like the three-year strike of the Bethesda quarrymen in 1900–3, which partly concerned his own constituents. He was forthright in condemning the autocratic role of Lord Penrhyn, his refusal to acknowledge trade unions in his quarries, and his wanton calling out of the militia to coerce the quarrymen back to work.[57] But Lloyd George was really out of his depth when confronting the continuing turbulence within the south Wales labour movement from the war years onwards. Even during the war, he deeply antagonized Welsh and other workers with the controls imposed by the Munitions of War Act, the enforcement of 'dilution' of skilled men and the imposition of military conscription.[58]

After the war, his 'anti-Bolshevik' rhetoric directed against the Miners' Federation, his apparent deceit of the Federation over the Sankey Commission in 1919 and again in resolving 'Black Friday' in April 1921, the widespread use of troops (and even the navy and airforce) in putting down striking Welsh miners during the national stoppage in 1921, the use of emergency powers as an anti-strike strategy, the government's support for neo-fascist police chiefs like Captain Lionel Lindsay in Glamorgan[59] – all this tarnished Lloyd

[55]Lucy Masterman, op. cit., 233–5.

[56]Keir Hardie, *Labour Leader*, 22 December 1905.

[57]Merfyn Jones, *The North Wales Quarrymen, 1873–1922* (Cardiff, 1980).

[58]C. J. Wrigley, *David Lloyd George and the British Labour Movement* (Hassocks, 1976), 149ff; Kenneth and Jane Morgan, *Portrait of a Progressive: The Political Career of Christopher, Viscount Addison* (Oxford, 1980), 62–6.

[59]See Jane Morgan, *Conflict and Order: The Police and Labour Disputes in England and Wales, 1900–1939* (Oxford, 1987), 190ff.

George's reputation amongst the Welsh working class, and fatally so. The coalition, allegedly a government of national unity, now seemed a class formation devised to suppress labour.[60] The most influential and representative Labour party leader of the day, Arthur Henderson, humiliated by the 'doormat' incident after his visit to Stockholm in 1917, became Lloyd George's most formidable antagonist.[61] Despite the sympathy with the TUC shown during the 1926 general strike Lloyd George lost in the twenties any credible claim to be a serious spokesman for the British workers. There was a powerful resonance in the young Nye Bevan's bitter attack on Lloyd George in the House in 1930 – reminiscent of the young Lloyd George's own onslaught on Joseph Chamberlain – 'better dearer coal than cheaper colliers'.[62]

Lloyd George retained a broad appeal for Labour spokesmen in north and mid Wales: witness his impact on rising young socialists like Cledwyn Hughes in Anglesey or Tom Ellis in Wrexham, both powerful supporters of the Lloyd George tradition and of the centenary appeal in 1990.[63] But for the serried ranks of working men and their wives in industrial south Wales, the Lloyd George tradition represented a world well lost.

Something of the same applied to the idea of nationalism, too. Lloyd George rose in the early 1890s as a vehement champion of the Welsh nationalism of his day: his election addresses in Caernarfon Boroughs in 1890, 1892, and 1895 were largely a rehearsal of the Welsh demands of the day. He was anxious to try to turn the disendowment provisions of the 1895 Welsh Disestablishment Bill into a means of promoting Welsh self-government, by creating a national council to administer the secularized endowments such as tithe and glebe.

But his nationalism did not last. He never really managed to produce a satisfactory sequel to the *Cymru Fydd* movement after its collapse in early 1896. He was involved, from time to time, in attempts to promote Welsh administrative devolution, such as the Welsh department in the Board of Education in 1907 (the first secretary being an old political ally, Alfred T. Davies) and the Welsh Board of Health in 1919.[64] He showed some interest in the notion of a Welsh secretary of state after 1919 and urged his fellow-countrymen to 'go for the big thing' in this regard,[65] but he seemed very distant from some of the newer nationalist ideas advocated by writers like W. J.

[60]Cf. Kenneth O. Morgan, *Consensus and Disunity: The Lloyd George Coalition Government of 1918–1922* (Oxford, 1979).

[61]See Chris Wrigley, *Arthur Henderson* (Cardiff, 1990), 112–20.

[62]*Parl. Deb.*, 5th ser., 235, cols. 24, 62–9 (27 February 1930).

[63]Personal knowledge; Emyr Price, *Lord Cledwyn of Penrhos* (Bangor, 1990).

[64]A. T. Davies, *The Lloyd George I Knew* (London, 1948), 51ff.

[65]*Welsh Outlook*, January 1921, 302.

Gruffydd and R. T. Jenkins in *Y Llenor* at this time. Neither did he respond particularly to the modest devolution proposed in the monthly *Welsh Outlook*, founded by his cabinet secretary, Thomas Jones, and largely financed by his former assistant, Lord Davies of Llandinam.[66] Plaid Cymru emerged in the later twenties, minuscule though it was, as an updated Europe-based, intellectual nationalism to replace the tired pre-war 'radicalism' of the Eisteddfod, the Honourable Society of Cymmrodorion and the Edwardian Liberal party.[67] The real outcome of this emerged after Lloyd George's death. The advance of Plaid Cymru after 1966 – starting with Gwynfor Evans's election triumph in Carmarthen, the former seat of Megan Lloyd George – reinforced the decline of Liberalism in rural Wales. Nor did Welsh Liberalism derive any particular bonus from its support of Welsh devolution in the later 1970s; the 1979 election saw the defeat of Emlyn Hooson in Montgomeryshire, though it is true that Rendel's old constituency later reverted to the Liberal faith in 1983.

Curiously enough, Lloyd George managed in the end to achieve a more final settlement with regard to Irish nationalism. His record in relation to Ireland has been traced by the present writer elsewhere.[68] It is full of twists and turns with a particular dark chapter in the 'troubles' of 1919–21 with the terrible policy of 'retaliation' against the IRA and the use of free-lances like the 'Black and Tans'. Yet in the end, he managed to produce a settlement with Sinn Fein, in the Treaty of December 1921. Warts and all, it brought a more peaceful period to Ireland than that unhappy island had known since 1798, a more tranquil phase which endured until the 1960s, even if Ulster was subjected to an insensitive one-party rule. Lloyd George managed, after a fashion, to reconcile the demands of Irish nationalism, the refusal to coerce Protestant Ulster, and the need to keep open new channels of communication between London and Dublin. He cannot be reasonably blamed for the intransigence of the Ulster Protestant ascendancy or the centuries-old gulf between the rival cultures or Ireland, both dating from the Plantations of James I's reign if not earlier. In Ireland there was, for a time, a settlement of a kind. But the more indirect, more subtle, claims of Welsh nationalism remained unfulfilled.

Finally, from August, 1914 there was the challenge of militarism. The war, of course, turned Lloyd George's career in radically new

[66]*Welsh Outlook* 1917–22 *passim*, and article by Gwyn Jenkins in *National Library of Wales Journal*, XXXIV, 4 (1986).

[67]See Saunders Lewis in *The Welsh Nationalist*, January 1932, 1, where he pours scorn on 'the ardent Welsh Nationalists' of pre-1914.

[68]Kenneth O. Morgan, 'Lloyd George and the Irish' in *Ireland since the Union* (Oxford University Press for the British and Irish Academies, 1989), 83ff.

directions. He moved on to become minister of munitions, secretary for war and in December 1916 prime minister of Great Britain. His commitment to conscription caused a breach with Asquith and other old Liberal comrades, and impelled him towards an unexpected alliance with leading Unionists, including imperialist zealots like Milner. He used the language of 'no surrender' and of 'the knock-out blow'.[69] In Wales itself, he used shamelessly sentimental rhetoric about the warlike tradition of the Welsh; the Welsh bowmen at Crécy and Agincourt were dragged out of history or folklore, and a Welsh Division created, which saw ferocious action later on at Mametz Wood.[70] A 'Welsh Mafia' emerged in Downing Street, from December 1916, both in the Cabinet secretariat and the Garden Suburb, featuring Thomas Jones, J. T. Davies, David Davies, Sir Joseph Davies and many others. Other pillars of Welsh Liberalism went even further than Lloyd George in producing nationalist 'anti-Hun' propaganda. Even detached writers and intellectuals like Sir John Morris-Jones and Sir Owen M. Edwards lent their talents to the cause,[71] while another prominent Liberal, the Revd John Williams of Brynsiencyn, Anglesey, caused something of a sensation by preaching in the pulpit in full military uniform. Prominent Welsh academics like Sir Henry Jones and Sir Wynn Wheldon took part in recruiting campaigns to boost the trenches on the Western front, while the eminent German scholar, Hermann Ethé, was hounded out of Aberystwyth after a disreputable campaign against him in the town.

Yet a reaction against this mood was discernible in Wales even during the war years. As we have noted, in the south Wales mining valleys, the socialist movement, fanned by the 1917 revolution in Russia, was vocal in denouncing a long and bloody war. Even in rural north and mid Wales there were important voices of dissent like the poets, Thomas Gwynn Jones and Thomas Parry-Williams, and the two remarkable journals produced at the University College of Wales, Aberystwyth, *Y Wawr* and *Y Deyrnas*.[72] After the war, it became clear

[69] See particularly the interview with Roy Howard printed in *The Times*, 29 November 1916.

[70] For Lloyd George's 'Welsh Army', see Colin Hughes, *Mametz* (Gerrards Cross, 1985).

[71] See, for instance, Sir John Morris-Jones in *Y Beirniad*, Hydref 1914, 217–24, and Sir Owen M. Edwards, 'Cwymp yr Almaen', in *Cymru*, Chwefror 1915, along with Hazel Davies, *O. M. Edwards* (Cardiff, 1988), pp. 45–7.

[72] Kenneth O. Morgan, 'Peace movements in Wales, 1899–1945', *Welsh History Review*, 10 (3) (1981), 409–13 (published in this volume, 84–116). The authorities at Aberystwyth closed down *Y Wawr* in 1917 and there was controversy in 1919 when one of its leading writers, the eminent poet, Thomas Parry-Williams, was appointed to a chair of Welsh.

that significant elements in the Welsh intelligentsia, appalled by the juggernaut of war-mania, were turning against their Liberal background. A sign of the times was the astonishing victory in the 1923 general election by the Christian pacifist, George Maitland Lloyd Davies.[73] Radical sentiment turned to Labour, perhaps to inter-party movement such as the League of Nations Union.[74] Some, like Lloyd George's long-term friend, D. R. Daniel, left political activity entirely.[75]

The irony was that after 1918 Lloyd George himself emerged as a foremost 'peacemonger' and a prophet of reconciliation.[76] He called for genuine attempts to bring the pariah nations of Weimar Germany and Soviet Russia into the comity of nations, culminating in the abortive Conference at Genoa in April–May 1922. He called for a radical modification of the provisions of war reparations, a moratorium on war debts, for naval disarmament, and (in the thirties) for international action to promote peace through the effective use of collective security. In the best sense he was the first appeaser. In 1939–40, the ageing Lloyd George was identified with a putative 'peace party' and was compared by Churchill with the venerable Marshal Pétain for his pains.[77] But it was all too late. Lloyd George's highly personal identification with a Great War which many of his radical countrymen regarded as a bloody betrayal of Liberal values was damaging, even fatal. Welsh Liberalism in many ways died at Passchendaele. Like truth, it was another casualty of total war, as young Welshmen said 'good-bye to all that'.

Lloyd George is obviously a key figure in the making of modern Wales. Throughout his career he was an innovative, radical figure, for all the 'centrist' tags often imposed on him. His quest for party 'fusion' in 1919–20 is often misunderstood. As far as Wales was concerned, though a master negotiator who 'could charm a bird off a bough', he was not really a consensus man. He focused on schisms, tensions, class conflicts endemic in the Wales of his time, and sought to find political solution for them. He thus played an essential part in defining the Welsh political identity. In many ways he was unfairly attacked, not only over his domestic life, but also over the friends he was liable to attract. To claim that 'he had no friends and did not deserve any' is hard to reconcile with the devotion of men like Sir Herbert Lewis or the preacher-poet Elfed Lewis, or indeed of equally respectable men

[73] Morgan, ibid., 417, citing the Davies papers in NLW, Aberystwyth.

[74] See Goronwy Jones, *Wales and the Quest for Peace* (Cardiff, 1969), 125ff.

[75] K. W. Jones-Roberts, 'D. R. Daniel', *Journal of the Merioneth Historical and Record Society*, V (1965), 58–78.

[76] For this see Morgan, *Consensus and Disunity*; Richard H. Ullmann, *The Anglo-Soviet Accord* (Oxford, 1973).

[77] After Lloyd George's last major Commons speech, 7 May 1941.

like H. A. L. Fisher and C. P. Scott of the *Manchester Guardian* in England.

His volatility and flexibility, as a Welsh outsider, was a major key to his triumphs down to 1914, or perhaps, December 1916. Thereafter, they became a factor in his downfall, by giving an image of untrustworthiness, as novelists such as Arnold Bennett or Joyce Cary were to portray.[78] In the end, the great symbol of modernity and of restless, perpetual change had become a survival from the past. The great Welsh democrat had become another Cromwell, the model of autocracy, perhaps of reaction. For many years past he had been removed from Welsh life, with his life with Frances Stevenson at Churt looming ever larger, and not many close advisers to 'mind the shop' as brother William had once done in his constituency. Indeed the kind of men with whom Lloyd George associated in the 1930s, ranging from Lord Lothian to Liddell Hart were almost totally removed from the humdrum processes of normal party politics. Never in his entire career had he been a machine politician or an organization man. In the end, on New Year's day 1945, the Welsh Great Commoner, member for Caernarfon Boroughs for almost forty-five momentous years, became an earl. At the very last, the establishment had captured him. After his death, his constituency was won by the Tories, and then was merged into a Labour seat. His son, Gwilym Lloyd-George, retained the hyphen and became a Conservative MP and Cabinet minister. His daughter Megan, hyphenless, went the other way, as had been long predicted, and was elected Labour MP for Carmarthen in 1957.[79] His other child, Lady Olwen Carey-Evans, alone remained in Cricieth as a custodian of the old values and lived on, bright and stimulating to the last, to reach the age of ninety-seven. The age of Lloyd George, and of the Welsh Liberal ascendancy which he symbolized, was truly over. The new Wales of post-1945, the Wales of Jim Griffiths and Nye Bevan, of the Welsh Language Society and the Welsh Office, was the product of different, and perhaps more appropriate, hands.

1991

[78] Lloyd George appears, thinly disguised, as Andy Clyth in Bennett's *Lord Raingo* (1926) and as Chester Nimmo in Joyce Cary's *Prisoner of Grace* (1952).

[79] See the present writer's entries on both Gwilym and Lady Megan Lloyd George in *The Dictionary of National Biography*, supplement for 1961–70 (Oxford, 1981). A biography of Lady Megan by Mervyn Jones appeared in 1991.

22

D. A. Thomas:
The Industrialist as Politician

In Wales, as in the United States, the 1870s and 1880s brought with them the politics of the Gilded Age. The political structure of Wales, like that of similar societies elsewhere, was subjected to unprecedented strains as a result of industrial and urban growth. In a society, if not composed of the 'tramps and millionaires' of the rhetoric of the American populists, at least marked by immense inequalities in social opportunity, the alliance of business and politics found totally new dimensions. In this crucial period, David Alfred Thomas, Viscount Rhondda, symbolizes the tycoon in politics, a dedicated and ruthless individualist in his political as in his industrial career. He is as typical of the politics of later nineteenth-century Wales as were Tom Ellis and Lloyd George, those symbolic figures of the peasants' revolt who have exercised so dominant an influence over the culture and mythology of modern Wales. In many ways, indeed, D. A. Thomas was more significant than either of them. Ellis and Lloyd George, like the American Populists, spoke for a remote and impoverished countryside, already losing population fast and being rapidly marginalized by an increasingly urbanized world. Thomas, however, represented a new Wales, an expanding and affluent Wales, the industrial and commercial society of the coalfield, which in the two decades before 1914 was growing as dramatically as any sector of the British economy.

Thomas, indeed, was a key figure in this process. Inheriting the Cambrian Collieries in the Rhondda and Aberdare valleys, by 1914 he had built them up into the massive Cambrian Combine, a huge oligopoly with a nominal share capital of £2,000,000, that dominated the Welsh economy almost as comprehensively as did the empires of

Rockefeller or Carnegie in the United States. By 1917, the list of collieries under his control seemed like a roll-call of the industrial revolution: the Cambrian Collieries, the Albion Collieries, David Davis and Sons Ltd, North's Navigation and many others, with a total annual output of 7,355,000 tons. His enterprises extended into steel and aluminium, into docks and railways; he seized extensive holdings in German-owned property liquidated by the Board of Trade during the First World War. He bought a controlling interest in the *Western Mail*, the *Cambrian News*, *Y Faner* and *Y Tyst*, until it seemed that the larger proportion of the social and financial capital of Wales itself was under his direct control. Like many other capitalists, he entered Lloyd George's wartime coalition government in 1916; unlike many of them, however, in that so-called 'businessman's government', he provided at the Local Government Board and in the Food Ministry a truly businesslike administration. When he died prematurely in July 1918, at the age of sixty-two, he was already a millionaire many times over, one of the best-known and best-hated men in the land.

D. A. Thomas represented a new phenomenon in Welsh history, the rise of a native capitalist class. In the first phase of industrialization, dominated by the metallurgical industries, it had been from England that most of the entrepreneurs and ironmasters had come – industrial colonizers like the Guests and Crawshays, the Baileys and Homfrays. However, as the coal industry expanded in the middle decades of the nineteenth century until it dominated the Welsh economic scene, more and more Welshmen began to shape the destiny of their native land. A new managerial class arose, with men like David Davies of Llandinam, David Davis of Maesyffynon and Thomas Powell of Powell Duffryn. Until the growth of the new 'county' schools in the 1890s, which increasingly deflected Welsh boys into bookish pursuits and professional careers, this new plutocracy dominated much of Welsh society, especially in the coalfield. Its members were often active patrons of local philanthropic and cultural activities. They largely financed the expansion of Welsh Nonconformist chapels, from which so many of them had sprung. Foremost among them was D. A. Thomas. His dignified estate at Llanwern, Monmouthshire, resembled the nerve-centre of a vast industrial empire, whose contacts extended to all the major markets of the world. South Wales, traditionally democratic and populistic, was becoming dynastic.

Thomas, however, differed from most of his fellow capitalists in one important respect. For most of his career, from 1888 to 1910, his major concern lay not in industry but in politics. He felt compelled to enter political life himself, unlike many businessmen and industrialists who felt safer negotiating with the politicians at long range, trading with the political commitments of others rather than championing any of their own. In this, as in other respects, Thomas was an eccentric. For over twenty generally frustrating years he spent huge reserves of time and energy as a Liberal back-bencher in the House of Commons; only after his retirement from politics in 1910 did he devote himself exclusively to building up his many industrial concerns. He soon made a reputation at Westminster as one of the most able, if most wayward, of the younger radicals in the Welsh Parliamentary Party of the later 1880s. But from the outset also it was recognized that Thomas's Welsh radicalism had a quality all its own. He was regarded equally as a spokesman for the newly emergent bourgeoisie of the south Wales coalfield, and as the champion of their interests. It would be more accurate, in fact, to see him as representing the coastal fringe of the great seaports of Swansea, Barry, Newport, and, above all, Cardiff. This was where he truly found his institutional and political base. For many years he was active on the Cardiff Chamber of Commerce, the forum of the new capitalist class of coalowners, shippers, exporters and insurance brokers, concerned with the distribution as well as the production of coal and iron, and thus in important respects at odds with the interests of the inland mining valleys. Thomas bitterly attacked his distant kinsman, Sir W. T. Lewis, for upholding a wasteful form of industrial competition that separated artificially the productive from the marketing side of the coal industry.

The south Wales chambers of commerce, however, dealt with far more than purely commercial considerations. Their members could form a powerful pressure-group for other demands as well; for social as well as for economic emancipation, free religion as well as free trade, visible liberties as well as invisible exports. Many of them were Nonconformist in religion and radical in politics (in contrast to Sir W. T. Lewis who was an Anglican and a Tory); disciples of John Stuart Mill, they linked their economic grievances with political protest. Most of them were dedicated to demolishing the ascendancy of the parson and the squire over so much of Welsh society, those anachronistic symbols of an older agrarian order that a generation of cumulative economic change should largely have swept away. The growing industrial might of the marquesses of Bute, which threatened to revive the old paternalism in a new form, added a keener edge to the campaign against the landlord and his clerical allies. And so, Clifford Cory, a leading shipowner in the 1890s, spent his energies in the Welsh Protestant League, crusading against clerical control of elementary schools. Rees Jones, who had worked his way through shipping and broking to become manager of the Ocean Coal Company, was also an ardent Welsh Baptist and for ten years (1883–93) a militant president of the Cardiff Liberal Association. As member of Parliament, D. A. Thomas, in his individualistic way, upheld the values of such men as these. He symbolized their cosmopolitan standpoint, rooted in the complex, quasi-American society of the coalfield, and their search for a new social status commensurate with their economic power. But he represented also a specifically Welsh outlook, peculiar to the coalfield, the 'free trade nationalism' of the first-generation bourgeoisie that gave him a political attitude peculiarly his own.

Not, however, until 1910, his last year in active party politics, did Thomas represent the metropolis of Cardiff in Parliament. For almost the whole of his career as an MP, his political base was the radical stronghold of Merthyr Tydfil. Here Thomas was returned unopposed at a by-election in March 1888 at the age of thirty-one. In many ways he was the natural candidate. He had been born and brought up in the constituency, at Ysguborwen near Aberdare. He was already prominent in the industrial life of the area, sales agent in the Cambrian Collieries of Thomas, Riches and Co., which his father had built up nearly twenty years earlier. He was prominent locally as a magistrate, a member of the Ystradyfodwg Board of Health, and an active freemason within the Loyal Cambrian Lodge. He had a university degree (a second in mathematics from Caius College, Cambridge), more respectable indeed than either Tom Ellis or Stuart Rendel whom Welshmen generally credited as being intellectuals in politics. His university reputation as a boxer did him no harm in the virile, masculine society of the coalfield. He had some nodding acquaintance with the Welsh language. He was reputed to be an active Congregationalist; certainly he was a generous patron of Merthyr chapels even though he left Cambridge a confirmed agnostic and reacted to the squabblings of the sects with little less than boredom. His Nonconformist connections probably ensured his nomination as Liberal candidate, in preference to the distinguished Liberal churchman G. W. E. Russell, who was thought to be less enthusiastic over Welsh disestablishment. In any case, with his extensive commercial connections, Thomas was an appropriate representative for the cosmopolitan town of Merthyr where Englishmen and Irishmen, Spaniards and Italians had long settled into the local community. So he was nominated and returned unopposed on 14 March 1888 for perhaps the safest of all Liberal seats.

Thomas's election, however, added some new cross-currents to the already complicated political structure of the Merthyr Boroughs. Ever since the 1868 election had seen the triumphant return of the famous radical and pacifist Henry Richard, Merthyr had been regarded as the most democratic constituency in Wales, with an unusual degree of popular participation. Richard's return was the outcome of two main factors: a powerful local Nonconformist pressure-group, headed by Dr Thomas Price, and an active working-class tradition that dated from the Chartist period. However, during the twenty years that had elapsed since Richard's first election, Merthyr Liberalism had undergone many changes. On the surface the constituency remained an impregnable Liberal bastion, dominated by Nonconformity on the platform, in the press and from the pulpit. In reality, though, a mass of local rivalries and tensions was barely concealed, linked especially with the explosive potential of labour as a political force. The long years of depression in the Merthyr and Dowlais ironworks from the 1860s onwards lent a background of depression and unemployment to the political strains of the Boroughs. By its very completeness Thomas's election victory intensified them. His personal domination helped to undermine the already struggling Merthyr Liberal Association. For the next twenty years, he maintained his own election machine and his own agents, one being J. M. Berry, father of the newspaper barons, Lords Camrose and Kemsley. Like the Guests in the 1830s and Fothergill in the 1860s, Thomas showed how a mighty industrialist could dominate even as radical a constituency as Merthyr. By helping to destroy the Liberal machine of Henry Richard's heyday, Thomas, ironically enough, was helping to pave the way for Keir Hardie and the rise of labour.

When Henry Richard died later in 1888, Merthyr Liberalism in its organizational form finally collapsed. After much delay the local association nominated Ffoulkes Griffiths, a Baptist solicitor from London prominent in the *Cymru Fydd* movement. Thomas campaigned hard for Griffiths in the by-election in October, 1888. But he had misread the political omens. His own reputation could not be transferred paternalistically to an alien middle-class import from London. Working-class electors in particular resented the failure to nominate a 'Labour' candidate, like Mabon in Rhondda. They turned instead to the itinerant adventurer, W. Pritchard Morgan, *yr aelod dros China* (the member for China) to his enemies, whose quest for gold had taken him as far afield as Queensland and Korea, not to mention Dolgellau. Morgan claimed to stand as a 'labour man', the local boy made good. He flooded the constituency with leaflets depicting himself as a young man, clad in the rough garb of a Welsh collier, a naked candle in his cap, appearing 'on behalf of the working-classes' like some refugee from the Victorian music hall. Morgan defeated Griffiths with some ease, and the Merthyr Liberal Association promptly disintegrated.

For years to come Thomas and Morgan maintained a bitter personal animosity. They fought entirely separate campaigns, yet they were elected time after time under the joint banner of Liberalism. For they represented, in their contrasting ways, different facets of the Welsh Gilded Age. Thomas for all his individualism was firmly rooted in the mercantile and industrial world of the coalfield. He operated from an institutional base. Morgan, a wayward speculator, half demagogue, half pantaloon, was out on his own, without the backing of chambers of commerce or employers' associations. Neither man could claim to be conventionally religious yet Thomas, as the cynical patron of local *cymanfaoedd*, and Morgan, as the unlikely son of a Wesleyan minister, seemed not improper heirs to the mantle of the Revd Henry Richard. The Welsh Liberal mystique could comprehend both the industrial dynast and the self-made freebooter. The bizarre partnership of D. A. Thomas and Pritchard Morgan in Merthyr testified to its resilience as well as to the seeds of its ultimate collapse.

In politics at Westminster and in Wales itself Thomas displayed the same erratic genius that stamped his career in industry. Politics, like economics, he regarded as being among the dynamic order of sciences. He was firmly identified with the radical wing of the Gladstonian Liberal party, an ardent advocate of Irish Home Rule, women's suffrage, reform of the House of Lords and anti-imperialism. At the end of 1888 he was appointed one of the whips of Stuart Rendel's newly formed Welsh Party – an ironic choice since he of all the Welsh members rebelled against the constraints of party. He was committed, therefore, to the stock Welsh radical programme of disestablishment, public and free education, land reform and temperance legislation. Already, though, he wore his Liberal rue with a difference. He showed little interest in the lengthy and repetitious debates on Welsh disestablishment and the tithe question between 1888 and 1892, and intervened not once in any of them. However, he did flare into life over a very different issue, namely local home rule.

He spoke out fiercely against his colleague, Alfred Thomas's cumbersome National Institutions Bill of 1892, which proposed among many other things to set up an elective National Council and a secretary of state for Wales. Thomas's line of attack foreshadowed the one he was to adopt in the *Cymru Fydd* controversy. He questioned the functions of the proposed Council and even more its composition. The more populous counties of Glamorgan and Monmouth, he complained, would be liable to domination by their rural neighbours, unless the balance of representation were changed. Thomas's criticism, which was echoed by many Cardiff Liberals and by their member, Sir Edward Reed, helped to bury Alfred Thomas's abortive measure. D. A. Thomas's stand, however, cannot be dismissed, as it is by Lady Rhondda, as a crude rejection of the idea of 'Wales for the Welsh'; this *simpliste* interpretation would make nonsense of Thomas's entire political career. He was not opposed to a National Council as such; two years later he was to advocate one himself. He saw rather that Welsh Liberalism was a more complex movement than it had seemed

to be in the heady days of 1868. In the coalfield and especially in the
coastal ports a very different society and culture were emerging from
those of the rural heartland. Llewelyn Williams, an ardent nationalist,
the son of a tenant farmer from Llansadwrn in rural Carmarthenshire,
spoke with bitter disillusion of the failure of his journalistic efforts to
strike nationalist sparks from the cosmopolitan, bourgeois, 'philistines'
of Barry and Swansea. Williams's brand of Welsh nationalism was even
more repellent to Cardiffians, and D. A. Thomas was their spokesman.
Certainly, Thomas's stand did him no harm in Merthyr Boroughs
either; in 1892 he and Pritchard Morgan were overwhelmingly
triumphant by more than 9,000 votes, a record for that or any other
Welsh constituency at the time.

The next few years form the crucial divide in Thomas's career. They
brought the time of testing for his species of radicalism. He was soon
at odds with his Welsh colleagues, dominated as they were by Tom
Ellis, with whom Thomas was never intimate. Thomas was a private
sceptic over the Welsh Land Commission which Gladstone appointed
in 1893. He thought many of the farmers' grievances over rents and
security of tenure would be proved illusory. Twenty years later many
Liberals agreed with him, but in 1893 the land question seemed a
basic test of Liberal orthodoxy. Over the formation of a University of
Wales, Thomas and Bryn Roberts led the unavailing opposition of
those who wanted to withhold the charter until students from
theological and other colleges outside the university could be admitted
to degrees. Thomas may have been right, but once again his attitude
stamped him as a maverick, set apart from the mainstream of Welsh
radicalism which was committed to a unitary, national university.

Thomas's most extreme gesture of defiance, however, found him in
alliance with three of his rural colleagues. The issue was Welsh
disestablishment this time. In April–May 1894 he joined Lloyd George
and two others in a rebellion; they threatened to reject the Liberal
whip if a Welsh Disestablishment Bill were not immediately introduced. Thomas, who had shown little enough interest in this question
hitherto, was a valuable if surprising ally for Lloyd George and his
rural friends. But it was clear that Thomas's approach was very
different from theirs. Lloyd George was mainly concerned with
disestablishment, the symbolic restoration of equality to Nonconformists as an excluded class; the terms of the financial settlement
could be left to later negotiation. Thomas, however, cared more for
disendowment, the way in which 'national property' such as tithe and
glebe would be transferred from the Church to the people of Wales.
The difference between Lloyd George and Thomas concerned ends as
well as means. Thomas saw disendowment as a means of providing
new social and cultural services in the urban and most populous

counties of Wales: work-houses and wash-houses, libraries, museums and art galleries. Endowments should be distributed on the basis of population, to the advantage of Glamorgan and Monmouth, instead of being frittered away in rural parishes throughout the land. This view was to lead to a basic division of outlook from his fellow 'rebels', to bring about the collapse of the 1894 'revolt' and ultimately of the *Cymru Fydd* movement as well.

Thomas's role in the break-up of the *Cymru Fydd* movement has often seemed puzzling. Some of the puzzlement has been contributed by the account given by Llewelyn Williams in Thomas's official biography, written in 1921. Williams was a major participant in the events he was describing, while by 1921, as an ardent Asquithian, he had developed an almost pathological hatred of Lloyd George. Yet Thomas's attitude surely seems intelligible, even consistent, when set against his views on other contemporary issues. The key is to be found in his opposition to the Welsh Disestablishment Bills of 1894 and 1895 over their provision for the allocation of tithe. Thomas pressed hard for tithes to be distributed by a national council on a national and not a parochial basis. His amendment on this point on 20 June 1895 saw the Liberal government's majority reduced to seven. The next day the ministry fell on the 'cordite vote' and Thomas was widely condemned for having fatally weakened its position the day before. Yet his objection, however intemperately expressed, was a basic one which sheds light on his wider political outlook. The injustices which were to be inflicted on the industrial areas of south Wales were so grave that he preferred to wreck the whole measure rather than see it go through as it stood. Cardiff, with a population of over 100,000 people, would receive only a few hundreds of secularized endowments, less than small market towns in Anglesey, instead of the £20,000 to which it was entitled. The county of Glamorgan would receive a mere £26,000 annually instead of the £90,000 which was its due. Disendowment in this form was an attempt to turn the clock back two centuries. Thomas wanted to see a disestablished Church, but in a prosperous, urbanized Wales, not a land in which wasteful subsidies were frittered away in depopulated and declining rural areas. That was not 'religious equality' as Thomas understood it.

Thomas maintained this attitude in the *Cymru Fydd* debate. At first he was enthusiastically in favour of uniting the Liberal Federations of North and South Wales with the nationalistic *Cymru Fydd* League. As president of the South Wales Liberal Federation (1893–7) he spoke out in favour of this policy. A national council, as advocated by *Cymru Fydd*, would be the means of doing justice to south Wales over the matter of tithe allocation. But the structure of the new league was the crucial issue; it should be a mechanism for promoting the buoyancy of the industrial south, not of stifling it. If effective autonomy were not granted to Glamorgan and Monmouth within the new Federation, it should be dismantled. It should be constructed from the bottom up, not from the top down. As early as 3 November 1894, he could write to the venerable Thomas Gee that 'few responsible politicians down here regard the new League seriously'. In the next few months Thomas and a growing number of allies continued their campaign against the proposed structure of the new Federation. Its structure was indeed their main objection to it. They were not afraid of Welsh Liberalism cutting itself off from English, since it was clear that Lloyd George himself intended no such thing despite occasional rhetorical excesses. When the Aberystwyth convention of 18 April 1895 formally merged the North Wales Liberal Federation with *Cymru Fydd* in a new 'Wales National Federation', Thomas and most south Wales Liberals held aloof. Thomas, in his already well-known polemical style as a newspaper correspondent, condemned the meeting as a 'fiasco'; the grandiose constitution of the new WNF had been concocted by a mere handful of delegates. South Wales Liberalism, he pointed out, was virtually unrepresented, save for a few highly untypical figures such as the Revd J. Towyn Jones of Garnant and several delegates from Aberystwyth. The disingenuous appointment of Mrs D. A. Thomas as president of the proposed Women's Divisional Council was a mere façade.

More and more Liberals in different parts of Wales agreed with Thomas's criticism of the artificial new Federation. He was told of revolts against it by loyal party members in Anglesey, Denbighshire and Montgomeryshire, while the South Wales Liberal Federation was firmly hostile. Even in Merioneth the local Liberal Association held aloof while Tom Ellis himself was noticeably cool. A meeting at Llandrindod Wells on 22 June 1895 seemed to restore a kind of unity between the WNF and the SWLF, and even Thomas himself seemed to be temporarily placated. In fact, however, the real divisions that existed could not be spirited away by Lloyd George's verbal formulae. Into the late autumn deadlock continued over a wide range of issues, especially over the powers of the four proposed provincial districts, of which Glamorgan and Monmouth would form one. There was a long hostile correspondence between Morgan Thomas, secretary to the SWLF and a close associate of D. A. Thomas, and Beriah Gwynfe Evans, the controversial secretary of the WNF. Bitterness was intensified when Lloyd George conducted a thinly-veiled missionary campaign to rally support in south Wales constituencies, under the pretext of giving a series of lectures on Llewelyn the Great, whom he claimed as a thirteenth-century apostle of *Cymru Fydd*.

At the decisive meeting of the SWLF at Newport on 16 January

1896, when union with the WNF was discussed, *Cymru Fydd* finally collapsed as the artificial rump it was. There was immense uproar; south Wales Liberals, headed by Robert Bird of Cardiff and Alfred Edmunds of Merthyr, insisted that Glamorgan and Monmouth 'were not to be dictated to by the isolated county of Caernarvon'. A centralized league was voted down by 133 to 70. Lloyd George, who claimed to be present as a delegate from Landore Liberal Association, was howled down and the *Western Mail* gleefully gave the 'radical bear garden' maximum publicity. Amid charges and counter-charges of packing, the *Cymru Fydd* League broke up and nothing like it has ever been revived. Throughout, D. A. Thomas had been Lloyd George's major adversary. Ever since, he has occupied a prominent place in the demonology of Welsh nationalists, a leading candidate for the chamber of horrors. But what is striking about the entire episode is how Thomas for once was able to find a wide range of support. In upholding the authority of the SWLF (however unrepresentative) against the (equally unrepresentative) *Cymru Fydd* League, he found support in all parts of Wales. He could represent *Cymru Fydd* as a racialist attempt to narrow the base of Welsh Liberalism by excluding Welsh Liberals of English birth, at the initial expense of the commercial society of the southern coastal fringe, but ultimately at the expense of Liberals everywhere. Llewelyn Williams's efforts to explain away the collapse of *Cymru Fydd* in terms of Lloyd George's intention of setting up a personal dictatorship thus miss the mark. It was far more basic than a clash of strong-willed individuals, though that played its part. It was far more even than a conflict between north and south Wales since the debate raged inside Liberal Associations in all parts of the country. It was basically the rejection, inspired by Thomas, of an attempt to shatter the varied coalition that made up Welsh Liberalism, by translating the harmless rhetoric of Welsh 'nationalism' into a real separatist organization. Thomas preferred to keep his Welsh Liberalism diverse and flexible, and his nationalism essentially sentimental. In this sentimentality, perhaps, Thomas and not Lloyd George showed the true realism, as the past sixty years have gradually confirmed.

After the *Cymru Fydd* débâcle, Thomas's influence as a Welsh politician went into steady decline. Lloyd George had the resilience to bounce back immediately and to patch up old quarrels after his defeat in 1896. Thomas, however, found his own victory a pyrrhic one; he could not ignore old conflicts and he became more and more isolated as a result. He retired from the Welsh Party after 1896, remaining a lone wolf on the sidelines, 'the most sinister figure in Welsh politics' in the opinion of the *Western Mail*. He ruthlessly analysed the weaknesses of the Welsh parliamentary group; they were, he asserted in 1908, 'a fraud and a failure . . . tame cats and needy knifegrinders'. The Welsh

Party was 'a sickly pretence' and the Welsh National Liberal Council 'a mere annexe of the Hotel Caernarvon'. He became a sceptic about democracy itself. 'It is easily swayed and led by the fluent speaker rather than by the man of caution and capacity. Froth rises to the top and the person who carries his brains in his tongue is the chosen leader.' By this time, however, Thomas's criticisms seemed purely destructive, the product of his own disgruntlement and disillusion; he was less successful in explaining in positive terms how the Welsh Party could exert any more influence than it did, while it seemed mere prejudice to allege that Welsh Liberalism since 1868 had been completely ineffective.

When the Welsh members were roused into new life in rebellion against Balfour's Education Act of 1902, Thomas ridiculed the result. He condemned their attempt to maintain elementary education through the chapels, after withdrawing pupils from Church 'National' schools, as financially unworkable. His colleagues wanted to impose one form of clerical domination upon another, instead of settling in a logical, businesslike manner for the secular solution. He voted against Runciman's Education Bill of 1908 on the same grounds, the only Welsh member to do so. Thomas also bitterly attacked the failure of the new Liberal government to introduce a Welsh Disestablishment Bill in 1906. The new Church Commission, he claimed, was a pretence to postpone the measure indefinitely; it was totally unnecessary, taking the evidence long after the verdict had been given by the Welsh people. Thomas articulated, in fact, what many observers sensed, that Welsh Liberalism was losing its vitality and its relevance, fighting battles of long ago that had already been won. Few, however, cared to have the weaknesses of Liberalism dissected with such ruthless candour. Many indeed wondered why Thomas remained in politics at all, since he seemed to find it all so distasteful and frustrating. When he resumed his managing directorship of the Cambrian Collieries in 1906 and joined the Coalowners' Association, it seemed strange that he had not concentrated earlier on building up his industrial empire. These critics had their answer, in part, in the campaigns Thomas waged in defence of his own thriving economic base in Cardiff and the south-east. After 1900 he had given up his directorships to devote his energies entirely to political affairs. He led his colleagues on the Cardiff Chamber of Commerce in a vigorous attack on Hicks-Beach's export duty on coal in 1901; it would undermine the natural advantages of the south Wales coalfield. He re-emphasized this in his famous paper on the coal export trade, read to the Royal Statistical Society in 1903. His ardent defence of free trade in 1903–5, in the face of Joseph Chamberlain's tariff reform campaign, made up for many earlier disappointments. Chamberlain's programme was economic nationalism of the narrowest type, a fiscal version of *Cymru Fydd*. Through parliamentary politics, Thomas could project his industrial and commercial philosophy. His position at Merthyr Boroughs meanwhile remained as impregnable as ever. Despite his aloofness from the constituency, in the 1906 election he ran well ahead of Keir Hardie and polled 77 per cent of the votes cast by its overwhelmingly working-class electors.

The major issue affecting his political and industrial career in these later years was the rise of labour. The harsh years of industrial bitterness that followed the six-months coal stoppage in 1898 were in the course of time to transform the political pattern of south Wales. The first fruits came in the 1900 'khaki election' when Keir Hardie was elected to join Thomas as junior member for Merthyr. Thomas, as one of the largest coalowners in south Wales, seemed an obvious target for the class rhetoric of the ILP and the other socialist bodies. He was deeply sceptical about the egalitarian message of socialism. It would never work: 'you must have captains – or anarchy'. Yet he faced the growth of labour with equanimity, and with considerably more resilience than most other Liberal capitalists, and with reason. He had an honourable and progressive record on labour matters; in the 1892 election the cause of labour had preceded even Irish Home Rule in his manifesto. He had pioneered a Conciliation Board in his own Cambrian Collieries. He was pledged to a minimum wage and to collective bargaining, with the reversal of the Taff Vale decision. Thomas had little quarrel with labour as such; it was disorganized labour that he feared, as he feared disorganized management also. His main objection to the syndicalist gospel of workers' control after 1909 was that it encouraged disunity amongst the miners and a rejection of leadership. He was contemptuous of class distinctions, which was one reason for his intense admiration of the United States. Rather than being divided along class lines, the entire coalfield seemed to him one gigantic 'interest' with common economic needs. He had long been a rebel in industrial relations as in politics, challenging the old prejudice against producers of coal being involved in its sale and distribution. In 1897 he presented to the Coalowners' Association, headed by his arch-rival Sir W. T. Lewis, a complex scheme for restricting each company's output to a fixed proportion of total production each year, owners who produced in excess of the agreed quantity contributing a specified amount as liquidated damages. It was a progressive attempt to control output, prices and wages, to substitute planning for the crudities of *laissez-faire*. But the coalowners rejected this attempt to interfere with the sacred laws of supply and demand; the coal stoppage followed in 1898 and Thomas bitterly denounced the owners for their intransigence.

In the 1900 general election, Thomas worked surprisingly closely with Keir Hardie, in opposition to his old enemy, Pritchard Morgan. Indeed, Hardie gained immeasurably from the appearance of running in some sense in double harness with Thomas. Hardie's strong opposition to the South African War caused Thomas little concern, since he was himself a caustic critic of 'Chamberlainism' and was usually reckoned by the press as belonging to the 'pro-Boer' wing of the divided Liberal party. After 1900, in fact, Hardie and Thomas co-operated quite amicably for several years, as befitted two singularly flexible and independently-minded politicians. Thomas also maintained good relations with Mabon, Brace and other miners' leaders. Even the growing tension in the valleys from 1906 onwards seemed to leave the traditional political and personal ascendancy of 'D.A.' largely unaffected.

But now he was well into middle-age, and more and more dissatisfied with the course of current politics. His advice was ignored and his talents neglected. The final humiliation came when Campbell-Bannerman's 1905 government, which included several Welshmen, could find no place for Thomas, the result of Asquith's influence it was said. Thomas's growing industrial empire absorbed more and more of his energies, together with such current political controversies as the Mines' Eight Hours Bill of 1909 about which he had many reservations. Then, quite unexpectedly, at the end of 1909, he yielded to pressure to leave his safe seat at Merthyr for the much less secure constituency of Cardiff, which perhaps he alone could hold for the Liberals. It was an act of self-sacrifice, especially as he had just recovered from a serious attack of rheumatic fever. His departure from Merthyr produced a minor political revolution there. The Merthyr Liberal Association was resurrected to nominate a new candidate, and a head-on clash between Liberalism and Labour was inevitably foreshadowed. In the election of January 1910, Thomas fought and won Cardiff in his last and greatest fight; he appealed to the city as a bastion of free trade and mercantile enterprise, on non-party lines. It was his last appearance as a candidate. Later in the year he announced his retirement from politics; consequently the Liberals lost Cardiff to the Butes at the election in December 1910. Though he continued as president of the Cardiff Liberal Association, Thomas was now wholly absorbed in the problems of the coal industry. His former amicable relations with labour leaders were a thing of the past now. He symbolized for them monopoly capitalism in its starkest form; he was the supreme autocrat, the tsar of the coalfield. In the year-long Cambrian strike in 1910–11, Thomas was the foremost target for the invective of miners' leaders, socialist and non-socialist alike, especially after the dispatch of troops to Tonypandy. Even Sir Nevil Macready,

the general sent to south Wales to maintain order, condemned Thomas
for his autocratic methods and for taking himself at his own valuation
as 'the little white father'. With the outbreak of world war in 1914
Thomas's industrial empire continued to expand inexorably,
culminating in the purchase of the Ferndale and many other collieries
in his *annus mirabilis* of 1916. His escape from the sinking of the
Lusitania added to the drama that surrounded his extraordinary
career. Then, at the height of the war, he was suddenly invited back
into public life by the new premier, David Lloyd George, from whom
he had been estranged ever since the *Cymru Fydd* fiasco. With the new
title of Viscount Rhondda, Thomas proved a brilliant success in
government office, especially in implementing the new system of food
rationing. He worked in harmonious co-operation with his assistant,
the socialist J. R. Clynes. As food controller, he directed the whole
supply of commodities from production to consumption, imposing a
total control over the entire economic process as he had done in his
industrial concerns. At last, on the national stage, until his death in
July 1918, Thomas's political genius found the platform it had so long
been denied in his native Wales.

The political career of D. A. Thomas is hard to sum up, so
contradictory seem to be so many of its features. The most hated
coalowner in south Wales, he was the friendly associate of Keir Hardie.
The most doctrinaire of anti-socialists, he introduced new extremes of
collectivism into British economic life. He could urge industrial co-
operation through governmental planning in one crisis, and
unregulated free enterprise, even industrial anarchy, in another. He
could denounce the Cymru Fyddites for Welsh parochialism and yet
stake his whole career on behalf of Welsh disestablishment. He voiced
the aspirations of the outward-looking, highly anglicized society of the
coalfield, yet most of his parliamentary career was taken up with the
immemorial grievances of the Nonconformists of the countryside. An
agnostic and a materialist, he championed religious equality and
temperance. Small wonder, then, that contemporaries found him hard
to assess and harder to work with. As Llewelyn Williams says, 'he
seemed the last of the eminent series of independent members',
doomed to plough a lonely furrow of his own.

The irony is that on so may issues time was to prove him right. His
insistence that only the secular solution could settle the controversy
over elementary education; his advocacy of a planned wages and prices
policy for the coalfield; his view that Welsh nationality was too flexible
a concept to be chained by the rigid structure of a *Cymru Fydd* league:
on all these and many other issues, the succeeding decades were to
prove him largely justified. He found, however, to his cost, that being
logically right was not the same thing as being politically right. In

politics, unlike industry, there could seldom be total victory or total defeat; conciliation and compromise were inevitable, and these were qualities that Thomas as a politician, however amiable his personal temperament, conspicuously lacked. For him it had to be all or nothing. The dictum that he applied to business could serve for his political career as well: 'I make it a rule never to touch anything that anyone else is after.' As a result his career as a party politician seemed a frustrating failure for the most part. Only in the party truce of the First World War, when his administrative genius could be expressed free from the trammels of intrigue and dogma, did he find a fitting arena for his talents. For the rest, like a somewhat similar personality, Lord Milner, he remained a 'pro-consul in politics', a tsar in search of an empire, and in a party system that breed is highly expendable.

It is too easy, however, to dismiss Thomas's political career as fruitless and ineffective. It is too simple for critics of the right to see him as a political opportunist, prepared to veer from extremes of individualism to near-socialism; and for critics of the left to condemn him as a ruthless tyrant whose mantle was inherited by the 'hard-faced' profiteers who exploited the country during the First World War. Certainly he was temperamentally ill at ease in politics, yet his political career had its creative and positive side. He played his part in advancing Wales towards national equality in the generation before 1914. Further, by consistently linking Welsh radicalism with the interests of the mercantile bourgeoisie of the coalfield, he helped to make the national movement in Wales truly nation-wide, and thus able to adapt itself to the twentieth century, instead of being simply the last hurrah of a declining countryside. In this, Thomas, and not Tom Ellis, is the truly prophetic figure in modern Welsh nationalism, since it was Thomas who preserved a broad-based national coalition. In defeating the *Cymru Fydd* League in 1896, in this apparently destructive act, he kept alive a real sense of national unity. Wales, as Thomas saw it, was a flexible structure, a complex of individual competing sections within a loose general framework, rather like his own Cambrian Combine, or the United States which he admired so much. Without this flexibility, the Welsh national movement would collapse. The ties that bound the urban, mercantile south to the rural areas would be snapped. Thomas's Wales was above all a federal union; either secession or excessive centralization would kill it. But at least the union must be preserved.

There is a further side to Thomas's career. If he gave much to the strength of the Welsh national movement, he contributed more to the awareness of things Welsh in his own mercantile society. The Welsh political career of a mighty industrialist like D. A. Thomas helped to turn the regional awareness of the coalfield into something approaching national pride. The civic consciousness of an already

anglicized Cardiff was linked with the growth of Wales as a nation.
Long before his death, a series of imposing buildings was beginning to
enclose Cathays Park, confirming the role of Cardiff as the major city
in the nation. After 1918, when Cardiff was dubbed 'the city of
dreadful knights', its self-satisfied bourgeoisie could well have recalled
the concern for social and cultural causes that Thomas helped to
kindle. A generation later still, when the BBC, the University, the
National Museum and other institutions were to form an oasis of
Welshness in the heart of so English a capital city, when a passion, real
or contrived, for Welsh affairs became a badge of social status,
Thomas's career found its true fulfilment. His industrial inheritance is
now disappearing; the collieries he owned are being closed down one
by one in the face of a newer technological revolution. D. A. Thomas,
the industrialist, in fact, is being fast forgotten, and perhaps deserves
to be. The legacy of Thomas the politician, however, lives on in the
Wales of today. He himself would have relished this supreme, final
irony of the tragi-comedy that made up his career.

1966

23

Mabon and Noah Ablett

South Wales was the cockpit of the British labour world in the early twentieth century. In the bitter, often violent, confrontations between the Miners' Federation and an obdurate Coalowners' Association – the era of the Taff Vale verdict and the Tonypandy riots – a new generation of labour leaders came of age. Already by the First World War, the socialism, even the syndicalism of the Welsh coalfield had become legendary. It had become, government spokesmen complained, a kind of 'El Dorado' for every kind of extremist doctrine. After the war, tension continued to mount. The Welsh coalfield threw up hard men like Arthur Cook, and later Arthur Horner. Through their influence, as well as through young neo-Marxist politicians like Aneurin Bevan and S. O. Davies, the passions of the pioneering years were kept alive and aflame during the unemployment and stagnation of the inter-war years as they had been during the expansion and industrial advance of the pre-1914 period. As south Wales went, so, to a degree, went the nation. It was the Welsh miners who largely swung the affiliation of the Miners' Federation of Great Britain to the Labour party in 1908. It was they also who carried industrial relations to unimaginable depths of class confrontation in the years up to 1914, during the war itself and on to the General Strike in 1926. Even after that, young militant unemployed miners carried the passions of the valleys to such unlikely places as Oxford and Slough, Coventry and Dagenham; the Welsh were catalysts of social revolution as the Irish had been in the past. In Glamorgan over this period, under the aegis of the fanatical chief constable of the county, Captain Lionel Lindsay, himself a product of the Egyptian army in the time of Sir Garnet Wolseley, with his frequent

recourse to troops and the new operational violence adopted by the
local constabulary, south Wales became the battleground of the class
war, British style.

Two men particularly symbolized the struggle within the labour
world for the hearts and minds of the Welsh proletariat – William
Abraham (Mabon), the very model of Welsh Nonconformist Lib–
Labbery, and Noah Ablett, the incandescent young Marxist ideologue
who erupted to leadership in Rhondda in 1909–10. The struggle
between the ethic of Mabonism and the ideology of *The Miners' Next
Step*, the neo-syndicalist tract published by the Unofficial Reform
Committee at Tonypandy in 1912, of which Ablett was the inspiration
and part-author, reached deep down into the psyche of the Welsh
working class. Through their dialectic, a wider battle was fought out
throughout the working-class movement in Britain as a whole between
the idea of class collaboration and of class conflict. The outcome was a
mixed one, in which both the aged Mabon and the young Ablett
emerged as part losers. But its course, and the violent passion that
accompanied it, dictated much of the nature of British labour relations
in the first quarter of the twentieth century.

Mabon was a typical product of the Nonconformist radicalism that
galvanized and democratized Welsh politics and society after the
general election of 1868, uniting tenant farmers in the countryside
with industrial workers in the mining valleys against the common
feudal, Tory enemy. He grew up during the first development of the
Rhondda coalfield in the late 1860s and 1870s. Born in 1848, he had
emerged, by the time he had entered his thirties, as a formidable leader
of the Cambrian Miners' Association, one of the fledgling unions in
Rhondda. He was a faithful Nonconformist, a deacon of Nazareth
chapel, Pentre, and a fluent and effective speaker in both English and
Welsh. His fine tenor voice, which won him the eisteddfodic *nom de
guerre* Mabon, was also of value in times of industrial tension. Mabon,
it seemed, had only to strike up the Welsh national anthem for the
most angry assembly of miners to be transformed into a peaceful and
united gathering. General Smuts was to marvel at Mabon's style of
musical diplomacy during the First World War. Ironically – and
significantly – when Mabon sought election to Parliament in 1885 as
the first Welsh working-class MP, the local Rhondda Liberal Association refused to endorse even so quietist and undeniably orthodox a
Welsh Liberal as Mabon. He had to fight, and beat, a Liberal
coalowner at the polls. But the episode left no bitterness. In
Parliament, he proved himself a wholly loyal supporter of the young
middle-class nationalist Liberals of the *Cymru Fydd* school, such as
Tom Ellis and Lloyd George. Disestablishment, land reform, education, temperance, even a vaguely conceived Welsh Home Rule were

Mabon's political priorities. His quiet recital of the Lord's Prayer in Welsh on the floor of the House of Commons shook many a cynical Tory back-bencher. Built like a prop forward, Mabon was the sturdy proletarian embodiment of the Welsh *gwerin*, the folk myth of his people.

In industrial relations, his outlook was moral rather than economic. He adhered, as Professor Arthur Beacham once wrote, to 'the simple truths of the New Testament, not the tortuous canon of Karl Marx'. Indeed, there was a prophetic, biblical quality about Mabon himself – 'five feet by four feet, correct measurement' (according to Keir Hardie), with his long black beard, and patriarchal appearance and mode of speech. The south Wales sliding scale on wages, agreed by the coalowners and the miners' leaders in 1875, was Mabonism in action. He was its vigorous champion against more militant critics who accused him of being a bosses' man, enjoying cigars and other hospitality in the managers' offices. In fact, the sliding scale was largely to the disadvantage of the colliers themselves. It depressed wages (without any limit stated) while maintaining the owners' profit levels. An agreed scale of wage rates was achieved at the cost of infrequent audits, small percentage increases, and a built-in tendency to depress the price of coal, on which wage assessments depended. The price of industrial peace was acceptance of the terms of the owners, with their casual, even criminal, disregard for the physical safety of their men. In 1880, even the minimum wage provision of the sliding scale was swept away, and Mabon was left to propose such dubious expedients as compulsory emigration to America.

However, the sliding scale and Mabonism held the field until the massive six-months' coal stoppage – in effect, an owners' lock-out – from March to September 1898. It was a shattering defeat for Mabon, a decisive turning-point in his career as in the history of the Welsh miners as a whole. Symbolically, 'Mabon's day', the miners' holiday on the first Monday of each month, was abolished in the holocaust. Mabon had indeed 'fought tooth and nail for his day'; but the owners were implacable. The South Wales Miners' Federation (popularly revered as the Fed) was formed shortly afterwards in 1899, shaking the valleys and pit villages into class unity. Mabon became its first president, with William Brace, (once an enemy of his) the vice-president. But it was clear that his influence, and the creed of Lib–Lab conciliation, were on the wane.

In the first years of the new century the remnants of Mabonism were rapidly cast asunder in a period of extraordinary industrial turmoil in the valleys. Coal production soared to unimaginable heights, and Cardiff became the major coal-exporting port in the world, followed closely by its *arriviste* neighbour, Barry; together, they dominated the international carrying trade. A third of the world's coal exports came from south Wales. But at the same time, a huge rise in immigration from England, and much sociological upheaval in the coalfield, reinforced an intense bitterness between owners and men. The sliding scale was formally rejected by the Fed in 1902. These years were a time of continuous retreat for Mabon – the merger of the Welsh miners into the Miners' Federation of Great Britain, and affiliation to the Labour party; a nation-wide campaign for a minimum wage; an explosion of anger at the effects on wage rates of the Mines Eight Hours Act; demands for the standardization of wage rates against the hazards of 'abnormal places' where the cutting of coal was difficult. Tension was built up still further by a series of appalling mining tragedies, from explosions and other mishaps, with the death of 439 miners at Senghennydd in 1913 the crowning tragedy. All this meant a decisive breach with the older chapel-reared Liberalism to which Mabon automatically subscribed. He was the venerable victim of the conflict that scarred the road that led to Tonypandy.

The Welsh miners were ripe for another Messiah. Indeed, the use of religious and eschatological terms comes naturally enough to an analysis of the coalfield at this period. The 1904 religious revival, which galvanized Wales in the next two years from its starting-point at Loughor near Llanelli, had a powerful impact on the consciousness of many young miners. They included men like Frank Hodges, Arthur Cook, Arthur Horner, S. O. Davies, and others moved by religious experience to become part of the vanguard of industrial revolt. One of these was Noah Ablett, the most remarkable Marxist ideologue to surface in any part of the British coalfield in this period. Born to a large mining family at Porth in the Rhondda in 1883, his early enthusiasm was kindled by the community life of the local chapels, and he was soon preaching the gospel in local pulpits. However, a pit accident, which prevented his moving on to a post in the minor civil service, led to his continuing as a working miner underground. Over the next few years, he became fired by the theory of socialism, and of the message of Marx's *Kapital* in particular. He was an outstanding student at Ruskin College, Oxford, in 1907–9, where he became closely associated with an older Welsh miner and fellow Marxist, Noah Rees. Ablett returned to Rhondda in 1909 a fierce and learned advocate of extreme socialist views, coloured additionally by the syndicalism of Sorel in France and the industrial unionism of Tom Mann now flourishing in Australia. Ablett was, indeed, a remarkable young man, a rebel of cosmopolitan, perhaps cosmic, importance. As an educator and ideologue, he was unique.

He now set up Marxist tutorial classes in the central valleys of the Welsh coalfield, the Rhondda and Cynon valleys in particular, using

the chapel Sunday schools he had known in his childhood as
something of a model. His Plebs League, founded in January 1909, led
to the eventual creation of the Central Labour College, a militant and
class-conscious organization which led to a fierce revolt amongst
working-class students in Oxford against the quietism of Ruskin
College. Between 1909 and 1912, Marxists such as Ablett and other
young ideologues like Will Mainwaring and Will Hay were ceaselessly
active throughout south Wales, contributing to Tom Mann's syndicalist
publications, expounding the truths of Marxist economics and
sociology, propounding a class-based attitude towards the industrial
controversies of the day. Ironically enough, Ablett was hailed locally as
illustrating the dialectical and philosophical skills of 'the Oxford man',
hitherto associated only with bourgeois institutions such as Jesus
College. His main activity focused on the Unofficial Reform
Committee based on Tonypandy, in the heart of Rhondda. It was
essentially a rank-and-file protest against the caution of Mabon, Brace,
and other older leaders of the Fed. It was also a revolt at the grass-
roots (or rather the pit-head) against the autocratic position of senior
miners' agents within the federalized framework of the miners' union
which emphasized local autonomy.

In *The Miners' Next Step*, published at Tonypandy in 1912, the
doctrine of Ablett (one of the six authors) was spelt out with
frightening clarity and language of Biblical intensity. Not only the
timeworn Lib–Labbery of Mabon was condemned. The Labour
party's call for parliamentary leadership and the state nationalization
of the coal-mines was equally rejected, in favour of industrial
unionism, workers' control, pit-head democracy and the running of
mines by miners' syndicates at the point of production. Public debates
that took place between Ablett and (ironically enough) Frank Hodges,
for the neo-syndicalists, and T. I. Mardy Jones and George Barker, for
the socialist nationalizers, were forums for a crucial debate between
the idea of 'the mines for the nation' and of 'the mines for the miners'.
Under nationalization, so Ablett argued at Trealaw in November 1912,
the same depressed wages, the same lack of basic safety provision, the
same absence of industrial freedom would prevail. 'Where there are
state workers', he proclaimed, 'there is always a condition of servility.'

In 1910–12, the battle lines were drawn up between the old ethic
embodied in Mabonism and the angry class ideology of Ablett and his
friends. The valleys were locked in intense ideological crisis. With the
background of the terrifying violence of the Tonypandy riots, almost
equally alarming events in Aberdare, the loss of life at Tonypandy in
November 1910 and then at Llanelli in August 1911 during a rail
strike, south Wales was the arena for an immense industrial turbulence.
The whole British labour movement seemed poised at a historic

parting of the ways. Ablett at this time was, by all accounts, a figure of Lenin-like charisma, a great teacher, a brilliant orator and pamphleteer. Young miners like Arthur Cook, Arthur Horner and Aneurin Bevan were swept up by his gospel of industrial revolt; they never forgot it throughout their subsequent careers. Within the SWMF, the fortuitous death of three members of the executive in a train accident, led to the election of three militants, Will John, John Hopla, and Tom Smith, in their place. Ablett himself was on the executive from early 1911, as representative of Maerdy. In addition, he helped launch a new publication, *The Rhondda Socialist*, the self-proclaimed 'BOMB of the Rhondda workers'. Renamed *The South Wales Worker* in 1913, it claimed a circulation of over six thousand. From his base in red Maerdy, where he still worked as a checkweigher, Ablett acted as the one-man Comintern of the coalfield.

Mabon by this time was becoming an increasingly ceremonial, even pitiable, figure. He remained MP for Rhondda until his retirement, at the age of seventy-two, in 1920. He stayed on the executive of the Miners' Federation of Great Britain, and travelled widely abroad. During the First World War, of which he was a powerful supporter, his public image reached a zenith of respectability. He entered the Privy Council and was conferred with a doctorate of laws by the University College of Wales, Aberystwyth. He was a powerful advocate of conscription. He also lent his name – and his beard – to the advertisement of tobacco and tomato sauce. He became a director and major shareholder of several insurance companies. At his death, his biographer, Dr Eric Wyn Evans, tells us, 'he was a wealthy man by any standards'. Ideologically he had outlived his usefulness by at least twenty years. The myth had consumed the man. He seemed an incongruous survivor from the years before 1898, the middle ages of mining trade-unionism. In plain terms, as the then syndicalist, Charles Stanton, told him bluntly at Aberdare in 1910, he should 'move on or move out'. Mabon did neither, and his irrelevance to industrial history was only the more vividly underlined as a result.

Yet the future in south Wales, and amongst the miners generally, did not really belong to Noah Ablett either. Despite the alarm raised by *The Miners' Next Step*, the Unofficial Reform Committee did not greatly extend its influence beyond its original power base in Rhondda. In 1912, the elections to the SWMF executive saw a marked reaction against the class-war militants like Ablett. Mainstream advocates of orthodox trade-unionism like Brace, Hartshorn, Onions, and Barker were elected instead. By 1914, the URC was a declining and localized splinter group. The early years of the First World War, in which patriotism was surprisingly rife in the coalfield and in which Welsh miners volunteered in vast numbers, also saw Ablett in eclipse. He remained, however, a powerful teacher and strategic influence. His role was an important one in the Welsh miners' official strike in July 1915, in which they defied Lloyd George and the government, and won a significant wage advance. In the latter stages of the war, Ablett returned to prominence as the Unofficial Reform movement resurfaced, especially after the excitement generated by the Bolshevik revolution in Russia. Ablett became miners' agent for Merthyr in 1918; he served on the MFGB executive from 1919 to 1926; and, with supporters such as Mainwaring, Cook, and S. O. Davies, he was active within the so-called 'minority movement' with the Fed, in effect proclaiming the industrial policy of the Communist party of which he was an early member. Reports from the excitable Special Branch, sent to the Cabinet, mentioned Ablett, along with Cook and S. O. Davies, as a revolutionary figure, bent on establishing 'the Soviet system of government' in south Wales. As late as the 1926 General Strike, he was prominent enough to be arrested. The legend of Noah Ablett, the guru of Marxist industrial economics and the prophet of the class war, lasted long beyond his lifetime (he died in 1935, a totally spent force at the age of fifty-two). Labour historians have faithfully recreated it anew in recent years.

But, for all his charisma, the future for the Welsh miners, and indeed for the British proletariat as a whole, did not lie with Ablett any more than it did with the antediluvian conservatism of Mabon. In part, this may be a comment on Ablett's own personal decline. Like other Welsh miners' leaders before and since, the pressures of his public role led to his succumbing increasingly to the solace of alcohol. In his later years, he was thereby effectively removed as a significant force in mining trade-union circles. This was the unspoken reason why Arthur Horner and other Welsh militants threw support behind A. J. Cook rather than Ablett in the election of a successor to Hodges as secretary of the Miners' Federation of Great Britain 1924.

Beyond these personal aspects, Ablett's appeal to direct industrial action, focusing on the localism of individual pits and valleys, cut against the class solidarity of the mining community. To many Welsh miners, Noah Ablett from Porth, translated to Maerdy, was simply parochial. In addition, his brisk dismissal of parliamentarianism, local government, the chapel ethos – the values of south Wales communal life as it had emerged over five decades – was too complete and total to win many converts, even amidst the storms of Welsh labour relations between 1910 and 1926. The Central Labour College itself folded up in the late twenties, with much bad blood (and allegations of financial malpractice) all round. As south Wales emerged from the maelstrom after the General Strike, defeated and embittered but with its pride and local institutions intact, the leaders of the miners, in the main, conformed to a different style. It was best personified by a man like Vernon Hartshorn of Maesteg, the outstanding Welsh miners' leader of the post-1918 era, who served in the first Labour governments of 1924 and 1929. Along with Hartshorn went other distinctly centrist figures like Arthur Jenkins, Enoch Morrell, Charles Edwards, Oliver Harris, and the coming man of the thirties, James Griffiths. All of them were pragmatists, practical negotiators rather than ideologues. With men like these, the appeal of community was fused with the call of class. Through the capture of community power, in local government, in the local branches of the Fed, in adult education and in a variety of local services, a new leadership élite was created. It was freed from the outdated ethos of Mabon and all his works, but it was totally detached from the adversarial creed of Ablett as well.

By all accounts, Noah Ablett was a remarkably selfless, sincere, devoted man. He died in October 1935 as he had lived, comparatively poor (he left effects worth £230), revered within Maerdy and his own local circles, but proudly contemptuous of the honours and blandishments of a wider world. As with the Scottish Clydesiders – or some of them – his very dogmatism was both his strength and his downfall. It led him into destructive paths, and into an unrelenting commitment to class stereotypes, from which even such a militant associate as Will Mainwaring finally managed to free himself. Mainwaring moved on to Westminster, and so later did S. O. Davies. The ethic of industrial unionism remained articulate in south Wales, especially in the Fed through men such as Horner and other gifted Communist leaders. But it proved to be too parochial and backward-looking to provide an effective critique for coming to terms with a world in which industrial technology, world markets, and a wider social culture were generating immense changes. In the new, more affluent circumstances that the Welsh coalfield experienced from 1945 to the mid-1970s, with full employment and industrial diversification, there was little room for the ideas Ablett had promoted. Even his disciple, Arthur Horner, who served as secretary of the NUM from 1946 to 1960 and became an indirect prop for the Attlee government during the first phase of nationalization, moved into more positive channels; the old poacher even briefly considered turning gamekeeper and joining the National Coal Board, but declined the offer after some thought.

Ablett will remain a romantic legend for the apostles of an 'alternative', counter-factual labour history, full of bravura, panache, and schizoid turbulence. In the more humdrum, real world, *The Miners' Next Step* proved to be a step too far.

1987

24

'The Red Dragon and the Red Flag': The Cases of James Griffiths and Aneurin Bevan

The main archives at the National Library of Wales on which I have worked over the decades have been the papers of Liberal politicians – Tom Ellis, D. R. Daniel, Herbert Lewis, Stuart Rendel, Arthur Humphreys-Owen and of course Lloyd George, whose letters I edited in 1973. This, of course, reflects the Liberal ascendancy in Welsh politics in the later nineteenth and early twentieth centuries. But it also reflects the fact that Liberals tend to come from professions which are archivally minded – lawyers, journalists, businessmen. The Liberal archives in the National Library are a celebration of the hegemony of the Nonconformist middle class. Labour archives are a much more difficult problem. Labour figures tend to be poorer, less well educated, ill-equipped with administrative or secretarial assistance in keeping their records.

But progress is being made. The journal *Llafur* admirably reflects the new seriousness being attached to Labour and working-class records and their preservation. The Political Archive in Aberystwyth has already acquired the records of organizations like the Welsh Council of Labour, and of many Labour politicians and grass-roots activists. It is partly to encourage this process that the present theme has been chosen.

James Griffiths and Aneurin Bevan have been to date the two outstanding figures in the Welsh Labour movement – authentic Welsh figures unlike arrivals like Keir Hardie or Michael Foot, or departures like Roy Jenkins. Both made a considerable impact on national and international politics. Both were at various times thought to be possible Labour leaders, especially Bevan. At the same time, they are usually thought to represent contrasting outlooks and stances. Griffiths is seen as a moderate, a Nonconformist, Welsh-speaking Christian socialist, close to the old radical traditions. Bevan, by contrast, is viewed as an agitator and an extremist, doctrinaire, an international socialist and an agnostic. They appear to embody two different approaches to socialism – and to Welsh socialism in particular. Griffiths's papers are mostly in the National Library in Aberystwyth. Bevan, characteristically, seems to have left no archive at all.

Well, how far are they contrasting personalities? Are the differences between them more apparent than real? And what was their relationship to the culture of Wales? I want to look briefly at five main aspects – their origins; their roles as trade unionists, party politicians and Cabinet ministers; and their attitude towards Wales. It may be that, if we look at them under these categories, a few surprises emerge and the received wisdom looks a shade less reliable.

As regards their *origins*, James (or, to give him his proper Christian name, Jeremiah) Griffiths grew up in an intensely Welsh-speaking community, the Amman valley at the turn of the century. His brother, 'Amanwy', was a noted local eisteddfodic bard. Jim Griffiths was much affected by the 1904 religious revival (when he was fourteen) and also by the preaching of the Revd John 'Gwili' Jenkins who preached a powerful brand of humanitarian, ethical Christian socialism, as Professor Beverley Smith has powerfully demonstrated.[1] Griffiths moved on into the Independent Labour Party, then much galvanized in eastern Carmarthenshire by the impact of *Llais Llafur*, edited at Ystalyfera by Ebenezer Rees (the great-grandfather of the 1989 Archive lecturer, David Marquand). Griffiths was a devoted Congregationalist and an advocate of temperance. He attended the 'White House' at Ammanford, a workers' forum for the discussion of socialist and radical ideas. It was a relatively peaceful background which left a legacy of consensual endeavour and also a regard for learning, focused on Coleg Harlech in his later years. The First World War and Griffiths's entry into the Marxist Central Labour College in 1919 did not really alter this inheritance.

Nye Bevan came from a notably different background – Tredegar in Gwent with echoes of Dic Penderyn, Chartism and the radicalism of the eastern valleys. Bevan, unlike his father, was not Welsh-speaking; in religious terms he was an agnostic, a devotee of 'the religion of socialism'. His reading was much more eclectic than that of Griffiths. It fortified his claim to have been a nineteenth-century romantic,

[1] J. Beverley Smith, 'John Gwili Jenkins, 1872–1936', *Transactions of the Honourable Society of Cymmrodorion*, 1974–5, 191–214.

whereas Hugh Gaitskell was an eighteenth-century rationalist.[2] It seems to have included works by Jack London, Thorsten Veblen and later the south American philosopher, José Rodo. Although seven years younger than Griffiths (he was born in 1897), Bevan seems to have been much more influenced by the Cambrian Colliery strike of 1910–11, the riots at Tonypandy and the neo-syndicalist pamphlet, *The Miners' Next Step*, with its call for direct industrial action. There was an atmosphere of social conflict, to which Bevan's incipient Marxism naturally related. He thus derived a very different lesson from the Central Labour College which he attended at the same time as Griffiths – modified by the fact that Bevan appears to have been a somewhat indolent student who found it difficult to get up in time for early morning lectures! In terms of their origins, then, Griffiths and Bevan certainly diverge, a distinction symbolized by their respective wives – Winnie Griffiths, a gentle Hampshire socialist of Christian persuasion, and Jennie Lee, a dynamic, Scottish Marxist firebrand.

As a *trade unionist*, Griffiths was always strongly committed. He worked his way up the South Wales Miners' Federation in the 1920s. Fortunately for him, he was absent from the physical violence of the 1925 anthracite strike at Ammanford (in fact, he was a Labour agent at Burry Port, not very far away). In due time, Griffiths became president of the South Wales Miners' Federation in 1934, where he worked well with Communists such as Arthur Horner. Griffiths, indeed, was part of that new generation of moderates – men like Arthur Jenkins, Enoch Morrell and Oliver Harris – that rose to power in the 'Fed' after the General Strike. As president of the 'Fed', Griffiths negotiated the first miners' wage increase since 1926, the so-called Schiller award, and also helped settle the disputes that arose at the time of the 'stay-down' stoppages in 1935. His bilingual wartime pamphlet *Coal [Glo]*, with a foreword by Will Lawther, recalled those years of struggle and solidarity. He always believed that the trade union alliance was the linchpin of the Labour party. He made much of this theme during the 1945 Labour government when he felt close to union leaders like Ernie Bevin. Griffiths was pushed by Hugh Dalton as a possible foreign secretary in succession to Bevin in early 1951, simply because Griffiths was the most able trade unionist around in the government. Even as late as 1963 Griffiths voted for the trade-union figure of George Brown as party leader,[3] even though Brown's behaviour must have strained the loyalty of a temperance advocate like Jim Griffiths to breaking-point.

[2]Philip Williams, *Hugh Gaitskell* (London, 1979), 206, citing Gaitskell's diary, of 21 November 1949.

[3]James Griffiths, *Pages from Memory* (London, 1969), 139.

Aneurin Bevan, by contrast, was not always at ease with the unions and their leaders. His background was syndicalist as much as socialist – he wanted workers' power rather than the bureaucratic rigidities of nationalization. He went into politics partly in reaction to the quiescence of the trade union leaders after the trauma of the General Strike. In the 1930s, now member for Ebbw Vale, he was often at odds with TUC leaders like Bevin and Citrine, mostly on the Labour right. Union bosses like Arthur Deakin and Will Lawther were foremost in the campaign to drive Bevan out of the party in 1944 and again in 1955. In the 1950s, Bevan saw the union block vote as the greatest single obstacle to promoting socialism within the Labour party. He proposed various reforms of the National Executive and other bodies which have recently again become fashionable. Bevan launched ferocious attacks on the union bosses in *Tribune*. He was, therefore, always somewhat deracinated from his own union roots as a miner, though it might be added that sentiment kept him friendly with an undeniably right-wing leader like Sam Watson of the Durham miners. It is at least a tribute to Bevan's syndicalist origins that he was almost the only minister in Attlee's government to raise the issue of industrial democracy during discussions of nationalization, linking it with wages policy.[4]

As a *party politician*, Griffiths always saw himself as a reconciler. There may have been an element of humbug in this, or so some people thought. Ian Mikardo's memoirs refer to Griffiths having 'both his hands on both his hearts'.[5] Griffiths was a centrist figure from the time he entered Parliament as member for Llanelli in 1936. On the NEC he was a staunch supporter of Attlee and the party leadership; thus he became front-bench spokesman on social security during the war. In the 1950s, Griffiths was undoubtedly a strong supporter of the Gaitskellite right, but he was also the only right-winger on the NEC constituency section to keep his place during the Bevanite upsurge. He tried to restrain Gaitskell from seeking to expel Bevan from the party in 1954–5. As deputy-leader of the party from 1956 (defeating Bevan for this post), he worked strenuously to heal the breach between Gaitskellites and Bevanites. He remained a great loyalist to the end. Thus in the 1966–70 period, although increasingly unwell, he stayed on in parliament to prevent a by-election in Llanelli that might have let in the attractive Plaid Cymru candidate, the rugby player, Carwyn James.

Nye Bevan, on the other hand, was a rebel from the very start. He

---

[4]See Bevan's contribution, Cabinet conclusions, 17 July 1947 and 2 February 1948 (PRO, CAB 128/10 and 128/12).

[5]Ian Mikardo, *Backbencher* (London, 1988), 127.

was never a reconciler or a sound party man. An early speech in the House in 1930, despite the government's dependence on the Liberals, contained a biting attack on the old titan, Lloyd George, for his record on the mines. Bevan flirted with Oswald Mosley's New Party in 1931 – in its pre-fascist days, of course. He became friendly with such unexpected companions as Lord Beaverbrook, Brendan Bracken and Lord Castlerosse. In the 1930s, he was a free-lance radical *par excellence*. He took a particularly aggressive line against the National Government on such issues as the means test. He greeted the transition from Baldwin to Neville Chamberlain in 1937 as follows:

> In the funeral service of capitalism, the honeyed and soothing platitudes of the clergyman are finished, and the cortège is now under the sombre and impressive guidance of the undertaker.[6]

Bevan, for a brief time, called for 'freedom brigades' to defend the unemployed and the hunger marchers against the assaults of the police and their bosses such as Captain Lionel Lindsay. In *Tribune* Bevan wrote vigorously on behalf of Labour's joining the Popular Front. He was expelled on this score, along with Cripps and Strauss, in early 1939 and was not re-admitted to the Parliamentary Labour Party until after the war had started.

Bevan came close to being expelled again in 1944 after a fierce attack on Ernest Bevin, the minister of labour. His pamphlet, *Why Not Trust the Tories?* in 1944, written under the pseudonym 'Celticus', warned Labour of the dangers of being too coalition-minded and too devoted to the wartime consensus. As Cabinet minister in 1945–51, Bevan had a double role. He was a key member of the government, but also a man with a unique hold over the annual conference and the party rank and file, an insider and an outsider at the same time. His resignation from the Attlee government over NHS charges in April 1951 sparked off the revolt of the so-called 'Bevanites'. It was a resignation deliberately provoked by Hugh Gaitskell, the new chancellor of the Exchequer; the future was to show that on the key issue of the economic cost of the rearmament programme, which had led to charges on dental and ophthalmic treatment, Bevan was broadly right. Years of internal conflict followed. The Bevanites were accused of being a party within a party. Bevan himself lambasted Gaitskell (his presumed target) as 'a dessicated calculating machine'. He came within a whisker of being expelled from the parliamentary party again in March 1955, when he was saved by the conscience of a Moral

[6]Michael Foot, *Aneurin Bevan*, Vol. I (London, 1962), 257.

Rearmer on Labour's National Executive.[7] By this time, Bevan was
falling out with former Bevanite associates like Harold Wilson and
Richard Crossman, too.

It is a stormy record – but not the whole story. In the end, Bevan
became something of a reconciler himself. It is debatable whether
Bevan was really a Bevanite at all. In 1956–7 he came together with
Gaitskell, somewhat uneasily; he became foreign affairs spokesman
and in October 1959 he probably saved Gaitskell, after the general
election defeat, by a magnificent speech on behalf of the party
statement on industrial policy. Bevan always had a strong commitment
to the party, however fierce the internal rows in which he was a leading
participant. He genially chided Jennie Lee for her political 'virginity' in
preferring the purity of the wilderness with the ILP to the realities of
power with the Labour party.[8] In 1949 he was quite prepared to see
the expulsion of Konni Zilliacus from the Labour party. As Bevan told
a Welsh comrade, Huw T. Edwards, it was because of Zilliacus's 'close
association abroad with the enemies of Labour and Social
Democracy'.[9] Bevan had a great faith in loyalty and, according to his
own lights, he practised what he preached. Socialists must use power,
not destroy it.

Bevan was certainly a much less disruptive or disloyal figure than
was Tony Benn in the 1970s. He always saw the path to socialism in
parliamentary, not in extra-parliamentary (let alone anti-
parliamentary) terms. As Bevan wrote powerfully in his book *In Place
of Fear* (1952): 'Parliamentary democracy is a sword pointed at the
heart of property-power.'[10]

As a *Cabinet minister*, Griffiths was always immensely competent. He
made an excellent impression as minister of national insurance in
1945–50 though he was, of course, on a pretty favourable wicket in
implementing the Beveridge proposals with measures for national
insurance, national assistance and industrial injuries compensation. He
made a highly significant move to the Colonial Office in February
1950. Here, the constructive side of development of the economic
structure of African and other Third World colonies went alongside the
hard side of fighting a ferocious war against Communist insurgents in
Malaya. His most controversial policy was his pressing for a federation
in Central Africa, consisting of Northern and Southern Rhodesia and
Nyasaland. Griffiths may have been over-impressed by the ex-boxer,
trade-unionist Southern Rhodesian spokesman, Roy Welensky, though

[7]Philip Williams, op. cit., 339 ff. The Moral Rearmer was James Haworth.
[8]Jennie Lee, *Tomorrow is a New Day* (London, 1939), 151.
[9]Bevan to Huw T. Edwards, 20 June 1949 (National Library of Wales, Huw T.
Edwards papers).
[10]Bevan, *In Place of Fear* (London, 1952), 25.

he was much less dogmatic on the point than was Patrick Gordon Walker.[11] When it became clear that black African opinion was solidly opposed to any federation, Griffiths promptly retracted and attacked the federation in its later, ghostly existence. Certainly Africa was a major point of reference for him thereafter – witness his concern with the Biafran tragedy during the Nigerian civil war in the late 1960s.

In his wider ministerial role, Griffiths was generally cautious, he retreated from some strong postures during the Korean War (for instance, in resisting the American 'brand China' resolution in the UN) and he failed to back up Bevan to the bitter end over Gaitskell's proposed National Health Service charges though Griffiths was certainly an early ally of Bevan's.[12] Wilson resigned along with Bevan, but Griffiths stayed on in the government. As secretary for Wales in 1964–6, the first holder of that office, now a septuagenarian, he pursued a largely exploratory policy. He was mainly concerned with setting the new department up. The test would have come over local government, still an unresolved issue when he left the Wilson Cabinet in April 1966.

Bevan was a more controversial Cabinet minister. He is indelibly associated with denouncing the Tories as 'lower than vermin', which caused a great stir at the time, perhaps excessively so.[13] Bevan often threatened to resign in 1945–51, over housing, devaluation of the pound and other issues. Yet he was always a brilliant and creative executive. The National Health Service was very much his own work since the Willink scheme during the war had proved abortive. Bevan proved very conciliatory over many health aspects, for instance in protecting private practice and 'pay beds' and in going very slow on health centres. Indeed, the broad scheme of the NHS was something of a disappointment to the Socialist Medical Association. But Bevan was, nevertheless, able to construct a powerful new health system and then dig in successfully to defeat the sabotage attempted by the British Medical Association, or at least its executive council. A vital key to Bevan's success was the remarkable alliance he struck up with the presidents of the royal colleges, notably Lord Moran, 'Corkscrew Charlie' of the Royal College of Physicians.

The NHS was far from immaculate in its conception. Its financial demands were underestimated from the start; prescription charges were discussed by the Cabinet in 1949 and charges on false teeth and

[11]Memorandum of conversation between Griffiths and Gordon Walker, 25 April 1951 (PRO, DO 121/136).

[12]Gaitskell's diary, 2 February 1951 (Nuffield College, Oxford, library) for the 'brand China' resolution; Charles Webster, *The Health Services since the War*, Vol. I (HMSO, London, 1988), 173–4.

[13]*The Times*, 5 July 1948.

spectacles in 1950. Supplementary estimates for the NHS were required in 1949 especially to meet the rising cost of the hospital service.[14] But overall the Health Service was a magnificent achievement, one which has survived the test of time. Unlike Christopher Addison (a Cabinet colleague of Bevan's) back in 1921, Bevan in 1945–51 found that his reputation was made by the needs of social reform. In 1956 the Guillebaud committee was to uphold the cost-effectiveness and efficiency of the NHS *en bloc*. More remarkably still, Mrs Thatcher was compelled to assure the electorate during the 1983 election that 'the National Health Service is safe with us'. (However, the government White Paper of February 1989 appears to place the universality of the facilities of the NHS in some doubt.)

On housing policy, another of his departmental responsibilities, Bevan was probably more effective than was often thought. After a slowish start, over a million well-built council houses were constructed, to a high standard. Great housing need remained but the explanation lies more in the underlying financial constraints of the time, including the inroads made by Dalton and Cripps at the Treasury into house building.

Bevan always saw his role in the Cabinet in a broader context than did Griffiths. He intervened very widely on a great range of issues between 1945 and 1951. He had much to say on steel nationalization, which he defended as a talisman of socialist intent.[15] As minister of labour briefly in January–April 1951, he gave his views on the wage-freeze and collective bargaining. He had a great deal to say, too, on foreign policy questions. In 1948, remarkably, he became quite hawkish and anti-Russian over the blockade of Berlin. On the question of rearmament and the new defence budget in 1950–1, it is totally wrong to allege, as Attlee, Gaitskell and others tried to do, that Bevan only raised the wider question at the very last moment.[16] In fact, he made powerful interventions on defence expenditure from August 1950 onwards.[17] In the ultimate crisis, Gaitskell, the economist, based his support of the huge new arms burden on political considerations – his staunch commitment to the American alliance. Bevan, ironically, raised a range of cogent economic aspects, the effect on the balance of payments, exports, labour shortages and much else besides. Despite

[14]The supplementary estimates amounted to £53m. See Sir Cyril Jones, 'Enquiry into the Financial Working of the Health Service', 15 July 1950 (PRO, PREM 8/1486).

[15]Cabinet conclusions, 24 July 1947 (ibid., CAB 128/10); cf. *Tribune*, 10 October 1947.

[16]See the footnotes cited in Philip Williams, *Gaitskell*, 247–8.

[17]Cabinet conclusions, 1 August 1950, and 15 and 25 January 1951 (PRO, CAB 128/18 and 128/19).

the Bevanite civil war that erupted from 1952 onwards, the main issue was resolved in Bevan's favour. In 1952 Churchill radically curtailed Labour's defence programme. In effect, and grudgingly, Churchill had become the ultimate Bevanite.

As a Cabinet minister, Bevan was undeniably an unpredictable figure. No doubt, too, ambition played its part in the clash with Gaitskell, a younger man who had overtaken him. Attlee is much at fault for not having given Bevan a post more major than the Ministry of Labour. In the last stages, from 1957 on, Bevan was a powerful shadow foreign secretary, a man with links with figures like Nehru, Tito and Mendès-France. It is intriguing to speculate how impressive Bevan might well have been as Labour's foreign secretary in the post-Stalin world where the cold war was thawing and the old rigidities breaking down.

Finally, there is the question of Griffiths's and Bevan's attitude to *Wales*. It is an old theme – the relationship of socialism to nationalism, 'Y ddraig goch a'r faner goch'.[18] Griffiths was, without doubt, strongly sympathetic to the national heritage. He spoke Welsh freely. During the war, he had advocated Welsh devolution during his time on the Welsh Reconstruction Committee. In the Attlee Cabinet after 1945, he urged that Wales should be treated as a distinct administrative unit in the nationalization of electricity.[19] He also pressed in vain for Herbert Morrison to give the Council of Wales stronger powers in 1949. At least he did secure the strongly nationalistic figure of Huw. T. Edwards as first chairman.[20]

Griffiths was also mainly instrumental, while party deputy-leader in 1956–9, in getting a Welsh secretaryship of state put on Labour's manifesto. He found James Callaghan sympathetic at this time. Finally, he became the 'Charter secretary' for Wales in 1964. There was not a great deal to show here, with the project for a new town somewhere near Caersws not destined to progress. Appropriately, in his last years Griffiths was a staunch supporter of devolution for Wales.

Bevan was, apparently, a strong critic of Welsh separateness, by contrast. In the first 'Welsh Day' debate in the Commons in 1944, he asked ironically how Welsh sheep differed from English sheep, and claimed that the whole idea of a Welsh debate was a waste of time. He

[18]See, for instance, T. E. Nicholas, 'Y Ddraig goch a'r Faner goch', *Y Geninen*, Ionawr 1912, 10–16.

[19]There is material on the Reconstruction Committee in the James Griffiths papers in NLW. For electricity, see Griffiths's 'Note on the Electricity Bill', 17 December 1946, CP (46) 21 (PRO, CAB 129/6).

[20]'The Administration of Wales', October 1948, CP (48) 228 (ibid., CAB 129/30); correspondence between Morrison and Griffiths, October 1949 (NLW, Griffiths papers, C/2/6–11).

was unsympathetic to supporters of the Welsh language. Alan Watkins has a story of how Bevan told the young Emyr Humphreys in the 1950s, when being informed he was a Welsh speaker, 'I s-s-suppose you want a job with the BBC'.[21] (In fact Humphreys was a BBC employee anyway!) Bevan often gave the impression of being somewhat bored by Wales, by the puritanism of the chapels, by the parochialism of village life. He seldom dined at the 'Welsh table' at the House of Commons. His intimates were altogether more colourful and cosmopolitan.

Yet Bevan's antipathy to Welshness can be overdone, and John Campbell's biography is at fault in largely ignoring Bevan's Welsh roots. In this as in other respects, Michael Foot's earlier work is a surer guide, for all its partisanship. Bevan, after all, grew up in the south Wales industrial world. Wales was a most important base throughout his career, not least during the Bevanite controversies. Bevan grew up in a homogenous Welsh working-class society, the pit, the working-men's club, the Medical Aid Society, local government, extra-mural education, in a way not really true, say, of Neil Kinnock whose early experiences were shaped by student politics in the post-1945 welfarized world. Bevan's remarkable speech at the 1958 Eisteddfod at Ebbw Vale shows how important his vision of Welshness was to him. What we now require is to relate Bevan to a wider cultural exploration of south Wales society as a whole, and in this respect Dai Smith's *Aneurin Bevan and the World of South Wales* (1994) is most valuable.

In comparing Griffiths and Bevan, there appears to be a basic contrast between a right-wing reconciler and a left-wing militant, *Socialist Commentary* versus *Tribune*, the Gaitskellite versus the Bevanite. Without doubt, they were men of different styles. Griffiths was a fairly conventional product of a Welsh mining background. Bevan was an aristocrat in outlook and taste – he liked to compare an aristocrat like himself with a humdrum bourgeois like Gaitskell (in fact, a man closer in temperament to Bevan than is often realized). Bevan had a lively interest in art and music (so had Jennie Lee, who was a marvellous minister for the arts after 1964); he liked expensive wines and food; he dressed with style. He was friendly with a social maverick like Beaverbrook. Brendan Bracken once chaffed that Bevan was only 'a Bollinger Bolshevik, a ritzy Robespierre, a lounge-lizard Lenin'.[22]

Yet, in terms of substance rather than of style, the contrast between Griffiths and Bevan may not be so stark. Bevan was a more centrist

[21]Article by Alan Watkins, 'Neil takes on Conference', and letter by Emyr Humphreys, *The Observer*, 3, 10 July 1988. Mr Watkins tells me that the story came originally from V. S. Pritchett.

[22]Charles Edward Lysaght, *Brendan Bracken* (London, 1979), 150.

figure than is often imagined. He merged Marxism with what he called 'relativism'[23] – perhaps pragmatism might serve instead. In 1945–51 Bevan's socialism was far from extreme – he accepted the mixed economy in which 80 per cent remained in private ownership. He supported NATO. He showed more loyalty to the party than ever Benn was to show in 1974–9 – witness Michael Foot's acid dismissal of 'Brother Tony' in his book *Loyalists and Loners*.[24] Bevan's old friendship with Stafford Cripps kept him reined in under Attlee's leadership. On occasion, Griffiths and Bevan (who did not particularly like each other as a rule) could work closely together, as when they both pressed unsuccessfully in 1949 for Labour to include the nationalization of the insurance companies in its next election manifesto.[25]

On foreign affairs, it is arguable that Griffiths might have been the more radical of the two, with his old pacifist sympathies. Kenneth Younger claimed that Bevan might have become 'a rather right-wing' foreign secretary.[26] On the 1951 rearmament programme, Bevan's criticisms were logical and based on fact. Unlike Griffiths, Bevan had a strain almost of imperialism in his make-up. Over the Suez crisis in 1956, he was almost a 'patriot' since he saw President Nasser of Egypt as a dictator and bully. Bevan's residual sympathy with Israel may have helped make him less aggressive towards the Eden government than were right-wing figures like Gaitskell and Healey in the crisis.[27] And, of course, in the 1957 party conference Bevan was even to break with a devoted friend and ally like Michael Foot over unilateral nuclear disarmament. Bevan was no pacifist and no unilateralist, and he claimed that the disarmers would only send Britain 'naked into the conference chamber', its international influence relinquished.

Jim Griffiths and Nye Bevan, to my mind, embody different aspects of the same Welsh Labour ethic. They reflect the attachment to community and a wider internationalism of spirit, humane pragmatism and creative imagination. There was no fundamental conflict between them. In 1945 Labour was to call its election-winning manifesto *Let us Face the Future*. To my mind, it will need the qualities of both those remarkable Welshmen, if it is ever to face the future with confidence again.

1989

[23]Bevan, *In Place of Fear*, 202.

[24]Michael Foot, *Loyalists and Loners* (London, 1986), 107–26.

[25]National Executive Committee minutes, 30 September, 30 November 1949; Policy Committee minutes, 30 May, 7 and 28 July, 24 October, 14 November (Labour party archive, presently at Walworth Road). Courtesy of Mr Stephen Bird.

[26]Kenneth Younger interview transcript, 67 (Nuffield College, Oxford, library).

[27]Bevan's article in *Tribune*, 3 August 1956; cf. Janet Morgan (ed.), *The Backbench Diaries of Richard Crossman* (London, 1981), 508.

25

Aneurin Bevan
and the Welfare State

Aneurin Bevan, incorrigible rebel, prophet and tribune of working-class power, appears at first sight an unlikely member of the pantheon of constructive architects of the welfare state. He is often recalled today as a dogmatic irreconcilable. During the 1930s he was an implacable critic of the National government. In the war years, he was a remorseless opponent of the wartime consensus and of Churchill in particular.

His years in the Attlee government, from July 1945 to April 1951, were scarred by bitter controversy. To his political opponents, he was a 'squalid nuisance', a 'Tito from Tonypandy', even 'the Minister of Disease'. No episode during the Attlee years caused a greater sensation than Bevan's remark, during a speech at Manchester in July 1948, ostensibly delivered to welcome the introduction of the National Health Service, that his Tory opponents were 'lower than vermin'. The fury of the Tories was, after April 1951, matched by the enmity of his Gaitskellite Labour colleagues. In the 1950s, Bevan re-emerged as a party rebel and trouble-maker. The 'Keep Left' group and the Bevanite movement became the symbols of savage, internecine conflict within the Labour party over foreign and defence policy. The formal reconciliation with Gaitskell in the last phase before Bevan's death in 1960 did not greatly alter the picture.

Nothing, indeed, could be more ironic than attempts sometimes made now to contrast the moderate character of the socialism of the Bevanite 'legitimate left' with the extremist excesses of Bennery or the Militant Tendency. Aneurin Bevan, in fact, is in danger of passing into prehistory, almost as forgotten a figure as Keir Hardie or George

Lansbury in the past. His childhood home in Charles Street, Tredegar, was demolished some years ago with remarkably little public protest.

Yet this stormy petrel was to prove himself, in his five and a half years at the ministry of health under Attlee, both a prophet and a great constructive pioneer. He was unusual, almost unique, in the British labour movement in combining a passionate commitment to socialist principles with rare creative gifts of practical statesmanship. He was to prove himself, no less than his fellow-Welshman, Lloyd George, an artist in the uses of power.

Despite all the hammer-blows of financial crises, governmental cutbacks and industrial troubles, the main edifice of the National Health Service still endures as a model of humane social engineering, admired throughout the western world. The NHS alone ought to be proof, if any were needed, that Bevan's contribution to British public life was both positive and creative. The need to propel him out of myth and prehistory into the living world of historical reality is an urgent one. A book on the founders of the British welfare state seems a highly appropriate place at which to begin.

Bevan's appointment by Attlee to the Ministry of Health in July 1945 was something of a surprise. During his earlier career, as MP for Ebbw Vale from 1929, and as a union activist in the south Wales coalfield for years before that, he had not been greatly involved in problems of health and medicine as such. In the 1930s, it was unemployment and the means test (later on, Spain and the threat of fascism) that absorbed much of his energy. At the same time, no one could emerge from the crucible of the Welsh mining valleys unaware of how disease, squalor and environmental deprivation enshrouded the lives of the miners and others in the community.

Indeed, a notable aspect of south Wales society from the turn of the century had been the creation of a large array of workmen's health clubs and medical aid societies in the coalfield, often with the aid of Miners' Federation funds through joint subscriptions to hospitals. The private club system worked well; yet it was always bitterly opposed by local general practitioners who resented the element of lay control. In the end, the operations of the National Insurance Act after 1911 killed off many of these private miners' schemes; the conflict between the professional status of the doctors and the social needs of the working-class community was already present in microcosm. One of these schemes, a local Medical Aid Society, survived in Tredegar in the 1920s, and the young Aneurin Bevan, along with other young socialists from the Query Club, served on its hospital committee in 1923–4.

Beyond this, Bevan's early involvement with health and welfare seems to have been somewhat indirect. The pressure for a non-contributory national health service to be included in the Labour party's programme, successfully achieved in 1934, came after all from the professional doctors enrolled in the Socialist Medical Association, men like Somerville Hastings and Stark Murray, rather than from the ranks of union representatives like Bevan at Ebbw Vale.

For all that, it would be wrong to conclude that Bevan emerged at the Department of Health in 1945 innocent of specialist knowledge of medical matters. The doctors themselves were probably misled by his jovial pronouncement at a medical dinner during his first months in office that 'I am a comparative virgin'. Medical matters frequently caught the attention of his enquiring and incurably active mind; so did they for his wife, Jennie Lee, herself from a Scottish mining district where similar social deprivation prevailed. Bevan, we know, was much stirred by the Clement Davies committee report on the anti-tuberculosis services in Wales in 1939, which depicted in graphic terms the consequences of damp, insanitary housing, environmental neglect and inadequate public services for lung disease in the valleys. He also had close doctor friends like Dan Davies of Pontycymmer.

More generally, Bevan's concern with the range of socio-economic issues during the 1930s provided him with a broad synoptic diagnosis of the interrelated character of employment, welfare, health, education and other components of a civilized society. They left him with a deep scepticism of the vested interests of middle-class groups such as the medical profession. Additionally, from his early days before 1914 when he was stirred by syndicalism and *The Miners' Next Step*, he inherited from south Wales a profound commitment to mass popular involvement and accountability in public services, and to the full panoply of democracy, political and industrial. It was not a bad equipment to bring to bear to the Ministry of Health in the heady days of Labour's electoral victory in 1945.

The National Health Service is invariably recalled as Bevan's major achievement in this period. At the same time, it ought to be noted here that there were other important areas where his role in the creation of the welfare state was crucial and decisive. One was housing. This is often thought to be a blemish in Bevan's record. Slow progress in house-building was attacked at the time, while Bevan himself gave hostages to fortune by observing once blithely (and quite wrongly) that he spent a mere five minutes a week on housing during his time at the Ministry of Health.

Certainly, the housing programme of 1945–51 began badly and had several endemic problems. There were endless difficulties of co-ordinating the housing drive, with responsibility diffused between the Ministries of Health, Supply, Town and Country Planning, and Works, with the Scottish Office having its own responsibility north of the border. There were frequent conflicts for building materials such as bricks, timber and steel between the competing needs of council houses, hospitals, schools and factories in once depressed areas. There was no agreed procedure for ensuring that building starts were kept in line with the availability of labour on a local or regional basis; the list of half-built houses grew steadily.

On the other hand, the crushing problems that Bevan faced ought also to be given due weight. There were ceaseless financial difficulties, culminating in the severe cutback of the local authority housing programme from over 200,000 to 170,000 in 1949. There were constant shortages of raw materials, notably softwood and other timber. There were problems of the allocation of skilled labour, far beyond the control of the Ministry of Health. And there was the legacy of the ravages of the wartime blitz which imposed a huge strain on the resources for urban development. In the circumstances, Bevan's achievement of 1,016,349 permanent houses constructed in the six years to 31 October 1951 (excluding Northern Ireland) comes out impressively enough. Again, given the circumstances of the time, the decision to concentrate on council-house building via the local authorities (who controlled sites and planning machinery) for homeless working-class families, rather than private housing for sale designed for the middle class, was surely right.

Another area where Bevan was much involved was the social insurance schemes intended to implement the Beveridge proposals. Here the main architect, of course, was another Welsh ex-miner, James Griffiths, minister of National Insurance from 1945 to 1950, a man as firmly on the Labour right as Bevan was located on the left. In fact, the two men worked well together, and waged a joint campaign on the Labour party Home Policy Committee in 1948–9 to have the nationalization of the private assurance companies placed on the party manifesto, to reinforce the legislative achievements in social insurance and health.

In the end, Herbert Morrison and others managed to achieve the watered-down proposal for 'mutualization', a scheme under which ownership would be distributed between policy-holders. This appeared on the nationalization 'shopping list' in the February 1950 election manifesto, but was subsequently buried. Only in the 1970s did Labour again turn to consider bringing the industrial assurance companies, with their huge, untapped investments, within the fabric of a comprehensive public social service.

But it was, of course, the National Health Service that was always Bevan's main preoccupation. Indeed, after the war years, with Beveridge, the Willink scheme of 1944, and several other proposals for revamping the health and hospital service, it was generally anticipated that a new publicly financed health service would be a major priority for the Labour government. And, on this basis, Bevan's initial dealings with the British Medical Association were amiable enough, while his relations throughout with the presidents of the three royal colleges (Surgeons, Physicians and Obstetricians) were even cordial, especially with Lord Moran of the RCP. Like an earlier Welsh politician, Bevan could 'charm a bird off a bough' when he tried.

But problems soon began to emerge. Some resulted, perhaps, from the advanced nature of some of Bevan's proposals. In health as in other spheres, it is wrong to make too much of the continuity between the wartime social consensus and the welfare politics of the post-war Labour government. Beveridge had its limits.

Bevan's schemes went notably beyond those of Willink in 1944, especially the latter's final watered-down version. Bevan markedly increased the overall central control of the ministry. He provided more encouragement for new group partnerships in 'under-doctored areas' and for local health centres. He was unambiguous that there should be a salaried element in the remuneration of the general practitioners, even though capitation fees would still be the main component of a doctor's salary. Above all, there was a decisive commitment to the nationalization of hospitals, with a comprehensive reorganization of the hospital governing system under regional boards. This was something of which the Willink scheme, with its tenderness towards smaller and voluntary hospitals, had always fought shy.

The nationalization of hospitals was the only issue which caused major dispute within the Cabinet. On 18 October, and again on 20 December 1945, Herbert Morrison, with his long experience of local government on the London County Council, led the resistance of those who sought to preserve voluntary and municipal hospitals under local rather than national control. Morrison urged that there was no authority in the party manifesto for such a proposal (which was true). He emphasized the role of civic and local pride, and voluntary enthusiasm. He also attacked the proposal to make the cost of the hospitals a full charge on the Treasury (to which Hugh Dalton, the chancellor of the Exchequer, had already agreed). 'There would be a very large transfer of liability from the ratepayer to the taxpayer.' Morrison was backed up by the home secretary, Chuter Ede. But the great majority of ministers, not only left-wingers like Ellen Wilkinson and Emanuel Shinwell, but more centrist figures like Arthur Greenwood and Tom Williams, backed Bevan strongly.

An authoritative voice was that of the aged Lord Addison, once Lloyd George's minister of health in 1919–21 and himself a notable founder of the welfare state, now leader of the Lords under Attlee. Addison had himself been an anatomist of immensely high professional reputation; he was also the founder, in effect, of the

Medical Research Council. He warmly supported Bevan now on the grounds that a nationalized system would assist the teaching of doctors and the training of nurses. Addison's voice carried much weight with his close friend, Attlee, and the Cabinet endorsed Bevan's plans overwhelmingly.

But the main reason for the problems that arose lay not in the radicalism of Bevan's proposals – which, when introduced, won the warm support of such notably non-socialist organs as *The Times*, *The Economist* and the *Lancet*. It lay rather in the mulish intransigence of the BMA and its spokesmen, the elderly Dr Guy Dain, chairman of the BMA council, and its serpentine secretary, Dr Charles Hill, who had won fame on the air as 'the radio doctor'.

The association recognized that Bevan had made many concessions, including the preservation of private practice, pay beds in hospitals (which Bevan himself regarded as detestable but inevitable), the waiving of limits on specialists' fees, and appeal procedures for doctors to NHS tribunals. Nevertheless, it regarded the threat of a full-time salaried service as posing a fundamental menace to the professional freedom and security of the general practitioners. The BMA and its *Journal* also claimed to view the new powers vested in the Ministry of Health, and of the executive councils which would supervise GPs, with alarm. Dr Alfred Cox, absurdly, even denounced Bevan as a 'medical Fuehrer'.

The outcome was that negotiation between the BMA representatives, largely drawn as they were from wealthier, suburban doctors, and the minister and his civil servants broke down. Although the Act to create the NHS was carried in Parliament by a huge majority, the BMA threatened the same campaign of intransigence and obstruction as it had done to another Welshman, Lloyd George, back in 1911. The *British Medical Journal* warned doctors that, like his Celtic predecessor, Bevan was both 'a bard and a warrior'. The emollient approach of the Welshmen (like that of the Scotsman, Ernest Brown, and the Englishman, Henry Willink, before him) could not be taken on trust.

The period from the summer of 1946 until the final capitulation of the BMA in May–June 1948, and its acceptance of the inevitability of the NHS, is an undistinguished interlude in the history of the British welfare state. Bevan himself struck the wrong note at times. In exasperation, on 9 February 1948 he launched a fierce broadside at the BMA representatives as 'a small body of politically poisoned people'. He condemned the 'squalid political conspiracy' which had led to the terms on medical salaries – now to be much augmented after his acceptance of the Spens report – being so misrepresented. But Bevan had been goaded beyond measure by the extraordinary negativism of the BMA spokesmen, an attitude which the *Lancet* frequently and outspokenly condemned, notably in its issue of 21 December 1946. There were grave doubts (voiced by Henry Souttar, a past president of the BMA), as to whether the views of the ordinary GP were necessarily being fairly represented by the BMA council. Furthermore, there was powerful pressure by Moran and Webb-Johnson, on behalf of the royal specialist colleges, to try to break the professional intransigence of the BMA. Eventually, Bevan ended the impasse by a tactical manoeuvre that made no concession of major substance. While retaining all the central features of the NHS scheme – the nationalization of hospitals; the regional boards and executive councils; the redistribution of practices; the abolition of the sale of practices – he agreed with Moran's private suggestion that an act might be introduced to affirm that no whole-time salaried service would be introduced by ministerial regulation, and that the fixed element of remuneration of £300 would last only three years and then remain optional only. He confirmed, too, that doctors would have complete freedom to publish their views on the administration of the NHS – not that this had ever seriously been in question. He looked forward to an era of 'friendly cooperation'.

After that, Dain's diehard obstructionism seemed out of touch, even with grass-roots doctors' opinion. A month before the NHS was to be launched, without their waiting for the official advice of the BMA representative body, it was announced that 26 per cent of English practitioners had already joined. Significantly, the proportion was much higher in Wales and Scotland. Shortly after the act came into operation, Bevan announced that 93.1 per cent of the population were enrolled under the NHS. The popularity of the service was henceforth never seriously in doubt. It was Bevan's, perhaps Britain's, finest hour.

Bevan's main preoccupation after that was to ensure that the NHS that he had created would be given adequate funding. As he commented, quite fairly, in his book, *In Place of Fear* (1952), he had given deep thought to the financial basis of the health service, and had strongly resisted any attempt to impose a contributory insurance system here. In fact, the financing of the health service proved to be a recurring problem, and one that somewhat damaged Bevan's reputation as an efficient social service minister.

In 1949, the NHS estimates proved to be inadequate, and supplementary estimates were brought in. Morrison and other ministers complained that economies elsewhere, in capital investment in industry, housing, education and the like, were not being matched by any such sacrifices on behalf of the sacred cow of the health service. With much reluctance, Bevan accepted the principle of a shilling charge on prescriptions on 20 October 1949, but it was understood that there was no immediate likelihood of this being implemented.

In March–April 1950 there was a fierce battle with Sir Stafford Cripps who had succeeded Dalton as chancellor and who now wished to introduce charges on spectacles and dental services. Bevan told the Cabinet on 3 April 1950 that 'the abandonment of the principle of a free and comprehensive health service would be a shock to their supporters and a grave disappointment to socialist opinion throughout the world'. Aided by Bevan's long friendship with Cripps, going back to Popular Front days, it was agreed to shelve the charges. A ceiling of £392 million was placed on NHS expenditure for 1950–1, and Bevan's own proposal of a Cabinet committee (including Addison) to provide a constant review of health finance was accepted.

A year later, the same issue blew up, fuelled by the huge cost of the rearmament programme adopted under American pressure during the Korean War. This time the outcome was disastrous. Cripps had gone; Gaitskell, the new chancellor, was relatively inexperienced and tactically inflexible, as well as being a target for Bevan's personal rivalry. With Attlee shortly to retire to hospital, and Morrison temporarily in charge, things went from bad to worse. The Cabinet committee divided on Gaitskell's proposals on dental and ophthalmic services, and on health appliances. In full Cabinet, Bevan was supported only by Harold Wilson and, somewhat mildly, by George Tomlinson. Even Addison now turned against him. The ailing Ernest Bevin's compromise scheme for a £400 million ceiling on expenditure fell by the wayside. Bevan himself, now at the Ministry of Labour and goaded elsewhere by trade union 'unofficial' militants, declared that, for the sake of a totally unrealistic defence programme, the government were 'departing from Labour Party principle' and from socialist idealism for the sake of a 'paltry' £23 million. When Gaitskell's view prevailed, Bevan promptly resigned and internal party bitterness of great intensity ensued for many years.

The whole episode was coloured by partisan and personal issues. In retrospect, Bevan's case looks a powerful one. The £4,700 million defence budget was unrealistic, as the next Conservative government soon confirmed. Churchill himself was to cut it back substantially that December. The health service charges (only £13 million for 1951–2) were a minute item in so vast a budget; Hilary Marquand, Bevan's successor at Health, actually complained on 26 April 1951 that any economy resulting from the new charges would be undermined by the huge and unprecedented rush for dentures and spectacles before the charges would take effect in the summer. Above all, a fundamental principle, bearing on the relation between public health and private means, had been eroded. The theoretical conception underlying one of the great achievements of the British welfare tradition had been weakened with permanent and damaging long-term effects.

Bevan's resignation in April 1951 was the pivotal moment of his career. It should be viewed not so much in terms of protest at the government's foreign policy or rearmament programme, but rather as a rearguard action on behalf of a fabric of comprehensive, single-standard welfare which Bevan himself, along with Griffiths, Addison and others, had largely built up. Beyond the smoke and fury of the controversies of 1951, which seem remote enough now, several points emerge. One is the solidity of the administrative and (for some years) the financial structure of Bevan's health service. The Guillebaud committee of 1956 gave the efficiency of its operations a broad endorsement. So have historians since, while an examination of the arguments for and against centralism and localism has appeared in Charles Webster's authoritative work, *The Health Services since the War*, Volume I, published in 1988 by HMSO.

Another conclusion is the health service's broad reasonableness. A genuine compromise was effected, in 1946 as in 1911, between state direction and professional independence. Generous provision had been made for both general practitioners and consultants within the framework of administration. Indeed, the Socialist Medical Association, with its call for a vast extension of health centres and an end to private medicine, openly voiced in its journals its disappointment at Bevan's relative lack of socialist zeal.

A final verdict must focus on Bevan's rare fusion of the talents of the visionary and of the constructive reformer. He always sought power wherever it resided, even if you 'always saw its coat-tails disappearing round the corner'. He upheld the 'principle of action' which would make socialism practically effective, rather than cherish his doctrinal purity in the wilderness of opposition. In power, as minister of health, he exemplified his own generous ideal, that 'the emotional concern with individual life is the most significant quality of a civilised human being'.

1985

26

From Eulogy to Elegy:
Welsh Political Biography

Political biography, like all biography, takes as its starting-point the famous text from *Ecclesiasticus*, 'Let us now praise famous men.' The Welsh like other European peoples have delighted to write in praise of their heroes, real or imaginary. But, just as Welsh politics as a concept developed relatively late, in the early nineteenth century – in the aftermath of industrial expansion, mass literacy, and the growth of popular democracy – so Welsh political biography, too, is a relatively recent growth. From very early times, there were Welsh authors to write about political notables, with some kind of Celtic context in mind, as in the case of Asser's Life of King Alfred (assuming he actually wrote it) *c.*AD 890. Again, Welsh saints or other religious figures inspired the same kind of devotional eulogy as their counterparts elsewhere – witness the many lives of St David from Rhigyfarch (*c.*1090) onwards. But there is nothing remotely resembling a Welsh biographical tradition visible in the works of Asser or Rhigyfarch. After all, Welsh political biography could hardly exist over the centuries from the eighth to the eighteenth because, in most political senses, Wales itself did not exist. When a late nineteenth-century bishop of St David's described Wales as 'a geographical expression', he was much abused by the Liberals and nationalists of his time. By then, such a view was becoming dated – and it was certainly tactless. But at least down to the 1850s, he was not far wrong.

Welsh political biography, then, began in the nineteenth century, in the imperial heyday of Queen Victoria. As in much else, it is a case of 'For Wales – see England'. In the early and middle decades of the nineteenth century, English political biography developed a settled form, that of the 'Life and Letters'. The purpose was to point out the exemplary and benevolent qualities of the man discussed. The emphasis was on public achievement rather than on inner exposure; feet of clay were kept decently veiled like the legs of Victorian pianos. At its worst, in the memorably abusive words of Lytton Strachey, the Life and Letters genre was 'as familiar as the cortège of the undertaker, and wears the same air of slow, funereal barbarism'. The biographer was a public moralist, almost a kind of butler, anxious to serve, celebrate and elevate his subject. At their frequent best – and Monypenny and Buckle on Disraeli are a fine example here – the authors weave together copious documentation to bring out a central dimension of the public man. The style became institutionalized and collectivized in the 1880s with Leslie Stephen's launching of that literary dreadnought, *The Dictionary of National Biography*.

In the light of this English model, Welsh political biography now began to emerge. In the Edwardian period after 1900, joint works appeared bearing such titles as *Eminent Welshmen* or *Enwogion Cymru*, or the Revd J. Vyrnwy Morgan's edited works on *Welsh Political and Educational Leaders* and *Welsh Religious Leaders in the Victorian Era*. Another was *The Welsh at Home* (1904), by William Johnstone, author of *Notable Men*. Of course, they were all anxious to show that their Welsh subjects were admirable and flawless, free from vice, sex and much else that makes life interesting and bearable. But in Wales there was another purpose as well – to show that Wales itself, climbing out of centuries of neglect and post-Edwardian defeat, was interesting and admirable as well, and that all famous Welshmen, whatever their beliefs or creeds, were bound together in some cosmic, organic union. Vyrnwy Morgan, indeed, a rare Nonconformist Tory, wrote with almost Darwinian zeal to argue that there was such a thing as a Welsh political type, a Welsh contribution to international 'thought-energy', almost a Welsh genius. Today, Llanystumdwy, tomorrow the world.

I propose to discuss in detail three broad categories of biographical writing. But note the omissions, too. First of all, I shall have nothing at all to say about Welsh *Tory* biography – for the very good reason that there is no such thing. Since the 1868 general election, Toryism or Conservatism has played only a marginal part, at best, in Welsh political consciousness, and as a result I am unable to think of any single biography which focuses on a Welsh Conservative. The literary tradition over the decades has just followed the election returns. It may be that the advance of the Tory party in parts of Wales in the 1980s may lead to change. We may in the future be reading a two-decker study of the life and times of Lord Crickhowell. But, at least down to 1988, Welsh Tories lacked their Boswell.

Nor shall I have anything to say about *women* politicians. Welsh politics over the centuries have been macho, chauvinist politics, with perhaps Lady Megan Lloyd George and now Ann Clwyd as the only women to penetrate the male fastness with any degree of success. Welsh political biographers have for 100 years praised famous men with gusto. But famous Welsh women have been ignored, and shamefully so. Finally, my last omission – there is, to my knowledge, no Welsh biographical *debunker*, no Cymric Lytton ap Strachey to pour scorn on the stereotyped form of the political biography. The Welsh are usually very good at laughing at themselves. But on balance, it seems to me, Welsh politicians who have 'got on' and have been suitably embalmed in print, have escaped almost scot-free, in the way Welsh rugby players used to do. Welsh political biography is usually straitlaced and straight-faced. To laugh at its pretensions would be rather like poking fun at Haydn Tanner or Barry John. So there are no Tories, no women and no jokers to record. Nor have there ever been.

First of all, Liberal biographies. Their standard form in the Victorian period was the *cofiant*, a monumental commemoration which usually followed a set form. The emphasis was wholly on the public achievement, the struggle to achieve fame and influence from a humble, usually rural, origin; the public seriousness and dedication copiously illustrated from sermons and speeches; the undying fame kindled in the hearts and minds of contemporaries. The *cofiannau* of Nonconformist eminences in the nineteenth century follow this pattern. Studies of men like the Revd John Jones, Talysarn, the Revd John Thomas, Liverpool, or the Revd Herber Evans played their part in sustaining the populistic upsurge which lay behind the dominance of Welsh Liberalism in the later Victorian period. A more interesting variant is the life of the Revd Michael Daniel Jones, founder of the Welsh settlement in Patagonia, by the Revd E. Pan Jones, Mostyn. The author was himself an angular, intense radical-socialist. Far from seeing the solution for Welsh agrarian problems in a peasant pro-prietorship for tenant farmers as most Liberals did, Pan Jones advocated land nationalization and an interim swingeing tax on the unearned increment. His *Oes a Gwaith Michael Daniel Jones* (1903) comes alive with rather more effect because it brings out the passionate class awareness and anti-English nationalism of M. D. Jones. It lacks the sentimentality of most *cofiannau*. Its very commitment gives it more insight.

Nonconformist ministers were the usual subject for these works of eulogy, naturally so when one thinks of the key role of the chapels in nineteenth-century society, rural and urban. Another, lesser subject was the radical journalist. The most notable of these works was perhaps Thomas Gwynn Jones's lengthy study of Thomas Gee, the radical editor and political crusader from Denbigh, published in 1913, fifteen years after Gee's death. Gwynn Jones himself was a remarkable man of letters, especially as a distinguished poet, and his *cofiant* of Gee is well worth attention. At the same time, it is somewhat disappointing, to my mind. Not only does he say virtually nothing on the family or personal side, which is regrettable since Gwynn Jones worked under Gee, that old editorial tyrant, on the staff of *Baner ac Amserau* for some years in the 1890s. It also contains no attempt to place Gee's social and political outlook in any kind of critical or comparative context. Thomas Gwynn Jones himself was, unusually, a socialist, a member of the Independent Labour Party, whose heroes included Keir Hardie and Robert Blatchford. In the First World War, he was amongst the courageous pacifist minority. No one would have been better placed to offer a critique of the mid-Victorian thought-world of a traditional Liberal Nonconformist like Thomas Gee. Gwynn Jones fails to do so. This failure on his part is, in its way, a condemnation of the *cofiant* as a literary form.

Apart from the ministers and the journalists, the notable Welsh politicians who began to stir the national consciousness from the 1880s onwards gradually found their biographers. Tom Ellis, the nationalist member for Merioneth who became Liberal chief whip and died in 1899 in his forty-first year, was perhaps the most beguiling of all. He has yielded two long biographies this century. The first, in two volumes by his son T. I. Ellis, published in 1944–8, was immensely valuable for the great richness of its documentation from the Ellis papers, now deposited in the National Library of Wales. It is still a book well worth reading in close detail. T. I. Ellis, the secretary of *Undeb Cymru Fydd*, a former headmaster, and a pillar of 'Round Britain Quiz' on the radio, was especially interested in conveying information on Welsh literature, education and religious life. But he stressed these somewhat at the expense of other topics that might interest an historical biographer, such as Tom Ellis's imperialism and his concern with social reform. That Tom Ellis's acquaintances should include both Cecil Rhodes and the Webbs is worth further examination, at least. The other major biography of Ellis is *The Forerunner* by Neville Masterman of Swansea, published in 1972. This compares Ellis, most fascinatingly, with particular types of unhistoric European nationalists, with Thomas Davis, Mazzini, Kossuth and Masaryk all brought in for comparison. Mr Masterman's penetrating insight and comparative historical learning enables him to bring out the rich complexity of Ellis's ideas and 'genial alchemy' as no other author has ever done.

Ellis's parliamentary contemporaries also attracted much biographical attention. Sir Herbert Lewis, member for Flintshire, was admirably recalled in a centenary book edited by his daughter, Mrs Kitty Idwal Jones, in 1958. His work on local government and Welsh education come out very clearly here; indeed, the book shows how a study of a second-ranking figure can be sometimes more revealing than a biography of a Napoleonic giant. Lewis, of course, was a professional man, a lawyer like many of his Liberal colleagues. A very different Liberal was D. A. Thomas, Lord Rhondda, the industrial tycoon who owned the Cambrian collieries but was also a maverick Liberal MP for Merthyr for twenty-two years from 1888 to 1910. He was an odd, unusual politician, the voice of the 'American Wales' of the south-east, and the biographies he has attracted reflect this quality. A commemorative volume produced by his daughter, Lady Rhondda, in 1921, has a pungent piece on Thomas's political operations by the former MP, Llewelyn Williams, then an Asquithian Liberal. He was partly concerned to settle old scores with Lloyd George and the result is a distinctly slanted version of Thomas's political views on Welsh Home Rule and other matters. Even so, inadequate though they are, the studies of D. A. Thomas do at least remind us that Welsh Liberalism in its heyday claimed Cardiff no less than Caernarfon, that its base was for long as secure in the industrial valleys of the south as in the rural fastnesses.

The outstanding Liberal topic for biographers, though, is obviously David Lloyd George. To date, he has inspired over ninety biographies, including alas more than one from the present writer; while there are multi-volume works by John Grigg, W. R. P. George, Bentley Gilbert and Don Cregier all currently in progress. The biographies of L.G. are most remarkable for their extraordinary lurches from one extreme of interpretation to another. In the earliest phase, from 1908 onwards when he became chancellor of the Exchequer, Welsh biographers such as J. Hugh Edwards and Beriah Gwynfe Evans wrote of Lloyd George in terms of an heroic populist tradition like the American Horatio Alger stories, telling how the 'cottage-bred boy' trod the primrose path from village green to Downing Street, slaying the lords, the bishops and sundry other philistines along the way. Nor were these romantic, 'log cabin to president' studies confined to Welsh authors. The English barrister, Herbert du Parcq, wrote no less than four strongly admiring volumes on Lloyd George in 1911–13. After the war, du Parcq, now a peer, a High Court judge and an Asquithian Liberal, felt so ashamed of what he had done that he left out all reference to these bulky volumes in his *Who's Who* entry. Nor does the entry on him in *The Dictionary of National Biography* mention these dire facts.

Down to December 1916, the biographical treatment of L.G. was romantic, perhaps epic. Thereafter, with the 'coupon election' of 1918, the coalition with the Tories and the split in the Liberal party, Lloyd George changed from superman to scapegoat. Writers like J. A. Spender or Charles Mallett condemned him for betrayal of his principles and his friends. J. M. Keynes, memorably, saw him as 'a vampire and a medium in one'. The youthful Gwyn Jones in *The Welsh Review* in 1939 called L.G. 'the sarcophagus of radicalism'. Public failures were accompanied by merciless private exposure. In 1960 the second Earl Lloyd George depicted his father as a philanderer and a faithless husband. In 1963 Donald McCormick, better known as Richard Deacon, went even further in *The Mask of Merlin*. He pursued L.G.'s private lapses, real or invented, from the Palace of Westminster to Cemmaes Road railway station, and used them as a kind of parable of the corruption and self-indulgence of the Welsh as a whole.

However, from the mid-1960s came a third phase, with the opening up of the riches of the Lloyd George papers in A. J. P. Taylor's magnificent Beaverbrook Library in London and later in the National Library of Wales. A much more measured phase of Lloyd George historiography now resulted, less moralistic, more genuinely scholarly. The inquiry into Lloyd George's private life has not abated, with the diaries of his mistress and future wife Frances Stevenson, published volumes of his letters with both Dame Margaret and Frances Stevenson, and the revelations of personal advisers like A. J. Sylvester. But the frenetic air of exposure has gone and historical perspective has returned. In any case, even in Wales we are perhaps no longer shocked by revelation of social or sexual irregularity or scandal. The permissive society has dawned even here.

On balance, it seems to me that, with this vast, apparently never-ending torrent of studies of Lloyd George, Welsh Liberal biography has reached new heights of sophistication. Awful though many of the books on him have been, they have generated real argument, whereas the old *cofiannau* were essentially uncritical. And yet – and I hope it does not seem ungenerous of me to say this – it seems to me that the enigma of Lloyd George's chameleon-like personality and style, so memorably portrayed by Keynes in 1919, has not wholly been unravelled by any single biographer to date. Each has contributed much; but each has found the going difficult. If his current biographers have freed themselves from dated moral stereotypes and old disputes over long-forgotten matters like the Maurice debate or the 'coupon election', they have encountered problems of a different kind. In particular, they have found constant difficulty in relating Lloyd George's political outlook to the culture of Wales. Bentley Gilbert, whose astringent transatlantic approach is a welcome change, rather oddly asserts that L.G.'s connection with Wales was of no more account than that of Napoleon with Corsica, surely a major misjudgement. John Grigg is quite admirable in dealing with the vicissitudes of high politics and shows an intuitive appreciation of the political world perhaps gained from his father, a distinguished member of L.G.'s 'Garden Suburb' of political advisers after 1918. On the other hand, he was somewhat uneasy in treatment of his subject's Welshness, at least in assessing his career down to 1906. When the Welsh Liberals of that period are dismissed as 'a tribal faction' it is hard not to feel that a major dimension of the subject is being disregarded. To be fair, the second and third volumes of Mr Grigg's study do redress the balance, while his National Library lecture on *Lloyd George and Wales* (1988) was admirably judicious.

Lloyd George is clearly a most difficult subject for a biographer in himself alone. But there is another problem – that he has been taken as the symbol for a wider theme. He has become a scapegoat for national decline, for the erosion of faith in our great institutions, for the undermining of accepted canons of behaviour in both public and private morality. In Wales, he is particularly linked with the undermining of that vibrant tradition of national achievement associated with the Liberal high noon between 1868 and 1918. In interpreting Lloyd George, Welshmen seem to be judging themselves, perhaps covering up their own uncertainty about their identity in the face of a man who was so transcendentally confident that he had got it right. More than forty years after his death, Lloyd George remains deeply disturbing and controversial – but also central to our perceptions of Wales and a changing world.

The tradition of Liberal biography did not die out with the downfall of Lloyd George's Liberal party after 1922. In Welsh biography, it has produced at least one posthumous legacy of enormous importance to historians and everyone concerned with the Welsh past and present. I refer to the *Dictionary of Welsh Biography*, published by the Cymmrodorion Society in Welsh in 1953 and in its more familiar English, extended form in 1959. Edited at first by Sir John Lloyd, then by Professor R. T. Jenkins, it is a marvellous cultural tribute to latter-day Welsh Liberalism, exemplary in its scholarship, covering an enormous range of Welsh personalities prior to 1940 in economical and lucid terms. There is no Scottish version of the *DWB* and our Scottish friends lament the fact. The strength of the *DWB* lies in its seriousness and its scholarship. The comparative weakness lies in its frame of reference. It is clustered with Nonconformist ministers, minor poets, teachers and preachers of all kinds. It is inexorably middle-class. Rebels, 'roaring boys', mavericks, above all working-class spokesmen of all kinds do much less well – as do Welsh women. It is a celebration of late-Victorian respectability. And yet, and yet – if one wants to see the Welsh biographical approach at its best, the *DWB*, orchestrated by that incomparable littérateur-historian, R. T. Jenkins, is surely the example one would choose.

Welsh Labour biography is a much more fragile plant. Until the 1930s, indeed, there can hardly be said to be a recognizable tradition of writing about Welsh Labour public figures. The earliest working-class pioneers were treated in a manner heavy with symbolism, a kind of secular martyrology. There tended to be a set pattern. Our hero would emerge from cruel poverty and exploiting employers, coalowners or whatever. Then there would be a climactic experience, a pit tragedy, the 1904 religious revival perhaps, or a decisive engagement in industrial conflict, such as the Cambrian Combine strike of 1910 which saw the Tonypandy riots. The final stage of the story would be a successful quest for conformity and acceptance by the establishment, a few honours, even perhaps a peerage. The nature of Welsh and British Labour biography thus mirrored the lack of militancy in the class it described. It repeated the values of the Liberal biographies of the past.

It has been hard to break out of this somewhat simple treatment. Thus many important Labour leaders in Wales are still desperately short of attention, though the devoted efforts of the Welsh Labour History Society since 1971 and its quite excellent journal *Llafur* have helped improve matters considerably. In particular, the Lib–Lab mainstream tradition, the dominant strain of Welsh working-class politics at least down to the 1920s has been sorely neglected. The only biography of a Welsh Lib–Lab I can recall is Eric Wyn Evans's life of William Abraham, *Mabon* (1959). But that has little personal or political material and is mainly useful as a study of labour relations in the coalfield between the 1870s and the 1914 war.

The Marxist or neo-syndicalist far left has done rather better, perhaps because of the implicit sympathies of many younger Welsh historians and researchers. A splendid, if strongly partisan, work is Robert Griffiths's study of S. O. Davies (1983), that stormy petrel from Merthyr, half nationalist, half Stalinist.

There are two major native Welsh politicians who may in the fullness of time inspire a more robust and coherent Labour biographical tradition, comparable with writing on Attlee, Bevin, Dalton and other English socialists. These two, of course, are Jim Griffiths and Nye Bevan. Jim Griffiths fits closely into the cultural and social context of east Carmarthenshire and the Amman valley and the collective study by Professor Beverley Smith and others (1978) deals superbly with that aspect. The way in which Griffiths emerged from an intensely vibrant Welsh-language world in the aftermath of the 1904 religious revival and the industrial storms of the 1910–14 period emerges most vividly. What is needed now is to build on this crucially important base, to see how Griffiths related his roots in a profoundly Welsh community to a wider sense of class, and to national and international solidarity. What was there in his background and outlook, for instance, that made him a remarkably effective colonial secretary and almost took him into the Foreign Office in succession to Ernest Bevin in 1951? There are some important personal clues in Mrs James Griffiths's privately-printed book *One Woman's Story* (1979).

Nye Bevan has been better served. He has inspired two considerable works so far, the two-volume work by Michael Foot and John Campbell's biography of 1987. Of these, Michael Foot's is a brilliant, breathtaking contribution to literature. It is a journalist's *tour de force* of the highest order which vividly conveys the compulsive magic of Bevan's personality. The author, of course, approaches Bevan's Welsh background as an Englishman; but at least in personal terms the mainsprings of political and industrial protest in the Monmouthshire valleys in the 1920s are made impressively clear, as befits an author who succeeded Bevan as MP for Ebbw Vale in 1960. The first volume, published in 1962, covers Bevan's career down to the 1945 election. The second, published in 1973, dealt with the bitter internecine conflicts within the Labour party after 1951 between Bevanites and Gaitskellites in which Foot himself, as editor of *Tribune*, was deeply involved. One effect, possibly, is that Bevan's radicalism is slightly overdone and the contrast with the Gaitskellites too stark. When the historian looks back at the Labour movement in Britain after 1945, especially at the record of the Attlee government, Bevan seems much more of a mainstream figure, a 'relativist' advocate of the mixed economy, a critic of trade-union militancy, sometimes a cold-warrior in those Stalinist times, almost a 'patriot' in condemning President Nasser at the time of Suez. More could be said, no doubt, about Bevan's record as minister of health with the public records now available: indeed Michael Foot once observed to me that he would have written about the post-1945 period somewhat differently now in the light of his own experience of ministerial office after 1974. For all that, Foot's is still an incomparably exciting and valuable book. It is the best biography any Welsh politician has yet received. It is to my mind, superior to John Campbell's work of 1987.

Campbell is a Scot, an outstanding political biographer, and he deals with the high politics of 1945 to 1960 in a most skilful fashion. He gives, indeed, rather more attention to Bevan's political ideas and writings than Foot does, though his approach to *In Place of Fear* is unduly hostile. But his book was concerned in part to demolish the errors and inadequacies of the 'mirage' of socialism as a creed in the 1980s, to lay low not only Bevan but also Michael Foot and indeed Neil Kinnock who is roundly attacked in a fierce peroration. It is written in praise of the SDP (Campbell once wrote a campaign biography of a very different Welshman, Roy Jenkins). By rooting his critique of Bevan in the mid-1980s, Campbell has made his book something of a period piece – the more ironically, indeed, since the period since the 1987 election has seen his own SDP crumble into complete oblivion. The other problem with the book is the almost total failure to relate Bevan and his philosophy to Wales. Indeed the Welsh aspect of Bevan is presented as background material disposed of in a mere twenty-eight pages in a book of 430. We still needed, then, a different kind of view of Nye Bevan, a study which relates the local and the central, the particular and the universal in Bevan's make-up, and which gives his Welsh roots proper emphasis. Fortunately, Professor Dai Smith of Cardiff has written precisely such a book, perhaps a cultural exploration of South Wales working-class life as much as a biography of the member for Ebbw Vale. It appeared in 1994.

Welsh Labour biography is patchy, episodic. It should be much extended. We need far more studies of lesser, local figures as well as the Griffithses and Bevans, men like miners' agents, WEA lecturers, or local councillors, to shed light on the wider problems of the rise of the working-class movement in Wales. If a modern biographical treatment were accorded, for instance, to the pupils of the Central Labour College after 1918 – who included Griffiths and Bevan, along with Morgan Phillips, Ness Edwards, Bryn Roberts, Lewis Jones and others of that inspired generation – the importance of that college in the Welsh socialist tradition would be much illuminated. We also need wider perspectives, to see Welsh Labour men – and women as well – as national figures in a British social and post-industrial structure, and to measure them in a wider international typology of Labour leaders, European and North American. We need a Welsh Egon Wertheimer or Maurice Duverger to provide a comparative, analytical treatment. Welsh Labour biography is, I think, an exciting area of discovery for younger writers and historians. To date, however, it has not had the intellectual impact of the Liberal historiography that preceded it.

The final strand of Welsh political biography needs much briefer treatment: I refer to the Nationalist tradition. Of course Plaid Cymru and other manifestations of nationalism or separatism, going back to the Cymru Fydd movement of the 1890s, have produced very few major politicians. The most influential and distinguished of them, Mr Gwynfor Evans, has not generated an important biographical study, partly of course for the excellent reason that he is still very much alive, partly because he is himself such a lucid expositor of his own credo. Most of the other nationalist figures that occur to one have largely been men and women of letters, Gwenallt, Waldo Williams, R. S.

Thomas and many, many others, and naturally have been considered by their biographers mainly as literary influences and personalities.

There is, perhaps, one notable exception, Saunders Lewis. He, of course, was primarily a littérateur, poet, dramatist, novelist and critic of extraordinary facility. But, as everyone knows, the pivot of his career was political nationalism. Not only was he the founding father of Plaid Cymru and its president down to 1939. Many of his plays deal directly with political themes. *Gymerwch Chi Sigaret?* (1955) deals with the clash between political obligation and personal conscience in the context of the cold war. *Brâd* (1958) examines the issues raised by the German generals' bomb-plot against Hitler in 1944. Saunders Lewis's writings are spattered with the treatment of aspects of political commitment and ideology. Hitherto, the many discussions of his life and works have focused on Saunders Lewis as man of letters. So far as Lewis's politics of nationalism come in, they tend to pivot on two heroic episodes – the burning of the RAF bombing school and Lewis's subsequent imprisonment in Wormwood Scrubs and dismissal from the University in 1936–7; and the old man's call to arms on behalf of the Welsh language in his famous broadcast of 1962. Now these two dramatic events have certainly been of seminal influence in the course of modern Welsh nationalism, but there is much more that should be said about Lewis's politics. One problem for his would-be biographers, no doubt, has been the embarrassing nature of some of his political opinions. The strong note of sympathy with fascist corporatism in the 1930s and even during the war is strong stuff for any biographer in a place like Wales. But more difficult, perhaps, has been the trouble in accommodating a complex, many-sided character like Saunders Lewis within the conventional framework of political biography. What we much need is a study of his political life set in terms of his evolving ideas. With his Francophilia, his fascination with right-wing nationalists like Maurice Barrès and the ideas of *Action Française*, his medievalism, his mysticism, his commitment to the organic concept of the Catholic Church, he stands outside the mainstream of Plaid Cymru itself. Lewis's basic rejection of the premises of nineteenth-century liberal democracy makes him quite distinct. A good intellectual biography of Saunders Lewis (say, something comparable to Bernard Crick's life of George Orwell) would indeed be a breakthrough in Welsh political writing. It is good to know, therefore, that Tecwyn Lloyd's and other volumes will shortly appear.

Biography, political or otherwise, is currently in turmoil. A symposium on the subject, to which I contributed, was entitled by the editors (or perhaps the publishers) *The Troubled Face of Biography*. Welsh political biography is in trouble for somewhat different reasons, because the culture that gave it birth is rapidly passing away. As a result, there is an elegiac note to all the main strains of Welsh political biography to which I have referred. The Liberal heyday of pre-1918 now seems excessively remote. Few authors seem to show much interest in disinterring the bones of such forgotten figures as Brynmor Jones, Llewelyn Williams, or Ellis Griffiths, all famous Liberals seventy or eighty years ago. Only Lloyd George retains his fascination – but he, of course, was prime minister for nearly six years and *sui generis* in so many other ways, too. Labour biography may be going the same way, perhaps, as the Labour party shows some of the same symptoms of social and intellectual disintegration as Liberalism did in the past. Whether Neil Kinnock will in due course generate a proper biography, other than the three ephemeral campaign biographies he has so far inspired, at present seems unlikely. And nationalist biography, as we have seen, has always been a fragile growth.

But we do urgently need a thriving political biography within the varied mix of modern Welsh literature, to set against biographical studies of such non-political Welshmen as Augustus John, Dylan Thomas or (of course!) Richard Burton. One of the most important features of the Welsh in the past hundred years, after all, is that they have been intensely political people, born orators, skilled committee men, 'fluid people' like Thomas Jones, 'able to charm a bird off a bough' like Lloyd George. Without a proper tradition of political biography, including such endangered species as Tories, women and immigrants, Welsh literature is singularly incomplete. What we particularly need is biography of different kinds, not a stereotype form of book which launches our hero on this earth on page one and, after a straightforward, chronological narrative of triumphs and disasters, kills him off on the penultimate page. We should have many more experimental types of biography, externalized and internalized, thematic, dialectical, flexible. To cite the works of a former principal of Aberystwyth, we need more 'Bundles of Sensations' and 'Chapters of Accidents'. We should certainly have many more political biographies written by writers or literary critics who are not themselves academics or professional historians. After all, some of the best biographies of American presidents from George Washington to Richard Nixon have been by such authors. We should bring into the realms of political biography a wider range of personalities and concepts not necessarily regarded as political at all. In this respect, the eclectic nature of Meic Stephens's marvellous *Oxford Companion to the Literature of Wales* is a model for us all. If there is to be, in any respect that matters, a living place called Wales in the twenty-first century, it needs *biography* as a source of reflection and renewal. Nye Bevan once told a famous parable of how he would retreat to the barren hills above Tredegar when lost in the swirling mountain mists above his home, to see precisely where he had come from. Like him, we need to retrace our steps to see where we are, to gain perspective on the difficult present, and, above all else, to point the way ahead.

1988

Index